Eder Jofre

Brazil's First Boxing World Champion

Christopher J. Smith

WIN BY
KO

Win By KO Publications
Iowa City

Eder Jofre
Brazil's First Boxing World Champion

Christopher J. Smith

(ISBN-13): 978-1-949783-05-6

(hardcover: 50# acid-free alkaline paper)

Includes footnotes and index.

Cover design by Javier Serrano and Christopher Miller ©

Manufactured in the United States of America.

Win By KO Publications

Iowa City, Iowa

winbykopublications.com

Contents

Preface

I have always thought about writing a boxing biography for several reasons. I am curious to know more about subjects that interest me, why those subjects enter the ring as a profession, and how their backgrounds change the sport and affect them personally. Boxing is an extreme sport, and it has been my favorite for a very long time. I can be found reading a boxing book at any given time. Over the years, I have read many boxers' autobiographies and some wonderfully researched and well-written biographies. As a fan, most of the fighters that I have gravitated towards have been Latino fighters. However, without a working knowledge of Spanish or Portuguese and limited archival materials, I have been less than satisfied when learning about some of those fighters.

The subject of this book, the legendary Eder Jofre, was one of the boxers I wanted to read more about. He came to my attention in the late 1990s when I was entering my mid-teens. I had been watching televised boxing matches for a few years already but started to become extremely interested in historical fights and fighters. Eder Jofre caught my attention one day when I was thumbing through *The Boxing Register: International Boxing Hall of Fame Official Record Book*. Several things stood out in his profile: his incredible record, his vegetarian diet, and the fact that he was from Brazil. At a time, when it was common for other great fighters of his era to record double-digit losses, Jofre, in contrast, had only two defeats in 78 fights over a career span of almost 20 years. His vegetarianism intrigued me. I could not imagine how any athlete, especially a boxer, could rise to the top without eating meat. And, I had never before noticed a Brazilian boxer. Growing up as an English football fan, I saw Brazil dominate on the international level with many wonderful players like Ronaldo, Romario, Rivaldo, Cafu, and Roberto Carlos; but I had never seen a Brazilian boxer compete in a big fight. Great Mexican and Puerto Rican champions I had read about, but Jofre was the first Brazilian boxer to whom I was exposed.

What further intrigued me beyond Eder's incredible boxing skills was that he is truly a national icon in one of the world's largest countries. Very few prizefighters can make that claim. Eder held the status as the world's best boxer pound-for-pound in one of the sport's greatest eras and this was at a hugely significant time in Brazilian history. This was a period when Brazil was becoming a modern country. The success of the national football team's multiple World Cup wins in 1958, 1962, and 1970 coincided with the country's growth in industry, technology, and culture. Boxing was probably only second to football in terms of global popularity when it came to sports at that time, so for Eder to have been its finest practitioner really showed why Brazilians still hold him in such esteem so many years beyond his career.

In the late 1990s, there was no YouTube. Online fight film was rare. Today, boxing enthusiasts can access boxers and their records at Boxrec.com or join countless boxing history forums and groups on social media. Before widespread use of the internet, research required tracking down old magazines and film collectors overseas. As a result, I spent large chunks of my "pocket money" to obtain those rarities. When I finally saw film footage of Jofre, I was hooked. His style was exactly what I liked to see in a fighter. He was intelligent, he was patient, he picked his shots well, he hit hard, and he went on the attack. He was an extremely technical and aggressive boxer. A complete fighter.

I needed to find more footage. Unfortunately, all I could find at this point were two of his bouts with Fighting Harada, his first bout with Jose Medel, and short highlight clips of his fights with Katsutoshi Aoki and the Medel rematch. When I managed to connect with some English-speaking fans in Brazil, they informed me that, sadly, in the 1970s there had been a fire at the Brazilian television studios that held Jofre's film footage. While some films survived the fire, in 1986, a second fire destroyed all remaining footage. This was bitter news as I was hoping to find dozens more recordings of this great champion's fights.

In 2000, an article written by Dan Cuoco for The International Boxing Research Organization (IBRO) sparked my interest even more about this fighter. Cuoco claimed that after Sugar Ray Robinson, Jofre was the second greatest fighter of all-time. For someone like Cuoco with his wealth of historical knowledge of the sport, to make such a claim, I knew this fighter was indeed significant. In part perhaps from Cuoco's work, in 2001, Eder was ranked number 19 among "The 80 greatest fighters of the last 80 years" by *The Ring* magazine. What makes these lofty positions so impressive today is that Eder competed in the bantamweight division for most of his career and rarely fought in America. None of his fights were broadcast on television or radio in America, so even hardcore fans can be forgiven for making the mistake of overlooking him. The fact that Eder is almost universally acclaimed as the greatest bantamweight in boxing history is no mean feat when considering that the bantamweight division is one of the original eight weight classes in boxing history and is a division often associated with Mexican dominance.

In 2004, I searched online hoping to find additional footage of this Brazilian fighter who fascinated me. Lo and behold, I saw that a documentary by Musart Music distributed by DVD Brazil had just been released, *O Grande Campeao (The Great Champion)*. I placed an order and waited patiently for the package to arrive. Much to my surprise and excitement, the DVD had English subtitles. I was elated to see highlights of many more fights than what I had at my disposal and a fascinating story to go along with a legendary boxing career. As an obsessed boxing fan, I watched it every day for a month.

Over time I was able to obtain more footage and discovered a documentary from 1986 called *Quebrando a Cara (Breaking the Face)*. In addition, I was able to access multiple major Brazilian newspaper archives and magazines and two books on Eder which were translated into English for me. Throughout this research, what I discovered was, that beyond being an amazing prizefighter, Eder Jofre was beloved for his exemplary sportsmanship and humanity. These were common themes from every person I interviewed. Eder Jofre was living proof that good guys can and do finish first.

Fortunately, I was able to locate Marcel Jofre, Eder's son. I reached out to both Marcel and Eder's daughter, Andrea; and in our many discussions, I learned of the fascinating family on Eder's mother's side. The Zumbano family comprises one of the largest numbers of professional boxers from a single family in South American boxing, and I would venture to guess, world boxing. The Zumbano and Jofre stories linked together families that began in Europe and ended up in Brazil and Argentina, families that were ultimately linked by a love of the sport of boxing. These families combined to create a unique part of boxing history and Brazilian culture. And while there were certain tragedies, the family was able to survive, backed by love, hard work, passion, and positivity, ultimately to witness the coronation of an icon.

In 2018, I wrote a detailed article on Eder for friend Jose Martino's website, *Boxeomundial*, which received positive feedback. Perhaps the best came from Dan Cuoco himself who reached out to say that he particularly enjoyed the piece. Several people requested more information on individual fights. One suggestion came from Kyle McLachlan, founder of *The Fight Site*. "Write a book," he said. I floated the idea around to friends, boxing historians, writers, and the feedback was the same: "Go for it!" Such is the beauty of the boxing community. While it is a relatively small community, it is one full of support and direct help to foster a new detailed biography on great historic figures.

Finally, and most important to this project, was the support of the Jofre family. His children and Eder himself were delighted and moved to hear that this book was in progress. I have been blessed to have had such co-operation of this wonderful family. I feel extremely privileged to bring this material to light. I can only hope that the reader enjoys reading this book half as much as I have enjoyed the reading, the writing, the research, and above all the friendships formed during the process. I hope that readers will see this fighter and his career in the light in which it deserves to be seen, shining upon one of the finest boxers in history and a man of honor, integrity, and decency.

Christopher J. Smith

Foreword

Knockout! This magical word transformed the life of a little boy who loved to draw superheroes, who did a course for architecture design, and became a locksmith. Everything in my father's life shaped him to be a boxer. This piece written by our dear friend Chris Smith will surely take the reader inside the boxing world.

A boxer deals in the four corners of the ring and this is what makes him a champion. I particularly think that every boxer's biography is a nice script for a movie, for these are lives carved with blood, sweat, and tears until reaching an explosion in the happiness of a victory. Eder Jofre – "Brazil's first boxing world champion," is a mirror of that pathway to glory. I am sure that the reader will not be knocked out when he meets Eder Jofre.

- **Marcel Jofre**

My father is my hero. I was born in the middle of this wonderful story. I saw and heard many things between camera flashes and autographs. Do not miss this opportunity to know the life of Eder Jofre.

- **Andrea Jofre**

It was a Saturday around 10 am on a sunny morning. Eder and I were going to a city in the countryside of São Paulo to deal with personal issues and as usual, I was asking him a lot of stuff. I asked what it was like to be in Japan on the other side of the world and if there was a boycott. He quickly told me he didn't see anything, then he burst into laughter and said "now that I think about it, they did sabotage me when I went there to face Katsutoshi Aoki and was looking forward to eating sweet rice, and they didn't know the dish or how to make it, so I asked the translator to order a bowl of cooked rice with no sauce, then I ordered milk and sugar and started eating it. It wasn't like Cida's rice, but it was sweet rice. Suddenly I realized they were all staring at me, startled, they had never seen that."

I am telling you this one occasion, chosen from so many I had with him. A few years later this story came back to my mind, one day going through registers of his career to write an article celebrating his birthday in 2017, something dragged my attention. The history did not match his background; it started with the title unification in 1962 against John Caldwell that would give him another title. I called Andrea and discussed with her already affirming he had a title that wasn't recognized, she agreed, and I said let's go after this. But I confess before the pursuit began, I was afraid because I thought it was impossible nobody saw this fault after so many years. After seeing it all over again with a lot of care, my doubt got bigger. He is not a two-time champion; he is a three- or four-time champion. So, we decided to ask the CNB (National Boxing Council) for help. The CNB, represented by President Geyza Caryny, was fundamental with Mike Miranda Jr. and Mike Miranda Sr.'s help, without them I don't think we would have got the recognition.

The sweet rice story is simply because, with that fight against Aoki, Eder became twice world champion and for some reason that I do not know, it wasn't registered! Now just so you know the results of that story and others. Enjoy the book!

- **Antonio Oliveira**

When I was a child, I thought of being a superhero. I did not imagine that one day I would earn a nickname by listening to my father's advice. With a lot of sweat, sacrifices, and discipline, today I am a two-time world champion. Do you want to know how I got there? Enjoy my story!

- **Eder Jofre**

Section One: Origins of a Champion

This section focuses on the family background of the Jofres and Zumbanos in addition to Eder Jofre's youth and amateur career.

Chapter One

Throughout the long and illustrious history of professional boxing, there are tales of fighters who came from humble backgrounds and found their way into the sport out of necessity for survival. They discovered their God-given talents. There are also examples like a young Cassius Clay, where fate played its hand in the form of a stolen bicycle. There are many stories of troubled young men who turned to boxing as a way out of the ghetto or simply to stay out of trouble. There are substantially fewer cases where a fighter was groomed before conception and was molded from the womb.

The subject of this story is a boxer from a unique background in the annals of ring history. Eder Jofre was not an exceptional case in that he grew up in an impoverished family and made it to the top, but he is unique because both sides of his family were involved in the sport before his parents even met one another, let alone tied the knot and started a family. His first toys were boxing gloves and his first hobby was boxing.

The story of Eder Jofre, Brazil's first boxing world champion, and national hero is a product of two immigrant families that shared a social status and a passion for the sweet science. The chance meeting of two ambitious brothers from Argentina with a struggling but hard-working Italian family would result in a permanent bond which resulted in a significant chapter in boxing history.

Brazil was going through a challenging period socially, politically, and internationally at the time. While the Jofres lived for boxing, the Zumbanos were also heavily involved in the Brazilian Revolution and the political struggles that ensued. What always kept the families bonded through these troubled times were their principles and ethics, and, above all, this ardor for boxing. It was a shared vision and sense of community that saw this friendship turn into family and ultimately influence a generation which resulted in the making of one of history's greatest boxers and a true Brazilian icon.

Brazil gained its independence from Portugal in 1822, but it was not until 1856 that people emigrated from other countries in large numbers in search of work as most of the immigrants until then were brought over for colonization purposes. There had been Dutch and Spanish settlers previously as the power struggle was played out with Portugal through the Sugar Age of the 1600s and the Gold Rush in the 1800s. The coffee crop was introduced in 1720. By 1850, Brazil was producing half of the world's coffee. The impact of coffee on the Brazilian economy was far greater than that of gold or sugar, as, by this time, Brazil was free of colonization and completely independent. By 1891, coffee accounted for 64% of Brazil's exports.

In the late 19th century, there was a large influx of Italian immigrants that were enticed over when propaganda material reached Europe just as slavery was abolished in Brazil in 1888. Between 1884 and 1903, Italians were the largest migrant group by far, accounting for 57% of the immigration into Brazil, which was 40% more than the second-largest group, which was the Portuguese. The promise of owning land and other riches prompted the large Italian movement to Brazil, particularly to São Paulo, where multiple huge coffee plantations suddenly found themselves understaffed. However, many immigrants soon became unhappy with the treatment they were receiving and likened their position to something of a modern type of slavery as they earned remuneration in the fashion of food rations, small living spaces on the working site, and certain necessities like medicine were paid back to the employer through a garnishment in wages or ultimately became debt.

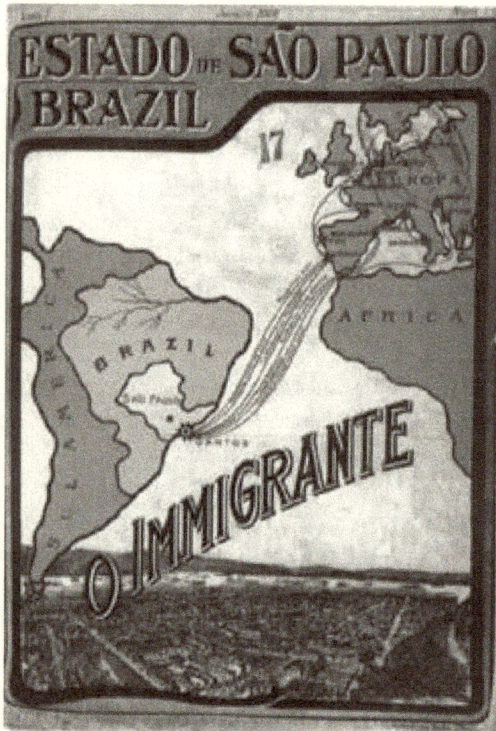

Many of these disgruntled settlers left those conditions and found land and business for themselves and built their communities. Others were not as fortunate and had to struggle with the rest of the population in this transitional period.

It is often said that poverty breeds the best athletes, and there is likely no sport that this rings truer for than boxing. At this point, Brazil was one of the world's largest melting pots and fastest-growing countries. Neighboring countries Argentina, Uruguay, and Chile were more connected internationally in the world of sports in the first quarter of the century. Their football federations were formed many years before Brazil's and their boxing was far more advanced. Brazil caught the football bug and it soon became a national obsession but the conditions for boxing were far more problematic. When it came to South American boxing, Brazil, the continent's largest country, was on the outside looking in. This challenging situation is what makes the story of the Jofres and Zumbanos so remarkable and the consecration of Eder Jofre so unlikely.

Argentina

Jose Aristides Jofre was born on December 31, 1903, in San Justo, Argentina. His mother, Lucrecia Temis, was born in Spain and his father, Olegario Jofre, was of French Basque origins but was born and raised in Chile. From Chile, they emigrated to Argentina. The Jofres did not lack essentials for survival, like many immigrants in Argentina at that time, and they provided a friendly environment for their five children.

San Justo was renowned for its sweet scent, oozing from the fresh flowers that littered the streets. The town was densely populated with cattle, and Gaucho cowboys dominated the population. San Justo is a rural town about 18 miles outside of the nation's capital city, Buenos Aires. Aristides' older brother, Armando, moved to Brazil in 1923 and started teaching physical education while Aristides worked on a large farm for a man known as Don Horacio, where he milked cows. Armando was born in Brazil, where his parents briefly resided before they eventually moved back to Argentina.

While Aristides did not view himself as a Gaucho, he mixed happily among them and made a lot of friends on the farm. Though he lived comfortably and enjoyed the beauty of San Justo, Aristides felt he was still young, and he could not see himself settling down there for the long term. Aristides wanted to see more of what life could offer; he knew that his options were limited in a small agricultural town. He would often receive letters from his brother in Brazil and always imagined the day that he would surprise him by showing up at his home in São Paulo.

A twist of fate expedited Aristides' decision to leave San Justo when one day, he and his two closest friends, Jose Rotondo and Jose Ataviti, decided to have some fun on their day off one Sunday in the summer of 1927. Every Sunday, the three amigos would go off to have fun together, take a few drinks, and flirt with girls. Aristides was a few years younger than the other two and was not a heavy drinker. In contrast, Rotondo and Ataviti were big drinkers who would enjoy drinking wine until somebody woke them up.

On this particular Sunday, Ataviti pulled up and said, "We are going to have a hell of a night," Rotondo responded as he lifted a bottle of wine and shouted, "We have drinks for the entire day." Rotondo jumped on his horse and led the way while Aristides and Ataviti jumped on the next horse together and followed. A few meters down the path, Rotondo spotted a group of cardinals in a tree and decided it would be funny to scare them by firing a few shots from a gun he was carrying. As he aimed and pulled the trigger, he slipped and lost his balance; the bullet strayed and hit Ataviti in the head. Aristides immediately jumped off the horse to try and revive Ataviti as the blood flowed across his friend's face. Rotondo, now in shock, came over still holding the gun, and Aristides shouted, "You dumb ass! What did you do?" Rotondo stood there, stunned, and speechless. Both of them picked Ataviti's body up and placed him on the saddle. "Let's go! Maybe he is still alive," Aristides said, hoping they could save their friend. Rotondo threw his gun in the bushes as if to hide the weapon, which could incriminate them. "What difference does it make? It was an accident, right? Everybody will understand," Aristides innocently said.

As they made their way back into town, they found everyone enjoying a beautiful summer day. The arrival of Ataviti's body attracted attention and a crowd of people soon gathered around the body of their dear friend. Ataviti was a local artist and was well known in the town, so the sight of his body was too complicated for people to comprehend. Aristides stood there sad, sober, and silent as the sheriff arrived on the scene, waiting for an explanation as Ataviti lay there dead with a bullet in his head. Aristides observed Rotondo, who gazed at the floor. Aristides could not bring himself to accuse Rotondo of murdering their friend before the crowd. Rotondo, in his drunken state, did not have the same compassion; he stepped forward and pointed at Aristides. "It was him, sheriff. It was him," he said as Aristides stood there shaking. As the onlookers stared in astonishment, one of Ataviti's brothers rushed towards Aristides and furiously threw a punch at him. As the sheriff held him back, Aristides finally spoke as he shouted at Rotondo, "Come on...Tell the truth!" "Sheriff, it wasn't me," Aristides pleaded as the sheriff dragged them along, taking them to the station and putting them under arrest.

Aristides and Rotondo were arrested and jailed. In the same cell, they noticed a colleague of theirs from Don Horacio's was passed out after a drunken bar fight. Aristides dozed off but was awakened by a frantic Rotondo who witnessed the man collapse and die on the spot. "You don't deserve my help. Let me sleep!" Aristides told him. As Aristides tried to get back to sleep, he had an idea that would make Rotondo confess what happened. He waited until he heard Rotondo crying in bed and then shouted out for him in a strange voice as if to mimic the dead man. Rotondo was still intoxicated and delusional, so he fell for it as he jumped up and shouted, "Who is that?" He went to Aristides to ask if he had heard the noise, but Aristides played dumb and acted like he did not know what Rotondo was talking about.

By now, it was dark, and Aristides threw the horsewhip from the dead man's body at him and then lit up a match. Rotondo sat there with his eyes wide open, guilt eating away at him as he shook in terror at what had turned into a real-life nightmare. Rotondo prayed and cried for a while, then confessed what happened to the sheriff, which meant that Aristides was released on the spot. Rotondo was also released, but it is not clear on what grounds he was released under or whether he was out on the same day.

Buenos Aires

1920s Buenos Aires

This tragedy expedited Aristides' decision to leave San Justo. Moments after he returned home, he packed his bags and bade farewell to his friends and family before embarking on a new life.

Although Buenos Aires was less than twenty miles away, compared to the small and sleepy town of San Justo it felt like a world away. A major city that was rapidly expanding and full of opportunities was exactly what Aristides sought, and he decided that he would move to the big city to kick off a new chapter in his life. The thought of Brazil was always in his head, but if Buenos Aires felt like a culture shock and a different world, then Brazil was another animal altogether.

As Aristides boarded a train to Buenos Aires, Rotondo was there to say goodbye. "You will never forgive me, right?" Rotondo asked. Aristides responded in jest, telling him, "Shut up, dumb ass! You are still drunk." The two friends hugged, and Aristides took a window seat on the train where he looked out, appreciating the beauty of the little farming town he would soon leave behind.

In Buenos Aires, Aristides met up with a friend by the name of Antonio, who owned a barbershop in the lively San Telmo neighborhood of the city. Antonio, who went by the nickname Tonho, provided Aristides with a place to live and gave him a job at his barbershop. It was during this time in Buenos Aires that Aristides came to terms with the fact that he indeed had been a Gaucho compared to the big city folk. He adapted to city life very well and loved the vibrancy of the town.

Aristides' career in boxing began when he became smitten with a pretty young girl who lived nearby. He was warned to avoid her because her fiancé was a local boxer and neighborhood tough guy who went by the name of Castro. Aristides did not care. He was convinced he was going to win her over, especially after she had noticed him looking at her and gave him a charming smile. Aristides said he did not care about the fiancé and that she was going to be his girl. The word soon got around to Castro. One day Castro saw Aristides on the street and approached him. "Look at me, little man. That girl is my fiancée," to which Aristides indifferently said, "so what?" Enraged, Castro grabbed Aristides and told him: "I am going to give you a chance, shorty. You will fight me at the gym in front of everybody," Aristides said to him that he didn't know how to box, but that didn't matter to Castro. "If you don't show up, I will break your neck in the streets. You have until next Saturday otherwise I will kill you," Castro warned him.

Aristides did not have much time to train, but he did not want to appear cowardly, especially since he saw it as an opportunity to impress the girl. He told Tonho about the situation he found himself in, and the two of them began to train at the barbershop where they made a ring, using the chairs to act as the ropes. Aristides learned a lot of moves very quickly as he worked furiously to make sure that he was not embarrassed. Aristides worked feverishly in a manner that would become familiar with any new task he was given. Tonho himself boxed a little here and there, and he was impressed with what he saw in his friend and admired Aristides's sponge-like mentality for absorbing new information.

Fight day, Aristides arrived first, after a restless night of tossing and turning worrying about the bout and what might happen. Castro entered the ring and immediately said to Aristides, "So you want to get hurt, right?" as the two stared at each other before the action would begin. The bell rang, and right from the start, Castro showered Aristides with punches in bunches and effortlessly avoided the few attacks Aristides could muster up. Castro was in complete control as he landed counterpunches while Aristides swung at air. At the end of the first round, Tonho offered to pull out his buddy, whose mouth was bleeding. "Forget about it, Tonho. I'm going to kill the bastard!" Aristides shot back.

The action in the next round was almost a replay as Castro landed punches at will, while Aristides fought like the novice he was. Castro connected a hard blow, which buckled Aristides' legs. As he followed up to go in for the knockout, the unthinkable happened. Aristides landed a perfect right uppercut, which dropped Castro. Aristides stood there confused, as the referee counted, but Castro did not move. The count reached ten, and the referee raised Aristides' arm in victory as Tonho ran into the ring to embrace him. "Tonho, Tonho, I think I am going to die," Aristides told him as he hobbled out of the ring, looking like a defeated fighter.

Aristides was an instant hero to many in the neighborhood who were disgusted by Castro's abrasive nature. The one person that Aristides wanted to win over most of all came up to him after the bout. It was Castro's fiancée. "I want to thank you for your interest in me, but..." she said. "But what? I would fight again to have you," Aristides told her. "Thank you sir, but he is my fiancé, and I love him with all my heart," she said to him. Aristides, sporting welts and bruises over his face and bloodied lips, looked dejected as Tonho praised him on how impressive his victory had been and how he could help train him for what he saw could be a bright future in boxing. Aristides perked up and asked Tonho if he felt dedicating his time to boxing was worthwhile. Tonho told him about all the riches available in boxing and how he could travel the world if he became successful. "You can be a world champion!" Tonho told him. "A world champion...What a beautiful dream, Tonho!" Aristides said.

Brazil

Aristides took boxing seriously and decided that this would be his career. According to Eder's son, Marcel, Aristides had at least a dozen amateur matches in Argentina, maybe as many as 20. The news of his exploits made its way out of Buenos Aires and to his family back in San Justo. From there, his sisters, Blanca and Eugenia, wrote to Armando in Brazil, informing him about his little brother's adventure in Buenos Aires. One evening Blanca brought a letter which was addressed to Aristides from Brazil. "Eugenia wrote to me about your fights. What a coincidence, brother. I am just opening a boxing gym. I believe in this business. The demand for the sport is huge. Why don't you come and help me? I offer you half of the equity of my company, and you can continue fighting. The boxing managers here are very generous if you are as good as Eugenia told me," Armando wrote.

Aristides read this letter repeatedly until he decided it was time for him to leave Argentina and surprise his brother. Aristides loved his country, and he was enjoying his time in Buenos Aires, but he was still seeking more out of life and sensed that the grass was even greener 1400 miles north in São Paulo. Aristides had been in Buenos Aires for less than a year and was extremely optimistic about his chances of becoming a professional boxer, but Armando's offer sounded so tempting to him.

1920s São Paulo

The decision to try his luck in Brazil was not without a heavy heart. He would be leaving behind his sisters, with whom he had a close bond. Also, he did not speak Portuguese, so he knew that things would not be easy for him once he arrived. However, Aristides was driven by his desire to make something of himself in boxing, and Armando's words of encouragement and the promise to appoint Aristides as co-owner of his gymnasium twisted his arm enough to make the move.

His three sisters were on hand to bid him goodbye at the port before he boarded a cruise ship named the Belvedere. It was an emotional affair as Aristides was leaving behind a family that loved him dearly. His sisters cried as they wished him luck on his new adventure. The first stop en route to Brazil was in the Uruguayan capital of Montevideo, and the city had an immediate impact on Aristides as he took in all the sights of the city in the short time he was there.

Montevideo had a similar effect on him that Buenos Aires did. The vibrancy, pace, hustle, and bustle of the city enforced his belief that he was making the right decision in moving to São Paulo, which was even bigger and more populated than both Montevideo and Buenos Aires. He vowed to himself that he would return to Montevideo in the future; only the next time he would go there it would be as a first-class passenger.

As he jumped back on board to sail from Uruguay to Brazil, he drank half a bottle of wine before going to sleep on the ship that evening but was awakened by the sounds of sirens as they passed the shores of Santa Catarina in the south of Brazil. The ship was rocking, and passengers were shaking, crying, and praying while Aristides was thinking to himself that this could be the end. It turned out that there was a problem with the rudder, and after a few hours it was fixed, and the panic was over. Aristides did not manage to get back to sleep, his nerves a wreck, but he returned to his cabin until the captain announced that they were docking at the port of Santos.

It was January 24, 1928, when Aristides walked off the ship and felt the cool breeze and beautiful sunshine of Brazil for the first time. Straight away, he felt the warmth of the Brazilian people and found them to be very energetic and happy people. While the Argentinians were more serious and sterner, the Brazilians appeared more playful and extroverted.

Aristides remained in Santos for a short time before boarding a train to São Paulo. The entire journey from Santos to São Paulo made Aristides feel as if he was in the jungle as the train went through nothing but rainforest for a little over 30 miles. Once he arrived at Luz station in São Paulo, he hailed a taxi down and gave the driver a crinkled piece of paper with his brother's address on it. He hopped out of the cab when the taxi driver pointed to the house, and Aristides made his way to the front door.

He had rehearsed this moment in his mind hundreds of times but was caught by surprise when a blonde lady answered the door. She had a stunned look on her face that made Aristides feel he had arrived at the wrong house, but when she called out to her husband, "Look, Armando! This guy might be your doppelganger," Aristides became assured that he wasn't wrong, and then Armando came to the door. The two brothers jumped into a firm embrace. They caught up to speed about how things were back in Argentina and what life would now look like in Brazil and what plans Armando had in store. Armando did not know that his brother was going to show up at his home, since the sisters kept it a secret, so it was a pleasant surprise to see his little brother make the brave move from Argentina.

Aristides stayed with Armando for a while as he settled into his new life and country. At first, Aristides missed Argentina and had a tough time communicating with people since the Brazilians could not understand his accent. While he learned Portuguese quickly, he had trouble getting his point across unless Armando was by his side to translate. For three months, Aristides learned Portuguese and gradually overcame his homesickness and the fact he missed his sisters dearly. "I will never forget Argentina, Armando, but I already love this country," he told his brother. One thing he did not like was that everywhere he went, he was called "gringo" and felt that he was being mocked. Armando's wife, Maria, told him that there was no real harm in this, and it was just because of his accent that they called him that and that it was more a term of affection than malice.

Chapter Two

At the turn of the 20th century, boxing was virtually unknown to Brazilians. The very few prizefighters in the country were immigrants with German and Italian backgrounds located in São Paulo state and Rio Grande do Sul. The first documented taste of boxing came to Brazil in São Paulo on March 16, 1913. A French sailor arrived and joined a theater group that was directed by Italian baritone Titta Ruffo. One morning, the cast went to visit Campo do Floresta, where they met an athlete by the name of Luis Sucupira, known as the "Brazilian Apollo" for his large, muscular frame. Sucupira weighed roughly 220 pounds and was an imposing figure with a keen eye for the ladies that were in the cast. He tried to win them over by posing and talking himself up and was suddenly challenged to a boxing match by the French sailor who had boxed in his native land.

The size difference was staggering, as the Frenchman weighed roughly 130 pounds, so the "Apollo" naturally ridiculed him. Sucupira agreed to the match and was handed a pair of boxing gloves by the Frenchman as a boxing ring was drawn up for them to do battle. In the first round, the "Apollo" moved forward, attacking furiously but was made to look awkward as he spent the round swinging and missing his attempts to land a blow on the Frenchman who moved swiftly with elegance. In the second round, after some light counter jabs and body punches, the Frenchman landed a hard right-hand blow to Sucupira's nose, which knocked him out and broke his nose in the process.

As the Frenchman celebrated, "Apollo" apologized for his actions and congratulated his conqueror before leaving and vowing to study the noble art of boxing. Sucupira learned that proper technique could overcome strength and size.

"Apollo" started to promote boxing, and in 1919, through sailor Góes Neto, who had learned boxing techniques in Europe, the sport was publicized and fully recognized in Brazil. After returning from a trip to

Europe, Góes Neto decided to do some exhibitions in Rio de Janeiro, where the nephew of the President of Brazil, Rodrigues Alves, fell in love with boxing. With the support of Rodrigues Alves' nephew, the sport flourished. Between 1920 and 1921, boxing academies were created, and it did not take long for boxing to become a regulated sport, with the creation of the municipal boxing commissions in São Paulo, Santos, and Rio de Janeiro.

By 1922, the first boxer to gain significant prominence was a powerful black heavyweight fighter by the name of Benedito dos Santos. Known as "Ditão," he started boxing at an academy in São Paulo and was said to possess heavy hands. He turned professional in 1923 and rattled off three consecutive knockout victories, all within the first round. It was not long until he attracted the interests of businessmen who saw him as a potentially lucrative investment.

On May 11, 1924, dos Santos was pitted against Italian heavyweight Erminio Spalla. The Italian was vastly more experienced, having won 34 of 41 contests and reigned as the European heavyweight champion. He was coming off a fight against Argentine Luis Angel Firpo before facing off with "Ditão" at Palestra Italia Stadium in São Paulo. "Ditão" started the match well as he knocked the Italian down, but unfortunately, that would be as good as it got for the local favorite as he was on the end of a brutal beating, which ended in the ninth round. "Ditão" had shown incredible courage and refused to quit but paid the consequences as he was left in terrible shape. For health reasons, he was forced to retire just four days later after a major stroke. "Ditão" eventually became paralyzed and later died of a stroke, which many attributed to the injuries he had sustained in his only defeat inside a boxing ring. The result of this fight caused a major stir, and there was a national campaign to outlaw boxing, which ended with the sport being abolished. The ban didn't last for too long and boxing was legalized once again in 1925. The first club to start hosting bouts after the ban was Esperia in São Paulo.

Kid Pratt

Armando Jofre was a professional boxer between 1924 and 1926 when he retired from the ring to become a full-time trainer. Just as he promised, he allowed Aristides to partner up with him as an assistant. Armando was addressed by the name "Kid Pratt," which was a homage to an Argentine boxer "Jess Pratt," whose real name was originally Jose Perez Garcia. Armando introduced new training methods and techniques that went beyond boxing. This led to his accreditation as a pioneer of the sport. With his background in physical education and an abundance of research, he started training his fighters in new breathing exercises, calisthenics, muscle training, roadwork, and more.

Aristides started to go by the name of "Kid Jofre." The nickname "Kid" was widespread in boxing in this period due to a large number of fighters with the same nickname in the United States. Another name his Brazilian friends affectionately called him was Aristo.

Armando was one of the leading trainers in São Paulo in the late 1920s, along with Celestino Caversavio, Batista Bertagnolli, and Sangiovanni. In the São Paulo boxing thesis, *Boxing in São Paulo from 1928 to 1953*, author Breno Costa de Macedo cited a 1931 interview in which Armando stated that his gym was the oldest in town, but Caversazio told of how he was the oldest coach in town and had even mentored Armando and Sangiovanni. In his book, *Mitos e Historias (Myths and Stories)*, Henrique Matteucci backed up this claim of Caversazio's that he had indeed mentored Armando. They cannot have worked together long because it is documented that by 1928 both were running separate boxing academies.

Armando Jofre aka "Kid Pratt"

During this power struggle into the 1930s, many other gyms would open and close, but it was Armando and Caversavio, who gained the most plaudits during this period and ultimately became the prominent two trainers on the scene. Armando ran the Paulista Gym after having worked alongside Jose Volpi as a coach at American Boxing Club, whereas Caversavio ran Caversazio Gym. Armando's gym was initially founded as Kid Pratt Gym before it was named Brazilian Gym, and ultimately, he settled for the name "Paulista Gym."

Initially, Caversazio had the more famous names in his stable with the most popular Brazilian boxer at that time, Italo Hugo being his prized pupil. The power did shift somewhat in 1931 when Hugo had a dispute

with Caversazio and moved over to Armando's gym, creating a sort of rivalry between the two coaches. Breno Costa de Macedo wrote in his thesis it was prevalent for Caversazio to separate from his pupils. Another famous boxer of the time, Attilio Loffredo, switched over to Sangiovanni's stable due to contractual disagreements with Caversazio since he was also a manager and matchmaker and not only the trainer.

Caversazio

Italo Hugo and Attilio Loffredo were perhaps the best known and most successful domestic boxers of this particular era. Hugo compiled a respectable record of 50 wins with 22 knockouts against 18 defeats, and 9 draws. In contrast, Loffredo retired with a ledger of 53 wins with 11 knockouts against 13 losses and 8 draws.

One day the Jofre brothers were walking to the gym to open up when a policeman approached them and raised his voice. "Hey gringos, you are under arrest." Aristides and Armando were very surprised, wondering what on earth they could have done to have warranted such attention. It turned out that there had been some robberies in the area the previous evening, and witnesses told the police that the two men who committed the crimes were foreigners. The Jofres spent three days behind bars before the Argentine government intervened on their behalf and had them released. Two weeks later, two Polish men confessed to being guilty of the crimes, and they were arrested. Upon their release, Aristides quipped, "Our police department is not easy to deal with," to which Armando replied, "Bravo Aristides! You are speaking like an authentic Brazilian now."

Italo Hugo came to visit Armando at his gym one day, and Aristides was in the middle of a sparring session. Hugo was impressed by what he saw, and he told Armando he should try to arrange a fight for him. Two weeks later, on a fight show scheduled for March 15, 1930, at the Antarctica Casino Theater, the promoters needed a flyweight to match against local boy Antonio Freitas. São Paulo being short of flyweights, and Armando encouraged by what he had seen of his brother, put his name forward, and Aristides' Brazilian debut was set. As Aristides made his way to the ring that evening, he felt nervous and intimidated, and it did his confidence no good when a man in the crowd was overheard saying, "Poor boy!" As the two boxers came to the center of the ring, Freitas was smiling as he sized up Aristides. Aristides told him, "We will see if you are smiling at the end," to which Freitas responded, "Calm down, little man."

In the first round, there were flashbacks to the time Aristides took on Castro back in Buenos Aires as Freitas banged him around the ring, bloodying his lip, dominating the action. He performed a little better in the next two rounds but was forced to the ropes on a few occasions and came back to his stool hopelessly behind after three rounds with only one to go. Armando asked if he wanted to quit, and that was immediately ignored as Aristides was determined he was going to get his man in the next round. In the final round, Freitas tried an uppercut with his left hand, which was blocked. Then Aristides landed a perfect counter-right uppercut to his opponent's chin, and he fell halfway out of the ring. The referee began to count as Freitas' body lay motionless as his mouthpiece hung out. The referee reached the count of ten and Armando ran into the ring to lift his brother just as Tonho had done back in Buenos Aires when he scored the improbable comeback victory over the neighborhood tough guy. Hugo, who had refereed the contest, came over to congratulate Aristides and complimented him on the power he possessed in his right hand. When Freitas came around, he got up and congratulated his conqueror. The audience gave Aristides a standing ovation as he walked from the ring back to the locker room.

Aristides was convinced he was going to become a world champion, but because of a shortage of flyweights in Brazil, his brother suggested he should stop fighting and help him full-time in running the day-to-day activities in the gym. Aristides disagreed at first and was willing to fight bigger men, even up to middleweight, but Armando's logic won out. Aristides retired after just the one professional bout in Brazil. "Brother, we have weight categories in boxing. Throughout the history of the sport, you can find a whole bunch of idiots who were destroyed by bigger fighters. You don't want to end up like that," Armando told his brother. The risk was not worth the reward, and it was agreed that Aristides could offer more in the way of developing fighters rather than being a punching bag for larger opponents for meager paychecks.

ACADEMIA DE BOX "KID PRATT"

AULAS DE GYMNASTICA DIURNAS E NOCTURNAS — TRATAMENTO DA OBESIDADE — CURSO ESPECIAL DE GYMNASTICA PARA ALUMNOS PARTICULARES — PREÇOS MODICOS

Director-instructor: KID JOFRÉ — Rua Libero Badaró, 40

Although his dream of becoming a world champion had been short-lived, Aristides was hopeful, and he felt optimistic about teaching the sport. He wrote a letter to Tonho back home in Argentina to inform him of how he had been coping in Brazil:

"My dear Tonho, you should have seen my debut in Brazil. I spent four rounds being punished like a horse stealer, but at the last minute, I remembered our training at the barbershop and threw that crooked uppercut, remember? It worked out well here too. I became a little famous around here, and a local champion repeated your words, said that I have dynamite power in my right hand. But I won't detonate that dynamite anymore. There are no flyweight boxers in Brazil, and my brother doesn't want me fighting bigger guys. So, I decided to stop fighting, and I am going to help my brother in his gym. You once said that I would be a world champion. I won't. But maybe, as a coach, I could make one, don't you think? Wish me well and write to me sometimes – Aristides."

Tonho would write back and often communicate with Aristides as he sent over training manuals from Argentina. Boxing had been in Argentina for longer than Brazil. As a result, the techniques were more advanced, so Aristides was driven to mix the best of both schools and help his brother expand the game in Brazil.

As mentioned earlier, Brazilian boxing was very much in its infancy, and with very little external influence, so it had been fated to grow organically. Aristides also shared his brother's beliefs in the importance of not only teaching boxing techniques but in training the body and the mind to be healthy and for boxers to be full-time athletes rather than only fighters. Despite São Paulo being one of the largest and fastest-growing cities in the world, Aristides felt they lagged far behind when it came to fitness and health programs taught to its public. He also thought that the will and courage taught through boxing were valuable attributes for young people to possess in all walks of life.

The scientific approaches that the brothers introduced were far beyond their time as they would listen carefully to the heartbeat of their pupils in addition to counting the pulses and studying the nervous system. Over his career, Armando worked many roles in boxing from trainer to referee to judge to a matchmaker. Because of the excellent reputation he had built as the head of his academy, he was recruited to work in the then capital city of Rio de Janeiro in 1932. At this point, Rio was the central boxing city of Brazil, so the arrival of Armando provided a lot of excitement for local fight aficionados there. Armando did not only teach boxing; he also coached wrestling and helped increase the popularity of that sport as well. Armando left Aristides to run his academy in São Paulo, which was an excellent opportunity for his little brother as he took to the responsibility well. This helped Aristides meet a family that would change his life and shape an essential history in Brazilian sports.

The Zumbanos

Left to right: Erasmo, Antonio, Ralph, Don Salvador and Dona Maria, Ricardo and Higino

The Zumbano family was from the town of Mococa, a small, humble place a little over 160 miles north of the megalopolis of São Paulo. They had moved to the state capital in 1930 in search of a better economic situation and way of life. In total, there were nine Zumbano siblings, born to Salvador and Maria, Italian immigrants from the coastal town of Calabria who arrived in Brazil in 1902. The Zumbano family was one of the many Italian families who were lured to Brazil in the early 20th century with promises of untold wealth and beautiful weather, but the reality was that life in Brazil was no easier than it had been in Italy. The first child of Salvador and Maria was Higino in 1908, and he had eight siblings by the names of Walter, Waldemar, Angelina, Olga, Antonio, Erasmo, Ralph, and Ricardo. Salvador was a very gentle and kindhearted man who encouraged his children to engage in sport from a young age in 1925.

The family had seen a movie called *Daredevil Jack*, a silent film released in 1920, featuring the reigning heavyweight world champion, Jack Dempsey. The movie featured many boxing scenes, and the family was hooked on what they saw. It inspired them to put up a makeshift ring in their backyard between two orange trees and two guava trees. From there, they put the ropes around it and started to box with each other. Higino was handy at working with leather, and he helped make a heavy bag and a punching ball. The family began to absorb all the boxing information they could, either on the radio or in newspapers and magazines. The classic Jack Dempsey vs. Luis Firpo match was one they discussed passionately. The story of how Dempsey was knocked out of the ring and landed on the press reporters and recovered to knock out the Argentine known as the "Wild Bull of the Pampas" was a hot topic of conversation. Other heroes such as Georges Carpentier and Gene Tunney increased their interest in the sport of boxing.

The sport was popular around this time in Mococa, with many children getting into boxing. A Swiss gentleman by the name of Walter Wolger came to help the Zumbanos. They saw their little gym grow from only a handful of kids to about 80 students within four months. The growth was staggering. Unfortunately, they lost these students after a man by the name of Hector Ragazzi defeated Wolger. Higino later said how this had been the death of boxing in the small town.

1920s Mococa

The Zumbanos were a hard-working family, but like many, they struggled to make ends meet. Salvador worked around the clock as a metallurgical technician to make sure he paid the rent, and his children could attend school. Maria baked cakes, which she sold at the local circus. A man by the name of Mr. Angelo ruled the town with an iron fist. He owned half of the homes in Mococa, a large amount of land, all the factories, and he was cozy with the local police. A lady that went by the name Zoraida was the only one he did not have power over. It was Zoraida who came to the Zumbanos rescue when Mr. Angelo was trying to kick them out of their home because they were late on rent.

The Zumbanos struggled with the loss of all their boxing students, and Angelo sent the police around to evict them from their house. Salvador was not going to go down without a fight and told the policeman that if he tried to come inside, he would never leave alive. Salvador bolted the door and instructed his kids to get axes and knives should the police try to force their entrance. The police officer was quite fond of Salvador and felt sorry for him, so he cut him a break. Rather than face the wrath of Angelo, they contacted Zoraida to tell her what was happening, and she instructed the Sergeant to hold off until Mr. Angelo arrived, and they would talk. Soon after, Mr. Angelo forgave Salvador and promised that he would not pursue the eviction on the condition that he made his payments on time. Mr. Angelo also promised Salvador that one of his boys would get a job in one of the factories he owned. Walter is the only Zumbano child who wasn't bitten by the boxing bug, so he began working in the factory and eventually became an industrialist who invented a gunpowder fixation tool.

Unfortunately, the Brazilian revolution of 1930 resulted in the closing of half of the schools in Mococa, and the town became a tough place to make a living besides being in a major state of depression. Salvador went to São Paulo and found work in his industry and then sent for his family shortly after. At first, they were amazed by the size of the buildings and pace of the city as they settled into their new home at 15 Rua Alfredo Maia with Maria's brother Marcelo Ziravello. "It was a big family, and we would starve. We were struggling back in Mococa; that's the ugly truth," Ralph explained in the 1986 documentary *Quebrando a Cara (Breaking the face.)*

Brazil was going through a crazy time at this point. In July of 1930, the governor of Paraiba, João Pessoa Cavalcânti de Albuquerque, was assassinated, and this created a great deal of unrest and contempt for the federal government and outgoing president Washington Luis. Pessoa was the vice-presidential candidate of Getulio Vargas. Pessoa had refused to back Julio Prestes, who then, in turn, led a revolt against Pessoa's state government. Pessoa responded by ordering raids of the homes on those he suspected had conspired against him, and this resulted in him finding love letters from a mistress of political rival João Duarte Dantas. These love letters were leaked to the press and came to light in the public eye, which infuriated Dantas.

Dantas murdered Pessoa while Pessoa was on an official visit to Recife. João Pessoa lost his life on a quiet evening at the Glória pastry shop. Pessoa had gone to Recife, the capital of Pernambuco state, to deal with issues on the war that his government had with rebels from the city of Princesa, which was led by colonels in the Paraíba countryside who wouldn't accept the increase of taxes that the government had implemented. Around 4 pm, Pessoa, along with a few of Pernambuco state's political leaders, went to photographer Piereck's studio, on Imperatriz Street, in downtown Recife. He was murdered as he walked to the pastry shop to have some tea before returning to Pernambuco.

The move to São Paulo did not bring instant prosperity for the Zumbanos, and the situation was hardly better than it had been back in Mococa as they struggled to earn a decent wage. While Marcelo helped them out with his home, he couldn't do much more than that as they struggled to find jobs. Higino, Waldemar, and Walter would hunt animals to bring home to help them fight off hunger.

Before Armando went to Rio, he met a young man who helped shape the future of Brazilian boxing, although, at that time, nobody would have any knowledge of what was about to unfold. Higino Zumbano initially just thought of ways he could make money to put aside and move back to Mococa to reunite with his girlfriend. Higino had been in a long-term relationship with a girl named Cleonice and could not stop thinking of her. Higino had wanted to finish his studies. One day, he took the day off to find a college course he could take in the evening following his shift at his factory job. Across from Praça da Sé, he saw a big multi-story building with a sign announcing, "Merchant College – Night Courses." Hence, he crossed over and looked around the building, trying to see if he could find any information, and by pure chance, he saw a boxing academy. Higino recalled his days in Mococa and the boxing scene that thrived there before his mentor, Walter Wolger was defeated.

As soon as he walked inside, he saw the boxing ring, the punching bag, and all the boxers working out. He sought the attention of the man who was supervising the gym. It was then that he met Armando Jofre and told him that he would be interested in boxing at the gym. Higino did not have enough money to afford the membership fee, but they worked out a price affordable to him. Initially, Armando was hard on Higino and would not let him fight. Armando put Higino through a rigorous training routine for a month before he granted him a chance to measure his technical skills against a sparring opponent.

Higino was tired after the first couple of days, and Armando warned him, "If you don't have balls, you will give up soon." Higino showed resilience, and after a few days, he would not get tired at the workouts as he worked out intensely. He never complained as he patiently waited to be called upon to showcase his boxing ability. In the first couple of days, Armando warned him that if he dared to step into the ring, he would kick him out of the gym, and he would not allow him to come back, a threat he took seriously. After a month of showing up, working hard, and doing as he was told, Higino pleaded to be given a chance to show what he could do in the ring. Armando and one of his other coaches tried to have some fun as they put him in with one of their better boxers, a man by the name of Orlando.

Left to right: Higino, Antonio, unidentified, Ralph &
Erasmo

The session did not go as anticipated, and Higino had Orlando groggy in no time. Armando was impressed with what he saw and knew that with such expertise, Higino could not have been a first-timer. Armando asked Higino if he had ever fought before, and Higino told him that he had but that he didn't have the chance to tell Armando since he would not let him. Higino then was able to spar with all the other fighters in the gym and impressed further and then told Armando that he had a brother named Waldemar who was just as good that he would like to bring along. This was music to Armando's ears who must have felt that his academy was about to secure the talents of two excellent boxers with great potential. Because of failing eyesight, Waldemar was in more of a hurry to begin a professional boxing career than Higino, who still had his mind on college. The more time Higino and Waldemar spent at the gym, the closer they became to Armando, and it wasn't long until they were formally introduced to Aristides.

Higino had been angling to move back home until he met the Jofres, and that kept him in São Paulo, where things started to look a little better for the Zumbanos. From there, the three would go and attend boxing shows at the Antarctica Casino, where they were able to see Italo Hugo up close. Higino started participating in amateur fights and, at first, began to struggle with mixed results but then found some consistency as Aristides worked with him closely. His first tournament victory came when he defeated an opponent from Santos by the name of Camilo. They fought to a draw the previous year, but this time Camilo was stronger than Higino and landed the first big punch, which looked sure to finish Higino, but to the astonishment of those on hand, Higino attacked ferociously in return and put Camilo down for the count. For his victory, Higino was given a small cash prize and a fancy winter coat, which was passed down the family to Eder Jofre many years later. Higino's interest in boxing slowly died down as the family suffered further financial hardships, and he spent less time in the gym as he became involved in politics. He went back to Mococa to see his girlfriend Cleonice and found that news of his boxing exploits reached home, and he was viewed as a hero.

Political Problems

After a short while, Higino came back to São Paulo with Cleonice but became caught up on the wrong side of the law. He was heavily involved in the revolution and was sentenced to two years in prison due to his involvement in the communist movement that was opposing President Getulio Vargas. Initially, the police couldn't find him as he was living like a drifter going from town to town, escaping the cops at every turn until one day they found him at his parents' home. He tried to escape and ran out of the back of the house as the police fired shots at him. He got further away, swimming through rivers and running through trees. Eventually, it was two construction workers who stopped him, and since he did not have much energy left, Higino did not put up a fight. The police finally caught up with him and took him to Rio, where they threw him in prison. In prison, he struggled with a lack of food, became sick often, and, upon release, was very skinny and suffering from tuberculosis.

Along with Higino, Waldemar was part of the revolution and was also detained by authorities and spent time behind bars. Higino and Waldemar both believed that communism would be the best path to create a better Brazil and sought to fight for freedom for all but matters only became worse during this period as the "Paulista War" played out. The battle lasted for over a decade. The problems with the law always loomed large over the brothers as they were arrested several times and beaten in prison.

The Paulista War was the uprising of the population of the state of São Paulo against the 1930 coup d'état when Getúlio Vargas forcibly assumed the nation's presidency. Vargas was supported by the military and the political elites of Minas Gerais, Rio Grande do Sul, and Paraíba. On July 9,

1932, about 35,000 men from two Brazilian federal states - São Paulo and Mato Grosso do Sul – rose in arms against the dictatorship of Getúlio Vargas, demanding the return to constitutionality and democracy. This movement became known as the 'Constitutionalist,' while its members became known as the 'Paulistas.' The Brazilian government reacted with brute force, deploying over 100,000 troops supported by heavy artillery and combat aircraft. The result was the most significant war ever fought in Brazil. It was the first-ever campaign to see strategic aerial bombardment conducted in the Americas in addition to seeing the first aircraft shot down in air combat, and the first battle to see night bombing operations. Following three months of bitter fighting – which often degenerated into trench warfare – the Paulistas were defeated. Indeed, the end of this conflict brought an end to a period of successive civil wars fought in Brazil since 1889.

Only in 1945, when Getulio Vargas issued a statement freeing political prisoners and pardoning those who performed political crimes during the last decade, could Higino and Waldemar feel free and clear.

Waldemar Makes His Point

Waldemar viewed boxing as more than a sport, but as an art form and an activity that could benefit and educate young people. He had turned professional in 1930, but due to his political activities, his career was somewhat hindered in the early days. Overall, he believed he had maybe as many as 200 fights, but this is difficult to quantify as it wasn't clear if he added the numbers of his amateur fights to his professional fights.

He once spoke on the subject of a potential bout with his friend Attilio Loffredo, who held the national welterweight title but said that he did not wish to fight Loffredo. He explained that he considered himself to be too close to Loffredo to swap leather with him due to their involvement in the revolution where they became very close. "The title is in the hands of my brother (Loffredo), a man I do not wish to fight. We were together in the revolution and formed an everlasting friendship. He is the only man I wouldn't have pleasure in confronting," he said.

With his name on the government's wanted list, Waldemar had the idea that he should adopt a different name for boxing so that he could avoid the law and make money to fund medical treatment for Higino. This was common during this time, with many boxers opting to use a pseudonym over their real name. The name Waldemar adopted was "Frank Eder,"

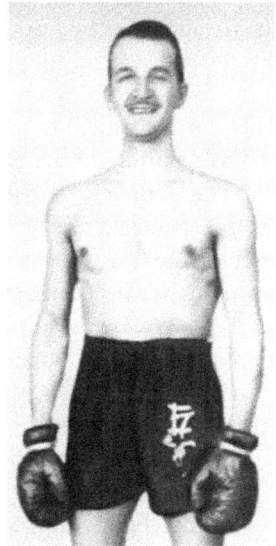

which was used after the name of a German boxer by the name of "Gustaff Eder." Perhaps these name changes are why it can also be challenging to validate the number of matches Waldemar claimed to fight. Waldemar often traveled and even competed in many fights at various circus tents around the country. His style of boxing was described as intelligent and precise.

While still an active professional boxer, Waldemar also acted in many other capacities. He was a referee, a judge, a trainer, and an author. Such was his passion for teaching boxing, and demonstrating the beauty behind the art form, he wrote a book called *"Boxing at everyone's reach,"* which was well received and used as a reference for several years. He had myopia which meant that the time he had left in which to make money with his fists was limited, but because of his passion for the sport, he knew he could spread his wisdom and make a living within the sport long after his eyes rendered it impossible to do such within the four corners of the ring.

In Guaranésia, southern Minas Gerais, Waldemar set up in the town square and preached bout the benefits of boxing and told people how it was the most powerful thing on earth. "Look at me. I only weigh 130 pounds, and I can't see shit with my sore eyes. However, there is nobody in this city who can beat me," he proclaimed. A large man in the crowd mocked him and told him that if he wasn't so blind, he would accept his challenge.

The people who gathered around to listen to Waldemar were amused by the spectacle and wanted to see him fight so a bout was arranged at a circus against a man named "Janjao." Though not a boxer, "Janjao" was a strongman who weighed over 200 pounds, and while boxing rules were used, there was no ring. A large formation of clouds threatened rain, which would make it almost impossible for Waldemar to move around. The owner of the circus introduced both men. "Janjao" was given a warm reception as members of the audience encouraged him to "kick his ass," while Waldemar was mocked as he was at such a physical disadvantage.

If the people did not believe that boxing was an effective art form before the fight, they would soon find out, as "Janjao" tried with all his might to connect hard blows. Waldemar was able to avoid his attacks and punish "Janjao" with his superior technical skills and movement. The storm kicked in, but the crowd didn't diminish as Waldemar lay a beating on his foe before punctuating the fight with a powerful uppercut, which laid the larger man out for the count. "Janjao" was rushed to a hospital while Waldemar quickly left the town as he felt it would not be the best time to convince the people that boxing was not a violent art form with rumors that "Janjao" was in a coma.

Chapter Three

Despite only being absent for a few months, Armando came back from Rio after having left his mark on the sport there, but he wanted to be close to his friends and family again. By now, Aristides had built a solid reputation for himself, in addition to some strong relationships with his boxers, and would remain the full-time head trainer as Armando shifted more into working the background as a manager and matchmaker in both boxing and wrestling. He helped bring a lot of wrestling shows to São Paulo. He was influential in the movement which saw São Paulo slowly overtake Rio as the nation's major boxing market.

Armando was well connected and as a result, created a large network that helped grow the sport between the 1920s and 1940s. Moreover, he was one of the biggest influences concerning the organization of amateur tournaments and the overall participation in boxing. He was perhaps the most responsible when it came to developing highly skilled coaches and teachers. He took a lot from his time in Rio and used what he learned to help the sport in São Paulo. He spoke about the difference between the two cities, and one of the major differences was that Rio had an arena dedicated to boxing, called the Brazil Stadium. In contrast, boxing was fading away gradually in São Paulo, with no designated stadium to host regular shows and a fast decline in the number of local shows. Most of the São Paulo boxers around this time had to take their talents on the road to Rio to compete and make money.

Aristides had become acquainted with the Zumbano family, and they were his closest friends in Brazil as their friendship extended beyond boxing. They truly made him feel at home, and he felt the love that he had so dearly missed from his sisters back home in Argentina. Aristides would hang out with the Zumbanos all the time, and they often invited him to their home. It took a while for him to agree to visit their home because he was painfully shy but one day, he needed to have a pair of gloves fixed and Armando said that Higino would be able to repair them. Armando was playing matchmaker and said to his brother, "You might even like the view over there." Aristides asked him what he was talking about and Armando told him that the Zumbanos have two sisters and that they are single. "And you waited until now to tell me this?" Aristides asked.

One casual Saturday afternoon lunch at their home would change his life when he expressed his admiration for their sister Angelina. Throughout lunch, he could not keep his eyes off her but could not work up the courage to say anything to her. Angelina was not quite as impressed, thinking that it was Armando who kept looking at her. "What a creep!" she told her brothers, blasting their friend who was a married man. The resemblance was so striking between Armando and Aristides that, just like when Armando's wife saw Aristides, they were mistaken for one another. Angelina's brothers explained to her how this was not Armando and that it was his brother who came over from Argentina. Angelina was embarrassed and vowed to treat Aristides with more respect the next time he visited. Aristides had spent the whole night thinking of Angelina and pondering what move to make and how to broach the subject to his friends.

The following day, Aristides went to the gym but couldn't take his mind off Angelina and even sang songs about her in Spanish. Armando noticed something was different about his brother and asked what girl had caught his eye. Aristides told Armando that it was Angelina, and Armando encouraged him to go and ask her on a date, knowing that she came from a great family and was a nice girl. Aristides would go to the Zumbano household every few days with a new pair of gloves for Higino to fix but the real purpose for these visits was to grab the attention of Angelina.

A month had passed since the time of the first lunch meeting, but Aristides had not forgotten about Angelina. One Sunday afternoon, Aristides dressed in his best clothes as he made his way to the Zumbano home for lunch. "Why are you so dressed up?" Salvador asked him. "You look like you are about to propose to a girl!" he added. "Yes sir. It's your daughter," Aristides told him. "Which one?" Salvador asked. "Angelina," Aristides announced to him. "Well, if she wants to, but you guys take it easy," Salvador responded.

At lunch, Aristides drank a little more than usual and got up to make a toast but mixed his speech up going back and forth between Spanish and Portuguese. "I want to marry her sooner or later, but I don't have money for the ring," he said. Salvador was confused as Aristides had said 'anillo' (the Spanish word for 'ring'), whereas the word in Portuguese is 'anel.' Waldemar is the one who pointed out that he was talking about a wedding ring. Once it clicked with Salvador, he slapped the table and said, "It doesn't matter. You are a good guy, and that is enough!"

Their courtship began there, and they instantly fell in love with one another, and it wasn't long before their relationship became serious. Aristides and Angelina tied the knot on November 7, 1933, at a registration office located at 177 Rua Benjamin Constant in São Paulo. It was a small gathering of close family, and from there, they went to a small ceremony  where everybody drank vermouth and danced the night away.

Aristides was back to work the following day at the gym as he had a team of boys to take to Rio de Janeiro for a tournament. This tournament solved the issue of the honeymoon as he brought his new wife along with him on the trip. The beauty of the Copacabana beach was a far cry from the working-class neighborhood from which they came. After a week in Rio, it was back to São Paulo where they furnished their new home.

Aristides took the new responsibilities of married life seriously and vowed that he would work harder and devote more time to boxing in the hopes of creating a champion. It was not long after settling into their new home that the Jofres were expecting their first child. Aristides hoped for a boy with his mind made up that he was going to make him into a world champion just as he had dreamed of becoming himself before dedicating his time to become a boxing coach.

The first child of Aristides and Angelina was born on August 12, 1934, and was a girl named after Angelina's mother, Maria, Lucrecia Maria Jofre. The following year Angelina became

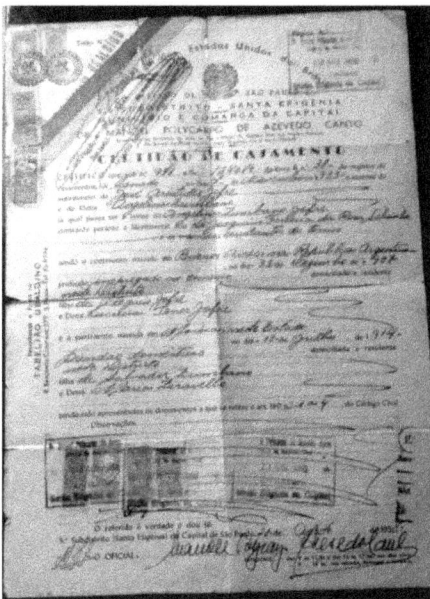

Marriage certificate of Aristides and Angelina

pregnant again, and Aristides bought them a new house that was located at the back of a new gym he was opening. Aristides was convinced this time it was going to be a boy and told Angelina they would keep trying for a baby until they had a boy.

In November of 1935, disaster struck as Aristides was carted off to prison while he was teaching his students at his new gym. He was accused of being a communist, and the police felt that he knew where Higino was located. Aristides was not into politics and was unaware of Higino's location, but the police thought he was lying and threw him in a basement in prison with a large number of activists and people involved in the revolutionary movement. After one month, he was finally allowed to have visitors, and Angelina came to see him.

Feeling depressed and lonely, Angelina suggested to Aristides that she would abort the baby. Aristides assured her that he would be out in a month, and she did not have to abort the child. "I will be out soon. Take care of our little champ!" he told her. After three months incarcerated, Aristides was released on March 10, 1936, and once the cell door opened, he walked outside and hopped on a trolley that took him home. He stepped inside the home and saw pregnant Angelina with her family around and a midwife by the name of Rosa. Angelina had been helped by Rosa through the pregnancy. Rosa taught her various muscle relaxation techniques and kept her calm and happy through this challenging time.

In the late hours of March 26, Angelina woke up and alerted her husband. "Aristides. It's time! Go get Rosa," she told him, and in a flash, Aristides jumped out of bed and put on his clothes. He ran two miles to Rosa's house and woke her up to bring her back to assist his wife in delivering the baby. "Where is your car?" Rosa asked. "I don't have a car," he told her. "Well, let's get moving because I don't have one either," she said. Rosa struggled to keep pace with Aristides as he sprinted back anxiously to meet his wife. Rosa finally arrived at the home and struggled to get through the boxing gym towards the bedroom in time to deliver the baby. "It's a boy Aristides!" Angelina said as she held the baby for the first time. "It's a boy! It's a boy!" he excitedly said. The next morning the Zumbanos came by the house to see the baby, and Salvador brought a bottle of wine. "Waldemar, what is that name you fought under?" he asked his son. "Frank Eder," Waldemar told him. "I don't like Frank. It's a gringo's name," Salvador said. "Eder is good," he added. One week later, the name of the child was made official: Eder Jofre.

Eder was a healthy and happy baby who spent a lot of his early days in the gym watching his father at work. If he was not in the gym, he was often taking a nap at any time of the day. Little Eder was a very sleepy baby. Angelina's mother, Maria, was always around the house in those days looking after the children when Aristides was working, or when Angelina needed to rest or to go somewhere. One incident gave Maria a little shock when Eder was sleeping. She accidentally touched his foot, and he raised his arms. She thought that was strange and tried it again and again, and he did the same thing as though he was doing a sit-up. "Look, Aristides, if you touch his foot, he raises his torso. Isn't that incredible?" she said to her son-in-law, who was amused. Aristides sat there and observed his son and said, "This boy will be a son of a gun."

There was a fright in early October of Eder's first year when one day, he woke up feeling very sick with a high fever. Aristides tried to find his friend Waldemiro, a local doctor and friend of the family. He could not locate him in time, so Aristides and Angelina took Eder down the street to a newly opened clinic and had the doctor examine him. The doctor told Aristides that he thought Eder had measles to which Aristides became upset and told the doctor it was something more severe. "Where did you go to school?" he asked. "The University, where else?" the doctor responded. "It doesn't seem like it. I am not a doctor, and I can see this is pneumonia," Aristides shot back. They left the doctor's office and luckily ran into Waldemiro, and he concurred with Aristides that Eder had contracted pneumonia.

For three days, Aristides stayed home by his

Young Eder

son's side with Angelina as they tried multiple homemade remedies, and Eder was soon back to normal. Within 12 months, Eder was walking and enjoyed spending time in the gym watching the boxers. He would imitate some of the boxers and even do chin-ups of his own and copied the moves which he saw. "No one remembers too early when you first are aware of your surroundings as a little child. I remember only that the gym was my kindergarten and my playroom. I was underfoot to all the cousins and uncles who were around there. But they were patient with me. They played with me, and they talked to me. I guess the first word I learned was 'fight,'" Eder told *Boxing Illustrated* in 1964.

At a young age, Aristides put the gloves on Eder and started teaching him techniques and punching patterns and the value of shadowboxing. It wasn't long before little Eder was jumping rope with the professional boxers. "I was a little monkey, and I imitated all the boxers I would see in the gym. It may sound stupid, but I was the hardest-training little boy in the world," Eder said about those days.

Moving and Shaking

Erasmo had shown great promise in boxing and music throughout his youth. He was a bubbly, outgoing kid that everyone liked. He did well as an amateur as he performed well through several tournaments and caused a stir in the gym when he knocked out a boxer by the name of Hans Norbert while sparring one day in 1937. "I have fought people forty pounds heavier than me, but this guy was in my weight class, and I would hesitate to fight him," Norbert said. Norbert was a professional fighter from Austria, known as "The Austrian Machine Gun." He had first visited Brazil in 1935 on his way to Argentina, where he had a couple of bouts but ended up back in Brazil, where he decided to settle down. He made a big impression on the Zumbano family, especially Waldemar, who he had bettered in a sparring session one day.

Norbert had come to the gym and, in broken Portuguese, asked if he could train. The Jofres and Zumbanos wondered who he was and didn't see him as someone who looked or acted like a fighter. They decided that they would have some fun with him and asked him to get ready so that they could see him in the ring. Waldemar observed how Norbert wrapped his hands, tied his laces, and prepared and thought that perhaps he wasn't such a soft touch after all since it looked like he knew what he was doing. That inclination proved accurate as Norbert left Waldemar with a bloodied nose, puffy lips, and a sore jaw before asking him, "Who are you?" to

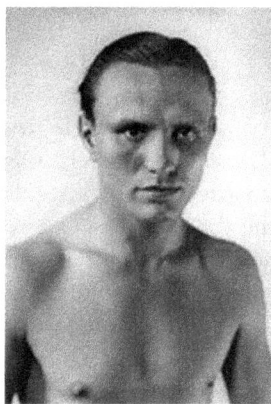

Hans Norbert

which Norbert responded, "I am Hans Novotny Norbert, from Austria."

Norbert became friendly with the Zumbanos and ended up falling in love with Olga. Olga was the third youngest of the Zumbano clan, and very early on, the desire to fight was burning inside of her, but she took up a different combat sport. She entered into wrestling and eventually became famous in Brazil, making a long and illustrious career for herself. When she was a kid, she would go along to the gym with her brothers, and it was one day where she walked upstairs and found women practicing boxing. "When I saw that, I thought, 'I am at the right place! I'll learn how to fight!' Olga said in *Quebrando a Cara*. She started to box, and because she was strong for her size, she soon ran out of opponents by the time she was around 11, so most of the practice she would get would be with her brothers. Although there were no laws against women working out and training in boxing, there were no competitions or leagues for women to compete in, so she gravitated towards wrestling.

Olga Zumbano

Olga took to wrestling quickly and saw a lot of success early on before committing herself to become a full-time wrestler in the form of Lucha Libre. Immediately, Olga clicked with Hans, they started courting and were married shortly after. Hans did not think that Olga should be wrestling as he thought women's wrestling was an ugly profession, so Olga made sure she did all her training in secret. Norbert had excellent results in Brazil and fought there until 1939 without defeat, but the breakout of World War II took him back to Austria, and he brought Olga with him.

President Getúlio Vargas was sympathetic to Nazi fascism when it took over Germany and Italy. He was also sympathetic to strong regimes in general, where the centralized government could run the country without any opposition. President Vargas's sympathy became apparent when he overruled the Constitution and became a dictator in 1937. President Vargas demonstrated an ambiguity concerning the Ação Integralista Brasileira Party. On the one hand, he took advantage of this party because it was against communism and did what he could not do as President. Yet, this party also started to create internal problems and had to be eliminated before it became so strong that it would undermine Vargas' government.

In 1937, Vargas outlawed the Ação Integralista Brasileira and Communist parties and ordered their dismantlement. He also banned Nazi political activity in all of the Brazilian provinces. At that time, Vargas, due to internal pressure, aligned his government towards a "nationalist policy," and he avoided familiarity with fascist regimes. Regardless of this alignment, radicalism was still evident within the Brazilian society, and the power of the Getúlio Vargas dictatorship increased gradually. After World War II, the Brazilian Army would play an important role in ending this dictatorship. Brazil had accepted large numbers of Italian and German immigrants for more than one hundred years before World War II, and their descendants had secured important positions within the Brazilian government and society, including the Brazilian Armed Forces. They had a significant influence on decision-makers. In the 1930s, German immigrants numbered more than 900,000, and the Italians more than 1,500,000.

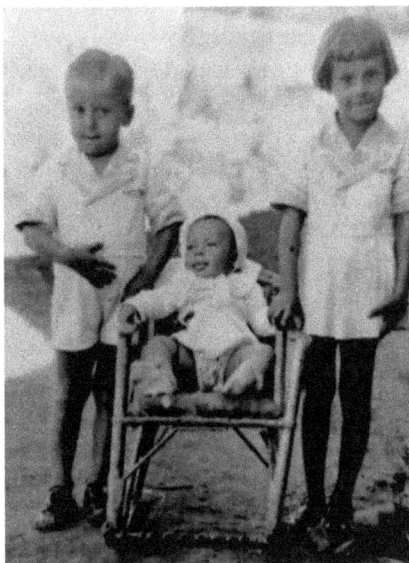

Eder and Lucrecia with a family friend's child

As the Jofre family struggled financially with these extra mouths to feed, Aristides felt they would make a fresh start in nearby Santos in 1938. In Santos, Aristides trained and managed local boxers and even built boxing gyms in the city. From here, Aristides was asked to train the popular Attilio Loffredo. Loffredo was from São Paulo, but now campaigning in Rio and was also training fighters and running a camp on the beach there. The family spent six months in Rio but moved back to São Paulo after one day at the beach when Eder almost drowned after running out of the sight of his family and into the ocean.

It was 1939 when Eder had his first-ever sparring session. There was a fight card at Luna Park in Santos. One of the promoters, a gentleman by the name of João Turco had been very impressed with the work he saw Eder doing on a punching bag, so he suggested that Aristides put him on in the preliminaries as a little show for the spectators. His opponent was his sister, Lucrecia. She was older and bigger and fairly proficient since she had spent a lot of time around the gym as well. She attacked and threw punches at Eder, but Eder was not afraid and was able to avoid punches with style, which thrilled the crowd greatly. "I think it was the first and only time I beat him," Lucrecia joked. After one round, Lucrecia was replaced by Eder's eight-year-old uncle, Ricardo Zumbano, and the two put on a great show. Aristides started to earn more money through boxing and was able to buy a bigger gym on São João Avenue back in São Paulo and moved into a new house on Rua Gabriel Covelli in Parque Peruche. Armando was devoting more time to the business side of the sport and also working in wrestling, so Aristides was coaching children, amateurs, professionals, and also teaching general physical fitness courses to ensure that the family made ends meet.

Zumbano III

Antonio, nicknamed Tonico, was one of Aristides' first pupils to turn professional, and despite making an indelible impression on Brazilian boxing, he probably did not live up to his potential due to his lifestyle and the infrastructure of Brazilian boxing at the time. He had been the third of the Zumbanos to pick up boxing after Higino and Waldemar. His professional debut is listed in 1937 on Boxrec but the Jofre-Zumbano family said that it was on Eder's birth date of March 26, 1936. His career spanned until 1950, but his activity was somewhat sporadic.

He was famous during his days, but this had as much to do with the life he lived outside of the ring as his accolades inside the squared circle. Tonico was a fiery character with a big punch, but he rarely came into the ring in optimum shape, and he was never able to get to the level of national champion. "If I had money, I swear, I would take Tonico to America. With those powerful hands, he would be a world champion in less than a year," Armando told his brother. Henrique Matteucci described Antonio as "impulsive and violent" and a fighter who carried the same personality traits into the boxing ring, which resulted in him being an excellent knockout artist.

Antonio spent many nights playing pool and cards and staying out until all hours, never getting enough sleep, which meant that he would show up to the gym hungover and late and even showed up to fights in the same condition. "If he didn't win the fight in four or five rounds, he'd get tired and lose the fight," Eder explained. Eder said that his uncle would spend roughly one week training for a fight, and as soon as the match would end, he would go straight to the club to dance, drink, gamble, and enjoy the fast life. "He didn't like working much," Ralph Zumbano said in *Quebrando a Cara*.

"A lot of times when there were like ten guys, he would knock all of them out in the street. He would punch them all. Other guys would have knives and guns but not him," Ricardo Zumbano recalled in *Quebrando a Cara*. Antonio was known in all São Paulo gatherings of this time. Everybody knew him from all walks of life from the pimps and prostitutes to the movie stars and people in high society.

One of Tonico's closest friends from the neighborhood was a notorious trickster by the name of Quinzinho. "Zumbano would fight in the ring as much as he would fight on the streets. He would pick any fight. Sometimes, he would just leave it, when he saw the guy wasn't worth it, he would tell the guy, 'Go on honey, say farewell, leave.' When it was a good fight, he would enjoy it. He would enjoy fighting on the street, but that would bring attention, and wherever he would hit, the hair wouldn't grow again. I know that because he punched me a bunch of times," Quinzinho said in *Quebrando a Cara*.

Ralph was one of the boxers in the family whom Eder looked up to the most as a child, but he felt that Antonio was the best of the Zumbanos. "He had a heavy punch, a hard right hand. I learned that punch from him," he said. While Ralph was more of a mover who relied on swift feet and quick moves to avoid blows, it was Antonio who had the most devastating punching technique. Eder said that how Antonio planted his feet and used his shoulders while also covering his chin was very impactful from a young age and helped form his technique. While Eder admired Ralph and felt his style was especially useful, it was Tonico's style he most tried to emulate when he would practice in the gym and mimicked his moves when shadowboxing. "He wasn't very tall, but he was powerful and hit hard with both hands. I think I got this from him," Eder added. Thankfully, the one aspect of Tonico that Eder did not pick up on was his lifestyle, which Eder acknowledges was his uncle's downfall.

Much like Waldemar's career statistics, it is hard to find out precisely what Tonico's final record was. Boxrec has him listed as 20-4-2 with nine knockouts, but in Henrique Matteucci's *O Galo de Ouro* book, he said that Tonico had 139 professional bouts, with 73 knockouts. However, Matteuci didn't specify the win-loss numbers. Many reports from this era point to the deadly punching power Tonico possessed, so it is not out of the realm of possibility that he did score a lot more knockouts than what Boxrec has listed.

Chapter Four

On February 22, 1940, Aristides and Angelina welcomed their third child when Dogalberto Jofre was born. Like his older brother, Dogalberto spent a lot of his early days in the gym, admiring the boxers and taking part in his little exercise routines. In 1941, Aristides and Waldemar worked together in tandem for a coaching course, which was designed to give other boxing teachers knowledge based on scientific studies and physical education. The course, organized by a physical education college, helped with the improvement of training and coaching mentality. Among the next generation of coaches who benefited from these teachings and graduated as coaches in 1942 were Oscar Davidson, Luiz Soares, Adriano Delauney, Italo Hugo, and Adrião Alves Nunes.

1940s São Paulo

The sport had been dying a slow death in São Paulo, which meant that local favorites like Attilio Loffredo became staples on the Rio scene and the most popular boxer of this period, Italo Hugo, had not fought since 1933. The Paulista Stadium had been São Paulo's boxing center but was closed in 1934, which led to some lean years with only five shows in 1935 and none in 1936, 1937, and 1938 compared to the 78 shows staged in Rio during those years.

A dream of Armando's was realized, with the opening of Pacaembu Stadium in 1940. Only then did things once again begin to look bright for the boxing scene in São Paulo. Pacaembu was not only a gymnasium used for boxing, as many other sports and activities took place there, but at last, São Paulo had its arena, which could produce regular boxing shows.

An initial fear was that the arena was not located centrally in the city and was hard for many to reach as it was in an area of town which was still being developed. The Boxing Federation asked that the council provide more bus routes from throughout the city so that people could find their way to Pacaembu much easier, and notices were displayed throughout the city on the many easy ways fans could find their way to the arena.

Until this point, all of the boxing venues in the city had been located centrally. But with the city growing at such a rapid pace, it was tough to find land in the center of the city. It was far more feasible to pay smaller costs and get more land in an area that would eventually be populated at the rate at which the city was growing.

In 1942, Brazil Stadium in Rio closed its doors, which helped shift more focus to São Paulo boxing and meant more Rio fighters would come to São Paulo instead of the other way around. A significant influence was that boxing was considered the sport of immigrants. With so many immigrants in São Paulo, it meant that interest in the sport soared, and this ushered in a golden era for Brazilian boxing where fights were well attended, and many big personalities helped increase interest in the sport.

From the 1940 inauguration of Pacaembu, boxing gradually worked its way back into the consciousness of locals with a scattering of shows throughout the first half of the 1940s with an average of about five events per year at the venue with several events in other venues such as Antarctica Casino and São Paulo Athletic Club Gymnasium. In 1946 there was not a single show in Rio, while São Paulo hosted 26, with 25 of those events at Pacaembu. Over the next decade, São Paulo averaged almost 24 events per year, roughly one every 15 days compared to the average of only three annual events in Rio.

Elsewhere, Brazil terminated diplomatic relations with Germany, Japan, and Italy on January 22, 1942, and started to prepare to fight in the Atlantic Ocean, North Africa, and Europe. Brazil gave up its policy of neutrality, overcame internal problems, and joined Allied Forces against the Axis in Europe. The "pendulum policy" practiced by Vargas for five years to take advantage of both sides was no longer effective. Vargas, pressured by public opinion and the Armed Forces, was also afraid of an invasion by Germany in the northeast region of Brazil and declared war against the Axis on August 22, 1942.

Even before, Brazil had authorized aerial bases in some areas in the northeast region to sustain Allied efforts against Axis in North Africa and to protect merchant ships on the way to Europe. Historian Joseph Smith summarized how Brazil could no longer maintain its neutrality and talked about its problems to join the Allied side. Vargas was under great pressure to abandon the policy of neutrality. The attitude of the Brazilian public towards the Second World War was similar to that shown at the outbreak of the First World War. Although opinion was generally in favor of Britain and France, there was no desire for Brazil to join the war.

Furthermore, the government and military leaders were only too aware that the country was militarily weak and ill-prepared. Nevertheless, it was known that Brazil could not avoid being directly affected by expanding conflict. A major concern was the inadequacy of the Brazilian Navy to protect the northeast coastline, or bulge, from external attack. There was also anxiety that disaffected pro-German elements in the south might provoke civil unrest or even encourage an opportunistic Argentine invasion. Also, there were adverse economic consequences caused by the establishment of a British naval blockade that virtually terminated Brazil's formerly profitable trade with Germany.

Waldemar's eyesight became worse over time, so he had to retire from the ring in 1942 and made it his mission to expand the sport and popularize it as much as he could. Along with Kaled Curi, he started a magazine called *No Mundo do Box (In the boxing world)* and sought to teach boxing properly and spread the word in written form. In 1947, he founded a boxing union and acted as president. Waldemar offered free courses such as a school for judges and referees in addition to trying to set up pensions for retired fighters. Even though Waldemar was retired, the Zumbano family still had many prospects active inside the ropes with Erasmo and Higino showing promise in the amateur ranks, and Antonio already engaged in the professional game. Ralph had also taken up the sport and was showing great promise.

After struggling for years in boxing and emerging in a generation when there was no government or council backing, things had finally started to look upwards for Aristides around the time Paceumbu opened. It was not long after the venue was opened that Gazeta Popular Championship started. In 1941, the amateur tournament was announced, and it meant that more of the football clubs would be involved with amateur boxing. This provided a financial break for Aristides and more pupils for him to work with if he could get hired by one of the clubs.

It could be argued that since Aristides was coming up in an era when boxing weeded out most people through lack of financial support and ultimately interest, that it helped him grow a thicker skin and sharpen his tools further so that in the event of such openings, he would be the right man to move the sport forward. Aristides was able to move Paulista Gym over to São Jorge Avenue in Largo do Paissandu. A lot of new faces came through the doors hoping that they could get some quality training with such a renowned teacher. Despite being the only academy that was not connected to one of the big football teams, sports associations, military departments, or workers unions, Paulista Gym had the second most fighters go to the first championship when they brought 23 boxers. Esperia Club was the most represented with 28 and the third-largest squad was the Civil Guard boxing team with 11.

Paulista Club performed very well during the first two seasons of the Gazeta Championship, placing second and then third in 1941 and 1942, respectively. It was this excellent work that brought Aristides and his club to the attention of the São Paulo Football Club, one of the biggest clubs in the city. They reached an agreement with Aristides in 1943 that he would be their boxing coach, and they promised to deliver him athletes from all over the city through their large scouting and recruiting network. For São Paulo Football Club, this was a big coup because, at this point, amateur boxing was now only second in popularity to football, and the tournament was attracting more interest.

Palmeiras and Corinthians were two of São Paulo's biggest football rivals, and now that rivalry expanded over to boxing as they fought for bragging rights. However, it was Esperia, now going by the name Floresta that was still the most successful boxing team. The first championship that São Paulo competed in saw them come in a respectable second place with four gold medals and four silver medals, but they lagged far behind Floresta, who picked up 17 gold medals and 13 silver medals. The reason why there were so many medals is that the eight weight categories were divided into separate competitions, such as debutantes, two different youth categories, and the veterans.

The good results for São Paulo garnered Aristides further praise, but it was Floresta coach, Oscar Davidson, originally from Estonia, who was selected to take the state team to the national championships. Waldemar Zumbano had been helping Aristides with the training and development of his fighters but left his gym in 1944 when Davidson stepped down from the Floresta Club and Waldemar replaced him. There was no falling out, and they remained as close as ever, understanding that it was business and both men had careers to expand and families to feed. Waldemar did not take any of the pupils along to Floresta. That meant all of his brothers remained with Aristides at the Paulista Club. The separation also served to improve the Jofre-Zumbano stranglehold on the city's boxing scene as now, the family ran the two most successful and highest performing clubs.

The year 1944 saw Paulista Club improve and achieve ten gold medals and nine silver medals, which saw them further break away from Palmeiras and Corinthians. However, Floresta still came out on top with 14 gold medals and ten silver medals. The São Paulo State Sports Department initiated a tournament in August of that year when it asked Paulista Club and Floresta to compete, and they invited a selection from Rio. This tournament, though not as prestigious as the Gazeta, was an important one that became of substantial historical significance when Paulista Club won it, which gave São Paulo Football Club its first amateur boxing tournament in only its second year of competition.

From this point on, they would hold the title of the most dominant club in the state and that established Aristides as the best coach in the region. That success was followed up by dethroning Floresta in the Gazeta, a title they would win for the next 13 years as Aristides was selected every year as the head coach for tournaments throughout the nation. Aristides and Waldemar would work against each other in local competitions but always joined forces for tournaments in Rio, where they had great success with their teams.

Aristides (third left) and his team. Ralph Zumbano is far right

Gym Rat

Eder was in the gym every day and sharing the ring with his uncles and other boys who were bigger than him. It was a valuable experience for Eder, and with his father's example of discipline and courage, he was able to focus on becoming a serious boxer at a young age. "Every day, as soon as I got back from school, I would get into the gym clothes my mother had made me and go to work. I would stand in front of a mirror and practice the things I saw the boxers do. Later, I would go out in the street and run block after block. The other children thought I was crazy and made fun of me. I felt like stopping and throwing a punch at them. But even then, I had self-discipline. I would say to myself they are fools. Why should I waste time with them? They just don't know about training," Eder recalled.

Aristides did not have to push his son to do something he did not want to do, nor did he have to remind him to do the work. Eder enjoyed it, and it was his passion. There are many cases of child prodigies in other sports or occupations where kids were forced into something they disliked and, consequently, lost their childhood or grew to resent their parents. This was never the case with Eder. His childhood was a happy one and years later he would say that he would not change anything. "It was a wonderful time. I had great memories. If I could ever come back to this world again, I would come back to Parque Peruche at a time there were no services and facilities whatsoever. To get to the closest means of transport, we walked 20 minutes from Parque Peruche to Casa Verde Bridge. The streetcar would cross the bridge, and that was where the last stop was. We had football courts, a park to play where we climbed trees to pick fruit, and where we ran after balloons and flew kites. A real child's youth. It was a wonderful time," he said.

Parque Peruche was one of the poorest neighborhoods in São Paulo around this time. Limited access to other points of town meant that the youth coexisted among potheads, thieves, and other outcasts. "I can't say they were criminals because I never saw them commit a crime," Eder said. With limited options in such an economically challenged part of town, it would have been easy to gravitate to the wrong crowd. The Jofres and Zumbanos were poor but they were hard-working, honest, and strived to make a better situation for everybody. "There was one thing that made me different than them (the outcasts): A father who educated me and wanted me to be someone," Eder said.

By the time Eder was seven, he was training like an adult and going to school. His closest friends were his cousin Sylvano, his uncle Ricardo and two other boys by the names of Tole and Gaeta. The boys were inseparable, and when Eder was not at school or training, he was playing in the streets, taking part in anything from flying kites to swimming in the river to playing football. Ricardo, now 11, was getting rather good at boxing and invited Eder to the gym to spar one afternoon after school. The two were boxing at a fast pace, and Eder moved Ricardo towards the ropes where Ricardo tried a counter-attack, but Eder was quicker and beat him to the punch as he landed a clean left hook which sent Ricardo sprawling to the canvas. Aristides heard the commotion and came to the ring and asked, "What happened?" to which Ricardo told him, "He knocked me down, Aristo. Damn. How hard does this kid punch?"

Eder encountered his first bully at school when another boy kept making fun of the backpack he would wear to school. After two weeks of bottling up all the barbs, Eder asked his father permission to beat the kid up. Aristides gave him his approval but told him to take it easy on the boy. The following day in school, as Eder passed his tormentor; he heard the boy joke and then proceeded to knock the boy down with a hard punch to his jaw in front of all the other students and the principal. The principal sent the boys home, and the next day, the other kids lauded Eder as a hero and started wearing the same backpack to school as he did.

By now, Higino had returned to the gym, and Erasmo was around more often. They consistently offered advice to their prodigious young nephew. One day, Erasmo coached Eder about receiving the opponent's punch, smiling to give off the impression he did not affect you. He demonstrated some footwork where he used a side-step to escape from the opponent. Eder interrupted him, showing him that he already knew the move. Erasmo was amazed and told Aristides, "Why don't you sign him up for a championship?" to which Aristides shot back, "Are you crazy? He is too young!" Erasmo said, "Why am I crazy? This little brat knows more about boxing than all of us put together."

Higino had returned to boxing after his ongoing difficulties with the law. Though he never advanced beyond the amateur ranks, he did have a positive impact and made it to the Gazeta Esportiva championship in 1941, where he was defeated by Artur Tacciolli and chose not to enter the following tournament. In 1943, Higino was arrested again alongside Waldemar and spent a little over three months behind bars, but this time they were treated better in prison. The brothers would teach literature and boxing to fellow inmates, and one of the prisoners, Romeu Barbosa, went on to become Brazilian national lightweight champion years later. Higino drifted in and out of boxing. He had a mental breakdown when it looked like he was going to lose his house and the land which he had bought for taxes that were owed.

By 1949, Cleonice, now Higino's wife told the family that he needed help because he wasn't talking to anybody and spent his nights staying awake and smoking. In 1950 he had electrical shock treatment and slowly recovered, and he started working on a lot of community projects for Parque Peruche and founded clubs for kids such as the Cultural Recreational Educational Social and Sporting Center (CRESC). There, he started up basketball, volleyball, and football teams with his brother, Ralph.

While Higino did not reach his potential in boxing, he proved himself as a genuine fighter and an inspiration for the neighborhood. He played a vital role in the Jofre-Zumbano boxing dynasty. In addition to the work he did in the community, he also helped Aristides out on several occasions and proved himself to be a competent coach. He once led São Paulo's team in a tournament in Rio against Vasco de Gama Football Club and filled in for Aristides from time to time when Aristides had to go overseas to coach a team in an international competition.

Erasmo's major downfall was that he would talk about how he lived for the moment, and as a result, he lived only to have fun no matter what the cost. He lost his focus on boxing, stopped training, and caused a lot of anguish to his family as he often found himself in trouble with the law and distanced himself from his family.

As he matured, Erasmo did get himself back into training more seriously. He was spending more time at the gym, which gave everyone a big lift. His personality would radiate and put everyone in high spirits. Kaled Curi wrote about a time when he sparred with Erasmo, and he came away thoroughly impressed. "He was spectacular. The first time I fought him, I looked at that skinny guy and thought it would be easy to knock him down. Erasmo called me 'Little Turkish' and asked if I sold socks and gloves. I didn't answer; I raised my guard and went after him. He deceived me, poising his left arm to a hook and I, instinctively protected my ear. That's when he threw a powerful and sudden right cross to my jaw. I lost the ground beneath me. I didn't know if I had drunk a gallon of liquor or if someone had hammered my head."

Erasmo's progress saw him improve so much that he entered the Gazeta Esportiva championship in 1942 when he was the only Zumbano representative. He came face-to-face with Artur Tacciolli, who had defeated Higino at the previous tournament, and things were looking great from the outset of the bout. Erasmo knocked Tacciolli down twice and almost won in the first round. In the second round, Erasmo had difficulty breathing and had to stop fighting. After the match, Erasmo entered the locker room, threw up blood, and was sent to see a specialist. He stayed in a clinic and was treated for tuberculosis. His family would come and visit him every Sunday. The better his health became, the more he felt the urge to go out into town and live it up. He would creep out of the clinic in the evening and then return in the morning. His health soon took a turn for the worse as the symptoms came back and started to get more aggressive.

Higino and Cleonice would visit him often, with Cleonice making healthy natural foods for him. One morning, she was unable to attend, so she gave the food to Higino. When Higino arrived at the clinic he found his brother wasn't there. He asked the staff where his brother was, and the nurse broke the news to him that he had passed away in the early hours of the morning. She took Higino to see his body, which was once vibrant and energetic but now was hard and cold. He was only 22 when he died, and his last words to the nurse were, "I just want you to tell my brothers that they don't need to worry anymore. I'm not coming back this time."

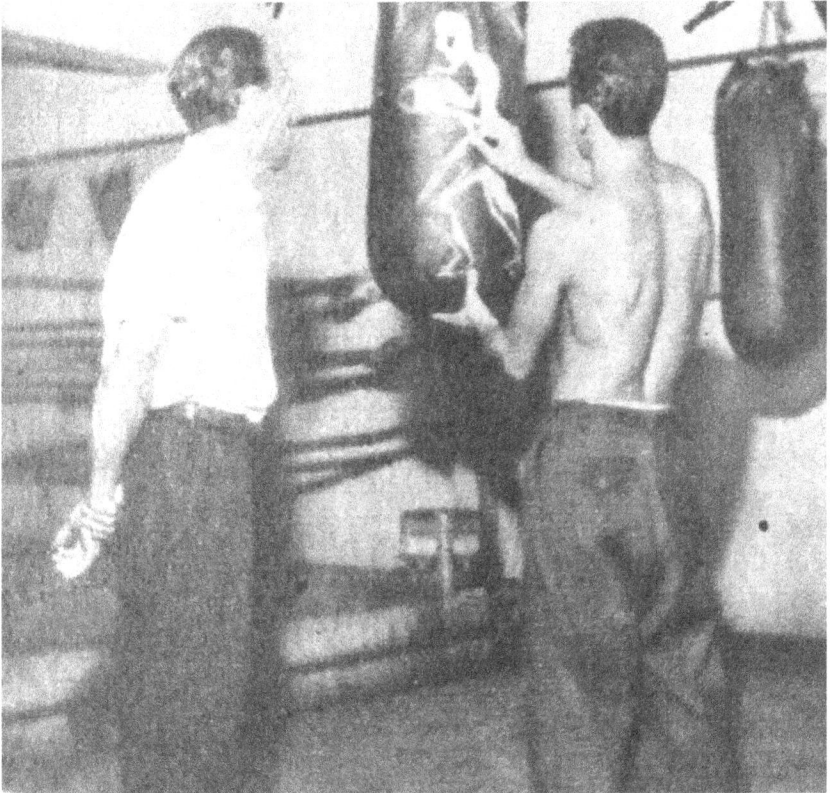

Aristides looks on as Eder paints the punching bag

Olga Returns

In Europe, Olga started to create her network of wrestling friends, but Hans was suffering from the side effects of injecting gasoline into his veins and was removed from the army. He suffered greatly from mental illness and returned to Brazil with Olga. She had the idea to support the family by showcasing female wrestling performers in her own circus.

Olga returned from Europe with 12 other ladies. She advertised in the local newspapers that she would be at a gym on Rua Santa Virginia with Aristides, and they would be providing lessons. "A lot of women showed up, and some that I saw could fight and we would spend the day training together," she said. Olga

MULHERES EM LUTA LIVRÉ

PELA 1.ª VEZ
NO BRASIL

HOJE no Pacaembú às 21 horas
(Quadra coberta de tenis)

INGRESSOS A VENDA: Farmácia Avenida (ao lado do Art-Palacio); Chaveiro Ralph Zumbano, à rua D. José de Barros, 35 e no Bar Bancario, à rua da Quitanda, 92.

invested in a circus and invited other women, mostly of different nationalities to come along, and she took the show on the road.

"I brought this art form to Brazil. We performed at Paceumbu for two months, but I didn't fight because it was forbidden for Brazilian women to fight, so we went to Bahia, and in Bahia, I changed my nationality," she added. Olga became Nina Olivera, and her nationality was listed as Spanish. These events significantly raised the profile of wrestling throughout the country and gained a lot of publicity. "I've been in 18 Brazilian states and have had 3,000 and something fights. Most of the time, with men. A few times with women. I would take the women with me for the demonstrations so the people would see what wrestling was. And there would be a challenge and any kind of fight was good," she explained in *Quebrando a Cara.*

In these circuses, Olga would often challenge the loudmouths or locate the town's bullies and take them on, usually winning. She took on men of all sizes, and no challenge was too big. Olga was nicknamed the "Queen of the Ring." With her growing reputation and fame, she was able to expand the circus empire and own multiple traveling circuses presenting these exhibitions. With her earnings, she started to purchase and sell other circuses, snapped up real estate, and began to buy and sell cars and boats. As she became older, she remained in the wrestling business but moved more towards choreographed matches, which she did until she was 60. At the age of 74, she trained actresses to play wrestling roles in soap operas.

Signs of a Champion

It was becoming abundantly clear to family members that Aristides' oldest boy had something special and could become an exceptionally talented boxer. "In time, I knew enough and boxed well enough so that all the Zumbanos and Jofres would watch me seriously. Some of them offered to correct me when I made mistakes. Some got in the ring and encouraged me to lead to them while they ducked and dodged to teach me how to hit a moving target. It wasn't long after my ninth birthday that we had a fight show in the gym," Eder said. His opponent was to be his cousin Ricardo, his closest friend from the Zumbano clan.

"The excitement I underwent before the bout was something I'll never forget. For a week, I trained extra hard. I ran extra-long distances. Every night when I went to bed, I dreamed that I was fighting. It was so clear - I would be going at it hot and heavy, then I would bring over a right-hand, and he would go down, the fight was over. On the night of the show, I was ready. I ate very early to have a clear stomach. I even took a nap in the late afternoon to be good and strong. When they introduced us, I felt a thrill up and down my spine. Then the fight began. Here all the nervousness went out of me. I was doing what I wanted to do. It all seemed like something I had done many times before. In other words, I was dream-fighting. And, you know what? In the third round, just as I had dreamed, I hit him a hard right-hand. Down he went, and he didn't get up. I had knocked him out. Inside of me, it was as if somebody had lit a fire. I was burning with happiness. My father climbed into the ring and effortlessly lifted me onto his shoulders. I couldn't have weighed more than 50 pounds. Everybody cheered, while my father danced around with me on his shoulders. But I remembered I had to be a good sport. I made my father put me down, and I went over to my cousin. He had been shaken up, but he wasn't hurt, and we embraced as he congratulated me on my good fight," Eder explained.

Although still a child, Aristides knew that Eder was destined to be a special man. One afternoon the family was together at the lake enjoying a lovely family day out when disaster almost struck. Angelina was tending to Lucrecia, combing her hair as Dogalberto played with a shuttlecock. In contrast, Eder played football, and Aristides dozed off under a tree. Out of nowhere, there was a big splash as Dogalberto fell into the lake and was unable to get out. A huge commotion followed by screaming and panicking while Eder ran in to rescue his brother and bring him back to safety.

On July 24, 1947, Aristides and Angelina welcomed another boy to the family when Mauro Jofre was born. He was the last child the couple had, and just like the other men in the family, he too was pinched by the boxing bug and spent his infancy around the boxing gym.

"I always took care of myself and my brothers. I don't know how many times I had to open the gym at six in the morning and only come back home at midnight. I would spend the night gluing posters to earn some money and get them used to eating not only rice and beans. That's not an athlete's diet," Eder told *O Globo* in 1973.

The Jofre clan: Eder, Dogalberto, Lucrecia and Mauro

Art and Football

Like most children, Eder was very impressionable and had multiple interests. Outside of his boxing, the two pastimes which he put the most energy into were football and artwork. He was a good student at school, and from a young age, he was very proficient at drawing, and the teachers loved his work. He learned to draw by watching fighters train at the gym. One of the coaches gave him a notepad, and he would draw the boxers or whatever came to his mind. At the age of ten, he saw a competition in a comic book to see who could draw the best Superman, and he sent his sketch in and ended up winning the competition, which gave a cash prize. Eder liked to read comic books and always would side with the good guys like Batman and Superman over the villains.

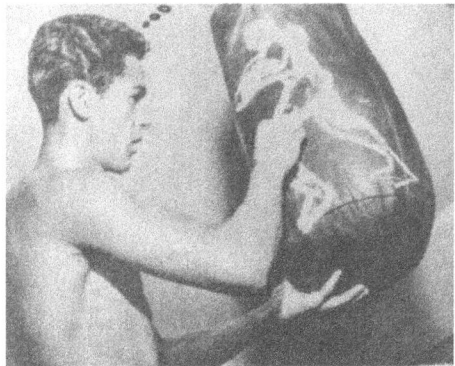

When he was only 11 years old, he attended classes at São Paulo School of Arts and Crafts. He was the youngest student by a few years and, at first, did not like the courses since they were teaching industrial design, which he was not interested in. Some of the older students would give Eder a hard time after he said that his goal was one day to teach art. In particular, one older student took to calling Eder names and made wisecracks. Eder did not take kindly to this just as had been the case of the student who made fun of his bag. He asked his father if he could come down to the school to talk with the guy. "He keeps calling me names, slaps my head all the time during the class, and comes up with new jokes about me every day," Eder pleaded.

His father told him that he would not be able to go down to the class and that Eder should teach the guy a lesson. The next time he went to school, Eder tried to avoid confrontation, but the bully kept tormenting him to the point that Eder put his bag down. "You better stop!" he said to the guy. "Or what?" came back the response. "You're not going to like it," Eder shot back. Everybody in the classroom started to laugh, and the bully said out loud, "You see that? The baby thinks he's a man." Eder clenched his fists and went towards the bully who, at this point, decided he was going to bring the youngster down to size. "Come here, you little brat. I'm going to teach you a lesson," he said. The bully threw the first punch, but Eder was able to slip it and counter with a left hook to his liver, and then as he was staggering, Eder delivered a right cross to his chin, which laid him out on the floor. "You son of a bitch! I'm going to kill you!" he said as he rose and tried to attack, and once again, Eder put him on the floor again in a flash, and everyone stood in amazement at the fighting skills Eder possessed. The bully got up and walked out of the class in humiliation and no longer attended any more courses at the school. When Eder arrived home that day, his father was waiting for him and asked how it went, and Eder told him, "It was a piece of cake, but I pity him."

Eder loved attending the classes and spent years pursuing this hobby and was even working on becoming a draftsman, but an accident at the school one day caused the roof to fall, and all the students' work and equipment were lost. "It was a shame because I bought all the material and stuff required for the classes. I bought all of that gear using the money that I earned as a locksmith," he said. As Eder did not have the money to replace all this equipment, he stopped attending the course, but he kept up the artwork to the point where he was working with a professor by the name of Walter Branco. However, Eder couldn't fully dedicate himself when he started to enter boxing tournaments.

In *Quebrando a Cara*, Eder's cousin, Sylvano, spoke about the focus which Eder had from a young age. "From six years old until he was 12, he would just fight with everyone verbally, not physically. He was a natural joker, and then when he turned 13 and started training seriously and going to championships, he did a 180. He wouldn't joke anymore, he became shy, and he wouldn't talk to anyone. We would call him and tell him we should go dance at the club, there are some cute girls there, but he isolated himself," he said.

The other sport in Eder's life was football, and he had aspirations that he would become a professional player one day and play for his beloved São Paulo Football Club. He played as a left-winger and was the highest scorer on his team. Eder's interest in football disappointed his father, who felt his son had what it took to make something special out of boxing. "For me, playing football was fun. But it was of disgust to my father. There was a time when I did not go to the gym, and I told him that I thought I was going to be a football player. He was hurt, he was like, 'Eder, you have a way for boxing. You're good; if you were not, I would not allow you to fight.' He encouraged me in this direction, and I ended up training again, for real," Eder said, reflecting on the influence of his father behind his decision to dedicate himself to becoming a full-time boxer.

Eder weighs up his sporting options

Aristides had been worried that his son was going to throw away all the hard work they had put into boxing to pursue football. Angelina asked Aristides if he was sure this was the best thing for Eder. "Think this through Aristides. What did boxing ever do for you? You and all my brothers. What have you guys got from it?" she asked. Aristides asked her if she wanted to see him fight, and she said she did but felt he had a better future in football. "Just so you know, this country is packed with aspiring football players, but nobody has ever seen a boxer as good as this boy," he told her. Angelina wasn't quite as sure and said, "How can you be so sure? He hasn't even had his debut yet." Aristides took her down memory lane a little bit when he asked if she had remembered when he ran down the street to get the midwife to deliver Eder. "Yes, I remember," she said. "Where did we live, Angelina?" he asked. "At the gym, my love," she replied. "That's it. That was his debut," Aristides said.

Eder as a teenager

The Big Time

Brazil sent a boxing team to the Olympic Games in London in 1948, and Aristides was selected as the head coach. This was an era when amateur boxing was not very organized in Brazil. Boxers throughout the country would do their training at their clubs and then would be selected and brought together when the team would travel to championships. This made things much harder for Brazil than other countries that had national headquarters where all the boxers trained, ate, and lived together, and the coach could see his pupils daily. Before the Olympics, Aristides worked with Waldemar and their team in the Brazilian championship in September 1947, followed by the Latin American tournament in November of that year.

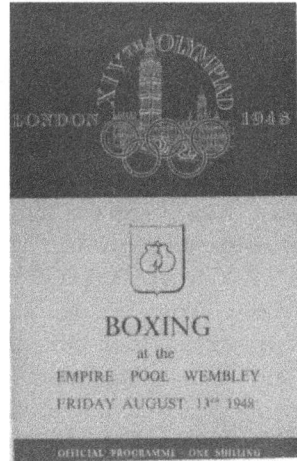

BOXING
at the
EMPIRE POOL WEMBLEY
FRIDAY AUGUST 13th 1948

The South American tournament proved to be a roaring success, as Brazil collected four gold medals and one silver medal. Kaled Curi won the featherweight gold, while Ralph Zumbano took the lightweight honors with Jorge Matuck clinching the middleweight gold and Geraldo Jesus took home light heavyweight honors. Curi and Zumbano were the two Paulista Club boxers who went undefeated throughout the tournament. Matuck and Jesus suffered defeats, but the championship was on a league basis where every fighter in

Aristides and Ralph

each division faced each other and the boxer with the most wins came out on top. Ralph was named the outstanding boxer of the tournament.

Such was the state of the amateur boxing program in Brazil at the time, the Olympic committee would only allow the Brazilian Boxing Federation to select four boxers. The Brazilian Federation had wanted to see fighters in all eight weight classes and felt that the excellent display in the Latin American championships had earned them that right, but the Olympic committee said that due to a lack of funding they could only send four boxers and that they only wanted athletes who stood a legitimate chance of winning a medal. The selection policy came down to a trial tournament between boxers from Rio and São Paulo, and after the elimination series, two fighters from each state qualified. Manoel do Nascimento and Jose Dias from Rio were the boxers in the bantamweight and featherweight divisions, respectively.

In contrast, Ralph Zumbano would be going in the lightweight division. Vicente dos Santos, known as Vicentao, would be competing at heavyweight. Jose Dias was injured on the eve of the tournament and couldn't compete, which left only three boxers remaining. Vicentao and Manoel were eliminated in the first round, but Ralph performed admirably in the Games. He displayed excellent skills and movement, so much so that the British press labeled him "The Brazilian Wonder," comparing his grace and movement to that of a ballet dancer.

Ralph advanced past the first two rounds, as he defeated Franz Ehringer of Luxemburg by second-round knockout before outpointing France's Auguste Caulet. Ralph's Olympic dream ended when he was eliminated by American Wallace "Bud" Smith in the quarter-finals. Smith would go on to lose his semi-final bout but turned professional later on and had a successful career which saw him become world champion in the lightweight division in 1955.

Although the Brazilian team did not win any medals at the Olympics, their participation was viewed as a huge success. Brazil had finally been able to send a team of boxers to the world's biggest sporting event, and at this point, amateur boxing in Brazil was more popular than the professional game. Events were well attended, featured heavily in the sports pages of the newspapers, interest was growing, and with Aristides leading the way, the sport remained in good hands. Aristides's three main pupils at this stage were Olympic hero Ralph, Vicentao, and Kaled Curi. Curi missed out on an Olympic place due to political issues. He had been critical of the federation and felt that they had then begun to bully him. He remained an amateur, but he was passed upon for the Olympic spot, which was the one that went to Jose Dias. Dias, as mentioned earlier, was injured, and didn't compete, but even before the tournament, he had no prior international experience compared to Curi's impressive performances at the South American championships. While Curi was in dispute with the federation, he went to Argentina and based himself in Buenos Aires for six months.

In 1949, Aristides' three prized pupils all turned professional, which helped raise the profile of the professional game in Brazil, particularly in São Paulo, where they would perform in front of lively crowds while carving out successful careers for themselves. Aristides was not only coaching Paulista Club's amateur boxers or state teams and national teams, but he was now heavily involved in the professional game, mixing his time between amateur and professional boxing. The infrastructure of Brazilian boxing was still far away from that in neighboring South American nations so international opportunities were still few and far between for Brazilian fighters. Zumbano, Curi, and Vicentao all became national champions within their weight classes, showing that Aristides was the best trainer of both amateurs and professionals in the country, but none of that trio was ever able to get a shot at a continental championship.

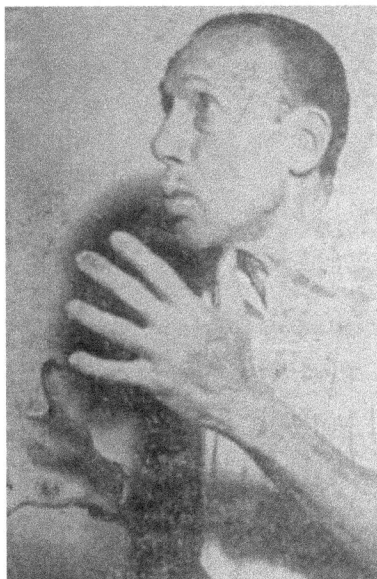

Aristides

A Terrifying Time

Some terrifying news hit the Jofre household when young Dogalberto, six, fell sick, and the outcome looked grim. Dogalberto had been complaining of body aches and pains, so Aristides and Angelina took him to the doctor and were floored when the doctor gave them his diagnosis. Dogalberto had bone cancer and was given roughly two weeks to live. Aristides didn't want to believe it and was defiant that his son would recover. The doctor apologized for being so blunt. He reiterated that it was best to tell them the truth, and the reality was that Dogalberto was terribly ill and did not appear to have long left to live. The doctor told Aristides that he wanted to run additional tests and perform surgery on Dogalberto, and that gave Aristides a glimmer of hope that perhaps he was not doomed.

Aristides and Angelina stayed at the hospital, and it broke their hearts to see their son not knowing how serious his illness was. The medical team took Dogalberto away to operate on him, and he asked his father what they were going to do. "Just an exam," Aristides told his son. As Dogalberto was being operated on, Aristides paced back and forth around the hospital, smoking cigarette after cigarette. When Dogalberto finally emerged from his surgery, he was asleep, and Aristides and Angelina waited for him to wake up. When he regained consciousness, Dogalberto pointed the finger, "You lied to me, Dad! They cut me up!" Aristides could do nothing but hug his son, and when he passed out again, he broke down crying as he felt helpless.

While Dogalberto was in pain, he could not understand why he was not allowed to play out on the street with his friends, but then the pain hit him harder and harder. Aristides had the idea to build him a cart so that he could play in that instead, and Eder went to the tool shed and began to assemble the cart. Once he was finished, Eder was pushing his younger brother around, and they were having the time of their lives until the pain became unbearable to the point Aristides took Dogalberto back to the hospital where they recommended radiation, but the price was far too high, and the Jofres couldn't afford it.

Aristides went home and sold furniture, old trophies, and other items so that he could pay for the treatment. The treatment initially bought Dogalberto more time as the two weeks turned into two months, and then finally, a miracle happened, and the sarcoma went away. Dogalberto was almost a healthy boy again. The next five years were to be crucial, and over time, he felt better and better, and except for the scars that he bore on his stomach from the surgery, he was void of any signs of cancer by 1954.

At the age of 14, Eder went to see one of his uncles in a professional fight for the first time when his uncle Higino snuck him inside Pacaembu to see Tonico fight. The date was April 22, 1950, and that was the last time Tonico fought as he was defeated on points by Osvaldo Silva. Eder was only able to see two rounds of the fight as he was spotted by security at ringside and then carted off to the locker rooms since children were not allowed to attend live boxing matches in those days.

For Eder, it was a rough experience as he held his uncles up as real-life superheroes, and to see his uncle taking punches was not a pretty sight for him. With his professional boxing career coming to an end, Tonico had learned how to become a locksmith from a Zumbano family friend by the name of Allan Telles. They soon opened their own company called Zumbano's locksmith in preparation for a life after boxing and a means for other family members to make extra income. Eder also worked as a locksmith with his uncles and cousins to help ease the financial pressure off his father.

Sadly, some unfortunate news rocked the family when Armando Jofre died from lung disease on November 25, 1950. Although he did not make a great deal of money during his lifetime, he left his mark on Brazilian boxing, but he appeared at a time when Brazil did not fully understand the sport. Armando was instrumental in not only bringing his brother over from Argentina, but in improving the way athletes lived. He was the primary link between the two most influential families in Brazilian boxing history. Armando's death was sad for all because he was loved and respected. He was admired by the Zumbanos, and his daughter Anita was married to Ralph Zumbano.

Ralph became the first boxer in the family to win a national title as a professional when he won the lightweight championship in 1951. Since most of the nation's finest boxers were coming out of the Paulista Gym, Ralph contested the title against his stablemate and friend Kaled Curi and won on points. This occurrence of Kid Jofre pupils facing off with one another would become commonplace in the next few years as more of his fighters made their marks in the professional ranks. Aristides would usually train one of the fighters, often, Ralph and the other boxer would go to another gym, and then after the fight, everything would be back to normal.

The Helsinki Summer Olympics of 1952 would represent the second time that Brazil sent a boxing team to the Games, but unlike London, Aristides was not selected as the head coach. It was not that his reputation had taken a hit. It was because Aristides was now just as involved in professional boxing, perhaps even more so. His pupils from the 1948 Games were now deep into their professional careers, and while Aristides was training an outstanding prospect by the name of Pedro Galasso, Luis Soares was selected as the head coach. This selection did draw widespread criticism as Aristides was seen as the undisputed best coach in Brazilian boxing while Soares did not have any of his pupils qualify for the Games.

Ralph Zumbano

Chapter Five

Records indicate that Eder's first official amateur contest took place on January 31, 1953, against Jose Duran Garcia. He also entered a tournament just a few days before his 17th birthday when Gazeta Esportiva featured boxers from the São Paulo area in a tournament called "Torneio Operario de Boxe," and Eder was successful as he came out on top in the flyweight division. On March 15, his first opponent, according to Henrique Matteucci, was Adilton Rodrigues, who came into the contest with a reputation of being a skilled and tough boxer of excellent pedigree. Rodrigues brought the fight to Eder from the start, but Eder skillfully avoided his attacks and was able to counter the boy at will. It was not long into the bout that Eder scored the first knockdown when he caught Rodrigues with a left hook and followed up with a hook to the body and chin that put him down for a count of six. Rodrigues survived the round, but in the second frame, Eder was all over him and attacking furiously, and the bout was stopped when Eder landed a hard right-hand straight down the middle of Rodrigues' guard.

The audience was in awe at what they saw and left the venue talking about what a prospect they had just seen. The newspapers of this time listed the opponent's name as Alberto Rodrigues and credited Eder with a first-round victory. According to Matteuci, Eder won his following two bouts and won the trophy. While this tournament is often referred to as Eder's first victory, his sister Lucrecia said she remembered him winning a championship called "Sesi Tournament" when he was 16.

Eder followed the Torneio Operario de Boxe success by winning another tournament hosted by *Gazeta Esportiva*, and he also won the little league and junior league championships. Eder would then go on to win the São Paulo state championship and the Brazilian national championship. At this point, Eder was unbeatable in his weight class, and nobody in Brazil could touch him, which was why he was chosen to represent Brazil on an international level at Ramon Platero's tournament in Uruguay in December 1953. This tournament was contested between Brazil and Uruguay and was named after a famous Uruguayan football coach who spent decades in Brazil coaching various professional football clubs. This tournament was considered a significant leap in class, and his opponent, Waldemiro Torres, was a highly regarded boxer who had competed very favorably with a lot of Argentinian opponents. Torres was no match for Eder as he was defeated with ease in the two bouts they engaged on December 17 and December 23.

It was around the time that Eder was making some waves locally as a precocious amateur talent that he laid eyes on the love of his life. Despite his success, he did not let the recognition or the praise get to his head. He kept the same friends and enjoyed playing football with them and walking the avenue. One day he noticed a pretty young girl who had recently moved into the neighborhood and saw her with her friends picking berries from a tree. The two noticed each other from time to time and often locked eyes whenever they passed and smiled at each other.

Upon returning from the tournament in Uruguay, Eder worked up the courage to ask the girl who he had taken a liking to on a date. "I used to pass her house every single day. One day I saw her there, and I looked at her, and she looked at me. When I turned around, she looked back with a smile, but I did not approach her. After three or four times this way, I finally gathered the courage to say hello and ask her on a date," Eder explained.

The girl went by the name of Cidinha, and like Eder, she was also timid. On their first date, Eder told her he thought about her often since the first time he saw her under the tree picking berries to which she replied she felt the same about him. Eder and Cidinha had been dating for about two

Cidinha

months but with Eder's busy schedule they were only able to see each other in the evenings after he finished his gym work. They would walk down the street together holding hands and one night a police officer stopped them and asked what they were doing walking down an unlit street. Eder said they had nowhere else to go so the officer said they would be safer at home and drove them to Cidinha's parent's home. "Don't worry, everything is fine. I just thought it would be safer if these two kids were at home at this time," the police officer said when Cidinha's mother, Ms. Josefa, opened the door. Ms. Josefa smiled and said that the officer was right and asked Eder, "Why don't you come and see her at home?" Eder was unsure if he had permission to do so and Cidinha's mother said that it was fine, and she would rather them be at home.

Eder described himself as a timid boy and said that at first, he hid his girlfriend from his family until one day he told his father he was seeing someone. Aristides told Eder that he should invite her to lunch with the family so they could get to know her. Eder had already met Cidinha's mother first and clicked with her family and then introduced Cidinha to his family. Cidinha was a nickname as her full name was Maria Aparecida Batista. She was born on December 24, 1938. Her mother's side of the family came from the Netherlands, and her father's side had come from Portugal.

In 1954 Eder continued winning and piling up the trophies until he suffered a fractured hand before a scheduled bout with Ari dos Santos on September 27 and had to pull out of the bout. Eder had already knocked out dos Santos on May 19, and after a few months out of the ring due to the injury, he was again matched with dos Santos. Eder knocked him out once more on December 18.

In 1955, Eder was much more active and again would win the São Paulo state championship on August 29 with a first-round knockout of dos Santos. He followed that success with the Brazilian national championship, this time in the bantamweight division. This tournament took place in Salvador and Eder started the competition with a second-round knockout victory over João Santa on September 10 before defeating Geraldo Magalhaes on points in the semi-final.

In the final, he defeated Valdemar Santos on points to secure the championship. Eder won the Golden Gloves in Rio the following month as his trophy collection grew. Before Eder left for Salvador to compete in the national championship, he received a letter from Cidinha, which threw him into despair. She wrote that she had to stop dating him because she was too young to get into a serious relationship. Eder decided he had to break his training and had to see her. He showed up at her house and knocked on the door. She answered and right away asked him where he had been lately. He explained there was a tournament he had to prepare for. "How long are you going to be gone for?" she asked him. When he told her that he was going to be away for 15 days, she ran into her room in tears. Eder waited at the door and asked Cidinha's mother if she could bring her daughter to the door as he had brought something for her. She came back, and he handed her a ring. "It's a memento so you can always remember me," he told her. After the tournament in Salvador, Eder came back, and Cidinha had changed her mind and wanted to be with him.

On one date, things almost got ugly when they were walking to Cine São Jose near Casa Verde, walking up Baruel Avenue when two guys were coming from a party and were being loud and offensive with their continuous swearing. Eder was upset and told Cidinha to walk ahead while he had a word with them. He tapped one of the louts on the shoulder and said to him that he was with his girlfriend and that the guy was being loud and talking trash and it was offensive. As Eder was trying to reason with the perpetrator, the other one came from behind and tried to attack him. Instinctively, Eder was able to block the attack with his arm and drop him with one punch. As the man went to the ground, the other one was agitated and reached for something, possibly a weapon that he was carrying. Eder acted quickly by throwing his jacket over the man's face and punched him in the chest, dropping him. He picked the coat off the guy and saw him struggling for his breath and decided to see how the first one was doing. He saw that the guy was struggling to deal with the effects of the punch, and Eder gave him another swift blow on the nose before walking away to get Cidinha.

Left to right: Lucrecia, Ricardo & Maria Zumbano, Angelina, Aristides, Eder, unknown, Gisleine, Claudio Toneli, Mauro Jofre and Silvia (front)

Eder was scheduled to go to the Pan-American championships in Mexico City in late February of 1956 but had to withdraw due to another fracture of his hand. This caused Eder to sit on the sidelines for a few months and when he was healthy again, he faced an opponent by the name of Acir Sereno on March 27. The bout was scheduled for six rounds which meant that some places recorded it as a professional match. Eder won in the first round and followed the victory up with what appears to be at least five more victories in bouts scheduled for six rounds.

On April 6 he outpointed Walter Valentim over six rounds at Pacaembu and then defeated Pedro Praxedes by fifth-round knockout on April 27 in what appears to be a tournament called "Professionals." A fourth-round knockout of Francisco de Lima on June 20 at Pacaembu and a six-round decision victory over Ataide de Oliveira on July 13 simply listed as in São Paulo were sandwiched by a June 30 three-round points victory in Rio over Luis Augusto Silva. The last victory that could be found was a bout scheduled for six rounds on September 21 against Osmar Crocicchia. A document which the Paulista Boxing Federation said was Eder's official professional record listed the bouts with Crochicchia, Valentim, and Sereno but only the Crocicchia date was accurate. The record shows the victory over Valentim to have taken place on January 5, 1957, and the Sereno fight on February 28, 1957. The venues and results match exactly from what the primary sources reported at the time, but they are roughly a year apart in their dates. It was not uncommon for amateur matches to be scheduled for more than three rounds, particularly outside of competitions and the language used by Aristides and Eder when discussing the start of his professional career would indicate that these were not professional bouts as would the newspaper reports when discussing Eder's matches after he participated in the Olympics.

The year 1956 would be Eder's final one as an amateur and one in which he drew valuable experience. Up to this point, he was undefeated and had won multiple championships but would learn to handle defeat for the first time when he went back to Uruguay, this time to compete in the Latin American tournament. Between October 9 and October 20, Eder scored three impressive knockout victories over Manuel Vega, Guido Granizo, and Goncalo Chavez and was faced with promising local boxer, Aniceto Pereyra, on October 23. Eder had previously defeated Pereyra in August at Pacaembu but was outpointed this time in Montevideo. The lesson that Eder learned was to never underestimate an opponent. Before the bout, Aristides told him, "You have already bested him, so let's finish this one quickly. Don't worry about analyzing him."

Henrique Matteucci described the bout in *O Galo de Ouro*: "It happened that Aniceto had a little something for them. He received a set of dirty instructions to follow and a certain funky strategy. During the first round, he avoided the battle at all costs, with his head down to the waistline illegally. The referee played blind about it. The next two rounds were about the same bullshit; except at the last ten seconds of each round, the Uruguayan initiated throwing combos at Eder. Eder didn't have time to counter because the bell rang when he was about to fight back. At the end of the fight, Eder was superior in all aspects of the contest. But the referee was playing the game, which ended up with Eder losing the title." There would appear to be validity to these claims as Eder was voted as the best boxer of the tournament by the local organizers. "At least they recognize something. It is compensation. I feel honored with that indication, but I would prefer that the fight result was fair, for this is what stays forever recorded in the background," Aristides said.

Melbourne

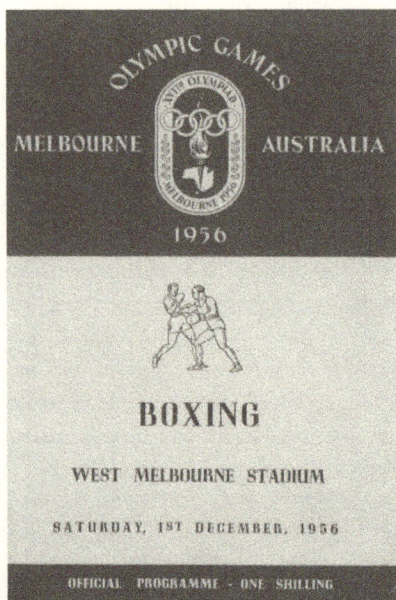

As soon as Eder arrived back from Uruguay, he got down to business and started training as he dreamed of winning Olympic gold in Melbourne the following month. As his uncle Ralph had done in the 1948 London Olympics, Eder was looking to make his family and his country proud in Australia. For Aristides, this was to be the second Olympic Games he had been selected as the head coach of the boxing team.

Previewing the Brazilian prospects in the boxing category of The Games, *O Globo* reported: "Brazilian boxing will be represented in Melbourne with only two athletes: Celestino Pinto (Carioca) and Eder Jofre (Paulista). Unarguably, those are the two biggest stars in our national boxing, and they have qualities not only to shine in their interventions but to fight for the accomplishment of one of the three medals. Joining them as head coach once again is old-timer, the competent Aristides "Kid" Jofre, the Paulista boxer's father, who with (the) Zumbanos, forms the most prominent boxing family we have heard of."

On November 8, the boxers went to the editorial room of *O Globo*, where they were given flags for the newspaper, and the team was asked about their prospects in Australia. Aristides explained that preparations were going well and that they would arrive ten days before the first round. That way, there would be plenty of time to acclimate to the time zone change of 13 hours. "Not even in London, when I took a huge team, including Ralph Zumbano, who lost under exceptional conditions, was I as confident as I am now. Celestino and my son can do what past Brazilian boxers weren't capable of and win an Olympic title. They are willing, excited, and forgotten of the injustices that they were victims of not too long ago," Aristides said. Eder was asked about the controversial loss he was handed in Montevideo against Pereyra and he chose not to dwell on it and instead looked to the future with a positive outlook. "The invincibility has to end someday. It's a past fact and now the important thing is to do well in Melbourne and justify our departure."

Eder was competing in the bantamweight division and in his first-round bout easily defeated Thein Myant of Burma (now Myanmar) on November 26, scoring two knockdowns en route to scoring a points victory. Eder made an excellent impression on the public and received wide applause as he left the ring. Unfortunately for Eder, the only other member of the team was lightweight Pinto, so the only sparring available was with a much bigger man. Eder suffered an injured nose during a sparring session the day before his next fight.

Eder jabs at Thein Myant in his W3 first-round victory

On November 28, Eder was defeated on points by Claudio Barrientos of Chile in his second-round match. "It may sound like excuses, but it's not. Celestino was about 20 pounds heavier than me, but I had practiced with him because there was nobody else. He struck me on the nose. It became swollen, and I could not breathe properly, so I was exhausted during the fight. That's why I lost, I believe," he said on reflection of this bout. Eder always felt that the match was even and that he would have won the gold medal if not for this injury. The controversy in this bout did not emerge from the Brazilian team. Eder talked about feeling comforted in his performance backstage when he was feeling sorry that his Olympic dream had been crushed. "I don't think I lost, and even in the locker room, I received a visit from other foreign boxers who came by to say hello, also disagreeing with the judges' decision," he said.

As was the case after the London Games of 1948, there was a lot of optimism now about the quality of boxers coming out of Aristides' stable. Eder was rightly seen as the most exciting Brazilian prospect, perhaps in history to this point. Ralph had retired, but Kaled Curi was still going strong. While Vicentao's career was winding down, he had been the national heavyweight champion. Pedro Galasso had turned professional and was going strong in his career. There was a pair of talented heavyweights by the names of Luiz Ignacio and Paulo Sacoma. Sebastiao Ladislau had also been the national lightweight champion but was just about entering the downside of his career in 1956.

Ralph had retired at a strong point in his career with his record standing at 27 wins with 2 draws and 2 defeats. His activity had started to slow down in 1953 when he became heavily involved in politics to the point that he was elected to congressman in 1954. In the documentary *Quebrando a Cara*, Ralph spoke with pride about what he was able to accomplish but felt that in a different era, he could have accomplished more in boxing. "Thank God I brought some glory to Brazil. At the time when I fought, I think I was one of the professional fighters that won most often at that time. Thanks to the press, radio, TV, and newspapers, I had a certain prestige. With the experience I have today, I believe I would do a lot better," he said.

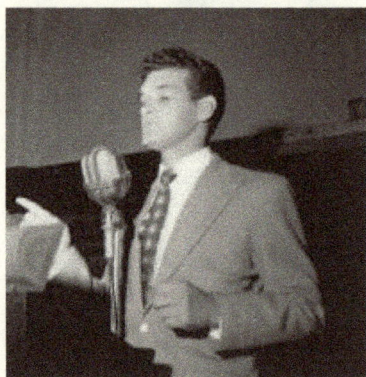

He was never knocked out in the professional game. He had a style of boxing that made a great impression on Eder, but this was at a time where Brazilian boxers still did not take part in too many international contests, so it was challenging to go beyond the national level. Without question, if Kid Jofre, Kid Pratt, and Waldemar Zumbano were three of the most influential coaches in Brazilian boxing, Ralph was one of the most influential boxers of that generation. He helped shape the future of the sport in Brazil.

Ralph Zumbano

Walter Zumbano

Vegetarian

It was in 1956, not long after Eder had won his last amateur bout that he decided to become a vegetarian, traditionally an unusual diet for most boxers.

In 1960, Eder's mother said that he never really liked meat when he was younger anyway. The clincher for Eder to go full vegetarian was when he educated himself by reading different dietary books. He read that it was harmful to the body and teeth to consume meat. He insisted on a diet that would contain vegetables, eggs, cereals, and a lot of fruit. "It was good for me because I always felt lighter and invigorated with this healthy diet, and it was easy to digest food as well as being rich in proteins and vitamins," he said. Even to this day, Eder has maintained that healthy vegetarian lifestyle.

Aristides told Eder that he should focus on turning professional in 1957 and that he ought to quit his part-time job at the locksmith to concentrate more on boxing. "I remember my father called me and said, 'Eder, let's talk seriously. As an amateur, you have already done everything. You have fought in the Olympics; you have won all these championships, so it is time for you to turn professional. As a pro, you will earn money, and you'll be famous,'" Eder recalled.

Now that he was entering the paid ranks, the training intensified for Eder as he would be training twice a day. The first training of the day would start at 5 am when he would get out of bed to go running before coming back home to rest, have lunch and then go to the gym in the afternoon. "Picture that, waking up that early with your body still sore from the day before, having all the muscles in your body destroyed and still getting out of the house to lose weight. Doing that drill every single day, no matter what, was crazy! Especially when you don't have a salary yet and a clear plan to start your career. It seems like a useless sacrifice." Those sacrifices and the example passed down from father to son on the virtues of hard work, dedication, and focus sowed the seeds early on and would serve as a staple for Eder for the duration of his career. Eder is one of the few champions from his generation who maintained that level of consistency and discipline throughout his entire fighting career.

"My father was a real man. He was friends with everybody, never meant to hurt anybody and always said to me: 'It doesn't matter if you want to be a politician, a priest or whatever, just don't kill anybody, don't steal from anybody who you envy, and always help others if you can.' My father made us, his children, real men. School is mainly made to learn mathematics and stuff, but family will teach you friendship, tolerance, to care for others, respect, and to deal with everybody," Eder said about the example his father set for him.

One coach that tried to get under the Jofre's feathers around this time was another trainer who had come over from Argentina and had settled in Brazil like Aristides. Eder told a story about a time this coach challenged him and his father. "There was a guy named Brito, who came from another academy. We had trained together a few times when he had different coaches and modesty aside, I broke his face. He then went with another coach named Molina, an excellent coach who had come from Argentina. He brought great boxers from Argentina and started training this guy, Brito. Then he started talking nonsense like, 'I am going to start breaking up Kid Jofre's gym and beat his son, Eder Jofre,' I was upset. My father fought all his life, a simple, humble, hardworking, honest man, and this guy says that? I said, 'Let's go. Let's do the fight,' and it was on. It was like a semi-professional fight. I was so angry that in the first round, I knocked him down twice, and the battle was over," said Eder.

A New Golden Era

In 1955, Wilson Russo Gym on Rua Consolação, close to Nossa Senhora da Consolação Church had opened. It became prominent in Brazilian boxing, much like what Stillman's Gym meant to New York City or what The Main Street Gym represented for the Los Angeles boxing scene. The gym was founded by a company owned by brothers Mateus and Nelson Russo who sold car motors and car parts. The brothers were keen boxing fans in addition to being close friends with Pedro Galasso. Initially, the gym was set up to enable employees of their company to exercise and learn boxing, but it became a beehive of activity with fighters of all levels from beginners to seasoned professionals. The location of the gym, by Roosevelt Square in the heart of downtown São Paulo meant that there was always a large crowd in the gym.

Waldemar became one of the leading coaches at the gym. Over time, other coaches who acted in the role of the chief trainer were Pedro Galasso, Nelson Garrido, and Fritz Seltenm. Wilson Russo was generally used by foreign fighters who came to Brazil to fight, especially when Eder fought an international opponent in his career.

Aristides still operated the Paulista Gym, which was initially located on Rua São João, at Largo do Paissandu. But in time as the demand increased and his stable increased, a new gym was opened by São Paulo Football Club at 176 Rua Santa Ifigenia in downtown São Paulo, close to Praça da Republica. "I used to go to the gym a lot when I was a child accompanying my father in training. For me it was fun, the perfect world because I was with my father and grandfather," Marcel Jofre said. The Paulista Gym would remain until just a few years after Eder finished his professional career when it was demolished. It was a classical boxing gym of the era in that it was not fancy.

Another venue that opened just in time for Eder's professional debut was Ibirapuera Gymnasium. The inauguration date was January 25, 1957, and much like Paceumbu, it hosted a plethora of different sports and would now act as the home of Brazilian boxing. About three and a half miles southeast of Paceumbu, it was located closer to the center of the city. It could house as many as 18,000 spectators, which was roughly four times the number that could fit into Paceaumbu. This was a real sign that the sport was still expanding in Brazil. It seemed almost like fate that it was opening just in time for the professional career of the man who would go on to become the greatest boxer in the history of the country.

Top: Eder's childhood home today
Bottom: The Zumbanos home today

Ricardo Zumbano

Angelina and Olga

Waldemar and Ralph Zumbano

Section Two: The Golden Bantam

This section focuses on Eder Jofre's professional career as a bantamweight. Eder earned the nickname "The Golden Bantam" and is widely believed to be the greatest bantamweight in boxing history. This section covers Eder's first 53 professional bouts which occurred between 1957-1966.

1957

Fight 1, vs. Raul Lopez, March 29, 1957
Fight 2, vs. Raul Lopez II, April 26, 1957

Eder Jofre's professional career began in his hometown of São Paulo, at a venue that became significant throughout his career – the Ginásio Estadual do Ibirapuera. Eder's successful amateur career, as well as his participation in the Olympics, created great fanfare and expectation for his professional career. His amateur exploits meant that he was held in high regard beyond the confines of his hometown. "I saw Eder Jofre's first amateur fights in 1953 at the Juventus football field here in São Paulo. From the beginning, you could tell he was a different fighter," said Newton Campos, the man often addressed as "The Bible of Brazilian boxing."

Jacob Nahun was entrusted with the responsibility of being Eder's manager upon the announcement of Eder's professional aspiration. It was understood that Eder had a rare talent that would need to be nurtured properly. Aristides knew that his son would not be thrown straight into bouts with champions, but also knew the caliber of opposition in Brazil was limited, so they had to be mindful of selecting opposition that would challenge him enough to develop his skill set at an appropriate pace.

Nahun came from a wealthy Jewish family that had succeeded in the coffee industry for decades. He was a merchant worker and also owned a bar on Rua São João called "Juca Pato" where many celebrities would hang out. He was also an avid sports fan who had been the São Paulo Football Club director from the early 1940s before getting involved in boxing. Since the club became interested in boxing, Nahun worked closely within the sport on an amateur level, and his influence grew. Through the São Paulo Football Club connection, he became close friends with Aristides.

People praised Nahun because, despite his business background, he was driven more by his passion for the sport rather than financial benefits. He was not opposed to losing money while remaining enthusiastic. Nahun became one of the first managers in Brazilian boxing to work with foreign

managers. He brought fighters from overseas to expand Brazilian boxing globally.

Eder had this to say about his early days with Nahun: "I grew up fighting in amateur leagues. After a series of matches, I decided to advance my career. In 1957, my professional career officially started. I only stepped up because I knew I was ready. In Argentina, there were a lot of good fighters back in those days. They were better than the Brazilians. I was anxious, but after a lot of training and conversations with my father, he told me: 'Eder, there is no other option right now; you've experienced the Olympic games, Brazilian championship, South American championship, so, it's time.'"

The opponent selected for Eder's debut was Raul Lopez from Argentina. Not much was known about Lopez other than his age. At 23, he was two years older than Eder. Lopez's win-loss record is tough to track, but the opponents he fought before facing Eder were of a good caliber. Lopez drew his match against the highly regarded Uruguayan, Ruben Caceres, but was defeated by the more experienced Argentine duo of Carlos Miranda (twice) and Ricardo Gonzalez. It is noteworthy that the records compiled throughout South America were disorganized and inaccurate unless the boxer turned professional with a great deal of fanfare and media backing. Many records reported more bouts and victories for some of these opponents through the national newspapers than databases such as Boxrec. This implies that the newspapers' reported records weren't 100% accurate since the records were mismanaged. Also, much information came from the management team of the boxer. The truth could often be somewhere in the middle.

Previewing the morning of the bout on March 29, *O Estado de S. Paulo* newspaper *(Estadão)* wrote: "The best Brazilian amateur in the bantamweight division turns professional against young Argentine Raul Lopez. According to the opinion of many, Jofre has great prospects and figures as a heavy favorite to get his first professional victory."

Eder did not disappoint that evening. He made his foray into the professional ranks with a fantastic all-around display of boxing. His performance was described as "excellent in every respect" as he dominated the action before winning by fifth-round knockout. Eder scored a knockdown in the fourth round and then finished the bout with two further knockdowns in the fifth round. In the locker room after the bout, Nahun said to Eder: "That's just the beginning, Eder. If you take this seriously, you will be a rich man."

Following the bout, Lopez stayed in town and, just two weeks later, would face another Brazilian debutante, Benedito da Silva. Lopez performed better as he managed a six-round draw against Eder's countryman, thus setting the stage for a return bout on April 26 back at Ibirapuera. Eder had it easier this time as the Argentine could not even complete two rounds at the prodigious fists of Brazil's new boxing star.

Fight 3, vs. Osvaldo Perez, May 24, 1957

Eder emerged rapidly as a favorite among the audience at Ibirapuera. His third fight came atop a Friday night bill on May 24. Eder's brother-in-law Claudio Tonelli won a bout on the undercard, which was described as boring. Eder's performance against Argentinian Osvaldo Perez saved the show and sent the fans home happy. This fight was described as pleasing as both fighters displayed an excellent array of skills. Perez's record was largely unknown, but up to this point, he had already stepped into the ring with opponents more experienced than Eder, such as Ricardo Gonzalez from Argentina and Arturo Rojas of Chile.

Eder was far ahead when he scored the knockout in the tenth round when he sent Perez tumbling through the ropes after a swarming attack that the local hero had launched. The visiting boxer could not recover from this volley of blows, and the contest was waved off by referee Jose Nicolo. *Estadão* reported, "The Brazilian made a magnificent impression and will soon be one of our boxing stars."

Perez came into the ring ranked as the 10th best featherweight in his native country. For four rounds, he matched Eder with the use of his excellent footwork and lateral movement. Perez shaded a couple of these rounds, but Eder displayed tremendous maturity and adaptability. He predicted Perez's game plan and then stepped down to put more power into his shots as he cornered Perez. Eder dominated the bout from the sixth round. He was composed when attempting to knock out his opponent in the seventh round. Eder punished the Argentine further in the eighth and ninth rounds. When the bout was halted in the tenth round, the Argentine was sent sprawling out of the ring.

The enthusiasm for Eder's performance was believed to be a potential blessing for a local fight scene suffering in recent times. Several recent shows recorded low attendance, mostly because of what was reported by

Estadão to have been "a bad quality of spectacles that the managers insisted upon imposing."

Fight 4, vs. Osvaldo Perez II, June 7, 1957

Only two weeks after their encounter, Eder and Osvaldo Perez were matched again at the same venue; this time underneath a card topped by Angel Bello's upset victory of local favorite Paulo Sacoma. As was the case with the rematch with Raul Lopez, Eder ended proceedings quicker in the return bout as he laid Perez out for a ten count in only the second round. The swiftness in which Eder dismantled an opponent who'd proven himself a worthy foil only two weeks prior pointed to the ring intelligence that young Eder possessed besides his rapid technical improvement.

Fight 5, vs. Juan Gonzalez, June 14, 1957

Almost as quickly as he walked down the steps after thumping Perez, Eder was climbing through the ropes again, but this time as the headline attraction at Ibirapuera. Eder was at the infancy in his career where the fights were coming rapidly, and he took no rest between matches. With this busy schedule, Eder welcomed the challenge of Uruguayan Juan Gonzalez merely one week after the Perez rematch.

Estadão reported: "We do not remember the last time when a fighter showed as much potential as quickly as young Eder Jofre. He has been developing very quickly under one of the best trainers in Brazil." Many press members noted how Eder was already looking like the best boxer in the country. Gonzalez was viewed as not being among the elite level but being a potentially formidable opponent due to his physical style and experience.

The contest was violent as Eder started full of confidence but soon discovered that he faced a determined opponent. Eder forced his strength on the Uruguayan but found the best course of action was to exercise caution. Eder used his jab to find the range and protect himself. He seized the opportunity in the opening round as he kept Gonzalez at a comfortable distance to control him. In the next round, Gonzalez used what was described as an "irregular style" as he smothered Eder's attacks. The fight intensified by the end of the second round.

However, Eder showed his class in the third round when he penetrated Gonzalez's guard and dominated the action. In the fourth round, Gonzalez felt the effect of Eder's punches and was warned twice by the referee for holding onto Eder's gloves in an effort to stifle him. Eder attacked more decisively with a two-fisted onslaught in the fifth round as he rained down left-right-left combination punches to shake up Gonzalez and then went downstairs as he mixed in hurtful punches to his liver. Gonzalez went down under a barrage of punches but willed himself up from the floor only to be flattened again. Gonzalez got up at a count of six, but by now was looking very dizzy as the referee looked closely before waving the action back on. Eder was back on top of him, and as the Uruguayan wilted once more, the bout was waved off. Eder was awarded a fifth-round technical knockout victory. He extended his perfect start to 5-0 with all wins coming inside the distance.

Fight 6, vs. Raul Jaime, July 5, 1957

On July 5, Eder faced off against another Argentinian opponent at Ibirapuera. For the first time in his career, he was extended the full distance and had to settle for a decision victory. The opponent was the more experienced Raul Jaime from Buenos Aires. Jaime, at age 23, had mixed it up with a better caliber of opposition but was not expected to offer much resistance based on Eder's recent brilliant displays. Among the opponents Jaime had swapped leather with was Roberto Castro, reigning national champion of Argentina, whom he had met four times over two years. Jaime had also fallen short against Ruben Caceres and Pedro Miranda, two of the top bantamweights on the continent.

The difficulty in this bout was that Eder had to force the action and could not quite pin down Jaime for a sustained period to impose his punching power or land meaningful combinations. Jaime used a lot of lateral movement, satisfied to last the distance irrespective that the decision would not go his way as Eder had carried the action. It was not all smooth sailing for Eder as he hurt his right hand in the first round and had to resort to mainly using only his left hand. Eder used the right to feint for left-hands and simply tap the Argentine when a right-hand opportunity presented itself. This bout had curbed some of the enthusiasm surrounding Eder's rise as some noted that he did not appear as polished as he had looked in his previous string of knockout victories.

Fight 7, vs. Raul Jaime II, July 19, 1957

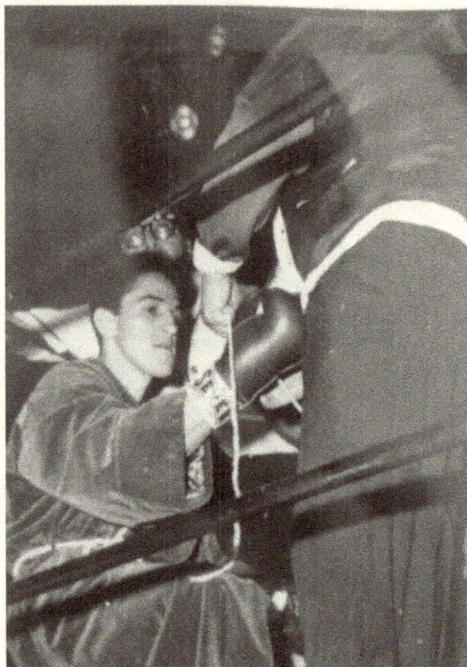

To improve on his last showing, Eder would rematch Jaime two weeks later, on the back of his first critical press. *Estadão* reported that Eder was "completely recovered" from his right-hand injury. In contrast, Jaime was expected to be more adjusted, and thus a better bout was expected.

Unfortunately, in what was described without exaggeration as "the worst of the night," the quality of the bout was labeled as being "terrible." The blame fell mostly with Jaime, who might as well have brought his track shoes as he offered little offense throughout the bout. In the rare instances that Eder pinned downed Jaime, the Argentine grappled excessively. He was warned on over ten separate occasions for these indiscretions and was told by the referee to make a fight of it, but he was not sanctioned. Not only content to run and hold, but Jaime also tried to sell the referee on multiple occasions that he had been hit with illegal blows. "That happened four or five times, and every time, Jofre would have finished the fight had he not been ripped off by the referee momentarily stopping the fight on those occasions," according to *Estadão*. The rounds belonged to Eder, but apparently, there was "not even one exciting second during the ten rounds."

The first three rounds saw both fighters study one another before Eder attacked with more purpose and intent in the fourth and fifth rounds. Eder got through, and one punch bent the knees of Jaime during the fifth round, and from then on, the action became worse. *Folha de São Paulo* reported: "The ten rounds of the fight showed the Brazilian chasing the Argentinian, without, being able to find the right distance to deliver precise and powerful blows. In the few times that Jofre managed to get closer, Jaime protected himself by grabbing Eder. He easily stopped the attacks of our boy who failed to demonstrate technical resources to apply hooks, clean punches, and uppercuts, which could earn him a knockout victory."

While Eder had not impressed during his two bouts with Jaime and the action in the contests was limited, he was less than six months into his professional career. These are the standards and expectations to which he was being held so soon. The experience of the rounds banked, and the different looks Jaime gave him compared to the first few opponents would serve as a valuable learning experience. The support system behind Eder with his father, the Zumbanos, and Nahun would make sure that Eder was always improving and facing different styles of opponent and fighters that held significant advantages in experience over him.

Fight 8, vs. Ernesto Miranda, August 16, 1957

In his next bout, Eder stepped up in the level of his opposition when he was pitted against one of the brightest prospects throughout South America in Argentina's Ernesto Miranda. Although Eder was criticized in his recent bouts, he had still dominated the action. Unlike Raul Jaime, Miranda was expected to come and try to win rather than simply survive.

Like Eder, Miranda was a successful amateur having won multiple national titles and was trained by his father. Miranda boxed in the provincial town of San Luis where his father took him to the gym at age 12. He took to boxing quickly and was fighting amateur bouts at age 13. Miranda had participated in twice as many fights as Eder up to this point; thus, he was considered the more polished boxer of the two. Miranda had also faced a tougher roster of opponents and had come to Brazil full of confidence. The prestige he carried in his homeland was comparable to that which Eder held in Brazil up to this point.

Miranda was a technical boxer who often used a lot of feints and possessed good movement and ring generalship. The local press was apprehensive coming into this showdown between hot prospects. This type of bout between rising young boxers with extensive amateur records would be unlikely to happen in today's game where the promoters and managers like to take few chances when steering their boxers towards possible championship bouts. This bold roll of the dice shined a light on the willingness of Eder and his team to step up to this level so soon after the harsh press received in the Jaime bouts.

Estadão previewed the bout with great anticipation on the morning of Friday, August 16:

"Another boxing gathering will take place tonight with a great final fight at the Ibirapuera Gymnasium. After the presentation of a series of mediocre fighters, the promoters for the current season decided to bring from Buenos Aires a valuable fighter, currently the second-ranked bantamweight from Argentina. It's Ernesto Miranda, number one challenger of Argentine champion Roberto Castro. Eder Jofre will have in the young Argentine, with no question, the hardest opponent of his career. If Ernesto Miranda repeats his performances from last year, he might even be the first to defeat the local boxer. Despite having had a few professional fights, Eder Jofre has been outstanding lately as one of the best national boxers. However, not too long ago, he became worse and didn't impress much. It is true that, for tonight's fight, Eder was submitted to rigorous training, and for sure, his condition will be better, meaning he should come to the ring in excellent shape. Anyway, he will box against a dangerous fighter. If he is in any way careless, he might lose his invincibility. Knowing the quality of his opponent, Jofre will probably fight carefully during the early rounds, and only after half of the fight, he might punch with no fear to offset the counter-attack that Miranda usually does. Due to the personalities of both boxers, the audience is likely to see a high-quality fight tonight since they both have more style than violence. That doesn't mean that the fight couldn't end with a knockout, but it's more likely to be decided by points."

Despite the qualities and ambitions of the two young upstarts, the bout was a disappointing one in terms of action. Both boxers fought cautiously throughout the first five rounds as they studied each other for weaknesses and openings. Miranda used a lot of lateral movement as both fighters struggled to muster any offense. The crowd whistled as they showed discontent, demanding both fighters to step it up and provide some action.

"Only from the sixth round on did the boxers decide to exchange punches with a small advantage for the local boxer," reported *Estadão*. After that, Miranda showed more class as he edged the next three rounds. In one instance, Miranda landed a clean right-hand cross, which removed Eder's mouthpiece, but he did not follow up aggressively. Eder forced the action in the final round as he pressed for a knockout, hurting Miranda, but he could not put him away. The bout went to the scorecards and was ruled a draw, which meant that Eder kept his unbeaten record intact but fell short of scoring a significant victory. Eder's chief criticism was that he was cautious for too long throughout the bout. Despite possessing the harder punches of the two, he lacked the precision and counterpunching of the Argentine. Despite the excitement surrounding the bout, it wasn't well-attended due to multiple days of torrential rainfall. Both boxers, disappointed with the bout's outcome, agreed to a return bout merely three weeks later, but at Pacaembu. This would be Eder's first professional fight outside Ibirapuera.

Fight 9, vs. Ernesto Miranda II, September 6, 1957

Despite the miserable artistic spectacle in the first bout, the return match garnered a massive buzz around town. Due to both rising pugilists' reputations, both boys' level of quality showed that they possessed elite talent when they were not fighting too carefully. While the second fight wasn't as monotonous as the first bout, it wasn't pleasing either. Once again, both boxers preferred to look for counterpunches, and only in a few rare moments did they exchange hard punches. Once again, the result was a draw, which all parties considered a fair result.

This was now the fourth consecutive bout in which Eder had been extended the full 10-round distance. Given he had to experience such resistance and adversity, it left the impression he would come out of this period the better for it as it exposed what deficiencies Eder and his father had to work on if they wanted to progress in the rankings.

Fight 10, vs. Luis Angel Jimenez, October 30, 1957

After a two-month stretch in which he completed forty rounds in four bouts, Eder took his longest break. While he no longer had an unblemished record, he was still unbeaten and most important, had received some crucial seasoning. The seasoning would benefit a young fighter far more than stringing up a run of early knockouts over opponents who didn't deserve to be in the ring with him.

It would be over six weeks until he stepped back into the ring against Argentinian Luis Angel Jimenez. At age 26, Jimenez had proven himself to be a worthy competitor as he had two draws with the upcoming Ruben Caceres plus a tie against the brilliant future world champion Horacio Accavallo. The highest class that Jimenez had been in was even greater than what Eder had encountered. He faced the legendary flyweight world champion, Pascual Perez, a few months earlier, losing a 10-round decision. The Jofre vs. Jimenez bout on October 30 served a useful purpose because it got Eder back into the KO column as he forced an eighth-round technical knockout. The bout was not considered a fascinating spectacle as the gulf in class was very apparent early in the contest. Eder won every round before punishing the Argentine with multiple hard right-hands in the eighth round, forcing Jimenez's corner to carry their man to the corner where it was deemed he could not continue any further.

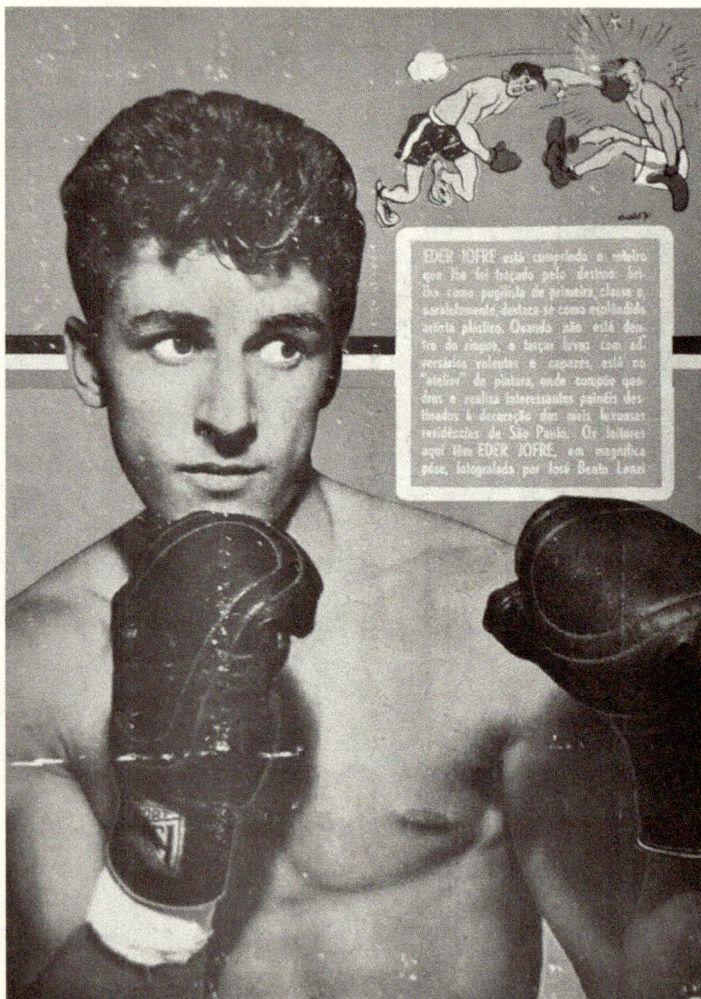

Fight 11, vs. Adolfo Ramon Pendas, December 13, 1957

Eder was back in action on December 13 when he took on Adolfo Ramon Pendas from Argentina. Pendas, 25, had more experience than Eder with twice as many bouts plus a sizable unbeaten streak but was not considered among the elite in his native country. Therefore, Eder was expected to polish him off without too much difficulty.

Eder was headlining the show and his uncle Ricardo was making his professional debut on the undercard, which meant an exciting evening for the Jofre-Zumbano family. Ricardo took on an opponent named Sebastiao Raimundo, who was also making his debut. Raimundo had been a solid performer in the amateur ranks but started his professional career losing to Ricardo when he was defeated on points over the six-round distance.

Eder was becoming more comfortable in his role as a headliner at Ibirapuera. He won his bout comfortably but had to settle for a decision victory as Pendas proved to be a durable opponent. Eder came out aggressively from the opening round as he sought a quick knockout, and he landed powerful punches that sent Pendas into a defensive shell. Pendas paced back and forth to dodge many of Eder's venomous attacks, and when hit cleanly, he took the punches well. Eder scored a clean knockdown with a short left hook in the third round, but Pendas rose quickly and shook off the cobwebs. The action slowed a little bit at this stage in the fight, with Pendas focusing more on not getting hit than on coming up with any attacks of his own. Eder had a strong round in the seventh as he dropped Pendas again before the round ended. Pendas provided resistance in the last three rounds but was beaten handily on the judges' scorecards.

Estadão described Eder's performance as "beautiful" as he fought well with great disposition throughout the contest. *O Globo* reported: "In one of the most hectic fights that pleased the audience who attended Ibirapuera Gymnasium, last Friday night, Eder Jofre overwhelmingly defeated Argentine featherweight, Adolfo Pendas, who had demanded a lot from the local. 'Jofrinho' was, at many times, about to knock out his brave opponent, but the Portenho's* class and goodwill took the fight to the end, under the audience's great excitement. Adolfo Penas (sp) hit the ground twice, for brief seconds, to get back with a lot of grit, demanding a lot of care from the local boxer."

*Portenho is slang for somebody from Buenos Aires.

Fight 12, vs. Cristobal Gavisans, December 22, 1957

The following week saw Eder fight outside of São Paulo for the first time as a professional when he headlined a Sunday afternoon show three days before Christmas in Rio de Janeiro at Auditório da TV-Rio. The opponent was featherweight Cristobal Gavisans, a Spanish-born Brazilian citizen who, at 27 years old, was Eder's senior by six years. Gavisans was familiar with the Jofres as he had faced Eder's brother-in-law Claudio Tonelli, losing a six-round decision. In this bout, Eder closed out his first year as a professional boxer with a routine 10-round decision victory to end the year unbeaten with a record of 10-0-2.

1957 Results

Eder Jofre KO5 Raul Lopez
Eder Jofre KO3 Raul Lopez
Eder Jofre KO10 Osvaldo Perez
Eder Jofre KO2 Osvaldo Perez
Eder Jofre KO5 Juan A. Gonzalez
Eder Jofre W10 Raul Jaime
Eder Jofre W10 Raul Jaime
Eder Jofre D10 Ernesto Miranda
Eder Jofre D10 Ernesto Miranda
Eder Jofre KO8 Luis Angel Jimenez
Eder Jofre W10 Adolfo Ramon Pendas
Eder Jofre W10 Cristobal Gavisans

1958

Fight 13, vs. Avelino Romero, January 29, 1958

After a brief rest over the Christmas and New Year period, Eder was soon back in the gym and getting himself into top fighting shape through an intense training regimen. Avelino Romero was the next opponent brought over from Argentina to face Eder back at Ibirapuera's friendly confines. Not a great deal was known about Romero beyond the fact he had recently suffered an eighth-round TKO loss to Ernesto Miranda.

Romero was keen to tell the press how well he had performed in defeating Chilean Conrado Moreira. Moreira was reported to have performed well in a decision loss to the great Pascual Perez at Pacaembu the previous month, but the Romero-Moreira bout does not show up in any record databases. Whatever the case, on the evening before the bout, Eder was described as in his best physical and technical form to date as he sought to score a more impressive victory over Romero than his nemesis Miranda had. The pre-fight predictions anticipated an entertaining bout but gave the Argentine no serious chance of victory.

The predictions proved accurate as Eder made quick work of Romero, demonstrating an excellent technique in dominating the bout from the start. Romero was described as having an "appreciable technique," but he could not avoid the punishment which the Brazilian rained down on him. Eder scored two knockdowns in quick succession at the end of the first round as the bell saved the Argentine. Sensing Romero was on wobbly legs, Eder attacked at the beginning of the second round letting off a volley of blows that sent the visiting boxer to the canvas again. This time he rose on unsteady legs at the count of seven. He sagged into the ropes, where he held on until the count of nine when referee Antonio Ziravello waved the contest off, awarding Eder an impressive second-round TKO victory.

Fight 14, vs. Cristobal Gavisans II, March 7, 1958

In a rematch of Eder's last bout of 1957, he welcomed Cristobal Gavisans to São Paulo at Ibirapuera on March 7. Since Gavisans' lopsided decision loss to Eder in Rio, he gained a credible draw with Eder's brother-in-law Claudio Tonelli, in a rematch. This earned his shot at redemption against the crown jewel of the Jofre-Zumbano dynasty. As was the theme with previous rematches, Eder once again showed his superior boxing IQ and ability to adapt as he improved on the previous victory. He scored a sixth-round TKO over the Spaniard. The report from *Estadão* expressed that the stoppage was a little harsh on Gavisans: "As expected, Eder Jofre found no difficulty in overcoming the Spaniard Cristobal Gabisans (sp), beating him by TKO in the sixth round. It must be said, however, that the referee was wrong to suspend the combat at that time since Gavisans was still in a position to continue."

Fight 15, vs. Ruben Caceres, May 14, 1958

Eder's positive momentum improved his technique and ability. For the first time in the professional game, he fought outside of Brazil when he traveled to Ruben Caceres' hometown of Montevideo, Uruguay. Early on Tuesday, May 6, Eder, his father, and Pedro Galasso boarded a flight from Congonhas Airport in São Paulo. Eder was cutting it close as his bout was scheduled for the following day. He received a notice upon his arrival that his bout would be postponed one week out to the following Wednesday due to inclement weather in the region. "The Paulista boxers have remained confident and hope to succeed, as they are in good technical and physical form, thus able to properly represent Brazilian professional boxing," reported *Estadão*.

The rescheduled bout took place at Palacio Penarol in front of a partisan crowd who cheered their local fighter on. A year younger than Eder at age 21, Caceres was riding a 16-bout unbeaten streak after losing his debut by disqualification and maintained that streak when he held Eder to a draw. Noticeable in the records of South American boxers of this era are several draws early in the fighters' careers. The reason behind this is, for a boxer to win a bout on a decision, he needed a lead of at least four points on at least two of the judges' scorecards. The purpose of this was to maintain a young fighter's prestige early in their career by not having them suffer too many losses. This ensured the best fighters faced each other and discouraged promoters and managers from protecting their fighters from facing the best opposition. You need only to look at the records of some other South American boxing legends like Carlos Monzon and Nicolino Locche to see multiple early draws on their records.

Eder and his father were disappointed with the verdict, believing they had done enough to go back to Brazil with the victory. The crowd also shared this opinion and acknowledged Eder was better despite their interest in a Caceres victory and they felt Eder deserved the win. "The audience booed the judges' decision loudly since they understood that the Brazilian fighter deserved the victory," reported *O Globo*.

It could have been worse, though, as Eder maintained his unbeaten record and gained valuable experience fighting in front of a hostile crowd. In what wasn't a pleasant trip, Galasso was knocked out by Eulogio Caballero four days before Eder's controversial draw.

Fight 16, vs. German Escudero, June 21, 1958
Fight 17, vs. German Escudero II, June 29, 1958

The draw that Eder received in Uruguay didn't do too much to dampen his spirits nor hurt his progress as he came back to Brazil to score back-to-back victories over German Escudero of Argentina. Escudero entered the ring with a rather modest-looking record but some good experience, having earned a draw with future world champion Horacio Accavalo and he was the first to defeat the highly regarded Paraguayan Kid Pascualito. The Argentine also owned a win and loss over Eder's rival Ernesto Miranda and was defeated on points by Jose Smecca, a fast-rising prospect making noise in Argentina.

The Jofre vs. Escudero bouts took place three weeks apart in June, with the first bout in São Paulo and the return in Rio with Eder getting a second-round knockout each time. On the fight in São Paulo at Ibirapuera on June 11, *Estadão* reported: "The final bout of the evening pleased those in attendance with an outstanding victory for the promising bantamweight Eder Jofre. Jofre scored a knockout in the first minute of the second round when he landed a violent right cross on Escudero's face. He followed up with a left hook to make his opponent fall to the floor. Escudero had already been knocked down in the first round; he tried to get up but did not possess the strength to do so before remaining still on the canvas after the 10-second count had passed. Eder attained another great achievement in his short boxing career."

The second Escudero contest took place in front of a jubilant crowd who awoke early that day to gather around their radio sets and listen to the Brazilian national football team win its first World Cup. The team, featuring the likes of Pele, Garrincha, Mario Zagalo, Gilmar, Didi, and Nilton Santos, defeated host nation Sweden 5-2 in Stockholm and put the country in a real party mode ushering in a golden era of Brazilian sport.

On July 8, it was announced by the Paulista Boxing Federation they were anointing Eder as the national champion in the bantamweight division. Eder had yet to face a domestic rival, but with no serious competition, Eder was handed the title without objection. Media members claimed that the title was long overdue. It was clear Eder was not only the best bantamweight in the country at that moment but arguably the best fighter the country had ever produced. In addition to Eder getting the title, brother-in-law Claudio Tonelli was anointed featherweight champion, and Fernando Barreto was awarded the welterweight title. It was believed that

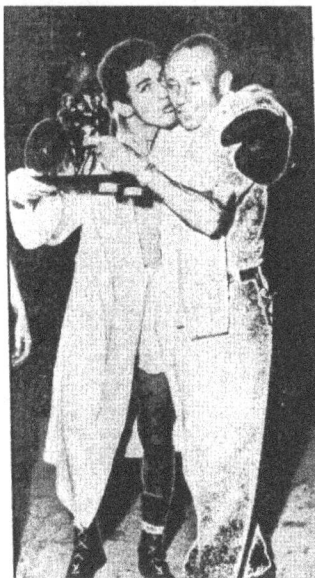

the awarding of national titles on a more consistent basis would move Brazilian boxing in the right direction.

O Globo reported: "Within the poor environment that national boxing still has – if we compare it to more advanced countries like Argentina, for instance – there hasn't always been the wished abundance of values for regular fights for professional Brazilian championship titles. So, by including in one of those categories someone much more outstanding than those currently fighting, it's no wonder the adjudication to such boxers, of the belt correspondent to their consecration as the 'King' of Brazil in their category."

Eder, Tonelli, and Barreto joined middleweight Milton Rosa, lightweight Pedro Galasso, and light heavyweight Luiz Ignacio as the national champions. All but Barreto and Rosa were trained by Aristides. This was considered an essential move because Brazilian boxers had often struggled to qualify for South American championship fights because they did not even have national titles, which meant that Argentine boxers often fought each other or opponents from Uruguay or Chile.

Eder expressed his desire to add to that silverware and issued a challenge to the current champion of South America, Roberto Castro of Argentina. This bout was not to happen soon however, as per the regulations of the South American federation, Castro had 90 days to decide if he wanted to accept that challenge.

Fight 18, vs. Juan Carlos Acebel, July 18, 1958

Rather than wait for his challenge to Roberto Castro to be answered, Eder focused on maintaining his recent activity by staying in the gym without breaks. He was back in the ring merely three weeks after the second Escudero win when he opposed Juan Carlos Acebal of Argentina.

Acebal, who started his career with a draw with Kid Pascualito and a win over Waldemiro Torres, was ranked 10th in his homeland's divisional rankings. He had mixed with some of the continent's finest bantamweights having gone toe-to-toe with bright young Uruguayan prospect and amateur star, Aniceto Pereyra and the superb Horacio Accavallo.

In the first round, Acebel showed some excellent movement while Eder showed more aggression. The opening round was described as even because the Argentine was very economical with his punches. When the bell sounded, signaling the beginning of the second round, Acebal stopped moving and opted to fight in close to gain the Brazilian's respect. In this round, Eder attacked Acebal's body, and with a strong left hook to the liver followed quickly by a violent right cross, he dropped the Argentine. Acebal struggled to his feet but was up at the count of five only for Eder to trap him in the neutral corner where he fired away, attacking at will. Acebal struggled to escape from the corner, so he tried to cover up but could not muster up the strength to resist the blows Eder rained down on him. Eder was attacking with left hooks and straight rights down the middle, which eventually dropped Acebal for a second time. Acebal could not beat the referee's count and had to be assisted to his stool by his trainer to clear his head and recover from the beating he had sustained.

Fight 19, vs. Roberto Olmedo, August 8, 1958

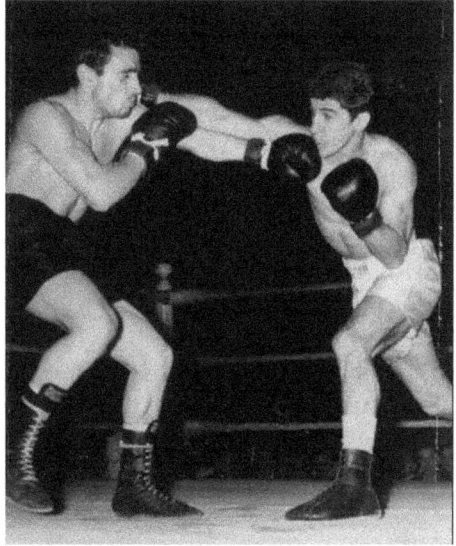

Behind Eder's impressive performances, his confidence was growing; it was a matter of when, not if Eder would win the continental championship. Once again, instead of resting on his laurels and waiting for Roberto Castro to accept his challenge, Eder continued to work on his rapidly improving skill set as he took on another Argentine import, this time named Roberto Olmedo. It was anticipated that Olmedo would borrow the tactics of his countryman Ernesto Miranda and avoid standing in front of Eder, which had been disastrous for those brave enough to face Eder head-on.

Olmedo did adopt those tactics as best he could and tried to negate the Brazilian's potent power punches. In the opening round, Olmedo stayed as far away as he could, looking to make sure that Eder couldn't test his chin early. These tactics carried Olmedo into the second round, but then he became brave and tried to take on Eder in close. Shortly after this change in tactics, the two traded blows in the center of the ring. Eder promptly scored the bout's first knockdown when he connected with a clean straight right-hand through the middle, which he followed up with a hard left hook. Olmedo rose quickly but was visibly shaken and opted to clinch as much as he could simply to make it out of the round.

In the next round, Olmedo appeared clueless. He came out defensively but once again opted to go into the ring's center to entice Eder into a toe-to-toe brawl. There would be only one outcome in such a fight. Eder beautifully sidestepped Olmedo's punches before following up with a hard left hook and right cross. Olmedo tried to fight back, throwing punches at Eder's body, but his efforts were blocked. Eder attacked again, which nearly brought Olmedo down as the bell rang to signal the end of the round.

The Argentine corner instructed their man to avoid contact. When the fourth round began, Olmedo tried to move around the ring and out of Eder's range. Eder closed the ring down on Olmedo with relative ease and worked his body before scoring another knockdown towards the end of the round. Once again, the Argentine was saved by the bell and bravely came out for the fifth round, but the contest only lasted a further 15 seconds as Eder cracked him with a left hook to the liver, which lowered Olmedo's guard and left him wide open and Eder smashed a short right-hand to the chin which laid Olmedo out for the full count.

After the fight, Olmedo complained about a clavicle dislocation, possibly caused by the final knockdown. Rather than blame the injury, Olmedo acknowledged that an excellent fighter had defeated him.

Fight 20, vs. Jose Casas, September 12, 1958

A seasoned boxer named Jose Casas came over to try and stop the tremendous momentum Eder had been building. Casas, 26, had fought many of the best boxers in Argentina and often gave a good account as he earned draws with Roberto Castro, Alfredo Bunetta, and Carlos Miranda, younger brother of Ernesto. He caused a stir four years earlier when he upset the highly touted Chilean fighter Arturo Rojas. Unfortunately, due to poor record-keeping, Casas's record was far from complete. He impressed in what little workouts the local press saw of him and was said to be a very classy boxer who possessed excellent mobility and sound fundamentals.

"Eder Jofre will reappear at the next professional boxing meeting of the Paulista Boxing Federation on the 12th, at the Gymnasium of Ibirapuera. Among the four fights, the main one stands out. This fight marks the return of the Brazilian bantamweight champion contesting with Argentine Jose Casas. Eder Jofre has been assiduously training, in an exceptional physical and technical condition and could gain another significant triumph for his record. As for his opponent, it is known that he is a boxer of good technical skill that enjoys a great reputation in his homeland. The results of his four recent fights, all fought with famous professionals, such as Roberto Castro, Alfredo Bunetta, etc. truly reflect his caliber," reported *Estadão* in previewing the bout.

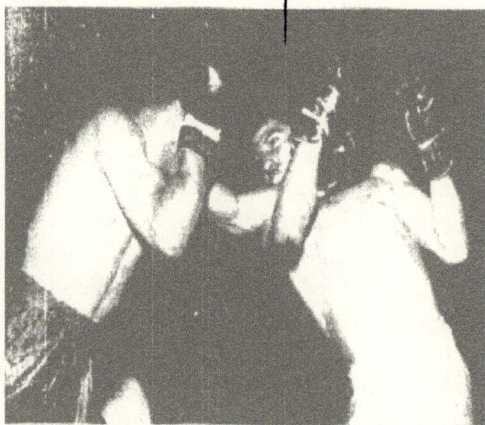

Eder is in the white trunks

Eder was made to work hard as he scored what was described as his most challenging victory to date. Eder won the fight, but he didn't have it all his way as he had to defend responsibly even late in the bout when he stepped on the gas in an attempt to get Casas out of there. *Estadão* reported: "When Eder chose to fight at a distance and use his well-schooled style with movement, the Argentine responded in great style with a lot of skill of his own. When Eder tried to close the distance and fight more aggressively, his opponent wouldn't run and fought on fairly even terms with the Brazilian boxer."

The fight was fairly close until the last round when Eder almost overwhelmed Casas with a vicious attack. Casas lost a point for blatant low blows after having lost a point in the eighth round also on multiple fouls. Eder claimed a decision victory in a vicious fight that pleased the fans. "To sum it up, the fight between the Brazilian bantamweight champion and the fighter who was able to tie with the South American champion (Roberto Castro) made the entire evening worth it. It offered technical skills to those who appreciate that style, and it also pleased those who prefer a harder fight as it had its violent moments. Eder won with difficulty, but it must be considered that Casas has been the best fighter to face him at Ibirapuera," summarized *Estadão*.

VITÓRIA DIFÍCIL A DE EDER JOFRE

O Argentino José Casas Foi um Adversário Perigoso Para o Campeão Brasileiro do Pêso Galo

Fight 21, vs. Jose Casas II, October 10, 1958

Only two weeks after his hard-fought defeat at the hands of Brazil's brightest boxing star, Jose Casas scored a significant victory by defeating Eder's brother-in-law Claudio Tonelli. It was a crowd-pleasing match. That victory earned him a further two weeks in Brazil and another crack at Eder. The rematch took place at the same venue, and fans anticipated another entertaining brawl between the two well-matched youngsters.

Eder left no doubts in the return bout as he clearly showed his superiority with a swift third-round knockout. Casas fought bravely but was outgunned from the onset and could not keep pace with an improved Eder. Eder didn't need too long to study Casas and seize control with a beautiful display of powerful boxing. Eder gathered the information from their previous bout. The ten rounds of action were enough for him to know what to expect from Casas and improve on that victory with a more positive outcome.

Casas accepted the fight which Eder imposed upon him. Despite landing a couple of nice punches early, he was punished towards the end of the first round. The Argentine could not bother Eder much with his offense and was quickly on the wrong end of a shellacking. In the next round, Casas did try to make it a wrestling match in close, but it didn't take Eder too long to break away and hurt Casas when he found space to punch cleanly. Eder landed a left hook, which forced Casas to back up and then quickly followed that up with a quick right-hand blow, punctuated with a short-left hook that knocked Casas down. Casas rose quickly but barely made it out of the round as Eder punished him. Between rounds, Aristides instructed Eder to attack the body of Casas before trying to finish the bout. Eder followed his father's orders and quickly turned Casas's liver, spleen, and stomach into his targets.

"He (Eder) gave him a left hook to the liver; Casas brought his guard down and received a right-hand punch to his face and went down. The referee Antonio Ziravelo counted to three. Before he could reach the count of four, the Argentine had already jumped up with his guard up. Eder didn't care. He resumed attacking in an even more brutal way. Casas kept stepping back periodically, not being able to avoid the punches that were landing all over his body. After a bunch of punches and hooks, Casas stopped stepping back. His muscles were tense; he was transfixed and couldn't breathe. Eder hooked with his left hand, punched with the right hand right after that, and Casas fell heavily on the ring floor. Stunned, with his eyes frozen, he couldn't get up, even after the referee counted ten seconds," reported *Estadão*.

Tennis superstar Maria Esther Bueno was as impressed as anyone in attendance. She came up to the ring after the bout to congratulate Eder. She talked about how she was a boxing fan and had seen one of the classic fights between Sugar Ray Robinson and Carmen Basilio. Eder was interviewed over the sound system as Bueno took her seat. He dedicated the victory to her. Bueno came back into the ring and hugged Eder. The audience broke out into loud applause at the gesture between two of the nation's brightest sporting talents.

Eder hoped he would secure a bout with Roberto Castro for the South American title. Instead, his old foe, Ernesto Miranda, was offered the title fight. Miranda defeated Castro earlier in the year with the Argentinian title at stake over the 12-round distance. Eder and Miranda were the two leading men in their respective countries. They were on a collision course to eventually settle the score from their two drawn bouts. Still, the Argentine had beaten Eder to the punch in getting to fight for the continent's top honors. The Castro vs. Miranda championship match was set for November 22 at Luna Park in Buenos Aires.

Fight 22, vs. Jose Smecca, November 14, 1958

With Ernesto Miranda challenging Roberto Castro, Jacob Nahun and Aristides were determined to find an opponent with some cache that would continue to help Eder's prestige grow. The reasoning behind this was that if Eder kept knocking everybody back and raising his opposition level, they would force the champion, whoever it may be, into facing him.

There were serious negotiations for a big fight between Eder and Paraguayan boxing hero Kid Pascualito for a bout in Corumba on November 22. The city of Corumba sits along the Paraguayan river in the southwestern part of Brazil. It figured to be a perfect location for such a bout as it would give Pascualito's fans the chance of a short trip across the border to see their man in action. Pascualito had forged a strong reputation for himself, running up an impressive record in his home country and Argentina. The location, date, and purse were agreed promptly by Aristides when they traveled to Corumba to iron out the details with local promoter Renato Pace. Still, they never received confirmation from the Paraguayan side. The deadline passed, so a bout was quickly agreed for Eder to face a dangerous Argentine boxer named Jose Smecca. Smecca, born only two months before Eder, was unbeaten and, like Eder, had desires to fight for the continental championship. He had been in training and had no problems accepting the terms and came to Brazil to face Eder in a quickly arranged show at Ibirapuera on November 14.

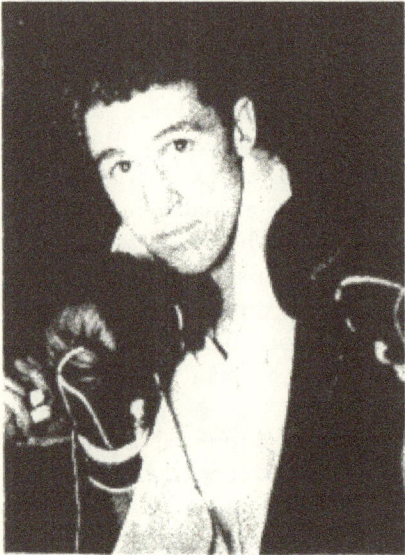

Eder had also been in training but had expected to be in action a week later against Pascualito. Smecca had earned a national ranking in Argentina. He ran up a string of impressive victories upon turning professional in 1955 but lost that ranking when he halted his career and spent 12 months in the army. Smecca was quite different from the other Argentine boxers that came to face Eder because he was shorter with a stocky build. He had the height of a flyweight but the upper body of a lightweight. Most of the Argentinians who faced Eder up to this point used their legs and moved around the ring, but Smecca preferred to fight in close and wear his opponents down with his formidable, accurate two-handed offense. His dangerous punch was the left hook. The local press expressed concern coming into this bout due to Smecca's unblemished record and strong reputation. The pessimism resulted from the perceived lack of adaptability by the local hero, and many felt that Eder would have to be at the top of his game and box patiently before going on the attack.

Eder suffered a rare moment in this fight when Smecca caught him with a fast right-hand, and Eder stumbled to the floor for a knockdown in round two. Eder admitted to becoming complacent after he had dominated the first round against his opponent. He also admitted that he felt nervous seeing Cidinha and his mother in the audience and was perhaps too keyed up with trying to impress them. In the corner, Eder asked his father, "What happened?" "He caught you with a right-hand," Aristides said. "How long was I down for?" asked Eder. "Four seconds," his father responded. The next two rounds were tough, especially the fourth round when both fighters went toe-to-toe and returned to their corners with some facial damage. Coming out for the fifth round, Eder quickly seized control of the fight and dished out a one-sided beating before the referee stopped the fight in the seventh-round awarding Eder a TKO victory.

The feeling of getting knocked down wasn't a good one for Eder, especially in front of his home fans. Eder took the weekend off and was back in the gym on Monday, working even harder and seeking further challenges as he was not only closing in on the South American title, but he was also closing in on a world ranking.

Fight 23, vs. Roberto Castro, December 12, 1958

As Eder stayed sharp, hoping to get a shot at the South American championship against Roberto Castro, the news came back to São Paulo on November 22 that Castro was dethroned by Ernesto Miranda over 15 rounds in Buenos Aires. It was the second time Miranda had outpointed Castro, but he was not ready to put his title on the line against Eder. Instead, it was the recently deposed Castro who would accept an offer from Jacob Nahun to face Eder in São Paulo merely weeks after losing his title. Despite Castro's loss, he was still considered in his prime and a dangerous opponent. For Castro, this was also a perfect opportunity to get back to the front of the queue because a win over Eder would make him the most logical challenger to the title.

Up to this point, Castro was by far the most experienced opponent the young Brazilian had been matched against despite his relative youth of only 24 years. Castro, a native of San Juan, a valley city east of the Andes Mountains, was coming to Brazil with something to prove after he was relinquished of his South American bantamweight championship. He proudly held that title for over a year after he avenged an earlier loss against Arturo Rojas of Chile. Other career highlights of Castro's were winning the Argentine title in only his fifth bout and when he pinned the first loss on the fast-rising Pedro Miranda in 1955. He again defended his title with a 15-round draw against Miranda the following year. Castro came to Brazil with a formidable record that consisted of 56 wins against five losses and eight draws.

In previewing the bout, *O Globo* reported on December 8 that if Eder defeated Castro, he would be getting a shot at Ernesto Miranda's title, but they felt this would be a legitimately difficult assignment for Eder. "Remarkable boxer and Brazilian bantamweight champion, Eder Jofre, will fight next Friday at Ibirapuera gymnasium, Argentine Roberto Castro, former South American champion of the weight category. The Argentine lost the continental title less than a month ago to his countryman Ernesto

Miranda, but is still one of the greatest men in the continent and may break 'Jofrinho's' invincibility. In the case of a victory over the former champion, Eder Jofre will have the right to fight in January with Ernesto Miranda in an official fight for the South American championship. The result will therefore be one of the most important ones for the Brazilian boxer, who will have a big chance to finally be acknowledged."

Eder would have been more concerned about Castro and his credentials, but he had another thing on his mind: Dogalberto's amateur debut. Eder screamed so much from the corner for his brother that he lost his voice, but the family was happy that Dogalberto won his bout. If Eder had not been focused as he might be, his father was taking no chances. Aristides brought film of Castro's recent matches, and Eder was taken aback by the speed of the Argentine. "Oh gosh…he's too fast for me," he told his father. Eder got down to business and was in the best condition possible for what he felt had just become a more difficult task than what was initially anticipated. During fight week, Aristides came down with a bout of the flu and could not attend the training sessions.

"Yesterday evening, Eder Jofre wrapped up his preparations for tomorrow's fight. He arrived at the gym on Rua Santa Ifigênia around 5 pm. With Kid Jofre absent, Higino Zumbano is the one in charge of all boxers, including the Brazilian champion Eder. And it was under his order that Eder did his last practice before the fight with Roberto Castro. Eder began with a gym session during which he forced his muscles, trying to stretch easily to get all his movements. The champion was doing well. Then, he started to hit the punching ball. He did it masterfully, showing quickness on the hits and a perfect view of his target. He came closer to the heavy bag, started punching it with both hands. He took about 20 minutes in each exercise, which goes to show how strict Eder's training is. The champion even jumped rope and shadowboxed before his uncle summoned him to the ring," reported *Estadão* before the bout. Eder had been sparring Pedro Galasso and Mario dos Santos.

While sparring with Galasso, Eder showed excellent form proving that he could fight on his toes. There had been criticisms in previous camps and bouts that while Eder was showing excellent fundamentals and technique, he had appeared a little bit flat-footed. In keeping with Galasso's movement and educated skill, Eder showed excellent movement. In the absence of Aristides, the teachings of Higino were praised as Eder was quick to absorb everything his uncle taught him. Showing off his versatility and variety of offense, Eder impressed while sparring with dos Santos. Unlike Galasso, dos Santos stayed in the center of the ring and tried to impose his size and power on Eder, but Eder took advantage of his limited defense and used the speed advantage he held over dos Santos.

"After the training, Eder was ready to leave the gym. While he was changing, he spoke about his strong will to win the fight tomorrow. By his side, Higino Zumbano and Attilio Loffredo would happily smile due to Eder's esteem. Both, by the way, complimented their pupil's focus during this preparatory phase, quoting his detachment and his disposition as factors that will be able to determine a great victory," concluded *Estadão*.

The Jofre vs. Castro fight was the top of the bill at Ibirapuera, but some of the excitement turned to concern because on the undercard, Eder's uncle, Ricardo Zumbano, was defeated by Geraldo Marques. However, Eder had excellent focus, and entered the ring determined to leave the arena on a positive note.

While Eder was the crowd's favorite and considered the brighter talent of the two, few expected him to destroy Castro so quickly and ruthlessly as he did when he put the Argentine out for a ten count at only 2:40 of the second round. Right in the first minute, the fighters engaged in a vicious exchange in the center of the ring. Castro was trying to pick up the pace of the fight, looking for a fast knockout. Eder blocked two of his punches and counter-attacked to his body. In the second round, Eder took the initiative as he forced the action further and attacked Castro, throwing punches to the body and head. The attack left Castro breathless, and he was ruthlessly knocked out.

Dogalberto had one more fight and then hung up the gloves. The pressure of being the brother of the great "Galo de Ouro" was taking a significant toll, and he lost his second fight. After that, he stopped fighting and decided to be a sparring partner for his brother. Dogalberto had been impressive to many who'd seen him to this point and displayed many of the same moves as Eder.

1958 Results

Eder Jofre KO2 Avelino Romero
Eder Jofre KO6 Cristobol Gavisans
Eder Jofre D10 Ruben Caceres
Eder Jofre KO2 German Escudero
Eder Jofre KO2 German Escudero
Eder Jofre KO2 Juan Acebal
Eder Jofre KO5 Roberto Olmedo
Eder Jofre W10 Jose Casas
Eder Jofre KO3 Jose Casas
Eder Jofre KO7 Jose Smecca
Eder Jofre KO2 Roberto Castro

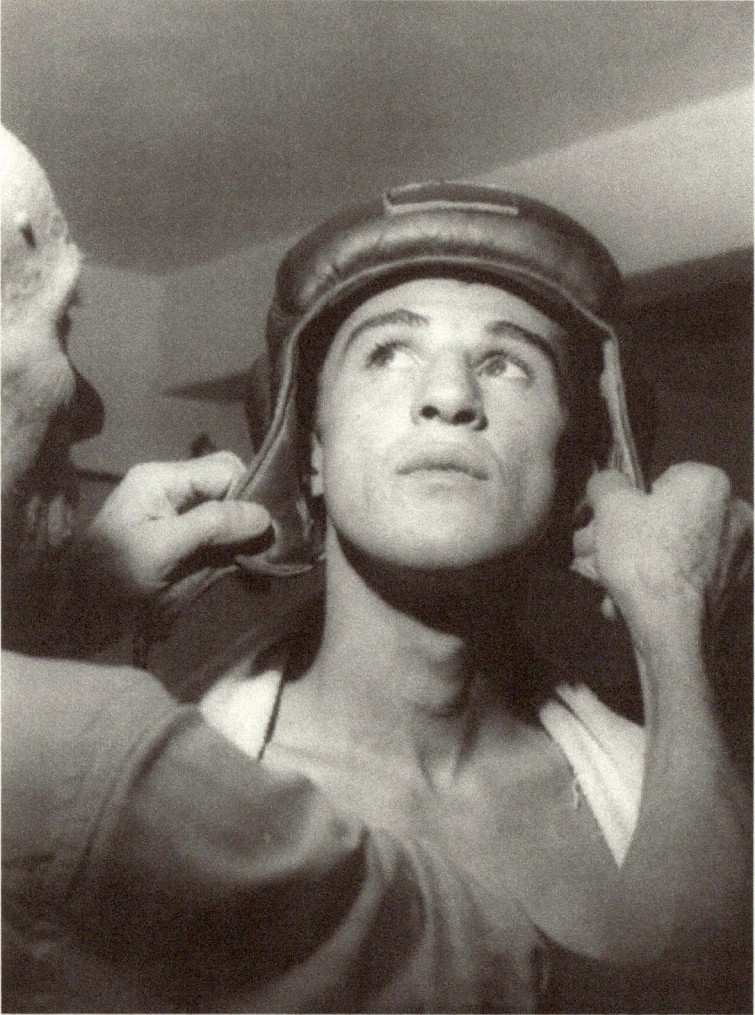

1959

Fight 24, vs. Aniceto Pereyra, March 23, 1959

Shortly after the impressive dispatching of Roberto Castro, Ernesto Miranda accepted Eder's challenge, and the bout was scheduled for January 23 in Buenos Aires at Luna Park. Unfortunately, on January 6, Miranda pulled out of the bout due to illness, so Eder was left without a fight. He stayed in the gym working daily to stay sharp as the managers worked on a date on which to rearrange the title bout with Miranda.

On February 15, Jacob Nahun took a flight to Buenos Aires to rearrange the Miranda bout but returned frustrated when the Argentine wouldn't agree to the fight suddenly. It was believed there was a change in their negotiation, and the promoters at Luna Park were not willing to put up enough money to satisfy Miranda to take on such a risky opponent. There was little persuasion in the fact that Nahun held the original signed contract. It was back to square one.

Instead of Miranda, the opponent who did agree to come to Brazil to face Eder was an interesting one in Aniceto Pereyra. Pereyra, 24, from Uruguay, boasted of an unbeaten record and was one of the brightest young fighters on the continent. He was one of only two boxers to have defeated Eder as an amateur. While this was not the fight Eder wanted, it was one that motivated him. Eder and his father had always felt he was given the short end of a bad verdict in their second amateur meeting back in Montevideo at the South American championships in October of 1956.

The professional bout turned out to be a dominant victory for Eder as he won every round, but due to a recent string of impressive performances, it was deemed a somewhat underwhelming performance overall. Pereyra fought defensively as he dodged the Brazilian's attacks but seldom tried to force any action of his own. Aristides demanded more pressure from his son. The crowd grew bored of the contest as Eder was very content to win the rounds with something to spare without extending himself in going for the knockout.

Eder sensed the crowd was growing restless in the final round, which persuaded him to go for the kill. He was met with multiple clinches as the Uruguayan did everything in his power to make sure he heard the final bell. Eder won a wide unanimous decision. "During the ten rounds, Eder played with his opponent. He could have finished the fight right in the early rounds but decided to hurt him until the end of the fight. The Uruguayan did not even touch Eder," wrote Henrique Matteucci in *O Galo de Ouro*.

After the bout, Eder instructed Nahun to try and re-negotiate a bout with Ernesto Miranda. Nahun tried to work with the Argentine but negotiations hit a snag. This time the promoters at Luna Park obstructed the long-awaited rematch. Miranda had been receptive to risking his title in São Paulo, but the promoters would not sign off on the bout, which left Miranda upset.

The worst part about this was that Miranda was so angry at the decision he announced that he would not even fight in Argentina. He intended to move to Europe where he would take on multiple fights. Miranda was joined by his brother Carlos as they settled in Italy, but he did not relinquish his championship. Despite the standoff between the Luna Park promoters, the Argentine Federation, and Miranda, they did not intend to strip him of the title. This perhaps was because they saw him as such a talented boxer and did not want to risk the belt finding its way out of Argentina or risk suffering an irreparable rift among the parties.

Fight 25, vs. Salustiano Suarez, April 20, 1959

One month after the dominant victory over Pereyra, Eder was back in action again at Ibirapuera. This time the opponent was Salustiano Suarez, the second-ranked Argentine bantamweight. Because he held this lofty ranking, the local press was concerned this could be a challenging assignment for Eder. It took only one training session at the gym of Palmeiras Football Club for them to discount the Argentinian's chances as he left a poor impression having said to have looked "really, really bad," according to *Estadão*. Suarez had split a three-bout series with Kid Pascualito, so the poor showings in training came as a surprise. Those sessions were carried over into the ring as Eder easily defeated Suarez.

"Eder stood out soon enough even though he wasn't fighting completely in order. After winning the first round, the Brazilian improved in the second round when he intelligently realized that Suarez's defense was vulnerable. Suarez lowered his guard whenever he threw the right-hand punch, Eder dealt punches at will, shadowing whatever move Suarez was trying to make. The Argentine finished the second round badly, bleeding excessively through his nose and breathing with difficulty, Suarez went to his corner. When he came back, he knew he was defeated. At a simple threat of attack coming from Eder, Suarez would clinch, stopping the fight. Suarez received a warning because of that, and other faults caused by his disorganization. Suarez didn't attempt to dodge as Eder landed punishing shots in close. In round four, the fight still had the same rhythm. At the moment when Eder decided to finish the fight, it was enough for him to push forward and let his hands go. One right cross, followed by a straight left, dropped Suarez to the floor. Referee Alfonso Araujo counted the ten seconds, and the Argentine remained still. It had been an easy victory for Eder," reported *Estadão*.

On April 23, it was confirmed that Eder would travel to Montevideo for a rematch with Ruben Caceres for charitable purposes. There had been major floods in Uruguay the previous week, so to raise funds to aid the victims, Uruguayan boxing promoter Roque Rolando wanted to put on a boxing showcase. Eder agreed to the rematch with Caceres in Montevideo at a week's notice.

Just before boarding the flight from Congonhas airport, Caceres had pulled out of the bout, leaving Eder with no opponent. He still traveled to Uruguay with his brother Dogalberto and their father. Stablemate Luiz Ignacio was defending his South American light heavyweight title against Dogomar Martinez. The Uruguayan Martinez defeated the Brazilian and retired after the bout. Eder took part in some sparring while in Uruguay before heading back to São Paulo, where they sent a proposal to Kid Pascualito for a bout on May 25 in São Paulo.

Once again, they did not hear from the Paraguayan and promptly agreed to terms on May 12 for a bout with the world-ranked Filipino Leo Espinosa for June 1.

Fight 26, vs. Leo Espinosa, June 4, 1959

Aristides wanted to extend his son's fame internationally. Through meetings with Jacob Nahun, they agreed to bring in Abraham Katzenelson to assist. Katzenelson had good international connections, including George Parnassus, the famous Los Angeles boxing matchmaker who later became a promoter. Parnassus was the matchmaker for Cal and Ailen Eaton, the lead promoter for the Olympic Auditorium in Los Angeles.

The Eatons were without question, the most powerful promoters west of New York, and as far as the lighter weight classes went, the most important by some distance, catering to the large Mexican population in Southern California. Parnassus had replaced Babe McCoy as the matchmaker after McCoy had been banned from boxing in 1956 for his involvement in arranging fixed matches from the late 1940s until the mid-50s. "George Parnassus was a good man and a powerful businessman with connections all over the world. He had every type of connection needed to do just about anything," said Rick Farris, former professional fighter and president of the West Coast Boxing Hall of Fame.

Parnassus told them that if Eder could beat the experienced Filipino Leo Espinosa, then he would gain a world ranking and be within reach of a world title shot. The official announcement of the fight against Espinosa made Eder doubt himself. He thought about his victories but knew that the Filipino was a significant step up in class and experience. He came up to his father and asked:

"Do you agree with that fight?"

"Of course, Eder," Aristides replied.

"Isn't it too soon?" Eder asked.

"No, Eder. It's about time to reach higher altitudes," Aristides said.

Aristides taunted him: "Well…if you are too afraid, I can still cancel it," he needled Eder.

"Afraid?" Eder stayed quiet for a minute and smiled: "You know what, I am afraid."

"Alright then, I will cancel," his father said.

"No Dad. That's the way it is, afraid or not. I am fighting," Eder said, confirming he was up to the challenge.

Aristides and Eder share a laugh

The world-class Espinosa represented Eder's biggest challenge to this point. Espinosa came with an excellent pedigree and was ranked number two in the world. At 29 years old, he came to town with a 44-11-1 record and the experience of having fought for the world flyweight championship twice, coming up short against Japan's Yoshio Shirai and the legendary Argentinian Pascual Perez. He had also failed in an attempt for the bantamweight championship when he was defeated by the popular Raul 'Raton' Macias in a Mexico City bull ring. Espinosa's impressive run included a win over Shirai plus impressive victories over Pone Kingpetch (future flyweight champion), Sadao Yaoita, and Speedy Akira. The confidence of Espinosa and his legendary manager Lope Sarreal appeared justified given the experience and track record the Filipino brought to Brazil.

On May 25, just a few days before boarding a flight from Venezuela where he fought the previous month, Espinosa's team asked if they could move the fight a few days from the first to the fourth of June to afford them an extra few days to acclimate. Their request was granted by Nahun.

At this time, the only Brazilian boxer who had ever fought a world-ranked opponent was Luiz Ignacio when he fought light heavyweight world champion, Archie Moore, the previous year. Eder expressed his delight at this opportunity stating, "I am very pleased. I know that Espinosa is a well-regarded boxer, which explains his high ranking in the world. I will immediately begin intense training."

The president of the São Paulo Boxing Federation, Vicente Saguas Presas Junior, declared that "Eder will now have the opportunity to show his value," while Nahun stated that he felt this historical event would usher in a fascinating time for boxing in Brazil.

Espinosa arrived on May 28 at 4:45 pm and was greeted by a crowd of sports media at the airport. He did not reveal too much but admitted that he knew little about the Brazilian. "I know nothing about him, nor have I read about him, but I was informed that he knocked out Roberto Castro, so it is clear he has quality," he said.

Espinosa had defeated Castro in October of 1955 on points in Argentina on his previous South American tour. When told by local media of Eder's power, Espinosa remembered a previous bout when he faced a highly touted puncher. "When I fought Young Martin (in 1953), I suffered a lot at his hands. Even though he isn't very technical, he is an excellent puncher and presents danger until the bell finishes the fight," he said. He wasn't sold that Eder would possess the same punching prowess that the Spaniard Martin had.

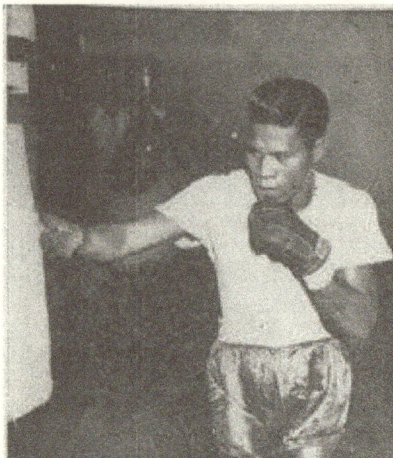

Leo Espinosa works the bag

On May 30, both fighters' training sessions were covered extensively in the local sports papers as they trained at different headquarters. Espinosa trained at Wilson Russo Gym, and many spectators gathered to see what Eder would be up against. Espinosa did not reveal too much as he did not spar. Instead, he performed several exercises, including three rounds on the speed ball and two on the heavy bag. He concluded his session with some impressive jump rope exercises and shadowboxing. Espinosa's manager Lope Sorreal said: "Leo is well prepared, and I believe he will win this fight."

Eder arrived at his training session at his father's gym in good spirits, having done his roadwork in the morning before getting some rest at home. His training was similar to the Filipino's as he worked the speed ball, heavy bag, and did his shadowboxing and skipping routines. Some noted that Eder looked sharper than he had for his previous fights. "I don't have any pre-studied tactics because we don't know the Filipino. Eder will fight accordingly with his conditions and according to how the fight goes," said Aristides.

On fight night, an excited crowd went to Ibirapuera, knowing that their man stood on the threshold of something vital. While Eder was the favorite, Espinosa's pedigree gave justified anxiety to many of Eder's fans. The first boxer to walk to the ring was Espinosa wearing a blue robe with blue shorts. The audience clapped, and he thanked them for their pleasant welcome by taking a bow. Eder came up right after him wearing a black robe with white shorts. The audience clapped for a long time when he entered the ring to let him know that their support was behind him.

Round By Round from *Estadão* and *O Globo*

Round 1
(*Estadão*) – Slow fight at distance with the boxers studying each other. Eder hit Leo's face once with a left hook. A small advantage to Eder.

(*O Globo*) – A study round, with feints and jabs thrown and avoided. Eder throws a strong left hook, beginning the hostilities. The audience incentivizes him, but there is not much action.

Round 2
(*Estadão*) – Leo attacked, and Eder stepped back, putting his left hand in front, using jabs, stopping his opponent from making any advances. Eder connected a straight right-hand punch and a left hook to Leo's face, and he (Espinosa) didn't fight back. Another attack by the Brazilian, shooting straight right-hand punches between the Filipino's gloves, connecting with his face. Leo attacks passively. He still hasn't touched the Brazilian. Further advantage for the national boxer in this round.

(*O Globo*) - A straight right-hand punch rocks Espinosa. With great left-hand work, the Brazilian keeps a distance. A straight left-hand punch completes Eder's advantage.

Round 3
(*Estadão*) – Eder used left jabs to keep Leo away. The Filipino hit the Brazilian's face with a straight right-hand punch. Eder got right back at him with two punches. At the end of the round, they fought at a short distance, exchanging light punches. The Brazilian won the round.

(*O Globo*) - The Filipino attacks but receives counterpunches. "Jofrinho" is cornered, avoids a bunch of punches, spins, and throws a right cross. More jabs and straight punches (from Eder) hit Leo's face again. The Brazilian won the round.

Round 4
(*Estadão*) – The Filipino went on the attack, and one of his punches took Eder to the ropes. The Brazilian went back to the center of the ring and hit back at the Filipino with crosses and uppercuts. Leo was warned for landing a head butt. The Filipino covered up and moved away to avoid the Brazilian's attacks. Before the bell rang, Eder shot a left hook against Leo's liver and completed the attack with two more punches. Eder performed better again.

(*O Globo*) - Eder lost control of the distance but soon recurred to a clinch. More studying from Eder, more initiative from Leo, but with no efficient punches. The Filipino won the round.

Round 5
(*Estadão*) – Eder attacked firmly. He hit Leo with various punches. Espinosa stepped back but couldn't avoid the punishment. After trying to clinch, the Filipino tried to fight at distance. One right-hand punch by Eder

made the Filipino step back, and he tried to get back at him right away. Eder avoided the counter-attack and hit Leo's chin with a hard left hook, sending him to the floor. Feeling dizzy, the Filipino heard the referee count and got up. He was in bad shape. He resisted well, however, to the punishment that Eder followed up with. When he (Espinosa) was close to the ropes, and under a lot of pressure, the bell rang, saving the Filipino from a dangerous situation. Fifteen more seconds would have been enough for him to fall again and lose by knockout.

(*O Globo*) – Straight left and right-hand punches followed by a hook, hit Espinosa's face. The Filipino reacts, but he is cornered on the ropes. "Jofrinho" punches him with violent hooks, crosses his right up, and sends him to the ground. The audience is delirious. The referee counts to eight, Leo gets up and gets punched several times. The bell rings, with the Brazilian's complete and spectacular domination.

Round 6

(*Estadão*) – Eder came back calmly. He didn't insist on attacking. He waited calmly for Espinosa's unpredictable attacks. When the Filipino let go a right-hand punch, Eder ducked and hit him with his left hand. Leo felt it, stepped back, and was knocked down by a hook. (Referee) Ziravello counted another eight seconds and Leo got up again. Another save by the bell for Sarreal's pupil. Eder won the round.

(*O Globo*) - The referee signals a head butt from Leo. Espinosa attacks, but immediately is retorted. In the middle of the ring, a left hook sends Espinosa to the canvas again. Eder harasses him. The Filipino turns his back to him, dazed, but he gets himself together. Eder's advantage.

Round 7

(*Estadão*) – Leo came back to the fight furious. He attacked and made Eder step back. The Brazilian didn't push it, always preferring to counterpunch. After the first minute, the round became dull. Neither one tried to hit hard. This round was better for Leo.

(*O Globo*) - The weakest round of the fight. Eder follows the instructions and keeps his distance, walking back, instead of attacking. He hits efficiently, but with no continuity. Again, Leo uses his head. No winner in this round.

Round 8

(*Estadão*) – Eder attacked, missing a lot of punches. Leo, calmer, ducked well, and hit back every time. The Brazilian retook a defensive position, leaving the attacks for Leo. When he tried to get back at the Filipino, Eder also missed a lot of punches. Round tied.

(*O Globo*) - Leo used counterpunches. He showed class but couldn't get past the Brazilian's left hand. The fight lost quality at this point, with too much caution from both fighters. There is no winner in this round.

Round 9

(*Estadão*) – Leo tried to undo the point difference, still favoring the Brazilian. He attacked Eder and landed a straight right-hand punch to his face. Eder stepped back to avoid another two crossed punches. Another straight right-hand punch from Leo hit Eder's face at the end of the round. The Filipino won the round well.

(*O Globo*) - The Filipino works well with both his hands. Eder gets confused and doesn't know how to react. Clear advantage for Espinosa.

Round 10

(*Estadão*) – Leo restarted the fight with the determination of someone who could only win by knockout. He pushed Eder on the four corners of the ring and hit him to the spleen. Eder hit back with two hooks. Another attack from Leo pushed Eder to the ropes. Eder took his stance as the audience was cheering for the bell to ring. Eder didn't run from the fight and hit back every time Leo would punch. When the fight was developing, the bell rang, signaling the end of the contest.

(*O Globo*) - The boxers try hard. The fight gets faster and more dramatic, but the punch exchanges don't offer any advantage to either fighter. No winner in this round.

Antonio Ziravello took the papers from judges Andrade, Bizarro, and Prado. Minutes later, he called Eder to the center of the ring and held up his right arm, declaring him the winner on points. Before the judges' final decision, Espinosa acknowledged Eder's advantage by raising his arm and pointing to him as the crowd cheered.

After the bout, Eder said that Espinosa did not hit as hard as he had anticipated. He expressed his happiness in defeating such a highly regarded opponent. Espinosa was gracious in defeat, acknowledging that he had been well beaten but asked for a rematch. He said that his ears were still ringing from the blows he had received during the contest.

Shortly after the Espinosa bout, Jacob Nahun made yet another offer for Ernesto Miranda to face Eder. Once again, the offer fell on deaf ears as it was proving increasingly difficult to deal with the Argentinian. On the plus side, the rousing victory over Espinosa did elevate Eder into the rankings as the number three bantamweight in the world. This represented the first time that a Brazilian boxer had ever held a world ranking in the sport.

This milestone moment was a source of great pride for Brazilian boxing aficionados and the media who had followed his progress since the amateur days.

Sensacional Vitória de Eder Jofre

O Globo wrote in reverence: "At first sight, 'Jofrinho' doesn't have any marks or signs of the fight on his face, he has a serene look, and he's smiling and communicative. He doesn't look like a puncher at all. It's surprising to know that this shy boy is the same one with whom big audiences fall in love and who always sends his opponents to the ground. He would even smile and not take it seriously when someone brought up the possibility to fight for the world title. Today, he hasn't changed. Amazingly modest, despite the publicity the papers have been giving him. He practices with doggedness, eats a vegetarian diet, drives around with a Vespa, and draws in his spare time. He is not only good at football and boxing. He is good at drawing, with light cartoons and a style of his own, using fighter movements. Clóvis Graciano wanted to teach him the technique that made him famous. 'Jofrinho,' however, didn't want to learn it. No, it's Aldemir Martins who is obsessed about teaching him his talent."

Only three days after the Espinosa victory, Aristides was in Rio with Pedro Galasso for a fight with Osvaldo Amburi of Argentina and was asked on the television show *Rio Ring* if he felt that his son was already ready to challenge for the world title, but he quickly shot that suggestion down and stated that Eder needed more experience. "It is too early. Even if they look for me, I won't sign a contract for this fight. It's still too early for Eder to try his best, which means the world title. There are still many opponents left to face him and give him experience, and it would be a shame and true insanity to throw him against (champion) Halimi now," he said.

He was asked if they would be giving Espinosa a rematch, but Aristides also shot down that possibility. "It would be ridiculous if we accepted a new fight in São Paulo, just to make money, and show the audience the same superiority that Eder already showed in the fight. In Los Angeles, as Espinosa has asked, it would be impossible and with no compensation. Eder is still unknown, and he would have to leave 40% of his payment to pay taxes," he added. Aristides said that the next logical big fight for his son was against Ernesto Miranda.

Recent Bantamweight History

Ever since South African Vic Toweel dethroned the legendary Mexican American champion, Manuel Ortiz, on May 31, 1950, the bantamweight division had not seen an American boxer hold its crown. That represented the longest streak in the history of the weight class to this point. It has typically always been the larger fighters from lightweight and above who have drawn the largest crowds and television attention. Due to these factors, there was less focus on the division in America, which had long been regarded as the Mecca of the sport. Throughout Latin America and Asia, the weight classes from featherweight and under have generally been the divisions that gathered the most interest.

Jimmy Carruthers had become a national hero in Australia when he took the title from Vic Toweel in front of 28,000 fans in Johannesburg, South Africa in 1952 before retiring in 1954 as champion. The decision to retire surprised many as Carruthers was at his peak at only 24 and figured to be a boxer who would stay around for a while and could dominate. "In my own heart, I know I am doing right, as I am only 24 years old. I feel that I am at my peak in fighting, and, in my opinion, that is the time to get out of it, not waiting till you are passing your peak. In my case, I will say I have been fortunate, in this respect, that I have made my money while I reached my peak, and I know that I am retiring 100 percent, physically and financially. When I won the world crown from Vic Toweel in South Africa, I knew I would defend my title three or four times more at most. As things turned out, I defended it three times and received big gate money for all title defenses," he was quoted saying in the *Sydney Morning Herald* on May 17, 1954.

Algerian-born Frenchman Robert Cohen claimed the vacant title when he defeated Thailand's Chamroen Songkitrat that year. He reigned until 1956 when he was dethroned by the popular Italian Mario D'Agata. Things get a little confusing here as Cohen was stripped by the National Boxing Association (NBA) for failing to defend his title against Raul "Raton" Macias of Mexico. Cohen remained the lineal champion and was recognized by the European Boxing Union (EBU) and British Boxing Board of Control (BBBC) as the champion before losing to D'Agata. D'Agata lost the title the following year when he traveled to Paris to face Algerian-born French favorite Alphonse Halimi, who defeated him over 15 rounds.

Songkitrat was given a crack at Macias for the vacant NBA title in 1955. He fell short as the Mexican stopped him in 11 rounds. Macias had become a national hero in Mexico, largely viewed as the first star of the television era in that country. That popularity was noticeable when 50,000 fans packed into the Plaza de Toros in Mexico City to see him defend the title against Leo Espinosa. Macias called for a unification bout with Cohen the whole time, but those calls went unanswered. "With this fight, I have shown my class. If Robert Cohen makes up his mind that he wants to fight me, he can come to look for it now," he said after stopping Espinosa in 11 rounds. Macias continued to run up an impressive string of victories and exciting performances before meeting Halimi in a fight for the undisputed title in November of 1957 at Wrigley Field in Los Angeles.

The Macias vs. Halimi fight had been one of the most entertaining contests of its era as the two waged war over 15 rounds. Halimi brought the fight to Macias from the beginning as he kept the pressure on the Mexican champion and imposed his strength. Rather than back up and try to box from a distance, Macias was willing to fight the Frenchman's fight at close quarters. Halimi dominated the latter rounds of the contest to earn the decision, and the Mexican fans were crushed. Macias conceded that Halimi had been the better fighter on the night and deserved his victory and expressed a desire to face him again to regain his title, but that rematch never came about, and Macias retired shortly afterward.

Halimi remained busy for the next two years but did not put his title on the line as he ran up six straight non-title victories in Europe.

Fight 27, vs. Angel Bustos, June 19, 1959

Merely 15 days after the stunning victory over Leo Espinosa, Eder was scheduled back in the ring at Ibirapuera against 24-year-old Angel Bustos of Argentina. Bustos was fresh on the heels of an impressive upset victory over Kid Pascualtito but was not expected to offer much resistance at the hands of the local hero. Bustos, though described as possessing excellent agility and brute strength, was shorter than Eder. Few felt that Bustos had much of a chance to enforce his position to win this bout. Opponents that fought Eder using the technique of distance and patience were being picked off and could not match his skills, but it was an even riskier proposition trying to get inside and make it a phone booth fight with Eder proving to be an excellent counter attacker.

The bout with Bustos turned out to be an easy one. Eder seemed to prolong the bout to benefit the audience as he carried Bustos through the first few rounds. He showed great accuracy but held back from putting his full strength into his punches. The crowd clapped and cheered through the entire contest in appreciation of the skills Eder displayed, and just as he was warming up to set Bustos up for a thrilling knockout finish, the Argentinian refused to leave his stool after the fourth round. The audience was happy with what they had seen from their local champion, but Eder himself was disappointed in Bustos' decision not to continue as he shrugged his shoulders and apologized to the crowd. Eder was far beyond this level of opponent already, and it was believed that unless he could entice another boxer inside the world's top five to face him, then this would be the pattern of most fights.

Fight 28, vs. Salustiano Suarez II, June 28, 1959

Only nine days after the Bustos victory, Eder took a return match with Salustiano Suarez in Rio de Janeiro. The result was even quicker than the last time he fought Suarez. Eder scored an impressive first-round victory courtesy of a hard left hook that left Suarez out for the count. Following the Suarez bout, Eder visited the editorial rooms of *O Globo* and thanked everybody for their encouragement. He was told that his name appeared in *The Ring* magazine's latest issue in America, and he did not believe it. He requested somebody show the magazine to him and felt a great source of pride in seeing the name "Eder Jofre" in the publication known as "The Bible of Boxing."

On July 8, at the Sports Arena in Los Angeles, world champion Alphonse Halimi put his championship on the line for the first time when he faced Jose Becerra. Becerra had idolized Raul Macias and was seeking revenge on behalf of his countryman when he took on Halimi and promised Mexico's President Adolfo Lopez Mateos that he would bring the title back to Mexico. In a classic fight, Becerra took the championship from Halimi in the eighth round.

"That was when the grandfather of all demonstrations took place. Pandemonium broke loose, the frenzied fans screamed hysterically. It was contagious. Even this hardened veteran of ring activity found himself cheering. Later a friend of mine, a sportswriter of a Spanish daily published in Los Angeles, told me that he had a wire from Guadalajara, Becerra's hometown – a city of 400,000 – that the city had gone stark mad. Thousands of people crowded around radios, and when they heard about the first knockdown, people started to embrace each other and weep for joy. When the end came – well, try to picture it: You've seen Mexican fans!" wrote Bill Miller for *The Ring*.

Fight 29, vs. Ruben Caceres II, July 31, 1959

A significant match for Eder was arranged when Ruben Caceres agreed to leave the comfortable confines of his hometown of Montevideo and take on the now world-ranked Brazilian at Ibirapuera. Eder took a couple of days off after his rematch with Suarez. He participated in some exhibitions and public sparring sessions between the third and fifth of July at the Odean Gym in São Paulo. Having taken on three bouts in June, the bout with Caceres, scheduled for July 31, was to be his only one of the month.

Caceres arrived for the bout with plenty of time to prepare after he landed on July 12. The local press reported Caceres' record standing at 33 wins with 3 draws and no defeats. Boxrec records show that the Uruguayan had two career losses before this bout, one of which had been reported as a disqualification in his professional debut. Caceres had earned two credible draws with Kid Pascualito in Paraguay since the first fight with Eder in Uruguay. There had been a great deal of anticipation around this fight as the drawn verdict the previous year in Uruguay was still something that didn't sit well with Eder, nor did what he perceived as a bad attitude that the Uruguayan carried. It was one of the very few bouts in his entire career that Eder admitted to entering the ring angry.

Estadão reported: "Last night at Ibirapuera Gymnasium, Eder Jofre knocked out Uruguayan Ruben Caceres in the seventh round and accomplished a victory with great meaning for his career. The apparent success of the Brazilian champion in this fight is the result of his current great technical and physical shape. More than Roberto Castro and any other South American boxer, Caceres made Eder's victory very hard. Not for having more technique but because he is very resistant, brave, aggressive, and very experienced. Undefeated until last night, Caceres showed he is terrific and did everything he could. He stood the weight of the punishment Eder gave him heavily until he fell after the Brazilian's punches were too much to bear."

Eder ended the bout in the seventh round, but he could have finished proceedings earlier. Eder came out to start the bout in a patient manner, not wasting any punches or rushing his opponent. He excellently used the jab early as he subtly moved around, trying to pierce the Uruguayan's guard. Caceres tried to use his jab and make use of the height advantage he held over Eder, but the speed of Eder quickly forced Caceres to change those tactics. Caceres tried to box at a distance but stopped pumping his jab out, instead opting to counter.

Eder fought with controlled aggression and precision over the first six rounds as he carried the action. While Caceres performed well enough, he was not much of a threat to Eder as he struggled to make his mark on the Brazilian with his attacks. By the seventh round, Caceres sported the look of a beaten fighter as he came off his stool with a lot of facial damage and blood running from his nose. The Uruguayan tried to make it a close distance fight, as he leaned on Eder and they exchanged punches in close. Eder's punches were stronger, and Caceres tried to back out of the exchange but could not escape and was dropped by a flurry of punches for an eight count. Caceres pulled himself together and bit down on his mouthpiece as he went back to fighting but was quickly dazed by a hard right cross that came after he had ducked two punches. Caceres stayed up but was on borrowed time, and Eder sensed the end was near as he doubled up on his attack with hooks and hard right-hands, which dropped his opponent for the full count. This had been a sweet victory for Eder since he had been determined to leave no doubt between himself and Caceres after their controversial draw in Montevideo.

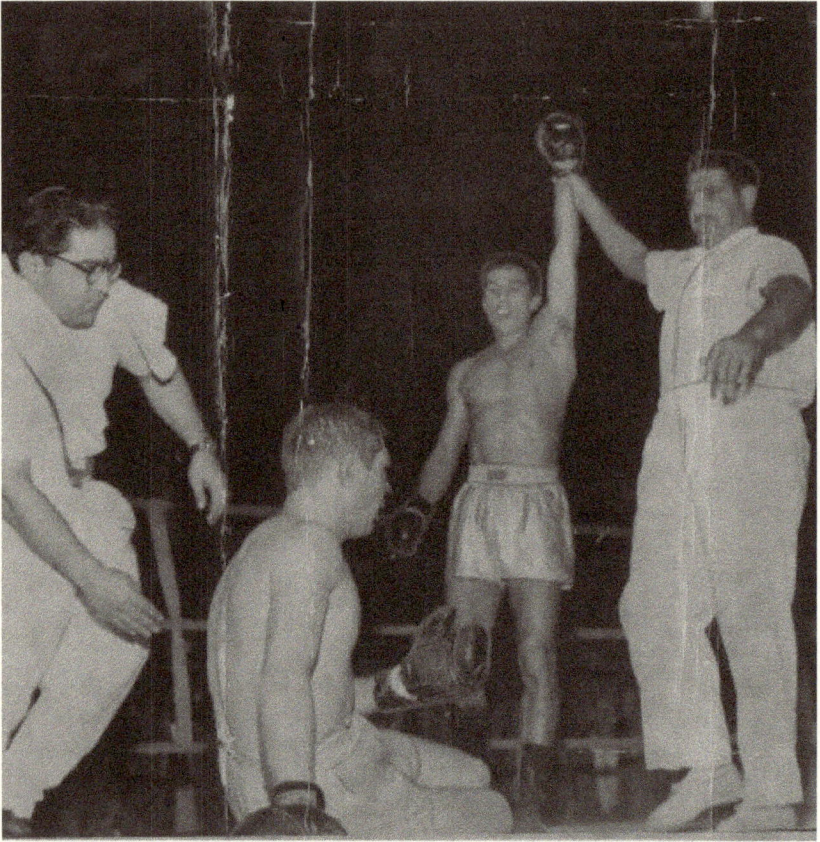

Referee Americo Cury counts Caceres out

A trip was organized by *Estadão* for Eder and his father to go on a multi-city tour of America to elevate Eder's name further in the United States. Mr. Geraldo Martins of the São Paulo Boxing Federation expressed his gratitude to the newspaper in stating: *"O Estadão* took a great initiative to sponsor this trip to the USA – the world boxing Mecca, for Eder Jofre to improve his technical skills. His father and coach Aristides will travel with him. This is, without a doubt, a great measure, and it will give 'Jofrinho' new technical knowledge whether watching exciting fights or training at the top gyms in the country. The results of this experience will show themselves soon since this is a man whose vocation for boxing is more than proven. If Eder Jofre knows how to take advantage of the teaching he will get from North American teachers, he will be able to bring soon, for the first time, a boxing world title for Brazil. This is not the first time this top-notch newspaper has given the means to improve the skills of a Brazilian athlete. Recently, as it is known by everyone, Maria Esther Bueno, thanks to *'O Estadao de São Paulo,'* brought the biggest Tennis title to Brazil. It is commendable under all aspects, and we want to give homage to *Estadão* for the noble initiative to sponsor our champion, Eder Jofre's trip to the USA."

The day before his departure, Eder went to the editorial room of *Estadão* to thank each member of the staff for arranging this trip for him, and, on August 23, he boarded a flight from Congonhas Airport to Chicago. Aristides was training amateur boxers participating in the Pan American Games, and Eder helped train the boxers and took part in plenty of sparring with local boxers. The trip also saw Eder visit New York and get to spend some time in Archie Moore's training camp out in California, where he met the legendary former featherweight world champion, Sandy Saddler. It was hoped that on the final leg of the trip, in Los Angeles, Eder would fight on September 4, but that did not come to pass. Despite that, the trip had been a valuable experience for Eder as he was able to meet a lot of the top officials at the NBA, took in some live boxing, and sparred with local boxers, which gave him a good chance to see different styles and give him a taste of what he would experience when he eventually did fight in America.

Fight 30, vs. Angel Bustos II, October 9, 1959

Kiyoshi Miura was in line to face Eder but was defeated by Angel Bustos, who remained in Brazil for additional fights after his loss in June against Eder. This moved Bustos in line for a rematch. Bustos' win over the Japanese boxer was considered an upset because Miura had previously won the Japanese title and was the Asian champion, owning a victory over the excellent Leo Espinosa.

Bustos, though credited with being strong and brave, was merely considered simply an opponent despite some solid showings in the past. To stay sharp to prepare for future assignments, Eder trained with amateur João Gutierrez.

Eder's second victory over Bustos came as expected as Bustos did not put up much resistance. Bustos was a little more aggressive than in their previous battle as he tried to get inside, but he did not last long as Eder was soon picking him apart with clean, crisp, accurate blows. As he had done in their first bout, Eder appeared to carry his over-matched foe during the opening rounds as Bustos struggled to get inside. Eder ended the contest in the third round and let his hands go as he scored two knockdowns. The final knockdown was from a left uppercut that didn't appear to land with much force, but Bustos went down and was counted out by referee Pierre Siaú. It appeared to onlookers that the Argentine had quit once again and performed a poor acting job as he did not rise before ten seconds.

Champion Jose Becerra made his first appearance as world champion on October 24 when he was welcomed by his hometown fans in Guadalajara. Unfortunately, this homecoming would be a tragic one that perhaps affected his career. Walt Ingram suffered a terrible beating and died just six hours after the bout. Ingram's corner wanted to pull him out after the eighth round, but the brave American insisted he was OK to continue and came out for the ninth round, where he was knocked out.

Fight 31, vs. Gianni Zuddas, October 30, 1959

Several exciting bouts were being lined up around this time to keep Eder busy against top opponents. On October 6, it was announced that discussions with the managerial team of the fourth-ranked Danny Kid of the Philippines were close to completion for a November bout in São Paulo. Piero Rollo was also mentioned as a possible opponent should the promotions stall. Rollo was ranked number two by the NBA, but it was believed that his management team would be more reluctant to risk their ranking on foreign soil than Danny Kid, who was already campaigning away from his homeland, having settled in California. The next boxer to face Eder was the Italian Gianni Zuddas at the end of the month. Initially, it was thought the bout would be postponed as the Italian team couldn't find a flight on October 10, but then they secured flights on October 16, which would give them a full two weeks to acclimatize.

Zuddas was an experienced opponent and arrived in Brazil full of confidence that his knowledge would carry the day. He had won an Olympic silver medal in the bantamweight division at the same 1948 London Games, where Aristides coached Brazil's first Olympic boxing team. Zuddas held a professional record of 57 wins against 14 defeats with 4 draws. He scored one of his signature wins earlier in the year when he beat the popular Spaniard Juan Cardenas. Zuddas had fought in many places around the world, such as Australia, Sweden, and multiple other European destinations, so it's unlikely that he was fazed by the prospect of performing in front of Eder's Brazilian fan base.

Eder had difficulty in getting down to the bantamweight limit and missed the weight by one and a half pounds when he tipped the scales at

119 ½ pounds. Because of this indiscretion, Eder was forced to wear the larger 8-ounce gloves. In contrast, Zuddas wore 6-ounce gloves to offset the perceived advantage that Eder would gain from the extra weight he carried. When a boxer drains himself so much to make weight and is genuine in his attempt to do so, he is at a greater disadvantage, especially in the days when the competitors weighed in on the morning of the fight. There was no extra time to re-hydrate, load up on carbohydrates, and come into the ring much stronger like the fighters can do today where they weigh in roughly 30 hours before entering the ring.

The local press had high hopes for their rising star, but they were also apprehensive coming into this bout, and Eder wasn't considered a strong favorite by any means. Once the bell rang, however, Eder calmed the nerves of the audience present at Ibirapuera when he took command early in the fight and showed a level of calmness and experience that defied his age. He boxed aggressively but economically.

Eder moved forward, landing clean hard jabs, and punished Zuddas with hurtful punches at a distance while displaying beautiful form. Zuddas was down for a brief count in the sixth round and spent most of the latter stages of the bout in retreat mode with little intent on trying to win. Eder took little punishment in this bout as he used excellent head movement whenever he moved into striking distance. At the end of the fight, Zuddas sported an assortment of bumps and bruises with one eye nearly closed from the punishment the Brazilian dished out. The scores were unanimous as Eder won by a large points margin and gained another feather in his cap by defeating such an experienced and well-schooled opponent.

Here is the report from *Estadão*: "Italian Gianni Zuddas showed last night, a new way of fighting with a much superior opponent without being knocked out. It is a strange and recriminate method because it should never be allowed that a boxer enters the ring only determined to run away from his opponent to simply avoid being knocked out. In the ten rounds of last night's fight, Zuddas backed off non-stop. He shut down like a land snail and did not attempt to dodge or block off the punches. He didn't, not even for a second, show any aggression towards Eder Jofre and didn't land any punches. Eder, on the other hand, didn't push the fight in the first five rounds, and in the next ones when he tried to punish the Italian, he was always stopped by the wrestling of Zuddas. Eder was even annoyed by Zuddas' procedure, which is why he missed several punches, making the spectacle even worse. Unhappy with Zuddas, who would always run, and with Eder's carelessness, for he would be comfortable and not fight hard, the audience booed a lot."

While it was already clear that Eder possessed serious power in both fists in addition to a complete skill set, if there was any "weakness," it was that Eder still had a hard time finishing off reluctant opponents such as Zuddas. This wasn't a weakness in the sense it would cost him a fight, but as a perfectionist, it was something Eder was keen to work on to make sure if the opponents didn't want to be there, then he would send them home early.

Fight 32, vs. Danny Kid, December 12, 1959

Only a couple of days after the Zuddas bout, the management teams of Eder and Danny Kid tried to iron out details to finalize a bout for later in the year. One of the sticking points had been the managerial contract of Danny Kid, as he was contracted to both Lope Sarreal and Pedro Estomago. Estomago, who claimed to have exclusive rights to the contract of Danny Kid, had received a commitment for a bout with Eder from Danny Kid, but the contract between the two was permitted only for Danny Kid's fights within the United States. The influential and worldwide respected Sarreal was the manager who had the global rights to his contract and thus was the one responsible for the negotiations for a fight in Brazil. Danny Kid was determined to face Eder as he had designs on getting a crack at the bantamweight title. He saw the opportunity to face one of the few fighters ranked ahead of him as the perfect chance to move closer to that shot.

Having recently turned 28, Danny Kid arrived from Los Angeles along with world welterweight champion Don Jordan on November 13 for a mouthwatering double-header scheduled for November 28 in São Paulo. Jordan was participating in a non-title bout against Eder's stablemate Fernando Barreto who had run up an impressive 27-0 record. For Barreto, this was a huge step-up in competition, whereas Jordan admitted upon arrival he knew little about Barreto. Danny Kid, by comparison, said that he knew a lot about Eder and knew his lofty ranking and fearsome reputation as one of the most talented fighters in the bantamweight division. Danny Kid stopped short of making any prediction or giving any assurances but did state he was greatly confident in his abilities and showed a

Danny Kid

level of confidence you would expect from a fighter of such pedigree.

Danny Kid was originally from the Philippines but, at this point, resided in California, and was the reigning champion of North America. Before settling in California, the Filipino had spent some time in Japan, where he became a national champion of that country, adding to the national title he had achieved in his homeland. His impressive track record included wins over Jose Medel, Toluco Lopez, Billy Peacock, and Dwight Hawkins. The victory over Medel earned him the North American title and a ticket to Brazil to move closer to the coveted world crown. In a thrilling fight at the Olympic Auditorium in Los Angeles, many in attendance felt the Mexican, Medel, had deserved to win based on landing the harder punches throughout the bout, which saw both fighters cut. While Eder had mixed in with some excellent competition, Danny Kid had been in the ring with an even higher caliber of opposition overall. Earlier losses by decision in Thailand against Pone Kingpetch, and Argentina against the great Pascual Perez only helped him further develop his skills. He had scored a knockdown in the losing effort against Perez.

November 16 was Danny Kid's first training session in Brazil. Unfortunately, he injured his left eye while sparring at Wilson Russo Gym with a young local amateur boxer named Jose Cruz. The injury re-opened a cut the Filipino had sustained in his last bout against Jose Medel on September 24; thus, the bout was postponed.

The match was pushed back from November 28 to December 12 to give his eye time to heal. Danny Kid's eye was fixed by a local doctor who said that the eye would heal in a week, which would mean that the fight being a month away, was more than enough time to heal, but his co-manager, Pedro Estomago did not share that opinion. "In Los Angeles, the commission gives the boxer four weeks to recover when his eye is cut. He shouldn't fight during that period. It would be unforgivable to risk his career in one fight. I have 29 years of experience in boxing, so I think I should know better," he said. Some joked in the press that Cruz could count Danny Kid among his victories as he had put the world-ranked fighter out of commission temporarily.

On November 17, a significant change was made in Eder's career as he signed a managerial contract with powerful Abraham Katzenelson. Katzenelson had worked with Eder and his team to bring Leo Espinosa but now was made official as not only a partner but as co-manager alongside Marcos Lazaro.

Born May 25, 1917, in Lithuania, Katzenelson had moved to Argentina as a child. He lived in Argentina until 1952 and then came to Brazil. He began as a manager for the Argentinian bolero singer Gregório Barrio. Also, he managed the career of Ângela Maria, who was a big name in Brazilian music. Katzenelson came from a Jewish family and spoke Portuguese through a thick-sounding Spanish accent. He is still considered one of the most influential boxing managers in South American boxing history and one of the most charismatic characters in Brazilian boxing history. He lived in the Santa Cecilia neighborhood of São Paulo, one of the city's wealthiest parts. Katzenelson had many good connections with promoters and managers in his native Argentina and was friendly with some of the biggest names in boxing.

These connections attracted Eder and his father to Katzenelson. They perceived they would move closer to the big fights and home in on a world title shot with his experience and vast network. "He is a great businessman and an honest man. Who wouldn't want to get help to reach a dream, such as getting to a world title?" Eder said.

The contract with Jacob Nahun was set to expire in January 1960, so Eder and his father were already free to negotiate with other management teams. Along with Katzenelson, Marcos Lazaro would act as co-manager. "Marcos was a famous manager among artists and became partners with Katzenelson. They were accommodating to me in the beginning because they were involved with important people and very competent in what they did. My first manager Nahun, who arranged my first fights and was good friends with my father, brought me fighters from Uruguay and Argentina. Why did I let him go? Because my father told me: 'Eder, we have to let him go because he doesn't have any connections in the United States. Got it?' Then we got to know Katzenelson and Lazaro. When I met Marcos, I sincerely thought: 'This is wonderful!' Because he was managing great artists like Roberto Carlos, Elis Regina, and Wilson Simonal," recalled Eder on his managerial switch.

As early as December 3, over two weeks since the agreement with Katzenelson, the Jofres saw his managerial expertise and use of secure connections. Katzenelson reached an agreement with Ernesto Miranda to face Eder once again. Eder was just over a week out from facing Danny Kid. This news came with great excitement as Eder now appeared likely to finally fight for the South American championship regardless of the upcoming bout with Danny Kid. The Miranda bout was proposed for February 15 at Ibirapuera, with Eder getting 30% of the bout's total income. Miranda negotiated a rematch clause to guarantee a return within 90 days if he lost his title. Though the bout was not official yet, it appeared to be a mere formality that the two sides would finally agree on everything. The two boxers would finally fight to settle the score.

The day before the fight with Danny Kid, *O Globo* gave some insight into the two training camps and felt that Danny Kid figured to be a challenging opponent and had been provided with a more ideal preparation for this match. "Danny Kid trained daily with Ricardo Zumbano, 'Jofrinho's' uncle, and is showing how fast he is to counterpunch, precise in his hooks and agile in the ring. Kid Jofre stated to the paper that Eder is in good condition, despite the lack of a quicker sparring partner in his practices. He trains with his uncle Ralph Zumbano, former Brazilian champion, who has a lot of experience, but is a little bit slow to help a bantamweight."

The newspaper reported on the day of the fight it would be difficult to determine a winner since Danny Kid had looked so good in the time he had been in Brazil. "There is no favorite to the fight that will gather tonight at Ibirapuera between bantamweights Eder Jofre, undefeated Brazilian champion, and Danny Kid, Filipino, who has many titles in Asia and the USA. If Danny Kid's counterpunches are strong and precise as it has been watched during his practices, it is also certain that his game is always short, which could make Eder's work easier. Less experienced, the local boxer has the quality and great technique, but he has, however, a stronger punch and may decide the fight on the first opportunity."

On December 12, Eder faced off with Danny Kid at Ibirapuera in front of an excited crowd. The bout was the main event on a Saturday night show, and the fans went from excited to restless as it took some time for the organizers to initiate the boxers to move towards the ring. Just before the fight, Eder expressed his confidence when interviewed in his locker room in saying, "I am in good shape. I respect Danny Kid, he is a good boxer, but I believe I will beat him." Eder's father showed more signs of nervousness when the microphone was put in his face as he simply said, "This will be a tough fight."

In the opposing locker room, they displayed a lot of confidence and downplayed Eder's much-touted power. "My pupil is in good shape. People say Jofre is a powerful puncher, but so is Danny Kid," claimed the Filipino's manager, Pedro Estomago. The visiting boxer made his way to the ring first wearing black trunks before Eder came to the ring wearing white trunks with a golden bantam cock stitched to them and his robe. As Eder entered the ring, a ringside fan pointed out his bucket with a bottle in it and shouted, "Champagne?" to which another of Eder's supporters responded, "Yes, for when 'Jofrinho' breaks the guy." 20,000 fans were finally ready to see their man face yet another highly ranked opponent.

Round By Round from *Estadão* and *O Globo*

Round 1

(*Estadão*) – At 10:49 pm they started the fight. The first movements were very cautious by the two fighters. Eder landed a right hook but without too much effect. Kid Jofre instructs his son, "Easy. This round is just to study the man." He instructs a team member, "We need ice. Go get some now," while he tells Eder: "Let your arms go now and start to attack."

(*O Globo*) – The audience watched silently as the boxers study until halfway into the round. A strong left hook by Eder is answered with a left and right from the Filipino, but Eder finishes with a one-two, with his left hook, up and down to complete the round.

Round 2

(*Estadão*) – The round began with a reasonable exchange of punches. Danny took the initiative and tried to pressure Eder. The fight heats up. Eder is looking for opportunities to counter-attack. Kid Jofre complains of a head butt, "This is wrong. This is not honest," he said. Ralph Zumbano tells Eder: "Easy, boy."

(*O Globo*) – Eder starts with big punches, hitting upwards, but the Filipino quickly reacts with left and right-hand punches through the middle. Danny Kid is dangerous with his counterpunches, but Eder lands the stronger punches. The Filipino initiates more but the superior technique and efficiency are in the Brazilian's favor. Eder's advantage.

Round 3

(*Estadão*) – The round commenced with a more violent exchange between the fighters. Eder took a blow to his face that caused a cut to his eyebrow. The referee stopped the fight for a while, cooling down the pace. The Filipino boxer crowds Eder, but with a strong left hook from the Brazilian champion, Danny goes down. The Filipino got up quickly, and the fighters were involved in another violent exchange of punches. Danny Kid shows fast recovery and no signs of tiredness. At the end of the round, Danny was standing in his corner, while Eder received treatment from his team.

(*O Globo*) – Danny takes risks in the exchanges. He feels a punch and bumps his head, opening Eder's right eye, but then Danny violently falls under a flurry of punches. A hard punch to the chin knocks Danny down for four seconds. Eder attacks him furiously, but the bell rings. Eder dominated.

Round 4

(*Estadão*) – The round continued with a more even attitude from the boxers. Danny is taking more initiative in this round, putting Eder against the ropes two times, but Eder knows how to protect himself from the attacks.

(*O Globo*) – Eder lures Danny Kid, hitting under, waiting for a counterpunch to land. Danny is caught, but he fights back and looks recovered from the punishment. Eder wins the round by a small margin.

Round 5

(*Estadão*) – After an exchange of punches, Eder dodged a punch and landed a strong punch on Danny, knocking him down for the second time. The Filipino bounces back up again, ready to hurt Eder, but Eder once again lands a good punch, bringing him down for the third time. Danny Kid gets up again and, as usual, is focused on attacking.

(*O Globo*) – Two violent punches from Eder send Danny Kid down. The first knockdown was with a left hook to his chin. Danny gets up groggy, is hit again, and falls one more time, waiting for the referee to count up to six. The KO looks imminent. Eder dominated and controlled the round. Easy round for Eder.

Round 6

(*Estadão*) – Danny Kid sought an opportunity to attack, while Eder kept him away as he landed hard punches. His father and coach, Kid Jofre, instructed him to look for a perfect punch that would knock Danny out, but against this advice, Eder prefers to stay away from Danny, keeping him at a safe distance with efficient long left-hand shots.

(*O Globo*) – Eder fights the way he wants. He lures the Filipino and lands strong, efficient punches. Danny Kid falls again. Great crossed punches and hooks from Eder hit the Filipino's head and body repeatedly. Eder's eye still bleeds. The Brazilian dominated the round.

Round 7

(*Estadão*) – Like always, Danny Kid takes the initiative, but Eder assumes control. Eder maintains the same strategy, keeping him at distance, landing good long shots. The Filipino boxer displayed his courage and attempted to change the course of the fight.

(*O Globo*) – Eder Jofre calmly dominates, not worrying about the knockout. A right-hand punch takes out the Filipino's mouthguard. He feels it. Again, with the initiative, Eder opens a cut over Danny Kid's eye with a straight right-hand punch. Eder wins the round.

Round 8

(*Estadão*) – Eder was instructed by his father to move faster, but he maintained the strategy used in the previous rounds, keeping Danny away with long shots. The Filipino lands punches on Eder that open a cut on his eyebrow. Eder's shorts are tainted with blood.

(*O Globo*) – Danny Kid backs up and clinches. Eder fights with no concerns, looking for an opportunity to land hard punches. Danny keeps his guard up. In the clinches, Eder avoids the Filipino's head and punches. In the end, Danny throws good counterpunches. A small advantage to the Brazilian in this round.

Round 9

(*Estadão*) – Eder Jofre persisted in his technique of fast long shots and fast step backs. The Filipino showed good endurance and is looking for attacks all the time, but Eder takes control.

(*O Globo*) – A 1-2-3 of Eder shakes Danny Kid. The Brazilian hits hard, but with no continuity. The referee gives the Filipino a warning due to another head butt, followed by a violent, illegal punch that hits Eder Jofre's kidney. He (Eder) wins the round.

Round 10

(*Estadão*) – Danny Kid continued attacking and tried to lock Eder against the ropes, but the Brazilian blocked and ducked all the punches thrown at him and even lands shots on his opponent. The round ends with a tremendous ovation for Jofre.

(*O Globo*) – Danny Kid violently attacks, trying to end the fight. Eder covers well, and shakes his opponent twice in a row, stopping, however, when he could continue. An attack from the Filipino is contained by the Brazilian, who punished him with left and right-hand punches. Another round was well won by Eder Jofre.

The clapping continued, even as the announcer came to the microphone to give the official verdict of the judges. The noise only heightened when Eder was announced as the victor, and he lifted his father. Danny Kid and his team greeted the Jofres and offered their congratulations. This act of sportsmanship brought applause from the audience.

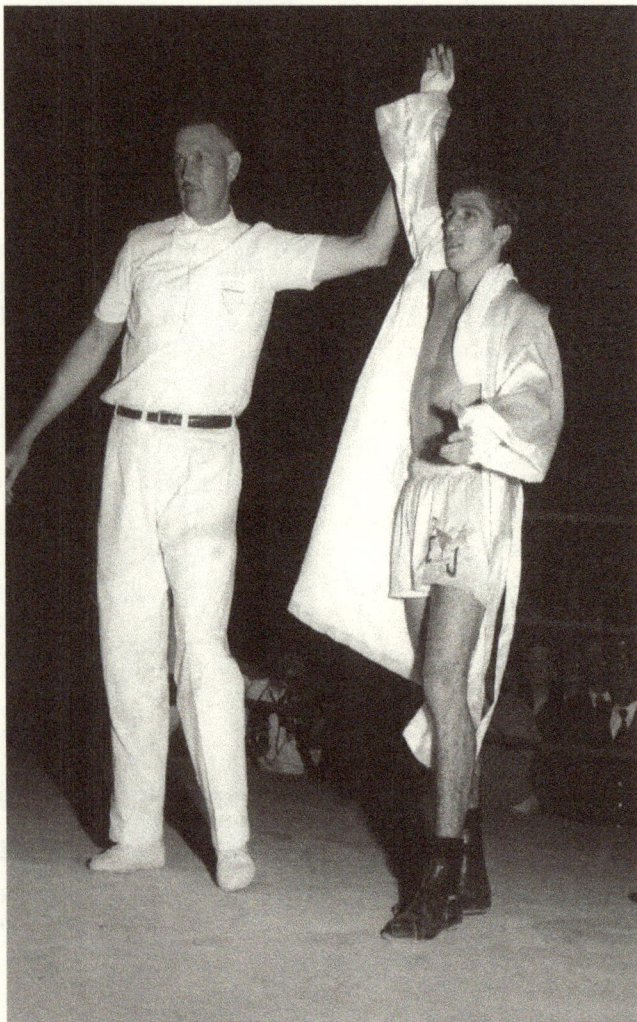

There was a party in the Brazilian locker room as many fans and friends came in to share the moment with Eder and his team. "I fought to win, and I did. Maybe I could have won by knockout, but a lot of times, I decided to spare myself because that man is dangerous, and I did not want to take too many chances. Danny Kid is one of the best fighters I have fought with until today. I hit him a lot, but the Filipino has an iron head. He is also very slick. A few times, he pretended he was dizzy to see if I would be reckless. I believe at a point that the dizziness was true though," Eder said.

The mood in the visiting locker room was understandably more somber as the excuses flowed. Despite his comments only an hour earlier, Pedro Estomago said: "My pupil went into the ring in bad condition and still had a cut on his eyebrow." He did offer some credit for Eder before claiming his man was still the better fighter as he said, "Eder Jofre is great. He is in a condition to fight anyone, but in a rematch, Danny would win."

Danny Kid was also not willing to admit he had been defeated by a superior fighter. "I fought in terrible physical condition; otherwise, I would never have been knocked down. In a rematch, I think I would win because I hit harder than him. In my career, I only ever fell once, and that was against Toluco Lopez, and I even won that fight. Tonight, I fell three times. Tonight, I had a bad night," he said.

The Filipinos said that they felt they deserved to win the fight and demanded a rematch, which brought a great deal of laughter from the journalists on hand. When this was relayed back to Eder, he said, "I will fight him again if necessary. What about the knockdowns? They don't count? Another fight is no problem. Just set the date. Though I am under the impression that they are kidding."

Aristides laughed at the claims from Danny Kid and his team and said that the most logical opponent for his son would be Ernesto Miranda. "Danny Kid's excuses, after all, have a reason to be. He doesn't want to lose his place in the world ranking. From that to sincerity, there is a long way. If they schedule another fight, Eder will win even easier," he said. It was believed that the Filipino camp was just trying to create a controversy out of nothing to drum up potential interest in a rematch that, in reality, served little purpose given the dominant nature of Eder's victory.

O Globo reported: "It wasn't only 'Jofrinho's' punch that decided the fight. The Brazilian imposed himself technically and showed the ability to face any other boxer in the rankings. Danny Kid showed himself a good boxer, quick, opportunistic, with a perfect sense of distance. His counterpunches were precise, but Eder, little by little, started dominating him, attacking him, and making him an easy target for his punches with both hands. He opened ways to a victory that might improve his classification in the world ranking, decreasing the distance that sets him apart from Mexican Jose Becerra. Danny Kid, on the other hand, valorized the Brazilian boxer's victory. Making him feel the punches and show capacity to fight. With no doubt, it completed 'Jofrinho' for other commitments already announced for the next season."

This emphatic victory further showed that Eder possessed many wrinkles in his game. His punching power and strength had been evident for some time, but in dominating such high caliber foes as Espinosa, Zuddas, and Danny Kid in the fashion in which he did, he showed that he could win fights with patience and box on the back foot and counter-attack effectively.

Another report in *Estadão* summarized the bout and labeled it "The most important victory" of Eder's career to date.

The Most Important Victory

"The Brazilian bantamweight champion achieved this mark last night at the Ibirapuera gymnasium, winning on points against the Filipino Danny Kid, North American bantamweight champion, and second-best ranked fighter worldwide. Besides his superior technique showed last night in nine of ten rounds, the Brazilian champ put him down three times during the fight. He just didn't finish him by knockout because Danny is a very persistent fighter, showing a fast and incredible recovery."

"Nobody could be disappointed by the spectacular fight put up by Eder against an opponent who can be considered the most dangerous of his career. Except for the fourth round, which the Filipino won slightly, Eder scored more than him in all the rest of the fight. Danny kicked off the fight taking the initiative, punching Eder all around the ring. The Brazilian kept control of his opponent, but without over-exposing himself. In the second round, with Danny throwing left jabs to open space for his right hooks, Eder accepted the fight and started to throw more punches. Also, Danny was mirroring Eder's game; that's why they were so equally matched."

"In the third round, receiving instructions to attack, Eder changed his style, landing two right hooks that made him back up. In the face of Eder's offense, Danny counter-attacked with hooks, but couldn't help but fall to the ground after two more strong hooks from Eder. Against all the odds, Danny bounced back up, focused on attacking, and retook the initiative, throwing several punches at Eder. In the fourth round, the Filipino was better than Eder, with fast left jabs, Danny could keep the Brazilian at a distance, occasionally landing some good right hooks, which were not a big deal for Senior Aristides' pupil. This round was Danny's. In the fifth round, Eder dominated his opponent. Attacking with great explosion and efficiency, Eder knocked Danny down two more times after hitting him with violent hooks and uppercuts. The Filipino wasn't the same anymore, fighting loosely, and a little bit lost in the ring. He wasn't even able to find his corner after the end of each round. But Eder cautiously noticed that Danny wasn't dead yet, so he kept him at a safe distance until the end of the tenth round. The fight was officiated by Antonio Ziravelo."

1959 Results

Eder Jofre W10 Aniceto Pereyra
Eder Jofre KO4 Salustiano Suarez
Eder Jofre W10 Leo Espinosa
Eder Jofre KO4 Angel Bustos
Eder Jofre KO1 Salustiano Suarez
Eder Jofre KO7 Ruben Caceres
Eder Jofre KO3 Angel Bustos
Eder Jofre W10 Gianni Zuddas
Eder Jofre W10 Danny Kid

1960

On February 4, 1960, Jose Becerra and Alphonse Halimi met again, this time at the Los Angeles Coliseum in front of 31,000 fans. This was the first title defense for Becerra, who had taken three over-the-weight bouts in Mexico. It had been another barn burner as Halimi was ahead after eight rounds and had scored a knockdown in the second round. He appeared to be close to regaining the title, and then in the ninth round, a well-placed left hook crashed against his jaw, and he was laid out on the canvas and counted out. The exciting finish sent the Mexican fans in attendance into a frenzy as they celebrated wildly, rushing for the ring to get close to their champion and throwing sombreros into the air in celebration.

Eder was experiencing increasing difficulty getting down to the bantamweight limit of 118 pounds, and some thought he should move up to featherweight in 1960. He consulted a dietitian named Dr. Francisco Pompeu do Amaral, who warned that Eder was sacrificing a lot and endangering himself by getting his weight down so low. "Eder Jofre's height, 5 feet 4 inches, determines the average weight of 133 pounds. Admitting a subtraction of ten percent from that limit, he will be 120 pounds, which is above the bantamweight limit, which is 118 pounds. He is strong, muscular, with no sign of fatness; he can't force to go lower. If he does, that effort will reflect on his physical, technical, and mental state, bringing disastrous consequences for his career," Amaral stated.

Aristides felt that his son could continue in the bantamweight division and said that he would not need to make the weight for every fight as many of the non-title fights were scheduled slightly over the weight limit. "With his practice intensified, as it must be for the big fights, Eder will easily lower his weight. That won't happen more than twice a year, which is why he won't be affected. To fight Ernesto Miranda, I can assure you guys that he will be inside the weight limit and properly strong for his commitment," he said. One man who felt this wouldn't be an issue was former South American welterweight champion, Martiniano Pereyra from Argentina, who sparred several rounds with Eder and said: "He hits like a middleweight."

Fight 33, vs. Ernesto Miranda III, February 19, 1960

While Danny Kid stayed in Brazil hoping to earn a return match with Eder, he accepted a bout with Ernesto Miranda. For Miranda, this was a vital bout as Danny Kid still held a high world ranking. It would also be a good gauge for him to compare his performance against the Filipino with Eder's impressive victory the prior month. The fight was scheduled for Ibirapuera and would be the first significant boxing show of 1960 in Brazil.

Despite the fight being contested by two foreign boxers with no titles at stake, the event gathered a lot of local interest and did well at the box office. Miranda had been in São Paulo with his brother Carlos as they watched the Jofre vs. Danny Kid bout from ringside. Miranda had been impressed with what he had seen and was generous in his praise for Eder when he went to the editorial room at *Estadão*. "In February, I will fight him for the title. I have already fought him twice, and I know it will not be easy to fight this guy. He is now much better than when we fought two years ago," he said.

Just three days after the bout, the Mirandas went back to Buenos Aires to spend the holiday season at home. Eder took a short vacation in Rio de

Janeiro, where he relaxed on a ranch with Cidinha for a week before coming back to begin serious preparation for the big fight with Miranda.

There had been talks of a rematch with Danny Kid, but Aristides opted to pass on that bout as he wanted his son focused on the bout with Miranda in February, and that is how the Miranda vs. Danny Kid fight was scheduled.

Inauguração da Temporada Profissional

Ernesto Miranda	NOME REAL	Florencio S. Olpiendo
Argentina	PAIS	Filipinas
23 anos	IDADE	28 anos
1,68 m	ALTURA	1,64 cm
52,500 kg	PESO	55,800 kg
35 cm	PESCOÇO	38 cm
86 cm	TORAX NORMAL	88 cm
91 cm	TORAX DILATADO	91 cm
71 cm	CINTURA	78 cm
27 cm	BICEPS NORMAL	28 cm
29 cm	BICEPS DILATADO	33 cm
24 cm	ANTEBRAÇO	24 cm
15 cm	PULSO	16 cm
25 cm	PUNHO	29 cm
47 cm	COXA	46 cm
33 cm	PERNA	35 cm
170 cm	ENVERGADURA	172 cm
Ernesto Miranda	NOME PROFISSIONAL	Danny Kid

Tale of the tape for Miranda vs. Danny Kid

The bout between Miranda and Danny Kid took place on January 23 and turned out to be a disappointing one as they heard boos from the crowd throughout the contest. The result was a draw, and according to the reports, it was a fair result as there had been little to separate the pair and minimal action in general. "It was a weak fight. Both boxers ran from the fight. Miranda had a physical disadvantage, but the Filipino, on the other hand, was technically inferior, for it's hard to hit Miranda," Eder said.

Miranda went back to Argentina after this fight, and Jacob Nahun, still managing Eder, traveled to secure a deal with him to finally defend his title against Eder. "If Ernesto Miranda won't defend his title in São Paulo, we will go to Argentina. Naturally, he tries to buy time. After all, the two ties that Eder got were when he was only beginning as a professional, and the recent knockout against former champion Roberto Castro in the second round, must be a burden. However, my son is the mandatory challenger, and the fight will have to happen," Aristides said.

The insistence on a fight with Miranda drew criticism because it was a fight Eder did not have to take. Although Miranda was the South American champion, he was ranked below Eder in the world rankings, and stood to gain more from it than Eder. Eder justified the bout when he told O *Globo,*

"When I'm abroad, besides being Brazilian champion and fourth in the (world) ranking, I hope I'll also have the continental champion crown, which is yet another title. It will avoid the classic question: 'But aren't you South American champion?' that they always ask me."

Since the two tied encounters with Eder in 1957, Miranda had run up an impressive streak of 25 consecutive victories before the draw with Danny Kid. Among the victims Miranda could claim were Juan Cardenas of Spain when Miranda was campaigning in Italy, Alberto Barrenghi, and Roberto Castro, who he defeated twice for the continental championship. Though an agreement had been made back in December, it wasn't until February 1 that the particulars were confirmed, and the Ernesto Miranda vs. Eder Jofre mega-fight had a date and a home of February 19 at Ibirapuera.

Both fighters had been in training and were already in fighting shape when they performed for the media in separate workouts. The following day a deal was offered for Eder to face former world champion Mario D'Agata of Italy. No date was set, but it was targeted for some time in March in São Paulo. "I think he will come in March. Nothing has been treated officially for now. But Eder is ready to face him," Aristides said.

There was a lot of talk in the press and among Eder's fans that scheduling fights with too many world-ranked opponents depicted poor management since Eder already had a lofty ranking and was close to a world title opportunity. The belief was there wasn't any need to face so many world-class opponents in such a short space of time, and this could only harm his cause. The Miranda bout was accepted, but a D'Agata fight was viewed as a waste and a risk they didn't need to take. The argument from the Jofre camp was that further seasoning could only benefit Eder's chances of moving forward so they gave their approval for the D'Agata fight.

It was in the buildup to the third bout with Miranda when Eder told Cidinha's mother, Josefa, his intentions to marry her daughter.

"You know I am dating Cidinha, right?" he told her.

"Yes, it's been a long time, right?" she responded.

"Yeah, but you have to know that I am a righteous man, and I love her very dearly," he said.

"That I know too," she replied.

"Well, after my next fight, I need to have an earnest conversation with you, OK?" he said to her.

Josefa understood that Eder would ask permission to take her hand in marriage.

Aristides wanted to make sure that Eder sparred with lighter sparring partners for the crucial contest with Miranda. He knew that Eder had seen the most significant improvement of the two boxers since 1957. Miranda was a classy operator who relied heavily on swift movements. "We did not have good sparring for the fight with Danny Kid. Usually, we can only count on men who weigh more, and that influences Eder's speed. The sparring, whom we will choose this time, will be lighter, quicker men, for that's the only way we can correct the mistakes from that fight," he said.

The proposed fight with D'Agata was scrapped because the Italian suffered a hand injury just two days before Eder's match with Miranda. There were whispers that bantamweight champion Jose Becerra would fight Eder, but only in a non-title affair. Aristides did not take kindly to such talk and said, "Joe Becerra wants to fight with my son from what I've read in the papers, without, however, putting the world title at stake. I disagree with that. Eder won't be a test for anyone. We are willing to fight him for the bantam crown. If Eder wins that fight, with no official aspect, can you think of how many obstacles they will put for a second fight?" Eder agreed with his father and said that if Becerra wanted to fight somebody in the world rankings, he should put his title on the line.

Advertisement for Jofre vs. Miranda III

As both fighters wound down their training, they gave the press a final peek into their training quarters and appeared very relaxed. Eder gave a light training session and didn't get out of second gear. "Tomorrow, I'll wrap up my preparations by walking a lot in the morning and doing some gym exercises in the afternoon. I will have a big lunch, but I won't eat dinner to keep my weight down below regulation before the weigh-in at 9 am on Friday," he said. "I won't chase Miranda around the ring," Eder said regarding how he would combat Miranda's style. "Miranda's tricks are already well known. He always tries to run from his opponent, runs a lot in the ring, expecting his opponent to chase him. He retreats well, and then he punches, making the opponent tired, but that's not going to happen to me," he added.

Having had such a strong training camp, Eder showed high confidence: "I know Miranda is game since we have fought twice already. He is no better than Danny Kid, who I defeated with ease. I will not miss this opportunity to become champion of South America," he said. This confidence was also felt by Aristides, who chipped in and stated: "If Miranda is willing to fight Eder with the same style he fought Danny Kid, this will be a short fight. My son has never been as good as he is now. He will win, even if Miranda runs all the time."

As the fight neared, Miranda's training sessions were much more intense than Eder's as he performed a rigorous exercise routine for 45 minutes before sparring with Raul Justo for four rounds. This all came after he ran two and a half miles in the morning. "Eder is more dangerous than Danny Kid, but I will beat him," said Miranda. "His style is like that of Juan Cardenas, who I defeated by knockout not too long ago," he added. The Argentinian's trainer, Hector Vaccari, also expressed his confidence in stating, "I strongly believe Miranda will win no matter how."

Both boxers comfortably made weight, and in a move that pleased both fighters, it was announced that the referee would be Alphonso Araujo from Argentina. The judges would be Juan Guasch, also from Argentina, and two Brazilian judges, Edmar Teixeira and Moacyr Andrade.

O Globo set the scene for the fight in the morning newspaper the day of the fight:

"Eder Jofre and Ernesto Miranda will fight tonight for the third time, this time disputing the South American bantamweight title currently held by the Argentine fighter. It will be disputed over fifteen rounds, and there is no favorite. On the two occasions when Jofre faced Miranda, even though he didn't have today's experience, the undefeated Brazilian champion wasn't able to get more than a tie. For the continental title, Eder will risk his position of fourth-ranked bantamweight in the world in the official classification."

"Although in the Brazilian boxing business, a convincing victory is expected from 'Jofrinho,' the experts don't hide the danger that Miranda's style represents for the national champion. Miranda is always defensive, hitting and leaving quickly, and using clinches in every situation that feels dangerous. With no worries whatsoever to give the audience a spectacle, he plays only for himself, trying to score and win the fight."

Eder Jofre	NOME REAL	Ernesto Miranda
Brasil	PAIS	Argentina
23 anos	IDADE	23 anos
1,64 m	ALTURA	1,68 m
53,520 kg	PESO	53,500 kg
35 cm	PESCOÇO	35 cm
89 cm	TORAX NORMAL	86 cm
94 cm	TORAX DILATADO	91 cm
75 cm	CINTURA	71 cm
26 cm	BICEPS NORMAL	27 cm
29 cm	BICEPS DILATADO	29 cm
25 cm	ANTEBRAÇO	24 cm
16 cm	PULSO	15 cm
28 cm	PUNHO	25 cm
47 cm	COXA	47 cm
35 cm	PERNA	33 cm
1,67 m	ENVERGADURA	1,65 m
Eder Jofre	NOME PROFISSONAL	Ernesto Miranda

Tale of the tape for Jofre vs. Miranda III

On February 19 at Ibirapuera, Eder showed everyone that attended that his development as a fighter was far superior to Miranda's since their two drawn matches three years earlier.

Eder fought aggressively throughout the fight as he continually forced the action. He attacked Miranda from every angle as he gave the Argentine little time to rest. Miranda fought in a defensive shell for almost the entire bout, occasionally looking for counter-punching opportunities. Not too many openings appeared for Miranda as he sometimes resorted to clinching and was deducted two points for deliberate head butts. Miranda's clinches were easily shrugged off by Eder, who showed not only his best technical form to date but also moved with grace and appeared physically stronger. Some spectators became dissatisfied with what they perceived to be a lack of action, especially by Miranda, who appeared to fight solely to last the distance. Overall, the audience enjoyed the display from their local hero as they willed him on by standing and screaming throughout most of the contest.

Round By Round from *Estadão* and *O Globo*

Round 1
(*Estadão*) – Eder and Miranda leave their corners and meet in the center of the ring. They keep a distance, studying each other. Both are fighting behind a tight guard. One Miranda left hook is avoided by Eder, who ducks his head. The Brazilian doesn't punch. Another two punches from the Argentine connect lightly with Eder's head. Eder counters with his attack. Miranda attacks and Eder backs off, looking for support on the ropes. Eder moves to attack from a defensive position, landing a long right-hand punch to Miranda's face. The Argentine provokes the first stop of the fight, wrestling the Brazilian to stop the attack. Eder takes one step backward and attacks Miranda with two straight punches before the Argentine can react. The bell rings, announcing the end of the round.

(*O Globo*) - The boxers study each other in the center of the ring. Miranda shows great movement. Eder sidesteps, trying to attack, with no result. A hard cross from Eder gets loose in the air, causing the audience to gasp. Tied round.

Round 2
(*Estadão*) - Eder attacked and tried to hit Miranda with a quick straight right-hand punch. Miranda ducks and fights back with two crossed punches, but he missed. Eder blocks two more punches from Miranda. The Brazilian fights back, forcing the Argentine to back off to the ropes, hitting him with many punches. Miranda gets off the ropes and tries to pay Eder back for the punishment. But Eder doesn't give him an opportunity and goes on the attack, forcing Miranda to wrestle to get rid of the critical situation he was in. A Miranda hook hits Eder's body. The round ends.

(*O Globo*) - Miranda shows great leg movement and excellent work with his left, in jabs, to step away. He always runs from Eder's attack, who tries to take him to the ropes. At the end of the round, Miranda attacks, but Eder blocks well. Tied round.

Round 3
(*Estadão*) – Eder attacks and Miranda backs off. The Argentine's guard is shut, and two of the Brazilian's crosses miss their target. Both kept a distance, and the fight became dull. Eder and Miranda hesitate to attack. One straight right-hand punch by the Brazilian hits the Argentinian's face but doesn't hurt him. Miranda reacts but misses two punches. End of the round.

(*O Globo*) - Miranda throws a one-two, blocked by Eder, who lets his left hand go, hooking. The Brazilian takes the initiative and attacks the Argentine, sidestepping perfectly, taking few punches. Eder's advantage.

Round 4
(*Estadão*) – It's the Brazilian who pushes for the fight, decisively attacking. Miranda backs off and doesn't seem to want to counter-attack. Two punches from the Brazilian hit the Argentinian's body. Eder hooked his opponent's liver, who felt the effect of his punch. End of round.

(*O Globo*) - Opening ways with his left, Eder violently attacks. Leaning on the ropes, Miranda receives a flurry of punches and he clinches. Cornered again, he grabs and is booed. Eder looks to be on his way to a KO victory. An advantage for the Brazilian.

Round 5

(*Estadão*) – With his left hand in front of him, throwing jabs, Eder prepares and executes his attack. Miranda backs off slowly and, when hit by the first punch – a straight left – he wrestles with the Brazilian and stops the fight. The referee warns him, demanding combativeness. Eder attacks and punches Miranda with two straight right-hand punches and a left hook that the Argentine shows he has felt. End of round.

(*O Globo*) - Miranda reappears with good leg work, moving non-stop. He blocks all of Eder's punches and doesn't give him the margin to react. An advantage for the Argentine.

Round 6

(*Estadão*) – The fight resumes at a distance. Eder waits for Miranda to attack. Seeing that the Argentine doesn't attack, Eder pushes forward firmly and takes Miranda to the ropes, throwing many punches. Miranda wants to pay him back, but Eder doesn't give him a break. There is wrestling and breaking apart. Two of Miranda's punches hit Eder's face. The bell rings, announcing the end of the round.

(*O Globo*) - Miranda backs up but Eder still lands punches. Eder fights lower, trying to get closer, but the Argentine dances and hits him with lots of lefts, with no efficiency. Miranda's advantage.

Round 7

(*Estadão*) – Eder attacks with his left hand in front of him. A straight punch by the Brazilian hits the Argentinian's face. Miranda fights back and hits Eder in the face twice. Miranda commits a foul and is warned by the referee, who doesn't take off any points. Eder begins another attack and forces Miranda to go back to the ropes. End of the round.

(*O Globo*) - Eder hits, Miranda's clinches, and the Brazilian leaves with his left eye bleeding. Miranda shoots punches in succession. However, "Jofrinho" reacts and hits hard, provoking a sensation. Miranda still has the advantage.

Round 8

(*Estadão*) – A straight punch from Eder is avoided by Miranda, with a slight movement of his head. The Argentine fights back and makes the Brazilian back off. In the center of the ring, Eder hits Miranda's face with two straight punches. The Argentine feels the effects of both punches, wrestles with the Brazilian, and almost makes him fall. Eder attacks again and hits Miranda's solar plexus with two hooks in a row. Both keep a distance, looking for a better position for their actions—the end of the round.

(*O Globo*) - Eder's initiative. Miranda, without the same speed, grabs to avoid being punished. He receives two hooks to his face but doesn't feel them. The Argentine clinched eight times in this round. Eder's advantage.

Round 9

(*Estadão*) – Eder attacked, and Miranda held his right arm to avoid a second left hook. Eder backs off and lands a violent straight right-hand punch against Miranda's face. The Argentine goes to the ropes, tries to contain the Brazilian's attacks by wrestling. Eder punches Miranda's head twice with right cross punches. Miranda goes back looking dizzy, and the bell rings for the end of the round.

(*O Globo*) - Miranda still runs but uses counterpunches that hit Eder Jofre's head. The Brazilian doesn't throw strong punches, but he has the advantage. Miranda ends the round on the ropes.

Round 10

(*Estadão*) – The Brazilian attacked again, making the Argentine run. Two straight right-hand punches to the head and a left hook hit Miranda's body as he backed off awkwardly. Eder makes a fresh attack, but it results in nothing, for Miranda, even cornered, ducks well. The Argentine tries to react and undo the points advantage that the Brazilian already has. He attacks Eder with two punches, but he misses. Eder fights back with a straight punch, and Miranda's head shakes under the impact of the punch. The round is over.

(O Globo) - Three crosses hit Miranda's head, who then takes a flurry of punches. He reacts when he looked beaten and suffers a new and violent attack from the Brazilian boxer. Eder won the round.

Round 11

(*Estadão*) – Eder attacked furiously. Miranda backed off under a flurry of punches and, despite being severely punished, resisted well. He felt dizzy but didn't fall. Eder persisted and pushed his opponent close to the ropes; Miranda grabbed Eder's arm and stopped the fight. The bell rings and marks the end of the round.

(*O Globo*) - A Monotonous round, with Miranda always running and Eder not knowing how to hunt him down. There is a good technical exhibition but little violence. Tie.

Round 12

(*Estadão*) – The boxers stopped in the ring and slowed the fighting pace. Neither attacked. They studied each other as if the fight were just about to start. Miranda decides and attacks. Eder backs off under a lot of punches. Then, he reacted decisively and forced Miranda to back off to the ropes. Two punches by Eder make Miranda dizzy. A straight right-hand punch marks a sequence of punishment that the Brazilian imposes on the Argentine. Miranda still resists, attempting to clinch at the exact moment when the bell sounds for the end of the round.

(*O Globo*) - Eder is cornered on the ropes and takes some punches. Eder uses a clinch, takes in another flurry of punches and after signing to his father, coach Kid Jofre, dominates the fight, shaking Miranda with lots of punches to his body and head. The bell saves the Argentine, who is on his way to his corner. Eder's advantage.

Round 13

(*Estadão*) – Eder left his corner with a decision to end the fight. Miranda backed off under intense punishment and moved to initiate another clinch. Miranda bumped his head against Eder's face. The referee stops the fight and tells the judges to take three points off the Argentine (one each). Eder keeps hitting Miranda, who finds himself in a critical situation. The fight stopped again when the referee tells the judges to deduct another point from the Argentine as he was again penalized for head butting. End of round.

(*O Globo*) – This round was too difficult to make out on the report. All that could be made out was, "A Miranda head bump is severely reprimanded by the judge."

Round 14

(*Estadão*) – Eder waits for Miranda in the center of the ring. The Argentine doesn't attack, forcing the Brazilian to move forward. Two punches shave Miranda's head, but a third punch – a straight right – hits the Argentinian's jaw. Miranda backs off again. Then, he fights back and hits the Brazilian's face with two strong punches. Before Eder gets himself together, Miranda hits him with a straight right-hand punch and a left hook. The Brazilian backs off and counter-attacks. A straight right-hand punch, followed by a left hook, makes Miranda back off to the ropes. Stuck in the corner, the Argentine is intensively punished. The round ends with Miranda dizzy.

(*O Globo*) - Miranda comes back recovered, and even exchanged punches with the national champion. The fight quality drops again, with the Argentine counter-attacking, but running and abusing the clinches.

Round 15

(*Estadão*) – Believing that Miranda is still feeling the punishment from the previous rounds, Eder attacks decisively. He hits him with left and right-hand punches, forcing him to back off to the ropes. Miranda doesn't react. He keeps his guard shut, blocking Eder's punches. Suddenly he fights back and hits the Brazilian with two straight right-hand punches. The fight is stopped, which is caused by Eder. After breaking apart, Miranda throws his body against Eder, but this time the referee doesn't punish him by taking points off. Eder attacks and hits Miranda with a straight punch. The bell rings for the last time, marking the end of the round and the fight.

(*O Globo*) - Eder spends his last energies looking for a knockout. Miranda also reacts with violence. The rest of the round report was ineligible.

Eder is in white, Miranda in black

At the end of the bout, when the announcer held the microphone, there were nerves from the audience with one ringside fan saying, "they have Argentine judges," but when the emcee announced Eder as the new champion, the crowd erupted with huge cheers from all over the arena. Miranda and his camp were not happy with the verdict as they'd hoped his defensive approach would be appreciated more by the judges.

As Eder tried to make his way to his locker room with his new title, he had difficulty working his way past the fans who wanted to get close to him and congratulate him on his victory. It took him 15 minutes to make his way back to the locker room where both he and his father were interviewed. "Sidestepping doesn't win fights," said Aristides. "I haven't counted the rounds that 'Jofrinho' won, but the decision was more than fair," he added. The Argentine referee Alfonso Araújo said that his countryman's loss had been "clear and inarguable" in response to the Miranda camp crying foul. Miranda left the ring and showed those at ringside he did not have marks on his face as if to show that avoiding a knockout was enough to have earned him the victory. "When a boxer has a title, he shouldn't just run, but defend it and try to keep it with his will and with his heart," Eder said.

O Globo reported: "The spectacle only shook the audience in the 7th, 10th, and 12th rounds when Eder found space to let his magnificent shots go, trying to end the fight. One can't say, however, that it was a disappointing fight. The technique was up to the two boxers' reputation. However, Miranda, as his temper is, has exceeded in the defensive game and abused the clinches, even causing six of them in the seventh round and nothing less than eight in the next round. That added to the head butts he applied many times. On the other hand, however, the Argentine revealed he is a magnificent boxer, worked exceptionally well with his left, was excellent in his movement, and didn't allow Eder to hit him in the middle of his face. Even cornered on the ropes, he knew how to avoid the shots."

"Miranda fought carefully and conveniently to avoid being knocked out. He thought if he tired Eder Jofre, he could take advantage of his fatigue during the late rounds. Eder, however, showed himself in exceptional shape, fighting well from the first to the last round. Eder utilized sidesteps and perfect blocking in an attempt to impose his strongest punches. He controlled the initiatives, always looking for an advantage, and just like Miranda, he didn't let himself get caught dangerously. Although the fight was balanced, the victory could never belong to someone else."

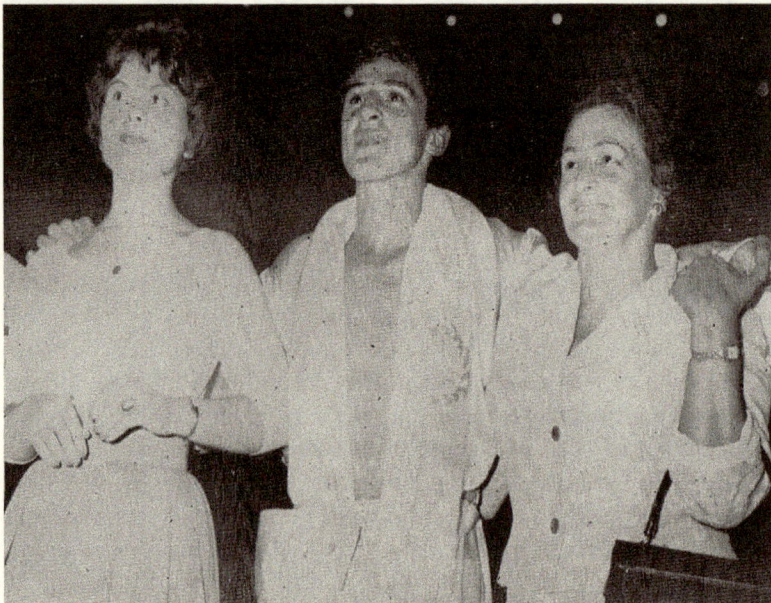

Eder celebrates with Cidinha and Angelina

Miranda, in a slightly delusional manner, was insistent that he had been robbed, stating, "I won most of the rounds because I landed more punches." As he was being interviewed, several members of his camp were shouting, "You were robbed." In the press conference after the bout, the fighters, their management teams, and families warmly greeted each other and shared their joy in the bout's having broken box office records at Ibirapuera. Miranda stated that he intended to activate the rematch clause and would be back in 90 days to regain the championship.

Between the third and fourth battles with Miranda, there was a significant change in Brazil when the capital city changed from Rio de Janeiro to the newly constructed Brasilia on April 21. Brasilia had been an idea that went back to 1827. Given it was centrally located, it was believed that it was a more appropriate location for what was becoming a powerhouse nation. Brasilia went from an idea to a plan in 1922, but it took decades to come to fruition and gain approval. The location was considered more regionally neutral compared to the northeastern placement of Rio, which had served as the capital city since 1763. Brasilia was a man-made city that took from December of 1956 to construct and was heralded as a masterpiece in modernist architecture.

Fight 34, vs. Ernesto Miranda IV, June 10, 1960

Now that Eder was the continental champion and ranked third in the world, it appeared a world title shot was not far off. Jose Medel's manager Lupe Sanchez proposed a Medel-Jofre fight in Mexico. That bout offered no real reward to Eder as Medel was ranked below him in the world rankings. Eder was set to make more money in the upcoming Miranda rematch, which he also was obligated to accept by prior contract.

At this time, Eder stayed in training and participated in several exhibition contests. Miranda took a tune-up fight back in Argentina at Ciudad Mendoza against countryman Ricardo Moreno. This bout ended in a 10-round draw. Miranda touched down in São Paulo on May 19 and, upon arrival, requested that the bout be suspended a few weeks from the scheduled date of June 10 as he felt he wasn't in ideal fighting shape. The request was denied, so Miranda knuckled down rather than lose out on the fight. He went to work at Record Gym. Miranda made the fight personal, hurled several insults at Eder, and even sent crude messages and letters to his family. This angered Eder, who couldn't understand why a fighter would act disrespectfully and take things to a personal level. Eder did not reveal the specifics of what Miranda sent to them, but he felt Miranda had crossed a line and vowed to make him pay for his distasteful antics.

In a reversal of roles from the first bout's conditions, Eder would receive 30% of the gate, while Miranda was to receive 20% as the challenger. This time around, the referee was the Brazilian Edmundo Lima, and he was joined by his countryman Ademar Teixeira, and the Argentinian duo of Hector Chaumont and Grazon Funes as the judges.

Just ten days out from the bout, Eder trained in front of the press, and between exercises, he was seen with a blanket covering his body as he was struggling to get the weight off. Intensified training with a lot of extra roadwork and some tough sparring helped get his weight down to a point he was on track to make the weight safely and healthily as the bout drew closer.

Miranda had rubbed many people the wrong way with his sour grapes from the last fight. Everybody outside of the Miranda camp had seen Eder dominate the action and beat Miranda handily, but the Argentine continued to tell the press how his title had been stolen. With two Argentine judges, he said he would not receive an unfair verdict should the bout go the distance again. It was anticipated that the two fighters would go the full fifteen rounds again, but Miranda made a statement in a sparring session days out from the fight, which further irritated the fans.

"Ernesto Miranda yesterday took in his last practice for tomorrow's fight with Eder, an attitude that caused revolt at Record Gym. He knocked out an inexperienced boxer who was practicing with him. During the practice, the Argentine would increase his potency in every round. At a certain point, after a sign from Vaccari, Miranda landed a hard punch on Filismino Barreto da Silva – the sparring partner – dropping him to the canvas. The former South American champion, with his head protected, reached the climax of the 'wave' he has been on since he arrived: trying to intimidate 'Jofrinho.' But we believe it all went wrong. His gesture against the young boxer only caused anger," *O Globo* reported on June 9.

Eder would not be drawn into a war of words and instead went to work as he performed his last training session. Some observed that he was probably still tight at the weight as he worked out in a woolen sweater, and between exercises, he wrapped himself in a blanket. He looked sharp as he sparred six rounds, three with Alencar Ribeiro, two with Jorge Sacoman, and one with his uncle, Ricardo Zumbano. There were a lot of cheers from the spectators on hand as he gave a show in which he displayed a full repertoire of punches with both hands.

"I feel really good. I don't want to be overly optimistic, but I have high hopes to win the fight. I know that Miranda said he came to São Paulo only to take the title. We'll decide that on Friday. I am prepared, and I want him to be too. We don't want excuses later," Eder said. Aristides appeared noticeably confident that his son would repeat his victory over Miranda, saying, "Well, one thing is to come to pick up the title, taking it is something else. While they talk, we'll keep on practicing. I always trusted the boy, and now I do more than ever."

The pre-fight taunts and personal jibes from Miranda continued into the arena on the night of June 10 back at Ibirapuera, where 20,000 fans packed inside to see a good old-fashioned grudge match between exceptionally talented world-ranked contenders. The tension between the fighters helped push further attention to the event as the bout profited Cr$4.235.000,00 (roughly BR$153999.85 in today's Brazilian currency or

$28,400.00 in US currency), which was a record for any sporting event in the state of São Paulo. Miranda, in a tasteless act, had found a photograph of Cidinha and cut out her face and placed it over the face of a naked woman in another photo, and threw it under Eder's locker room door in an attempt to further destabilize the Brazilian's mindset.

The crowd was in high spirits throughout the preliminary bouts, and as the main event drew closer, the excitement grew. The audience was described as being well dressed with an abundance of different colors on display. There were also many women in the audience. Sometimes, a rocket would be fired in the stands, further adding to the fervent atmosphere building. There was a large crowd of fans outside of the arena, but there were no seats available besides a minimal amount at ringside, which were still priced at top dollar. Many fans stayed around outside, chanting for Eder, also hoping that the stewards would let them in or give them a

Angelina cheers as Cidinha and Claudio Tonelli look on

special deal, some fans yelling "Two tickets for the price of one," since it was only the premium pricing left.

A prolonged clapping greeted Eder when he emerged with his father. They passed by the audience and stepped into the ring to thunderous applause. Despite the provocations he had received before the fight, Eder came to the Ibirapuera ring calm and confident about what lay ahead. He patiently waited as Miranda took ten minutes to get to the ring amid a torrent of abuse and a chorus of boos and catcalls. This treatment began the moment he put his robe on and opened his locker room door and only intensified the closer he got to the ring.

The audacity of his pre-fight bravado, coupled with the poor sportsmanship he exhibited after the defeat last time, had turned the Brazilian boxing aficionados sour towards the opposing boxer. Miranda appeared nervous as he asked on the microphone for a minute of silence for the victims of a recent disaster in Chile. On May 22, the largest earthquake ever recorded, known as the Valdivia Earthquake, shook Chile to its core. Miranda's wishes were answered. But during this silence, a man yelled: "Go, Eder!" Before the fight, the two boxers exchanged their country's flags.

Round By Round from *O Globo*

Round 1

Eder takes the initiative, but Miranda avoids his approach, working quickly with his left. An attacking attempt from the Argentine is opposed with a strong right-hand punch that reaches his face. On the ropes, Miranda reacts and hits the body of the Brazilian. Round with no winner.

Round 2

Eder hits strong without any aggression. Miranda works admirably with his left hand and attacks and lands jabs on the Brazilian's head. Eder retakes the initiative and shows a more efficient attack, making Miranda clinch. Round with no winner.

Round 3

After many passes with no danger in the attack, Miranda receives a violent counterpunch from "Jofrinho." The Brazilian corners him on the ropes. He hits Miranda's liver with a hook. He shuts his eye with a left hand, hits him with an uppercut. Miranda crumbles, gets up, and walks to his corner, dizzy, in no condition to defend himself, obliging the referee to reach the count of ten seconds.

Eder, perhaps anticipating that Miranda would, once again, try to fight on the back foot, came out aggressively and went after his foe. Much to the audience's surprise, Miranda was willing to stand with Eder and try to catch the defending champion by surprise. Eder possessed superior technique and strength and got the better of the fight in the first round and brought the crowd to their feet as they cheered after he went for Miranda. The pattern continued in the second round as Eder turned up the heat on Miranda further.

In a brave but ultimately foolish act, the Argentinian refused to back down as he had done so often in their last fight, but after two rounds, it was clear who the boss was. Miranda again would not abandon his newly established aggressive tactics in the third round while Eder was looking for the perfect moment. That moment came two minutes into the round when Eder hooked Miranda, which forced him into a corner. Miranda tried to escape but was met by another left hook. He fell and grabbed hold of his right eye in pain. Miranda grabbed the rope as his eye bled, but he remained unresponsive for the full count of ten, and Eder was awarded an impressive third-round knockout victory over his fiercest rival to date.

O Globo reported: "Friday's fight was the fourth between Eder and Miranda. On the two first occasions, with Eder starting his professional career, there was no winner. Since the third fight, and the Brazilian's victory on points, Miranda must have understood how hard it was to overcome or eliminate the opponent's strong punch. His habitual game, hitting and quickly leaving, working with his left, and avoiding any punch exchanges, could take him standing to the 15th round, but wouldn't be enough to turn him into a winner. That's why on Friday, he even tried to surprise (Eder) in the first round. Eder, like everyone else, expected the Argentine to try to come on in the second half of the fight. Miranda, however, went on, and in the second round, he even tried to attack. Still, this time his plans didn't work. At the first opportunity, 'Jofrinho' opened his guard and hit him with punches that brought him down. Sensitive to the punishment, the Argentine fell, got up when the counting was coming to three, but the pain in his eyes and his mouth prevented him from returning to the fight before the referee reached the KO counting."

Miranda was a sorry sight in the ring when he gave his interview after the bout. Sporting a swollen eye, cracked lips, and three wobbly teeth, he said that he had gone dizzy and was having difficulty with his visibility but stated that he would like another chance to fight Eder.

After the bout, the Jofre camp celebrated and the fans chanted his name in joy. The Argentinian showed poor sportsmanship just as he had in their previous encounter when he said he was robbed again. The injustice he claimed this time was that a head butt took him out. "He gave the excuse so quickly it was though it was rehearsed," wrote *Estadão*. In *O Grande Campeao*, Eder laughed off this excuse when he said (pointing to his left hand), "Right. This is my head." Miranda was lucky to escape the arena without more damage as an angry mob tried to attack him on his way to the locker room. Miranda's trainer, Hector Vacarri, assaulted a young fan who was only smiling as they made their way backstage. The poor sportsmanship and excuses out of the Miranda camp again left a bad taste, and the press collectively shook their heads when they pointed the finger and said how a head butt had settled the fight and not a punch.

Despite their rivalry, Miranda later admitted that it had been an honor and privilege to have shared the ring with Eder Jofre. Eder also expressed a level of respect for his rival's qualities and defensive skills. "I fought four times against him; (the) Argentine had excellent technique and tremendous energy. (I had) great difficulty getting through his defense," he said.

Fight 35, vs. Claudio Barrientos, July 15, 1960

On the heels of the impressive thrashing of Ernesto Miranda, Abraham Katzenelson contacted George Parnassus in an attempt to get a fight for Eder against world champion Jose Becerra. Eder was considered the most logical and dangerous challenger to Becerra's throne. Alphonse Halimi was ranked as the number one contender, but he had been knocked out by Becerra twice. Eder had cleaned out an exceptionally talented generation of South American bantamweights and had dominated high-quality international boxers such as Danny Kid and Leo Espinosa, but his name didn't quite have the same cache in the boxing Mecca of the United States. Eder had shown himself to be a complete boxer entering his peak at age 24 with an undefeated record of 33-0-3, having defeated every man he had faced in dominant fashion. When asked if Eder would be comfortable going to fight Becerra in front of his Mexican fans in Los Angeles, Eder said, "For the world title, I would go to Los Angeles or the moon."

He was making headlines in Brazil and held the hopes of a nation, but to North American boxing fans, he was more of a curiosity, a fighter whose name appeared in the rankings and the win columns but not in their rings or on their television screens. The victories over Danny Kid, Zuddas, Miranda, and Espinosa had been received well globally and pointed to Eder's quality, but the reality facing Eder was that Becerra being a famous Mexican champion, had great options fighting in Southern California against the likes of Jose Medel, Jose "Toluco" Lopez, and Ignacio Piña. All highly regarded and popular boxers who figured to be lucrative opponents for the champion in the Mexican boxing hotbed of Los Angeles.

On June 16, it was reported in *Estadão* that Becerra was almost set to finalize an August bout with Medel, which could leave Eder out of world championship opportunities until the following year. A bout still rumored for Eder was one with Mario D'Agata, but this was considered a waste of time as D'Agata had seen better days and was no longer ranked among the world's top ten bantamweights. Aristides responded to growing criticism they didn't need to take so many fights since it was clear he was close to being offered a title shot. "We shouldn't keep him locked in a jar," Aristides said. Aristides felt it was beneficial for his son to keep up a high level of activity. "They (extra bouts) will even help the kid get ready," he added.

The speculation regarding Becerra vs. Medel raised little attention as Parnassus contacted Katzenelson regarding the possibility of a Becerra vs. Jofre bout in Brazil where he said they would save a lot of money on taxes. The negotiation lasted for a few days as an offer of $30,000 was made to Becerra, but it was promptly rejected. Parnassus came up with a plan to have an elimination tournament in Los Angeles between the leading bantamweight contenders and have the winner earn the shot at Becerra.

To stay sharp as he closed in on the title shot, Eder took a bout with Claudio Barrientos on two weeks' notice. Becerra also accepted two non-title bout tune-ups as he waited for his next big money title defense. Jofre vs. Barrientos represented an interesting promotional angle. The memory of the defeat by the Chilean Barrientos in the 1956 Melbourne Olympics was still a thorn in Eder's side, and he sought revenge to prove that the judges had it wrong in Australia and that he was the superior fighter of the two.

Barrientos, 25, arrived in São Paulo at 3 pm on July 2 from Santiago and came with his manager Pino Barrientos. His training began the following day at 10:30 am at Academia Record Gymnasium, but in two days, he was pleading with the promoters to push the bout back a week, stating that he needed more time to acclimate. Barrientos' appeal was granted, and he continued with his intensive training regimen. Barrientos showed good form in his practice but stopped short of making any promises of what he could produce on fight night as he remained reticent throughout the buildup to the bout.

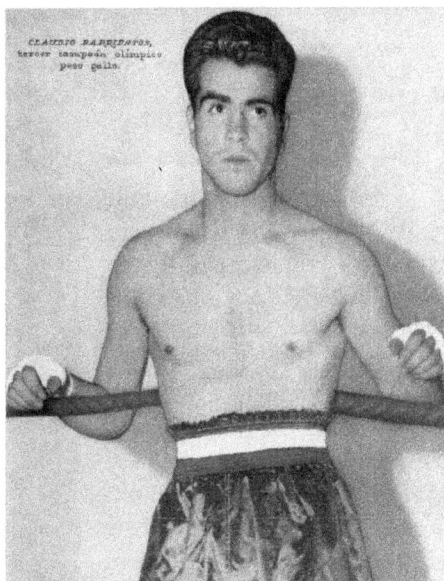

Eder also made no brash predictions but had an air of confidence about him as he wowed spectators at the final public workout sessions. While Eder remained focused on his Olympic revenge match, behind the scenes, the wheels were in motion for his next bout to be for the championship as it was reported from Mexico that Becerra's management team received an offer from Brazil worth $50,000, which was a significant improvement from the offer just a couple of weeks prior. The manager of Becerra, Pancho Rosales, countered that they would not accept a penny less than $60,000.

On fight night, the trajectory of each boxer's career proved quite different when Eder finally had the opportunity to even the score with Barrientos. Eder started the bout by boxing cautiously as he looked for openings and tried to find weaknesses in the Chilean's game. Barrientos moved well, and Eder struggled to find the right distance and could not quite nail Barrientos with his best punches in the early going. Barrientos, boxing a defensive fight, landed light punches as Eder reached in. The first three rounds were close, and it looked like Eder was not quite at his best. He did warm to the task in the fourth round as he displayed his intelligence and adaptability when he

picked off Barrientos with more regularity. Eder gradually began to dominate as the rounds passed. He dropped Barrientos eight times. The Chilean, to his credit, was an immensely proud and resilient fighter as he would rise each time. Despite his grogginess, he would engage Eder to get back into the fight rather than move away and go into survival mode. At the end of the eighth round, the Chilean corner informed referee Americo Cury that their man had suffered enough and threw in the towel. Soon after the bout, a telegram came through from Los Angeles from George Parnassus, it read: "Get ready to fight Joe Medel in L.A. next month. The winner will meet Joe Becerra for the world title."

Aristides wrote a special feature in *O Globo* which gave a behind the scenes look into what was going on in their training camp, the strategies implemented around this "Olympic revenge" match, and future plans:

"The fight story between Eder Jofre and Claudio Barrientos started four years ago. My son and I left, taking a lot of hope to bring back from Melbourne, the first Olympic boxing title to Brazil. In the beginning, it was a strong fighter, a Thai man who opened up our way to victory. Right after that though, a cold Chilean, Claudio Barrientos frustrated our victory hopes. Eder came back, started as a professional, and Barrientos remained, besides Uruguayan Aniceto Pereyra, against whom we had an unfair result, the only one to beat Eder. With Aniceto, we got another fight and erased the past. Only Barrientos was left, and fate wanted him to meet Eder again for first place in the world ranking, defending his prestige as an undefeated champion."

We can't be reckless

"Eder's position in the world ranking doesn't allow him to be reckless with any opponent. Maybe that's why we fed no wishes of revenge for the Melbourne result. We did want to beat him, just like any other opponent. During the practices, I warned my son not to get too excited about the revenge that the audience and the press demanded. I advised him to fight carefully, not being exposed, study Barrientos' style, and wait for the best occasions to put himself in an advantage. I never doubted that Eder would win the "rematch," which doesn't mean I would underestimate a man who never kissed the floor and who counted only one defeat in 150 fights as an amateur and as a professional.

What I did in the corner

Eder came up to the ring, calm as always, smiling and saying hello to his friends. Angelina, my wife, Cidinha, my future daughter-in-law, in the first rows, looked more nervous than us. Before the bell rang, I told Eder: "Be careful. Work with your left and let the man get confident." Barrientos was vulnerable to his solar plexus, and after the round was over, I told Eder to let go straight rights followed by left hooks. In that round, we already felt that victory was inevitable. A left hook punch hit Barrientos' chin, and from that moment on, he stopped being a boxer who never kissed the ground.

Beginning and end of the punishment

"Force him, Eder. Take him to the ropes, and don't let him run. Hit fast and strong and he won't be able to take it." - That's what I suggested before the third round. I confess, however, that after that round, I was surprised by Barrientos's resistance. The little man would take punches and punches, some more violent and in his vital points. Someone else, less strong, would have fallen soon. Barrientos, however, was brave and didn't want to surrender. He would fall, get up, take other punches, and always get up before the counting was over. I lost count of how often he fell; it was eight, according to what they told me later. I kept telling Eder to squeeze him and work quickly because I knew that resistance had to end, as happened in the eighth round. Before that, there were plenty of opportunities. The Chilean boxer did not lack resilience.

He was not in danger

Friday's fight, although with no title at stake and with little importance, was accepted by us as preparation for the world title. Until then, Eder needs to have other fights and not miss the ring. We weren't too concerned about his weight, although four pounds over his category meant Eder did not have the same speed. The bad weather, the fog, and the cold stopped his morning running. That's why I told him to control himself in the first few rounds and not force the KO that the audience was asking for. I concluded that Eder loses a lot of his mobility when weighing more than usual. It doesn't seem like it, but from 118 pounds to 122 pounds, as he weighed on Friday, it's a big difference he can feel in the ring.

We will go to Los Angeles, no doubt

Lastly, I think more than an analysis of his fight with Barrientos; the audience wants information on the dispute of the world title with Becerra. I will tell everything to O GLOBO readers. The telegraphic agencies have been informing that Joe Becerra's coach, Mexican Pancho Rosales, won't let his pupil come to São Paulo to put his title at stake. He demands to fight in Los Angeles, and I don't deny him that right, for, after all, Becerra is the champion and defends at his conveniences. We will, however, go to Los Angeles when he wants. There will be no fight in Mexico because the financial conditions don't even answer to Becerra's interests. Also, the altitude and the weather conditions are unfavorable. Will Eder win the title? We have our hopes up. A lot. Watching Becerra's fight with Japanese (Kenji) Yonekura on film, I found the Mexican vulnerable. He uses his punch, but from what I've seen and from what they tell me, Eder might beat him by KO."

In his personal life, Eder by now had been long engaged to Cidinha, but his busy schedule had pushed back the proposed wedding date. Eder vowed that he would marry Cidinha after he won the world title and give her the title as a gift. There was still more work to do, but he assured Cidinha's mother not to worry and that they would be married no matter what.

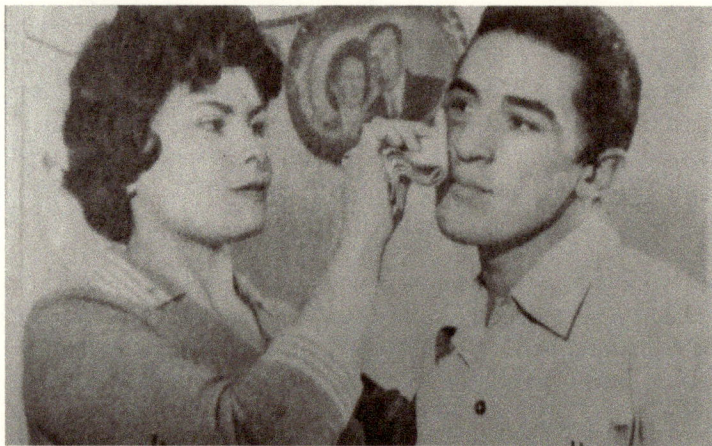

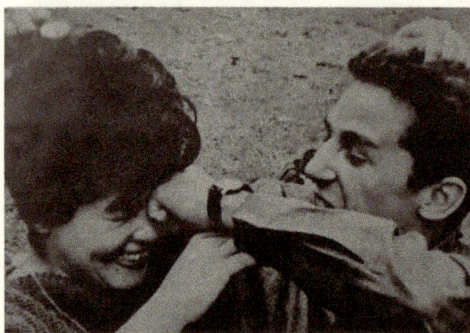

Fight 36, vs. Jose Medel, August 18, 1960

Eder had earned the top ranking in the division and was ready to face Jose Becerra, but negotiations between the two camps hit a snag. Eder and his team felt they were the next logical challenger for Becerra and were prepared to do anything to get a shot at his championship, but the Mexican camp insisted that Eder had to face the fearsome Jose Medel to earn a shot at their man. "Manager Katzenelson's attempt to schedule a fight between Eder Jofre and Mexican Jose Becerra for the bantam world title was unsuccessful. Instead of disputing the title, Eder will have to fight Mexican Jose Medel on August 18 in Los Angeles, and only then, if he wins, will he fight the world champion. Although Eder Jofre is officially Becerra's number one challenger, the managers announced this was the way they found to guarantee a future fight for the world title," *O Globo* reported.

Aristides accepted the 12-round contest with Medel for his son and asked the Brazilian Federation to select another coach to take the Olympic boxing team to Rome since he had been selected as head coach but would be preparing his son for this fight.

Becerra, with his crowd-pleasing style, had become a national hero in Mexico, particularly in his hometown of Guadalajara. He had proven himself to be a grand world champion because he too had come up the hard way having to defeat Jose Medel, Dwight Hawkins, Mario D'Agata, and Billy Peacock before he lifted the title from Alphonse Halimi in a thrilling bout in July 1959.

Tragedy struck when Walt Ingram died as the result of injuries sustained at the hands of Becerra in what was supposed to be a celebratory homecoming fight in front of his Guadalajara fans. Becerra defeated Halimi again before holding onto his title in a tough bout in Japan with Kenji Yonekura.

Becerra vs. Jofre seemed a natural fight given both fighter's styles, their excellent records, and the fact that they were the same age. Becerra must have known how tough Medel was since they had faced each other three times when they were both prospects coming up in Mexico. It was an excellent opportunity for the Mexicans to assess the Brazilian as it would be his first bout outside South America, and they could get a proper gauge of what they would be up against should Eder defeat Medel.

Medel was born in 1938 on Calle Caridad in the heart of the Barrio Bravo neighborhood of Tepito, one of Mexico City's roughest areas. Tepito was the home of one of the first Mexican boxing icons when Kid Azteca rose to prominence in the 1930s. The proud boxing tradition has existed in Tepito ever since, as they have churned out some of the best fighters in Mexican boxing history, particularly in the bantamweight division. It has long been a neighborhood where fighting, whether one-on-one fistfights or gangs fighting with knives and guns, was rampant.

The second of five children, Medel worked selling lemons and oranges on the bustling streets of the Mexican capital to help support his family as a child. On these streets, Medel learned how to defend himself and gained a toughness almost innate among Tepito boxers. His first experience in the ring occurred when his friend Leonardo Lopez was competing and a fighter failed to turn up, so he volunteered his services. It was love at first sight for the young Tepito boy as he soon trained at Gloria Gym in the neighborhood where he was from, and he could not get enough of it.

As a child, Medel had seen other people from the same neighborhood make it in boxing and become heroes and would often pray to God to afford him the same success. Medel was given the nickname "Huitlacoche" by his trainer Antonio Aznar due to his dark skin complexion. Huitlacoche is a sort of fungus that grows on corn and is sometimes served as a delicacy in Mexican dishes.

Jose Medel

The 1950s has been described as arguably the most exciting in Mexican bantamweight history. Raul Macias was the first Mexican national to win a bantamweight world championship. Jose Becerra followed him, not only as a world champion but also as a national hero. Though they weren't the only fighters to gain a fan base among boxing aficionados in Mexico. There was Ricardo "Pajarito" Moreno, German Ohm, and the very popular Jose "Toluco" Lopez. Moreno was a "do or die" type banger with no amateur experience. He thrilled crowds with his wild style and incredible punching power. He scored 59 knockouts in his 60 wins but soon outgrew the division and lost almost every time he stepped up to the world-class level. Ohm perhaps never reached Moreno's popularity, nor did he fight for a world title like "Pajarito," but he was a steadier performer. He was good enough to avenge a cut eye defeat by dominating Jose Becerra in a rematch, but he later succumbed to a defeat against Boots Monroe before retiring at age 21.

Toluco Lopez was perhaps the most popular and successful of the fighters never to win a world title. He ran up an impressive string of victories over fighters such as Billy Peacock, Boots Monroe, Carlos Cardoso, and Danny Kid as he claimed the Mexican bantamweight title in addition to the North American title. Medel emerged at the forefront of the division towards the end of the 1950s.

He turned professional at age 17 in 1955 with limited amateur experience. Initially, it was tough for Medel as he fought, more often than not, against opponents who had more experience. The most notable rival of his early days was Jose Becerra, whom he met three times in one year. He couldn't pin a loss on Becerra as he was defeated each time on points, but

he did score some impressive wins around that time when he defeated Raul Leonos and Dwight Hawkins. Hawkins had defeated Becerra in a knockout victory in Los Angeles. Medel was a streaky fighter at this point in his career as he would win some and lose some but could never gain a consistent run of victories. He fought often and attracted the attention of Don Lupe Sanchez, who had successfully managed the career of Ricardo Moreno and later guided Pipino Cuevas and Rodolfo Martinez to world championships.

By the time Medel was ready to challenge for the Mexican bantamweight title, he was 21 years of age, had a record of 37-13-3, and had recently scored an impressive victory over the highly touted Cuban, Johnny Sarduy. Sarduy had run up an outstanding record in Cuba but was blown out in three rounds when he took on Medel in Mexico City.

That triumph was followed up with three comfortable wins before Medel was pitted against the famous Toluco Lopez. Toluco had run up an impressive record of 60 victories against only nine defeats and was in the prime of his career at 27 years of age. He'd been champion for some time and was expected to turn back the challenge of Medel without too much difficulty. Medel failed to read the script as he dominated Lopez over the 12-round distance and earned a unanimous decision victory. The fans of Lopez didn't take this defeat kindly as they attempted to invade the ring and then went into the cantinas to drown their sorrows. Medel did not have Lopez's charisma, and several fans turned on him because of what he had done to their beloved Toluco. Medel was back in action the next month as he scored a knockout victory over Pimi Barajas in Monterey before hitting a three-fight losing skid. Among that losing streak was an unpopular split decision defeat against Danny Kid in a bid for the North American title.

"Danny Kid of the Philippines retained his North American bantamweight title by gaining a split decision over Jose Medel of Mexico City in 12 rounds last night. Among a crowd of 5,500 people at the Olympic Auditorium, the majority booed the decision, thinking Medel had landed the harder punches, though both boys suffered eye cuts. There were no official knockdowns," reported the *Associated Press*. The referee, Mushy Callahan, had missed a knockdown in the fifth round when Medel floored

Kid with two right-hands, but Callahan judged it to have been a slip. Following this setback, Medel was then defeated by Ignacio Piña and Eloy Sanchez in his last two bouts of 1959.

Medel was a highly skilled boxer, who was adept at fighting off the ropes and was a dangerous counter-puncher. His inconsistency was attributed to a somewhat nonchalant nature. Medel was always dedicated and in fighting shape but was said to be reasonably passive in many of his bouts. The higher the stakes, the better fans would see of Medel, and that was consistent throughout his career. In 1960 he had an immediate turn of fortunes as he was able to avenge the losses to Danny Kid and Sanchez to shoot his way up the bantamweight world rankings.

Although most felt Eder deserved to be fighting Becerra, he accepted the Medel fight in Los Angeles at the world-famous Olympic Auditorium for August 18. Anthony Maceroni, president of the National Boxing Association (NBA), said that if Eder lost to Jose Medel, he would be entitled to a rematch in São Paulo. "At most," he said, "Eder will fall to second or third place in the world ranking in the event of a defeat. Regardless, a win or draw will guarantee a fight with Becerra for the title." The purse for Eder in this fight, according to Maceroni,

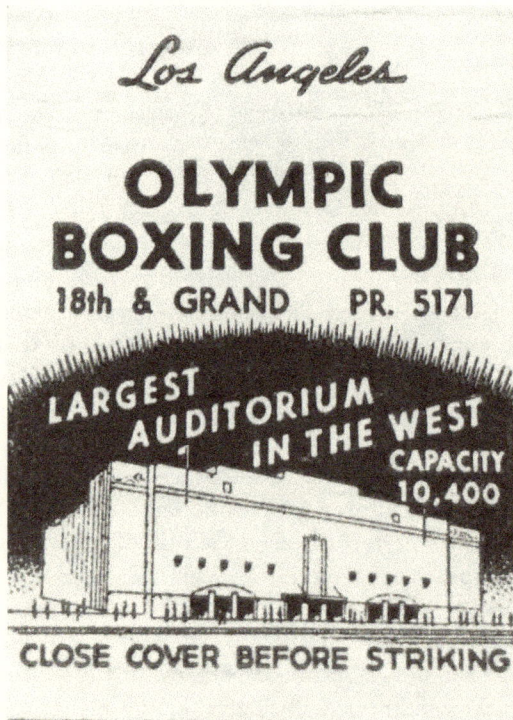

would be 20% of the total gross revenue. If the income would be less than $ 15,000, the income tax would not exceed 22.5%.

Eder had been to America before when *Estadão* helped take him over on the multi-city tour the previous year, but the bout with Medel would represent the first time he was fighting outside of South America. For many young fighters, that would be a daunting task, but Eder relished the task at hand. The added prestige of fighting at The Olympic further inspired Eder. The venue on the corner of 18th Street and Grand Avenue in downtown Los Angeles right off the Santa Monica freeway was built in 1924. Over the years, it had been the most critical boxing venue west of Madison Square Garden. With a seating capacity of 10,400, it had hosted such fighters as Sugar Ray Robinson, Willie Pep, Henry Armstrong, Archie Moore, and Manuel Ortiz. Rick Farris shared with me his experience of performing at this venue. "It was a dream come true for me to box at The Olympic. (Jack) Dempsey had broken ground for its construction in 1924. All the legends had fought there. I remember the energy when the place was sold out, coming down the aisle to the ring. Once you passed from under the balcony into the view of all the fans, the place would explode, literally shaking the walls. It was a magical moment!"

On August 5, Eder participated in an exhibition contest with former foe Cristobal Gavisans in Salvador. They boxed eight rounds which the fans enjoyed. He was already deep into his training schedule for the big fight in America.

On August 9, only nine days out from the fight in Los Angeles, Eder did his final training session for the Brazilian reporters as he sparred with a middleweight named Mantegna. Eder was in high spirits and dismissed the notion that he could be out of his element in California, which held a sizable Mexican audience. "I won't be out of place. I will meet several South Americans in Los Angeles and some boxers like Kid Pascualtito and Ricardo Gonzalez," he said. In this final session, some observed that Eder was training in heavy clothes and a coat when he was doing his various exercises. It was believed he had not done enough roadwork at home in Brazil, but he insisted that as soon as he arrived in Los Angeles, he was going into a rigorous training routine and would add plenty of roadwork, so he could make the 118 pounds limit.

On Wednesday, August 10, Eder, and his team took a 7:30 pm flight from Congonhas airport to Los Angeles via New York City. Eder told the press on hand he was "confident in my ability, and I won't be afraid of Medel or the audience in California."

In a statement for *O Globo,* Eder addressed his fans through the newspaper: "Through O GLOBO, I want to tell the audience from Rio de Janeiro and Brazil that I'll go to LA focused on representing Brazilian boxing well in this first commitment abroad. Disposition, goodwill, and unshakable wish to get to the end of the journey have never lacked in me, and I hope to count on, as always, the press support, and especially the support of the Brazilian people, the most important factors in my career."

After the long journey to Los Angeles, Eder and his team were greeted at LAX airport by George Parnassus, Anthony Petronella, and some journalists. A Brazilian named Manoel Rodrigues Pineda was also on hand and introduced himself to the Jofres. "I am Brazilian. Thank God. I live here with my wife, and I will be your guy. Anything you need just hit me up," he said. Manoel had been brought along by Parnassus and became more than a helper; he became a friend and a part of the training camp. Pineda was to get Eder out of bed every day at six in the morning to start his morning training by getting his roadwork in early.

Awaiting Eder and his team was a telegram from Ernesto Miranda who wrote to wish his former rival well. "We are sure you will do well, for neither Medel nor Becerra will be able to beat you," it read.

In George Parnassus' office

Aristides and Eder

Eder set up camp at the famous Main Street Gym near Skid Row at 318 Main Street. The Main Street Gym was as renowned as any boxing gym in the world and at the entrance was a sign that read, "world-rated boxers train here daily." Like many of the great gyms, there was nothing pleasant about the Main Street Gym with its creaky floorboards, the mixed aroma of liniment and sweat, and the sound of an old gong sounding every three minutes. Eder hired Kid Pascualtito as a sparring partner to help prepare him for the bout.

Eder also put some quality work in with two highly regarded South American boxers as he worked with Ricardo Gonzalez and the legendary Pascual Perez. Gonzalez's pedigree was excellent. He had a lot of experience and had previously held the South American featherweight championship before being stripped of the title. Perez had been flyweight world champion from 1954-1960 but had recently lost the title to Thailand's Pone Kingpetch. He was in Los Angeles preparing for his rematch with Kingpetch at The Olympic, and the two men were happy to help get each other in excellent condition ahead of their significant matches coming up.

At a public workout on August 15, just three days out from the fight, Eder was asked which of his hands is most powerful, and he responded, "I have two arms, and I can use them both." Eder appeared relaxed and in good spirits as his father talked to the press about how Eder was born to be a champion. When asked to strike a fighting pose for the cameras, Eder stood like John L. Sullivan with both arms extended and his fists in the air.

It was reported in the *Los Angeles Times* that both fighters had looked in fine form, and the local boxing aficionados were expecting a great fight.

Eder was a 2-1 favorite against Medel, but there were concerns in the Jofre camp as he struggled to get down to the weight. His father put him through the paces in Los Angeles, but the last couple of pounds would not come off. It would appear the lack of roadwork in Brazil was coming back to haunt them. Eder took off the remaining pounds on the morning of the fight through some strength-sapping methods such as wrapping his whole body in plastic and spending long periods in the sauna. After 55 minutes of hopping on and off the scale, Eder finally made weight. Medel, by comparison, made the weight easily and quickly departed to grab a big lunch.

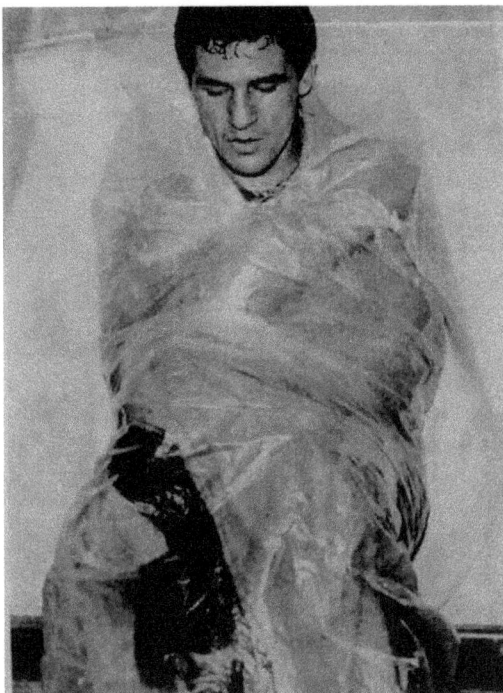

Eder sheds weight

Aristides had a feeling that someone was trying to play dirty tricks on them. He said that he had brought his own scales with him and that Eder was under the weight limit in the hotel room and had put nothing in his body from there until the weigh-in. But how could he prove that the scale was wrong? After a life of suffering, Aristides finally had a boxer on the verge of a world title, and everything could be lost because of sabotage or by ruffling the wrong feathers.

This was not ideal preparation for what would not only be the most hostile crowd Eder would encounter to date but also the most formidable opponent. "I had to lose a lot of weight on the day of the fight. I had to lose approximately four pounds. Can you imagine someone who's already slim and in shape having to lose four pounds on the day of the fight? By the time of the fight, I was exhausted, but it was the opportunity of a lifetime, so I did my best," Eder said in *O Grande Campeao*.

Merely a few hours before the bout was set to take place, Eder was starving and went to eat after that terrible weight cut. He felt tired but didn't have time to sleep. At night he was sitting in a car with Pineda, and then he felt muscle cramps. Hundreds of Brazilians were waiting for him at The Olympic Auditorium in anticipation of another victory, which would move him one step closer to the pinnacle. Eder entered the arena, and at this moment, he asked for some time alone backstage: "I want to take a rest Dad. If I stay alone, it is possible that I can take a nap," he told his father.

Aristides left Eder alone in the massage room. As he lay on the table, doubts crept into his mind: "I'm not going to be able to handle it. I'm too tired!" The thought of losing the fight scared him: "I need to handle this…" he thought about the millions of Brazilians depending on him and felt the size of the expectations put on him. From the massage room, he could hear the roar of thousands of Mexicans in the arena. Eder recalled the time when his uncle, Ralph, became Brazilian champion. He was still a kid when he stared at his uncle and looking at his reflection in the mirror, he was thinking: "When I grow up, I will become the champion of the world." It seemed like they turned up the volume of the audience, and Eder opened his eyes. He then came back to the reality of facing Medel. Aristides was outside, pacing around. He had been smoking non-stop since he left his son alone in the massage room. In half an hour, he smoked an entire pack of cigarettes. When he opened the door, he found his son overcome by emotion and with tears in his eyes.

The crowd of 5,000 created an excellent atmosphere as the two fighters took to the center of the ring to listen to the instructions from referee Mushy Callahan, former junior welterweight champion of the world.

The fight started with both boxers circling each other, flicking light punches, mostly jabs. Eder, fighting out of a crouch, attempted the harder blows, whereas Medel was not giving much away as he boxed cautiously from an upright position. The action was mostly cagey in the early going, with Eder throwing a nice body shot, before stepping around and aiming a left hook which prompted Medel to fire back with his own shots to the body. The fighters went back to circling one another as they looked for openings. Eder felt he had found one as he landed a clean left hook, which he attempted to follow up on but fell just short of connecting again.

The second round saw both fighters again showing each other respect and trying not to give too much away. Medel was the first to throw with any hurtful intent as he missed a right-hand to which Eder countered with a nice left hook right under Medel's elbow. The pace picked up as Eder landed a clean right-hand and then used his footwork to maneuver Medel to the ropes where he could follow up with some clean shots. The Mexican escaped and fired back with some body shots to briefly slow Eder's momentum as he moved towards the ropes. Eder escaped quickly, but Medel showed more aggression as he responded to a clean right-hand by Eder with a hard left to the body.

In round three, the action sped up as Eder landed a nice left hook while Medel tried to work behind his educated left jab. Eder leaped in with a big left hook, and the two boxers briefly exchanged punches in the center of the ring. Eder moved Medel to the ropes where he hammered away at the Mexican, but Medel fought back with gusto. Eder looked for some big shots whereas Medel attempted to attack the body. A good counter left to the gut by Medel briefly moved Eder to the ropes, but the Brazilian fired back with a nice left hook that registered cleanly on Medel, who moved back to the ropes. Medel tried to fire back with body shots, but a clean left hook by Eder momentarily stopped him in his tracks before the bell sounded.

There was a pause in the action at the beginning of the fourth round as the crowd and fighters regained their breath. The respect between the two men was evident at this point as both fighters showed great poise and technique. Medel was fighting economically whereas Eder semi-crouched as he threw long left-hands which connected. Eder mostly kept his left hand out as he probed for openings while expertly moving his head as he avoided the counterpunches coming back in his direction. Eder landed a right-hand punch on Medel and followed up with a combination of punches of which Medel could block only a few. At this point in the contest, the rounds were close, but Eder appeared to hold a slight edge based on landing the cleaner shots and showing more effective aggression.

The fifth round started with both men going toe-to-toe on the ropes with a lot of body punches mixed in. Medel perhaps got the better of the initial exchanges until Eder turned him around and then worked him over with a flurry of hard punches. Medel was quick to fire back to take the play away from Eder until Eder connected a hard left hook to the body, which visibly hurt the Mexican fighter. Medel regained his composure and attempted to work his jab until a big right-hand from the Brazilian stunned him again, and then Eder followed that up and hammered away at Medel in the corner until the bell ended the round. In what was a great round, both fighters had shown plenty of toughness to go with their technique.

After the war in the previous round, both fighters come out cautiously at the start of the sixth as they went back to circling each other, but there wasn't much distance between the two men as they both stayed within striking range. Eder was working behind his left jab and having some minor success with it as Medel fell short with his shots as he searched for counter-punching opportunities. Eder fired some big left hooks out of a crouch, but Medel kept a tight guard and avoided them. Medel had averted the near-disaster of the previous round and was back to fighting competitively with Eder, with the bout still up for grabs.

The technical skill of both fighters was on display in round seven with Eder the more aggressive of the two as he moved Medel to the ropes, but the Mexican did have success in landing beautiful counter shots as he pushed the fight back to the center of the ring. Eder was the one using more variation in his attacks, but Medel pumped his left jab with success as Eder moved forward to gain control.

The crowd booed at the start of the eighth round as both fighters circled each other in search of openings. The crowd, perhaps wanting to see a repeat of the vicious fifth round, failed to appreciate two master boxers struggling to gain the upper hand. Eder wasted little movement as he subtly moved while also extending some accurate hard right-hand punches, whereas Medel came back with a nice body shot. Eder was searching for the bigger shots but was also landing enough clean shots so the Mexican couldn't get set enough to throw back any hurtful punches.

Both fighters came back out for the ninth round at a faster pace as Eder pushed Medel back with a body shot to which Medel responded by moving Eder to the ropes. Eder landed a nice counterpunch, which then pushed Medel to the ropes, and then he began to lay into the Mexican with a two-handed assault. The two fighters exchanged blows closely as they stood forehead-to-forehead without giving an inch. Punches to the head and body from both fighters were met with wild applause from the crowd. Medel landed a hard left-hand, which visibly hurt Eder and forced him back. Eder showed immense fighting spirit as he fired back, attempting to take the play away from Medel. Medel was the one landing the stronger punches at this point as he moved Eder back again and hammered away at the Brazilian who appeared to be in trouble and then suddenly, an incredible counter left-hand from Eder landed cleanly, and Medel was out on his feet as Eder went in for the kill only for the bell to sound signaling the end to a thrilling ninth round.

Eder sported a severely damaged nose but was back in control at the start of the 10th round as he went after Medel. The Mexican tried to fire back, but his punches lacked power. Eder displayed expert poise and intelligence as he knew he couldn't afford to be too aggressive. Eder crowded Medel, landing some brutal body punches, and then went about patiently stalking the Mexican before landing a nice right-hand shot, which stopped Medel. Eder then expertly raked Medel to the body to take the wind out of his sails before going back upstairs with a huge right-hand punch, which landed clean and hard on Medel, dropping him to the canvas where he was out cold as the bell rang. Medel was rushed back to his corner where his cornermen tried everything they could do to revive him, but he couldn't regain consciousness, and the corner had no choice but to throw in the towel on behalf of their brave warrior.

The fight had been an entertaining one as the stocks of both men rose. Writing in *The Ring*, Bill Miller stated: "Jofre and Medel staged a savage brawl. The Brazilian, making his U.S debut, is aggressive and colorful: hits hard with both mitts. This was his 23rd knockout in 36 pro starts, an imposing figure for a banty." Eder was ahead on the cards at the time of the stoppage. Referee Mushy Callahan had him out in front 96-90 while Charley Randolph and Dick Young each had it scored 97-93.

Words of Wisdom from Kid Jofre

It was at the end of round nine that Eder credited his father with winning the fight for him. "I went to my corner bleeding, my nose was hurt. I couldn't even breathe right. There was blood going down my throat, and my liver was in pain. That's when my father said, 'Eder, sit down. How are you feeling? I said I don't know if I can, he said 'Yes, you can. You can. Breathe deeply,' he then started fanning me with the towel and massaging my stomach. I started getting better. He cleaned me up and everything and then said, 'Eder, come down hard on him because he felt your punch. The Brazilian people are cheering for you. Your mother is cheering for you. You can win.' After feeling such support, I went back to the ring very well protected," he said.

"I looked back and saw the guy (Medel) there jumping around in his corner waiting for the next round, and then I asked: 'Throw some water on my head,' and my father threw me the best shower of my life. That cold water somehow gave me an extra life, and I said to my dad: 'Here I go.' So,

I crowded Medel and started to throw punch after punch and landed one on his liver, I felt that I hurt him when he went to the ropes, and I finished him with a single punch, POW! Hit his chin, and he fell slowly with his head in the canvas. The referee started to count: 'one, two, three…' but was interrupted by the bell getting to the number of four. When the bell rang, I thought to myself: 'Now I'm dead, because I gave all that I've got.' But he didn't get up; he was in his corner, barely sitting straight until the referee ends the fight by TKO in the tenth round. That fight was the most remarkable for me because it was the first time a Brazilian boxer made it to the world championship fighting in the USA, and it was a hard fight. I almost lost it, and suddenly, I won by a knockout! It was the most beautiful thing that happened in my life," he reflected.

In the locker room after the bout, Eder asked his father, "Becerra now. Do you think all Mexicans are tough like Medel?" to which Aristides responded: "I think we better start training today. They say Becerra is twice as tough as Medel," to which Eder responded in awe. "Oh my God," he said.

On August 20, *O Globo* reported the scenes from São Paulo and the Jofre household, having been on hand as the family gathered around to listen to the fight on the radio.

"The celebration that took place yesterday morning was a party in this city due to Eder Jofre's brilliant victory over Mexican Joe Medel. As soon as the stations announced the Golden Bantam's spectacular knockout; screams, singing, rockets, and the continuous noise of car honks filled the central streets in São Paulo. One would think that a civil victory was celebrated, a world championship, or that the whole population had gotten lucky...if Jofrinho's admirers were cheering and triumphant with the victory, the Brazilian's family did that much more, notably his mother and young Cidinha, his fiancée. At Eder's house, since yesterday, countless people, acquaintances, friends, relatives, and journalists would see, gathered the emotion of Ms. Angelina, Cidinha, Ms. Maria, Eder's grandmother, and his other relatives. Before the fight, the famous boxer communicated to his mother and his fiancée through a Paulista broadcaster. He only asked: "Mom, trust your son."

The mother cheered, and the fiancée cried

During the 10 rounds: "I've never seen such long rounds," said Ms. Angelina – Cidinha cheered for her fiancé, crying nervously. Ms. Angelina and her mother-in-law, Maria, nervous, squeezed their hands, asking everyone to stay calm. The request, however, couldn't be answered...

The family's reaction

Nobody would move or speak during the first round. While Eder and Medel exchanged their first punches, the Jofre-Zumbano dynasty would pray. Cidinha would cry and bite her nails. Ms. Angelina immediately complained: "The Mexican is already grabbing Eder..."

The punches that 'Jofrinho' would take and feel would either hurt or seem to hurt more to those who were at the Parque Peruche household. Ms. Angelina would get up and walk through the entire room, and Cidinha would cry...Maria, 71-year-old grandmother, took a few glasses of water with sugar. "Be careful, my son."

When the broadcaster announced that 'Jofrinho' was bleeding through his nose, Cidinha instinctively brought her hands to her ears, as if she had also been beaten. The boxer's mother and grandmother continued to pray, and then, as if the boy could hear her, Ms. Angelina instructed him: "With your left, Eder, with your left. Be careful, my son; watch out for the man..."

In the tenth round, the nervousness at the home on Rua Gabriel Covelli increased. No one could stand still. Higino Zumbano, Eder's uncle, said: "You guys need to calm down. It's going to be over soon. Eder knows what he is doing."

And he did. Right after it, the announcer would scream loudly:

Medel hit the ground. Eder wins by knockout.

The final explosion

It was a joyful explosion, with smiles and hugs. Champagne bottles were opened, beers, sodas. Ms. Angelina hugged and was hugged by everyone. The old lady Maria had her first thought after the victory: "I wonder if Eder is OK."

Right after that, the Golden Bantam would come to the microphone and send a hug to everyone. The crowd went nuts, and the party went on. Cidinha then stopped crying..."

When reflecting on his career, Eder selected Medel as both his hardest fight and his toughest opponent. "He was the most complete opponent I fought. He provided me with the necessary security to become champion of the world," said Eder. "He was a damn good fighter. He hurt me in that fight," Eder added. Eder concluded that fight had given him the belief that no matter the opponent he was against, he would be victorious. "After that fight, after what my father told me, that morale booster, I said without arrogance 'There is no boxer who can beat me!' I was really full of determination. I had put my mind to that. I really trusted in my abilities and believed I could beat anyone," he said.

After the victory over Medel, Eder and his team took four days of vacation in Los Angeles to enjoy some sightseeing before boarding a flight from LAX back to São Paulo. They arrived home on August 23 to prepare for the impending world title challenge against Jose Becerra.

His celebrity had grown, preventing him from leaving his house without receiving requests for autographs and small talks with fans and members of the public. The reception which greeted Eder at the airport was exciting as thousands lined up to greet him as though he had already won the world championship.

On August 25, *O Globo* reported: "Despite the intense cold and the incoherent news on his arrival, a big audience attended yesterday morning at Congonhas to welcome Brazilian and South American bantamweight champion Eder Jofre. VARIG Caravella landed exactly at the planned time: 8:35 am. As soon as 'Jofrinho' came down off the plane, his admirers carried him in their arms, from the land track to customs, under intense applause. Later, journalists, cameramen, photographers, announcers, and other people surrounded the boxer and his father, causing serious disturbance to Congonhas employees who couldn't avoid the track from being invaded. The last people to say hello and hug Eder were his dearest relatives: his mother and his fiancée. By the way, it was a very touching scene. Ms. Angelina and Cidinha would cry, rubbing off on old Aristides Jofre and other people from the family."

Eder and Aristides took a little over an hour to make their way out of the airport as they were greeted by admirers and media. Eder was given a bronze statue of a boxer in a fighting pose, and as they left the airport, there were explosions of fireworks to celebrate his arrival. All the way from Congonhas to the TV Record studios, Eder was tailed by other cars, and people on the sidewalks waved at him and shouted his name as he went past.

Eder was right there now and had his shot at the title guaranteed following the thrilling battle with the excellent Medel. Eder felt on top of the world and invincible, convinced nobody could get in his way of becoming Brazil's first boxing world champion. Rumors had it that the Jofre and Becerra camps reached an agreement they would hold a match in Brazil with a rematch clause in place should Eder win. The agreement stipulated that if Eder won the title, he would have to do an immediate rematch in California.

That arrangement of bouts was never officially announced, but it was declared that Eder would be challenging Becerra, and a venue would be worked out soon. Ultimately, it was determined that Los Angeles would serve as the host city. Becerra took some convincing when it came to signing off on the bout. He had threatened retirement, and it was only an all-time bantamweight highest purse of $75,000, which got him to agree to the fight. Eder was set to receive $20,000, which was a significant jump from the $3,000 he had received in the Medel fight. Eder's highest purse to date had been close to $4,000 for the fourth encounter with Miranda. In contrast, he had turned professional earning roughly $400 per fight.

Eder was promised a new car as a bonus from the promoters in addition to the proposed $20,000 for the upcoming title bout, should he win the title. Eder had to let Cidinha know that their wedding would need to be pushed back until the following year due to his upcoming world title challenge. *O Globo* sat down and spoke to the family and reported that Cidinha appeared a little sad that the date had to be pushed back, but she understood that it was necessary. Angelina said to Cidinha, "If Eder wins, he will have a nice car to give you as a gift," and she smiled. Eder said to Cidinha, "Anyway, you are coming to Los Angeles with me when I fight for the title, is that OK?" and again she smiled and nodded.

Aristides appeared even happier than Eder that he would soon be challenging for the world championship. "This opportunity is the biggest aspiration of my son's career besides representing an excellent chance for Brazilian boxing. Eder is in condition to face this big responsibility, and I even go beyond that: I believe his chances to have a sensational victory are huge," he said.

Aristides added that while he knew the credentials of the Mexican champion, he felt that his son had what it took to take the crown away. "I saw Becerra fight when he was an amateur in the Pan American Games in Buenos Aires, in 1951 and more recently, I watched the film of the fight he had with Japanese (Kenji) Yonekura. With no shenanigans, not underestimating the merits of the world champion, I think his style is very favorable to Eder. Becerra is too aggressive, and that may help my son a lot, since, as everyone knows, he can hit hard with both hands." Despite the status Becerra held, Aristides did not feel it was necessary to switch things up too much and said there would be no difference from the preparation he undertook for the fights with Danny Kid, Leo Espinosa, and Ernesto Miranda. "Of course, Eder will have to start his exercises far in advance for the fight and take them seriously. However, I don't think of making any fundamental change in the preparation he usually does. Maybe a short concentration, two weeks before the fight would benefit him. We shouldn't forget though, that Eder is used to being home, and changing his habits suddenly wouldn't be good from a psychological point of view," he said.

A couple of interested spectators from the Medel fight had been Konji Yonekura, the Japanese contender who had met Becerra and was rumored to be a potential future opponent for Eder, and Kid Pascualito's manager Lazaro Kossci. Both said that they felt Eder would dethrone Becerra when they meet for the title. "He will certainly beat Beccera," said Yonekura while Kossci said: "From my part, and I've seen Becerra fight many times, I do not doubt that Eder will be world champion. I'll bet on him. He is more of a boxer, he has more qualities than Becerra does, and he will certainly be the next champion." Jose Medel also opined that Eder had everything it takes to become champion in saying, "He is a very strong young man, a great puncher, who can resist well and will be perfectly able to become world champion."

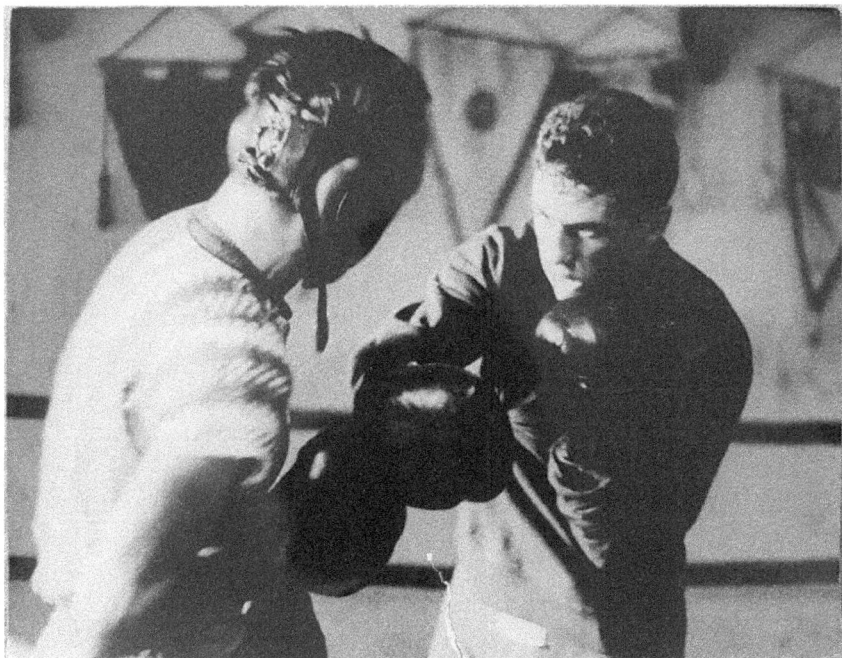

Eder had barely returned to working in the gym when the news came that Jose Becerra would not be fulfilling his side of the agreement as he'd been knocked out by Eloy Sanchez in a non-title bout on August 30 and would retire immediately. "There was much speculation about Jose's abrupt retirement from the ring. Some believed he quit because of his loss to Sanchez. Others believed that Jose lost much of his fire after he killed Walt Ingram. They pointed to the fact that his vaunted hook had been coming across with less assurance since the Ingram fight. And then there were rumors that he retired because of eye problems. The rumor about the eye problems was never substantiated, and Jose was too much a man to retire over a knockout loss. The opinion here is that Becerra retired because he just lost the fire in his belly for fighting after the Ingram fight. Jose was a humble man who came from a deeply religious family and never sought the adulation of the crowds that most fighters missed when their fighting days were over," wrote Dan Cuoco for *International Boxing Research Organization*.

Becerra had been an even more popular champion than his idol Raul Macias, who had also retired at the tender age of just 24. Macias featured in Mexican movies and become a celebrity outside of sporting circles, whereas Becerra lived a more private life. It would be almost a decade before the popularity of these two popular bantamweights was matched in Mexico. For Eder, it was somewhat of a bitter pill to swallow as he'd admired Becerra and imagined that he would face him for the title.

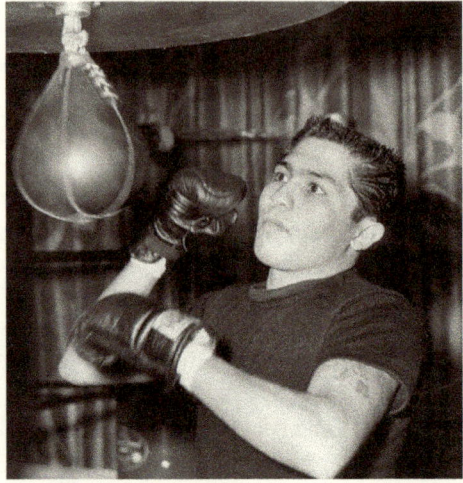

Jose Becerra

"When I was coming up in Brazil, (Jose) Becerra was the world's champion. I kept reading about him in our Portuguese-language newspapers in São Paulo, what a slam-bang little puncher he was, and how he'd knocked out Alphonse Halimi in a wonderful fight for the title in Los Angeles. It was my ambition to fight Becerra, I didn't care where. But Becerra was unlucky enough to be responsible for the death of Walt Ingram, whom he had fought in Mexico. I don't think he had wanted to fight too much after that. He continued for another year, or until he was knocked out over the weight in Mexico by Eloy Sanchez. Then he did retire," he said.

The title would be vacant since the Sanchez vs. Becerra fight had been set above the bantamweight limit. The NBA announced that a bout between Eder and Sanchez would determine their champion. In early September, Anthony Maceroni announced that the Jofre vs. Sanchez bout was for the title and added that the winner would have to meet the winner of an upcoming bout between Freddie Gilroy and Alphonse Halimi proposed to happen in Europe. "Sanchez proved his right to fight for the title after defeating (Jose) Becerra by knockout. Jofre, however, is the number one contender, so a fight between the two of them is completely justified," said Maceroni.

George Parnassus, speaking at an NBA conference in Mexico, also announced that his venue in Los Angeles would still host the world bantamweight championship. "There was a fight agreed upon by Jose Becerra and Eder Jofre, who defeated Jose Medel, for the bantamweight world title. This fight, according to signed contracts, was due to take place in November or January. However, since Becerra retired, I will promote his conqueror, Eloy Sanchez, as a replacement," he said.

The NBA was the real world's championship but had been losing credibility due to multiple scandals in boxing. The NBA had worked in compliance with the European Boxing Union (EBU), and BBBC (British Boxing Board of Control) and effectively acted as the one true major sanctioning body in boxing, but the EBU and BBBC had created distance from the NBA. Influential British promoter Jack Solomons had other ideas and, working with the BBBC, and EBU, announced that a bout between Alphonse Halimi and Freddie Gilroy of Northern Ireland would be for their version of the world title.

That was a ridiculous assertion since Eder had gone up the rankings and earned his number one placement before he had even gone through the hell of having to beat the highly regarded Jose Medel. Eder was to be Becerra's next title defense, and Halimi had fallen twice at the hands of Becerra. The NBA title carried more clout and was recognized globally as the true world championship, but there was a little fragmentation here, and that was slightly unsatisfactory.

On September 16, Eder signed his part of a new contract to fight in Los Angeles for the world championship. There had been talks that the bout could end up in Mexico, but through negotiations and reference to the previous contract (for Eder and Becerra at The Olympic Auditorium), Abraham Katzenelson reached an agreement with The Olympic and Parnassus with approval from the NBA. "This should end every discussion about the place where Eder will fight," he said. Promoters in Mexico had suggested at the NBA conference in Mexico City that Mexican fighters were no longer welcome in California due to what they perceived as maltreatment their fighters received there.

The Mexican authorities took a hard stance on the matter several days later when they stated their intentions to no longer recognize any Mexican boxer who fought in California. This complicated the situation since the Jofre vs. Sanchez bout was between the top two contenders for the belt, but the agreement was made before this radical stance by the Mexican commission. The Mexican commission made things difficult for Sanchez, as he had clearly earned his right to fight for the title with such a great win over the defending champion but also as he did most of his fighting in Mexico so, in effect, he could be taking food off his own table especially if he failed to defeat Eder. Macaroni said Sanchez could be suspended by the NBA if he refused to comply with the contract to fight in California with Eder. "If this is true and if Sanchez has not even committed to Parnassus, then I will have to consider Alphonse Halimi to fight Eder Jofre instead, as it seems to me that the Mexican will be unavailable."

Fight 37, vs. Ricardo Moreno, September 30, 1960

While the mess over what would happen with the world championship was being sorted out, Eder kept himself busy ahead of the championship bout and accepted a tune-up fight with 19-year-old Ricardo Moreno from

Argentina. Moreno had earned a draw with Ernesto Miranda back in Argentina earlier in the year. There does not appear to be much else known about Moreno's record before his bout with Eder. However, a scouting report from Argentina stated that he was unbeaten in 25 bouts, having scored 11 knockouts under the name Arturo Desiderio Moreyra. He was said to be one of the brightest young talents in Argentina.

The Argentine Boxing Federation showed a record of eight wins and two draws in ten fights for Moreno with the two draws being with Ernesto and Carlos Miranda. Moreno and his trainer, Hector Vacarri said there had been four drawn fights with Ernesto Miranda. Maybe his record was harder to track down because the promoters at Luna Park had essentially blacklisted Moreno because of a dispute Vacarri was having with them. Most of Moreno's listed bouts took place in Mendoza and Cordoba. The Jofre vs. Moreno fight was scheduled for September 30, which meant Eder had about six weeks from his last bout and would have about six weeks at least until his title bout.

The bout was scheduled above the bantamweight division, but Eder still attempted to get as close to the 118 pounds limit as possible. On September 26, only four days before the bout, Eder was seen in a coat and a fleece sweater, working out, as he went through his paces in training. To finish his exercise routine, he skipped rope for six minutes. He then sparred four rounds with Antonio Zumbano and two rounds with Sylvano Zumbano. The report in *Estadão* stated: "Even though he tries to show he is in good shape; Eder currently has excess weight and is moving slowly. It is possible to see his complete lack of concern about the fight (with Moreno). He appears convinced of his superiority. On the one hand, that shows that Eder has reached a champion's maturity, but on the other hand, he shows too much optimism, which can be dangerous."

Aristides confirmed to reporters that his son would do another full practice later that afternoon and wake up early for a jog. Moreno did show himself to be an adequate boxer when he worked out in front of the press. *Folha* reported: "Not more or less than Miranda. Moreno has been impressive during his training since the day he landed at Congonhas. He is quick, with fast hands, presses the fight, and has a style that might please the audience. However, seen and analyzed in cold blood by some experts, in their opinion, he cannot do a lot when it comes to Eder. 'He is better than Miranda in some aspects and worse in others,' they have informed us. Rumor has it that Moreno is not as quick as Miranda. However, he has more 'fighting spirit.' He should lead more, precisely what the audience and Eder Jofre wish. His carelessness may be a threat because it can cost him the first knockout in his career. There were flaws in his defense for the left counterpunches, and we cannot forget that it as with his powerful left punch that Jofre opened up his path to world ranking."

The comparisons between Moreno and Miranda stemmed from the fact that both men were trained by Hector Vaccari. Vacarri bragged to the press in the days before the bout that his protégée was the best fighter to come from Argentina, in addition to possessing a unique style that would upset Eder's plans. "Ricardo is more positive, more aggressive, like Eder. He is very young, with great will and faith to defeat 'Jofrinho.' I also feel like that and I even think it's good that the audience, the press, Eder, and Aristides Jofre don't show trust in my pupil," Vacarri said.

Vacarri stated that if Moreno won the fight, then they would be prepared to go to Los Angeles to fight Eloy Sanchez for the world title and that if his boy was to lose, then it would serve as a valuable learning experience. "We'll go to Los Angeles (if we win), for if Eder defeated Joe Medel, almost unknown and now will dispute the world title with Sanchez, even more unknown. I think that Ricardo Moreno, in case of victory, also deserves to dispute the bantam crown. If we lose, we will go back to Argentina aware we fulfilled our obligation, for 'Morenito' lost to the first man in the world ranking, and that is not a shame for anyone," he added.

On the eve of the bout, Moreno worked out for the press and said that he was not overly impressed with Eder and his credentials and showed little fear of his punching power. "I watched the film of the last fight between Jofre and Ernesto Miranda. To be honest, I didn't like him. I found him slow, with no leg shifting. He fights with his arms almost still. He moves too little, with a uniform style during the whole fight. I don't deny that Jofre has powerful punches, but he must hit me, and it won't be easy. He likes to chase his opponent, just like the dog and the hare. But he doesn't do it quickly," the young Argentine said.

O Globo looked into Moreno's training camp and reported on the morning of the bout:

"During his practice last Wednesday, he sparred for four rounds. Two rounds with amateur featherweight Jasmenon de Oliveira and two with promising professional bantam Raul Justo. The latter had to fight with 16-ounce gloves and the Argentinian, with ten ounces. In the first movements, Justo hit 'Morenito' hard, which earned him a few recommendations: be calmer, less aggressive, and more guarding than attacking…and they reminded him it was the Argentine training to face 'Jofrinho.' Ricardo Moreno didn't leave a good impression. It's clear his guard is a flaw. He has the concern to run from tougher combat, and his condition is not great. Raul Justo, before the 'recommendations,' hit him with good punches. We asked the sparring partner what he thought of the Argentine: 'He is good. He is not as bad as he looks. He punches hard.'"

Various reports claimed that the Moreno bout would serve as one of two hometown tune-up bouts Eder would take before jetting off to America to fight for the title. A bout with Dutchman, Sugar Ray was briefly discussed, but in consideration of the weight problems from the Medel bout, Eder's team felt it would be smarter to set up their training quarters in America with enough time to acclimate, get a full training camp and make the weight with minimum fuss.

The bout itself was a foregone conclusion as Eder had defeated many boxers of this caliber and higher with ease. The concerns of Eder's apparent lax preparation came to light somewhat early in the contest as he appeared to move slowly and could not catch Moreno in the first round as the Argentine paced around and edged the round. From the second round on, however, the distance between the pair grew closer as the fight took place at mid-range. When the Argentinian's legs became weaker, Eder let his hands go as he broke Moreno down with a strong body attack. Eder took control in the second round and punished his opponent in the fourth and fifth rounds, as he switched the attack upstairs and beat Moreno to a bloody pulp. At the end of the fifth round, Moreno was a sorry sight as he bled from the nose and sported a nasty cut over his right eye. Moreno informed his team he could not go on. The crowd booed the Argentine for surrendering the fight. On the way back to the locker room, Vacarri got into an altercation with a fan just as he had done when he was leaving the ring the last time Eder had defeated Miranda.

Eder attacks Moreno

Abraham Katzenelson had not been ringside for the bout as he had been in America securing the deal for Eder to finally fight for the world championship. He arrived back in São Paulo on October 1. He showed the press a copy of the contract for Eder to face Eloy Sanchez in November in Los Angeles. The contract also stipulated that if Sanchez should refuse the bout, then Parnassus would nominate a substitute to face Eder for the title.

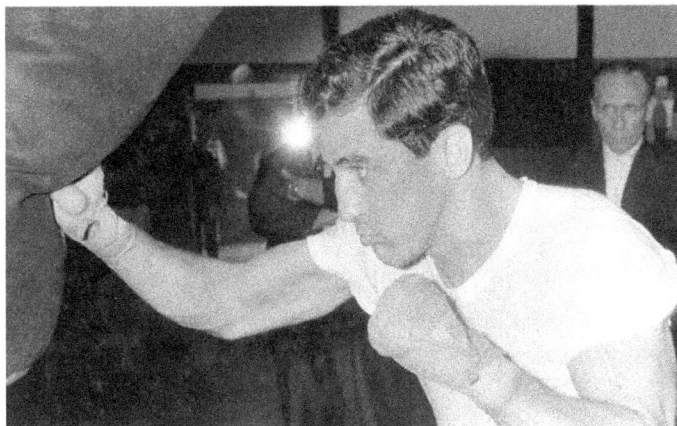

Departing for Los Angeles: L-R (top) Dogalberto,
Cidinha, Angelina, and Abe Katzenelson
(front) Eder, Mauro & Aristides

Fight 38, vs. Eloy Sanchez, November 18, 1960

Using the experience of the weight problems from the bout with Jose Medel, Eder and Aristides adjusted their pre-bout schedule. They boarded a flight to Los Angeles on October 17, a month away from when the title bout was scheduled. The trip was naturally an exciting one for Eder and his father as they would be joined by Eder's mother, Angelina, who would be preparing and cooking his meals. Also joining them would be Cidinha, and Eder's brothers Dogalberto and Mauro. They had a light sendoff at Congonhas airport. A small gathering of photographers and journalists wished them well as they departed for Los Angeles. "I am dedicating my campaign for the championship to Brazil," Eder said. "I want to show my gratitude for the support my countrymen have given me by becoming Brazil's first world champion," he said. In Los Angeles, Eder was welcomed once again by Manoel and Tereza Pineda, friendly acquaintances from the Medel fight in August.

Eder, Aristides and Cidinha look over their travel tickets

In Eloy Sanchez, Eder was coming face-to-face with the man who had effectively beaten Jose Becerra into retirement, so he knew that he had an opponent who could not be taken lightly. Sanchez, a former blacksmith with ambitions of owning his own sporting goods store, would have been considered an unlikely world title challenger when Eder had last fought in Los Angeles. But boxing is the theater of the unexpected, and now he stood in the way of Eder's attempt to make history as Brazil's first world champion. His business partner and manager, Manuel Moreno, said: "Not underestimating the qualities of other bantams, as former Mexican champion Jose Toluco Lopez, or current Mexican titleholder Jose Medel, I believe that Sanchez has better possibilities in front of Brazilian Jofre."

Eder set up camp back at the Main Street Gym. For his previous bout in Los Angeles, Eder sparred with Kid Pascualito, but the Paraguayan could not make this trip as he was scheduled for an assignment in Buenos Aires. Eder once again secured the services of Ricardo Gonzalez and Pascual Perez. Gonzalez, who'd already fought in Los Angeles five times, had a bout scheduled for Texas in November. Perez had lost his rematch with Kingpetch but decided to stay in Los Angeles for a little while and was excited to help Eder get into fighting shape ahead of his big moment. Eder and his family rented a large house with a swimming pool in Santa Monica in a charming chic neighborhood.

The Jofre camp had only been in Los Angeles for less than 48 hours when they received the news that the Mexican commission was not budging, and Eloy Sanchez, although agreed to the bout, had not been given the Mexican commission's blessing to travel. Luis Spota, working for the Mexican commission, had substantially discussed the matter with George Parnassus and convinced him that the Jofre vs. Sanchez bout would be better set for Mexico City, given the climate of affairs.

Parnassus felt that an accusation of inadequate treatment to Mexican boxers by Spota was ridiculous, and he even had the contract to host the bout, so it came as a big surprise he approved the bout to go south of the border. Katzenelson stood firm and pointed to the signed articles for his man, and with the backing of Anthony Maceroni, they could simply find another challenger. Eder would not fight anywhere else for the title. "I have many fond memories of Mexico, but my pupil, Eder Jofre, will only fight for the title in a neutral venue, which means Los Angeles, where I have a contract with George Parnassus. If Eloy is stopped from competing for the title against Eder, then we will wait for the winner of Halimi vs. Gilroy to compete for bantamweight supremacy. Personally, as a Brazilian promoter, I might as well push for this fight to take place in São Paulo, but I would rather be equanimous. I am grateful to Parnassus for his kindness, for he offered me the freedom to take Eder wherever it's more convenient for me; however, I prefer to fulfill my obligations," Katzenelson said.

There was a tense meeting between Katzenelson, Aristides, and the infamous mobster Frankie Carbo on how things worked in America when title fights are made. Eder recalled a story kept from him during this trip: "This fight was arranged by my manager (Katzenelson) with someone who was enemies with Frank Carbo (Parnassus), who was the boxing kingpin in the U.S. He was unhappy to know that someone outside his area was arranging fights behind his back, so he called Katzenelson for a little chat. My father went with Katzenelson, and at the building entrance, they bumped into a big, bad-looking guy who was waiting for them. Inside the apartment, there were two more big guys. My father once told me that while Carbo was eating, he didn't even have the courtesy to look at them while talking. He kept eating with a gun on the table. He said some things about the way that fights were arranged, creating a scary atmosphere in the room. That was enough to scare the shit out of my father and manager."

TODAY—IN PERSON—FREE

JOE BROWN

World Lightweight Champion training for his title bout next Friday vs. Cisco Andrade.

EDER JOFRE

No. 1 Bantamweight contender from Brazil training for Nov. 17 title bout with Eloy Sanchez.

No Admission Charge . . . Workouts Start at 1 pm

Olympic Auditorium, 18th & Grand Ave.

IMPORTANT NOTICE

3000 reserved seats at $5 and 2000 reserved seats at $10 go on sale at 10 a.m., today at the Olympic for next Friday's Joe Brown-Cisco Andrade 15 round world title match . . . NO TV OR Radio.

Eder was staying sharp in the gym, getting in some excellent sparring. One sparring session caught the eyes of onlookers as Eder trained with Ricardo Lara from Mexico. The sparring became so heated that many others in the gym stopped what they were doing to watch the action. Onlookers said it was one of the most violent sparring sessions ever seen at the Main Street Gym. Eder cornered Lara on the ropes several times, but the Mexican fought back aggressively and landed his own shots before Eder punished him to the body and head. Eder's impressive display prompted some on hand to compare him to the great Manuel Ortiz, who reigned supreme in the 1940s as one of the greatest bantamweight champions. Aristides told the observers they hadn't seen the best of his son. "He never really shows his best in training. He prefers to save his best for the fights," he said.

Around this time, there were many requests from Eder's fans back in Brazil to get visas and make the trip over to support their man in his attempt to become a world champion. Travel agents remained busy and made sure those fortunate enough to afford the expensive excursion secured the paperwork and flights to Los Angeles.

Luckily, Eloy Sanchez received the approval needed so he could travel to California guilt-free and contest the title. He arrived on October 28, three weeks out from the scheduled date of November 17. On November 1, it was announced, due to massive interest in the bout from Sanchez's fans in Mexico, that the bout had been pushed to the next day, the Friday nightspot. This would also give the fans extra time to make their travel arrangements. The formal ceremony announcing the bout took place on November 10 at the Alexandria Hotel. Both fighters met with the great former bantamweight champion Charles "Bud" Taylor and the legendary Sugar Ray Robinson to pose for publicity shots. Sanchez was asked how it felt to have knocked out his idol in the upset win over Becerra, which earned him this title shot. "Terrific. It was a great honor to be in the ring with him, but once the fight started, it was hit him or be hit by him. Naturally, I wasn't there to get beat, so I started swinging," he said. Eder was asked if he expected to win by knockout, and he replied, "I'll do my best to win by knockout, but I'll be satisfied to win by decision." Sanchez was asked what round he expects to win the bout in, and he responded, "That's a tough one, so I won't attempt to say. I have hopes, of course, that I can knock him out, but I'll be out to win any way I can. Winning is what counts."

Both boxers with Sugar Ray Robinson at contract signing

Eder and Sanchez share a laugh with Robinson and Charles "Bud" Taylor

The Jofres were well received by the press on this trip. One area of fascination was that of Eder's vegetarian diet. Jeane Hoffman of the *Los Angeles Times* interviewed the family in their rented home and spoke with the women behind the champion. Cidinha talked of how they planned to be married soon, and when they tied the knot, she would no longer serve meat in their home. "Eder is a strict vegetarian. I am not. We have agreed that when we marry, I will serve no more meat in our home," she said. "So, I shall just have to learn to cook a vegetarian dish, that's all. Senora Jofre has been doing Eder's cooking for years. I hope she can teach me her culinary secrets," she added.

Angelina cooked Eder's meals and made sure she kept his weight down. She talked a little bit about the history of boxing in her family. "Jose (Aristides) is also Eder's manager and trainer. How long has this been so? Ah, about 21 years because Eder was only three when my husband first put boxing gloves on him. You see, we are a boxing family. Jose's brother ran the boxing academy in São Paulo for 33 years, and when he died, Jose took it over. My six brothers, all professionals, learned boxing there. That's where I met Jose. So, you see, we know our boxing," she said.

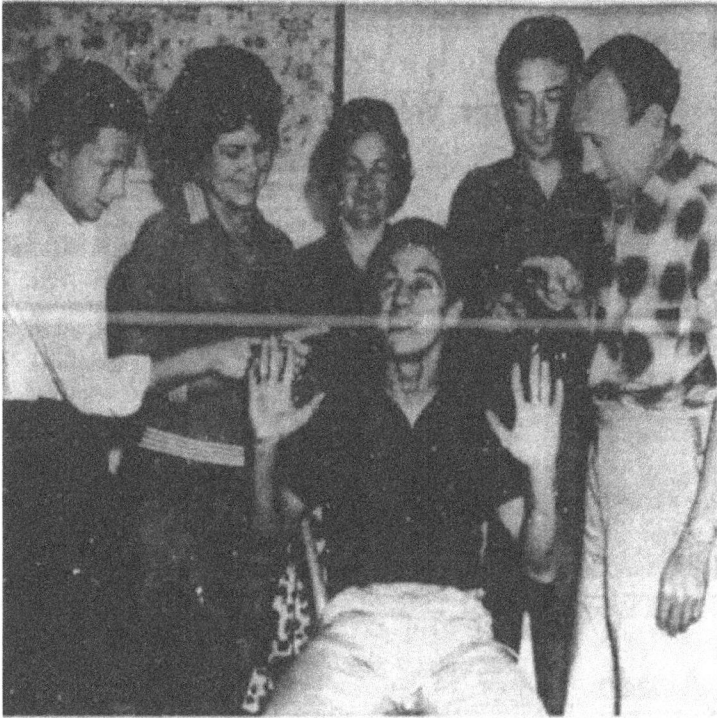

Left to right: Mauro, Cidinha, Angelina, Dogalberto, Aristides and Eder (front) posing for the Los Angeles Times

The Other Champion is Crowned

A little over three weeks before Eder's title bout, Alphonse Halimi and Freddie Gilroy fought at Wembley Arena for the EBU title. Coming into that bout, the Irishman, Gilroy had suffered a humiliating defeat at the hands of Mexican southpaw Ignacio Piña. At 21-0, Gilroy was considered one of the brightest talents in the bantamweight division following his bronze medal at the same Melbourne Olympics where Eder had lost in the second round. He had been in the running for a shot at Becerra's crown. With the backing of the powerful British promoter Jack Solomons, it was believed he was close to securing that shot until Piña put a spanner in the works in Manchester, England on April 25. The Mexican scored a knockdown in the opening seconds of the bout and boxed with calmness through the 10-round-bout as he claimed a decision victory to stake his title claims. Piña, however, was defeated by the man whom Gilroy had lifted the British title off in his next fight when he fell to a decision loss at the hands of Billy Rafferty of Scotland.

A crowd of 10,000 dominated by Irish fans packed into Wembley. They anticipated their man would become the first fighter from the British Isles to win a world title since Randolph Turpin's victory over the great Sugar Ray Robinson in 1951. Gilroy started the faster of the two as he got off his punches first and carried the fight to Halimi in the early going. Halimi was able to briefly slow the fight down when he caught Gilroy with a stinging left-hand punch. The Frenchman grappled to sap the Irishman's energy and use his experience in close, but Gilroy

Jack Solomons PRESENTS THE

**BANTAMWEIGHT
CHAMPIONSHIP**
OF THE
WORLD

ALPHONSE HALIMI   FREDDIE GILROY

EMPIRE POOL WEMBLEY
Tuesday, 25th Oct. 1960

OFFICIAL PROGRAMME
TWO SHILLINGS AND SIXPENCE

was moving ahead in the fight with his superior energy and work rate. In the 13th round, Halimi turned the fight on its head when he dropped Gilroy with an excellent right-hand shot, which had Gilroy struggling to come to his senses. Luckily for the Irishman, the bell sounded, potentially saving him a heartbreaking knockout loss. *Boxing News* reported: "Oh, how that hushed the crowd! You could almost hear Halimi's heart pound with excitement."

Gilroy survived the last two rounds, much to the excitement of the crowd. Still, they were soon subdued when the referee raised the Frenchman's hand, indicating that he had won the title. A chorus of boos and missiles from the crowd came with screams of "robbery." A jubilant Halimi celebrated and was full of praise for his defeated foe. "Gilroy was a powerful fighter, very courageous; he was a gentleman in the ring, and he gave me a tough fight," he said. As the new champion was basking in the glory, Gilroy lamented the verdict of the referee. "I forced the pace throughout; that knockdown must have given him the edge," he said.

Only a week out from the Sanchez bout, on November 11, it was reported that Eder took part in an intense sparring match with Ricardo Gonzalez. The two went hammer and tong at each other to where Aristides had to tell both fighters to calm down. In the same gym, Sanchez worked out, and his trainer Manuel Moreno stated, "I am satisfied with Eloy's physical condition. Within a week, he will give the boxing world another surprise." Sanchez was in excellent condition, having trained hard in Mexico as the complications over the bout were being handled. Aristides remarked that his son was in perfect condition and could go "20 rounds" if necessary.

Over the next few days, as both fighters trained in the same gym, Aristides and Mauro were able to see Sanchez train on multiple occasions.

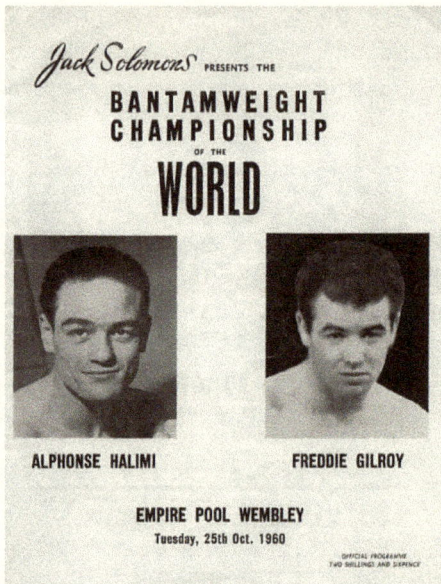

"My father and I saw him in training two or three times and came to the conclusion that if he fought like that, he would be knocked out by Eder," Mauro said on *Quebrando a Cara* when reflecting on those gym sessions.

Sanchez looked healthy and was already at the weight a week before the bout, but with his short reach and propensity to want to fight inside, it was believed he was tailor-made for Eder. This sentiment was echoed by the odds-makers with Eder as a 10-6 betting favorite. The odds did not deter Sanchez, who was confident that he could win the fight and take the title back to Mexico. Sanchez was under no illusions though and conceded, "Eder is the favorite. He is a solid fighter, and he has never been beaten."

When he defeated Becerra, Sanchez, 24, had overcome odds as high as 10-1 but dominated his countryman. Sanchez had dropped Becerra with a left hook in the fourth round before dropping him in the sixth round with a devastating right cross. A left-right combination put the champion down for the count in the eighth round as the audience watched in astonishment. "He was out cold," said Sanchez. Becerra was rushed straight from the ring to his hotel room to be treated after that bout. "He hurt me with some hooks in the second and fourth rounds, but I was connecting too," he added.

Becerra arrived in Los Angeles on fight week as he was on hand to present the bout's winner with the world title he had vacated in the light of that stunning upset loss. Sanchez was viewed as a fierce competitor but didn't have Becerra's profile. It was considered such a big upset when he knocked the champion out in eight rounds. However, Sanchez did boast impressive performances, including a win and draw with Ignacio Piña and a split pair of bouts with Jose Medel.

The extensive preparation and utilization of extra roadwork in Los Angeles meant Eder did not have to struggle as badly as he did in the Medel fight in getting down to the bantamweight limit. In one of his final training sessions before the bout, Eder sparred with Ricardo Gonzalez again and focused on his defense during the session. Eder worked on this to prevent any potential injury and because Sanchez was strong, and the knockout of Becerra had proven that he was a dangerous opponent who deserved the respect of a champion.

Eder, Jose Becerra & Eloy Sanchez at weigh-in

Before the fight, the Los Angeles boxing scribes were polled on who they thought would emerge victoriously:

Rodolfo Garcia, *La Opinion*: "I will have to choose Eder Jofre because his record is impressive."

John de la Vegas, *Los Angeles Times*: "In cases like this, simply because he has never suffered defeat, I am obliged to pick Eder as the favorite."

Jack Hawn, *Hollywood Citizen*: "Few have Jofre's skill, and because he has dynamite in his right hand, I choose him decisively as the winner."

Sam Schnitzer, *Los Angeles Examiner*: "Both Jofre and Sanchez are magnificent boxers. I am almost inclined to believe that the one with the greatest physical endurance will be the winner, but I cannot resist the temptation to choose Jofre. He fights very hard and is tremendously fast. It looks like Sanchez, however, is an underrated fighter."

Bud Furillok, *Evening Herald and Express*: "Eder Jofre, in my opinion, is too strong at this weight class. As brave as the Mexican is, I don't think he can go 15 rounds. Eder will win by knockout."

John Hall, *Los Angeles Mirror*: "This boy from Brazil is fast and powerful. In my opinion, he will take down Sanchez before the 10th round."

Luis Magana, public relations manager at The Olympic Auditorium: "This will be one of the busiest fights to be witnessed at this venue. I believe in a triumph for Eder Jofre, not because he is unquestionably superior to Sanchez, but because of the state in which the Mexican's eye is currently."

Terry Rand gave his opinions on the bout, having sparred rounds with Eder and seeing Sanchez up close every day in the gym. "Jofre is an outstanding fighter. He boxes well, but what impresses me most is his strength. He can stay in there and swing all night. He may miss quite a bit, but sooner or later, he nails you. Yes, I think he has the punch to stop Sanchez. This Mexican boy is good, don't get me wrong. He has a very unusual style. He's aggressive, moving in all the time, and he slips a lot of punches. Like I say though, sooner or later, Jofre will nail him," he said.

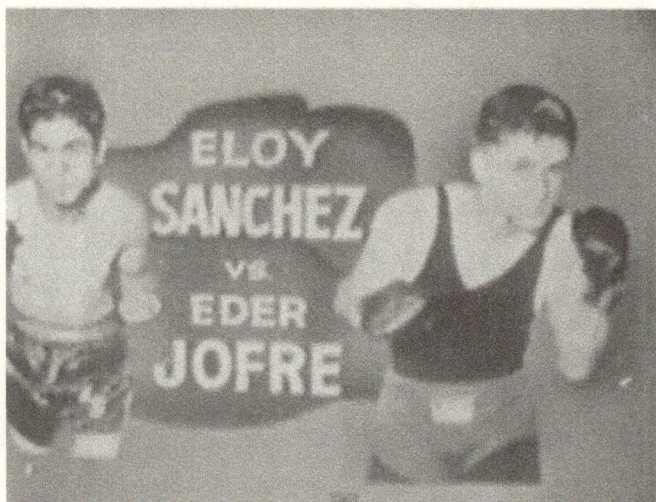

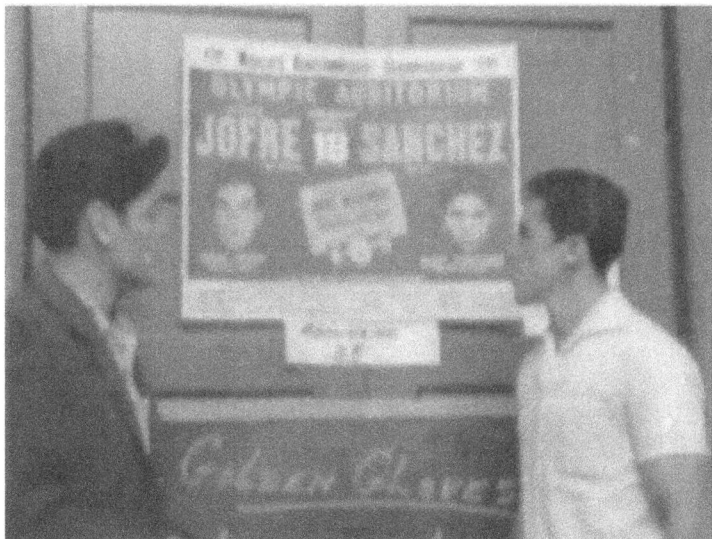

A crowd of 10,000 fans was expected on fight night, but a transportation strike in the Los Angeles area dropped that number to 6,500 fans who could make it to the event. Although The Olympic was not full the evening of Friday, November 18, the *Los Angeles Times* remarked that it was "the noisiest crowd of the year." The venue was shaking, and in the locker room, Aristides told his son: "They will boo you," Eder said: "I know they will. I can take it." Eder entered the ring to some hostility from the Mexican fans who shouted to him, "Jofre, Sanchez will kill you!" "Sanchez is going to knock you out!" which affected the visiting fighter not one iota. Eder smiled and waved to his small cheering section and located Cidinha and his mother and gave them a wave. Describing the atmosphere that evening in *O Galo de Ouro*, Henrique Matteucci wrote: "When the bell rang, you could hear the lighting of a match in its box. It was just a brief quiet moment, and soon things got real."

Jofre 10-6 Over Sanchez Tonight

BY JOHN DE LA VEGA

Delivered to winning Brazil's first world boxing title, Eder Jofre is a 10-6 favorite to realize his dream tonight when he clashes with Mexico's Eloy Sanchez at the Olympic.

There will be no local television or radio broadcast of the 15-rounder for the NBA bantamweight belt. It goes on sharply at 9 p.m. to accommodate a radio audience in Mexico and Brazil.

The weigh-in will be at the Olympic at 11 a.m.

Besides the prestige of winning this continent's recognition to the vacant

Tale of the Tape

	John		Sanchez

throne, there's even bigger glory and gold awaiting the survivor. The victor will be matched with France's Alphonse Halimi, who recent...

TITLE SEEKERS—Mexico's Eloy Sanchez, left, battles Eder Jofre for NBA version of world banty title tonight at Olympic. Winner fights Alphonse Halimi.

SANCHEZ		**JOFRE**
24	**AGE**	24
118	**WEIGHT**	118
	HEIGHT	
5ft.4in.		5ft.4in.
	REACH	
65in.		66in.
	NECK	
14½in.		14in.
	CHEST NORMAL	
36in.		35in.
	CHEST EXPANDED	
38in.		38in.
	WAIST	
29in.		29in.
	THIGH	
20½in.		20in.
	BICEPS	
13in.		12in.
	CALF	
12in.		13in.

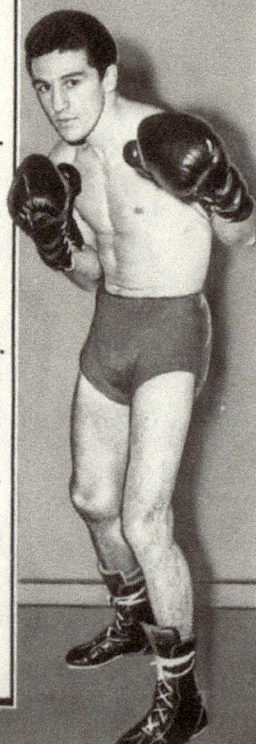

Round By Round from *Al Folha*

Round 1

Eder attempted a left-hand punch, but it is blocked. He brings his opponent to the center of the ring and tried a few jabs. They observed one another, circling with precise movements. Eloy throws his left hand, but Jofre blocks with his shoulder. The Brazilian maintained his distance and tried to attack with his left hand. He launched a right-hand punch on Sanchez's face, but it was too weak to have any effect. Eder worked with his left hand in front of him and turns Sanchez, not allowing him to define the distance. Both fighters display their defensive prowess and cannot land effective punches. Eder Jofre displayed confidence, but he couldn't accomplish much during the first round. Tied round.

Round 2

Eder attacked with three punches; finishing with his left hitting Eloy's jaw. The Mexican backs up and defends himself, putting his left glove up. The Brazilian takes the initiative and hits Eloy with a right-handed punch. The Brazilian starts pushing, and the two boxers fight intensively. The Brazilian is ahead. Another good right-hand punch from Eder hits his opponent. Eder feinted a blow with his left, but he hits with his right hand, and the Mexican defends himself. Jofre dominates the round, imposing himself in the attack. He hits with a hook, hits a right-hand punch, followed by another left, which the Mexican avoids. Jofre is on top. Eder hits with a hook and tries to throw a right cross, but the bell rang. The Brazilian had a clear advantage.

Round 3

Eder moves, searching for control of the fight. Even with little forward movement, Sanchez moves well and avoids the attacks to his left side. The Mexican throws a hook that landed on the Brazilian's spleen. The boxers grab each other, and Jofre hits Sanchez with a left hook. Eder ducked Sanchez's dangerous left punch and hit his opponent repeatedly with right-hand punches. Jofre's left punch is avoided by Eloy. The Mexican pressures Eder in the corner, but the Brazilian evades him. The boxers clinched as the referee intervened to declare the end of the round: the bell rang—a small advantage for Eder.

Round 4

Eder backs up a little from the center of the ring, and he dodges well in front of the first attacks of his opponent. The Mexican tried to use his left hand but is neutralized by Jofre's good notion of distance. They grab each other, and the Brazilian tries to bring his opponent down with a lot of punches to the waistline. Then Eder punches with his right hand from which Eloy defends himself. The Mexican resists well and goes to the center of the ring. Eder measures the distance and receives a precise counter-attack from Eloy, who tries to take him to the ropes. The round is over. The action became harder due to the diminishment of Eder's aggressive rhythm. The Brazilian waited for Sanchez to attack more, which didn't happen often. Tied round.

Round 5

Eder tries to establish an ideal distance. He has his hands up and waits for the attacks. He lets Eloy jab with his left and throw a right-hand punch. Eloy pushes Eder to the ropes. The Brazilian reacts and hits Sanchez with a right cross, which sends him to the canvas for eight seconds. The Mexican gets up dizzy but resists the Brazilian's desperate attacks. At the anxiety of attacking, Eder slips and falls, and the referee cleans his gloves. Eder advanced and got careless; he received several punches from his opponent, who defends himself desperately. A wide advantage for the Brazilian in this round.

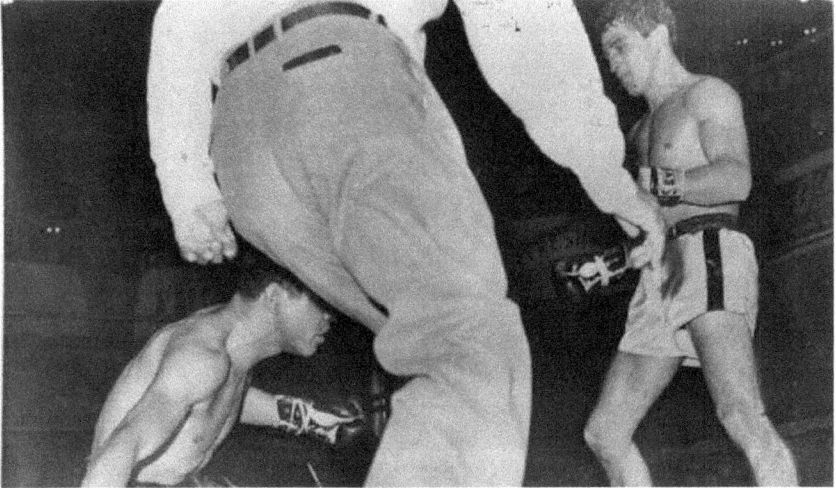

Round 6

The action continues to develop in the same violent rhythm as the previous round. Eloy corners Eder and "Jofrinho" looks in bad shape in front of the Mexican's attacks, but out of the blue, he counters vigorously with a right-hand punch and sends Sanchez to the canvas. The referee counts, standing next to Sanchez, but the Mexican doesn't recover in time. The fight is over. Eder Jofre won by knockout, as he was declared the new NBA bantamweight world champion.

In summary, Eder got the better of the early rounds as the two fighters boxed patiently, seeking openings in the other man's defense. Eder stepped up the intensity in the fifth round and started viciously attacking the Mexican before dropping him after a heavy onslaught. Sanchez surprised many in attendance by getting up from the knockdown and surviving the round. Sanchez realized that he was losing the bout in the sixth round, so he advanced more aggressively and connected with an uppercut that knocked Eder's mouthpiece out. He followed up throwing with a flurry of punches, but the Brazilian landed a perfect counter right cross that separated the Mexican from his senses.

Veteran referee Mushy Callahan counted Sanchez out and raised Eder's arm as his vanquished opponent lay motionless on the canvas at 1:30 of the sixth round. The first person to run into the ring and congratulate Eder was his brother Dogalberto who shouted, "I can't believe I am the brother of the world champion!"

In the ring, Eder was interviewed and spoke through an interpreter: "I am now as much a world champion as is Halimi. I have been awaiting a chance to fight for the world title, now I have the championship – at least on this side of the world. I am eagerly awaiting the fight with Halimi that Mr. Parnassus and my manager have told me will take place either in Brazil or in Los Angeles, preferably in my country where we can get a tremendous crowd during January or February, our summer. I feel confident I can do to Halimi what I accomplished in my bout tonight. I expect to win by a knockout."

Eder had expected the fight to go longer. "I was surprised when he stayed down. I did not expect him to get up in the fifth round, but when he went down in the sixth round, I was expecting him to get up," Eder told the ringside press as Jose Becerra put the belt around his waist. Eder was now the first Brazilian boxer in history to win a world championship. Eder said that while this bout had been his most thrilling moment, it was not the hardest, but he did pay respect to the grit of the Mexican. "He is one of the bravest men I have ever fought," he said. Sanchez reciprocated and was full of praise for the man who had just halted his championship dreams. "I heard the seconds counting, and I tried with all my strength to get up, but I couldn't. The last punch of the fight was the most powerful I ever received," the Mexican said. "He's the hardest puncher I've ever met. He'll knock Halimi out," he concluded.

There were roughly 200 Brazilians in attendance among the crowd of 6500, and many of them approached the ring and were screaming congratulations in Portuguese at the new world champion. A police escort was needed to shield Eder from the throng of fans and guide him back to his dressing room where he would field questions from Brazilian pressmen and celebrate with friends and family. "I am beyond happy," he told the reporters. "I wouldn't have been able to win without the moral help of all my countrymen who made me feel as if I were in São Paulo. I dedicate this victory to Brazil and São Paulo and all Brazilians," he added.

Telegraphs came flooding in from Brazil, offering their congratulations to Eder for making history. President Juscelino Kubitschek wrote: "At the moment in which a valuable athlete enriches the Brazilian sports patrimony with another glorious international title, it is with sincere satisfaction that in the name of the Brazilian people, I send you my effusive greetings and wishes of new and great triumphs following your brilliant sports career." Mr. Carvalho Pinto, the state governor of São Paulo, offered his congratulations with the following telegram: "Transmitting the joy of the people of São Paulo, I greet the great Brazilian boxer for the achievement of becoming world champion."

Eder, as gracious as ever, gave credit to Sanchez for being a worthy opponent. "He was a tough kid. In the fifth round, I caught him with a real barrage and dropped him. I thought it was all over, but he came at me like a little tiger. He put on a rally in the last few seconds of the round, and in the sixth, he tore in again," Eder said. "He had me bleeding from the nose. I didn't mind that. A bloody nose was an old story for a guy who begun taking his lumps in our family gym as a little fellow. I just kept looking for an opening for a straight right. The round was almost half over when I saw it. I dropped it into the jaw, nice and short. He went down hard, and it was the end for him – and the beginning for me as a champion," he said.

After he showered, Eder joined his friends, family, and some of the Brazilian reporters who had made their way to Los Angeles. They went back to the house in Santa Monica, where they enjoyed drinks as they celebrated the championship win. As they enjoyed the luxury and the moment, it was not lost on Eder where and what he came from to reach this moment. "To think where I'd left, where I lived in Parque Peruche. There was nothing there. The nearest bus was far away. My God from heaven, 25 minutes and from there to the tram, which also took a long time," he said.

Eder and Cidinha had been dating for seven years by this time and announced their intention to get married in March or April. A jubilant Eder said: "She said she would marry me anyhow, but I want to give her the undisputed title as a gift."

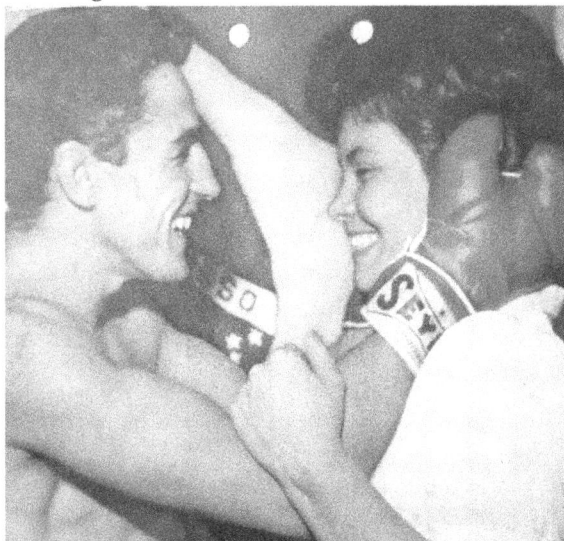

The family enjoyed five days of vacation in Los Angeles and did some sightseeing in the days following the bout before flying to New York. Eder and his family said farewell to Manoel Pineda and his wife, Tereza. The couple waved at Eder from the airport lobby as he went to board his flight. In New York, they enjoyed an extra couple of days of sightseeing before they boarded a flight to Congonhas Airport on Monday, November 28.

At Congonhas, a huge parade awaited them. Over 100,000 fans showed up at the airport to welcome their returning hero as he hopped aboard an open-top bus. A crown of laurels was placed upon his head, and he moved slowly through the city, waving to his people and proudly displaying his championship belt. The procession went all the way through Eder's neighborhood in Parque Peruche. "After 20 hours or so flying back to Brazil, I was exhausted, but I missed my country. I got to São Paulo and went up in a fire truck to a parade that was organized; after the parade, when I arrived in my neighborhood Parque Peruche, everything was different, decorated with Brazilian flags. These are beautiful memories that stuck in my mind forever," Eder said, reflecting on his homecoming. Sitting atop the fire truck, seeing everywhere decorated with Brazilian flags, Eder joked with a journalist: "This was my wildest dream," the journalist responded: "Being acclaimed by your people? "No...the fire truck. Since I was a kid, I have always wanted to be in one of these," the champion said.

There was no time for Eder to rest as he had to make multiple stops to accept the many honors being bestowed upon him. He stopped by the *Estadão* offices to accept various awards before he was presented with a commemorative golden medal at the city hall. He was also given another medal as he was awarded the title of "São Paulo Emeritus Citizen."

The following day the honors did not stop as both Eder and his father traveled to Rio de Janeiro, where President Juscelino Kubitschek met them. While in Rio, additional honors were given in recognition of the prestige they had brought to Brazil with this world championship. A few days after returning home in São Paulo, Eder received an honor from the Rotary Club of São Paulo. The latter declared, "This honor is to recognize the qualities of Eder and the significance of the victory he conquered. Eder is a valuable example for Brazilian youth."

On a special presentation in 2010 to commemorate the 50th anniversary of this bout, *Globo TV* network in Brazil had Sanchez flown in from Mexico to reunite with Eder and discuss the fight. Sanchez was very complimentary, discussing the talents and merits of the Brazilian: "He was a great champion. He was powerful, unyielding, his technique was perfect, and he was a consistent boxer with heavy hands." Sanchez expressed sadness at being unable to win the world title but continued his praise for Eder: "It's always sad to lose, but the title was in good hands. Eder was a tremendous fighter. I have a lot of affection for him. For sure, he was the toughest opponent of my career in the form of striking and withstanding punches. He fired tremendous punches and eventually knocked me out."

By becoming Brazil's first world champion, Eder became a national icon. "Back in the day, we didn't have any Brazilian boxer who became world champion. We didn't even think about it. The closest that we (Brazilians) got was the South American championship. For me, when I had the opportunity to fight for the world title in the United States, it was a huge and incredible happiness. I say incredible because I am the first Brazilian in history to get to that level," Eder proudly stated. Eder knew at this moment that his life might never be the same as he was now a genuine national hero and an integral part of Brazilian sports history. "My

life changed with all that fame; I can't deny it. It's a crucial point in your life because you can lose touch with your roots, there is always an event going on, an interview, parties to attend, so, you are committed to all of this," Eder reflected in *Gente*. Eder did always make a point of visiting his old neighborhood and maintaining the friendships he kept from his youth. He never wanted to stray away from his roots, although he was one of the most recognizable people in his country.

Brazil was entering a momentous period of its sporting history, which has perhaps never been topped since. Eder was Brazil's first boxing world champion. The national football team was world champions with Pele universally acclaimed as the world's most outstanding player. Maria Esther Bueno was sitting on top of the Tennis world after winning back-to-back Wimbledon titles to add to her 1959 US Open title.

Éder Jofre Campeão Por K.O.!

No 6.º "Round" a Queda Definitiva de Eloy Sánchez, Que já Fôra à Lona no Assalto Anterior — Seis Mil e Quinhentas Pessoas Assistiram à Luta — Um Cruzado de Direita no Queixo do Mexicano Foi o Sóco Decisivo — O Brasil Alcança, Assim, Pela Primeira Vez, um Título Máximo no Boxe
(Telegramas e Radiofotos na Primeira Página da Segunda Seção)

O GLOBO

FUNDAÇÃO DE IRINEU MARINHO

Diretor-Redator-Chefe ROBERTO MARINHO · Diretor-Secretário RICARDO MARINHO · Diretor-Tesoureiro HERBERT MOSES · Diretor-Substituto ROGÉRIO MARINHO

Flagrante do "Knock-Out"

O pêso-galo mexicano Eloy Sánchez estirado na lona, pôsto fora de combate por Eder Jofre um minuto e meio após o início do sexto assalto da luta que estava programada para 15 (Radiofoto U.P.I. — Exclusivo para O GLOBO)

Já Campeão

Eder Jofre p.ssa alisando entre sua mãe e o seu "manager" após colocar "Knock-out" o mexicano Eloy Sánchez no sexto assalto da luta de ontem em Los Angeles (Radiofoto Associated Press — Exclusivo para O GLOBO)

RECONTAGEM

BOMBA EXPLODE EM HAVANA

Eder Jofre é campeão mundial

Taticas e tecnicas no futebol

Vitória!

PLATÉIA: 6 MIL PESSOAS

As primeiras declarações do novo campeão

Fight 39, vs. Billy Peacock, December 16, 1960

The focus at this point had shifted to getting Alphonse Halimi into the ring to decide the undisputed championship. Halimi said he was not surprised Eder defeated Sanchez to become NBA world champion and stated that he would fight Eder even in São Paulo if the money was right.

Eder received glowing references in the American boxing publications and was widely seen as the best fighter in the division as he drew comparisons to some of the all-time greats. Henry Kraweic, writing for *Boxing Illustrated*, wrote: "Jofre looks somewhat like Manuel Ortiz, a former bantamweight champion now retired to his artichoke farm in California. He punches like a hammered-down Joe Louis, who retired to the position of boxing's elder statesman. And he boxes like a young Ray Robinson, who just keeps on retiring."

January 24 was the date proposed for the Jofre vs. Halimi unification bout to take place, but the Frenchman and his team quickly thwarted these attempts as they rejected a rather generous $40,000 offer and stated their intentions to participate in a few bouts in Europe before making any significant decisions on fighting for the full championship. Eder said: "If he is afraid to fight me here in Brazil, I will go to France to fight him," but that fell on deaf ears as did a lucrative $15,000 offer to Freddie Gilroy.

Meanwhile, Eder accepted a non-title bout against Billy Peacock from America. Peacock had fought a veritable who's who of the bantamweight division and had been a fan favorite at The Olympic. Unfortunately, he had hit a losing skid and was on the downside of his career; falling from top contender to journeyman, despite being only 27 years old.

The bout was set for Ibirapuera on December 16, which would give Eder a chance to appear in front of his hometown fans for the first time as a world champion and national hero. George Parnassus came to town to meet with Eder and to scout potential venues and gauge what the boxing market looked like. Parnassus arrived on December 10 and announced his intentions to stage a Jofre vs. Halimi mega-fight in São Paulo. With Halimi and his team playing hardball over participating in the unification bout, the NBA proposed Piero Rollo as the highest-ranked challenger for Eder to make his first title defense against. Rollo, however, would not be ready to fight in January as he was recovering from an injury he suffered to his left hand in a recent win against Mario D'Agata for the Italian championship.

Abraham Katzenelson was in discussions to have Eder go fight in Buenos Aires at Luna Park in January, but nothing was finalized. A few days before the Peacock fight, Eder appeared to be in good shape, fresh from the celebrations and good life he had lived after his championship win. He participated in a public training session where he worked out with a full gymnastics routine followed by six rounds of sparring with his uncle, Ricardo, who also had a bout scheduled on the Ibirapuera fight card. Peacock also trained in the same gym after Eder and the pressmen on hand noted that he appeared to adopt a very defensive style with plenty of covering up and movement mixed in with some counter-attack combination punch displays. Some noted that he did appear to be slow, which prompted forecasts of a comfortable victory for Eder.

The fight wasn't competitive as Eder moved comfortably in the first round on the balls of his feet. He went after the American. Eder boxed behind his jab without overexerting himself. Peacock could not get in any shots as he struggled with the speed of the Brazilian. Peacock, as the shorter man, tried to make it an inside fight but was picked off every time he tried to get in close. Eder displayed an excellent variety of shots, from straight right-hands to left hooks and punches delivered in combination.

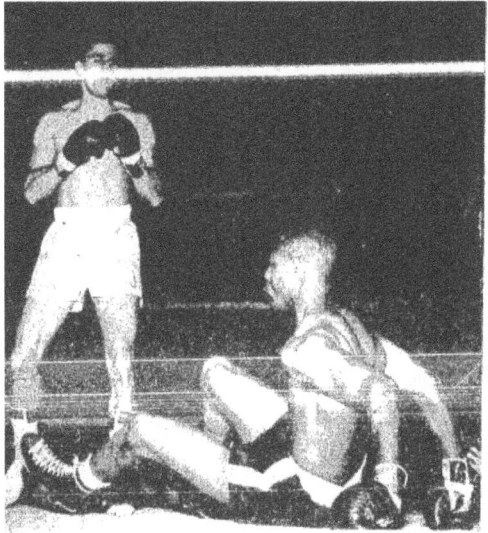

Peacock backed off and assumed a defensive position to get out of the way of the deadly blows raining on him. To start the second round, Eder decided he would end the bout early. Once again, he delivered several punches from his arsenal as he drove Peacock to the ropes with a mix of left hooks and right crosses. On the ropes, he mixed those punches in with some violent uppercuts as the American wilted under pressure. The first knockdown came due to a vicious left hook to the liver followed up by a left hook to the jaw as Peacock was now in a groggy state. He rose from the knockdown and tried to muster an attack. Eder ducked as he stepped aside and landed two left hooks before dropping Peacock again with a right cross. The American collapsed on the floor for the full count.

In the days following Eder's victory over Peacock, as they were lining up his next bout, Parnassus abruptly left Brazil in a foul mood. He had intended to stay in town into the New Year as they sought to arrange Eder's first title bout back home but was left dumbfounded and frustrated at what he perceived to be a terrible marketplace. Parnassus had been staying in a hotel. He had intended to rent an apartment and fly his wife over but said there was no room for a boxing market in Brazil. He lamented that TV was free, radio was free, and even at the boxing shows, he noticed that tickets were being given away. Parnassus said, "Eder Jofre vs. Piero Rollo can happen in Los Angeles, Rome, or Milan but not here." Parnassus added that the NBA would dictate where Eder's next bout would be but remained firm. He wanted nothing to do with promoting a show in Brazil.

1960 Results

Eder Jofre W15 Ernesto Miranda
Eder Jofre KO3 Ernesto Miranda
Eder Jofre KO8 Claudio Barrientos
Eder Jofre KO10 Jose Medel
Eder Jofre KO6 Ricardo Moreno
Eder Jofre KO6 Eloy Sanchez
Eder Jofre KO2 Billy Peacock

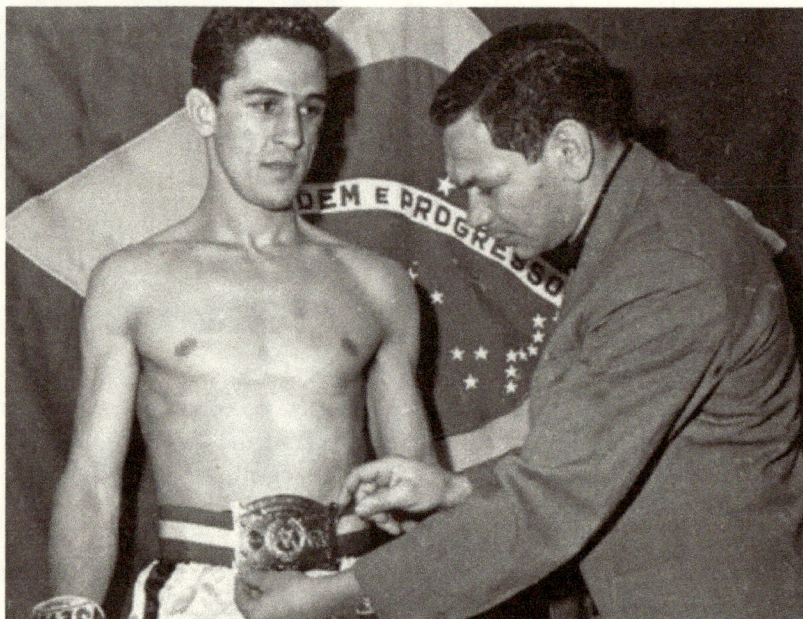

1961

Fight 40, vs. Piero Rollo, March 25, 1961

Piero Rollo was believed to be the most likely choice as the next opponent, and *The Ring* also announced that they would recognize the winner of a Jofre vs. Rollo bout as their publication's bantamweight champion. Rollo said he felt joyful when he was proposed as the lead man to fight Eder for the title but re-iterated that he could not be ready by January.

The bout was proposed for March, which would give him enough time to heal from his hand injury. Eder did not intend to take any tune-up bouts and would focus solely on defending his title in his next fight. George Parnassus' stance on Brazil complicated matters. Rollo's hometown of Cagliari was mentioned as a possible venue for the bout. The Italians felt it would be profitable to fight in Cagliari as they had a football stadium that could house 40,000 spectators. As the negotiations seemed to hit a wall, it emerged from Mexico that a rematch between Eder and Eloy Sanchez could take place in Tijuana.

Ramon Arias from Venezuela was also proposed as an opponent, so it was clear Eder had options which perhaps played a hand in the Rollo camp's swift agreement to travel to Brazil to face Eder rather than push further for Italy. Another factor was that Eder intended to marry Cidinha towards the end of March or in April in São Paulo, and from there, they planned to embark on a one-month-long honeymoon beginning in Buenos Aires before traveling to Europe where the plan was to visit multiple countries.

Parnassus had cooled down on his stance with Brazil over time and accepted that the bout would happen in Eder's homeland. Rather than the show going to Ibirapuera as initially intended, some suggested that the bout would be held at Estádio de General Severiano in Rio de Janeiro which was the home to Botafogo Football Club.

The bout was announced on February 15 and was scheduled for March 25. The famous Maracanã stadium was believed to be the front runner for the event, but Estádio Severiano was a more logical venue as it had enough seats to satisfy the public demands. Eder was happy that his first title defense had finally been arranged since he had been growing frustrated at how long it was taking. "I hope there are no obstacles now. I'm looking forward to coming back to the ring for I have been stopped for two months since my fight with American Billy Peacock. I don't think this is good," he said.

Eder said that he had been training but was conscious not to go full throttle until he received an official announcement that a title defense was confirmed. "Training continued daily but not as intense. I rested a few days after my last fight and went back to the gym but only did one or two rounds a day, a little gym work, a little bit of rope, and that's it. There was nothing certain, a lot of contradictory news, and we thought it was better – my father and I – to wait for what was next," he added.

Eder was set to receive around $35,000 while the challenger, Rollo, would be paid $10,000. Aristides felt that his son had reached a certain status now where they would only fight for significant purses moving forward. "We have to face reality. Eder has reached as much as a boxer can aspire, which means the world title. It's fair that now he must face things on the more practical, more commercial side. A football player, for example, each time he renews his contract, he tries to do it on a better basis than before. I think my son already has conditions to impose certain demands since he has that title that wasn't easy to achieve," he said.

Eder said that he had major plans beyond the Rollo fight. He signaled his intention to squeeze one more fight in after the defense against Rollo and then said he would become "a serious man" and tie the knot with Cidinha on April 22. *O Globo* broke the news on February 16 that Ernesto Miranda helped Rollo prepare for this title fight by sparring with him in Italy. Aristides was not pleased by this and suggested that it indicated poor sportsmanship by the Argentine. Eder was not concerned by this news, nor did he think it would have any impact on the outcome of his fight. "That's silly. If Rollo wishes, I'll accept to train with him as many times as necessary. He can study me as much as he wants. The fight will be decided between the ropes and not all of my punches are the same in every fight," he said.

ASSISTA NO RIO A LUTA

EDER JOFRE x PIERO ROLO

PELO TITULO MUNDIAL

Sabado – Dia 25

Estadio do Botafogo

Saida de São Paulo às 13 horas em ônibus pullman da BREDA regressando após a luta. Patrocinio da Empresa Brasileira de Desportos. Ingressos e lugares numerados.

PREÇO POR PESSOA COM TUDO INCLUIDO A PARTIR DE

Cr$ 2.500,00

Informações e reservas:

BREDA TURISMO

S. PAULO - Praça da Republica, 203 Telefone 37-8091
SANTOS - Praça Mauá 9 - Fone: 2-2121
SANTO ANDRE' - R. Cel. Oliveira Lima, 41 - Fone: 44-4294

The Jofre vs. Rollo fight was the first world title fight ever scheduled in Brazil. Jacob Nahun, former manager of Eder and co-promoter of the event along with Abraham Medina, was asked what he felt about the status of the championship since the EBU and BBBC recognized Alphonse Halimi as champion. "90% of the acknowledged boxing associations recognize the NBA. The European title is clearly based on commercial interests and local boxer's enhancement. Alphonse Halimi has already received the best propositions made to a bantamweight to fight. He didn't want to accept them, for his interest is to exhibit in Europe and take advantage of the name he still has without the risk of being destroyed by Eder. That's why (the) NBA chose Piero Rollo as the first challenger. Halimi's title is nothing but a lie," he said.

Rollo, at 34, was a veteran of 65 bouts and had been the Italian and European champion. He was fighting outside of Europe for the first time and making his maiden world title bid. He had run up an impressive resume throughout his career as he defeated such fighters as Mimoun Ben Ali, Pierre Cossemyns, Jackie Brown, Alphonse Halimi, and Mario D'Agata. Rollo had an entertaining, aggressive style of boxing. He wasn't a big puncher, but he was a busy fighter who liked to work inside and defeat his opponents by throwing a lot of leather. Rollo was on a ten-bout unbeaten streak since he had been annexed of his EBU title at the hands of Freddie Gilroy in a good 15 round contest at Wembley Arena back in 1959. Rollo confessed that several people advised him not to fight with Eder as it would be a career-ending defeat. Rollo expressed he couldn't turn down a world title bout. He was confident in his ability and felt he received some excellent experience when he sparred many rounds with Ernesto Miranda when the Argentine set up camp in Italy in the latter part of 1959 and to prepare for this championship bout.

On March 1, it was reported that Eder arrived at the gym looking overweight at 123 pounds, but Aristides said he was not concerned as he had an intense training regimen planned for his son. Eder stated that he respected Rollo and his record and felt he was a dangerous opponent. "It will not be easy, but I will try to end the fight quickly," he said.

Working feverishly, as usual, Abraham Katzenelson was in Europe working on some interesting future proposals. Although he could not get the Halimi camp to enter serious negotiations, he talked to the management team of Mimoun Ben Ali while in Madrid. Ben Ali, originally from Morocco but now based in Spain, was ranked in the world's top ten, so would be accepted as a viable title defense for Eder. A bout was agreed in principle to take place in July in Madrid either at the Palacio del Deportes or the Plaza dos Toros. When Katzenelson arrived in Brazil, the news came in that Ben Ali had been defeated by Ramon Arias in Venezuela. Arias, another potential foe for Eder, had now moved up the list of possible future opponents as he was also on a good run of form.

On March 4, there were rumors through the media in São Paulo that Eder was sought after by American managers to handle his career. These claims were quickly shot down by Aristides, who said that he would rather see his son retire from the sport than see him submitted to foreign managers. The stance was clear that they would fight in the USA, Mexico, Europe, Japan, and other places but Eder would be handled exclusively by a Brazilian team who would prioritize his son's interests. "There is no money that can buy our contract because I, Eder, and Aristides get along very well," added Katzenelson.

Eder's training intensified as the fight day became closer. He trained six days a week, and even on Sundays, he would get in some roadwork. He sparred many rounds with local amateur Minorof Rodrigues, his cousin Raul Jofre and his uncle, Ricardo Zumbano. There was a lot of emphasis on getting right back into the shape he was before his fight with Eloy Sanchez and tightening up his defense. Aristides told the media on March 10 he was pleased with his son's physical and mental preparation and praised

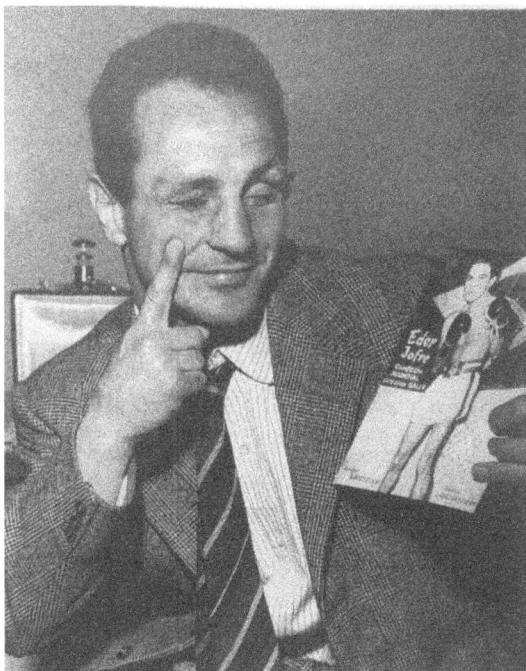

Rollo poses with photo of the champion

his professionalism. "He is in excellent condition and will get down to the weight limit easily as he will do some extra roadwork," he said.

Rollo arrived in Rio on March 16 after a slight delay from Rome, where there was a strike by Alitalia. Instead, he had to re-arrange his flights and board an Air France flight. As he left the airport in Rome, Rollo declared that he was in excellent condition and had prepared well for this opportunity. When he arrived in Rio, he said that while he didn't know Eder on a personal level, he respected him for his achievements. "I came to win. I know that Jofre hits hard with both hands, but I'm prepared to win the title and take it to my country," he said. "Boxing itself taught me not to be cocky. However, I know that I'm well prepared and I can perfectly win the fight on the 25th. I've been a professional since 1950, and the experience I acquired during that time will certainly be useful in the fight with Jofre. I don't know what his style is. I haven't even seen film of his fights. Gianni Zuddas, who fought with him in São Paulo and lost only on points, is my 'Squadra' buddy and told me a few things. The tactic I will use, however, will be decided in the ring depending on what Eder starts doing," the Italian added.

"Rollo has waited for the chance to fight for the title until now. He spent many years in line, like our countryman Duilio Loi, who waited for ten years," Rollo's coach Umberto Brancchini said. Brancchini added that he had been trying to get a fight with Alphonse Halimi, but the Frenchman refused to put his claim to the title on the line.

On March 17, Eder and his father conducted their final training session at their home gym before visiting the newsroom at *Estadão*. They told the newsmen they would be traveling to Rio with Dogalberto the following day, and they would be staying at the Copacabana Hotel. While in the newsroom, Eder saw a photo from his bout with Jose Smecca and remarked how he remembered being confused while on the canvas after being knocked down and how he listened to his father's advice to overcome that moment of adversity.

Jacob Nahun announced that the fight would not be televised in Rio in an attempt to bring as many people to the stadium as possible and he also said that they had turned down good offers from the São Paulo television stations in anticipation that a large contingent of Paulistas would make their way to Rio to see their champion in action. "We didn't even accept the excellent offers that were made to us from São Paulo because we believe that a huge audience will come from there," he said.

Pela primeira vez no Est. da Guanabara!!! Disputa do campeonato mundial de box (PESO GALO)

EDER JOFRE PIERO ROLLO

Cidinha joins Eder in the gym

On March 19, Eder and Rollo met for the first time at TV Rio Auditorium, where they came to watch a fight between Fernando Barreto and Eder's old Olympic teammate Celestino Pinto. Barreto won the fight by ninth-round knockout to win the vacant Brazilian welterweight title. The meeting between Eder and his Italian challenger was cordial as they shared smiles and hugs and posed for photographs. Both men felt the warmth of the crowd, who gave them a great reception.

Two days later, the fighters went to the offices of *O Globo* and spoke about their upcoming fight and then had a promotional lunch where both teams appeared to get along well with each other. *O Globo* reported on the meeting: "The Italian boxer arrived a little bit late, but after saying hello to those present, he went to hug 'Jofrinho.' All were talking about the activity of both boxers outside the ring when Rollo said that for 15 years, he has been an employee of Work Minister in Cagliari and that he needed a special license to leave the country. He does bureaucratic services – he has a college degree – and produces geometric drawings. Eder talked to him for a long time, remembering the times when he worked as a locksmith, with his uncle Ralph, and as a designer, a profession he left to dedicate himself entirely to boxing."

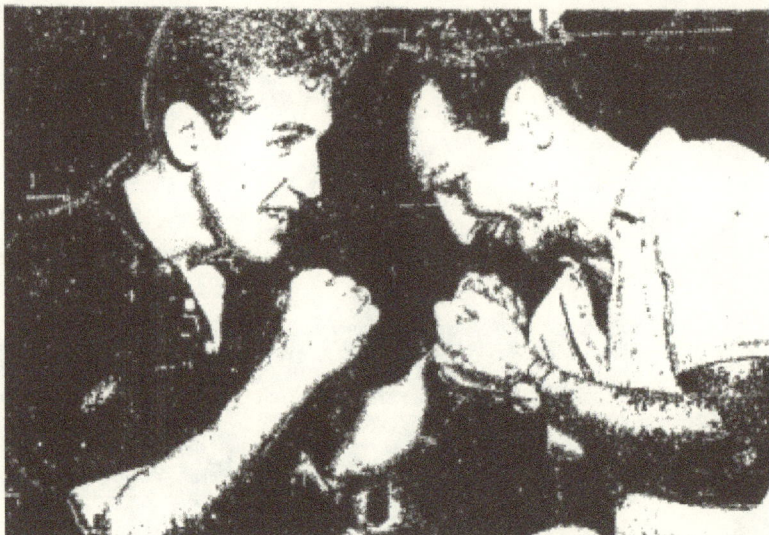

The two men also shared a passion for football, as Rollo said he admired Brazilian football and said they had many great players. Cidinha was also at the luncheon, where she confirmed that she was excited about the wedding on April 22. She was asked what frame of mind she is in around Eder's fights and said: "Naturally, I'm nervous and unsettled, but I fight with myself not to accept the thought that Eder might be defeated."

When Eder was asked if he would make the weight with no problem, Angelina cut in and said: "I take care of that. I'm responsible for his food, and I can guarantee that on Saturday, Eder will be weighing less than 118 pounds."

Two days before the bout, Eder had an issue with his shoulder. He was advised to rest up under the sun and make sure that the area was massaged thoroughly so the arm would be functioning back to normal on fight night. Luckily for Eder, he was already down to 116 pounds, so there would not be a major last-minute struggle to shed any excess weight.

On March 23, Rollo knocked out a local amateur named João Cirilo in the second round of a sparring match. Rollo did the damage with a left hook and an uppercut. "Showing extraordinary violence and aggressiveness, Piero Rollo winded up, unexpectedly knocking out his sparring partner João Cirilo, during his last exercises for tomorrow's fight with Eder Jofre. Rollo practiced like he never had before, showing a lot of speed, nice sidesteps, great defense, and magnificent combinations in the attack. Halfway into the second round, when obliging the sparring partner to defend himself, Rollo hit him with a short right hook in the stomach, immediately followed by a left uppercut to his chin. Although the punch was hit with heavy twelve-ounce gloves, João Cirilo fell asleep and took some time to get himself together. The episode was purely accidental and Rollo, showing to be deeply surprised and upset, was the first to assist the sparring partner who was taken to the corner. He immediately asked to stop the practice, to which his manager Umberto Brancchini disagreed. He didn't do any more sparring, however, limiting to jumping rope, shadowboxing, and hitting the sandbag. He then submitted to a massage and made a point to explain to everyone surrounding him that the accident had been a surprise even for him," *O Globo* reported on March 24.

Some noted Rollo had appeared to keep his cards close to his chest and not reveal too much in his training sessions, but this session showed that he was a dangerous opponent and a legitimate threat to Eder. Rollo said that he was very regretful of what had transpired in the sparring match: "It wasn't my fault; it didn't even cross my mind that I could knock him down. The uppercut got out automatically, with no intention to catch him hard. I'm sorry that this has happened to a young man who has been so useful for my preparations and who I care a lot about."

On the same day, Eder was also involved in a violent sparring session as he gave poor Jose Neves Martins, a flyweight from Rio, a real working over. After the session, Martins bent over in pain from the blows he absorbed and was bleeding from the mouth. Aristides confirmed Eder did have a muscle complaint in his arm towards the left shoulder and had been to the Army Escola de Educação Física (Army Physical Education School Gym) to get some last-minute treatment on the sore area and said it would not be a problem when Eder stepped into the ring on fight night.

O Globo previewed the bout in the morning newspaper: "Eder Jofre, for many reasons, comes up as a favorite, deserving the absolute trust of our sports audience. However, it's undeniable that Eder never faced anyone with the experience and credentials of Piero Rollo. Not even Leo Espinosa, Danny Kid, and Ernesto Miranda, who took 'Jofrinho' to the world ranking, or Joe Medel and Eloy Sanchez, against whom he got to the world title, gathered such an impressive background as the European who tonight will try to take his bantam crown."

"When showing the qualities he showed in his last practice, Piero Rollo will be a hard obstacle for the world champion. Rollo has in his favor, besides experience, speed, leg work, and splendid work with hooks and crosses, indispensable arsenal for the game at a short distance that he certainly will try to eliminate Jofre's span. His punches are hard and well put together, his power is extraordinary. His big flaw, revealed during practice, is an impetuous reckless nature to 'fight,' forgetting to keep his guard shut. That might constitute a great triumph for 'Jofrinho,' whose punch is considered unequaled. However, it's not too much to remind that Rollo, until today, was never knocked out, despite having faced other punchers."

Both boxers weighed-in at 10 am the morning of the fight at Nossa Senhora de Copacabana Avenue 750. Eder was just inside the weight limit at 117 ½ pounds, whereas Rollo was a pound lighter at 116 ½ pounds. On fight night, over 29,000 fans made their way into the stadium in Rio to see Eder defend his title. Captain Nelson Bezerra dos Santos directed 250 soldiers from the military police to be present on fight night to stop people sneaking into the venue without tickets.

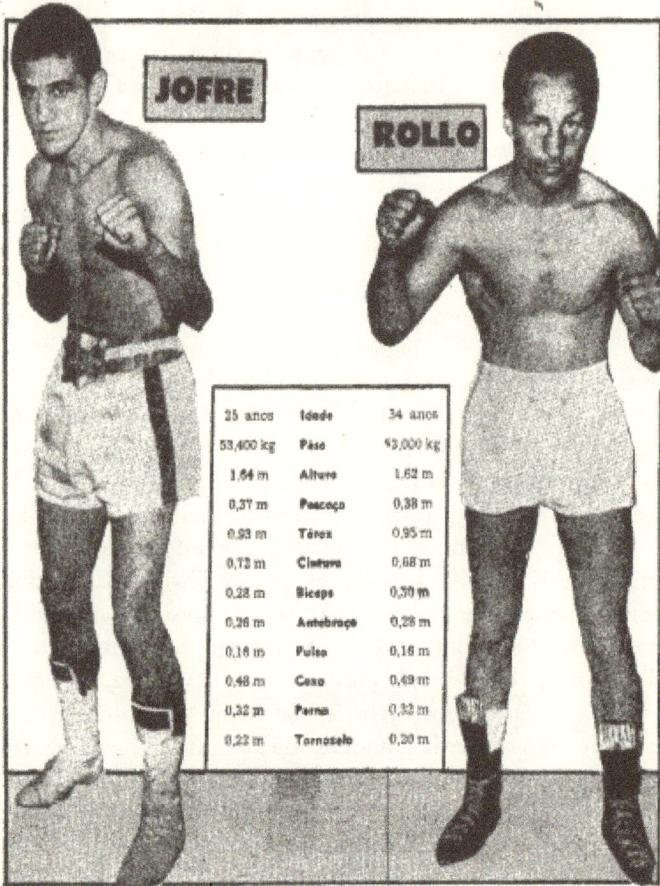

25 anos	Idade	34 anos
53,400 kg	Pêso	53,000 kg
1,64 m	Altura	1,62 m
0,37 m	Pescoço	0,38 m
0,93 m	Tórax	0,95 m
0,73 m	Cintura	0,68 m
0,28 m	Biceps	0,30 m
0,26 m	Antebraço	0,28 m
0,16 m	Pulso	0,16 m
0,48 m	Coxa	0,49 m
0,32 m	Perna	0,32 m
0,22 m	Tornozelo	0,20 m

At 10:50 pm, Rollo came to the ring wearing a yellow robe with a black collar and took in the light applause from the audience before undressing down to his blue shorts and black shoes. He stood with his team as the Italian national anthem played out over the speakers. Eder received thunderous applause as he emerged at 10:55 pm in a light blue velvet robe designed by famous artist Aldemir Martins. Eder's name and a golden bantam cock were attached to the back. Eder was wearing white shorts and white shoes when he took the robe off, and he stood calmly as the Brazilian national anthem played. The action started at 11 pm, which was about half an hour later than anticipated. The undercard featured a few bouts that went longer than had been expected.

Round By Round from *Estadão* and *O Globo*

Round 1

(*Estadão*) The two boxers studied each other for a while. Rollo tried to attack first but was brutally warded off by Eder. The contender throws a combo with hooks to the solar plexus and head but with no effect. The round is over.

(*O Globo*) Studying and precaution from both boxers. Eder tries a right cross that only grazes. Rollo tries to approach, but Eder shuts down and doesn't let him work. A few hostilities until the end. TIE

Round 2

(*Estadão*) Eder and Rollo get into an exchange at the beginning of the round. Eder wants to keep a safe distance and throws calculated punches. Rollo tries to close distance with hooks to the body. The champion throws a hard punch at him, landing on his eyebrow. This round belongs to Eder.

(*O Globo*) Eder tries for the initiative, keeping Rollo far away with jabs. Left-hand punches from the Italian hit the champion's head with no efficiency, and he fights back with hooks. Rollo tries to fight toe-to-toe but can't find the distance and grabs Eder to avoid an exchange of punches. EDER, 20-19.

"When finishing the second round, Eder got to his corner smiling and told manager Katzenelson, who was one of his seconds: "This one is easy. I already figured the man out." His father, Aristides Jofre, immediately protested against the excess of confidence and said that Eder hadn't quite seen Rollo's fight yet. That he would have to force the fight to truly figure the Italian out," O Globo.

Round 3

(*Estadão*) Eder changed his strategy and took more action; he threw a combo of jabs followed by three punches to the body. The contender reacts with a cross to the head, which Eder dodged and countered with a straight punch. Eder's round.

(*O Globo*) Eder starts violently punching. Straight shots and hooks land on Rollo, who looks for an exchange. The referee gives Rollo a warning because of a head butt, and he apologizes. Eder gets back to attacking, the ropes catch one of Rollo's gloves, but the champion doesn't take advantage of that. EDER, 20-18.

Round 4

(*Estadão*) Rollo involves himself more now while Eder just protects himself. Eder reacts and responds with two precise crosses. Rollo seems astonished by Eder's power; slowly he backs down a little bit. Another round to Eder.

(*O Globo*) Rollo starts well, hitting the body. He lands a violent punch to the champion's face. Eder gets an uppercut wrong and then throws more punches. He goes back, however, to violently hitting the Italian champion, obliging him to grab again. EDER, 20-19.

Round 5

(*Estadão*) Seeing that Rollo became vulnerable, Eder pressures him. Looking to put an end to the fight, Eder throws big combos with jabs and shots to the body. Round goes to Eder.

(*O Globo*) Rollo spins in the corner after feeling one of Eder's punches, followed by a spectacular punch. The audience gets up feeling the KO is about to come. Rollo, however, resists and avoids the most powerful punches. Rollo passes his gloves close to his eyes, to see if there's blood at the end of the round. EDER, 20-18.

Round 6

(*Estadão*) Rollo starts well, punching Eder's torso, but the champion throws the same combination with jabs and heavy shots to the body. After the exchange, the fighters save some energy until the end of the round. Round goes to Eder.

(*O Globo*) Eder starts with a sensational hook and other punches. Rollo resists heroically. He bleeds a lot from his left eye, throwing two good swings at Eder's face. He tries to not give up ground under the champion's terrible punishment.

Round 7

(*Estadão*) The boxers are showing signs of fatigue, but Eder is still punishing the Italian with his left hand. The Italian is forced to clinch. Round to Eder.

(*O Globo*) Rollo looks to avoid the exchanges. In an untidy manner, he (Rollo) moves forward and closes Eder's distance. He works with hooks and grabs. Rollo slips, falls, and gets up quickly. Eder looks to spare his energy. He was passive, (only) letting his hands go a few times.

Rollo, 20-19

Round 8

(*Estadão*) Rollo starts the round with a violent cross and tries to take control of the fight. Eder answers with right-hand punches and left hooks to the body. Rollo guarded himself well and, for the first time, takes the advantage in this round.

(*O Globo*) Eder comes back violently, but Rollo replies with a fierce right cross. The fight gets violent and hectic. Rollo goes to the ropes; Eder tries to punish him from underneath. It looks like the end of the fight, but the Italian unexpectedly reacts with a quick attack. He is practically blind-sighted, bleeding a lot.

Round 9

(*Estadão*) Eder punishes the Italian brutally with punches aiming at the eyebrows. Rollo bleeds heavily as the knockout seems close, and Rollo is avoiding the fight.

(*O Globo*) Rollo receives a spectacular crossed punch. Eder chases him down. The blood covers both boxers' shorts. Hooks and crosses from Eder demolish Rollo, whose knees bend. The Italian took incredible punishment.

Round 10

(*Estadão*) At the beginning of the round, Rollo's coach tells the referee that Rollo cannot continue the fight. Eder is declared the winner by TKO.

(*O Globo*) The bell rings, and referee Jaime Ferreira raises Eder's arm. In the corner, Umberto Brancchini had called the FCP doctor, Aloisio Caminha, who was examining Rollo's eyes. He immediately determined the fight over. Jofre keeps the bantam world title.

O Globo repeated some comments heard from the audience that stood out in the next morning's newspaper. Here is an excerpt:

"Hit him, Eder! If that Italian wins, he'll wind up opening a pizza place on Atlantica Avenue!"

"Come on Bantam! Hit him in the eye!"

"That Italian's face is all crumpled already. After the fight, only a light houseman can fix it!"

"Hurry up, Eder! If it's not in this round (the fourth), I'll miss my flight…"

Eder had given a magnificent display. He proved too fast and complete for Rollo as he dominated the contest from the start. Rollo tried to test the young champion early by fighting aggressively initially, which proved to be a mistake as Eder slipped and blocked his attacks and punished him in return. Eder rocked the challenger twice with left hooks in the fifth round and opened nasty cuts on Rollo's face. Using his intelligence, Eder took a lot of the energy out of his rival by landing multiple hurtful body punches throughout the contest. "I took my time with him. I am never in a hurry," Eder said.

At the end of the ninth round, with blood flowing down the beaten challenger's face, the commission, with his manager's consent, halted the contest declaring Eder a winner by TKO. Despite the dominant victory, Eder was not satisfied with his performance. "I fought very badly. I know I could have done more. On top of it, I hurt my left hand and was even in pain when I would do the stronger jabs," he added. The champion was asked when he would be putting his title on the line again, but he said that was not on his mind. "It looks like they will schedule me against Mexican Jose Toluco Lopez or Venezuelan Ramon Arias. But I don't want to think of that for now. My problem now is to be knocked out by Cidinha, getting married April 22," he concluded.

Rollo left the ring with tears coming down his eyes, having felt sad that he could not take the championship from Eder. "I lost because, in fact, there is no bantamweight who overcomes Jofre. He is better than everyone else," he said graciously. "I wanted to fight on, but I just couldn't see him after he cut me in the ninth round," the beaten challenger added.

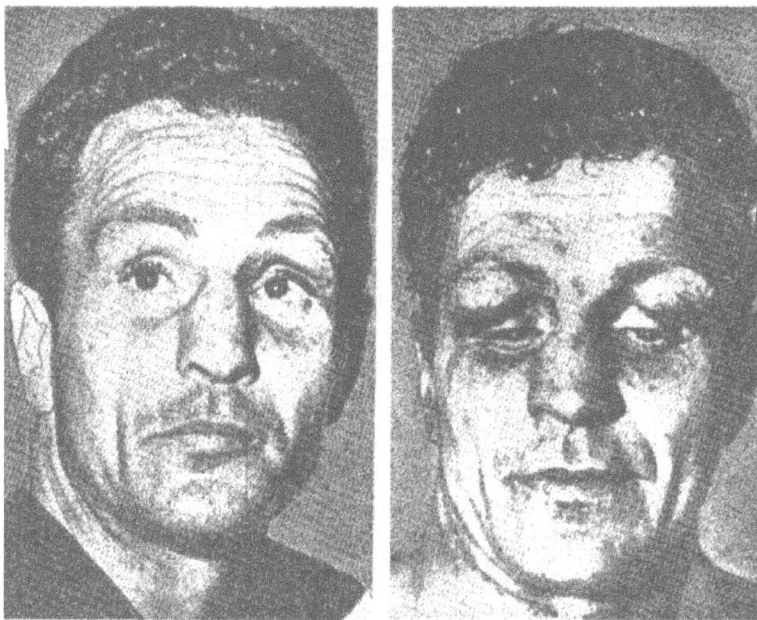

Rollo before and after the fight

Eder was confirmed as *The Ring* bantamweight champion by Nat Fleischer who reported from ringside: "Under the circumstances, there can be no doubt that Eder's knockout over Rollo entitles him to recognition as world champion. *The Ring*, to clear the atmosphere, presented Jofre with its championship belt. It is up to the European Boxing Association now to do justice to the Brazilian by granting him the recognition he deserves due to the exorbitant demands of Halimi and Gilroy. Rollo, a veteran with a record of 53-6-6 (21) had the experience, but against his more youthful, fast stepping opponent, he was made to order for Jofre. He tried to trade punches with Jofre, but like all the others who have fought Eder, he learned quickly that it was not proper procedure. The victor, known in South America as the Golden Bantam, had the upper hand almost from the start."

"The first five rounds were loaded with action, the Italian striving for a quick kayo. But he found his master in Jofre, who caught many of the Italian's blows on the arm or shoulders and quickly countered with perfect jabs and speedy hooks to the face. Twice in the fifth round, Rollo was staggered with left hooks, and in the same session, a long, swishing right caught Jofre on the chin and put him off balance. He spun around, speedily recovered his equilibrium, and retaliated with a right that cut a deep gash over Rollo's left eye. The next round was another bad one for the Italian. His eye began to close, but good corner work enabled him to come out for the next two rounds. He made an excellent comeback in the eighth. Rollo realized his only chance was to win by knockout, and he forced the issue during the first portion of the round."

"Jofre dominated the game by assaulting him with left and right punches to the body and head throughout the last minute. When the bell sounded for the ninth round, Jofre rushed out of his corner prepared for the "kill." He staggered Rollo several times with hard punches, and his defensive work was excellent. Rollo tried hard to fight back, but his smart opponent kept up a constant volley that forced the Italian to retreat. Blood trickled over his face, which, before the round ended, was a crimson hue. The flow blocked his vision, and he became a setup for Jofre's stinging lefts. The new champion, with an assortment that only veterans possess, made it extremely uncomfortable for the Italian who, when the bell clanged, ending the round walked warily to his corner. The contest was stopped between rounds by the commission doctor with the consent of Rollo's manager."

After the fight, the fans rushed into the ring to get close to their champion as Nat Fleischer struggled to put *The Ring* championship belt around Eder's waist. Rollo declared that Eder had been one of the best boxers he had ever met when he was interviewed backstage in his locker room. Sporting several nasty cuts and heavy bruises, he said that he felt he could have given a better show if his features had held up better. "Jofre is very good and deserves the world title. I don't believe that another boxer can defeat him currently. I'm happy I didn't fall and didn't disappoint anyone," the Italian said.

A jubilant Eder was pressed on whom he would prefer to face next if he had his choice. He expressed his desire to consolidate the championships with Halimi. "I am not afraid to fight him, but his refusal to accept the large sum to meet me shows that he's afraid of the outcome."

As a gift, George Parnassus presented Eder with a 1961 Chevrolet Impala after the bout. The following day it was Eder's 25th birthday, and he attended a banquet held at Monte Libano, a Lebanese restaurant, where 400 people were on hand to honor the fighters from the previous evening's bouts. The champion stated that his preference was to get Halimi in the ring and unify the titles to clear up the confusion as to which bantamweight was the top man. He also wanted to say kind words about the man with who he had shared the ring the previous evening. "We had lunch together. He was very lovely, and I think I won a friend despite the punches we exchanged. When I get married, I intend to go around Europe and visit him in Cagliari." Eder was asked where he would rate Rollo among his best opponents, and while he said he was not quite as good as Jose Medel or Ernesto Miranda, he was "smarter than everyone."

Rollo and his team attended a boxing show on the Sunday after the fight at TV Rio Auditorium. He sat towards the back of the arena, wearing sunglasses to cover his eyes, and was spotted by fans who gave him warm applause. Rollo and his manager Umberto Brancchini were thrilled with the reception they received. The boxer said that made him happy, and Brancchini commented: "The Brazilian audience knows how to make justice. For us, the visit to Rio will always be a reason to be proud and happy."

Rollo was complimented on his bravery and asked about what prospects Eder had going forward. "He is the best bantamweight in the world. He boxes well and has a great punch; nobody can beat him. Halimi wouldn't stand a chance before Jofre. I don't believe he would end the fight standing," Rollo said. Freddie Gilroy was mentioned as a potential foe, and the Italian felt Gilroy had even less chance than Halimi. "Much less (chance than Halimi). I fought with him, and I know his game. I know he would resist much less than Halimi," he added.

Eder stayed in Rio for three days after the fight and received invitations all over the city to various events. "I'm obliged to think of and talk of boxing all day long. Invitations come up from everyone for meetings, dinners, celebrations of this or that. If I don't answer them, they say I have a mask on. Everyone who meets me wants to know how the fight was, what I do, what I think. Then, there are letters to respond to, autographs all the time, a world of things that saturate us and to which we have to submit. Sometimes, I think it's not worth it to be a champion," Eder said.

O Globo reported on March 29: "Eder Jofre ran away from the invitations and had a lot of fun in the last hours he spent in Rio. He watched the Vasco da Gama vs. São Paulo game – not enjoying his team's defeat – and then went to a nightclub where he remained until 4 am with his mother, Ms. Angelina, and his fiancée Cidinha. He tried out a whiskey dose, with a lot of water. He didn't like it and finished his supper with mineral water and a lot of joy."

Eder wrote a thank you letter to the fans that had supported him during his time in Rio, and that letter was published on March 29 in O Globo:

"Through O GLOBO, I would like to profess, the day I return to São Paulo, my profound acknowledgment to the Carioca audience for the manifestations of endearment and incentive I had during these days I spent in Guanabara. I hope to be back soon – to fight – and continue deserving the trust of that audience that incentivizes me so much, and that is responsible also for the success I have been able to reach. To all of you, thank you very much.

-Rio, March 28, 1961, Eder Jofre."

Despite a good crowd turnout, Abraham Medina said that he had lost roughly $50,000 on the event. He was not unhappy, however, as he said that the main initiative had been to shine a light on boxing in Rio and test the waters on what the market looked like. The lack of television in Rio and São Paulo had undoubtedly been a money breaker, but Medina was upbeat. "I am entirely satisfied with the promotion. The press coverage was magnificent and brought a lot of people from outside of Rio," he said. He said that he would love to stage more of Eder's fights and was interested in staging a contest for Eder against Alphonse Halimi for the undisputed championship.

Fight 41, vs. Sugar Ray, April 18, 1961

Although Eder already had his wedding date booked and had just gone a full nine championship rounds in defense of his world title, he was determined to squeeze one more fight in as he had a lengthy honeymoon planned. Katzenelson quickly scheduled a non-title affair against a Dutch boxer, originally from Suriname, who went by the name of Sugar Ray. Originally named Henri April Richenel, Sugar Ray, 32, was the Dutch Bantamweight champion.

Because the event had been so quickly arranged, there were issues, and it required last-minute adjustments to make sure the bout went through. The show was scheduled to take place at Pacaembu gymnasium, but the venue had been double booked as the São Paulo indoor football federation had an event. Ibirapuera was booked, so it couldn't be used, so the indoor football federation transferred their tournament to Banespa gymnasium. The event was on, but there was a frantic finish to get the ring in and organize the seating accurately for a boxing event.

Eder was rushed around from Brasilia to Rio de Janeiro as he had sponsorship obligations and last-minute wedding activities that needed to be tended to. He arrived in São Paulo on the eve of the bout after a 10-hour journey from Rio and was tired and not in ideal condition. Since the bout was a non-title affair, it took place above 118 pounds, so at least weight was not a concern.

Eder knocked out Sugar Ray in a fight that couldn't have been any easier. Eder's technique was on display as he easily avoided the Dutchman's punches in the first round to start dominating the action. Towards the end of the round, two left hooks and a right cross put Sugar Ray in a world of trouble as he barely made it out of the round. In the second frame, Eder continued where he left off and quickly took his opponent to the ropes, where he dropped him with a right-hand shot. Sugar Ray held his right eye in pain, seemingly from an earlier shot, since the finishing blow came from Eder's right hand which landed on the Dutchman's left temple. He was counted out and then taken to the doctor who took a closer look at his right eye.

On April 22, 1961, in São Paulo at Coração de Jesus church, Eder and Cidinha were married in front of a large gathering. The wedding brought out a sizable press contingent, and fans of the champion gathered outside the church. It was a wonderful occasion as all of their closest friends and relatives were on hand to celebrate the event. Eder and Cidinha took a trip to Europe for their honeymoon, where they visited Italy, Portugal, Switzerland, and France over a month. While they were in Paris, Eder met Alphonse Halimi in a friendly lunch brought together by the newspaper *L'Equipe*. Eder said that he liked Halimi a lot and thought he was a lovely guy, but he reiterated that he still desperately wanted to face him in the ring.

When the married couple returned from their honeymoon, Eder bought a new house for them to live in and purchased a new home for his parents on Rua Santa Eudoxia in Parque Peruche. It was only a street away from where his parents had been living, and Eder made the point always to make sure that he regularly visited them. "I opted to get married and have my wife come live with me because I wanted that life. Every person who gets married soon comes back and will visit their parents more often but then this sort of decreases. Still, I remember very well that I visited them a lot. My parents were everything to me. My mother was a very playful woman; she always told jokes and lived happily. My father had a frowning face but a big heart," Eder fondly remembered.

On their European honeymoon

John Caldwell Snatches Halimi's Crown

John Caldwell had fought at the same Melbourne Olympics that Eder did in 1956. Caldwell, boxing in the flyweight division, actually went further than Eder in the Games and won a bronze medal at the tender age of 18. The 1956 Irish Olympic team was successful in winning one silver and three bronze medals. The team was heralded when they came back to Ireland, and Caldwell was touted as one of the brightest prospects, having compiled an amateur record of 265 wins against 10 losses.

Initially, the plan for Caldwell was to stay in the amateur ranks for a while and gain more international experience, but he was given an attractive offer to turn professional under the management of Sam Docherty. Docherty, a wealthy bookmaker from Glasgow, Scotland, had been a fight promoter, but his interests lay in managing the prodigious Caldwell. In Caldwell, he saw a potential gold mine given the popularity of boxing in Ireland. Caldwell turned professional in 1958 and would undertake his training camps in Glasgow.

The Belfast boy rose through the ranks, and he soon caught the interest of Jack Solomons, the biggest and most important promoter in British (and European) boxing. In 1960, Caldwell captured the British flyweight title, but it came as a surprise when Freddie Gilroy was overlooked for his proposed rematch with Alphonse Halimi, and Caldwell received the unexpected title shot in May of 1961. Caldwell was still seen as a developing young fighter, and he had never fought in the bantamweight division.

John Caldwell

It was believed that a rematch between Halimi and Gilroy was a formality and that they would soon sign articles to set a date when Caldwell was given the shot at Halimi's crown. The announcement shocked the boxing fraternity and was a bitter pill for Gilroy to swallow. Gilroy and Caldwell had been friends, but this turned their relationship sour as Gilroy felt Caldwell had wrongly skipped ahead of him in the queue. The Halimi vs. Caldwell bout was scheduled for Wembley Arena on May 30, and Caldwell, making his debut in the bantamweight division, exuberated confidence despite the odds against him. "I am convinced Halimi is past his best, and I will succeed where Freddie Gilroy failed," he said upon the announcement of the bout.

Caldwell boxed a brilliant fight in front of a buoyant Irish crowd as he pulled out into a big lead as Halimi struggled to work his way into the fight. Caldwell became excited, sometimes opting to go toe-to-toe with the dangerous champion but resorted back to his boxing on the instruction of his corner. Sensing the title was within his grasp, Caldwell took no chances and brought the fight to Halimi in the final round and punctuated his performance with a knockdown of the defending champion. When the decision was announced, the fans inside Wembley Arena went wild when Caldwell was given the verdict and was crowned champion.

Halimi was just as gracious in defeat as he had been in the victory against Gilroy when he said, "Caldwell is a gentleman. He is a great boxer, and I have no quarrel with the verdict." Years later, Caldwell reciprocated Halimi's kind words as he said: "Halimi was a very, very dangerous man and a hard hitter, and I know that well as he caught me many times throughout the fight. He was constantly at me – in and out all the time – and I couldn't take my eyes off him for a split second: The fight was one of the hardest of my career. I remember that after a terribly hard struggle, I eventually knocked him down in the last round, and that got me the decision in the end. I felt as if I was on top of the world – which literally I was – and knew, as an Irishman, that it had been a great sporting achievement. I was the first fighter to win a world title since Rinty Monaghan, and that was everything that I could have wanted to achieve."

Fight 42, vs. Sadao Yaoita, July 26, 1961

Following a three-month break after the blowout victory over Sugar Ray, Eder kept busy with another non-title bout, but this time against dramatically improved opposition. Sadao Yaoita of Japan was scheduled to face Eder on July 19.

Yaoita, once the number one ranked flyweight contender in the world, had made a name for himself, becoming the first fighter to defeat the great Pascual Perez in January 1959. Perez was the dominant flyweight champion of the era and one of the greatest in divisional history. Yaoita easily defeated the Argentine legend who entered the ring with an incredible record of 51 wins against 0 defeats with 1 draw. Unfortunately for Yaoita, this bout took

place half a pound over the flyweight limit of 112 pounds, and thus, no title was at stake. He would get a crack at the Argentinian's world title ten months later and would give a good account of himself once again but succumbed in the late rounds against Perez's attack and was stopped in the 13th round of a terrific contest.

The Japanese fighter was only a few months older than Eder at age 25. He was an energetic boxer who liked to use the ring, often bouncing on his toes and delivering a volume of punches from a distance. Yaoita was the number two ranked flyweight after Perez lost his titles to Thailand's Pone Kingpetch. Ahead of Yaoita in the rankings was Venezuelan Ramon Arias, who'd outpointed him in Caracas only two months before his bout against Eder.

The Jofre vs. Yaoita bout was set up to give Eder the best possible opponent he could find that would not require him to boil down to 118 pounds and put his title on the line. He had verbally accepted an offer to go to Caracas to fight Ramon Arias. That bout was already penciled for the following month. The Yaoita fight was postponed from July 19 to July 26 after Eder had a bout of the flu at the end of June. His training restarted on July 4 after taking a week-long break when he rested and recovered from his illness. The following day it was reported that Eder did not look 100%, which was expected as he went through his training regimen. As Eder worked towards his top fighting condition, it was announced on July 12 that Eder's next title defense was officially set. He was scheduled to go to Venezuela on August 12 to take on national hero Ramos Arias. The contract stipulated that should Arias defeat Eder, there would be a return bout within 90 days back in Brazil. When asked about the upcoming bout with Yaoita, Eder said: "I want to put an end to the fight as soon as I can. I have no interest in exhibitions."

Yaoita arrived on July 15 at 11 am in São Paulo. For the first two days, he took some time out to go sightseeing and conduct multiple interviews. He felt welcomed in São Paulo due to the large Japanese community in the city. One week out from the bout, on July 19, the two boxers met at the Japanese embassy in São Paulo for a celebratory barbecue. When asked about his famous opponent, Yaoita said that he recognized Eder had "great power and fast recovery."

Since Eder had been playing catch-up in training, he overextended himself and felt some muscle pain as the fight neared. Rather than keep up his demanding morning runs, he toned it down and went for brisk walks

Sadao Yaoita

instead, and after two days, he felt back to normal. *Estadão* reported that the Japanese boxer was training harder than Eder in their respective training sessions. Eder took it a little easier on his sparring partners. In contrast, Yaoita was going full throttle in his training and sparring sessions. Yaoita displayed his excellent speed and skills as he performed in front of a packed Wilson Russo Gym. It was noted that while he possessed a lot of qualities, he did tend to leave himself open, which was believed to be a recipe for disaster against Eder.

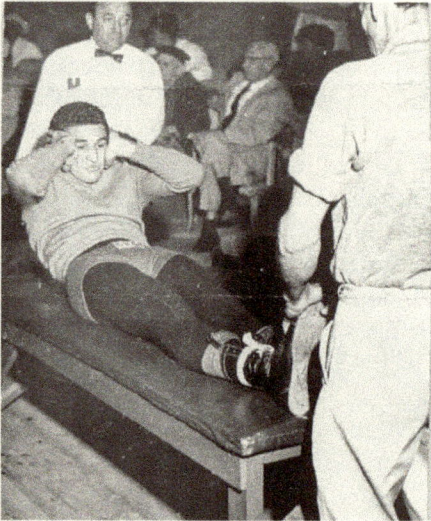

One of the last times the boxers worked out for the press was on Saturday, five days before the contest. Eder let up on his training, sparring with amateur flyweight Juvenal Dias for three rounds. He used Dias to practice his defensive game as Dias had comparable speed and style to Yaoita. Eder mainly focused on avoiding the attacks of Dias while also working on the positioning and movement of his feet. He then sparred three rounds with light heavyweight Jorge Sacomã with an emphasis on offense and throwing a variety of combination punches, while focusing on his punching power. Yaoita worked with flyweight Jose Neves Martins for three rounds, but Martins was unwilling to get into any exchanges with Yaoita. The Japanese fighter was not happy with his workout, so he added shadowboxing for six rounds before working on the speed ball. He said that he would be counting on the support of the Japanese counsel in São Paulo, Takoshi Ishi, and the many Japanese people he had encountered since he arrived in São Paulo.

Eder and Yaoita meet

Round By Round from *Estadão*

Round 1

Sadao started with a left hook followed by two rights blocked by Eder; the champion makes space using his jabs and drops a right cross to the face (of Yaoita). Eder stops in the center of the ring and observes Sadao, who is continuously shuffling around. With a left hook, Eder starts again, and Sadao backs away for a second and bounces back again. End of the round.

Round 2

Eder takes the initiative throwing jabs. Sadao responds with three left hooks, which Eder dodges and fires back a hook. Another left hook by the Japanese landed on Eder's face; the Brazilian shows no sign of pain or dizziness. Eder lands a sharp left hook to the head and traps him in a corner throwing combos; the Japanese just protects himself until the end of the round.

Round 3

Eder uses his jabs, making space for his deadly straight right punch. Sadao dodges it and crosses his left fist and lands it on Eder's face. The boxers get in a vicious punch exchange, and Eder lands a beautiful shot to the chin; the Japanese backs away and is saved by the bell.

Round 4

Eder tried a straight right-hand punch, blocked by Sadao, who answers with two hooks and a cross. Eder responded and landed a powerful shot to the face. Sadao feels the punch and backs away. The entire audience applauds Eder's attack. The Brazilian doesn't stop and lands two more punches to the face before the end of the round.

Round 5

Eder threw jabs and left hooks at Sadao, who suddenly tries to surprise Eder with a left cross. He (Yaoita) misses but lands a great shot to the liver, followed by two left-hand punches. Eder reacts with a straight right-hand and left hook blocked by Sadao's gloves. The Japanese suffers another attack and backs up after a right-hand punch to the chin. End of the round.

Round 6

Sadao tries to attack first now, but Eder deters him with a right hook. Sadao tries again and exchanges punches with Eder against the ropes. Sadao backs away when hit by a sharp right cross. Eder stays in the center of the ring, waiting. Sadao tries another attack, but with no success. Eder lands a violent right straight to the Japanese's face, which hurt him. End of the round.

Round 7

Eder crowds the Japanese with a violent combination of punches. The Japanese clinched him to avoid being knocked down as the Brazilian continued punishing Sadao, and the crowd applauded. One more clinch by the Japanese. Sadao, although not fully recovered, tries to attack but is punished by Eder's straight right. The bell rang.

Round 8

Sadao attacks with two left hooks, Eder reacted with right hooks. Both not efficient this time. Against the ropes, they engage in a violent exchange. A straight right by Eder hits Sadao, who gets a little groggy. Trying to attack, Sadao gets hit two more times in the face and clinches again. Getting out of the clinch, Eder almost lands a shot that could end the fight.

Round 9

Eder takes the initiative and goes ahead and attacks Sadao with a straight right-hand and left hook. Sadao clinches six times in a row to avoid going down. The referee warns the Japanese, and the crowd goes wild. Eder lands a hard punch to the chin, Sadao is groggy now. The bell rings.

Round 10

Sadao goes all in, trying to prevent a sure loss. Eder takes two steps back and suddenly drops a deadly shot to the liver. Under the pain, Sadao kneels, the referee counts, but he stands up. Eder crowds him against the ropes. Defenseless, Sadao gets hit numerous times. The Japanese is hit by a heavy punch and drops to the canvas. There is no way back now— victory by KO for Eder Jofre with 30 seconds to the end of the fight. A much-appreciated battle, thanks to the quality of Sadao Yaoita, the Japanese champion.

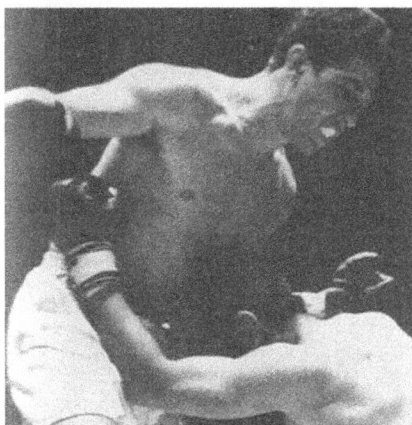

O Globo summarized the fight: "Sadao Yaoita impressed well during the early rounds, keeping the attacking initiative and letting his arms go against Eder. The latter, although not feeling any of the punches, had to study his opponent well to be able to find the gaps to commit himself to the counter-attack, for Yaoita took care of himself and would frequently exchange toe-to-toe. From the sixth round on, Eder showed himself to be more combative, chasing Yaoita around the ring, trying to finish the fight, and the knockout became just a matter of time as his opponent began to grab and hold Eder every time he was hit to delay the inevitable conclusion. Many times, the referee had to stop the fight, to call Yaoita's attention, which then limited his strategy to just avoiding the decisive fall. At the beginning of the 10th and last round, Eder landed a left on Yaoita, who suffered the first knockdown of the night, getting up after a count of three. The world champion then had difficulties knocking his Japanese opponent down again, for the latter tried to run to avoid a knockout. However, at two minutes 25 seconds, Eder was able to open up Sadao's guard with his left and landed a burning left that put him on his back, completely destroyed. Yaoita tried to get up, but it was useless, he was counted out, and it was a brilliant victory for Eder."

After the bout, Eder said: "I am happy with the result of the fight. Yaoita was a hard opponent. (He) is an honest, strong, and tough fighter." After taking some rest, Yaoita offered some words that were translated by his interpreter: "I fought two world champions in my life, Pascual Perez, who I beat up and Eder Jofre. The Brazilian is the best fighter I've ever faced; I am not upset with the outcome. I did my best." Yaoita also said that he felt Eder would be able to easily defeat Ramon Arias in his next title bout. This was a significant opinion because Yaoita had fought both men within a short amount of time.

Eder quickly switched his focus to the upcoming title bout he had scheduled in Venezuela against Arias. Yaoita had served as a very useful tune-up opponent because he also liked to use the full diameter of the ring and was a world-class opponent. Eder showed that the flu symptoms were out of his system as he was made to fight at a fast pace to score the knockout. It was reported by *O Globo* that Eder's purse for the Arias title defense was to be $35,000 plus flights, accommodation, expenses for five people, and a rental car during his time in Caracas.

Fight 43, vs. Ramon Arias, August 19, 1961

Eder's second title defense saw him take his show on the road against Ramon Arias in Caracas, Venezuela. Just as Yaoita had lost in a title bid to Perez, so too had Arias, who'd been the first Venezuelan to box for a world title. The challenge of Perez occurred in 1958 when Arias was only 22. The decision to award the Argentinian the verdict was met with disapproval from the Venezuelan crowd in Caracas.

The bout had been a thrilling one, with Arias dripping blood from the fourth round to the final bell as the result of an unintentional head butt by Perez. Arias used his legs and left hand to pile up points and stay with the champion all the way. Arias claimed he was close to retiring after this defeat. "I cried in the ring and after when I got home because I didn't feel like a loser. I always felt like a winner. I thought about retiring from boxing, but not because I felt defeated, but because I felt hurt by the decision. I constantly had my jab and my left hook in his face. I don't think it was fair, and if they had given a draw, it wouldn't have been fair either because I still wouldn't have won the title," he said.

Arias learned a lot from that bout, going on an impressive run of victories, which included Yaoita, Billy Peacock, Edmundo Esparza, Mimoun Ben Ali, and Ramon Calatayud, which set him up for the challenge of Eder's title. Arias was in line for a shot at the flyweight title held by Pone Kingpetch, but no offer came from Thailand, so the opportunity to bring over the bantamweight champion from Brazil provided a chance for the Venezuelan. Arias described his style as being very European, using a lot of feints and technical boxing but also with a lot of lateral movement. He adopted some of the more North American methods such as infighting and liked to use a cross-arm defense in the manner of the great Archie Moore. He was not a heavy hitter, so he preferred to use his length and mobility to keep fights at a distance more often than not and was often praised for having excellent defensive skills.

On July 28, Eder brought his family to Caracas, and just before they took to flight, Aristides informed the press on hand at Congonhas that the champion should start his practice later that day when they arrive. He stated: "Eder had no contusions in the fight with Yaoita. Only a head butt on his left arm with no serious injuries. This meeting with the Japanese boy was useful. It was a great test for Eder." According to Aristides, the champion left Brazil weighing 121 pounds with the last three pounds to be dropped in Caracas.

Along with his family and Katzenelson, Eder came with Fernando Barreto, Sebastiao Nascimento, and Raul Justo. Barreto would be staying in Caracas for a week and afterward would be heading to New York for a fight on August 26 at Madison Square Garden against Mexican fan favorite, Gaspar Ortega. Nascimento was signed to fight the Venezuelan featherweight champion, Carlos Hernandez. Justo was also hoping to schedule a bout as he worked as Eder's sparring partner.

The Venezuelan press was divided; some put Arias as the favorite based on his fast recovery and agility. Several local pressmen felt that Arias was in too deep against the more prominent, more powerful Brazilian champion. Rafito Cedeño, manager of Arias, boasted: "Ramon is the most extraordinary fighter I have ever seen," warning the Brazilian press that their man's reign would be a short one and would end in Venezuela. Eder had received hostile receptions in the past when he had fought overseas, such as in Los Angeles when he won the title against Eloy Sanchez, but some of the backstage shenanigans attempted on him in Caracas took it to a new extreme.

Eder had been socializing with some locals, and one particular individual took it upon himself to gain an edge for Arias. "That fellow was treating me super nice. He spent time with me at a cocktail party, playing around, singing, and being friendly with us. A few days before the fight, it was 107 degrees Fahrenheit, so I asked for lemonades from the room service. And I started to notice something weird. I was feeling tired and sleepy all day. I realized that they were putting a substance in my drinks. I told my manager about it, and he decided to drink one of my lemonades and felt sick, got terrible diarrhea. Upon recovery, he went to the fight promoters and gave them an ultimatum: 'First of all, we are going to eat our own food, nobody gets in our bedroom anymore. Don't worry; we can take care of ourselves.' Another thing that happened in Venezuela was a series of mysterious phone calls threatening to kill my wife and me. Every time that the phone rang, and I answered, it was a Spanish speaker saying something like: 'Es Jofre quien habla? Escucha, si tu ganas la pelea te vamos a matar, y a su mujer (Hello, is it Jofre? Listen, if you win the fight, I will kill you and your wife.)' I told my manager about it, and he took the telephone out of my room. On fight day, they almost canceled the event because they found a guy bearing a knife close to us. Supposedly that knife was for my wife," he said. "It was a good thing that my father didn't tell me that they threatened my wife with a knife in the hotel hall. I would have killed Arias," Eder said.

A big issue for Eder was that he was not provided with a regular gym to train in, and when he finally was provided with a gym, they would find that the facilities were far below par and lacking basic running water. Due to a heavy downpour for some days, it was also difficult for Eder to do roadwork before the scheduled fight date of August 12. "Jofre is feeling well, I don't believe he's going to have problems with the scale," asserted Katzenelson.

Only four days before the fight, it was announced that the bout would be postponed by a week to August 19. Ticket sales had gone well, and demand was high, so the promoters of the show moved the bout from the original 13,000-seat Plaza Del Toros to a 35,000-seat outdoor baseball stadium. Katzenelson was happy with the postponement as it would give Eder some extra time to get proper workouts in as he could not do so up to this point in Venezuela.

After the extra week, Eder did reach a peak in training, and by the end of the training camp in Caracas, he had sparred 86 rounds and completed 50 miles of roadwork during the two weeks. On the Venezuelan side, Ramon Arias, according to his manager Rafito Cedeño and many sports chroniclers, exceeded himself in the last few weeks coming into the fight. There was the impression he found himself primed to score an upset and bring Venezuela its first world champion.

His coach, Jorge Medina, was extremely optimistic about his pupil's physical condition and stated that the reach advantage which Eder possessed would be neutralized by Arias. He added that the Venezuelan trusted in applying a lot of pressure and had worked hard on short hooks and high volume in close. The night before the fight, hundreds of locals located Eder's hotel room. They stayed outside all night, playing loud music, banging drums while they chanted and sang to make sure he could not get proper sleep.

The intimidation tactics by the locals continued all the way up to the event at Estadio Universitario. As Eder traveled to the stadium, the hostile Venezuelans crowded his car, throwing rocks and punches at both him and his crew. "The fans tried to beat me before the fight. His fans said that I was nothing before the fight, and they rocked the car. I just thought, let's see inside the ring who's good," he said.

Aristides told *O Globo* after the fight how hostile it had been for them in the days and minutes leading to the bout. "The press and the public opinion were completely against the fight, under the argument that Arias – the biggest local idol – wouldn't have a 'chance' to win. Because of that, we had much shame. On the eve of the fight, Lucio Inácio, already designated as a judge, received threatening calls. And at the stadium entrance, our car was even kicked and crushed by the crowd that wanted to assault us. With the police protection and a lot of effort, we were able to escape, after pushing and being pushed a lot," Aristides said. On his walk down the aisle before stepping into the ring, fans threw many things at Eder, from plastic cups to peanuts and cigar butts.

Round By Round from *Estadão* and *O Globo*

Round 1

(*Estadão*) Both fighters studied each other for a minute, and then Eder threw five shots. Arias responded with two right-handed punches. Jofre takes the offensive and hunts Arias around the ring. Round goes to Eder.

(*O Globo*) The studying phase was disrupted by Eder Jofre, connecting five punches with both of his hands. Arias answered with two straight punches, but he had to back up in front of the champion's aggressiveness. Eder was winning the round when the bell rang.

Round 2

(*Estadão*) Jofre started with a one-two combo. Arias dodged the punches and threw a combination. They got in an exchange, which resulted in Arias getting the best out of it.

(*O Globo*) Jofre started with lefts, followed by two quick and strong rights. Arias immediately fought back with two rights and exchanged punches at mid-distance, working with more efficiency. Arias won the round.

Round 3

(*Estadão*) The champion wanted to finish the fight, so he crowded Arias in a corner and brutally punished him. Round goes to Eder.

(*O Globo*) The champion went back to attacking with powerful left and right-hand punches. Arias stepped back, getting punished. His fall was expected when the bell stopped the fight—wide Eder Jofre advantage in this round.

Round 4

(*Estadão*) Eder started with two right-hand punches, Arias was trying to keep the distance using jabs, but Eder was vicious and kept the pace throwing deadly hooks. Round to Eder.

(*O Globo*) Two hard straight right-hand punches by Eder Jofre couldn't be contained by the challenger who tried to jab. With violent left-hand punches, Eder worked Arias' waist, looking for the knockout. His victory was evident in this round.

Round 5

(*Estadão*) Eder kept throwing powerful punches. Ramon's nose is bleeding now; he is on the defensive, trying to run away from Eder.

(*O Globo*) Jofre's attack continues. To contain him, Arias limited to stepping back and shooting jabs to avoid exchanging punches. Jofre won the round, and he was looking for the knockout.

Round 6

(*Estadão*) The Brazilian intensified the attack, landing violent hooks at Arias, who is now stranded against the ropes. Due to the punches landing, Arias loses his mouthguard and gets knocked down. As soon as Ramon got up, Eder crowded him again. The bell rings, saving Arias from a knockout.

(*O Globo*) The Brazilian intensified his attack, hitting violent punches to the Venezuelan, who already looked like he would sleep while standing up. A bunch of rights and lefts make Arias fall. The challenger gets up with difficulty, but two crossed punches in a

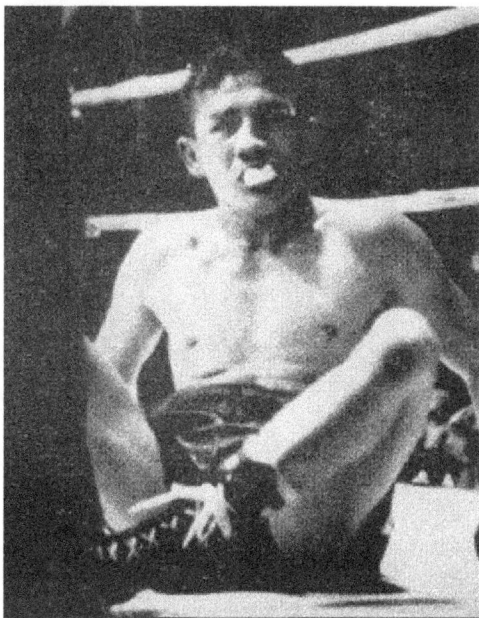

row knock him down again. He's almost knocked out, but the bell saves him again. Eder dominates.

Round 7

(*Estadão*) Jofre started slowly with no intention to end the fight but soon punished Arias against the ropes again. Arias is in bad shape trying to survive another round. After another knockdown, Ramon's coach throws in the towel.

(*O Globo*) Eder restarted, not looking willing to finish the fight. Halfway into the round, however, he again threw his power punches. Arias was destroyed, about to fall, when his trainer threw the towel to the ring, finishing an unequal fight. The referee immediately accepted the towel and proclaimed Eder's victory by TKO.

The Ring magazine founder and boxing historian Nat Fleischer traveled to Venezuela as one of the three judges for this bout and waxed lyrical about the performance of Eder, comparing him to some of the greatest fighters in history. "He is by far the best the division has had in many years. Clever, a powerful left hooker, a stand-up boxer who has learned much of the technique of past masters; Jofre stands out as did Ray Robinson for many years in the welter and middleweight divisions. He can give and take punishment, blocks well, and like Benny Leonard can make his opponent fight the way he wants them to. Watching Jofre against Arias, champion of Venezuela, I was reminded of the days when the bantam class boasted a score of top, hard socking fighters," said Fleischer in his ringside report for the magazine.

Another significant glowing review came from referee Barney Ross, the all-time great three-division champion who said: "I just thrill at that boy's performance. He is a marvel of boxing perfection. He does things in the ring that I never expected to see again. There is nothing he cannot do."

Arias showed his toughness in the fight maintaining a high pace, but ultimately, the harder, more accurate blows dished out by Eder slowed him down. In the seventh round, the Brazilian unleashed a painful blow to

the body which put the brave challenger on the canvas as his trainer came into the ring to concede defeat. It was the third knockdown in the bout, and Arias had the look of a beaten fighter as he bled from the nose and mouth and sported nasty cuts over both of his eyes. After the bout, many angry fans jumped into the ring to attack Arias' manager Rafito Cedeño which caused the riot police to fend them off. The mob fought back but eventually subsided as the police used batons to enforce law and order.

Eder was not impressed by his opponent, and perhaps angry at the treatment he had received, gave a scathing assessment of Arias. "He's so weak that I couldn't even believe it. He is slow and doesn't have any power in his punches; even my young brother Mauro, only 13 years old, can punch harder than him. He fights like he is scared, trying to avoid the exchanges," Eder said.

There was a lot of criticism in Venezuela aimed at Cedeño. Many felt he had pressured Arias to fight with Eder. "That's not true. Rafito had nothing to do with it. Rafito offered me the fight, and I said, 'Show me a film of him.' He offered me a lot of money, and because I was having economic problems, I took the fight, but Rafito never forced me to fight with anyone. I said, 'This is boxing, let's do it.' He (Eder) was a great world champion, but I also believe a lot in aberrations. I couldn't rule out that there could be an aberration. If that happened, then I had a great opportunity to become a world champion," Arias said.

The Venezuelan newspaper *Ultimas Noticias* ran the cover story "Juan, this man is going to kill me" referring to what Arias said to his corner before the end of the bout. Most newspapers in Venezuela explained how the fight had been a massacre and gave Eder a lot of respect and explained how he was a "phenomenon." Some Venezuelans struggled to come to terms with such a resounding defeat for their idol, and this was never more evident than when one newspaper ran the ridiculous headline the following day: "American Gangsters Fixed Fight: Mob Out To Lynch Arias' Manager." Arias showed exemplary sportsmanship as he visited Eder and apologized for the article. He stated he was satisfied that he didn't belong in the same class as the champion and would remain in the flyweight division.

The hostility did not end in the ring as Eder had to be escorted out. When locals spotted him before his flight back to Brazil, a large number shouted at him, calling him an assassin and a butcher. It appeared that Eder was not supposed to win, and the locals were angry that he went in there and did his job. When Eder arrived back in Brazil, he connected through Galeão Airport in Rio and spoke to the press from *O Globo* at the airport. "It was one of the easiest fights I ever had. Arias didn't punch hard or have enough defense to run from my punches. However, he was brave, showed a lot of resistance, was willing, and wished not to let his fans down," Eder said.

He also said that he did obtain a slight injury during the contest, but it was not from his opponent. "I hit him so hard my hands were swollen, but he resisted while he had strength and conscience," he added. It appeared

Eder had been a little kinder and more selective of his words when talking about Arias at this point after having some time to reflect on the fight and calm down from the hostile treatment he received from the Venezuelans.

After the bout, a message from Bangkok arrived, stating that the Thai government was prepared to offer Eder $50,000 tax-free to face flyweight champion Pone Kingpetch to benefit the military hospital. This was an offer they said they would accept, but things soon went quiet on the Thai end, and the bout never came to fruition.

A special guest on hand in Caracas had been Harry Markson, managing director of boxing at Madison Square Garden. The fight had been an entertaining affair, so Eder felt he would get some offers from America for him to appear on television so he could showcase his skills to the largest boxing audience in the world. Markson told Katzenelson he would love to make them an offer for Eder to appear on American television but said that he couldn't work it out because the sponsors and backers wouldn't put up the money to show bantamweights.

Markson was full of praise for the qualities Eder displayed in the ring, "Mr. Markson came to see me in the dressing room and, through an interpreter, said a lot of nice things. He told me: 'You're a complete fighter, just awfully, awfully good. I haven't seen a bantam champion in your class since Sixto Escobar in the 1930s. You box, you punch, and you always know what you are doing,'" Eder said.

Eder felt slighted by the powers that be that prevented him from being able to show his abilities in the homes of so many American boxing fans and spoke for many of the hardcore boxing audience when he said: "Generally they won't sponsor a telecast for anybody under lightweight regardless of who it is. That's not very smart. I've read enough about fights in the U.S. to know that once the bantamweight and featherweight champions were almost as important as the big champions, especially the featherweights. Willie Pep was the first big star they had on television. The fights he had with Sandy Saddler still are being written about and talked about. One of their championship fights drew nearly 34,000 people. Would that mean nobody cares about featherweights? Now, getting down to my own case, Mr. Markson had come to Venezuela to watch me fight. He would go home thrilled by my fight. And, being the top man in Madison Square Garden, which makes the matches for television, wouldn't you think his word would mean something? But no, here he was, still in Venezuela and admitting he couldn't give me a chance to fight on television. I think it's unfair; it's wrong. It is the sort of thinking which keeps boxing from becoming the greatest sport in the world, which it should be. Size is only relative. If you have two good fighters scrapping it out, it doesn't matter if they're 110 pounds or 190. That there are weight classes is what makes boxing for small men as big as big men. Those people are just not taking advantage of an opportunity to show all the good boxing available."

Arias, a once-promising young fighter, would never fight for a title again but remained popular in his native land beyond his retirement. The two title shots he had received, at flyweight against Pascual Perez and at bantamweight against Eder, could not have been any more difficult with both fighters having universal recognition among the all-time greats in their respective weight classes. Arias did score a pair of remarkable victories against Mimoun Ben Ali, but he fell short against the top contenders such as Bernardo Caraballo as he fell further down the rankings.

Caldwell-Halimi II

John Caldwell gave Alphonse Halimi a rematch back at Wembley. The rematch proved to be an ugly affair with the fighters far below the standard of their first match. It had been an unsatisfactory fight full of clinching and wrestling and was greeted with a lukewarm response. Abraham Katzenelson had been an interested spectator and said he had "no doubts" that Caldwell would be Eder's most difficult fight to date. "He is a great boxer. He is extremely quick, hits well, and is strong with both his hands, despite preferring the left, and has an excellent notion of distance, which makes it a lot easier for him to sidestep," he added.

Caldwell had defended the title, but it had been a night to forget for just about everyone. Freddie Gilroy fell further behind in the shadows as he was hammered to defeat by Pierre Cossemyns in Belgium.

Caldwell usually trained in Scotland under the tutelage of Joe Aitcheson, but the underwhelming display in the Halimi rematch was the straw that broke the camel's back for Caldwell. He was never particularly fond of training in Scotland away from his home and family, and the relationship with Aitcheson had been deteriorating. Caldwell was often a reserved and quiet character who kept things to himself, but to those close to the camp, it was acknowledged that he appeared to be rather down and unusually quiet before the Halimi rematch in October.

Unlike Halimi, Caldwell shared Eder's belief that a unification bout had to happen, and there should be only one champion. Less than two weeks after Caldwell had defended his title in the rematch with Halimi, he instructed promoter Jack Solomons to secure a deal to fight Eder early in 1962. Jack Solomons was joined by Sam Docherty as they flew from London to meet with Katzenelson in São Paulo. "There are a great many loose strings to be tied up – from deciding a venue for the fight down to arranging a seat for the Brazilian president," Solomons told the *Belfast Telegraph*. The Brits stayed in town for almost a week on Caldwell's behalf as they ironed out most of the particulars on the mega-fight, which would be happening in January.

Solomons and Docherty had been doubtful that Brazil had a great boxing market. This opinion was shared by the experienced George Parnassus. A lot of the proposals from Katzenelson and local promoters were on a percentage basis, which meant that the fighters would be paid on how well the event sold. Eder's fight with Piero Rollo had been the only world title fight to be staged on Brazilian soil, and a Jofre vs. Caldwell championship match would be the first-ever to be staged in São Paulo.

Although the Rollo fight had been well publicized and well attended, it had operated at a loss. The British team did not want to chance this and were worried that the local organizers might not handle something as big as Jofre vs. Caldwell. The Brazilians had slightly more leverage because it was acknowledged that Eder was the more accepted world champion. He was the boxer ranked as the number one in the division by all the publications and held the lineal claim as champion. The NBA title was also accepted throughout the world as the more legitimate, so a Jofre vs. Caldwell fight belonged in Brazil over Britain provided the money could be raised.

Jack Solomons was firm they would only agree to the fight in Brazil if there was a guarantee on the money as he was not interested in a percentage based upon the commercial success of the event. He also wanted to make sure that the radio and television broadcasters agreed to pay the taxes. Solomons and Docherty said that a contract for a rematch was just as important as a contract for one fight stating that they wanted to have a return match in London.

They were adamant that if they couldn't get these guarantees, then London would be the best place to stage the contest. "If there is any difficulty in São Paulo, I will promote the fight in London, offering Eder a guarantee of $40,000, tickets, and stay for him and his escorts. I'm sure it will be one of the greatest promotions in recent times, especially due to the trust that the audience has in undefeated Caldwell," Solomons said.

Docherty said there wasn't even "the slightest chance" that Caldwell would be defeated against Eder. He added: "He (Caldwell) has excellent technique and intelligence to overcome Jofre's punch, whose style I know through his films. As an amateur, Caldwell had around 250 fights and lost only four. As a professional, he has 25 fights so far, with no defeat or tie. I don't believe there is a bantamweight able to defeat him. And as for Jofre's punch, I have no fear of that, for Caldwell has faced other men who can hit hard."

Fight 44, vs. Fernando Sota, December 6, 1961

As representatives of the Jofre and Caldwell camps were discussing the unification match, which would determine bantamweight supremacy, Eder wanted to stay active with a tune-up bout before the end of the year. Caldwell fought three matches since Eder had defended against Arias, so he and his father felt it would be wise to stay sharp and get rounds in before the anticipated mega-fight in 1962.

The opponent brought in was Fernando Sota, often referred to as Fernando Goncalves. He was a 28-year-old Portuguese boxer based in the Los Angeles area. While the official agreement was not yet in place, it was accepted by both sides that Jofre vs. Caldwell would be happening in January in Brazil, and that whatever differences, they were not far apart and that it would be easy to get it over the finish line.

When Sota arrived two weeks out from a scheduled December 6 date, he requested that the fight be pushed back two weeks, insisting he felt he should take a tune-up fight before he faced Eder. Those demands were not met as Eder was already on a tight schedule with the holiday season coming up and a full training camp needed for the demanding bout with Caldwell. Aristides switched up the training for Eder and had him sparring a different partner every day so he could stay sharp and not get too comfortable facing the same style of opponent.

Round By Round from *Estadão*

Round 1
The Portuguese attacked while Eder was merely trying to get under his shots. Eder answered with hooks and straight punches. Fernando tried to attack again, but with no results. Eder responded with a left hook. The fight was unfolding at a fast pace.

Round 2
Eder waited for Fernando to start the action, but the Portuguese kept the distance and just went forward after Eder tagged him with a straight punch to the face. Fernando put Eder against the ropes and threw good

punches. Eder throws jabs to find space for the deadly hook, but he misses, and Fernando felt the threat and clinched him until the end of the round.

Round 3

Sota puts Eder on the ropes again; the champ responded with a right hook, they engaged in an exchange, in which Eder landed a shot to Fernando's chin.

Round 4

The fight slows down a little bit; Fernando throws jabs at Eder's face. Eder counters with two left hooks that knocked down the Portuguese. After that, Eder went back to his defensive exhibition.

Round 5

Eder knocked Fernando down one more time, landing precise left hooks. The Portuguese stayed down for eight seconds.

Round 6

Eder played with Fernando. Eder performs a total exhibition of good defensive skills. Two punches blocked by Eder, who responded with hooks, and after that, the champion decided to only use his left hand to fight.

Round 7

Eder attacked with two left hooks, Sota backed away with no counters. Eder stopped in the center of the ring, waiting for Fernando, who avoided him.

Round 8

Eder vigorously attacked Sota, who clinched again. With his left hand, Eder landed a strong hook, followed by a shot to the liver. The Portuguese fell to the ground and was counted out.

Eder looked like he could have finished the fight in the early rounds, but the Portuguese showed great endurance. Eder didn't want a quick fight; he wanted to give the audience their money's worth. The champion had fun in the ring as he bobbed and weaved under Sota's attacks and switched between orthodox and southpaw as he controlled the distance and poked away at his opponent.

It had been a successful evening as Eder gave the crowd a spectacle, and he put in some valuable rounds ahead of his January mega-fight. Eder said after the fight, this had been one of his most nerve-wracking nights in the ring because it was the first time his grandmother Maria Zumbano had attended one of his fights. "It was a frightening moment for me seeing her here. She has heart problems," he said.

1961 Results

Eder Jofre KO9 Piero Rollo
Eder Jofre KO2 Sugar Ray
Eder Jofre KO10 Sadao Yaoita
Eder Jofre KO7 Ramon Arias
Eder Jofre KO8 Fernando Sota

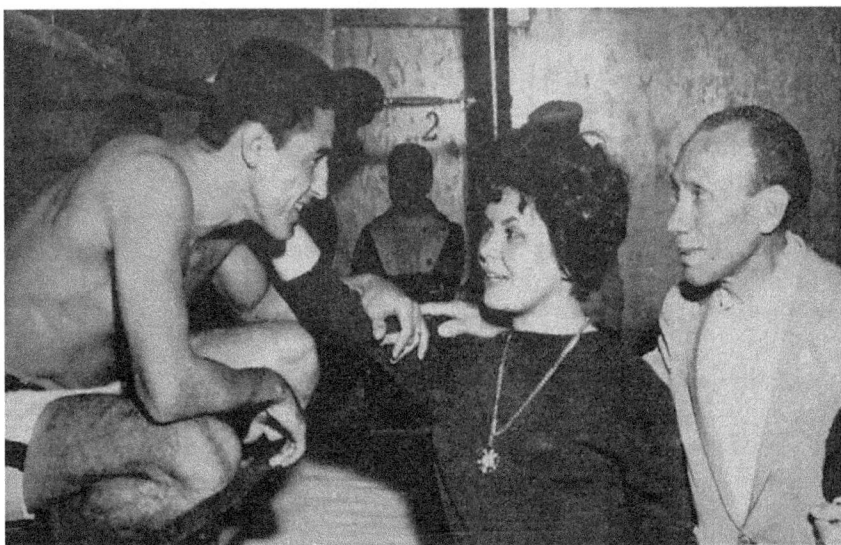

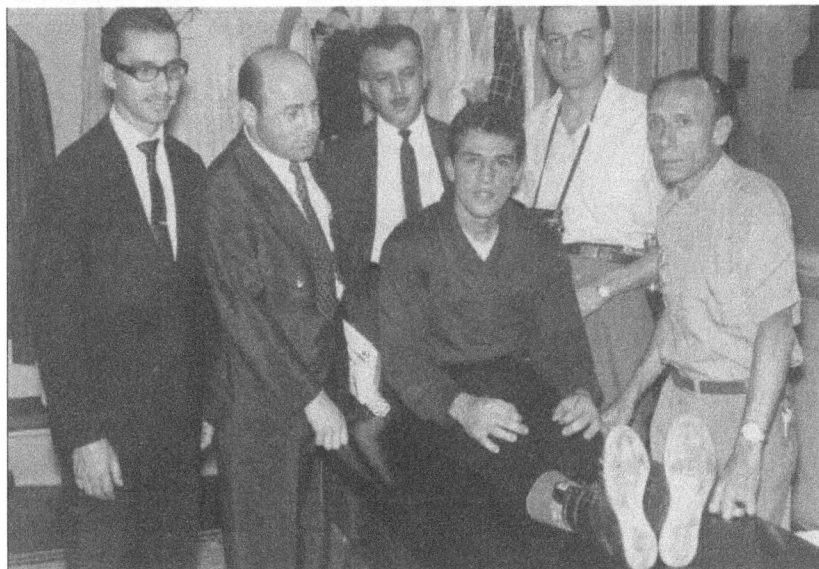

1962

Fight 45, vs. Johnny Caldwell, January 18, 1962

Even before the fight with Eder was confirmed, John Caldwell trained at home in Belfast and was noticeably in a better frame of mind and a better mood than he had been in before the Halimi rematch. On December 15, Tom Phillips of *The Daily Herald* reported:

"John Caldwell turned up at the Thomas A. Beckett gym yesterday, and for the first time I can remember, he wouldn't stop talking. Caldwell, who will fight Eder Jofre of Brazil in São Paulo on January 18 for the undisputed world bantamweight title, has already done a fortnight's training at home in Belfast. Caldwell said: 'Aye, I've heard about Jofre being a hard hitter. I'll find out in the fight because I haven't watched him in films. I never do. I like to sort my man out in the first round. I've read that they're betting two to one on Jofre, and I've tried to back myself with £1,000 of my own money, but I can't get it on.' Then Caldwell added: 'Every time you get into the ring, it is a gamble. Anything can happen in a fight. But I'm confident. I wouldn't try to bet £1,000 of my own money if I wasn't.'"

Eder confessed that it would not be easy getting down to the weight limit of 118 pounds and that it would require a lot of sacrifices, but he was confident he would not lose his title on the scales. "The other times, I also had that problem, and I was never defeated on the scale. It won't be this time that will happen. What will happen is that I will have to spend Christmas and New Year's Eve dry. No liquids or pasta. I will go back to my greens," he said. Aristides said that Eder relaxes his diet between fights but wasn't concerned because they knew what to do to get inside the weight limit and perform at a high level. Eder's typical weight between fights was 123-127 pounds.

DISPUTA do TÍTULO MUNDIAL dos PESOS GALOS
no GINÁSIO ESTADUAL do IBIRAPUERA
FEDERAÇÃO PAULISTA DE PUGILISMO
18 de Janeiro de 1962, às 21 hrs.
Jack Solomons
EDER JOFRE
CAMPEÃO MUNDIAL VERSÃO E.B.A.
versus
JOHN CALDWELL
CAMPEÃO MUNDIAL VERSÃO EUROPA
Cr$ 100,00
LUTA EM 15 ASSALTOS DE 3 X 1 MN.

The day after Christmas saw Eder and his father get down to serious work as they prepared for the January 18 unification bout. In the morning, Eder would run in the woods of Parque Peruche, completing three miles in sprint bursts. The afternoons would consist of going to the academy, where he completed various exercises, shadowboxed, and worked with two sparring partners. Eder and Aristides watched the films of Caldwell's fights against Halimi and came away impressed. Eder said that he found Caldwell "very agile and quick" but said that "you can't evaluate all of his qualities from a film."

Eder felt all opponents were dangerous in the ring and said that he trains for all stylistic scenarios. "I never practice only defense or only attack, for every opponent we use a new technique, and depending on his reaction we remain in the defense or attack, and we only see this after the fight has begun," he said.

Aristides commented that the Irishman appeared to be a very brave fighter who possessed a lot of speed. "He is a good boxer, and he hits well with his left hand," he added. Aristides also said he could see flaws in Caldwell, but he would not reveal them until after the fight because he was concerned if he gave a full analysis, Jack Solomons would pull his fighter out of the fight. While Aristides said that he had no doubts that his son would emerge victorious in the big fight, he refused to say that Caldwell would be an easy opponent.

Up to this point, Caldwell had essentially been training himself at home, but Danny Holland joined the team when he traveled to Brazil for the big fight. Caldwell spent Christmas at home with his family. On December 27, he flew to São Paulo, accompanied by Holland, Solomons, and Sam Docherty. One immediate shock to the system was that in December, it is summer in Brazil with temperatures closing in on 90 degrees plus humidity, compared to the almost freezing temperatures in Belfast. When asked if the heat will be too much for Caldwell, Solomons said it would not be an issue. Docherty agreed, stating that temperatures would be significantly cooler on fight night.

John Caldwell

Caldwell also felt that the temperature change would be of no concern, referencing the late start time. "The heat can be intense at times, but the fight is at night when it's cool – a blessing indeed," he said. On January 2, Caldwell impressed the Brazilian press during his first public workout session at the Wilson Russo Gymnasium. His footwork and punching technique are what drew most praise, but it was still believed there was no question the local man possessed the stronger punch of the two men.

O Globo reported: "Caldwell showed to be very fast with his hands, excellent left-hand work, and opportune, efficient counterpunches. He almost didn't allow the action at a short distance. He preferred to hit and work with both hands, always keeping the sparring at a distance. His guard is open underneath, especially when he lets his right hand go, but in the general sense, his defense is excellent, always followed by counterpunches, which show intelligence and a perfect notion of distance. The general opinion of the coaches and journalists who watched the European version world champion practice is that Eder Jofre will have the hardest fight in his entire career."

With the fight two weeks away, both men weighed slightly over three pounds above the bantamweight limit. Solomons remarked how he had seen Eder on a previous trip to São Paulo, where he appeared to be tight at the weight. "I found him sweating it out for an overweight fight, wearing more clothes than I was. When it comes to getting the extra pounds off, I fancy he may find it hard work," said Solomons. Having his first look at Caldwell, Eder was indifferent without being dismissive when he said: "He looks more like a playboy than a fighter, but he must have many qualities to have arrived at his present position."

Eder explained that he takes every opponent seriously, and anybody expecting him to fight like other boxers would be in for a surprise. "They came here thinking I'm just another fighter but soon find out differently. Anything can happen in the ring, and a champion must approach each fight, even non-title bouts as if his career were at stake," he said. With the Jofre camp taking no chances with Caldwell and treating him with the respect a fellow world title claimant deserved, Aristides hired sparring partners heavier than Eder. He was worried that the flyweight and bantamweights might not give a realistic

impression of what they would be facing on fight night. "Only the bigger guys come forward to exchange punches with Eder," he said.

The following day an argument over which gloves would be used had to be settled. The Caldwell camp refused to use the Brazilian gloves, and Eder would not use the English gloves proposed by the Caldwell team. After some negotiation, they reached a compromise and agreed to use the Mexican Reyes gloves, which were commonly used in North America.

Soon, the next drama unfolded as stories broke in the press that Solomons had ripped up the contract and would be taking Caldwell home and calling off the bout. He was unsatisfied with how the Brazilians were handling the payments they would be receiving for the event from television and radio. It was believed that the fight would draw 20 million television viewers outside of São Paulo. According to Solomons, they had an agreement they should receive £14,200 by this point and had yet to see a penny or any attempt of that deal being honored. Vincente Saguas, president of the São Paulo Boxing Federation, attempted to cool the fire by stating he was confident everything would be sorted with no fuss and that an agreement was simply a couple of days at most away.

"I refuse to do business with people who fail to keep their word," Solomons said. "As far as I am concerned, the fight is on. That is if the conditions of the radio and TV contracts are completed today. Everything depends on the TV and radio people. I'm tired of waiting to see the color of their money. I've given them until tonight to complete the terms of the agreement they have with me," he added. This conflict did not last long either, and the issue was resolved as quickly as it was raised.

Caldwell gave an impressive performance at another public workout on Tuesday, January 9, with around 300 spectators watching him go to work. He sparred four rounds with Brazilian lightweight champion Pedro Galasso before wrapping up his session by skipping rope and working the heavy bag. Dogalberto attended with Waldemar, and Ralph Zumbano. Waldemar spoke briefly to the British press and was generous in his praise of Caldwell. "Caldwell is excellent. His combination punching is fast and accurate," he said.

When pressed on Caldwell's capabilities, Waldemar smiled and said: "I don't know," he said. "He fought on the offensive the whole time as far as I could see." Caldwell's training sessions had been drawing large crowds, and he impressed everyone though Eder remained a heavy favorite. Ivan Cipriano, who sparred rounds with Caldwell, gave some insight into what he thought of both fighters. "Caldwell is faster than Jofre, and he jabs splendidly with his left and follows up with his right at precisely the right moment," he said. He did say that Eder was the much more powerful puncher of the two boxers.

On January 8, local broadcasters announced that they would be depositing $7500 for the rights to distribute the fight outside of the city. Radio stations Difusora, Bandeirantes, and Panamericana all agreed to transmit the fight for $4000 each while stations outside of the state of São Paulo were paying $2000 each. As the event gathered more attention internationally, offers came in to broadcast the match in Uruguay, Mexico, Argentina, and Venezuela.

It was speculated that Caldwell was set to receive a guaranteed $35,000 while Eder would be paid 25% of the event's profits. At this point, it was guaranteed the event had reached profits of $55,000 with estimations pointing towards the event earning up to $300,000. The reports on Caldwell's purse had been falsely reported with O Globo reporting on January 17 that the Irishman was also receiving the same percentage-based cut as Eder. The contract stipulated that the winner would be gaining a higher percentage in a future rematch.

With the bout only a week away, the excitement around the city was growing. High ticket demand prompted Solomons to fly in eight trained guards to man the entrances if fans tried to force their way in. Solomons said: "Everything is going to be just right. Not even the boxers will be able to get in without tickets." The ticket demand had been so high that last-minute plans were approved to fit more seats into the arena. Ticket sales had moved quickly, and it was estimated that they were already at $35,000 in sales one week out from the event.

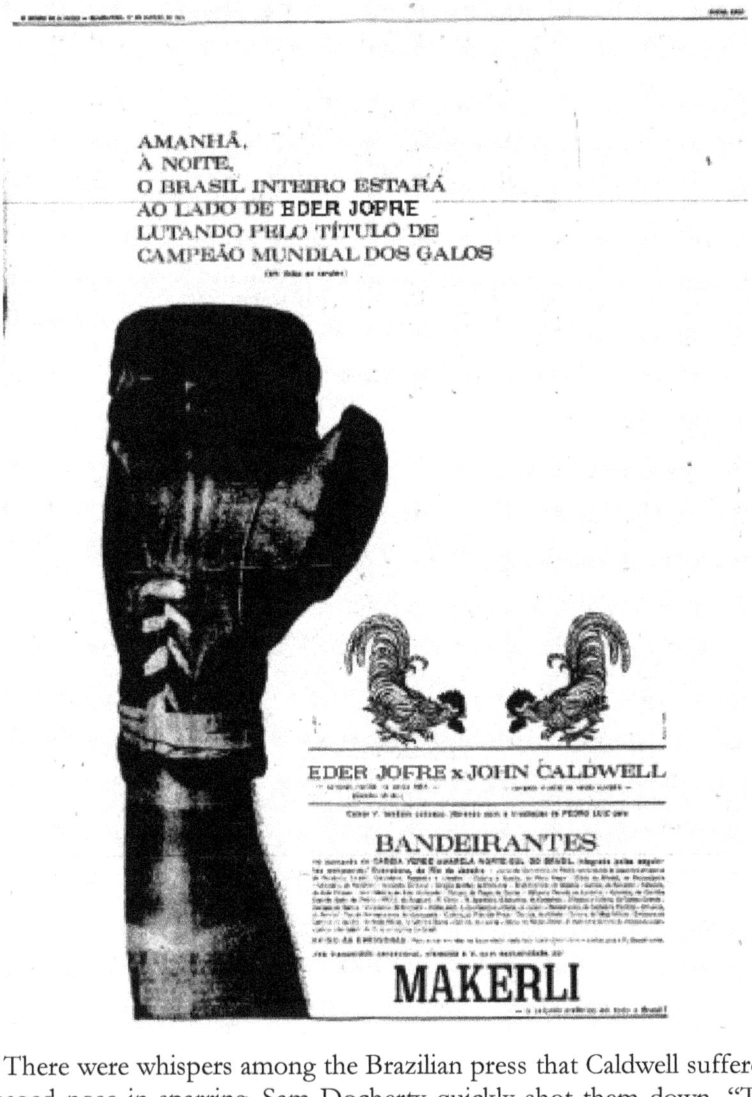

AMANHÃ,
À NOITE,
O BRASIL INTEIRO ESTARÁ
AO LADO DE EDER JOFRE
LUTANDO PELO TÍTULO DE
CAMPEÃO MUNDIAL DOS GALOS

EDER JOFRE x JOHN CALDWELL

BANDEIRANTES

MAKERLI

There were whispers among the Brazilian press that Caldwell suffered a damaged nose in sparring. Sam Docherty quickly shot them down. "They are off their heads. Our lad is doing just fine," he said. He also added that they planned to intensify their training program in the next few days. Another rumor to surface through the local media was that Eder was contemplating early retirement from the sport, possibly as early as the end of 1962. The rumors emerged when Eder openly talked about his ongoing struggle in making the bantamweight limit of 118 pounds.

One week out from the bout, Eder spoke to Peter Wilson of *The Daily Mirror* while heavily clothed in ballet tights and a woolen sweater despite temperatures well above 80 degrees. In this interview, Eder confessed to Wilson, "I have too many sacrifices to fight bantam." Wilson grabbed the attention of Abraham Katzenelson, sucking on his trademark cigar, and asked if these rumors were created to con Caldwell into a false sense of security. Katzenelson assured Wilson they ran a legitimate operation and that he was a man of the utmost integrity. "We would not pull a shabby trick like that."

That same day Caldwell appeared happy and relaxed as he worked out, which was a far cry from the sullen figure that trudged around his training camp for the rematch with Halimi. Docherty commented on an influx of Irish fans in town from Britain, Canada, and America. They had put up £5000 in betting money on their man to win. "Good luck to them. They are no mugs," said Caldwell. The Caldwell camp claimed a psychological edge on the Monday of fight week when they had the weigh-in moved to later in the day. Peter Wilson reported that the Caldwell camp had "already won round one" when the local rules were overthrown. Rather than 9 am as was customary for weigh-ins in São Paulo, it was confirmed the boxers would weigh-in at noon.

Eder was not the only man wearing woolens in town that week as Caldwell also was forced into wearing excess clothes as he went for his morning runs. The observers at Caldwell's training sessions had generally treated him well and spoke in reverence of him. On the other hand, passers-by were hostile towards him as he undertook his roadwork. His morning runs were often tracked by photographers, motorcycles, and fans shouting at him as they passed by. There were no significant incidents, but the booing he was subjected to was a sign of things to come. The crowd that would attend the event would never be as civil and polite as the press members.

Caldwell's brother, Paul, and his father joined on fight week after a long journey, which started in Belfast and saw them go through London, Paris, Dakkar, Recife, and Rio before finally landing in São Paulo. Caldwell's son, Paul, shared some of his uncle's memories of the trip with me. "He remembers being mistaken for my father on the flight out of Paris by a crew member. The person informed him that he was at the first Halimi fight in London," he said. Paul still laughs at some catcalls hurled at his brother and their camp but said nothing was malicious or upsetting. "He recalled to me what he calls true boxing fans waiting around the hotel to get my father's autograph and that it was always a civil encounter. He also met Jofre and said he was a very nice man," said the younger Paul.

On Monday of fight week Peter Wilson reported for *The Daily Mirror* after visiting both training camps over the weekend as they were closing in on the huge bout:

"Over the weekend, I saw the two of them in action. Jofre trains in a dingy, sleazy, grimy, greasy, jam-packed sweatbox over a shoe shop. It is on the third floor, with no lift, and then dirty marble steps have chips out of them, making them look like the teeth of an old beat-up fighter. There are dirty old artificial-silk pennants on the walls, bronze statuettes grey with dust, and a ring with dirty, dusty, pink ropes, surrounding a dirty pink canvas floor. There are lithographs of old-time fighters in crude colors on the dirty walls, old fight posters, and a few green lockers.

There are fat businessmen sweating tallow through bare hairy chests, some lean hard negros, and some South American Indians with carved stone faces. It is a place where I wouldn't willingly spend ONE three-minute round. It's a muscle factory, a prison for punchers – where you fight or get out.

Finally, Jofre arrives. He is an alert, intelligent, handsome, unmarked young man. He does two consecutive recorded radio interviews- speaking more fluently than the interviewers- then slides through the ropes like a craftsman settling down at his lathe. He boxes three rounds with a clownish spar mate who tries to grin when it hurts. Jofre is a fierce fighter. He operates on the principle, 'Cry, clown, cry.'

In the first round, he lands a left hook – reputedly his best punch-very low and follows with another below the Plimsoll line. He looks like an excellent fighter. Why wouldn't he be? His old man is known as the father of Brazilian boxing.

We switch to Caldwell. He trains in a big seat-ringed gym with one wall open to the fresh air. Against his first sparring partner, Raul Justo- a turkey rather than a bantamweight, Caldwell punches well but is hit too often. Then he tangles with Jose Fernandes, amateur bantamweight champion of São Paulo. In the first round, John isn't impressive - slapping. Leading with the right and boxing open-mouthed. In the second, a man with a mobile battery of dazzling photographic lamps flashes at the wrong moment, and Caldwell is put halfway through the ropes by a left hook. But he's as icily calm as ever. And when one of his supporters suddenly bereaved, has to fly home, John says: "Never mind, you may miss this fight, but you can always come back for the return which will be here after I've beaten him the first time.'"

Later that Monday evening, former featherweight world champion Willie Pep arrived from New York to work as the third man in the ring for the bout. There to greet Pep at the airport was none other than John Caldwell, and he talked one-on-one with the legendary ex-champion, who shared his wisdom with the Irishman. Caldwell explained that Pep had been his boyhood idol and what a thrill it was to have met him. In the build-up to the bout, Brazilian television was hyping the bout further by showing Eder's championship victory over Eloy Sanchez. When asked if Caldwell took a chance to see what he would be up against, he said he had not watched the bout. "I will see enough of him on Thursday night," he said. Pep shared his enthusiasm for what he felt would be a great championship fight. "It's going to be a great fight – the greatest. Both these boys are good – in fact, the best – so it's bound to be a thriller," he said.

The bout was gathering so much attention locally it was compared to any big football match, and even the "King of Football," Pele would be ringside for the fight. Irish fans were making their way into town, and a lot of international press arrived on fight week. A dozen British press members were on hand and were joined by media from Argentina, Uruguay, Peru, Germany, France, Norway, and Italy.

Sam Docherty was still trying to play mind games when he kicked up a fuss at the selection of Brazilian judge Edmar Teixeira, director of the Federation of Brazilian judges. Docherty said that as the Brazilians had selected Anthony Petronella, past president of the NBA, which recognized Eder as world champion already, he couldn't be regarded as neutral. According to Docherty, adding a Brazilian official loaded the scales against Caldwell too heavily. Docherty demanded that Pep would be the referee, and Peter Wilson would be the judge, but he wanted to see if he could get more things in his fighter's favor. He did calm down, and the following day said that since so many fans had made the journey from Britain and Ireland, he would not object any further to the officials selected. "I'll do the next best thing to getting a neutral judge. I'll just tell Caldwell to knock him out. That will save all the arguments," he said.

Two days before the fight, Caldwell gave a vicious beating to sparring partner, Raul Justo. Caldwell had perhaps been ticked off by the stories printed in the press that Justo had given him a bloodied nose. Also, the Caldwell camp felt Justo displayed arrogance. Justo was a young featherweight with only three professional fights under his belt. Roughly three hundred people were on hand as Caldwell unloaded on the sparring partner, and despite shouts from Docherty to "go easy on him," Caldwell did not hold back and gave Justo a thorough pasting. Caldwell said that he felt he had persuaded Justo "to not be naughty in the future."

The subject of Eder's weight had been constant in the build-up to the fight, especially with a drop in temperature days before the match. A rainstorm hit the area, and the temperatures had dropped to as low as 65 degrees, with many speculating that Eder could struggle to shake off the last few ounces at the weigh-in. He was insistent that he would have no problems making the weight and was quoted as saying he even had the pleasure of treating himself to a bowl of pasta on the Monday of fight week.

O Globo took a look inside both boxers' camps during their last public training sessions and reported:

"Eder Jofre and John Caldwell wrapped up their practices for tomorrow's great fight. Yesterday, while the Irishman was limited to punching the sandbag and jumping rope, the Brazilian would do rounds with two boxers from a higher weight category. But if Caldwell's final practicing didn't offer a bigger interest, Eder's demonstration was impressive. Using 14-ounce gloves, in the third round against amateur middleweight Edmundo Furtado Leite, he seriously shook him, and when realizing the state of the sparring partner, he stopped the sequence of punches to avoid the knockout. After that, against professional lightweight Leônidas Sacomã, in the second round, he obliged him to kneel, giving up after forcing the fight also to avoid the knockout. The spectators were impressed with the demonstration, and for our part, we guarantee that the great Eder's shape couldn't be better.

No problems

During his practice, Eder used his habitual shirts – a cotton one, a plastic one, and a wool one – but didn't cover up with the blanket during the round breaks anymore. For tomorrow's weigh-in, at noon, Eder and Kid Jofre guarantee that the fighter is within the category limit, not needing the second call two hours later."

While Eder remained a strong favorite to win the bout, Caldwell had performed well in his training sessions, and several local boxing experts felt that if Caldwell couldn't beat Eder, then he would at least prove his most challenging opponent to date. The well-publicized struggle which Eder had to go through to keep his weight down besides Caldwell's speedy style and excellent boxing pedigree pointed to a difficult stylistic match-up. The feeling was that while Caldwell didn't have the power to hurt Eder, his stick and move style could make Eder tired towards the middle point of the contest.

The constant speculation and noise from the Caldwell camp and the British press regarding Eder's struggles with the weight are why it came as such a surprise when he made the weight with no issues at the official weigh-in ceremony, but Caldwell needed additional time in shaking off a little excess weight. Caldwell went for a run and returned within the weight limit about 30 minutes later. Danny Holland said: "Caldwell was four ounces inside the limit when he was weighed on special scales in the hotel this morning, and he has not eaten before the weigh-in," claiming that the scale was slightly off.

Docherty was asked if forced exercises could hurt Caldwell's chances. "No. It will not weaken him. In fact, it might do him good. It will make him good and mad," he said. Eder was pleased with making the limit and displayed high confidence. "I am going to win like I always do. I am in good shape. I am only waiting now for the fight to start so I can get undisputed possession of the world title," he said. After the weigh-in, Caldwell took a walk around town to clear his mind and have some time alone before going back to his hotel room, where he rested and watched a movie in bed. Eder went home to relax before the fight.

Fans waited outside of the venue for 12 hours leading to the bout, hoping they could get tickets to the hottest event in town. The atmosphere outside the arena was so boisterous it was left to the imagination how euphoric it would be inside the arena. The atmosphere awaiting Caldwell

257

was very intimidating as he made his way to the ring. He was whistled at and booed wildly with audience members throwing items such as rolled-up papers, candies, and popcorn at him.

Caldwell later described the crowd as "real enemies" such was the cauldron they created for him. Eder was given an incredible reception from his adoring public as he was cheered all the way to the ring. He even had a microphone put in his face where he said a few words transmitted over the radio. The fans sang his name, and the audience could not have been any more encouraging in their outpouring of love to their champion.

Round By Round from *Estadão* and *Folha*

Round 1

(*Estadão*) At a safe distance, the fighters looked at each other and threw no punches. A straight and right cross thrown by Caldwell was dodged by Eder. The Brazilian feints to throw jabs at Johnny, but he restrains himself. Both fighters stay in the center of the ring, studying each other. The

Irishman goes on an offensive attempt again, but Eder dodges everything and doesn't respond, he just bobs and weaves. Caldwell attacks again, Eder hits the backpedal, and clinches. End of the round.

(*Folha*) Movements began with both boxers watching. Eder tries with his left hand to define the distance. His guard is perfect, and with his footwork, he avoids while the Irishman stays at a distance. Caldwell displayed good defense. Defensive round. Tie.

Round 2

(*Estadão*) Both fighters are poised for a punch exchange. Eder goes off and slightly touches Johnny's face. The Irishman tried to answer, but again Eder dodges all his punches.

(*Folha*) The defensive strategy is over, and Eder tries to prepare, with his left-hand jab, and throws hard with his right hand. Initially, Eder Jofre connects a good punch on the Irishman, but Caldwell also hits Jofre, however, Jofre is not affected. Eder's round.

Round 3

(*Estadão*) Caldwell threatens to attack but backs away when seeing Eder coming at him. Eder lands a right cross and a left uppercut; Caldwell has his back against the ropes. Eder tries a left hook and misses but lands a good right hook. Caldwell clinches again while Eder pulls himself away.

(*Folha*) Caldwell tries to reduce the distance, sometimes successful, and that results in clinching, making the referee interfere. Eder avoids it and, even though he is caught with a hook on his liver, he applies a good right cross and straight punches against his opponent, who bleeds from his nose. Eder's round.

Round 4

(*Estadão*) Eder is attacking; he tries a left hook but misses. Caldwell backs up, Eder misses two more hooks. Using left jabs, Eder is setting up a new attack. Caldwell hit Eder's body with two hooks. Eder fires back and lands a punch to his jaw.

(*Folha*) Putting himself at a short distance from Eder, to avoid that he (Eder) uses his better skills, the Irishman tries to reach the Brazilian with hooks that have no effect. With his left hand, Eder hits his opponent twice. Eder won the round.

Round 5

(*Estadão*) Caldwell started off clinching. After that, he tried a straight right. Eder countered with two hooks. Caldwell throws a combination at Eder and holds his arms to avoid the counters. With six jabs in a row, Eder made Johnny's head spin and almost made him fall with a straight punch. Eder lands a strong punch to the liver, making the Irishman fall to the canvas.

(*Folha*) Caldwell's biggest concern is sticking to Eder, pushing him against the ropes, and causing constant warnings from the referee. The Brazilian works with jabs with his left hand and sends Caldwell to the canvas for the first time, for six seconds, with a straight right punch and a left punch to the body. Eder's round.

Round 6

(*Estadão*) Caldwell goes all in, desperately trying to attack Eder, who just backs up and lands two hooks to his face. Caldwell is bleeding right now.

(*Folha*) Eder goes decisively against the Irishman and hits him with another straight right-hand punch. Cornered on the ropes, he (Caldwell) pushes his body against Eder's repeatedly, even locking the Brazilian's arms. Eder wins the round.

Round 7

(*Estadão*) The fight is taking a different pace right now. Eder is attacking, and Caldwell is running away. Eder traps him in a corner and punishes him heavily; the Irishman bends his knees to avoid more punches.

(*Folha*) Left jabs from Eder take the Irishman to the ropes. Also, left hooks and a right cross from the Brazilian make Caldwell sort of escape. The Irishman looks tired, but Eder also slows down. Eder's round.

Round 8

(*Estadão*) Caldwell tries two crosses and misses. He tries again and head butts Eder; the referee takes a point away from him. Eder goes forward and lands three powerful hooks at him, the Irishman, exhausted, clinches again.

(*Folha*) Eder's opponent is tired. However, he is still blocking the Brazilian's attacks. Eder's right-hand punch gets lost in Caldwell's blocking. Another left uppercut from the Brazilian hits him on the liver—Eder's round.

Round 9

(*Estadão*) Eder attacks with a hook and a straight right, making his (Caldwell's) nose bleed. The Irishman doesn't know what to do; he tries to respond to Eder's attack but receives a hurtful hook to the body.

(*Folha*) Caldwell tries to hit with his right hand, but Eder defends well. Eder connects a straight right-hand punch followed by a left hook. A right-hand punch from Eder and another hook. The Brazilian hits under with his right hand and does a "one-two" on the Irishman's liver and spleen. When the bell rings, the Irishman is dizzy. Eder's round.

Round 10

(*Estadão*) Eder starts this round punching with more power. He throws a violent hook to Caldwell's face, pushing him against the ropes. Caldwell runs to the center of the ring, but Eder goes after him throwing powerful and precise punches. With a straight right-hand to his head, Eder knocks him down to his knees. After four seconds, Caldwell gets up again, but he's groggy. Eder doesn't waste time, goes after him throwing a vicious combination, he stops just when Caldwell's coach waved the towel to the referee.

(*Folha*) Eder goes to his opponent's jaw with a swing, showing determination to wrap up the fight. A new sequence of punches brings Caldwell's guard down. Right. Left. Right again. The Irishman folds his knees, and the referee counts to eight. Caldwell gets up already defenseless, retreating. Eder hits again with his right and his left, in a rapid sequence of punches, sending the Irishman to the ropes. Two right hooks and a left hook (by Eder) against the opponent's jaw. Eder lands with right-hand punches and left hooks. Caldwell's assistant shakes the towel outside the ring. Willie Pep, the referee, finishes the fight, giving the victory to Eder Jofre by technical knockout.

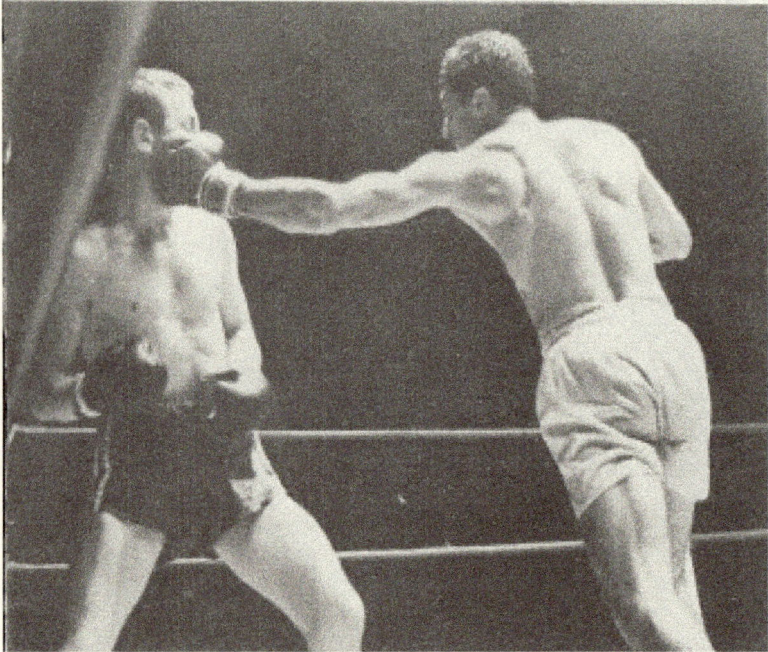

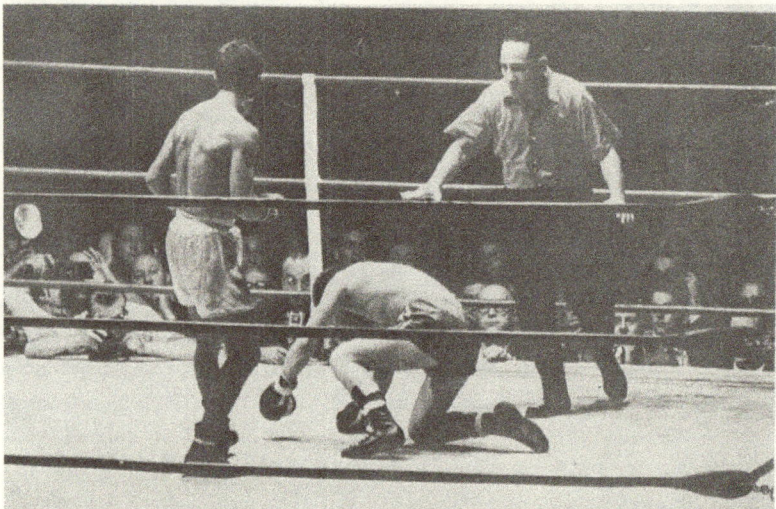

Willie, shown refereeing the Jofre-Johnny Caldwell bantamweight title fight in Brazil, is a most competent official whose services are in demand all over the world.

Here is the round-by-round report of the British judge, Peter Wilson:

Round 1
Caldwell started with a tentative left jab against his nervous opponent. Both fighters circled cautiously, with Caldwell taking the initiative. Jofre was getting in good left jabs, with the crowd already booing because of a lack of action.

Round 2
Jofre landed two body blows to Caldwell's stomach. Caldwell came back with a sharp one-two, bobbing and weaving against his lighter opponent. At the end of the round, Caldwell's face appeared slightly reddened.

Round 3

Jofre commanded the initiative in quick exchanges. Caldwell was booed for holding. A vicious left rocked Caldwell, who pulled away but came back to put Jofre on the ropes.

Round 4

Jofre opened by landing several left hooks, but Caldwell came back to sink in heavy punches to Jofre's body, doubling him up in pain.

Round 5

Jofre attacked, and a right hook caught Caldwell in the mid-section. The Irishman's head was jolted back with another hefty punch, but he rallied back to pin Jofre on the ropes with two hard left jabs to the stomach. Caldwell got in some good close work, but Jofre battled back to put the Irishman down for a compulsory count of 8.

Round 6

Jofre came out hitting, caught Caldwell on the chin, and then forced him to the ropes. The Irishman seemed a little dazed but quickly recovered.

Round 7

Caldwell still retained his speed, but Jofre looked in control of the fight. He landed heavy blows, but Caldwell recovered well and then sought safety close in.

Round 8

Spurred on by the partisan crowd, Jofre now appeared to be in complete, calm control. Against his constant aggression, Caldwell relied on speed. The Irishman tried gamely to fight back, but several times he looked in trouble. Towards the end of the round, Jofre seemed to tire and slowed down, and, as Caldwell sought to get close in, the Brazilian held. At the end of the round, however, Jofre was ahead on points.

Round 9

Caldwell was forced to hang on. Jofre, using his longer reach to advantage, jabbed away forcefully and halted Caldwell as he tried to get close. Caldwell took a hard left and went into a crouch. These constant clinching tactics by the Irishman annoyed the crowd, who loudly booed each time he got to grips. Caldwell continued his policy of fighting inside. Although Jofre made it clear he preferred to dictate matters from long-range.

Round 10

Jofre went after his man, and from a flurry of left hooks, sank Caldwell to the canvas. He had taken plenty of punishment throughout the contest, and this fresh barrage was too much for him. With 15 seconds remaining in the round, his manager decided that Caldwell had had enough, and the plucky out-punched Irishman retired.

The ring was a scene of mayhem minutes after the end of the bout as fans rushed to the ring, hoping to get closer to Eder to congratulate him on his victory. The ring got overcrowded, and Eder was tumbled to the canvas before security came in and cleared out the ring. Luckily, Eder was not hurt and gave a quick interview. "It feels good to be the real champion. Now we have everything in Brazil except icebergs," he said. When asked about his opponent, Eder gave credit to the bravery of Caldwell. "I thought I would win quickly after knocking him down in the fifth, but Caldwell surprised me, showing impressive powers of assimilation."

"I accepted Caldwell's retirement from the corner – but by God what a game kid that is," referee Willie Pep said. Caldwell offered no excuses and said: "He is a fine boxer and a great puncher. Nevertheless, I want to meet him again." For Eder and the Brazilian fans, it was a night of celebration as the crowd from inside Ibirapuera made their way out into the streets and celebrated with fans who weren't lucky enough to be inside the arena. Sam Docherty said he hoped that Caldwell could do better in a rematch but conceded that the better boxer had won. He stated that he had "never seen a fighter so good" as Eder. George Parnassus offered the opinion that Eder may already be "the best of all-time in his weight class," calling him a "true champion."

Peter Wilson spent one-on-one time with Caldwell and Solomons backstage after the bout. While they acknowledged the brilliance of Eder, they also still spoke with defiance regarding a possible rematch. "I'll always have another go at anything. He's a great fighter. He can hurt you with either hand. But I'd like to fight him a return, only never here, never here again," Caldwell had told him. "The fight, from what Caldwell told me, was decided between the locker room and the ring, for before the audience reaction, my pupil was under the impression that he would be lynched if he defeated Jofre," Solomons said.

The hostile atmosphere had soured Caldwell, and he did not sound all that keen on returning to Brazil to face his conqueror. Solomons said: "I'd like to put them on again in Britain. I don't think Jofre would be as strong there, and Caldwell wouldn't have to fight the crowd as well." Whether Solomons believed that a return would be any different or if he was simply trying to instill confidence in his fighter is hard to tell. Eder already proved he was a world champion who could perform anywhere and not just in front of his fans. Proof existed when he went to Los Angeles to knockout the fearsome Jose Medel and when he destroyed Eloy Sanchez for the title.

Irish bookmakers Matt Graham and George Long, who had traveled from Belfast, went to visit the offices of *O Globo* in Rio before they went back to Ireland. Graham said that while he felt Caldwell could do better in a British ring, he admitted that Eder simply operated on too high of a level for their countryman to defeat. Long said that it didn't matter where they fought and that Eder would defeat him just the same. "We've seen the best bantam in the world fight and never knew of a punch so violent. Only that punch on his liver, when Caldwell was still wholesome, was enough to evaluate the Brazilian bantam's quality. It's really a spectacle. Eder Jofre would beat John Caldwell anywhere in the world, at any time and under any circumstance," he said.

The two bookmakers agreed that the odds would double from 2-1 to 4-1 on anyone wanting to bet on Caldwell in the proposed rematch. Long also said that he would make Eder the favorite to defeat Davey Moore for the featherweight world title if he were to move up and challenge the American even with no warm-up bouts.

In *Quebrando a Cara*, Eder's uncle Waldemar says that he only saw Eder angry in three bouts: The return bout with Ruben Caceres, the fourth encounter with Ernesto Miranda, and this bout with Caldwell. Eder confirmed that he did fight with more anger than usual as he was upset at some of the noise coming out of the Caldwell camp.

In the 2004 documentary *O Grande Campeao*, Eder again stated that he fought with a wave of unusual anger. He said that he was upset before the fight that Caldwell said: "I haven't come across the Atlantic to lose my title to a bunch of monkeys. I come from the home of boxing." Reflecting on this fight, Eder said, "I worked so hard to put Brazil's name on the map and for this guy to come here talking all that crap? I kicked his butt, and I did it on purpose."

Eder, a proud Brazilian, had taken exception to the comments and admitting to prolonging the beating. "I was hitting him so badly and laughing so hard from inside. I remember allowing him to recover just so I could punch him more. I wanted to really hurt him; I was not interested in finishing the fight quickly," he was quoted as saying in 1976. However, it is not entirely sure that those comments came directly from Caldwell's mouth as they seem uncharacteristic of the man he was. Caldwell could be cold, but he was mostly quiet. His manager, Sam Docherty, was generally seen as the loud one and the one most likely to stir up interest and attention in such a way.

O Espetáculo de Ibirapuera

Caldwell never quite reached the same level again after his defeat in Brazil. However, he did take part in some major bouts like his domestic battle with Freddie Gilroy. He remains a great source of pride for sports fans in his native Belfast, where a statue of him was erected in his honor shortly after he died in 2009. Years after their bout, Caldwell was full of praise for his conqueror: "Eder Jofre was the greatest bantamweight and the hardest hitter for his weight of all time," he said. "I remember the place was packed to the rafters, and there were many thousands locked outside the arena. I just couldn't get to terms with him on the night, maybe it was the heat of the crowd, but it was an unbelievable occasion which I will never forget. As it turned out, it was my first defeat as a professional, and it was tough for me to take."

I spoke with his son Paul on numerous occasions, and he told me that his father had always thought highly of Eder. "I remember my father talking very fondly of Jofre, and I admit, you did have to chip away at him to get him to talk; he was a quiet man. He had such respect for Jofre, definitely considered him the greatest bantamweight ever. I vividly recall when chatting with him once about the Jofre fight, he said, 'I'd never been hit so hard, and he was the only man to hurt me,' - not something you want to hear your father say, that's why it sticks with me. The hotel scales were something that he mentioned - he did not appreciate having to skip and run off one pound at the official weigh-in. He felt the hotel scales were 'off' and did tell me that on return to the hotel, the scales had mysteriously disappeared. These, he told me, were official scales used daily to check his weight. Obviously, some fight decisions have rankled with my father, but not this one; he knew he was in with the greatest. He would smirk when I was annoying him for information, but I never heard him say a bad word about Eder Jofre," Paul said.

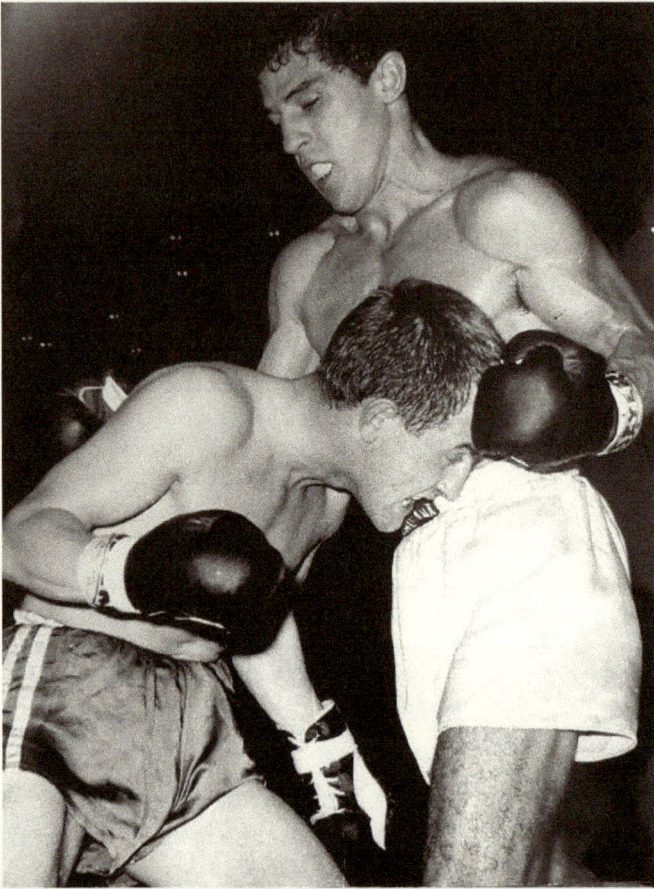

Featherweight Move Explored

In early 1962, *Boxing Illustrated* ran a story in which Edward Brennan interviewed Madison Square Garden matchmaker Teddy Brenner at Gallagher's Steakhouse on 52nd street in New York City. The topic of discussion was which fights Brenner would make above all in the sport if he had his way and could cut out all the politics that prevented certain matches. The matches Brenner selected were Floyd Patterson vs. Sonny Liston, Floyd Patterson vs. Eddie Machen, Sugar Ray Robinson vs. Terry Downes, Joe Brown vs. Carlos Ortiz, Emile Griffith vs. Benny Paret III, and Dick Tiger vs. Gene Fullmer. He finished with the match he proclaimed he'd most like to make and that was Davey Moore vs. Eder

Jofre for Moore's featherweight world title. "In case you don't know it, Jofre is the bantamweight champion of the world, and in my book, he's the best fighter, pound for pound, in the business. He's from Brazil. In Davey Moore, who is the featherweight champion, Jofre would be going against the best featherweight since Willie Pep was in his prime. Just look at Davey's record. He goes all over the world to fight his top contender's right in their own backyards - and he belts them over as fast as they keep turning up. In 1961 Moore won nine out of nine, four by knockout, which is par for any course. Moore is head and shoulders above everyone in his class, but I'm not so sure he can lick the guy who is champion of the class below his - Eder Jofre," Brenner said.

While moving up and challenging for the featherweight title was a realistic option, Eder felt as the undisputed bantamweight champion and widely received as the best boxer in the world pound-for-pound, that he did not want to build his way up in another weight class and would go straight to the champion or he would not move up. The paydays and the fame that came with being the world champion were good, and Eder was a hot commodity in Brazil. He was a national icon held in the same breath as Pele. He gave an interview to Natalicio Norberto for *Boxing Illustrated* soon after the Caldwell bout and suggested that he was almost ready to hang up the gloves and move onto new pastures.

The pressures and the sacrifices seemed to take their toll when Eder said, "I think I have the qualities to take me to the top in other pursuits besides boxing, and once I have given up boxing, I will become the Eder I was before I began my fighting life." He explained how it had been such a

Spartan life that he had lived and that so much sacrifice went into his career that it had taken its toll not only physically but emotionally. "I have lived a dedicated life as a fighter. It's been a tough struggle keeping to my fighting weight of 118 pounds. You can't imagine. I have not been able to partake in the good things my ring earnings can buy. What good is it? Why do I need it? I have given up just about everything to be a fighter. Yes, I am the champion, but what have I got? I can't eat what I want to, I can't go where I want to, and I'm not allowed to do what pleases me. Can you understand the turmoil that is inside me?" he pleaded.

He told of how he had to live a largely sheltered life and spent too much time away from Cidinha, who was pleading with him to retire from the ring. Eder appeared close to retirement but did reveal he had plans to box for the rest of 1962, at least. "My plans call for a return match with Caldwell and also a fight with Herman Marquez in California. Then two or three more fights and finally, in December of 1962, I will announce my retirement," he said.

Fight 46, vs. Herman Marquez, May 4, 1962

With a rematch contractually agreed to, Eder and Caldwell were set to go again but next time in Britain. The one-sided nature of their unification bout was such that a return bout figured only to benefit Jack Solomons in his bank account. For Eder, there was more to gain from defending his title in California or at home against a new opponent. Caldwell didn't stand to benefit much as another hammering defeat would figure to derail his once-promising career. But Caldwell was a fierce competitor, and despite recognizing the astonishing ability of his conqueror, he wanted another crack at the man who was now the undisputed bantamweight champion.

For some weeks, there was a lot of back and forth and speculation as to whether the fight would happen in Belfast or London. Solomons was very vague about when the bout would happen. The rematch clause was only eligible for a limited time. If it was not agreed upon promptly, then either side could go another way. Solomons held the ace, but he did not have the luxury of time, so any potential games he would try to employ stood only to hurt his interests.

As Solomons dragged his feet on a rematch for Caldwell, Katzenelson agreed on a bout for Eder with Herman Marquez, which would take place at the Cow Palace in San Francisco. Initially, the bout was scheduled for February 26, and Eder was back in training on February 6, just two weeks after the Caldwell bout. Eder came back to training almost four and a half pounds over the bantamweight limit, but this was of little concern to his father, who felt it was an average weight gain, and he had ample time to squeeze back into 118 pounds. Eder injured his left hand only two days back into his training routine and had to push the fight back, with Katzenelson proposing a date of March 12.

The injury to his hand was caused when he was working on the heavy bag. He connected awkwardly and then put the hand in ice. It was determined that it was a little too soon to fight time with training and weight loss still required before the bout in San Francisco. After talking with George Parnassus, it was agreed upon that the title defense against Marquez would happen on March 20. Eder was back in training on February 13. The left hand was working fine, but this news about different fights lit a fire under Solomons. The British promoter threatened legal action to prevent Eder from going through with that voluntary defense and even threatened a lawsuit as large as $100,000. Solomons was standing by the date of March 30 for the Jofre vs. Caldwell rematch, but Katzenelson wanted a date of April 12 since Eder would have only ten days between the Marquez fight and the Caldwell rematch, and that would require a trip across the Atlantic. The timing was just far too close for comfort and an unreasonable date for Solomons to demand. Issues regarding the venue were discussed with Solomons initially pressing for Belfast. Katzenelson wanted London before Solomons offered Athens, Greece as a potential destination for the return bout.

Since they had a contract, this gave Katzenelson little choice on what to do, and he had to inform George Parnassus they would have to put the Marquez bout on hold for the time being. Parnassus argued that the contract was void since Eder had won by knockout, but that stipulation was proven not to be in the contract. Now Parnassus threatened action against Eder's team since he had agreed to defend his title in California. Still, the money from Solomons' threatened lawsuit was a great sum. On March 7, the rematch was then swiftly agreed upon for April 10 at Wembley Arena in

London. Parnassus said he would take no legal action. He demanded that Eder's next world title defense should be held in California and under his company's promotional banner should he defeat Caldwell again.

With this whole mess settled once and for all, it didn't take long for Solomons to complicate matters. Still smarting from what he felt was a raw deal on the TV rights in January, Solomons said that he had yet to receive money owed to him. This made him push back the bout until June, but that meant that the timeframe for the contractually obligated rematch had passed, and rather than continue to deal with the headaches, the Jofre camp went back to Parnassus and confirmed that they were all in for Eder's third Californian bout and a date of May 4 was confirmed.

° VA A SÃO FRANCISCO VER A SENSACIONAL LUTA
° EDER JOFRE X HERMAN MARQUEZ
° FAÇA A EXCURSÃO DE OURO
° CONHEÇA LOS ANGELES - SÃO FRANCISCO - NOVA YORK -
NASSAU (BAHAMAS) - MIAMI - MEXICO.
° 22 MARAVILHOSOS DIAS
° TODAS AS VANTAGENS ASSEGURADAS
° TOTALMENTE FINANCIADAS

INFORMAÇÕES:

O T A L — Organização Turística Universal S. A.

RUA MARCONI, 53 — 7.º ANDAR — TELEFONES 35-7385 — 36-4065 — SÃO PAULO

Advertisement for Jofre vs. Marquez vacation packages from Brazil

This was the first time for Eder defending the title as the universally accepted undisputed bantamweight world champion. Marquez brought an unremarkable-looking record of 19-8-1, but the record was somewhat misleading as Marquez had proven himself to be a very competent performer and national champion in addition to winning multiple difficult elimination bouts to earn this opportunity.

San Francisco promoter, Lou Thomas, in previewing the bout in the official fight program for Eder Jofre vs. Herman Marquez, stated: "It took a long time to put this one together, but we finally made it. Eder Jofre and Herman Marquez should be a great fight. Jofre's record speaks for itself. The man's never been beaten. Those who have seen him say he's one of the greatest ever to hold the 118-pound crown. I'm taking a little credit for helping, in some way, getting Marquez this championship shot. When other promoters didn't want his services, I brought him into my club in Kezar Pavilion, where he fought a great battle with Jimmy Abeyta. People around here said it was the best fight between little men in San Francisco in 20 years. I used him again with Ronnie Perez. He stopped Perez. Because of these two solid wins, he got calls for Los Angeles fights. They wanted somebody as an opponent for Jofre. Carlos Hernandez looked like a hot choice. They matched him with Marquez, and Herman upset him in 12 rounds. With Hernandez out of the way, they brought Ignacio Piña in from Mexico with the thought in mind of getting Jofre for him if he beat Marquez. This time Herman turned the trick again. He beat the southpaw. Naturally, I was happy. Here's a fighter out of my club now in a position to fight for the title. It was then I joined with George Parnassus, who first gave Jofre his chance at the crown. Together we worked on this big attraction."

"As you know, we had plenty of headaches caused by postponements and delays. After we set a February date, Jack Solomons, British promoter, threatened to sue the Brazilian Federation if it allowed Jofre to fight Marquez before taking on Ireland's Johnny Caldwell in a rematch. Jofre agreed to give Caldwell the return and asked us to move the Marquez fight to another date. Then the London fight with Caldwell was rescheduled, even without Jofre being notified. That's when he became angry. He said he fulfilled his obligation to meet Caldwell, and as far as we were concerned, he was through with the London fight. A new date was set here, and everybody was glad when the champion got to town."

Herman Marquez was born in Sonora, Mexico but had moved with his parents and siblings to Stockton, California as a youth. He worked in fields picking vegetables around the time he was 12 before turning to boxing. He explained, "I never had the opportunity to be someone else. Boxing is clean, and it keeps you from doing a lot of things you shouldn't. 'Herman,' an old man told me once, 'you won't get hurt in the ring. The ring doesn't hurt you. The outside does.'"

Marquez enjoyed success in the amateur ranks winning the Diamond Belt Amateur Championship in Stockton in 1955, the Golden Gloves Amateur Championship in San Francisco in 1957, and the AAU Amateur Championship in Boston in the same year. As a professional, he was matched with tough competitors from the beginning. He scored a superb victory in only his seventh bout when he defeated the excellent Billy Peacock. Within his first dozen bouts, he had also taken on formidable opponents such as Boots Monroe, Saul Becerril, and Dwight Hawkins. Following a failed bid of Hawkins' state championship in 1959, Marquez scored a victory over Danny Kid

Herman Marquez

to lift the title after Danny Kid had dethroned Hawkins.

Successful defenses against Mario Macias and Manny Elias were followed by an agonizing split decision loss to Jose Medel on March 21 in San Antonio, Texas, for what was now known as the North American championship. *The United Press International* reported: "Joe Medel of Mexico City reigned today as bantamweight champion of North America. He grabbed the crown Tuesday night from Herman Marquez of Stockton, Calif., with an unpopular split decision at the Coliseum. Marquez staggered Medel with a booming left hook in the second round, but after that, neither fighter was hurt. Marquez jabbed effectively with a flicking left that kept Medel off balance most of the night. When the decision was announced, many of the 4,000 fans on hand protested loudly."

Medel had agreed to give Marquez a rematch, but nothing ever came of that, and Medel never defended the title again. Instead, he focused on trying to win the world title. Marquez would regain his championship when the belt was vacated. He defeated Carlos Hernandez and Ignacio Piña in elimination bouts while earning the Max Baer Memorial Award for being the best boxer in Northern California for 1961. At 28 years old, preparing for his first world title opportunity, Marquez was hungry and in his prime.

Eder began serious training for the May 4 bout on April 13 in São Paulo and worked out for the press wearing thick woolen coats, and he stated that his weight was a little over 123 pounds. He conceded that it was getting increasingly more difficult sweating down to the bantamweight limit and that he only intended to fight "three or four more" fights. Eder took advantage of some quality sparring with middleweight Fernando Barreto which Aristides said was of great value to both boxers. He said that as a middleweight, Barreto demanded a lot of physical effort from his son, whereas Eder's speed meant that Barreto had to work extra hard to get his shots in. Barreto also had a fight set for the undercard of the Jofre vs. Marquez show.

Eder arrived in San Francisco on April 24, having flown in from Los Angeles; and from the San Francisco International airport, he took a helicopter with George Parnassus to the Ferry Building where they met the press. Eder talked about the sacrifices he had taken to reach the top of his chosen profession. "To get where I have, I have sacrificed everything; partying, not enough food or drink. This dedication is not compensated for by money, which has a relative value," he said. Marquez expressed gratitude and beamed as he talked about the opportunity that had fallen his way. "This is the biggest break I ever had. I'm going to try hard to do a good job. This is the fight. Not only for myself—I'm not selfish. It is also for my wife and my seven kids and the one that's rounding third and sliding home," he said about his family and a new baby on the way.

A topic of curiosity among press members and event coordinators was that of Eder's vegetarianism. "I will admit being a vegetarian leads to funny experiences. George Parnassus, the promoter, arranged a big welcome. We were met at the airport and brought in by helicopter. There was a parade through the city, and then Mr. Parnassus had scheduled a big signing dinner at the Hotel Whitcomb in downtown San Francisco. Well, they had a lot of people there, including A. K. Cabral and Max Reynaud, diplomats of the Brazilian Consulate in San Francisco. Almost everybody ordered steak. When my wife and I tried to order, the waitress was all disturbed. She called the headwaiter over and said: 'I don't understand, there are supposed to be steaks for all, but this gentleman and his wife say they only want lettuce, beets, peas, and tomatoes, how can that be?' I finally got our message across. But, wherever I go, I run into the same thing. Frankly, I don't like to tell people how to live or what to eat. But I think many of you would enjoy better health if you followed eating habits like mine. I have never had an upset stomach, and I never feel sluggish," he wrote in *Boxing Illustrated*.

Eder set up his camp at Newman's gym at 312 Leavenworth Street, and his chief sparring partner was former Marquez opponent, Ronnie Perez. In the first training session Eder held, he sparred four rounds with Perez, and onlookers noted that he seemed to hold back and didn't show his full repertoire. Some felt he looked a little sluggish, but this was attributed to the fact he could still be suffering from jet lag after his long journey. One week until fight night, Bud Tehaney of *The Oakland Tribune* reported that Eder suffered a scrape above his right eye as the result of an accident he sustained in sparring. He had been sparring with Jesse Alaniz from Houston, and the head guard that Alaniz wore was not sufficiently padded. It scraped on Eder's eye as the two engaged in a clinch.

Eder and Cidinha get in some roadwork

Eddie Mueller took a look at Eder and reported for *The San Francisco Examiner.* "In gym clothes, Jofre resembles (Manuel) Ortiz. The present champ is fairly tall, has a long reach, and has power in his right-hand punch. Jofre doesn't delight in putting the slug on hired hands, merely to please onlookers. He's at the gym for a workout, not to entertain customers. Old-timers will like Jofre, for he doesn't wear a head guard. He feels it works as a handicap. Without one, he keeps moving his head to duck punches and has to be alert every moment he's in the ring."

On the subject of not wearing a head guard, Eder was rather blunt. "I learn how to avoid punches when I don't have a protector on my head. I don't wear one during a fight, so why should it be different in the gymnasium?" he said.

Eder was a clear favorite for the bout, but that did not bother Marquez, who insisted that he thrived in the underdog role. "If I'm not a short ender, I just don't feel right. When I beat Carlos Hernandez and then Ignacio Piña at The Olympic, I was on the short end of 2 to 1 odds," he said. Marquez made a case for himself, suggesting that he was more suited for the long-distance he anticipated that the bout would go. "Look at Jofre's record, and you'll find that he has only gone over ten rounds once in his career. My record will show I fought a 15 rounder and six 12 round fights," he added.

Just a week before the fight, Eder took two days off to rest and not risk further damage to his scraped eye. His father insisted that the rest would do him good and that he had sparred many rounds back in Brazil and was in excellent fighting condition. Eder was back in the gym on Sunday before fight night, and Eddie Mueller reported on the public workout of both boxers. "Marquez continued his boxing chores at West Coast AC today. He went through five rounds of boxing yesterday, three with undefeated San Francisco bantam Mike Galo and two with 142-pound Jonny Bermudez. Galo was instructed to throw right-hand punches and nailed Marquez with a couple of dandies. However, the Stockton boy fought right back without blinking an eye. Jofre boxed five fast rounds with Ronnie Perez, Stockton bantamweight, concentrating on speed and timing rather than power. However, he shook Perez with two hard rights in the final round."

Many press members felt Eder worked under wraps in the buildup to the fight, but that changed during this session when he dropped Perez before a crowd of 300 onlookers. "Now I know he's a cutie. He waited until the joint was packed before he leveled with his best weapon," Art Benjamin said in *The San Francisco Examiner*. Marquez's co-manager Shig Takahashi dismissed Eder's punch. "What if he's a puncher? He won't be the first one Herman's fought. I'm willing to bet Jofre doesn't punch harder than Dwight Hawkins or Boots Monroe or even Billy Peacock. All of them tagged Herman, but none of them ever put him on the floor. Jofre won't either," he said.

Both fighters were examined by Doctor Don Lastreto of the state athletic commission. They were two of the calmest fighters he had ever examined. "They were almost identical. Their blood pressure was 120 over 64. The pulse rate is 64. Reflexes fast and normal," he said. Both fighters had fun in front of the cameras. They participated in some publicity shots before Eder left for lunch, where he ate a large salad. Eder had no problems making weight for this bout as he kept a routine of only two meals a day – lunch and breakfast. Marquez was the same as he adhered to a strict and healthy diet with the only meat consumed being raw fish.

Takahashi talked about all the rounds Marquez trained and remarked that his charge was in the best condition of his career. He sensed the fans were in for a change of champion. Leo Leavitt, a local boxing promoter, concurred and talked about the times he had seen Eder perform. Earlier in Leo Leavitt's career when he was in Brazil publicizing a touring basketball team, he saw Eder fight. "That night, he knocked out Raul Lopez, who was also a good fighter," he said. He also noted that he couldn't believe Eder made 118 pounds and suggested that the vegetarian diet was based upon necessity. The next time he saw Eder box was when Eder defeated Danny Kid. "He rocked the Kid often, but he couldn't put him away. I saw Marquez play with the same Danny Kid in Stockton," he said before suggesting Marquez would finish stronger than Eder and come away with the victory.

The omens looked good for Marquez as every world title bout since Eder's victory over Caldwell saw a new champion with Emile Griffith regaining his welterweight title in a tragic match with Benny Paret, which saw the loser die because of injuries sustained in the fight. Terry Downes surrendered his middleweight title to Paul Pender, and Carlos Ortiz defeated long-time lightweight champion Joe Brown in the other two bouts. Eder appeared relaxed to the press but gave little away. He simply said that he had not seen Marquez fight and had no real set strategy on what he would do. He said that he would consider what Marquez had in the ring and fight accordingly.

Well aware of Eder's fearsome reputation as a heavy hitter but still confident, Marquez said, "This idea of standing there slugging and forgetting defense is OK for a street fight but not in the ring. You have to throw punches to win, but you don't have to stand there wide-open waiting for your opponent to bomb you." Marquez had appeared confident all week and had been impressing onlookers as he performed well in his training sessions, so much so the odds moved from 3-1 to close to 2-1 by fight time as local fight fans backed their guy.

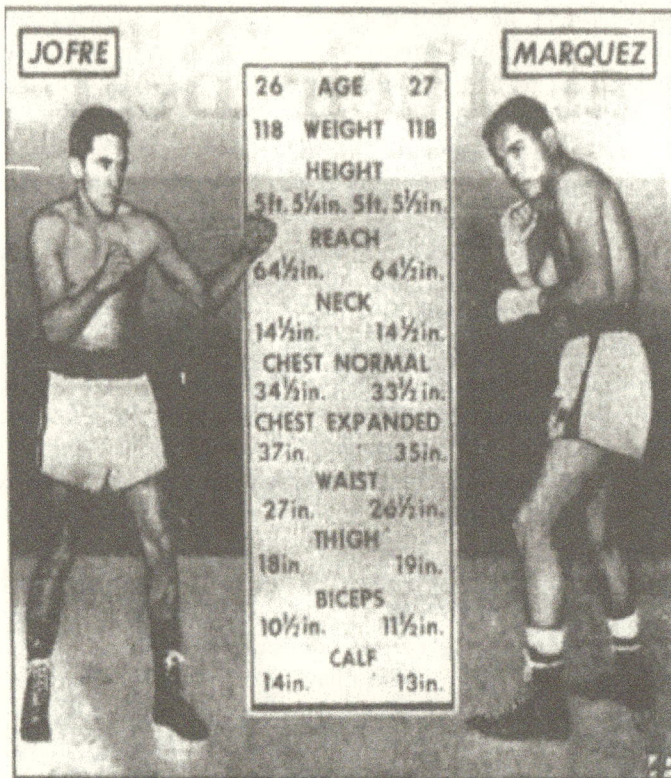

JOFRE / MARQUEZ

	JOFRE		MARQUEZ
AGE	26		27
WEIGHT	118		118
HEIGHT	5ft. 5¼in.		5ft. 5½in.
REACH	64½in.		64½in.
NECK	14½in.		14½in.
CHEST NORMAL	34½in.		33½in.
CHEST EXPANDED	37in.		35in.
WAIST	27in.		26½in.
THIGH	18in.		19in.
BICEPS	10½in.		11½in.
CALF	14in.		13in.

Approximately 6,000 fans attended the Cow Palace to see if the local challenger could overcome the odds and defeat the visiting pound-for-pound great.

Round By Round from *Estadão* and *O Globo*

Round 1

(*Estadão*) The boxers move around cautiously, and Marquez takes the initiative. The contender fires a straight right at Eder, who responds with a left hook. More walking around and studying when Marquez tags Eder's nose with a jab. Eder tries to counter it but receives another two shots, one to the body and one to the head.

(*O Globo*) A cautious beginning with Marquez shooting a short right and receiving a right hook from the champion. The challenger looks for distance with jabs, hits a right to Eder's body, but receives a left to his head in return.

Round 2

(*Estadão*) Marquez lands a nice "one-two" combo and receives the first strong punch of the night right to his chin.

(*O Globo*) Jofre provokes Marquez. He (Jofre) attacks, throws his left, and feints with his right, getting back at Marquez with a left and right combination to the body. At the end of the round, the challenger takes a strong right-hand punch to the chin from Jofre.

Round 3

(*Estadão*) Eder starts with jabs, but Marquez counters with his right hand. Marquez attacks Eder with two hooks to the body. Eder crowds him against the ropes throwing violent punches.

(*O Globo*) Actions already accelerated with Jofre's jabs, and he hits a hook to Marquez's head. Two strong Jofre jabs make Marquez move back, and then he comes forward afterward, with right-hand punches to the champion's stomach and head.

Round 4

(*Estadão*) Marquez lands a shot to the body while Eder was busy throwing jabs. Eder tries to trap him again in the corner, but Marquez gets away. Jofre lands a punch to his head and body.

(*O Globo*) Marquez throws his right to the champion's body and continues moving well and moving his head to avoid Jofre's jabs. He (Marquez) leaves his corner but receives a right to his body and another one to his head, but he fights back and lands a right to Jofre's head.

Round 5

(*Estadão*) Eder picked up the pace of the fight. He calls Marquez to exchange, but Marquez doesn't fall for that. Eder tries everything to close the distance but without a lot of success.

(*O Globo*) Jofre moves towards Marquez to attack him, but the challenger doesn't move forward. Two Jofre punches miss the target, but in the center of the ring, he lands a strong left hook followed by a right-hand punch to the head. Marquez lands a good punch to the champion's body, who then twice gets him (Marquez) to the body and the head, in a combination of punches. Marquez bleeds from his left eye.

Round 6

(*Estadão*) When the fighters meet in the center of the ring, Marquez lands a shot to Eder's head. Eder answers with a combo. Marquez keeps

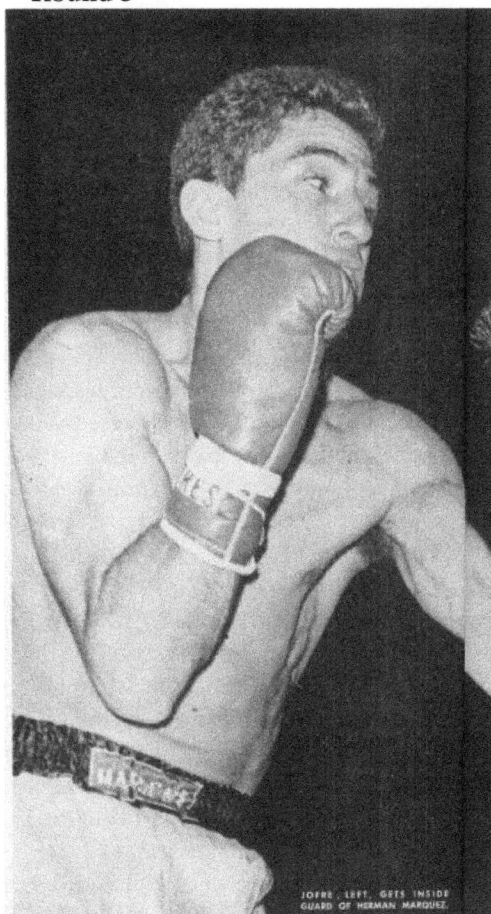

moving around quickly, fearing the chance of being a fixed target for Eder. Eder insists on aiming the shots to the head, and he caught Marquez with a left hook and a right cross.

(*O Globo*) Marquez starts with his left, but Jofre goes forward with his strong jabs. The challenger moves well and puts together good punches to the champion's body. The champion insists on hitting only to his opponent's head.

Round 7

(*Estadão*) Marquez goes first, throwing jabs at Eder's head, who is waiting for him in the center of the ring. The champion absorbed those shots showing no kind of problem. Eder is back up against the ropes, but he throws a combo at the mid-section of Marquez. Up to now, the referee has had an easy night, both fighters respecting each other and not clinching.

(*O Globo*) Marquez's jabs were well received by Jofre, who took, however, three in a row to his face and a right to his body. There was an exchange of punches. Jofre attempts to attack with no consequences, however.

Round 8

(*Estadão*) Eder fires two good straight punches at Marquez, who moves around and throws hooks to try to keep Eder at a safe distance. They got into a violent exchange in the center of the ring. Both fighters get hit. Eder hits Marquez with an uppercut; Marquez throws Eder to the ropes again with a straight right-hand punch to the chin.

(*O Globo*) Jofre, crouched, throws right-hand punches, but the challenger avoids those punches and replies with left hooks. An uppercut from Jofre is answered with a right on the chin, which throws the champion to the ropes.

Round 9

(*Estadão*) At the beginning of the round, the fight seems balanced. The champion's face and body are marked with the shots he has received from the challenger. The round goes on like that, both fighters hitting and getting hit.

(*O Globo*) The fight appears balanced. Marquez hits rights and lefts; (he) receives a right-hand counterpunch but hits the champion's head hard before the bell rings.

Round 10

(*Estadão*) Halfway through the round, Eder knocks Marquez down with an excellent one-two combination. The challenger got up after five seconds, but after another attack, Marquez went down to the ground again. No coming back now.

(*O Globo*) Jofre left his corner quickly, but his first punches were blocked by Marquez. Two rights received by the challenger were replied with punches to the champion's body. Jofre's left and right knock Marquez down, who gets up when the referee gets to the counting of eight seconds. Jofre throws himself ahead, violently hitting a bunch of punches with both his hands. Marquez falls again, and referee Apostoli, without counting, stops the fight, giving Jofre the victory by KO at 2 minutes 15 seconds of the tenth round.

The action started relatively slowly as the two spent the first round sizing one another up, flicking the odd jab while trying to maneuver for positioning and probe for openings. "For once, nobody was telling me I had to make good to be recognized as champion. Maybe it wasn't so good this way. I wasn't stirred up to show anybody. I fought even more deliberately than I usually do. Marquez was fast, but he was in there to jab and run, like a mosquito. I couldn't get my sights lined upon him. I didn't throw a right until the third round," Eder said. The pace picked up in the second round as both fighters showed more attacking intentions. Eder threw a big right-hand, which missed its target but staggered Marquez with a hard right cross in round three. Marquez was tangled in the ropes, but Eder showed exemplary sportsmanship when he afforded the local favorite the time to remove himself from a potentially compromising position. "He staggered back half out of the ropes. I guess some fighters might have gone after him while he was tangled there, but I don't fight that way. I let him come back before I did anything," Eder said.

In the fourth round, it was Marquez's turn to be the aggressor as he threw more shots in the Brazilians direction as Eder was happy to patiently look to pick his spots while measuring Marquez with his jab. In the fifth round, it appeared Eder downloaded all the information on Marquez he required as he began to up the ante. "The next round showed why many observers consider Jofre the finest prizefighter of any weight now in the ring. In it, he launched a rich variety of blows, and hard ones, too, both in combination and singly; he feinted deftly with head, shoulders, and hands and defended with remarkable resourcefulness. It seemed then as though he could finish Marquez whenever he took a fancy to," wrote Gilbert Rogin for *Sports Illustrated*. Eder continued to work towards a stoppage in the sixth round but found a stubborn opponent in Marquez, who fired back jabs to work his way back into the fight.

Marquez took the seventh round with a higher punch output as Eder waited for the right moment to land. In the eighth round, Eder emerged, trying to connect on Marquez with his right hand but was momentarily stunned by the Mexican, who moved in, sensing this was his moment of glory. At the end of the round, Marquez showed confidence as he raised his glove, whereas Eder sat down and inhaled smelling salts.

Marquez got the better of the ninth round as he threw punches intending to try and take the crown. "I continued to lie back, waiting for the openings. Marquez must have taken it to mean I was afraid of him. In the fourth round, he came to me with some good flurries. I figured he needed a little leather to teach him his place. In the fifth round, I went to work on him, left, right, left, right. I think I could have finished him then and there. But I'm a fighter in no hurry, as I've said time and again, and I didn't do much until the eighth round when I drove him back with several rights. He surprised me with a good right that I don't mind telling you stung me. This really got his wind up. In the ninth round, he sailed into me like he was going to do the finishing. The crowd was whooping it up for him, too. I was calm. I knew there were still six rounds in which to go to him," Eder said.

The tenth round showed what separates good fighters from the great ones as Eder kept his composure and turned the fight on its head suddenly. "Like so many of life's endings, this one, too, was unexpected, even startling. The 10th round began as the ninth had ended; no one, save perhaps Jofre, was in the know. Then Jofre struck Marquez with a right, but no more impressive a right than quite a few he had hit all along; certainly, it didn't have the visible effect of the one which carried Marquez through the ropes in the third round. He followed it, however, by a right uppercut like Popeye's, and two lefts which sorely shook Marquez. Then, unopposed, Jofre battered Marquez with a sequence of swift, incisive, and telling punches, about 10 of them. As Jofre paused before hitting him again, Marquez discreetly sat down. It was not valorous, but it was wise," reported *Sports Illustrated*.

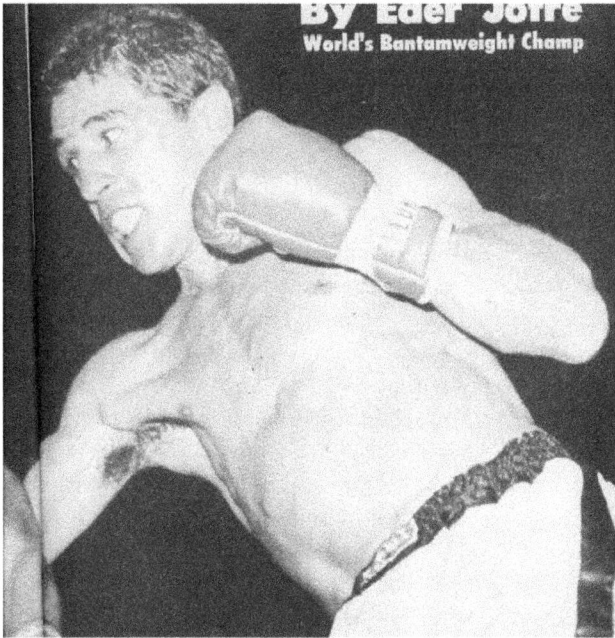

By Eder Jofre
World's Bantamweight Champ

Marquez later said that he was not hurt and that he was taking a rest, but it wasn't long after that breakthrough that Eder scored his second knockdown. Marquez was in trouble by this point, and though he was struggling to his feet, referee Fred Apostoli waved off the fight, preventing Marquez from what would have been a brutal ending. On the second knockdown, Marquez's attempt at rising was stuttered. His initial reaction was to get back to his feet, but then he briefly went to sit down again to further compose himself before pushing himself back up. That was all the incentive Apostoli needed to look out for the safety of the fighter as the bout had quickly turned into a one-sided massacre. Apostoli had Eder ahead by a score of 5-3 when the bout concluded, but the two judges Fred Bottaro and Vern Bybee, had him behind by scores of 0¼-7 and 1-5, respectively.

In his summary of the finish, the champion said: "In the tenth round I measured Marquez and caught him with a right. I followed up with a right uppercut and then two lefts. Now he was in real bad shape. I put together a string of solid punches, there must have been about ten of them, and he plumped down. He took a count of four, waited out the rest of the mandatory eight. I charged him and pounded him some more with both hands. He fell to the floor, and he tried to get up and then went down again. Then the referee stopped it. Some people in the crowd booed. Why? I only would have kept knocking him down. There is no reason why an outmatched, brave boy should be hurt."

"I'm not a bad loser," Marquez kept saying in his dressing room. "I'm just telling the truth. I wasn't hurt. I was robbed! Jofre didn't knock me out. He didn't even knock me down. The officials told me before the fight I could take as many eight counts as I wanted, and I was doing just that. I went down deliberately. I was playing it smart," he said. "Apostoli was influenced by Paret's death," said co-manager Al Avila, about the recent tragedy in the rubber match between Emile Griffith and Benny Paret, which saw Paret fatefully die as the result of the injuries sustained in that bout.

Nat Fleischer agreed with the stoppage of the bout, saying that Apostoli was "well within his rights when he called a halt with Marquez on his knees." Fleischer said that while he felt Eder was in front in the contest, he felt he was well below his best form. Fleischer added: "They saw Jofre suddenly lash out with a vicious attack that dropped Marquez twice. When he went down the second time, he rested helplessly on his knees, and one look at the fighter was sufficient for Apostoli to call a halt. When the referee started walking towards Jofre to raise his hand, the count of eight had been reached, and the challenger was still on the canvas. It is doubtful he could have regained his feet in time. Bringing the Paret death into the picture as an excuse was a bad taste on the part of Marquez and his handlers."

The knockdowns suffered by Marquez were the first time he had ever been off his feet in a fight. He had performed admirably and was praised for the fight he put up in his challenge to Eder's title, but the champion had a little too much class and proved his worth when he turned the tables on Marquez.

Wilbur Adams, writing for the *Sacramento Bee*, had the fight scored one-sided for Eder at the time of the stoppage scoring only one round for Marquez. In his report of the bout, he said the only round where Marquez did something significant was in the ninth.

In the days following the bout before Eder left for Brazil, he was offered $60,000 to return to California and defend his titles in a rematch with Jose Medel in Los Angeles. It appeared this would come to fruition until the Jofres arrived back in Brazil and Aristides shot down the idea that his son was going to defend his title in America anytime soon. He felt Eder had not been given a fair shake on the scorecards in the fight with Marquez, and there was a plot to take his title from him by the powers that be. "Eder was fighting easily against Marquez without extending himself fully. The advantage that the two judges gave in favor of Marquez was without coherence, ridiculous, and completely unrealistic. We have been alerted in this respect, and we concluded that the North American promoters intended at any price to take the title away from Eder. For this, it would be enough for one of his opponents just to hold up until the end of the fight without being knocked down. Eder won't risk his world championship in the United States again," he said.

Eder was not so scathing of the judges and simply said that he felt he performed below his best. "It just wasn't my day. It was a hard fight but not my toughest," he said. The quotes by Aristides took Parnassus by surprise. "Jofre's father must have been misquoted," he said. "It's ridiculous. I've got no comment. I won't dignify the story with a comment. It's not worth paying any attention to...It's just not true. Everybody who saw the fight thought Marquez was ahead. Jofre simply wasn't at his best, and Marquez put up his greatest fight. I can't believe his father would say such a thing. They were treated like royalty in San Francisco," Parnassus added.

Marquez did not stick around too long in the sport after the heartbreaking defeat against Eder as he defended his North American title one more time before losing a non-title bout against Jorge Salazar before focusing his time on his job as a longshoreman and raising his children. He retired later in the year with a final record of 20-10-1 with six knockouts.

Elsewhere in Brazilian sport, the national football team succeeded in defending its World Cup in June when they became the first (and still only) team to defend the tournament. Although star player Pele had been injured early in the tournament, Brazil was too powerful as they eliminated England and host nation Chile before defeating Czechoslovakia 3-1 in the final.

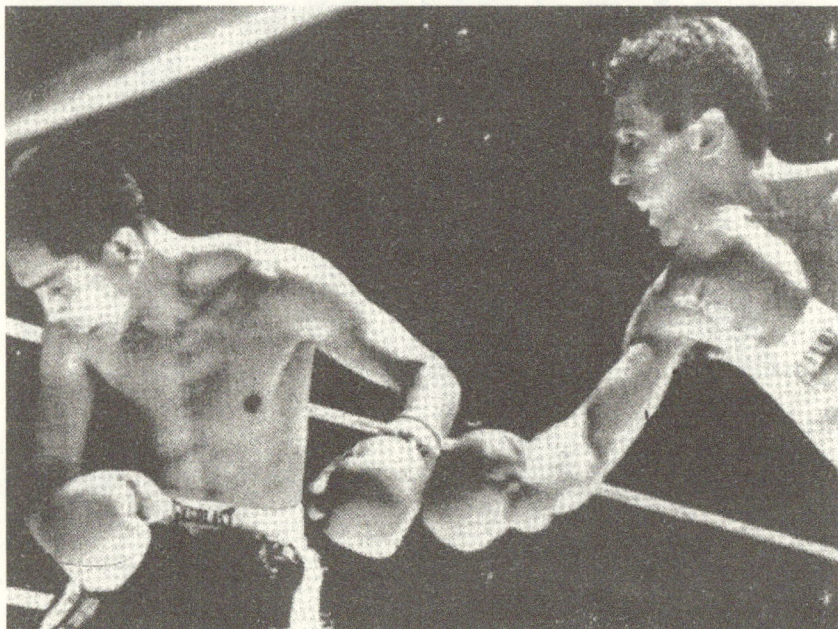

Fight 47, vs. Jose Medel II, September 11, 1962

After the Marquez victory, it had been confirmed that Eder's next title defense would be against top contender Jose Medel. George Parnassus flew out to Brazil on June 24 to convince the Jofres that the bout should be staged in Los Angeles or Mexico. Tijuana emerged as a potential venue as Lupe Sanchez, manager of Medel, had pleaded with Parnassus not to have the fight go to Brazil. A lucrative $65,000 was the offer to go to Mexico, but, as the champion, Eder and his father played hardball. "If they offer me double of what I would make fighting in Brazil, I will accept fighting abroad, but nothing less than that," Eder was quoted saying by *Estadão* on June 24.

PEDRO LUIZ

TRANSMITE HOJE

O LOGO APÓS À MEIA NOITE

EDER **JOFRE** X **MEDEL**

BANDEIRANTES

FOLHA DE S. PAULO

Aristides went further in saying they simply would not be leaving Brazil for this bout, stating: "Even if Eder receives half of the purse, we want the fight here." While Katzenelson, Aristides, and Sanchez went back and forth with Parnassus acting as the mediator, Eder was busy playing football with friends. He was confident his team would get him a good deal and that he would be defending his title in Brazil. During a cocktail party held at the Othon Palace Hotel in downtown São Paulo, George Parnassus confirmed the fight between Eder and Medel for September 6. The championship bout was announced and would be held at Ibirapuera. Eder's share of the purse was set to be around $50,000, with Medel set to receive $10,000 plus expenses, accommodation, and airfare for his team.

The rematch was significant in Brazil. The classic encounter two years earlier in Los Angeles was only heard on the radio by most Brazilians. "As an athlete, I gave him a chance. He requested a chance to fight me again, and I agreed but this time in Brazil," said Eder. Eder had not forgotten how brutal the fight in Los Angeles was, as he recalled how Medel was his most formidable opponent. Eder had three significant differences in his favor. He now fought at home before his fans instead of in front of the Mexican crowd he was up against in California. Due to that grueling victory, Eder said he felt nobody could beat him, and last, he had less trouble boiling down to the bantamweight limit this time. Eder had gone back into training camp on July 1, which would give him a little over two months of training. Helping him with his sparring was younger brother Mauro, now 15 and training as an amateur in the flyweight division.

Since the first fight, Medel had been very impressive, going unbeaten in ten matches. He wasted little time after that defeat. He was back in the ring and defeated Manny Elias only two months after the 1960 elimination bout. He closed out that year by once again beating fan favorite Toluco Lopez, which caused further ire among Mexican fight fans. Lopez had run an impressive string of victories since losing his Mexican title to Medel. Among his victims were Danny Kid, Eduardo Guerrero, Manny Elias, and Eloy Sanchez. Medel broke their hearts when he knocked Lopez out in what was heralded as a classic fight by local fight fans. Medel's thrilling knockout victory was especially painful to Lopez and his fans as it effectively finished him as a serious contender for world honors. Unfortunately, this signature victory for Medel hurt his popularity among his countrymen. "That was his mistake, to have beaten Toluco. The public never forgave him," recalled former bantamweight world champion Raul "Raton" Macias in 2001.

The year 1961 had been an awe-inspiring campaign for Medel as he gained a consistency he had lacked earlier in his career. He started the year off with a draw against Hiram Bacallao of Cuba before lifting the North American championship against Herman Marquez. A couple of tune-up fights in Mexico were followed up by an impressive two-fight tour of Japan. He scored an impressive knockout victory over Mitsunori Seki in five rounds on August 31. This fight grabbed a lot of attention in Japan as Seki was fresh off a split decision loss against world flyweight champion Pone Kingpetch of Thailand. Seki had defeated the future world champion Chartchai Chionoi, also of Thailand, and had defeated Leo Espinosa. *The Associated Press* reported: "Jose Medel, Mexico's bantamweight champion, Thursday night dropped Mitsunori Seki of Japan for a six-count in the second round, and then put the inexperienced Japanese down for good in the fifth of a scheduled ten-round fight here. Seki, 19, started a fifth-round flurry in the corner, but the Mexican landed a solid right hook to the jaw that spun the Japanese fighter around three times before he dropped. He was counted out 36 seconds after the round started. The game Japanese fought from the third round with his left eye closed."

That victory was followed up with a win over Haruo Sakamoto, who was fresh off a victory over Chionoi. Medel closed out the year by returning to Mexico to defend his national title when he avenged an earlier loss by knocking out the impressive Ignacio Piña, who had been on a stellar run of his own. On March 29, Medel was back in Japan, this time scoring an impressive victory over one of Eder's former opponents, Sadao Yaoita. Medel used his jab in swelling both of the Japanese fighter's eyes as he claimed a close, but clear decision in front of 9,000 fans. Due to his showings in Japanese boxing rings, Medel had become quite a fan favorite and was far more adored among Japanese boxing aficionados than he was in Mexico.

Medel arrived in Brazil on August 15, giving him plenty of time to acclimatize. He said that he knew Eder well from their first fight, so he would not need to do any special training. Medel conceded that he knew the champion was a great fighter, but he said he was confident in his ability, and he hoped that he would take the title back to Mexico. His manager Lupe Sanchez said that before the knockout blow Eder landed in their previous encounter that the fight was balanced and that his fighter had the Brazilian in trouble three times during the contest.

Medel said that he wished to see Pele play while he was in Brazil, citing that he was a big fan of the player. His training camp was headquartered at Wilson Russo Gym, and one of the main sparring partners was Ivan Cipriano. *O Globo* had a look into his training camp and reported: "Talking about his practice, he had the opportunity to reveal that he always exercises around noon, which is the opposite of most boxers, who prefer to do so in the evening. Every day, besides his morning running, he practices for an hour and a half, doing rope rounds, sandbags, punching ball, sparring, and a little gym work with no worries about his weight, which is usually 54 kilos (119 pounds)."

Medel arrived on Father's Day and Eder was spending the day at his father's gym. He sparred with Oripes dos Santos and trained in thick woolen coats and wrapped himself under a blanket between exercises. Aristides said that Eder was weighing around 123 pounds and would have no issues getting down to the weight limit. Eder talked about the first fight with Medel and acknowledged that while the Mexican had improved since that night, he had confidence, and he could take advantage of the home crowd behind him this time. "The fight day I had to take off an excess of three pounds, making the bantamweight limit, also facing the fans, which in Los Angeles were completely favorable to Medel. Now, calmer and fighting at home, I have the impression I can win, although I know that Medel advanced a lot in these two years," he said. Aristides said that he was expecting an even more difficult match than the one in Los Angeles and pointed to the quality that the Mexican possessed in his left hand in addition to his body attack.

Medel showed himself to be in excellent condition as he worked out in front of George Parnassus on August 25, going through all of his exercise

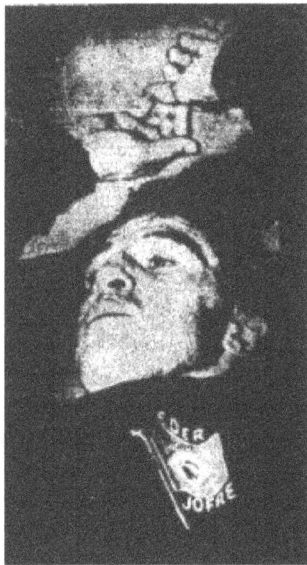

routines and sparring four rounds. Parnassus had caught a cold, perhaps due to torrential downpour in São Paulo, but toughed it out to see the Mexican up close, and he was very impressed with what he saw. "Jose is in great shape. It's not going to be easy for Eder," he told the local scribes. Those on hand at this training session remarked that Medel appeared to be in better condition than he had been in Los Angeles two years earlier. The same day, Eder faced two new sparring partners, lightweight Angelo Gutierrez and middleweight Furtado Leite. With each, Eder went three rounds; Gutierrez, being the smaller of the two, helped make him move around faster, whereas Leite, taller and heavier, forced Eder to go for harder exchanges.

On August 23, the National Boxing Association changed its name to the World Boxing Association, so Eder was no longer the NBA world champion but the WBA champion. The victory over Caldwell had cemented his status as the only world champion in his weight class, but now the title had a different name. On this day, Dogalberto went to see Medel in action at Wilson Russo Gym, and he was impressed with what he saw. He said that he was impressed with the speed and precision of the Mexican and that he appeared to practice a counter-punching strategy when he sparred with Ivan Cipriano.

On August 26, both fighters went to watch a big local football match between city rivals, São Paulo and Corinthians. Medel, like Eder, was a big fan of football, so he also attended the derby match. The game, played at São Paulo's Morumbi Stadium, ended in a 1-1 draw.

Popular Argentine lightweight Jaime Gine was booked onto the undercard to face Sebastiao Nascimento for the South American Championship. He insisted on getting in some sparring with Eder ahead of the show. Gine had recently lost in a bid for the national title in Argentina when he was defeated by Nicolino Locche but held a significant size advantage over Eder. The sparring was said to resemble a real fight as the two went back and forth. Eder said it was the best sparring he had received.

The following day, on August 28, Eder put some much-needed roadwork in as the skies cleared up. Then he sparred with another Argentine, this time Ricardo Gonzalez. Gonzalez was also in town due to appear on the show where he would be facing Eder's stablemate, Oripes dos Santos, for the South American featherweight title. Gonzalez had also been one of Eder's sparring partners for the first encounter with Medel back in Los Angeles. Once again, it was another hard sparring session as they went toe-to-toe for four rounds with Eder having Gonzalez backing up in the fourth round before winding down his exercises for the day. The session was said to have been a good one with both fighters getting in beautiful shots early, but Eder started connecting in combinations and ultimately began to hurt the Argentine.

Eder was still a little overweight due to a lack of roadwork the previous week. In contrast, Medel was underweight and feeling healthy. In the afternoon, Medel completed his training at the gym, first sparring two violent rounds with featherweight Antonio Luiz Paiva before he sparred with amateur bantamweight Joel Gomes. He wrapped up his day with speed ball exercises and a few rounds on the heavy bag before winding down with some jump rope. At a public workout on August 30, Eder confirmed that he was now at the correct weight after doubling down on his training. He added: "Now, I am going to have a good dinner followed by a bowl of yogurt," when he finished his workout. Medel had an easier session as he was a little slower with his jump rope and sparred half the rounds as he was trying to avoid losing too much weight.

On September 2, *Estadão* ran a story saying that while Medel had looked sharp and strong in the gym, Eder appeared below par. They reported that he sparred four rounds with Gonzalez again, but this time, he struggled to connect on his sparring partner while receiving some body shots in return. This came as some surprise as Eder had been looking sharp in the preceding sessions.

As the fighters wound down their training, the news came on September 4, only two days out from the bout, that the event would be pushed back a week. Abraham Katzenelson and Aristides said that Eder had suffered a shoulder injury.

Rumors circulated that the delay was because the bout had not yet sold out despite being advertised as the biggest boxing event ever staged in the country. The noise out of the Mexican camp was different, however. They felt that Eder was struggling to make the weight and was using a "dirty strategy" to buy time. Those comments were shot down by Aristides. "It's a stupid accusation. There is no foundation at all. I feel sorry that the Mexican press present in our daily activities has not sent the correct news. It's been ten days since Eder made the weight for this fight." Eder agreed with his father's opinion: "They just want to provoke me. They aren't going to succeed. I'm relaxed."

Eder returned to training the following day, and O *Globo* reported:

"With a coat on, Eder Jofre restarted his practices at Academia Brasileira do Boxe, doing four rounds with Ricardo Gonzales (sp), South American lightweight champion. He also did two shadowboxing rounds covered up with thick blankets and a plastic cover. In his practice with 'Gonzalito,' Eder shook him with a hook to the liver in the third round and a hook to the chin at the end of the practice. In a general way, Eder left a good impression."

Medel said that the postponement wouldn't affect him and that he was in excellent condition. "I waited two years to fight for the title, so I can wait an extra five days," he said.

The delay gave Parnassus an extra couple of days to promote the event. He said that he felt Eder was an almost unbeatable fighter and that the only boxer capable of defeating him was Medel. He noted that Eder was in the best shape he had ever seen him, whereas Medel was incredibly determined to win the title. The weather rendered training plans problematic days before the re-scheduled date, so roadwork was cut short for both teams.

However, since both fighters were already at weight, they worked in the gym.

Eder was very relaxed on fight week, confident that now he had Medel in front of his own fans and that he was not in a panic to make weight. Many believed this fight would be as difficult as the first bout due to both boxers' improvement. Medel, now 24, had found some true consistency for the first time in his career and by consensus was the number two fighter in the division.

On September 10, the day before the bout, Eder stayed in bed longer than usual because he wanted to watch a football game on television. He did his final workout from 10 am until around 5 pm when he finished with a massage. Some members of the media felt that Eder could benefit from a more intense workload leading to his fights. That notion was shot down by Aristides, who knew his son put everything into his sessions and was a true professional. "It was suggested to us to adopt a practice routine with a one-hour interval between morning running and some more in the afternoon. Eder practices for less than half that time and has never been out of breath except for his first fight with Medel when special circumstances obliged him to spend more energy outside the ring than in it," Aristides said. He also pointed to his son's excellent physical condition, great temperament, and lack of vices.

Roughly 150 of Medel's fans had traveled over to Brazil from Mexico and California in support of him and were on hand for his last training session on the eve of the bout. The Mexican performed 12 rounds of various exercises from shadowboxing to the punching bag and announced to the press, "I am ready."

Eder: menos altura e mais envergadura

A biometria de Eder e Medel identifica-se em determinados pontos: o torax de ambos (normal e dilatado) tem medidas iguais, bem como o tornozelo. Ambos calçam sapatos do mesmo tamanho. O mexicano é ligeiramente mais alto que o "Galo de Ouro" mas tem envergadura menor. O campeão mundial tem seus membros (braços e pernas) mais desenvolvidos. Eis a ficha biometrica dos dois boxadores:

	EDER	MEDEL
Idade	26	24
Altura	1 m 64	1 m 65
Pescoço	39 cm	37 cm
Torax (normal)	91 cm	91 cm
Torax (dilatado)	97 cm	97 cm
Envergadura	1 m 67	1 m 64
Biceps	31 cm	29 cm
Antebraço	28 cm	25 cm
Pulso	17 cm	16 cm
Cintura	75 cm	77 cm
Coxa	49 cm	40 cm
Barriga da perna	33 cm	31 cm
Tornozelo	22 cm	22 cm
Pé	39	30

Tale of the tape

...E O ESPETÁCULO SE REPETIRÁ:

Medel não veio só pela bolsa:

CAUTELA, EDER!...

CARTEL DE JOFRE
Lutas 46 - Vitórias 43
33 por KO - 10 por pontos
Empates 3 - Derrotas 0

Giné x Nascimento

CARTEL DE MEDEL
Lutas 73 - Vitórias 52
34 por KO - 18 por pontos
Empates 4 - Derrotas 17

Gonzalez x Oripes

--- PROGRAMA ---

1.ª LUTA - Meio-Médios - Jorge Saciman x Rodolfo Moyano.

2.ª LUTA - Médios - Abrasão de Souza x Miguel Aguero.

3.ª LUTA - Pelo título Sul-Americano dos Pesos Pena - Oripes dos Santos (brasileiro) x Ricardo Gonzales (argentino).

4.ª LUTA - Pelo título Sul-Americano dos Pesos Leves - Sebastião Nascimento (brasileiro) x Jaime Giné (argentino).

5.ª LUTA - Pelo título Mundial dos Pesos Galo - Eder Jofre (brasileiro) x Joe Medel (mexicano).

297

On fight night, Medel was the first of the two boxers to show up at the arena and went straight to his locker room. Eder arrived around 10 pm with Cidinha and his mother and other relatives. The first thing he did when he arrived was to see that they were situated. He then went to talk to some of the press reporters backstage before going to his locker room to get ready for the bout. *Folha* was behind the scenes to look into the camps of both of the contestants:

"Lupe Sanchez stopped his pupil's rest to prepare his hands for the gloves. Medel lifted, partially, with his muscles contracted. His coach kept himself serious and focused. Everything they did in the locker room was uncontrolled and nervous. To those who would come to him (radio broadcasters and reporters), Medel would always give the same answer, almost rehearsed, trying hard to keep control: (In Spanish) 'Tough fight...but I'm prepared, more experienced...' On Medel's locker room seat, there were four medallions of popular saints: San Martin, two Holy Mary pictures, and a scene of Christ's crucifixion. There was a big silence in his room, and then someone told him: 'Nice shoes, Medel.' 'My dad made them,' he answered with a serious face and the voice of a shy boy. In Eder Jofre's locker room, it is a mess. Many people, intimate friends, journalists, and the champion, laughing and telling jokes. Someone asks if Eder knows that Medel is asleep. 'No, I didn't know that. But to me, it would be better if he slept later.' Everyone laughs. Eder laughs too. A lot. He gets agitated, jumps, and moves his head in every direction, laughing hard with little purpose. The champion curves his body to tie his shoelaces. We ask him if he is nervous. 'We always get nervous when it's time to fight,' he said. Really? Afraid? We ask. Then he raises his voice to answer: 'Yeah. At the end of the day, we always need to go there and do what it takes,' he responds."

"Then, Eder continued talking, always loud, always laughing. The more his fight time approached, the more he laughed. Lupe Sanchez, Medel's coach, suddenly opened Eder's locker room door before the boxers were called to the ring. He walked up to the champion, grabbed Eder's fists with both hands, and put them together, locking them, and spoke to Eder in Spanish. 'Good luck. May the best man win,' as Eder's team looked on surprised, Sanchez continued. 'You know you have all our sympathy,' and then Eder thanked him before Sanchez left the room to get his fighter ready to walk to the ring. 'What a great guy, huh?' Eder said out loud to his team."

Medel entered the ring at 11:30 pm wearing an elegant black velvet robe over his black shorts with red stripes and handmade black-suede shoes. Eder entered the ring three minutes later to thunderous applause as he wore a blue velvet robe with a gold bantam cock stitched to the back. He took off his robe and unveiled his ring attire for the evening, which consisted of black shoes and white shorts. The two boxers met at the center of the ring, where they posed for photos as they listened to the referee's instructions before touching gloves.

Round By Round from *Estadão* & *O Globo*

Round 1

(*Estadão*) Eder and Medel touch gloves and stay far away studying each other. They poised themselves and exchanged a couple of jabs. Eder tries a right cross; Medel blocked it and countered with a hook. The Brazilian tries a one-two without success. Eder lands a cross at Medel's face as Medel touches Eder's face. The round ends in a draw.

(*O Globo*) Long studies at the start of the round. Medel tries a hook that Eder blocks. The study phase is disrupted by Eder's violent left hook that Medel defended with his elbow. Tie.

Round 2

(*Estadão*) They keep a little distance between them; Eder, with his left hand upfront, tries to close the gap with jabs. Medel is avoiding the fight. Eder throws a straight right-hand punch and lands. Medel counters with a punch to his head. They stayed apart for a while towards the end of the round before Eder lands a strong right cross. Round goes to Eder: 20 to 19.

(*O Globo*) Eder's quick and strong left connects on the challenger's head, and then he follows with a sequence to the body and head combined with a one-two, up and down. A right cross lands on the Mexican's head, who replies by slightly touching "Jofrinho's" face. Eder won the round.

Round 3

(*Estadão*) Medel tries an attack; Eder backs away, throwing jabs. Medel goes off again, throws a punch but misses and receives a light blow to the face in return. Medel tries the midsection and lands a shot at Eder's liver. Eder counters but misses. Medel throws hooks. Eder responds, and Medel blocks. They exchange jabs with no effect. Eder attacks and Medel hits the backpedal. He is against the ropes. The Brazilian tries a straight right but misses. Medel walks away from him to the center of the ring. Eder goes after him again and puts him against the ropes. End of the round which goes to Eder: 20 to 18.

(*O Globo*) Eder continues with the initiative, and Medel, with no sidestepping, but with perfect blocking and notion of distance, avoids the hardest punches. Twice the challenger hits Eder's liver, who at the end of the round attacks him again with insistence and efficiency. Eder's round.

Round 4

(*Estadão*) Medel and Eder keep fighting from a safe distance. They feint each other. Right after it, Medel lands two shots and touches Eder's face. Eder swivels around Medel, stops at his left side, and lands a right hook followed by two cross punches. Eder tries a long right-hand punch, and Medel dodges it. Eder throws another right cross and misses again. The Mexican attacks but receives a left hook in return. The round goes to Eder: 20 to 19.

(*O Globo*) Eder tries his famous "shotgun punch" but is countered with two hooks. He takes the Mexican to the ropes and three times they exchange punches with no advantage for either fighter. A good left hook from Eder gets a quick response from Medel. Tie.

Round 5

(*Estadão*) Eder attacked. Medel runs around the ring alongside the ropes and avoids a straight punch but doesn't respond. Eder keeps coming at him and crosses his left, blocked by Medel. Eder hits him with a jab. The two boxers get into a violent exchange of punches. Eder hits Medel with a straight right, and Medel backs away to the ropes. The Brazilian keeps coming. Medel quickly escapes from the ropes and lands two crosses on Eder. The Brazilian also lands a cross and two more shots. They engage in a vicious exchange; Medel lands a powerful shot at Eder, which throws him to the ropes. The Brazilian lands a left hook and a straight right. The Mexican stays against the ropes, where he takes a combination of left and right-hand punches. Medel bleeds. One punch lands exactly on Medel's chin, and he goes down to the canvas. The bell rang when the referee was already counting seven—Eder: 20 to 16.

(*O Globo*) Medel gets back with his hair and body wet, but the referee doesn't notice. Eder starts impetuously, cornering him onto the ropes. Eder lands four hard punches in a row with his right hand to Medel's head. Eder hits him, then takes him to the corner, and lands an incredible violent barrage of punches. Medel falls. Referee Joaquim Arvas starts counting, but the bell rings on the eighth second. Eder won the round easily.

Round 6

(*Estadão*) Eder takes advantage of his opponent's condition and goes after him, pinning him against the ropes. The Mexican escapes and keeps running away from him. Medel tries to respond but gets hit by a left hook and a straight right. Eder misses a straight right but lands two right crosses that put Medel to sleep. Knockout.

(*O Globo*) Medel, still shaken, returns bravely to the fight. He doesn't grab and he avoids punches. Eder forces the fight, hitting him violently. Eder corners him onto the ropes and lands another series of punches. The challenger falls for the second time, already out of mind, and the counting goes to 10. Eder Jofre won by KO after 1 minute and 11 seconds!

Despite Medel's excellent form since their Los Angeles bout two years prior, Eder was much more dominant in the rematch. Eder scored a more straightforward victory than was the case in the first bout. The fight started with the two boxers boxing patiently, waiting for openings. They examined each other to see if there were any differences from the previous encounter.

The action wasn't thrilling in the early going. The São Paulo fans watched on the edge of their seats in anticipation that a firefight could start at any moment. Eder warmed up and took the initiative in the fourth round with a vicious attack using all the punches in his arsenal. He showed incredible ability as he was dishing out the punishment. He was expertly avoiding the Mexican's famed counterpunches. Eder scored a knockdown at the end of the fifth round. He moved in and punished Medel with blows, punctuated by a short-left hook that dumped the challenger in the corner of the ring.

At the halfway point of the sixth round, the challenger worked Eder into a corner and caught him with a tremendous hook. For a moment, the Brazilian fans held their breath in fear. Their hero remained on his feet and responded with combinations that pushed his opponent back to the center of the ring. At this point, Eder finished him with a devastating cross that turned off Medel's lights before he had even hit the canvas. Remembering the rematch victory over the Mexican, Eder said, "Poor man. I say that because, on the day of the fight, he even cried. He saw me up there totally fit. I didn't have to lose weight. This fight was much easier than the first one."

Given the manner of the victory and the fact that the match was much less complicated than their previous encounter despite Medel's improvement, Eder proved he was a fighter for the ages.

Eder visited Medel in the locker room after the fight, and the two shared a warm embrace and exchanged pleasantries. "Medel, you are the greatest boxer from Mexico," Eder told him. "Yes, but out of luck," the Mexican responded. Eder asked, "Why out of luck?" "Because I had the luck to be contemporary with you Eder. You are invincible."

Renato Pires reporting for *The Ring* from São Paulo wrote: "Although statements have appeared that Jofre is having weight trouble and will vacate the throne to enter the higher division, he disproved the rumors by easily making 117 1/2 for the Medel bout and displaying his usual strength and speed. Medel was half a pound less. The victory was the thirteenth consecutive knockout for the champion. The 26-year-old title holder was a 3-1 favorite and proved the odds were reasonable by how he handled his opponent, who had fought ten fights without a loss since his last meeting with Eder."

Medel and the Mexicans were very gracious in the aftermath, offering no excuses, only praise for the champion. "He is a strong young man, and his right hand is very powerful. In front of Eder's punches and the speed with which he applied them, I felt like I should accept his violent fight. That's what I did. He, however, caught me twice in a row, with a series of very strong punches, and it wasn't possible to recover the second time," Medel said.

"Eder is a good puncher. I don't believe there currently is a boxer as good in the whole world, with such a punch. For this reason, I believe that if he continues to fight, the Brazilian will keep his title for a very long time," said Medel's manager, Lupe Sanchez. "I effectively told Medel to keep his distance from Eder. I believed that that was the most efficient way to face him. However, I should also say that Jose fought very well. It's tough to fight back against Eder's punches," he added. When the subject of a potential third installment of this series was brought up, Sanchez didn't seem so optimistic. "I don't think there is a chance," he said. Medel's trainer Enrique Huerta broke down crying in the locker room, saying the bout had been "a fatal surprise" to him.

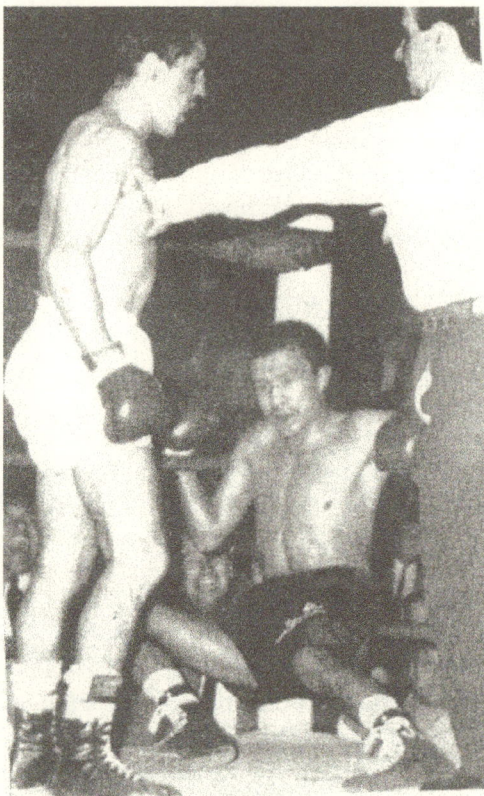

For referee Joaquin Arvas who'd come from Argentina to officiate the bout, it was his first time seeing Eder in action, and he was extremely impressed: "Eder is a champion that should last much longer. He is a true champion," he said. He commented that the bout was one of the easiest of his career to officiate, such was the class and sportsmanship of both fighters. "I had no work. The fight was very clean, with no fouls. I didn't need to set the boxers apart, not even once, or to warn them about anything. It's pleasant to work in a fight like this between two great athletes," he said. Arvas praised the efforts of the beaten man, stating that he was a dangerous fighter and a good boxer.

For Eder and his camp, it was pandemonium on the way from the ring to the locker room where Aristides and Waldemar had to tell fans and media they could not enter. Eder stood outside, answering questions and signing autographs before taking a shower. Eder was asked questions on whether this would be his last bout to which he said he did not know. "We'll see…it's been only 10 minutes since I left the ring…I need time to think about what I'm going to do. Anyhow, when I think it's convenient to stop, I won't hesitate," he said.

Eder also offered praise for his gutsy opponent. "He (Medel) was very demanding. He is a great boxer and was well prepared. However, fortunately, I also came up to the ring in excellent condition. I think that you guys, chroniclers, can analyze better than me how the fight was. What I can say is that I made decisions as quickly as I could. When I realized that Medel was dizzy, I didn't waste my time. I attacked him with strength because I had the Los Angeles experience and knew that he could get it together. By the way, he was able to get up after the punishment I gave him at the end of the fifth round. In the second half of the second round, he hit me with a left on the liver, which reminded me of the drama in Los Angeles, but he did not realize, and he gave me time to get it together," he said.

Folha reported on what had been described as the greatest night for Brazilian boxing in a story titled, "This right hand is worthy of a crown."

"Knocking out Jose Medel in the sixth round, Eder Jofre kept his world bantamweight title in the middle of the most glorious night of Brazilian boxing. A little bit before, in the previous fights of the program in front of an audience that was only half of what was expected, Brazil had accomplished another two titles: Oripes dos Santos became South American featherweight champion, beating Argentine Ricardo Gonzalez by points in 15 rounds and Sebastião Nascimento became South American lightweight champion, beating Jaime Guinê by points in 15 rounds, the most thrilling ones for our audience. In the first fight of the program, Brazilian Abrão de Sousa defeated Miguel Aguero from Argentina by a large points difference over 10 rounds and on the final fight of the program (after the world title contest), in front of an audience that was only sort of interested in the ring because it was celebrating Eder's victory, Jorge Sacomã, another Brazilian in the world ranking, knocked out Argentine Rodolfo Movano in the middleweight division. Ibirapuera gymnasium had a party atmosphere. Not completely crowded, there were a lot of women in the audience and the venue was even explored for a political campaign: folders and posters talking about how wonderful the candidates were. But the life of the party was Eder, whose right hand is worth a crown."

ASSIM ÉDER DERROTOU JOSÉ MEDEL NO 6º "ROUND"

Medel Poderá Abandonar o Boxe!

Alterações na Equipe do Flamengo

SEM PROBLEMAS AS ESTRÊLAS

The day after the bout, Eder and Cidinha drove down to Rio de Janeiro, where they would take a week's vacation. Medel had planned to stay in Brazil to visit Rio for four days before heading home. He appeared in good spirits the day after the bout as he woke late and went for lunch before enjoying the city. Later, he boarded his 7 pm flight, which would see him connect in Rio before arriving home in Mexico City.

Medel said that he didn't feel bad about the fight and that "Eder is a stupendous fighter, a champion for all his merits and the best bantamweight in the world." Medel's mother, Esperanza Guevara de Medel, passed out when she heard the result of the fight and said she hoped her son would retire. "He had promised to leave the ring within a year, but because of what happened, who knows if he will leave earlier? I would rather be poor and hungry than to suffer again in every fight my son has," she said. Medel had to cut his time in Rio short after he received a telegram from his pregnant wife. She was not feeling well, so he went back to Mexico a little earlier than planned.

1962 Results

Eder Jofre KO10 John Caldwell
Eder Jofre KO10 Herman Marquez
Eder Jofre KO6 Jose Medel

1963

Before the Medel rematch, there was an agreement in principle for Eder to defend his title in Japan if he defeated Medel. This had come amid much speculation that a Jofre vs. Halimi fight would finally come to fruition. Due to Halimi's refusal to meet Eder when he held a claim to the title, Katzenelson, perhaps administrating a dosage of spite to the Frenchman, swiftly accepted the offer from Japan to defend the title against Katsutoshi Aoki. Another opponent floated about as a potential foe for Eder was Ismael Laguna, an 18-year-old boxer from Panama. Ultimately a bout with Laguna did not bring the prestige or financial gain they could get in Japan.

Katzenelson had been interested in setting multiple bouts for Eder to maintain his activity and cash in on the world championship before Eder retired. He fielded an offer to fight Ignacio Piña in Tijuana, Mexico, for late May after the Aoki match, but settled on a proposal to compete in the Philippines after the Japanese bout. The Filipino promoters wanted to secure Eder's services for multiple bouts but could only come up with enough currency to get them one. They proposed their leading contender Johnny Jamito as a future opponent.

Fight 48, vs. Katsutoshi Aoki, April 4, 1963

On February 14, 1963, the World Boxing Council was founded in Mexico. Now two major sanctioning bodies were operating in boxing. Since Eder was already the undisputed and lineal champion, he became the inaugural champion of the WBC.

Eder agreed to a pair of fights that would take him to Asia for a mini-tour. The first stop would see him travel to Tokyo, Japan, to take on the precocious 20-year-old Katsutoshi Aoki. Eder's purse for the Aoki fight was set to be $40,000 after-tax, and this included all expenses for the entire team. The bout was set for April 4, and on March 14, Eder flew to Los Angeles. He stayed for a little over one week, training for the contest at the Main Street Gym while waiting for

Eder arriving in Tokyo

his father to arrive from Buenos Aires, where he had been working.

The Jofres were taken aback when they arrived on March 23 at Tokyo International Airport, where they were greeted by a large crowd of well-wishers. Aristides joked, "I've never seen so many bantamweights in one place!" Aoki, already a popular local attraction, had built up a record of 33 wins against only one defeat and one draw. A little over a week out from the contest, Aristides said Eder was roughly seven pounds over the weight limit and had work to do to get his weight down but was not concerned as they had planned for a strict training schedule.

On April 1, *O Globo* reported from a press event where both fighters drove through the city. "Tokyo – Brazilian Eder Jofre, bantamweight world champion, joined by his wife and his father, and by Japanese Katsutoshi Aoki, the challenger for the title in the fight to take place in this capital on April 4, went through the city today in a convertible car, causing a true parade for the crowd which in some moments stopped the traffic."

"The parade started, with spring weather in front of Kuramae stadium where the fight will take place and finished at the Tokyo Broadcasting Company building downtown. During the path, which lasted one hour and fifteen minutes, the champion and the challenger, who is the Oriental bantamweight champion, would shake hands and smile, saluting the crowd of fans throughout their way. The car stopped for ten minutes in Ginza, Tokyo commercial center, where more than a thousand people surrounded the car. During the parade, the traffic was stopped for an hour, and the police had to interfere in order to spread the attendants."

The buildup to the bout was energy-sapping as Eder was obligated to appear on television and at various events while also being photographed everywhere he went as the public showed the visiting champion a warm reception. Aoki, for his part, announced that he would perform hara-kiri in the ring if he were defeated, and this brought further publicity to the bout, appearing on the front page of national newspapers.

Eder and Aoki take part in some publicity shots

The Japanese press did not give Aoki much chance of winning with the consensus being that his only shot was to catch Eder by surprise early and land a lucky punch. They compared Eder to a machine and called him a perfect fighter after attending his workouts and sparring sessions. Eder was well supported in Japan with some newly acquired Japanese fans and members of the Brazilian embassy, and a small section of Brazilians who had made the long trip from South America.

The Japanese daily newspaper *Nikkan* reported on March 26 that even though Eder was using 14-ounce gloves in sparring, he made noses bleed and rocked two training partners. Former Japanese champion and Eder victim, Sadao Yaoita, complimented Eder on his defensive skills and said that he is a perfect boxer when asked to appraise the Brazilian's qualities.

Eder asked the local boxing commission if they could provide him with some left-handed sparring partners since Aoki was a southpaw. The chief sparring partner Eder was working with was former rival, Ernesto Miranda. The latter had joined the camp and had many bouts lined up for himself in Japan.

While Eder avoided heavy rainstorms in Tokyo by resting in his hotel room with his family, there was a lot of speculation that he was struggling to get down to the 118 pounds limit. Eder had been doing his roadwork in Meiji Garden, but due to rainy weather, he missed a couple of days. To supplement the weight loss required, Eder skipped a couple of days of meals, but even with this development, the Japanese press felt that his experience and class would be far too much for Aoki.

American promoter Leo Leavitt was part of the promotional team that made the bout. While the Jofre camp tried to keep the weight problems quiet, Leavitt confirmed to the press that Eder was struggling to cut the weight. "If he was a meat-eater, it would be much easier, but how can you cut weight if your diet is already based on fruits and vegetables?" he asked. In the last two days leading into the bout, the rain did ease off, so Eder put in some necessary roadwork and relaxed on the eve of the bout by getting a haircut before retiring to his room to watch TV with Cidinha. He arrived the following morning at the weigh-in ten minutes early and quashed the speculation regarding his weight by hitting 118 pounds precisely at the first attempt.

Along with Masahiko "Fighting" Harada and Hiroyuki Ebihara, Aoki was considered among the hottest talents in this boxing-rich country on his way up. Despite an earlier setback against Ebihara, Aoki had proven his worth with quality wins against Leo Espinosa and Piero Rollo. He was stepping up to a much higher level when he met the visiting champion, but that did not minimize the excitement of 10,000 wildly partisan Japanese fans who packed into the Kutamae Sumo Arena to see if their boy could upset the odds.

Round By Round from *Estadão*

Round 1

Aoki is the first one to punch. He hits Eder slightly with a left jab, but the Brazilian counters with an uppercut. Aoki dances around the champion with his guard still high. Eder has more strength and applies jabs to keep his opponent far at distance. Aoki shortens the distance and hits the Golden Bantam with two straight punches to his head, however, with no effect. Aoki backs up, and Eder continues to keep him at distance with left jabs and straight right-hand punches. Aoki attacks with a left jab, but Eder is quicker and hits first with two punches to the Japanese man's chin. The Brazilian moves forward and misses a straight right-hand punch and then the Japanese man sidesteps and goes to the ropes. There, Eder misses two punches. Aoki goes on the attack and punches again. He applies a 1-2 to the champion's head, but it does not affect the champion.

Round 2

Eder stays in the center of the ring. Aoki uses a left jab, a right cross, and another left jab. Eder attacks with two jabs. Aoki tries to counterpunch with his guard open. Eder neutralizes it by moving his waist. The Brazilian adjusts well to a hook that Aoki had landed against his liver. Aoki goes on the attack, but the Brazilian sidesteps, avoiding two straight punches, fighting back with a one-two. One of Aoki's eyes is already swollen. Eder dominates and controls the fight momentarily, and Aoki reacts with two crosses at short distance. The referee gives Aoki a warning due to an involuntary head butt. The Japanese hits the Brazilian with some success, and the champion is disoriented. Aoki hits Eder's body, but Eder avoids two left uppercuts. The champion hits his challenger with a sharp left punch, but Aoki keeps attacking. He (Aoki) threw a left hook and a right cross, which the Brazilian avoids. Eder goes to the ropes where he hits the Japanese man with three punches on his chin.

Round 3

Eder now dominates the fight. He retreats from punches and jabs from the Japanese man. He doesn't swerve, however, from two crossed punches with the left and right, which hit him on his chin. He is confused again but quickly punches back. Eder lands a sequence of hooks on Aoki's liver and connects punches to his head. The Brazilian connects a good left hook on the Japanese's chin and finishes with a powerful left hook to his liver. Aoki falls. He gets up almost at the end of the counting and bravely fights back. Eder hits his liver even more. He continues to punish him with hooks. The fight is over seconds later, with another left punch to his liver. The challenger gets up at nine seconds, but the referee ends the match. Aoki is in no condition to take more punches.

It was a surprise for the champion to face such an aggressive rival since most opponents fought carefully against him due to his immaculate reputation and fearsome punching power. At the end of the second round, the crowd rose to their feet in excitement. Eder went back to his corner and sat with a puzzled look on his face as his father shouted orders. This was a stark contrast from the Japanese corner where Aoki had an excited grin on his face as he was ready to come out and continue taking the bout to the champion. Much like the Marquez fight, where Eder had appeared to have encountered a spot of bother, he showed why he was regarded as the greatest fighter in the world when he produced a breathtaking third-round display.

Working as a judge for the bout, Tony Petronella wrote: "Jofre, who had just squeezed under the 118-pound limit, moved out cautiously as the bell sounded for the third, and for about a minute the challenger continued to rip into him. Then the flashy Brazilian started stepping up the pace. This was more like him. Aoki, 117 3/4, sensed the change and tried to pour it on. Suddenly, Jofre nailed him with a booming left that sent him crashing to the canvas. The punch was a beauty. It traveled only a few inches, but Jofre followed through with a wide sweeping motion - like a pitcher whipping a fireball across the plate. Getting up groggily at the count of five, the surprised Japanese wobbled on rubbery legs while taking the mandatory eight-count and threw a couple of feeble blows at Jofre's head. Stepping back, the champ carefully measured his foe and crumpled him with another sledgehammer left to the side. The blow knocked the last puff of steam from the game challenger, and he was counted out at 2:12."

The suddenness of the knockout momentarily silenced the crowd who'd roared so vociferously three minutes earlier. That deafening silence soon turned into pleasant applause for a grand champion. In typical Japanese custom, they threw cushions into the ring as a mark of respect to the man who had defeated their countryman. Seemingly in awe of the champion, Aoki was gracious in defeat and said: "I felt the first knockdown punch, but I didn't know what hit me the second time. That man has a terrific punch."

This fight was another prime example of just how complete a boxer Eder was and why all the plaudits were justified as he showed he can handle any style with class. Aoki had employed roughhouse tactics and was a little overzealous in some of his attacks, which did seem to agitate the champion who seemed to decide it was time to teach the young challenger a lesson and then crushed Aoki.

Eder confessed to feeling nervous that fans would demand Aoki to follow through on his hara-kiri promise if he lost. "After the fight was over, the crowd went off throwing pillows at the ring, forcing him to keep his promise. I got tense, imagining that someone could bring a sword so he could kill himself right there in the ring," Eder said.

Aoki left the ring with his head down in shame whereas Eder paraded around the ring with a trophy the Japanese organizers had made for the bout and was in good spirits when interviewed after the match, joking that his victory proved "raw celery and carrots are more potent than sukiyaki and tempura." Katzenelson spoke about how he knew Eder would win but was surprised he ended the bout as quickly as he did. "Aoki was a tough fighter. I was expecting that Eder would knock him out in the fifth round because he always takes his time to warm up. However, he took action faster tonight," he said.

The Eder Jofre love-in didn't stop in the arena. His escort from the fight venue to his hotel was followed by his newly acquired fan base, and a large group of locals waited outside of his hotel and sent him gifts and messages of congratulations. Eder reciprocated by making several balcony appearances to acknowledge their affection.

Back home in São Paulo, the streets of Parque Peruche were deserted around 9 am local time as everyone was tuning into their radios to listen to the fight. Only Aristides and Cidinha had made the voyage to Tokyo with Eder, so the family gathered around in Eder's parents' home. Also with the family were friends in the press. Here is the report from *Folha* on the scene at the Jofre household on that morning:

Eder's family celebrates KO with champagne and carnival

"Eder Jofre's victory over Aoki in Japan was celebrated with champagne by his family. Dona Angelina, who didn't leave the radio side and who cheered with her son's knockout, got the party started. 'Claudio, grab a champagne bottle.' Claudio Tonelli, former boxer and the world champion's brother-in-law, went to grab it. Among laughter and joy, they made a wish for health to the great Brazilian fighter. Everyone was happy. Dona Angelina, Eder's mother, and Ms. Maria Zumbano, his grandmother, only stopped when the broadcaster announced Eder Jofre would say a few words. They both curved their bodies in front of the radio and almost cried when they heard him. If the receiver had the power to bring people closer like they do to their voices, they would probably get a kiss on their cheeks.

Angelina pops the champagne

It was at 9 am. The broadcasts from Tokyo started, and Ms. Maria Zumbano couldn't control herself. 'Change it to another station, this one's not good.'

Ms. Angelina, continually rubbing her hands, said: 'It's taking forever to begin.'

The broadcaster announces both boxer's backgrounds. Ms. Maria Zumbano, who was curved in front of the radio, sits on a chair, looks up, and prays. She only left that position when the fight started. She seemed overexcited.

Ms. Angelina couldn't keep it together.

Ms. Maria was paying attention to what the broadcaster would describe, commenting on the punches that Eder would hit: 'Right on the liver, now he let go his right hand.'

In the first round, 'He is still not interested in this fight,' pulling Ms. Angelina through her arm.

The bell rang. Angelina exclaimed: 'Thank God.'

The second round began. The Japanese accepted the fight. Aoki takes Eder to the ropes. Everyone got nervous. Eder got away from the ropes. Ms. Maria was calmer. Her voice was almost prophetic: 'Let him let his right hand go.'

Eder did. The Japanese man felt it.

Eder's brother-in-law said: 'I bet a lunch that this would go up to the third round. Eder won't let it pass this round.' Dogalberto would calm his mother and grandmother: 'The broadcaster is exaggerating. He let his left hand go, but Eder defended it,' and would make the gestures lifting his hands in front of his face.

The third round began; Ms. Angelina was vibrant when Ms. Maria pulled her again through her arm: 'It was him who hit Eder.' She stopped. It wasn't true; Eder was punishing him. He sat down again. When the broadcaster announced the knockout, she jumped and yelled.

'We won! We won! My God, it's over. Eder won!' The joy took over. They would hug and jump, happy."

Eder and his team stayed in Japan for a month, training for the assignment in the Philippines with Johnny Jamito. The Jamito fight had not been officially signed, so Eder opted to stay in Japan, where he enjoyed the hospitality and culture. Not until April 27 was the bout made official when young Filipino millionaire Jorge Araneta guaranteed Eder a purse of $40,000. Araneta had made his fortune in property development, hotels, and the entertainment industry in the Philippines and saw the opportunity to bring the world's best fighter to their shores to take on a popular local as an excellent opportunity to further his empire and get into sports promoting.

Eder and Cidinha took a few days to enjoy the sights before he went back into serious training. The boxing fans in Japan were well and truly in love with Eder for the fighter he was and also with the class and grace he carried himself with. As Eder left town, a group of 5,000 Japanese fans came to give him a true champion send-off at the airport and told him they wished he would come back to fight there again.

Fight 49, vs. Johnny Jamito, May 18, 1963

On May 4, Eder had moved on to the Philippines to take on 23-year-old Johnny Jamito. Much like Aoki, Jamito had built up a respectable record of 32-3-2 and had suffered a loss to Ebihara, when he lost on a majority decision in Japan.

One of the most striking differences between Tokyo and Manila was the weather. In Tokyo, the weather ranged from mild to warm, but Manila was stifling hot. Eder had difficulty coming to terms with the humidity, which hit him the moment he walked off the plane. Only three days into his time in Manila, Eder confessed that the weather was troubling when interviewed by the Brazilian media that made the journey. "I feel tired very easily due to the weather," he said. When asked if the weather could make the fight difficult since it was scheduled outdoors, he said, "I'm having a hard time right now, but I will adapt to this. There is no such thing as an easy fight. I heard Jamito is a good boxer."

With the temperatures proving to be hard to handle, Eder moved his workouts to the evening. However, it was still an issue as the humidity remained in the air. During the first few days in Manila, Eder trained a little less than he had wanted to because of the searing heat. On Tuesday of fight week, Jamito invited the media to his gym to watch him work. He gave them a show as he boxed two rounds with a sparring partner before performing 20 minutes of exercises. He was in excellent fighting condition for what was the opportunity of a lifetime.

Though Jamito was ranked in the world's top ten bantamweights, he had not been expecting a call-up for a title fight since Eder had other options in Japan and America. The challenger offered no predictions. Instead, he stated that he would need all the support of his fans. "I can't tell you how the fight will go down," said Jamito. "I can tell that I am going up to that ring not only for me but for my people."

The love that Eder had felt in Japan was not on hand in the Philippines as he was given a dramatically different reception, receiving death threats and hissing when he appeared in public. Days before the fight, Eder felt bouts of nausea and sickness, which promoted belief within the camp he

was being drugged at the hotel in Manila. This brought back memories of Venezuela and the nefarious attempts to undermine his title defense against Ramon Arias. His team then made sure not to let anyone into the room and paid extra attention to what was going in his body.

Eder was a half-pound over the 118-pound limit at the weigh-in but quickly shed the excess weight with a brisk 15-minute walk under the searing Manila sun. Later that day, in front of a partisan crowd of 25,000 who gave him a very unwelcoming reception, Eder met the young Filipino challenger in the suffocating Manila heat.

Round By Round from by *Estadão*

Round 1
Eder and Jamito saluted each other in the center of the ring and threw punches right away. Eder was throwing jabs and opening space for his deadly left hooks. The Filipino backed away, trying to counter-attack. Right before the end of the round, Eder missed a violent attempt to hit his opponent using his cross punch.

Round 2
Jamito came back more aggressively and tried to hit Eder's midsection. The champion countered it with a powerful left uppercut. Another left uppercut to the jaw makes Jamito back away in fright.

Round 3
Eder takes action, throws a strong shot at Jamito's liver. Before the Filipino can react, Eder hits him with a hook to the chin. Jamito throws two punches at Eder, lands the first but misses the second. Before the end of the round, they engage in a violent exchange in the center of the ring.

Round 4
Jamito goes first and hits Eder with a straight right. Eder kept his guard high. Jamito scored more points in this round just by throwing more punches.

Round 5
Jamito wants to keep attacking, but Eder blocked his punches and countered with two left hooks. The Filipino went to the ropes and dodged several shots thrown by Eder.

Round 6
Eder punished Jamito several times with hooks and crosses, but the Filipino landed good right uppercuts.

Round 7
Eder misses a shot at Jamito's head. The champion tries again and lands a straight shot to the head. Jamito clinches him; Eder lands a punch to Jamito's nose while they are inside right before the end of the round.

Round 8
Eder attacks first and traps Jamito against the ropes. Jamito clinched two times, trying to buy some time, and threw a few jabs to keep Eder away.

Round 9

Moving and dancing around, Eder left Jamito dizzy and made him easy prey. A violent left-hand shot followed by two right crosses almost finished Jamito. Jamito clinches him again, trying to stay on his feet.

Round 10

Jamito tries to go first, but Eder counters immediately. The end is near. Eder makes a punching bag out of Jamito.

Round 11

Eder's looking to end the fight and throws several punches at him, with only three seconds to the end of the round; Eder lands a powerful shot to the face.

Round 12

When the referee Ziravello calls the fighters to the center of the ring, Eder came, but Jamito couldn't stand up, so (referee) Ziravello raised Eder's arms, giving him the official victory.

Jamito showed to be a smart fighter. He tied Eder up when he was close. Eder was biding his time, slowly taking over the fight before landing a murderous left hook in the ninth round which shook Jamito to his core. Jamito barely stayed upright from the effects of this blow and was never in the contest from that point on. In the 11th round, Eder landed a vicious right-hand to the Filipino's body, which pushed him back to the ropes where all he could do was attempt to clinch to avoid further punishment. The energy had been sapped out of him, and Eder easily fended off the clinch as he pushed him away before landing an explosive left hook to the body which floored the brave challenger. The bell sounded, saving Jamito from being counted out, but he was a beaten fighter as he slumped on his stool. His corner had no choice but to throw in the towel on behalf of their fighter.

This type of bout had proven to be a consistent theme with most contenders who challenged Eder. They were talented and earned their shot at the title, but once Eder warmed up and turned up the gears, few could survive the onslaught. Eder credited Jamito with being a talented young fighter worth keeping an eye on. "He (Jamito) is a brainy fighter. He uses his head. I did not expect him to be such a good fighter. It will take a good boxer with a good punch to beat him," Eder said after the bout. He also said that the heat had been a big obstacle. "You don't want to do anything, let alone fighting. Maybe that's why the fight went on until the 12th round, for I was fighting in slow motion," he added.

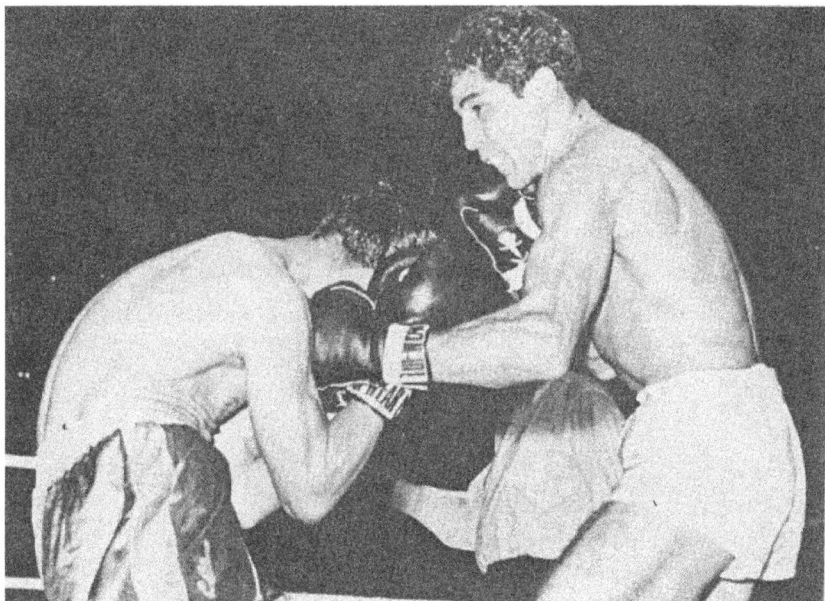

Jamito would remain a competitive fighter for some years but would never again fight for a world title. He went on an impressive run where he beat the likes of Ray Asis and Hiroshi Kobayashi, but was defeated twice on points by future featherweight world title contender Mitsunori Seki.

Days after defeating Jamito, Eder expressed his desire to fight for the featherweight world title against recently crowned champion Ultiminio "Sugar" Ramos. The Cuban-Mexican Ramos won the title when he knocked out Davey Moore, who died due to injuries sustained in their bout at Wrigley Field in Los Angeles on March 21, 1963. Eder and Cidinha spent some time in Los Angeles before arriving back in São Paulo on May 26. The champ said that he felt he had run out of opponents at bantamweight, and it was the right time to move up in weight.

"It is despair for me to have to deal with two opponents at the same time, and the worse of them has always been the scale," he said. He explained that he and Cidinha were expecting their first child and stated his intention of fighting Ramos. "I made a lot of money this season in Japan and Manila, but I had to go back to São Paulo, for Cidinha is expecting our baby and has been crying a lot, she is homesick. Dad stayed in Tokyo with Oripes dos Santos. My old man is teaching a few classes to the Japanese. He will come back soon, also, to take care of me for the fight against Sugar Ramos," he added.

Aristides was offered a lucrative deal to spend six months in Japan training their boxers, but he had to decline because he felt he had obligations to his fighters back in Brazil and felt that it would be a conflict of interest if he were training fighters who could eventually meet other Brazilian boxers. Aristides did confirm that he was to be the new trainer of Ernesto Miranda since Abraham Katzenelson had signed Eder's former rival to a management contract. The intention was for Miranda to soon be contesting Pone Kingpetch for the flyweight world championship in Thailand or Los Angeles.

George Parnassus said that he was prepared to offer Eder $75,000 to fight Ramos at The Olympic Auditorium in Los Angeles. A deal was not closed between Parnassus and Katzenelson in time, so Ramos took a voluntary defense in Mexico against Rafiu King. Aristides claimed that the offers being presented to them for a Sugar Ramos fight were around $40,000, which was far from what they would be willing to take. He said that while he was confident in his son's technical ability, the boxers at featherweight would be much stronger, so it made little sense to take on such challenges when they could earn the same amount defending the bantamweight title. There had also been talk that Cidinha was pressuring Eder to retire from the ring, especially now with their baby on the way. Aristides and Katzenelson felt it was best to let Eder and Cidinha have their own space and not push for the Ramos fight any further at this stage.

Eder was getting some pressure from the WBA about putting his title on the line with time moving along. The rules stipulated that a champion must defend his title every six months. While opponents like Jesus Pimentel were mooted, nothing was close to confirmation. Other potential opponents included a rematch with Piero Rollo and Alphonse Halimi, both long past their best by this point. Aristides argued that Eder should not have to defend his title for the rest of the year since the Medel, Aoki, and Jamito fights had all happened within eight months. Eder was considering the featherweight title. It was believed that a deal could be made, so they wanted to take a profitable non-title fight over the weight limit as their final bout of 1963.

Jack Solomons had finally reached a deal for Eder to box in a British ring, but the opponent was not to be John Caldwell. The latter's career was on the wane, having suffered multiple losses since the defeat in São Paulo. Instead, Eder was set to participate in a non-title bout with featherweight Billy Calvert on October 22 at Wembley Arena in London. The card was a blockbuster event with world lightweight champion Carlos Ortiz featured in a non-title bout with Maurice Cullen and Gomeo Brennan, and Mick Leahy to face off for the British Commonwealth middleweight championship. Eder stayed busy, waiting for his next fight. He participated in several exhibition matches in Brazil to aid the Brazilian Red Cross.

A great moment of joy hit the Jofre household on August 20, when Eder and Cidinha had their first child, Marcel. Eder's brothers suggested the name. They felt the name would pay homage to the late great former middleweight world champion Marcel Cerdan. This fantastic event in the champion's life gave him a new commitment and responsibility. He soon advised Katzenelson he would not be fulfilling the Wembley bout as he wanted to be by Cidinha's side and enjoy as much time with Marcel as he could before he competed in championship matches again. Jack Solomons still hoped that the bout would come off, and he would see Eder in October. Katzenelson informed him on September 8 that Aristides told him he would spend time with Cidinha and Marcel. Solomons understood that, and rather than sue the Jofre team for a breach of contract, he replaced Eder on the card with Sugar Ramos and intended to feature Eder on a show in late November. That card never materialized, and Eder took the rest of the year off.

In October 1963, Eder received *The Ring* magazine's ultimate compliment when it featured him on the cover of its 500th issue. *The Ring's* managing editor Nat Loubet penned an article entitled "Jofre a Small Sugar." Here are excerpts from the article:

"Ever so seldom the ring produces a fighter about whom it is said that he is the greatest in decades for his poundage. Such a standout was Ray Robinson. Now, with Sugar Ray on the wane, there is another spectacular scrapper on whom that "pound-for-pound" label of superiority and domination looks good. That man is Eder Jofre, the Brazilian, who holds the bantamweight championship of the world. There have been bantamweight champions galore since the days of Charley Lynch, who ruled the class as far back as 1856. The division has boasted such all-time greats as George Dixon, Kid Williams, and Johnny Coulon. But none have dominated the class in their time with more considerable elan than Jofre crowds into his reign as champion."

Harry Markson, boxing director of New York's Madison Square Garden, was also quoted as saying, "This Jofre man is the greatest guy for his weight since Sixto Escobar. He is a real scorcher; I wish he were some 20 pounds heavier. I'd bring him to New York and let the TV viewers see a great fighter."

1963 Results

Eder Jofre KO3 Katsutoshi Aoki
Eder Jofre KO11 Johnny Jamito

Marcel plays with his dad's title belt

Eder and Marcel

1964

O Globo reported on January 23, 1964, this was likely to be Eder's final year in the ring. He had $30,000 offers to defend his title in Belgium against Pierre Cossemyns, and in Italy against Piero Rollo in a rematch. The intention was to accept those fights and a rematch against Sadao Yaoita in Japan with the world title on the line. Katzenelson was taking Eder's retirement talk seriously and intended to cash in as much as possible while Eder was still active.

Promoters in Rio wanted to get Eder to put his title on the line there and offered $15,000 to fight Waldemiro Pinto or Raimundo de Jesus. Aristides said that his son would only fight for twice that amount. Teti Alfonso, acting on behalf of the Rio boxers, said he would be prepared to structure a deal based on television rights and profits from ticket sales, proposing that the fight would happen in May. Pinto and de Jesus had a match scheduled for Pinto's South American bantamweight title, and Alfonso felt that the winner against Eder would be a great fight for Brazilian boxing. Aristides stood firm on $30,000, and the talks died. The Pinto vs. de Jesus fight eventually was scrapped. Perhaps the dropping of Eder's name was merely to drum up interest in that bout because the fight was not rescheduled and there was no further dialogue about a fight for Eder in Rio.

On January 24, Eder opened a clothing and fabric store at 208 Rua Bresser in São Paulo. Before the store was officially unveiled, the business was profitable because of Eder's name. He partnered with Orlando Funcia, who had been in the business for years. Eder said his new business would not affect his boxing career because he would only visit the store when he was not training for an important fight. His brother, Dogalberto, would manage the store in his absence. Eder intended to buy a farm and house in either Rio or Santos after taking fights in Japan, Italy, and Belgium. He announced that while he was still active as a fighter, the end was near and that he intended to expand and open more stores and maybe open a sports clothing store. He planned to get out of boxing on top. When that day arrived, he would already have thriving businesses in circulation that would keep expanding as he transitioned from boxing champion to businessman.

On March 6, it was reported in *Folha* that Eder would not renew his managerial contract with Abraham Katzenelson. They had no rift or disagreement but because Eder was set to retire from boxing. "Eder has been announcing that he wants to quit boxing for the last two years. Now, however, he will retire," the article stated. The report pointed to Eder's recently opened fabric store doing tremendous business. While Eder had been genuinely serious about exiting the sport on top, he was tempted to stay in boxing for just a little while yet and soon renewed the terms with Katzenelson.

On March 31, the military overpowered the government with the aid of the United States. By April 1, Brazil was under military rule. There had been a growing concern that President João Goulart was pushing Brazil towards communism. Despite the Kennedy Administration's attempts to work with Goulart, they didn't get anywhere in convincing Goulart to remove what they felt were extreme leftists, ultra-nationalists, and anti-Americans in the government. According to US ambassador Lincoln Gordon, it was feared that Brazil was headed toward becoming "the China of the 1960s."

Ranieri Mazzilli was appointed as the acting President on April 2 before electing the Army Chief of Staff, Marshal Humberto Castelo Branco, as the President. He spent the remainder of Goulart's term in office. Branco was sworn in on April 15 as the 26th President of Brazil. He promised to deliver a united nation to whoever his successor may be while Goulart had fled the country to Uruguay on April 2.

An April 24 date was being discussed for Eder to compete in England finally. It looked to be all set with the opponent being the excellent Howard Winstone at featherweight, but more lucrative offers to defend his bantamweight world championship came in. Eventually, the London bout faded away. Masahiko "Fighting" Harada in Japan was one profitable possibility, as was the attractive option of facing Jesus Pimentel in America. Aristides' stance had softened from his 1962 comments about not wanting his son to box in America again and was happy for his son to face the Mexican.

Waldemar Zumbano would see his political history become the source of controversy once again when leaving for the Tokyo Olympics in October of 1964. Waldemar was leading the Brazilian boxing team but was stopped at Congonhas Airport and placed under arrest. He was told that he was being denied the right to travel due to being a communist. Sylvio de Magalhães Padilha, President of the Brazilian Olympic Committee, ensured Waldemar would not be held back and kicked up a fuss. He issued an extreme ultimatum that left the airport police with no choice but to let Waldemar travel.

Padilha said: "This is not a matter of military rank. Because if it were, mine is superior to yours, and I could give the release order. The issue here is different. This is an Olympic Delegation, which is under my command. I am the president of the Brazilian Olympic Committee, and I order that Professor Waldemar Zumbano be released immediately and travel with us. If you do not do that, I will leave here and send the entire delegation back home. I warn you that Brazil is no longer going to the Olympics in Japan. And I will tell them that you are to blame. Either Professor Zumbano travels, or Brazil won't go to the Olympics because of you." After such a bold demand, Waldemar was allowed to get on the plane with the Brazilian team. While the three-man boxing team earned no medals in Tokyo, João Henrique showed some promise in getting to the quarterfinals.

By 1964 the most exciting potential opponent in the bantamweight division was Jesus Pimentel. Pimentel, a Mexican-born fighter based in Los Angeles, was nicknamed "Poison" and possessed incredible one-punch knockout power. A Jofre vs. Pimentel fight was a natural fit.

The colorful manager of Pimentel, Harry Kabakoff, beat the drums for the match at the start of the year. "It's been nine months since Jofre defended his title for the last time; the WBA's rules require a title defense every six months." The money being offered to Eder was $40,000, but Katzenelson was firm that Eder would not be defending his title for any less than $50,000. Eder had other options, including the featherweight division or retirement. The sacrifice to get down to 118 pounds to put his title and prestige on the line was worth no less than $50,000, Aristides argued.

Pimentel had to get past former flyweight world champion Masahiko "Fighting" Harada of Japan in a bout scheduled for May 5 at the Coliseum in Los Angeles and would then be free to fight Eder in Los Angeles. Civic Sports Enterprises (CSE) was promoting the Pimentel vs. Harada elimination bout and expressed an interest in having the winner fight Eder under their promotional banner.

Only days out from the bout, Pimentel pulled out with a sore stomach. CSE Promoter Leo A. Minskoff sent Pimentel to see Dr. Martin Levy, a Beverly Hills specialist in internal medicine. Levy diagnosed the illness as being a virus within Pimentel's bloodstream. It was also being reported that the ticket sales, which were expected to be around 19,000, were not moving quickly and Harada had been working out under wraps at the Main Street Gym with a hand injury. All parties were happy with the postponement of the bout.

Kabakoff said he heard from reliable sources that Harada appeared "way over the weight limit." Harada went back to Japan while Pimentel got better. Shortly after, the Pimentel vs. Harada bout was rescheduled for July 6 at LA Sports Arena. CSE flew Eder and Katzenelson in from Brazil to attend the fight and booked a hotel in Beverly Hills for them. Minskoff was trying to secure the proposed bout between Eder and Pimentel at LA Sports Arena, whereas George Parnassus was interested in promoting the bout at The Olympic.

Once again, Pimentel pulled out of the Harada bout at the last minute, citing stomach pains. This development was met with skepticism by the promoters used to Kabakoff and his antics, so they scheduled tests for Pimentel to undertake to prove if he had been unfit to fight. The tests came back negative, and Pimentel was then in hot water with the California commission.

The Harada team was furious and they threatened to sue Pimentel's team since they had trained for the bout and were already in Los Angeles. Ray Asis of the Philippines was brought in as Pimentel's replacement and was defeated by Harada by unanimous decision. Harada suffered a nasty cut to his left eye in the second round and bled throughout the contest.

CSE insisted Pimentel was contractually obligated to them so they had the rights to his next fight. Minskoff was upset at the appearance of Parnassus "wooing" Eder at the Harada-Asis fight. Eder sat with Parnassus and was seen with him for most of the evening. Eder was impressed with Harada. "He's fast but can't punch," he said before offering his opinion that he felt Pimentel was a better fighter than the Japanese contender. With Harada's eye needing time to heal, Parnassus moved quickly to make the Jofre vs. Pimentel championship bout.

As if matters couldn't be complicated further, the California commission suspended Pimentel from fighting in the state. They also suspended Kabakoff from working in any managerial capacity within California for his involvement in the farcical circumstances surrounding this latest pull-out. This meant that the Jofre vs. Pimentel fight would need a different venue.

Harada's team stood firm and demanded that they get the fight with Pimentel, but this didn't come to fruition, and instead, terms were met between Parnassus and Kabakoff in early September for the Jofre vs. Pimentel bout to go to San Antonio, Texas, in late October. Eder would not be getting the $50,000 that Katzenelson was holding out for, but they did receive an offer for a $40,000 purse plus free travel expenses. Pimentel's cut of the purse was to be $15,000. The fight was set for October 28. On October 9, Eder came with his family and team as they flew to Texas, giving them a little over two weeks to train in San Antonio.

O Globo reported from Eder's camp on October 19: "Eder is in very good shape. He has been training regularly, keeping his weight down, and he is very easygoing for the fight with Jesus Pimentel. Eder will earn $40,000 after taxes, with all expenses paid for, including tickets and hotel, whether he wins or loses. Eder, wife, son, and his father are staying at the Gunther Hotel in San Antonio."

WORLD BANTAM WEIGHT TITLE BOUT
WEDNESDAY, OCTOBER 28, 1964—8:30 P. M.
15 ROUNDS — 118 LBS.

EDER   JESUS
JOFRE   vs.   PIMENTEL
World Champion   Mexico-Challenger

JOE FREEMAN COLISEUM
SAN ANTONIO, TEXAS
Promotors
Tony Padilla and George Parnassus
Admission $18.27
Tax 1.73

RINGSIDE

Total . . . $20.00

WORLD TITLE BOUT

Wed. Oct. 28, 1964

EAST

RINGSIDE

Row __6__

Seat __15__

Only days before the scheduled bout, Kabakoff did the unthinkable and called off the match. "I told Parnassus that San Antonio hadn't drawn $25,000 for a fight in its history," Kabakoff said. "It didn't make any sense. The whole thing was a setup. Jofre weighed 140 pounds and couldn't have made the weight if they cut off one of his legs. Everybody but me knew it. Then his manager, Abe Katzenelson, comes to me and says there's no money in the bank, no advance sale, and he's worried. I go nuts and start screaming. The fight is called off, and I get blamed and suspended. Now we are suspended by everybody everywhere except in Mexico. Beautiful. Now I am not a vindictive person, and I would never wish for someone to drop dead. But I did pray a little that a few people would spend the rest of their lives in an iron lung," he added.

Kabakoff was known as "The Mad Russian" due to his eccentric nature which was consistent with incidents like this throughout his career. The claim he made of Eder weighing 140 pounds was spurious as Eder never even touched 140 pounds when on the sidelines, so with a fight so close and the professionalism of Eder and his team, the possibility he was over 20 pounds over the limit was bordering on impossible. This claim was merely a deflection tactic from Kabakoff, who knew that he would be in hot water for yet another contentious cancellation of a significant promotion that saw one boxer go through the trouble of coming from a different continent.

In an interview given to Joe Rein many years later, Pimentel shifted the blame away from Kabakoff. "The real story was the fight was canceled not by us but the promoter, George Parnassus. And the reason was: Even though Eder Jofre was a world champion, and I was the number one contender, Jofre never fought in North America, and I, as the number one (contender), had never fought in San Antonio. Neither did Jofre, so there was not that kind of interest for a title fight, knowing it was for the bantamweight championship. So, that's why the promoter canceled the fight. But then, he accused me of being afraid of Jofre, and he had advanced me $10,000, which was wrong. I got suspended by Luis Spota, who at that time was the President of the World Boxing Council. Now, I wish that at that time, Don King and the recent President of the World Boxing Council, Jose Sulaiman, were around. I would have been the champion of the world. George Parnassus and Luis Spota used to eat out of the same plate. Parnassus told him a false story, and he suspended me for a full year," he said.

Those claims weren't accurate as Eder had fought three times in America. It did seem that San Antonio was perhaps not the right place to stage the bout despite a sizable Hispanic population. Several years later, Pimentel would finally fight for the championship in 1971 when he was scheduled to face Ruben Olivares. Still, Parnassus had a suitable opponent in Rafael Herrera on standby if Pimentel would pull out again because of the past indiscretions. For his worth, Pimentel was a superb fighter, one of the better bantamweights of his era but unfortunately, due to these managerial issues, only fought for the title when he was already beyond his prime as a fighter.

Fight 50, vs. Bernardo Caraballo, November 27, 1964

Due to the debacle of the botched Jesus Pimentel fight, Eder had endured by far his longest layoff to date. In the time between the Jamito fight, it had been 18 months when Eder accepted an offer to defend his championship against 22-year-old Colombian national hero Bernardo Caraballo. One of the major selling points of going to Colombia was that Eder would be guaranteed a tax-free $50,000. The bout was set for Friday, November 27, at the Colombian national football stadium, Estadio El Campín, in Bogota.

There is always an added spice when South American rivals face one another, particularly when Brazil is involved. This occurs in all sports and is natural as Brazil is the only South American country whose citizens speak Portuguese and is the largest country on the continent. Brazil is also the economic powerhouse of the region and the dominant force in international sports.

Caraballo was born in the port town of Bocachica, where he worked as a fisherman in his youth. His family moved to nearby Cartagena, where he shined shoes for tourists. He was taken to the gym by an older brother who had boxed a few years earlier. Caraballo would soon get noticed as he would win multiple regional and national titles.

On paper, the Colombian represented a tough challenge even without the added circumstances working against the champion. He was an athletic boxer who excelled in using his legs and lateral movement to dominate his opposition. He possessed a lot of speed, was adept defensively, and could box well at a distance. His record was 39 wins with no defeats and one draw. At age 22, he also had youth on his side. He had built up an excellent resume of names as he climbed the rankings. He turned professional at age 18, just three days before Eder won the world championship against Eloy Sanchez. He moved quickly and beat Ramon Arias after only one year in the paid ranks. He repeated that victory when he rematched Arias in Caracas before claiming the Colombian flyweight title in 1962. Caraballo attributed the wins over Arias as the bouts that made him an idol in his homeland.

"He was an excellent and swift fighter. I beat him in Colombia, and then he asked for a rematch in Venezuela, and I beat him again in a tremendous fight. I talk a lot, but I also back that up in the ring," Caraballo said. He also defeated another Venezuelan favorite in Ramon Antonio Calatayud before defeating the capable Mimoun Ben Ali in 1963. That would prove to be a banner year for the Colombian as he also defeated Piero Rollo and Carlos Miranda and scored his signature win when he defeated the legendary Pascual Perez, now campaigning as a bantamweight.

In 1964 he went to the Philippines and defeated future world champion Chartchai Chionoi and also earned a decision victory over Manny Elias. The fight with Chionoi had been a war as Caraballo had to dig deep to come back home with the victory. "It was ten tough rounds. When I got out of the ring, my right eye was swollen shut, and I had a cut in the eyelid of my left eye. I told my wife to pass me a mirror. I kept looking and said: 'now I look like a boxer.'"

That tough run of competition and impressive consistency would be more than enough to become a world champion multiple times over in a different era. In the days of one champion and fewer divisions, it was common for a fighter to go through multiple challenging assignments to earn the right to challenge for a title. Caraballo was the fifth-ranked contender in the division at this point, sitting behind Masahiko "Fighting" Harada of Japan, Jesus Pimentel, Jose Medel, and Manuel Barrios, all from Mexico. Pimentel had burned his bridges after the episode in Texas, and Eder had knocked out Medel twice. In contrast, Barrios had gone 1-1-1 with Medel, the last of those bouts being a victory for Medel. Barrios was an exceptional fighter but did not carry the cache that Caraballo did as a national icon.

It was a tempting offer that convinced the Jofre camp to cross over into enemy territory when they agreed to face the undefeated Caraballo in front of an anticipated hostile public in Bogota. The guarantee of a $50,000 tax-free payment was an attractive deal for a champion who had lost a year of his prime through no fault of his own. "There are many men for me to fight, and I want to fight them all," Eder said. "At first, I would have fought for nothing. Now I do it more for the money, but I love it."

Eder was afforded a warm welcome when he arrived in Bogota on November 7 with his family. More than one thousand fans and media showed up to greet the champion. Several Brazilian press members were already on hand in the Colombian capital, and Eder told all the media he would be hosting a press conference the following day from his hotel.

The buildup to the fight had been friendly, and Eder's training sessions were well attended, and the locals treated him well. Despite Eder's excellent showings in his training sessions, there was a sense of optimism among Colombians that their man was about to take the crown. Eder had not fought in a long time, and it was believed that the altitude could become an issue for him, especially if the fight went into the later rounds. Bogota sits

8675 feet above sea level compared to São Paulo's 2493 feet. Caraballo's style of using a lot of movement also prompted many to believe that the bout would indeed enter the latter stages.

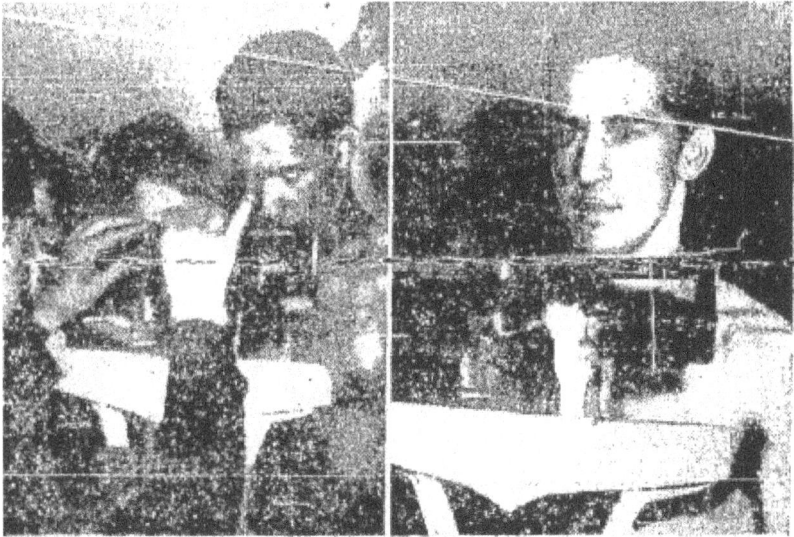

32,000 fans packed into Estadio El Campín, hoping their countryman could make history and claim the championship.

Round By Round from *O Globo*

Round 1
Right at the beginning of the round, Caraballo tried to run, but he slipped and fell. The Colombian boxer sidestepped while Eder kept his distance, almost as if waiting for a better opportunity. A jab by Eder almost hit Caraballo, who crouched in a nice sidestep. In the end, Caraballo was on the ropes, defending himself. Tie.

Round 2
Eder took the initiative. Eder tried to decide the fight and (he) hit his opponent often. Two punches, one with each hand, shook Caraballo, who attempted to clinch. Eder's round.

Round 3
Although always with Eder doing better, Caraballo, boxing with good movement, was avoiding punches. Often, he pushed, making referee Barney Ross intervene. At the end of the round, he slipped and immediately got up—Eder's round.

Round 4
Eder's chasing of Caraballo went on with some disadvantage for the Brazilian. In this round, the Colombian boxer hit Eder's face with a powerful left. Eder's superiority manifested in the last seconds when he hit

Caraballo with a punch right on the target to his chin, and he (Caraballo) felt the impact. Eder's round.

Round 5

More balanced round with good punches from Caraballo. Remarkably, a left hook shook the Brazilian, who wound up recovering and connecting counterpunches. Eder's round.

Round 6

Eder increased his attack, surrounding Caraballo, who often locked his opponent's arms, and the Colombian slipped. Eder's superiority was evident. Eder's round.

Round 7

Clearly, Caraballo wouldn't last much longer. Eder started the final hunt, surrounding his opponent who was hit in every way possible. Caraballo was backing up, and suffered two powerful punches, falling and remaining on the canvas while listening to Barney Ross' counting under excited applause from the audience, who was thrilled about Caraballo's invincibility ending after 43 fights. Even after the counting, he was still down.

From the beginning of the fight, Caraballo could not come to terms with Eder's attack and was hopelessly outclassed. Eder attacked from the start with long left jabs, hard right-hands, and punches in combinations. Despite the 18 months Eder had been out of the ring, he was on top of Caraballo early, showing his class and status as the best fighter in the world pound-for-pound. Early on, Caraballo's defense and reflexes were severely tested as Eder applied educated pressure and moved with cat-like grace.

In the first four rounds, Eder alternated between assassin and matador as he battered the Colombian to the body and head with thumping body shots and stiff jabs but then moved out of range effortlessly as Caraballo tried to inflict some damage of his own. Even those who felt Eder would successfully defend his title had to be surprised at how quickly he asserted his dominance, given that Caraballo possessed excellent boxing skills. Eder usually liked to take his time and study his opponent before going for the kill and was never too concerned about losing early rounds.

Boxing Illustrated correspondent Pete Vaccare wrote in his ringside report from Bogota: "By the fifth, Jofre had his man sized up, and astute ringsiders could see that the end was only a matter of time. Satisfied that Caraballo couldn't hurt him, the champion stepped up the pace in this round and began pinpointing his punches. A barrage of lefts right before the bell had Bernardo gasping. The storm continued through the sixth and into the seventh as Jofre poured on the coals. Easily riding safely through a volley of desperation rights early in the seventh, Jofre sandbagged his now groggy opponent against the ropes, shot across a blazing left hook to the head, and followed with two blurring rights that exploded against Caraballo's chin and dropped the stunned hometown fighter seat-first on the canvas for the fight's first-and-last-knockdown."

Despite the friendly welcome Eder received in Colombia before the bout, he received hell for beating their fighter. Initially, the Colombian crowd chanted "Champion! Champion!" when Eder celebrated but this show of respect didn't last long. Getting from the ring to the locker room was not easy as they required the police to stop an angry mob and escort him to his locker room where he waited for two hours for the thugs to subside. Marcel Jofre said, "Years ago, my father told me what a scene this was. The locals were not happy that Caraballo could not win the championship after they built up the expectation that he would defeat my father and become world champion."

The ugly scene after the bout notwithstanding, it had been a marvelous evening for Eder as he showed top championship form and registered one of his most impressive victories over such a well-regarded opponent. As an added cherry on top of the cake, it was confirmed Eder would be going back to Brazil with a $15,000 bonus due to the impressive turnout the bout brought.

Backstage, a heartbroken Caraballo was interviewed and said: "I did my best. It wasn't enough," as he cried in his locker room. Having averted the danger of the irate public, Eder was naturally more upbeat. "It was an easy fight. I knew I had him when I hurt him with that left hook in the fifth round. I was feeling him out and trying to tire him in the first four rounds. Everything went according to plan. Caraballo is a good fighter, but he has lots to learn," he said. The total professionalism which Eder always exhibited enabled him to give such a strong performance despite the ring rust and the continued struggle to get down to 118 pounds.

Experts marveled at how well Eder dispatched such a tricky opponent with the deck stacked so heavily against him and wondered how he could still perform at such a high level of excellence. "Eder is a good boy. He has a fine wife and son. He doesn't drink, smoke, or gamble. There is no running around. He is no trouble at all. He trains very hard. He is the best fighter in the world, and nobody can beat him," Aristides said when asked about the secrets to his son's success. Newton Campos, acting as a judge in this bout, said that it was the finest performance of Eder's career.

Eder initially intended to fly back to Brazil the day after the bout on Saturday but had to stay in Colombia until the following Tuesday. There had been confusion over taxes to be paid to the Colombian government. This was a matter which was supposed to be handled by his management team as per their contractual agreement, and Eder was told he was guaranteed the $50,000 free of tax, but the Colombian government needed proof before Eder could leave. During the extra days in Bogota, Eder contracted a small bout of the flu caused by an ear infection. One story waiting for Eder when he arrived back at Congonhas Airport with Cidinha and Marcel was that he had some sort of brain injury.

This report was no doubt embellished further since Eder did admit to feeling dizzy while in San Antonio in October. Eder dismissed the reports, insisting there were no such problems. "I am surprised by how my illness was reported," he said. "Those are some serious cases of criminal disinformation, aiming to destroy Eder's career," Katzenelson said, adding that Eder was in the prime of his career physically and mentally.

Eder greeted his fans in a familiarly warm manner upon his return at Congonhas and spoke about his latest title defense. "The knockout is a consequence of the fight. It can be casual, but it should always be worked. Anyone of us, if they could, would have knocked down the other in the first round. Caraballo is too young; he had a difficult childhood and won in boxing. He was, however, too confident. Maybe that's why my work was easier. Anyhow, he was a brave opponent, one of those who never gives up. His defeat against me won't take him away from boxing, where he can still be very successful since he is so young and talented," Eder said.

Eder was asked what it meant to be a world champion after all this time and said, "It doesn't have a price. Maybe it is worth much more in joy than in the dollars it gives." When asked how much that was, he smiled and said, "It's enough to excite us to think of the next fight." That next fight was already being talked about, and it was Masahiko "Fighting" Harada who was believed to be the frontrunner. Eder said that while he would be putting his title on the line again, extended rest and vacation with Cidinha and Marcel would be next before signing off on any bout.

Caraballo, for his part, returned to winning ways after this humbling defeat and ran up an impressive set of victories, including one over the undefeated Brazilian Waldemiro Pinto, who came into the contest with an impressive unbeaten record of 52 wins and three draws. Years later, Caraballo would make a rather spurious claim he felt the scales were tampered with. "I weighed myself on the morning of the fight and was only one pound over the weight, but a couple of hours later, when I arrived at the weigh-in, I was further over the limit. I had to go and lose the weight in the sauna, and that weakened me too much," he said. Why Caraballo felt he was sabotaged in his own country on a show promoted by his countrymen is a mystery and points to sour grapes and the fact that he simply couldn't come to terms with the fact he was not on the same level as the champion.

1964 Results

Eder Jofre KO7 Bernardo Caraballo

Marcel joins Eder for roadwork

1965

On March 9, 1965, Eder arrived in New York City for the "Grand Award of Sport" ceremony at the New York World's Fair, which was the following day. Eighty-three of the world's leading athletes, professional and amateur, across 20 sports, were chosen by journalists from *Sports Illustrated* and *ABC Sports*. Eder was up against Muhammad Ali, Joe Frazier, and Willie Pastrano in the boxing category and came out on top. The award was presented to him by astronaut Colonel John Glenn in an event hosted by Bing and Kathy Cosby at the Unisphere in Flushing Meadows.

Fight 51, vs. Masahiko "Fighting" Harada, May 18, 1965

With universal status as the world's finest pound-for-pound practitioner in the sport and arguably the greatest bantamweight of all-time, Eder was in hot demand. A bout with Jesus Pimentel was still a possibility and promised to make a lot of money, as did the opportunity to finally fight in England, perhaps against Alan Rudkin or Scotland's Walter McGowan. Eder accepted a return trip to Japan, where he would face former flyweight world champion, Masahiko "Fighting" Harada.

The bout was signed on March 23 for May 18 in Nagoya. Soon after Eder arrived back from New York with his Grand Award of Sports, he began training. Initially, it was proposed that the bout would be in April, but with Eder's other commitments, Aristides felt it would be best to push it back to May to give him and his son enough time to get his weight down and prepare. The purse Eder accepted was the smallest one he had received in recent times with a guarantee of $30,000. Harada would be getting $3,300. Eder was considered a favorite by odds of 3 to 2.

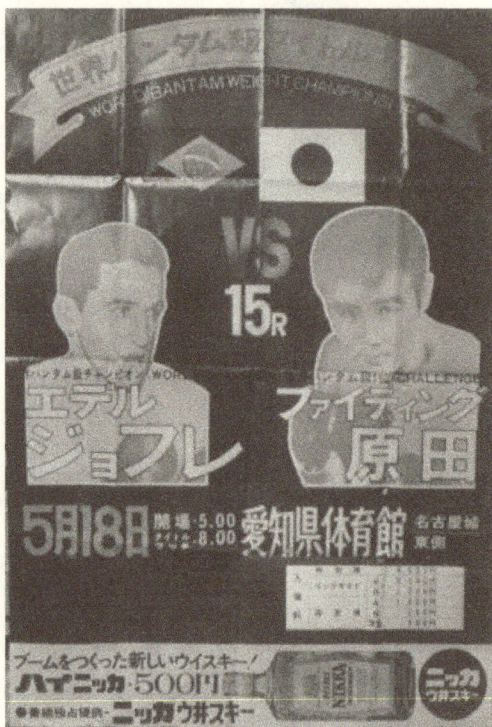

Harada grew up in a vastly different country than the Japan of today. He came up in an era where most families struggled and lived in poverty. When he finished middle school, Harada went to work to help carry some of the burden for his parents. "When I was 15 years old, I started working at a rice store near my house. I had to carry and deliver a lot of rice bags which were more than 100 pounds," Harada said. The family still struggled to make ends meet, and that is when Harada found another way that could move the family out of their difficult financial situation. "My father told me when I was young that there were three paths to success: to go to school and study hard, to create a successful business of some kind, or to achieve a great victory in some activity and he was talking about boxing."

"When I began boxing, in the late 1950s, Japan was poor. The gyms were full of young men like me, who saw an opportunity in boxing. When I started out in boxing, this was a poor country," he told Earl Gustkey of the *Los Angeles Times* in 1988. "No one owned much of anything," Harada added. Harada had no amateur fights and went directly into the professional game a few months before he turned 17. "When I was a little boy, I liked to play baseball. I was an outfielder, but I was too small to play baseball. In that time in Japan, baseball, boxing, and sumo wrestling were very popular sports. In my house, there was no television, so I went to other houses in the neighborhood to watch sports. When I saw boxing for the first time, it attracted me. The work from the rice store was very hard but it was very good because it helped me to train my arms, my feet, my legs, and my waist," Harada said.

He found Sasazaki Boxing Gym and learned to fight, working with Takeshi Sasazaki. Harada confessed that he did not think he was a natural talent. "I do not believe I was born with a fighter's talent and skill. When I first started boxing as a professional, there were three of us in the flyweight division that were rivals. Katsutoshi Aoki, Hiroyuki Ebihara, and myself. They called us the three crows of the flyweights. Among the three of us, I believe I was the least talented. Ebihara had his 'razor punch,' and Aoki had his 'megaton punch,' named after their powerful punches. I think I was able to beat them by training harder than anyone and not losing the will to win," Harada said. Part of that hard training of which Harada spoke was his commitment to roadwork. While most boxers generally do not enjoy this necessary but often tedious part of training, Harada relished it. He would run a minimum of 15 miles each day. Harada was a great student and dedicated athlete from a young age. "I did not have any boxing heroes, but my manager and coach Takeshi Sasazaki had fought Tsueneo 'Piston' Horiguchi, the former featherweight champion of Asia, before the war. Although I had never seen Horiguchi, he was a superstar in Japan at that time. Sasazaki respected Horiguchi very much, so he taught me Horiguchi's style," he said. His nickname "Fighting" Harada came about after he won an all-Japanese flyweight rookie tournament in 1961. He defeated Hiroyuki Ebihara in the final. His manager wanted to name him "Giant" after the Tokyo Giants, a popular baseball team, but the nickname "Fighting" was what was settled on since most people felt "Giant" was a peculiar name for a flyweight boxer.

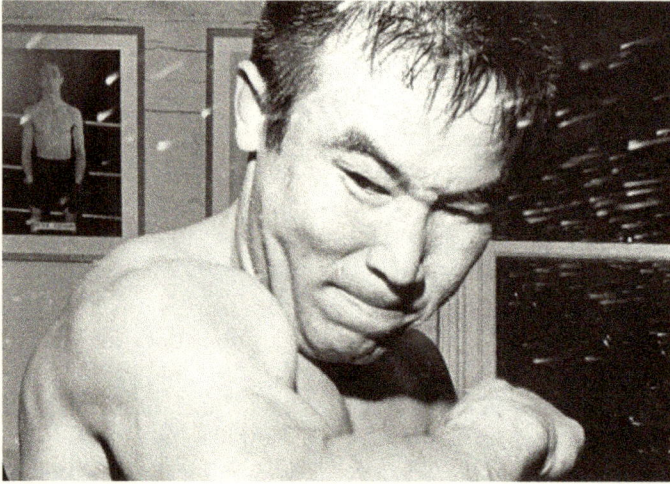

Fighting Harada

Harada, at only 22, had excellent credentials, having won and then lost the flyweight world title against Pone Kingpetch. When he dethroned Kingpetch, he did so in a devastating display of non-stop offense, which the Thai champion had no answer for as he was pummeled into defeat inside 11 one-sided rounds. Harada was only 19 and would lose the title on a controversial decision in a rematch in Thailand before his 20th birthday. Harada was growing and was having a torrid time getting down to the weight limit. "I would have just little sips of soup here and there," he would say about getting his weight down.

After that disappointing loss of his title, Harada had grown out of the flyweight division and settled into the bantamweight class, scoring victories over Ray Asis and Katsutoshi Aoki. On September 26, 1963, Harada would face Jose Medel. In what is undoubtedly one of the most significant victories ever recorded by a Mexican boxer, Medel shocked Harada and the Tokyo crowd with a thrilling sixth-round knockout. The bout

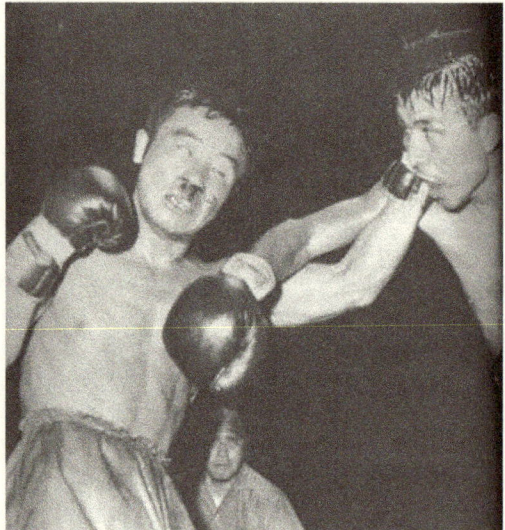

Harada (left), Medel (right)

was classic Medel as he waited patiently despite the ferocious onslaught by Harada and picked his shots carefully.

Harada took the opening two rounds with his patented whirlwind attack before Medel timed him and landed nice punches of his own, particularly to the body in the third round. Harada took the play away from the Mexican in the next round and was all over Medel like a cheap suit and led by fair margins after five completed rounds. The wonderful counter-punching of Medel came to the forefront in round six as they traded leather; he landed a cracking right-hand to the jaw, which put Harada down and almost out. Harada got up groggy but still tried to force the action as he appeared to fight on instinct. Medel expertly put him down again before Harada rose and attacked only for Medel to put him out of his misery with another thumping right-hand, which ended the bout.

"His quick counter-punches were invisible. Medel was great. He hit with a fast and accurate jab. He was not fearful if you did not go to him. It was not so much the power in his punches, but the ability to time the counterpunches. He was a defensive fighter, and if you did not throw punches, you had no fear of being knocked down – but there would not be a fight, either. So, I chose to be the aggressor," Harada told *The Ring*.

Medel floors Harada

When Eder returned from Colombia after the Caraballo fight, it was believed that he could be champion for as long as he wanted, such was his dominance. Aristides told the media Eder would do only one or two more fights before retiring from the ring. Although retirement plans were merely a fight or two away, a provisional agreement was in place for Eder to meet Walter McGowan in England in the fall. The stipulation was that Eder would need to defend his title successfully against Harada and that McGowan would not lose in the meantime. McGowan, however, accepted a difficult challenge when he risked this by agreeing on a bout against Jose Medel, scheduled for two weeks after Eder's fight with Harada.

On April 19, Eder had one of his final training sessions in Brazil when he sparred for the public with Miguel Araujo. Aristides told the press on hand that the goal was for Eder to be around 124 pounds before they left Brazil. Although Eder did not push himself too hard in this session, *O Globo* noted that he looked in excellent technical condition. He finished his training session by skipping rope and doing various jumping exercises.

Eder left São Paulo on April 24, where he spent a few days in Los Angeles before traveling to Japan. In Los Angeles, he helped Hiroyuki Ebihara prepare for his world title rematch defense against Mexico's Efren Torres.

Eder arrived in Tokyo on April 30 after the long journey from Los Angeles. The plan was to arrive long enough before the bout to give himself enough time to get acclimated to the 16-hour time difference between the two countries. After five days of training in Tokyo and filling in his media obligations, Eder traveled 220 miles to the host city Nagoya.

Eder's biggest concern was getting down to the weight as he was now approaching 30 and had fought only one bout in the last two years. Eder had been squeezing himself into 118 pounds since the Olympics almost a decade earlier when he was 20 years old. He was finding it increasingly more challenging to get down to the weight. This did not seem to factor in with the Japanese people expecting that their fighter would fall short. Eder was held in high esteem in Japan and was a boxing idol to many there.

When Eder defeated Aoki in 1963, the Japanese said, "The boxer who can beat Eder Jofre has not been born yet." Few expected Harada could last beyond six rounds with his aggressive style, which left him open, and they believed that he lacked the punching power to gain the Brazilian's respect. Eder said that he expected a problematic bout, pointing to the speed and precision of Harada's punches besides his ability to go the distance at a fast pace. Eder also knew that it would be challenging getting down to the bantamweight limit and was seen running in extra layers of clothing and sitting in the sauna in plastic wraps.

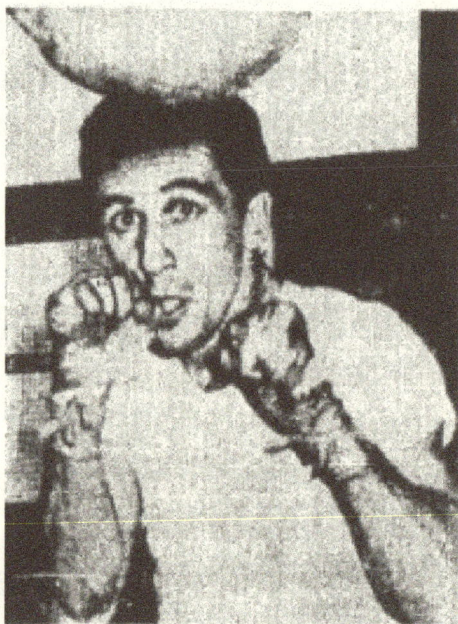

"I had to go for hours without eating. I had to train in sweat clothes and plastic covers, jump rope, and endure that unbearable heat under all those clothes, and this was not good. After some time, I found that I was losing water from my body, the necessary water and not the fat," Eder explained.

On May 11, Eder gave a public training session in Nagoya and left a great impression on the Japanese fans that still held Eder in reverence from the previous bout he had in their country in 1963. "Confident and optimistic, Eder Jofre is perfectly adjusted to Japan. Yesterday, the day of the first public training of his opponent, the Brazilian champion said he has no interest in watching Fighting Harada's practice. He stated he is training every day, with 30 minutes in the morning, and eight rounds in the afternoon. His public training has been watched with great interest and curiosity by his opponent's coaches, who have been crazy about finding the secret to Jofre's huge punch since the boxer is already a myth in Japan," wrote *O Globo*.

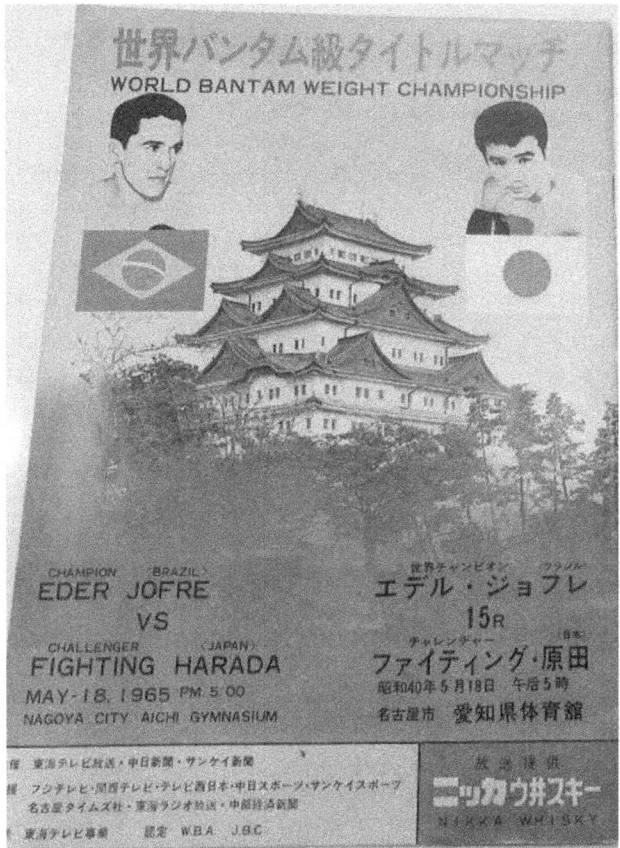

Aristides said that he wasn't too concerned that Harada's team had been watching his son training, nor would they pay too much attention to Harada's public training session. He said that Eder seldom gives his best in sparring and that he purposely tells him to hold back and save his best punches for the fights. When asked about the positive reaction his son had received from the fans in Japan, Aristides said, "The treatment that the Japanese audience has been giving us is great. They have been very nice. Therefore, Eder feels like he's at home."

He added that he felt Eder had even more fans in Japan than Harada did. *O Globo* noted that the fans they encountered felt a great deal of warmth for Eder over his humble nature and chivalry. Eder said that he was interested in the May 13 bout between Jose Medel and Katsuo Saito in Tokyo. He said that if Saito won, then he would be very interested in scheduling a match with Saito in Japan should he emerge victorious from his title defense against Harada. Medel was set to leave for England right after the Saito match for his upcoming fight with Walter McGowan.

Before the fight, Harada was respectful of Eder, claiming that he was "a great fighter" before adding that he "wasn't scared of him." Harada did not talk up his chances too much, saying he would give it his best but that he was not sure if he would win. Aristides had a few gripes before the fight, from the sparring partners to the gloves. He believed that the Japanese purposely sent bigger sparring partners, who were a few weight divisions heavier than Eder, to inflict a lot of physical punishment to his son.

"They were much heavier, and I don't know if they were ordered to hurt Eder. Thank God it didn't happen," he said. The second issue that Aristides had was with the selection of gloves. He was not happy with the Japanese Winning gloves. He felt they were not as friendly to punchers and that they were far too padded. He requested that Eder be able to use the usual Reyes gloves, but that request wasn't answered as the boxers had to use the same gloves. It was speculated that George Parnassus had simply forgotten to pack the gloves when he departed from Los Angeles.

Three days out from the bout, the Japanese were already hailing the Jofre vs. Harada match as the biggest fight ever held on Japanese soil. Some insiders picked Harada because the weight problems that Eder was having were well documented, and because the Jofre camp refused to entertain any speculation he may be tight at the weight. This was seen as a sign they were concerned about his weight. At the public workouts, Eder did give excellent performances. The Japanese press concluded that Eder was much stronger and far more confident than Harada. Yoshiro Shirai, former world flyweight champion, said that Eder "has dynamite in his fists." Harada declared in an interview he can never get enough sleep the nights before fights but told the press he was in excellent condition. "I trained hard. I carried to the letter all the instructions given by my coach Sasasaki. I will do what it takes to win that fight," he said.

At the weigh-in, the Brazilians in the room were apprehensive that Eder may miss the weight, but he lightened the mood by cracking jokes. He hopped onto the scale and came in just under the 118 pounds limit and then said he would be resting up in the afternoon by playing cards before heading to the arena for the fight.

On fight night, 12,000 fans packed into Aichi Prefectural Gym in anticipation of the mega-fight between a Japanese national hero and the best pound-for-pound boxer in the world. Both fighters received a good response from the crowd as they were introduced before getting their pre-fight instructions from referee Barney Ross.

Round By Round from *Estadão* and *Folha*

Round 1

(*Estadão*) Harada goes first and lands on Eder's chin with a right cross. Eder hits him back in the face. After the referee separates the fighters from the clinch, Harada lands a shot on Eder, who quickly counters with a left hook. Harada's eyebrow is bleeding.

(*Folha*) The boxers meet in the center of the ring, and the fight starts with an exchange of hooks; Jofre fails with two straight punches, and Harada makes him back up to the corner, but he receives a violent right blow to his face. They observe each other, and the bell surprises Jofre, who was punching his opponent's face with his right hand.

Round 2

(*Estadão*) Harada tries to hit Eder's midsection but gets caught clean by a punch in the face. They engage in a violent exchange of punches; Eder is working his jabs and uppercuts.

(*Folha*) Harada quickly attacks, but Jofre's left uppercut hits his body. The Japanese protects himself with his gloves in the center of the ring and tries to get back at him with two right uppercuts that don't hit the Brazilian. The Japanese's right eye is red.

Round 3

(*Estadão*) Long-range punch exchange. Eder throws a violent uppercut, which Harada successfully blocks. The Japanese goes for a brawl and traps Eder in a corner and lands several inside punches. Eder tries to get away from the corner. It's a tied round.

(*Folha*) The boxers exchange short, straight punches, and Jofre lands a left uppercut against his opponent's body, which is blocked. Harada makes the world champion back up to the corner; Jofre hits him with a right-hand punch, and Harada fights back with punches, using both hands.

Round 4

(*Estadão*) Harada shows great leg agility, Eder lands jabs to Harada's head. The Japanese catches Eder by surprise by hitting him with a strong right-hand punch. The crowd goes wild, screaming for a KO, Eder clinches. End of the round, which goes to Harada.

(*Folha*) Jofre gets upset, hits with his right hand, and Harada tries to get back at him, with no success. There is an exchange of right-hand punches, and the Japanese's face and nose bleed. Harada throws himself against his opponent, giving him "one-two" punches to the head. The Brazilian looks surprised by the attacks, but he grabs his opponent, while the viewers yell, thrilled. This round was favorable to Harada.

Round 5

(*Estadão*) Harada goes off, throwing jabs and hooks. Eder protects himself and throws uppercuts, which get blocked. Recovered, the champion throws one-two combos, hitting both body and face of his opponent. Harada bleeds from the nose. Eder hits him hard; the Japanese is groggy. Round goes to Eder.

(*Folha*) Harada starts the round by hitting a right cross punch to Jofre's face, who fights with his guard up to avoid his opponent's attacks. Jofre stays in the center of the ring; there is an exchange of punches. Harada lands a left uppercut on Eder's chin, who fights back with a right-hand punch, shaking the Japanese, and then the bell rings. Jofre's advantage.

Round 6

(*Estadão*) Punch exchange in the center of the ring. Harada resorts to clinches, which is something that he's been doing often in this fight. Eder bleeds on his eyebrow but keeps the pace. It's a tied round.

(*Folha*) Harada throws two left-hand punches, with no result. Both boxers show a slower rhythm in the center of the ring. Right-hand punches of Harada on Jofre, and a "one-two" from the Brazilian but the bell rings.

Round 7

(*Estadão*) They both look more cautious now. Harada receives a strong left and clinches again. Before the end of the round, Eder lands two more uppercuts on Harada. Round goes to Eder.

(*Folha*) After a quick exchange of short punches, the boxers grab each other and move slowly. Harada takes Jofre to the ropes, but the champion gets out with a left-handed punch. The Japanese sidesteps. The round ends with a toe-to-toe fight.

Round 8

(*Estadão*) Harada goes first. Eder keeps his guard up high. The Japanese throws Eder against the ropes with strong left and right-hand punches. Eder lands a powerful left hook, and Harada backs away. Another vicious exchange and the crowd goes wild. It's a tied round.

(*Folha*) The boxers attack and, in the center of the ring, Jofre guards himself, while Harada, attacking, takes him to the ropes. Eder uses his left hand and stops the Japanese's attack, who takes a right-hand punch, blocks him with his gloves, and goes back to attacking.

Round 9

(*Estadão*) Jofre moves around the opponent, lands a good right-hand punch but misses the follow-up. Harada hits the body and face. They both clinched each other. Masahiko works his one-two combo. A strong left by Eder makes the Japanese hit the backpedal. Round goes to Eder.

(*Folha*) Harada starts with a right-hand punch, which Jofre counters back with a punch to his opponent's body. The fight gets faster and more violent. The Japanese attacks Eder, who grabs him, and the referee separates them. The Brazilian finished the round with a fierce left-hand punch before the bell rings.

Round 10

(*Estadão*) The agility of the Japanese is something amazing to see. They both dance around each other in the center of the ring. Harada attacks and Eder counters it. Another tied round.

(*Folha*) Like in the previous rounds, Harada leaves his corner like a thunderbolt. They exchange punches, and a Jofre uppercut hits the Japanese's jaw. Harada gets back at Eder with a straight right-hand punch, with little effect. When the bell rings, they are both exchanging blows toe-to-toe in the center of the ring.

Round 11

(*Estadão*) Harada is dancing and hitting Eder's face. They both move with class, exchanging long-range punches. The Japanese blocks Eder's attempt and hits him back. Round goes to Harada.

(*Folha*) Once again, Harada is more aggressive. He lands many punches to Jofre's face and body; The Brazilian fights in his corner and receives another series of punches without landing his own shots.

Round 12

(*Estadão*) Harada goes first and lands a powerful shot to Eder's face. Eder responds with a one-two combo but gets caught by an uppercut. Harada throws Eder against the ropes again. A drawn round.

(*Folha*) Jofre starts this round with a right-hand punch on his opponent's body, who fights back with left and right-hand punches. Again, Harada takes Eder to the corner. Jofre's face shows pain, and he resists the attack, grabbing his opponent.

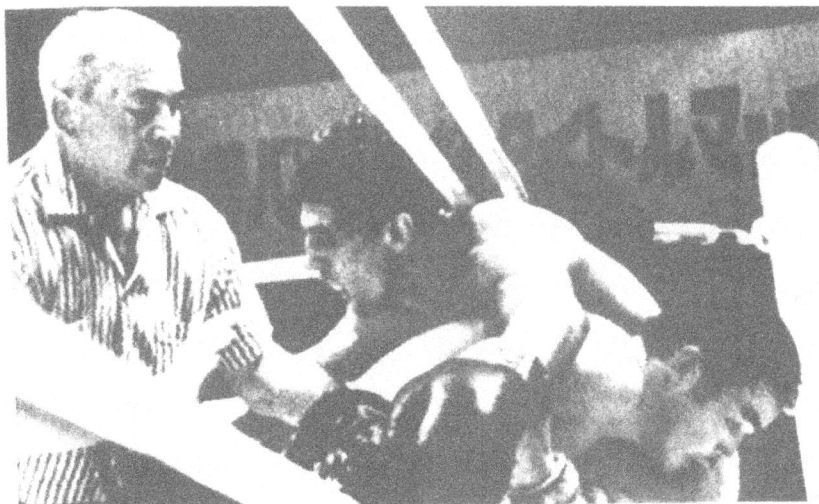

Round 13

(*Estadão*) The Japanese goes after Eder and hits him hard. They both show signs of tiredness. Harada keeps attacking Eder. Round goes to Harada.

(*Folha*) Once again, Harada shows himself more aggressive. He throws a lot of punches against Jofre's body and face. The Brazilian fights in his corner and receives another series of punches, without landing back in return.

Round 14

(*Estadão*) Harada keeps the pace, looking to attack Eder. Eder responds with a shot to the chin. The Japanese tries to react, but he slips and falls to the canvas. Round goes to Eder.

(*Folha*) Harada attacks again and, when he throws himself over Eder, he slips and falls. But the referee doesn't count. Jofre hits him with a punch to his body. Harada fights back with a one-two. Jofre grabs him.

Round 15

(*Estadão*) Jofre touches gloves with Harada and shortly after, hits him with a right-hand punch to the face, followed by a left hook. Harada backs away, throwing mid-section shots. The Japanese uses his jabs to keep Eder away. Eder surprises him with a strong right-hand punch to his face. Harada is bleeding again from his nose but throws Eder against the ropes again. The crowd applauds. Round goes to Harada.

(*Folha*) Harada attacks and hits Jofre with one-two punches, taking him to the ropes. Jofre fires back with a right cross. They move, exchanging hard punches, being clear that they are looking for a knockout. Harada attacks, forcing the champion to his corner. The viewers cheer "champion" until the bell rings. The fighters hug each other in the center of the ring. It's the end of the fight.

It had been a great fight from start to finish between what history tells us was not only two of the greatest bantamweight boxers of all-time but two of the greatest pound-for-pound fighters of all-time. Harada exceeded the pre-fight expectations of the Japanese public as he stood with Eder the whole way and delivered a thrilling and competitive fight.

Harada showed some great maturity in this bout by proving he was not only an aggressive brawler who threw punches in bunches. Instead, he showed that he could adapt his strategy and implement different ways of fighting as the two struggled to gain the upper hand throughout the contest. Eder was hurt badly in the fourth round and appeared to fall behind but rallied in the next round and had a badly hurt Harada on the brink.

Harada's jabbing confused Eder throughout the contest. It made it hard for the champion to pin Harada down, but Eder was the fighter consistently landing the harder, cleaner blows through the contest. The fight had been a close one, so not surprisingly, the decision went to the hometown fighter as the championship changed hands. Jay Edson from America scored the bout 72-71 for Eder but was overruled by the Japanese judge, who had his countryman out in front by a

	Jofre			Harada		
	加藤 Kato	エドソン Edson	ロス Ross	ロス Ross	エドソン Edson	加藤 Kato
(1)	4	4	4	5	5	5
(2)	5	5	5	5	5	5
(3)	5	5	5	4	4	5
(4)	3	4	4	5	5	5
(5)	5	5	5	4	3	3
(6)	4	5	5	5	4	5
(7)	5	5	5	5	5	5
(8)	5	5	5	5	5	5
(9)	5	5	4	5	5	5
(10)	5	4	4	5	5	5
(11)	5	5	5	5	5	5
(12)	5	5	4	5	5	5
(13)	5	5	5	4	5	5
(14)	5	5	5	4	5	4
(15)	4	5	4	5	5	5
	70	72	69	71	71	72

score of 72-70, and referee Barney Ross who scored the contest 71-69 to Harada. *The Associated Press* and the *Pacific Stars and Stripes* both had Harada winning by the slimmest of margins with several ringside press from Japan believing that the champion had done enough to hold onto his title. The Brazilian media felt that Eder had been robbed of his title. In reality, it was a close fight, with some challenging rounds to score, so it could come down to a matter of preference in what you are scoring the bout on.

Harada was consistently more aggressive and active, whereas Eder was more accurate and authoritative. If the bout was staged in Brazil, it is highly likely that the verdict would have gone the other way since the crowd did make a lot of noise almost every time Harada let his hands go. Years later, when reflecting on his great career, Harada gave Jofre the utmost respect stating, "I am most proud of the fact that I was able to beat a great champion like Eder Jofre." Harada gave a lot of credit to the resolve and the power that the Brazilian had, adding, "I had him on the verge of a knockout in the fourth, and he came out in the fifth to have me on the verge of being knocked out. He was a fierce opponent. Jofre's power-punching was beyond description."

Eder showed great sportsmanship after the bout and did not protest the result in the ring. "Harada is excellent, quick, and brave. He grabbed me many times and bumped his head against me. I almost brought him down, but he made things very hard for my game," he admitted after the bout. "My opponent avoided at all cost the mid-range combat, which is my best strategy. To avoid it, he clinched me several times, and deliberately head-butted me. That really impaired me. I had a hard time trying to strike him as the fight unfolded. I was self-conscious that I couldn't land many good shots," he added.

Regarding the gloves, Eder did say he couldn't get used to the Japanese brand he was forced to use. "They don't fit me. They obligated me to make a fist to force my hands in it, I fought with my hands tight closed the entire fight," he said.

A large portion of the Japanese fans felt that the champion had done enough to retain his title, an opinion which seemed reasonable to Harada, who said he wasn't sure he deserved the decision. "I was lucky to win. It was a very close fight. I was fighting hard all the time," Harada said. "I think my uppercuts to Jofre's body and chin hurt him the most, but I will make a more sober statement later," he added. Despite Eder's exemplary sportsmanship, he did say he felt he had deserved the decision. "I thought I had won by a one-point minimum point advantage. I was already kissing my family and celebrating," the former champion said.

Aristides did not take the defeat in the same stride that his son did and was visibly upset when the announcement was made in the ring. "Eder didn't lose. Harada didn't do much more than holding and head butting," he said.

Katzenelson agreed with Aristides and felt that Eder had been robbed before offering his prediction on what would happen in a rematch. "If Eder faces him again, he will knock him out," he said.

Harada said that he would be happy to fight Eder again despite not having any contractual obligation to do so. "If the boxing authorities believe Jofre is entitled to a chance to regain the championship, and he wants that chance, I shall give it to him as I did when I won the flyweight crown from Kingpetch and engaged in a return fight with him," he said.

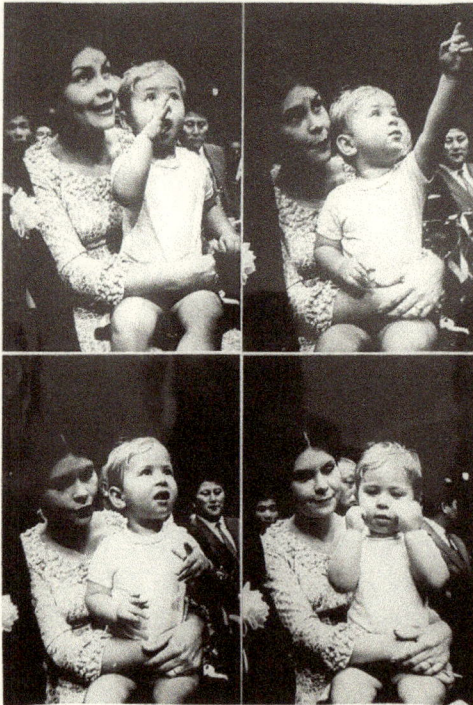

Cidinha watches with Marcel

Backstage, it was a sad affair as Eder had finally been defeated after 50 fights and was no longer champion. While Aristides and Katzenelson complained about the official decision, Eder was philosophical. "There is a time for winning and for losing. Losing the title is not like losing money but to me, the title means a lot," the former champion said. Listening on the radio back in Brazil, Eder's mother Angelina gave credit to Harada. "The result was fair. Harada fought well. No boxer has managed to stay on his feet for 15 rounds with my son. If Harada did, it is because he was in shape to win," she said.

When asked what Eder planned to do following the fight, he said that he would take a few days off in Hong Kong before heading to Los Angeles for a little vacation before returning home to Brazil.

After having some time to look back on the fight and review it again, his view did become stronger. "I won that fight clearly. Japanese people would come up to me and say, 'you won' which helped me with the pain of losing the title." Eder was also critical of the refereeing of Barney Ross. He claimed that Ross missed many head butts and failed to penalize the Japanese fighter for what he felt was too much holding. "Harada is a great champion. I must recognize that. He knew how to close the distance, always bobbing and weaving. Adding to that, he was the master of head butts. He gave me a lot of head butts. He opened a cut on my eyebrow, he also hurt my mouth and nose. He overreacted with the head butts. Clinching too. He clinched more than 100 times. All of that screwed me up. I couldn't fight. He was holding me, scraping, holding, giving head butts. That practically killed me," Eder said.

Eder said that the problems he was having in getting down to the bantamweight limit of 118 pounds was a significant factor in the defeat. "The truth is that I was very weak. He (Harada) was on top of me all the time, and I had been struggling to make the bantamweight limit for some time. I spent 12 hours without putting a drop of water in my mouth. I was dehydrated and exhausted," he said.

O *Globo* reported on what was a sad scene in São Paulo in the hours after the fight: "The environment in São Paulo was of profound sadness, showing despondency for the Golden Bantam's failure. Mayor Faria Lima commented on the unexpected defeat, saying he was upset about Eder Jofre's defeat but couldn't help but give his compliments to brave Harada. On the other hand, the Japanese colony partied the new champion's victory, especially because rumor has it a rematch can be scheduled again here in São Paulo, and the Nisei will be able to meet Harada in person."

George Parnassus, acting as a promotional partner for Harada, expressed an interest in hosting Harada's next title bout and pointed to Ismael Laguna as the preferred choice of opponent. He also said that he was happy to stage a rematch between Harada and Eder. Harada's manager, Takeshi Sasazaki, did not wish to think too far ahead; instead, he wanted to focus on the historical victory of his fighter. "This is not the time to think about it. I must thank Harada's Japanese fans before I think about the next plans," he said.

Eder and his family returned home on June 17 after two weeks' vacation, and Katzenelson said that he had a film of the fight and was still greatly confident in his contention that Eder had been robbed of his title. With no contract in place stipulating that a return bout was mandatory, Katzenelson said that he would be using the film as evidence there must be a rematch. By lobbying the WBC and showing the film, he felt this would give them no other choice than to enforce a rematch.

Fight 52, vs. Manny Elias, November 5, 1965

Despite the protests and lobbying from Katzenelson, there had been no rematch clause for the bout with Harada, so Eder would not be contesting the title he had lost in May. Instead of sitting idly while Harada defended his title, Eder took an over-the-weight, non-title bout with Manny Elias at Ibirapuera. Elias, a native of Phoenix, Arizona, had almost been in line to fight Eder the previous year but was defeated in an elimination contest by Bernardo Caraballo. Elias, at age 28, was an accomplished performer who had held the North American bantamweight title for several years and was a fierce fighter. He was short, defensively sound, and exceptionally durable. He presented his opponents with few openings as he moved forward. He had never fought in the class that Eder had and was not expected to be much of a challenge as Eder sought to stay sharp as he worked towards a rematch with Harada.

Eder missed some training with a stomach issue but showed to be back in good technical form when he sparred with national flyweight champion Jose Severino on October 20 after a morning run at Pacaembu. His weight was reported to be around 124 pounds. Elias set up his training quarters at Wilson Russo Gym. His chief sparring partner was a local boxer named Claudio Silva. His first public training session on October 22 showed that he had come to Brazil not simply to serve as cannon fodder but that he was a serious opponent. "Manny showed remarkable power in his right hand. His fighting style is slow but dangerous," reported *Estadão*. Elias's coach Paavo Tekonen said that his man was in great shape. Their only concern was the weather, with it being a different season in Brazil than in Arizona. Elias kept up a strong training schedule of working the heavy bag, speed ball, jumping rope, and shadowboxing before his five-round sparring sessions with Silva.

While Elias impressed onlookers with his constant aggression and savvy boxing skills, his short stature had locals believing that Eder would win easily. For Eder, the task was simple: win and get the rematch with Harada, mooted for January. George Parnassus said that the fight could go to California, and there were offers of $70,000 to Harada to risk the title in Brazil.

The Jofre vs. Elias bout was getting a lot of attention in São Paulo, with it being the first time Eder had fought in Brazil in over three years. On the morning of the bout, *O Globo* previewed the contest: "The two boxers wrapped up their preparations on Wednesday, and their respective coaches said they were in excellent condition. The experts see in Elias a boxer who resists punishment and is a good puncher according to what he showed when he sent his sparring partner to the canvas during practice. On his end, everyone knows Eder Jofre. What's left to know is if he will be as good as before he lost the fight in Japan, including psychologically. The experts say that Jofre should win by KO around the sixth round."

Round By Round from *Estadão* & *Folha*

Round 1
(*Estadão*) Manny looked to fight on the inside from the beginning. Eder hits the body and face of his opponent. Two uppercuts are thrown by the Brazilian. Nothing compared to what Eder can do but it got the audience excited.

(*Folha*) Elias attacks with short punches, however, with no effect because Eder calmly neutralizes all his crosses and hooks. Eder puts his left hand in front of him and applies a right uppercut and other hooks to the body, which make Elias back up. Eder had the advantage in this round.

Round 2
(*Estadão*) Manny closes the distance and throws a good combo at Eder's midsection. Eder slowly tries to keep the distance and throws jabs at

him. Manny keeps the pace and carries on with his punches; he throws punches too in counter-attacks.

(*Folha*) Eder punches right on the liver at the beginning of the round. He has no difficulties blocking Elias's punches. Eder gives the impression he could easily defeat Elias. It was the former champion's advantage again in this round.

Round 3

(*Estadão*) Eder is warmed up now and is a little faster on his feet. He successfully keeps Manny at bay, throwing good punches with both hands. Manny tries to counter it but can't hit Eder. The Brazilian has a massive advantage in this round.

(*Folha*) Eder throws combinations of straight and bolo punches; with his left hand always in front of him. Eder neutralizes Elias and wins the round well.

Round 4

(*Estadão*) Manny stays steady in the center of the ring and accepts the punching exchange. He showed little power but, for sure, was a lot faster. Manny ducks and tries to protect himself from Eder's punches. Round goes to Eder.

(*Folha*) The round begins calmly. Eder blocks his opponent's short punches and lands a sequence of right and left-hand hooks to the body. He completes the round with crosses to the head and wins the round.

Round 5

(*Estadão*) Eder gets his nose busted and breaths with difficulty. Manny breaks through Eder's defense and keeps attacking. Round goes to Manny.

(*Folha*) Elias fights back, not afraid of his opponent, attacking him non-stop within the short game that Eder takes in. The fight twists. Elias drowns "Jofrinho" with his style and makes the "Golden Bantam" feel a left uppercut and a left hook. Tied round.

Round 6

(*Estadão*) Manny keeps the same strategy, traps Eder against the ropes, and closes the distance. Eder looks worn down, and Manny scores more points in the exchanges. Manny wins the round.

(*Folha*) Eder takes a disadvantage. He receives a right uppercut from Elias, feels it, and continues always cornered. Eder takes in the short game, which isn't convenient for him. Elias wins by applying good punches to the body and head, without feeling "Jofrinho's" reply.

Round 7

(*Estadão*) Eder gets his act together and comes back hitting hard; the crowd is cheering for him now. Eder goes off on a violent attempt to put the American down. But Manny is not intimidated, he hits him back. Round goes for Eder.

(*Folha*) This round was Eder's because he put different combinations of punches to the body and concluded them satisfactorily with punishment to the head. Elias wasn't successful in his attacks this time.

Round 8

(*Estadão*) Manny keeps the same pace and closes the distance again on Eder, who can't apply his mid-range game. The American shows better speed and initiative.

(*Folha*) Tied round because Eder doesn't show speed or punching anymore. He becomes vulnerable to the short right-hand punches of Elias. Eder tried to get back at Elias, staying a little bit away, hitting from a distance.

Round 9

(*Estadão*) Manny goes first and hits Eder to the body and head non-stop. Eder reacts and hits him back hard to the body; the crowd felt the taste of a knockout, which seems close. The round goes to Eder.

(*Folha*) Despite Eder's reaction, in the last 30 seconds, the round belonged to Elias. "Jofrinho" had some moments of distress, initially, when he felt a few punches on his chin. He fired back with combinations to the body and head, but Elias won this exchange. "Jofrinho" reacted in the end.

Round 10

(*Estadão*) Eder goes for the body, looking to finish the fight. The American gets confused by Eder's attempt and accepts the fight. It's a tied round.

(*Folha*) Eder shows caution at the start of this round. He gives in to the opponent's attacks – with short punches – and loses the round again, due to the uppercuts and hooks to his chin.

Eder won the bout on all three scorecards, but due to the bizarre scoring method often used in South America, he had to settle for a draw as he did not hold a lead of four or more points on at least two scorecards. Olivier Bontempi had him up by five points with a scorecard that read 197-192, but the other two judges had it closer with Hedeo Kanashiro adjudging Eder the winner by one point at 196-195 whereas Fausto Martins Garcia had it 197-195. As referee Antonio Ziravello raised both boxers' arms, signifying the draw, Elias broke down into tears as he celebrated what for him had been a tremendous result.

Eder didn't like his performance, and right after the fight, even before knowing the verdict, he stated: "I don't know what's happening with me. Nothing seems to go right. This can't work. It didn't." When he heard about the tie, he spoke again, finding the result was fair. On Elias, he said he was a good boxer. "He hit me with a lot of head bumps, but they were all involuntary, given his style," he added. Eder couldn't put his finger on what he felt was going wrong with his performances, but his comments seemed to hint he had gone past his peak as a boxer. "I don't know what's going on, but my arms don't obey me like before," he said.

This is natural for all boxers to pass their primes almost overnight. Eder had never shown a decline, and while he had lost his title in Japan, he had performed well against a great fighter in Harada. It is only natural that after years at the highest level and the sacrifices Eder had to go through to maintain that level, he was past his brilliant prime. Eder's uncle, Waldemar, was not too impressed by Eder's performance and suggested that "fame doesn't win fights."

Aristides felt that his son deserved the victory but added that he was below his normal standard. "Eder didn't move in the ring like a boxer that fights often. He needs to have at least another hard fight like this one to be in good shape. He stayed away from the ring for too long, and that had a lot of influence." As for Elias, Aristides considered him "a good boxer and a tough opponent." He added that he felt Eder deserved the decision "by at least a point."

Katzenelson didn't like the decision and stated: "Eder was harmed by the judges in Japan, and that happened again here. It wasn't only Eder's loss, but also to Brazil. There was no reason for a tie, and it looks like they are willing to take Eder away from the title." He gave an interview to the TV broadcasters after the fight and said that he felt it would be more difficult now to get a return match with Harada and that the Japanese may defend the title against Elias instead.

Elias said that he was happy with the judges' verdict and that "Eder fights very hard." He also said that he was very thankful for the warm welcome he had received in Brazil and would hope they would have him back.

O Globo summarized the bout: "Manny Elias was not the hardest opponent Eder ever faced. However, he showed to be in shape and to be very strong, besides having the smart game of an experienced boxer. As for preparation, one could say he could even have gone another five rounds beyond the ten he had, the opposite of Eder, who finished tired, psychologically affected, hoping for the final bell. The fight showed sensational perspectives, especially due to the two boxer's differences. Manny Elias always tried to keep the game short and was able to in a way not give distance to the former champion's dangerous straight punches. He was worried about getting hitting to the body, sidestepping the worst of the Brazilian's impacts, and almost went for the victory in the second half of the fight. If it wasn't for Eder's famous will, his resistance, and stubbornness to gather forces and try the KO, the result would have been a lot different. Only that stubbornness and his will to overcome and win is that made Jofre get the judges to give him at least the tie."

Many fans noted that Eder appeared disinterested as though his only purpose of being in the ring was to fulfill a contractual obligation to certain sponsors or sentimentality to the directors of the venue. Most felt that Eder deserved to win the fight based on points but that he had been below par, and the draw was not a terrible verdict.

On November 11, *O Globo* wrote that Eder had probably lost his passion for fighting and had a lot more going on in his life at this point to focus on boxing the way he had when he was a young and hungry up-and-coming fighter.

The Champion's Decline

"Eder is not done, but on the other hand, he has no will to fight. A man of moderate life, entirely dedicated to his family, he has never been involved in scandals or excesses that harmed his boxing career. In the ring, he never received punishment able to shake him. He is, therefore, 'whole' like the boxing slang says. Eder, who was never eager for boxing, need not fight to survive anymore. Of modest origin and with little ambition, he quickly found the fortune way and became today a comfortable man who doesn't have the concern to get richer. Back when he had to, he was never a boxer who trained or sacrificed a lot for the sports. As a champion, he could have defended the title ten times more, but he preferred the tranquility of an apartment at Guarujá by his young wife's side, Cidinha, and his son, Marcel. To those who waved at him, he would answer he only wanted to live well. Lately, everyone knows he was connected to boxing only for sentimental reasons. To answer his father, his more intimate friends, and his contributor's requests. He would frown when thinking of the next fights, in the sacrifices to lower his weight, in the training routine, in the predawn, the running to recover his breath. His decline, physically, can only be explained by the lack of ambition of a man who is already comfortable in life. Many champions stopped being champions exactly when they didn't need to make money anymore."

1965 Results

Fighting Harada W15 Eder Jofre
Eder Jofre D10 Manny Elias

1966

Fight 53, vs. Masahiko "Fighting" Harada II, May 31, 1966

The noise out of the Harada camp did not look promising for Eder as it was being touted that Harada may opt to defend his title against an assortment of other opponents. He notched his first defense of the crown when he turned back the challenge of the excellent Liverpudlian Alan Rudkin. Harada had started strong and dominated the early going, but Rudkin fought his way back into the fight and gave a great showing, but the decision deservedly went to Harada.

Harada's manager, Takeshi Sasazaki suggested that Eder's draw with Elias was all the proof needed that he was not the best challenger and that Manuel Barrios was his preferred choice of opponent for their second title defense. Bouts with Jose Medel, Bernardo Caraballo, and Jesus Pimentel were all mooted too. Sasazaki was adamant that Harada would only fight in Japan and clarified his man would no longer be fighting for the meager purses he had earned for his flyweight title bouts and the first match with Eder for the title.

Despite this talk from Sasazaki, it was announced on February 9 that Harada had accepted a rematch with Eder, which would take place on May 31. Eder had been in heavy training in anticipation of the fight. His training since the Elias bout had consisted of the full gym routines in addition to sparring. The Jofre camp knew that it was tough getting the weight off, so did not want to take any chances this time. They hired a nutritionist and took on an even more grueling exercise and dietary regimen.

世界バンタム級選手権試合
WORLD BANTAMWEIGHT CHAMPIONSHIP

15 Rnd

世界バンタム級チャンピオン
ファイティング原田
FITING HARADA JAPAN

世界バンタム級第１位
エデル ジョフレ ブラジル
EDER JOFRE BRAZIL

Aristides closely studied the film of the first fight and noticed what he saw as a weakness in the champion. He felt Harada would lose his composure and drop his guard when he was hit, so he felt that Eder's strategy should be to study him in the first round and then open up to get clean looks. He felt his son would need a knockout to win as he felt it was difficult for foreign boxers to win fights in Japan on points. Eder held his last public workout in Brazil on May 7 as he performed an exhibition against three sparring partners. After the session, the opponent's comments were: "Very fast" and "he's hitting hard."

Estadão wrote, "The Golden Bantam showed first and foremost to be in great shape, not having problems with the scale." Eder's last private training session in São Paulo was on May 11, where he sparred with Jose Severino, who would also be fighting in Japan a few weeks after Eder's title challenge. *O Globo noted* that Eder was in "the best physical and technical shape" during this session.

Taking no chances with the change in time zones and differences of environments, Eder and his team left for Tokyo on May 12. "You can write it down, for all the Brazilian people to read; I am going to Japan to recover my title. I never felt so good and ready in my life," Eder confidently told the press at Congonhas Airport. In the four months he trained for the bout, Eder had trained 313 rounds in various exercises, 183 rounds of sparring with nine partners, and 80 miles of roadwork. "With a little more training, he could get to the flyweight division," Aristides said.

After the long journey, which included a refuel in Los Angeles, Eder told the Japanese press: "Everything that I can say right now is that I am going to give all that I have to recover the title." Katzenelson wasn't conservative with his predictions when he said that Eder would win by knockout in the seventh round. One day after he arrived in Tokyo, Eder surprised the Japanese press on May 16 at Kyoei gymnasium when he trained for 16 rounds and showed no signs of tiredness despite the long journey. After that training session, over 500 people were on hand to see both boxers sign the official contracts and pose for publicity photos for the event.

Eder worked out for the public on May 17 and once again expressed that he felt he was in top condition. "I am feeling great and capable, as good as it gets," he said. The champion also showed great confidence when he was interviewed. "They say Eder is in the best shape. I don't care. There will be blood, and I'm going to win," Harada said.

Eder missed a few days of sparring as his only sparring partner, Jose Severino complained of a migraine for several days, but he was on form when he worked out for the press on May 23 at Korakonen gymnasium.

"Tokyo – Without using the head protector, Eder Jofre did four rounds with sparring partner Eigo Takagi, fifth-ranked Japanese bantam and who has fight characteristics similar to Harada. Eder did a brilliant exhibition, although diminishing the rhythm of quick movements in the fourth

round, which seemed to be an order of his coach and father, Kid Jofre. Right after that, Eder worked the speed ball doing almost fifteen minutes of practice, and about five minutes of shadowboxing, showing great physical ability for the fight on the 31st and again leaving the commentators impressed. Tatsuo Shimoda, one of the most famous commentators, at the end of yesterday's practice, said that Eder should recover the title he lost on May 18 last season, thinking that the Golden Bantam looks to be in better condition, while Harada has weight problems and needs to improve his technique to face the Brazilian," reported *O Globo*.

Japanese newspaper *Nikkan* opined that Eder would likely win the fight sometime between the sixth and ninth rounds.

On May 25, it was reported that Eder dropped Severino in the fourth round of a sparring session and looked to be in excellent condition. "I'd be surprised if Harada walks out from that fight still with the crown on his head. Eder lost the first fight because of too much self-confidence, but now, looking at him, he's focused. I can't even imagine how Harada is planning to stop him," said George Parnassus who was in town as co-promoter of the event. "Eder is in excellent condition and will knock Harada out in either the sixth, seventh or eighth rounds. We have no problems whatsoever about his making the 118 pounds weight limit. He scaled 116 pounds now," Katzenelson said. He also reiterated his stance that Eder had not lost the first encounter the previous summer. Takeshi Sasazaki, manager of Harada, got a kick out of Katzenelson's comments and felt that his man had the upper hand. "I don't see how Katzenelson can figure that Jofre, a 30-year-old fighter who has passed his peak, can knock out Harada, who is only 23 and has certainly not reached his peak yet," he said. "Harada will win even more convincingly this time, and I look for him to score a knockout," he added.

Eder brought his son Marcel up to the stage at the weigh-in, and Marcel walked on the scales before Harada, which drew great laughter from the crowd on hand. Harada made the weight, scaling just a couple of ounces under the 118 pounds limit. Eder came in slightly under 116 pounds. It was announced that the fight had drawn 15,000 ticket sales and was anticipated to be packed full. Once again, the boxers would be wearing the same Japanese gloves they had worn in the first bout.

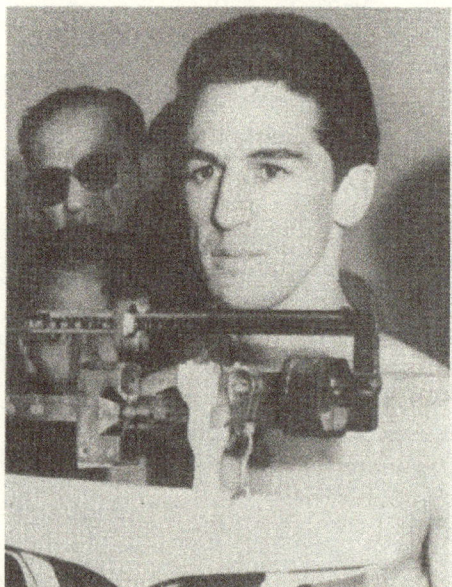

The rematch started with both fighters exhibiting excellent technique and ring intelligence as Harada boxed on his toes. At the same time, Eder worked well behind a high guard and jab. Both fighters went to the body in a close round, which Eder appeared to shade on the virtue of landing some nice right-hand shots. In the next round, Eder was still working well behind his jab as he tried to find hooks to land before the action went to the ropes where Harada tried to work, but they found themselves in the middle of the ring in little time. Harada went to the body and landed well, which was answered when Eder came back with an uppercut followed by a hook. Towards the end of the round, they exchanged punches at a fast pace but become tangled up as the round ended.

The third round began with both men moving well and looking to land their big shots as Harada forced the action more, and Eder was moved to the ropes where they exchanged punches before Harada tied Eder up and connected a couple of head butts before they moved away from the ropes. Harada succeeded in jabbing to the body, whereas Eder missed big punches.

Eder was sticking to his jab, and it was working well for him in the fourth round as Harada moved on his toes, trying to find a home for a hook. Harada worked Eder over to the ropes where they exchanged punches, and Eder landed hooks with both hands before moving back to the center of the ring. They exchanged punches at a fast pace in the middle of the ring with Harada landing a nice right to the body, and Eder landed a clean right-hand up top as the round came to a close.

In the fifth round, they both came out cautiously boxing again before Harada exploded as Eder was near the ropes. Harada threw everything as he tried to manhandle the challenger, who fired back, landing nice shots but Harada took them well. Harada landed a nice right to the body before the round finished with them boxing on relatively even terms.

In the sixth round, Harada was on his toes jabbing and trying to mix in body blows while Eder was playing it safe and looking for single big shots. As Eder went for an uppercut, Harada tied him up, and they wrestled inside before Eder landed a nice hook to the belly before Harada was back on his toes. This round was the sloppiest of the fight up to this point as a lot of it was spent with the two tied up as a result of Harada's clinching.

Towards the beginning of the seventh round, Eder landed a nice left uppercut before the two men worked inside and then went back to trying to outjab one another. They circled each other and probed for openings, and then Eder landed a beautiful right uppercut which landed cleanly although Harada took it well. As they boxed for openings, Harada missed with a jab but landed a big right-hand, which caused the sweat to go flying off of Eder's head, but he took the punch in stride. As Harada attempted to get inside and close the distance, Eder fended him off, landing his left hand before Harada smothered him, and then referee Nick Pope took a point off of Harada for persistent charges with his head.

In the eighth round, they both took turns fighting well off the ropes as Eder landed a lovely one-two to Harada's head. At the same time, the champion focused on attacking the body. As the action got in close, Harada clinched and then landed a sweet right, which was answered quickly by a hard left from Eder. Harada wrestled again as the round closed out. Harada started the following round firing jabs and right-hands before tying Eder up, forcing the action to the corner of the ring where Eder clubbed him with a hard left-hand before they went to the center of the ring. They probed for openings again as Eder set Harada up by measuring him with his left hand before landing a great right-hand to the head which forced Harada into a corner where the champion used his smarts and tied Eder up. Eder landed a strong hook as they were set free, and they jabbed before Eder landed another nice hook, but he was tied up again. Harada worked the body near the end of the round, but Eder was landing more punches as they finished the round exchanging jabs.

In the tenth round, they began by circling each other with jabs before Eder snuck in two right-hand punches to the head. The pace slowed down somewhat, and Harada landed a hook to the body before pumping his jab towards Eder's face. Harada mixed in some right-hands before getting caught to the body. Then Harada tried to work Eder by the ropes but received an uppercut before landing a great right uppercut of his own. Harada was then back on his toes and initiated another clinch before the round ended.

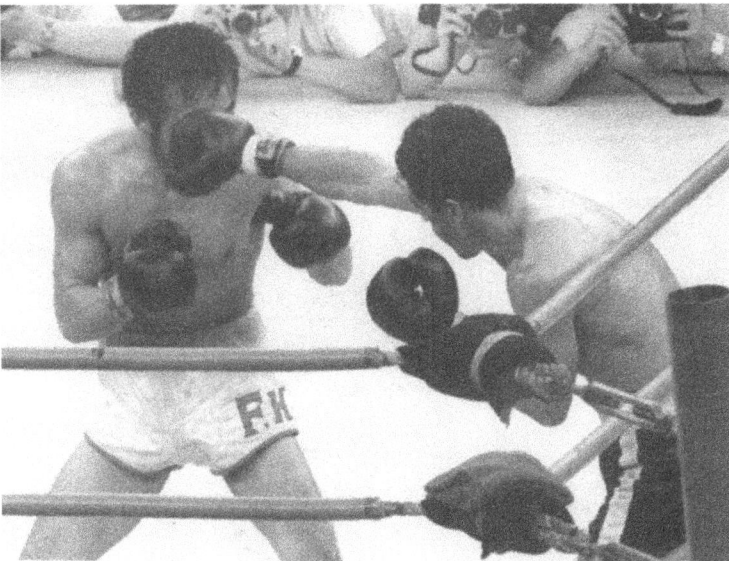

The 11th round was perhaps the most frustrating of the two fights between the pair as few punches were landed, with a lot of mauling, initiated by Harada. Both fighters struggled to gain the upper hand in close. At this point, Eder was visibly frustrated and looking to the referee after taking more head butts from the champion.

Perhaps sensing he was falling behind; Eder came out aggressively to start the 12th round landing forceful single blows as he avoided Harada's punches. Harada was boxing more defensively as Eder landed some slashing right-hand punches and strong left-hand shots. Harada started the 13th with urgency as he worked well to the body as Eder was boxing cautiously, trying to work off of his jab. Harada tried to force the action to the ropes, where he attempted several jabs but missed the majority before they tied up again. The action remained in close as Harada successfully smothered Eder's attacks and got more of his punches off.

To begin the 14th round, Eder missed a wild bolo punch and was punished by a right uppercut but answered quickly with his right-hand from underneath. Harada used his jab more as he was caught with a right-hand, which forced him to go to the body. Harada sensed Eder was tired, so he followed up and landed a few head butts, and as Eder tried to get away from the corner, they tangled up again where Harada connected another head butt, which forced Eder to wince in pain. Rather than separate the fighters, the referee let the action continue. At this point, Harada attacked furiously with both hands as blood flowed from Eder's eye. Before the round ended, Harada landed yet another head butt. The 15th round was another somewhat sloppy one as Eder tried to jab, but there was a lot of holding. The contest ended with a continuation of the head clashes as Harada had more energy and attacked, pushing Eder back as they went toe-to-toe to end the bout.

The rematch, though an exciting fight that did feature a lot of skill and changes in momentum, was not as aesthetically pleasing as their initial contest the previous year. Harada did not appear to have been as energetic as the first bout, and Eder looked old and more tired as the contest wore on. For Eder, the weight difficulties were something he had been put through for the best part of a decade, and Harada was also outgrowing the division.

The return match also featured substantially more clinching and head butts from Harada, which made some of the action a little too sloppy when compared to the first fight. The styles did match well for the most part as Eder was equipped at fighting toe-to-toe and taking Harada on at his own game. Harada proved himself excellent in his technical skills, which very few thought was possible.

The decision went to Harada again, but unlike last time, it was unanimous. Referee Nick Pope adjudged Harada the winner by a score of 69-68 with the two Japanese judges, Hiroyuki Tezaki and Takeo Ugo, scoring a little wider at 71-68, 71-69 respectively. This decision was considered less controversial than the first bout. Although Eder started the stronger of the two and raced off into an early lead, it was down the stretch that the younger man took over and grabbed the majority of the rounds, especially the last three, which he appeared to sweep, giving him the victory.

The head butts did seem to play a part, as Eder was visibly a frustrated fighter, having to deal not only with Harada's excellence but also the plethora of head butts and the excessive clinching. Many of the head clashes could be attributed to a clash in styles as Eder liked to box out of a semi-crouch. Harada wanted to come in quickly, and being the shorter man, he would lead with his head moving upwards, and since much of the contest was fought in close quarters, that invited these clashes of heads. There was significantly less talk of Eder being robbed of the bout this time, with most agreeing with the verdict of the judges. *Pacific Stars and Stripes* scored the contest 70-68 for Harada, whereas *UPI* had it a dead heat at 69-69, and the *Associated Press* had Harada out in front at 73-68.

Harada remarked that he felt that Eder appeared stronger in this bout than he was in Nagoya the previous year. He felt the power in the shots, but overall, he felt a drop in performance from the former champion. "Eder's shots were powerful but not very precise," he said. Eder said that perhaps it was time to finally move up in weight, and he said that he would not be pursuing another match with Harada in Japan. "I'm not done yet, but I want to take care of my family now." He said he would consider a third contest with Harada, but only outside of Japan, where he felt the champion was favored.

The whole family came out for the match, and they shared their grief. "Everybody cried a lot backstage: My father, my wife, our friends, my brother, everybody. My mother was there as well, and she cried a lot too. I remember hearing my mother cheering for me in her high-pitched voice; it was easy to identify her voice among all that mayhem. 'Go, Eder, get him, go again.' It was good to hear her voice. I already had my son Marcel. He was with us, and occasionally during the fight, I could glance at him. I always tried to keep my attention to my father's voice, who was instructing me," Eder reflected years later.

The talk among the Brazilian press who made their way to Japan was the probability that this was Eder's last fight. When asked before leaving the arena, Eder stated, "It's hard to say what I'll do. I'm tired, and I'll think about that later." He also stated that he felt weaker than usual and could have won the bout in the seventh round when he caught Harada and dazed him momentarily. "I couldn't follow-up and missed my opportunity," Eder said.

Katzenelson said that he felt Harada fought a dirty fight and if the head butt hadn't occurred in the 14th round, the result would have differed. He said that he would recommend that Eder retire, but a little later that evening said, "A great boxer never retires. Jofre won't retire and (he) is not happy about the decision of tonight's fight."

Unlike the first bout, Eder did not have problems getting down to the weight limit this time, but it was clear that getting down to a healthy 118 pounds was beyond his reach. The bones on his face appeared a little tighter for the rematch, and it's likely that through this more challenging workload, Eder whipped himself into good shape, but had nearly burned himself out. The work he put his body through during the preparation for this fight meant that he more than likely left his best performance in the gym.

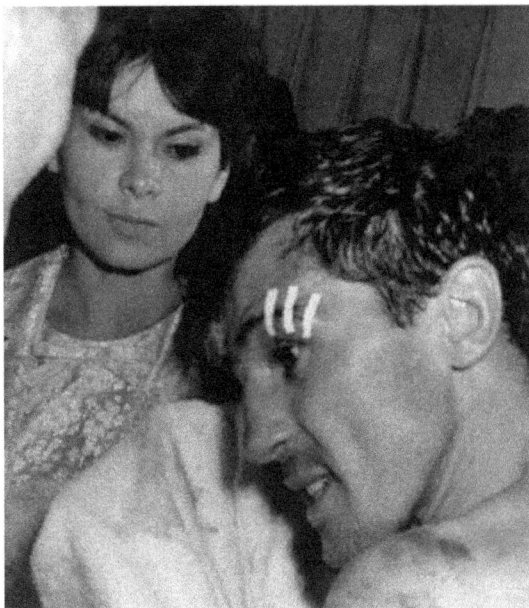

He had essentially done the equivalent of three times his usual workload in one training camp. "I was given a diuretic before the fight to help my problems with my weight, but this weakened me. Even after being on weight, the diuretic did not stop, and I ended up weighing almost a kilo below the limit. I was almost like a flyweight. Again, I was too weak, and I lost," Eder reflected.

Eder had come up short in his bid to regain his championship, and it appeared the magic had gone. For Brazilian sports, it had been a golden age over the last decade with the successes of Maria Esther Bueno on the tennis court, Eder in the boxing ring, and the heroics of the national football team. Eder was recognized universally as the best fighter in the world pound-for-pound, but now his title reign was over, and that glorious chapter appeared to be closed during what was also a very challenging time in Brazil due to the problems with the dictatorship.

Henrique Matteucci felt that Katzenelson had mishandled Eder's career and that he should have never stayed at bantamweight for as long as he did. "The two losses in Japan and the suffering and pain could have been avoided if Eder had gone to the next weight category after winning against Caldwell. This was his (Eder's) idea but (he was) deceived by Katzenelson, who was only thinking about the money. Eder stayed in the bantamweight division. Katzenelson didn't care about Eder's health. He didn't want to risk a steady sort of income. Around this time, he was making way more money than Eder, signing outside contracts behind his back," he said.

The weeks turned into months, and Eder still had yet to make any official announcement regarding his future. He made his decision official on December 29, explaining that he would be retiring from boxing. "Now I only want to dedicate myself to my home and my business," he told *O Globo*. The tough demands of his boxing career came at a cost and Eder felt it was the right decision to focus his energy elsewhere. "The daily workouts, as a matter of fact, all of the preparation that a fighter must undergo called for an enormous sacrifice for me and my family," he added.

Eder had been deeply saddened to come back to Brazil after the return match with Harada when there was nobody on hand to greet him at the airport since he had been defeated again. This lack of empathy and the years of struggle and sacrifice helped Eder make his decision to retire from boxing and focus on other business opportunities, his artwork, and his family.

To add salt into the wounds of Brazilians, the national team had endured a torrid time in the 1966 World Cup in England, where they went for an unprecedented three-peat. While Pele was back, he had a tough time as the Portuguese team kicked him off the field in a crucial elimination game that saw Brazil go down 3-1. Pele vowed never to play in another World Cup. England would lift the trophy that year, with many predicting a bleak future for the Brazilian national team. Esther Bueno was defeated in the Wimbledon final the same summer but salvaged some pride for Brazil when she won the US Open that September. That title victory was her seventh and final Grand Slam victory in her illustrious career. The Tennis Channel would rank Bueno the 38th greatest overall player and 15th best woman's player in history in 2012.

On January 20, 1967, Eder participated in what was labeled "The fight of the century" in Brazil. It was not a professional fight, but it was an exhibition fight against Nelson Gonçalves. Gonçalves was probably the most famous Brazilian recording artist of all-time. To this day, he is the second best-selling Brazilian musical artist of all-time, but he had fallen on hard times. The "fight of the century" talk was merely for promotional purposes as everyone knew it was not a serious match. Gonçalves released hit records from the start of the 1940s until the late 1950s, but he fell under

the evil spell of cocaine and alcohol. He was consuming as much as ten grams of cocaine daily and had snorted away his earnings.

He had lost his apartments, cars, and friends. Gonçalves had been an amateur boxer before he made it famous as a singer. He had picked up the sport at 16 after he was beaten up during a football game and then scored 24 knockouts in the middleweight division. He won a state championship but didn't pursue a boxing career as his music career took off and brought him great fame and fortune.

João dos Santos, Nelson Gonçalves and Eder

After years of abusing his body, Gonçalves, in poor health, decided he wanted to get better. He told his wife he had enough and would bring an end to the abuse. He instructed her to pour the drugs into the toilet, and then he locked himself in a small room inside of their home. His wife would feed him by knocking on the door and giving him his meals until he was ready to go outside for the first time in four months. "I'm the singer from hell," he told his wife, realizing that the damage done to his body had harmed his talent to sing.

Eder was the most high-profile person to lend a helping hand as Gonçalves sought rehabilitation. The singer was frail physically, and his face had a skeletal appearance when he hooked up with Eder. Eder offered moral and financial support to his friend and had him enroll in his father's academy. Slowly but surely, with Eder and Aristides training him, Gonçalves was in good condition. "Nelson was struggling to strengthen his body, but he was a disciplined boxer," Eder said.

The "fight of the century" was an event for charity and also served the purpose of showing the fans of Nelson Gonçalves that he was back, and he had turned a new leaf. "He did that (the event) to prove to the public and his fans that he was able to face the microphone again and go back to being that wonderful singer he'd always been," Eder told Orlando Duarte in *O Grande Campeao*.

The exhibition filled Ibirapuera as fans of Eder and Gonçalves saw their idols box a few rounds. Gonçalves admirably worked himself into excellent condition and put a lot of force into his punches. At the same time, Eder played around a little bit and allowed the fans to enjoy the spectacle. "His right arm was heavy, and he hit hard!" Eder said of Nelson's punching prowess. In the third and final round, Eder scored a knockdown, and when Gonçalves rose he grabbed the microphone and sang some of his old songs. It was a great emotional scene for the singer's fans and showed the public he could still thrill an audience and showcased Eder's big heart and kind nature to help others.

On April 29, 1967, it was reported that Eder would be returning to the ring after a year away and would be facing Mimoun Ben Ali of Spain, followed by a return match with Manny Elias, but these bouts never came to fruition, and Eder remained retired.

1966 Results

Fighting Harada W15 Eder Jofre

The Bantamweight Scene

In Fighting Harada's next title defense, he came face-to-face with the only man to that date who had scored a knockout against him when he welcomed Jose Medel to Nagoya. Harada had learned his lessons from the first bout in which he became a little too excited and ended up on the wrong end of a sixth-round knockout.

This time he used a more measured approach and resisted the urge to go on the all-out offensive. Not that he didn't go after Medel, as the two participated in some furious exchanges and were nip and tuck for most of the 15 rounds. Harada had built up a lead, but in the final round, disaster almost struck again when Medel visibly hurt him near the end of the bout, but Harada used his experience and held on to make it to the final bell to win a unanimous decision. Following the match, Harada was full of respect for the Mexican.

"This was my toughest fight of all four of my title fights so far," he said. Medel and his team accepted the loss with grace and acknowledged that Harada deserved to retain his title. "Medel was good tonight, but Harada was a better fighter," Lupe Sanchez told the press after the bout. "I admit that Medel was defeated. Harada showed himself to be a much better fighter than three years ago when Medel defeated him in Tokyo. Harada won without question."

Harada would again take on a previous victim of Eder's for his next title defense when he faced Bernardo Caraballo in Tokyo in July of 1967. This bout featured a very lively beginning as the Colombian attacked Harada and even rocked him in the early moments but soon found himself on the canvas. Caraballo fought mostly on the defensive and made things difficult for Harada as he used clever footwork and movement to win some rounds. There were no complaints from the Colombians when Harada was given a deserved unanimous verdict, but it was clear he had been in a problematic bout.

"He is a fast and good boxer. I still have lots to learn from the boxing trade after looking back on tonight's close match," Harada said after the fight. "Tonight, the best man won. I was in the best fighting condition of my career, but the champion was the better of the two of us. I want to fight him again, but it has to be in Los Angeles," Caraballo said. Before the bout, there had been a lot of concern among the press in Japan who felt that Caraballo could be the one to dethrone Harada since Harada was having such a difficult time getting his growing body down to 118 pounds.

Those fears were not there for Harada's next bout when he took on the largely inexperienced Lionel Rose in February of 1968. Rose, an Aboriginal Australian, was only 19 and took the fight on three weeks' notice when Jesus Pimentel pulled out of fighting for the title again. In a stunning upset and one of the most significant victories ever scored in bantamweight history, Rose boxed an incredible fight as he kept his cool and outpointed Harada on a unanimous decision in front of a surprised Tokyo crowd.

Rose kept the title for 18 months and scored three excellent title defenses. His first defense was back in Japan when he outpointed Harada's countryman, Takao Sakurai. Then he beat Jesus "Chucho" Castillo on points in front of a partisan Mexican crowd at The Great Western Forum in Inglewood, California. The audience did not take kindly to the verdict of what had been a close fight and took the shine off what had been a great championship fight between two world-class boxers. Rose then made a title defense back home in Australia when he turned back the challenge of Alan Rudkin on a close decision in Melbourne.

Despite the wild crowd reaction from the Chucho Castillo bout, George Parnassus raised enough money to satisfy Rose to bring him back to California to make his fourth title defense. This bout would result in the end of the Australian's short but impressive title reign as he was hammered in five lopsided rounds by Ruben Olivares. A new star in boxing was born, and Olivares would become one of the greatest bantamweights in history and one of the greatest fighters in the illustrious history of Mexican boxing.

Cidinha exercises at home

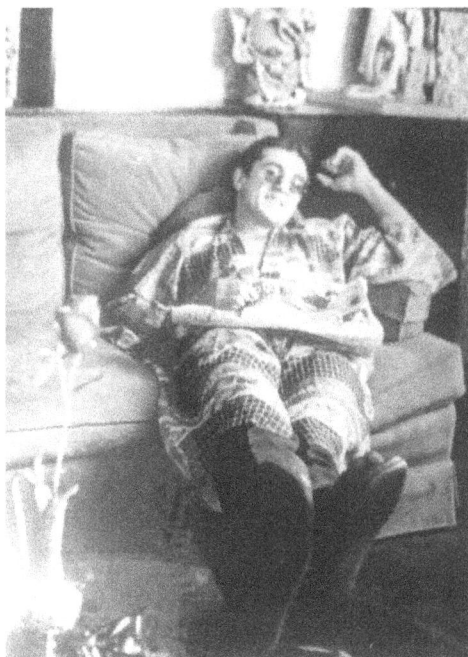

Eder relaxes at home

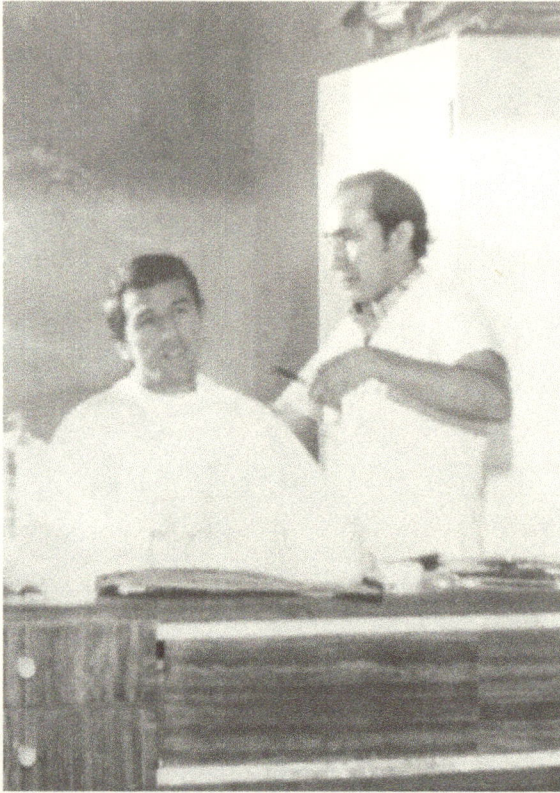

*Marcel climbs the punching bag as Newton Campos looks on
and Eder gets ready to go to work*

Eder with Marcel

Eder teaches Marcel the basics

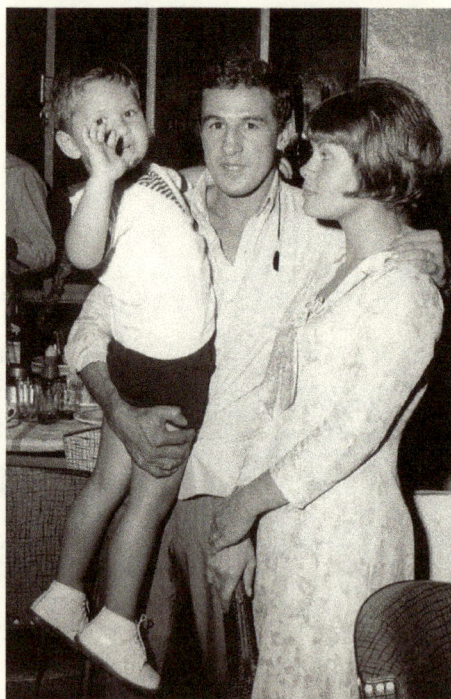

Eder, Marcel and Cidinha

Section Three: The Comeback King

This section focuses on Eder Jofre's return to boxing and career as a featherweight. Eder's comeback is widely considered to be one of the most successful in boxing history. This section covers all 25 bouts Eder participated in between 1969-1976.

1969

Brazil was going through a difficult time politically with the military dictatorship restricting civil rights. President Humberto Branco had overthrown the opposing parties and announced that elections would be indirect. He later had to step down for health reasons and was replaced by Artur de Costa e Silva in 1967. Branco died later that year in a mid-air aircraft collision.

There were protests from students, artists, politicians, and intellectuals, resulting in mass arrests and violent interrogations. A high school student, Edson Luís de Lima Souto, was murdered by military police on March 28, 1968, at Calabouço Restaurant in Rio for protesting the high price of meals for low-income students.

The fallout from this incident brought a lot of pressure on the regime. It sparked further protests, which resulted in more violence. On June 21, protests staged outside the US embassy resulted in 28 deaths, hundreds injured, thousands imprisoned, and 15 police cars set ablaze in what became known as "Bloody Friday." What began as a peaceful protest by the students turned into a bloodbath as the military police became violent, and office workers and construction workers joined to help the students.

The torturing and intimidation tactics used to crush those against the regime increased as interrogation methods included kidnapping, rape, and castration. There were many cases of bodies "disappearing" and a slew of "accidental" deaths before President de Costa e Silva issued the AI-5 (Institutional Act Number Five) in an attempt to stabilize the country and end the turmoil in 1968.

Several tragedies rocked the Jofre-Zumbano family. On May 12, 1967, Walter Zumbano's son, named after his uncle, Waldemar, died in a car crash with his daughter Maria, who was only six years old. Waldemar's wife and four-year-old son Itamar survived the accident. Itamar recalled, "When I was in the ambulance and treated in the hospital, Eder and my uncle Sylvano arrived to pick me up, but my mother remained hospitalized."

At the time of this tragedy, Waldemar was part owner of a company specializing in manufacturing metallurgical products. The company was named Walsywa, which had been founded by his father, Walter. Walsywa, which is still in business today, was named after Walter, who owned 50%, and his sons, Sylvano and Waldemar, both of whom held 25% ownership.

On July 2, Eder's uncle Higino died after suffering from amnesia, which was attributed to the mental problems and various treatments he had back in the late 1940s and early 1950s.

After these tragedies, an exciting moment in Eder's life brought a moment to rejoice on August 17, 1968, when he and Cidinha welcomed a new addition to their family with the birth of their daughter Andrea. Eder was still in retirement, and he spent a lot of time with Cidinha at home to enjoy Andrea's first year. Eder had his business interests but felt he was spending too much time at home. One day Marcel innocently asked him, "What do you do for work?" and Eder had a hard time explaining how he differed from the fathers of Marcel's friends with typical day jobs. "I had to explain to him that my job was boxing. He accepted my answer, but I think he considered that way of life unusual," Eder said.

This little interaction pushed Eder to want to train, and soon he was helping his aunt Olga in her circus tents. Olga was touring the country and felt that Eder would bring further prestige to her shows. These circus performances were successful in drawing thousands of spectators

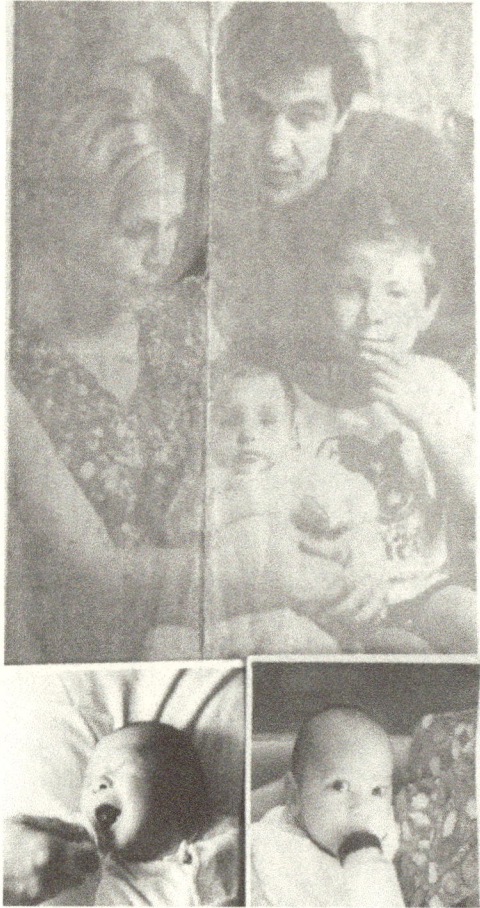

Cidinha, Eder, Marcel and baby Andrea

wherever they performed. Eder boxed mostly with Oripes dos Santos, one of Aristides' best pupils. The shows also helped Olga's business since the spectators got to enjoy a mix of boxing, wrestling, and showbiz. The spectators loved what they saw and asked Eder if he would fight again. Marcel said, "My father was invited by his aunt, Olga, to perform at a circus, which ran all over the country. It was at one of these exhibitions that my grandfather and the president of the Paulista Boxing Federation, Newton Campos began to plant the seed about him making a comeback."

That Eder was traveling and performing created rumors that he was struggling financially, but that was far from the truth. He enjoyed lending his spare time to offer support to his aunt. He enjoyed the interactions with the public. Eder aimed to make himself available for people throughout the country to see him. Not everyone had been able to afford to travel to São Paulo or overseas to see him in action during his heyday. "I went throughout Brazil up to cities on the border with Paraguay, to show the poor people, where I came from, what I knew how to do. Those who couldn't go to the stadiums saw me at the circus, at low-cost prices. People criticized me about wearing myself out, but I didn't care much because I was pursuing an important ideal," Eder said.

The public response to his appearances revealed that Eder remained in people's memories and was still loved by the fans. "My father was the co-owner of a fabric production company on Rua Bresser in the Brás neighborhood, and then he went back to boxing because his pleasure was not in the area of commerce but in boxing," recalled Marcel. Aristides was still training boxers full-time in his gym. Eder told him he wanted to come back at 33 and was serious about being a full-time boxer again. Eder would be returning as a featherweight. It was now impossible for him to make the bantamweight limit of 118 pounds.

The odds were highly stacked against Eder's comeback being a success given he was 33 years old, which was ancient for a boxer back in 1969, especially in the lower weight classes. No fighter ever improved by not fighting for three years. The task's scale can be put into perspective because the last bantamweight world champion to win the featherweight world championship was Terry McGovern back in 1900. McGovern was only the second boxer to have achieved that feat, following in the footsteps of George Dixon. The latter won the featherweight crown in 1892.

Dixon was 26 when he completed this feat, whereas McGovern was just a few months away from his 20th birthday. Both boxers were considered all-time greats, much like Eder, who had secured his legacy as one of the finest bantamweights of all-time. But in an era where being a world champion actually meant being the best in the world, the chances of seeing lightning strike for the third time appeared remote. For Eder, this was not of any deterrence as he was logical in his thoughts. He was coming back because he enjoyed boxing and missed it. Eder was in total faith that if he prepared himself to the best of his ability, his results would reflect that, and he was simply happy to be back doing what he did best.

There was neither brave talk of becoming a world champion right away nor any sense of entitlement that as an all-time great, he deserved to jump the queue. Eder knew he had to hone his skills and get to the back of the line and become a contender once again. "I think the years away from the ring were good for him to have a longer career, but at the same time, Eder lost his best years," opined journalist Wilson Baldini Junior.

The Featherweight Picture in 1969

When Eder was world bantamweight champion in 1960, the man who sat atop the featherweight division was the popular American, Davey Moore. Moore had been an excellent champion for several years until he died tragically after a fight when he was knocked out by Sugar Ramos in 1963. Moore had been the last fighter from America to wear the featherweight title, the longest drought the Americans had in this division up to that point in the 20th century. What this meant was a more international and diverse division but also limited television exposure to American audiences.

Ramos also proved to be an outstanding champion and carried the title with dignity and pride before he was battered to defeat by the relentless Vicente Saldivar in 1964. A crowd of 24,000 fans packed into a Mexico City bullring to see the 2-1 underdog hammer Ramos to take the title. Saldivar, from Mexico City, was nicknamed "El Zurdo de Oro" (The Golden Lefty), and he proved to be one of the greatest featherweight champions in history.

Saldivar made two defenses of his title before he ventured over to Great Britain to face the outstanding Welsh contender Howard Winstone. Winstone, one of the classiest British boxers of any era, possessed a tremendous left hand and exhibited impressive boxing skills behind his jab. Saldivar retained his title in an exciting fight in front of a packed house at Earl's Court, London, before turning back the challenges of Floyd Robertson and Mitsunori Seki, whom he defeated twice.

A rematch with Winstone occurred in the summer of 1967, this time in front of Winstone's Welsh fans in Cardiff. It was an even better fight this time as the two gave an incredible display of skill, but it was Saldivar's notorious late rounds surge, which pulled him away on the scorecards. "Saldivar came on strong in the final rounds against Winstone to take the decision, which was greeted with displeasure by a large section of the crowd. Winstone used a stinging left jab and good combinations to pile up points in the first eight rounds, but he was soon tired, and the stronger Saldivar took advantage of the opportunity. Saldivar almost finished Winstone in the 14th round after he floored the Welshman with a non-stop attack on the body. Winstone arose from the onslaught with his hands at his sides and took another savage beating but somehow managed to stay upright," reported the *United Press International*.

Winstone's trainer, Eddie Thomas, was among those who felt their man deserved to claim the title that night as he said: "I went out to raise Howie's hand. I took it for granted he had won. Up to the 11th round, I had Howard well ahead, and I know he lost the 13th and 14th rounds. But what do you have to do to become a world champion?" Winstone and his countrymen felt he had been robbed of victory this time, but that is not a commonly shared opinion outside of Britain as it was clear to most that the Mexican deserved his win.

The pair took a third fight to Mexico City, where Saldivar was more dominant as he scored a 12th round knockout victory over a gallant Winstone. After this fight, Saldivar retired from the ring, which resulted in the division left in chaos. In a statement after the victory, Saldivar said: "I had already planned to retire when the time came, although I had not made the decision yet when I stepped into the ring. I will take some rest and decide what to do in my new life." Winstone was then matched with Seki for the WBC world championship, and Winstone finally won on his fourth attempt when he stopped the Japanese fighter on cuts. Saldivar was on hand to present Winstone with the title after the bout.

The Ring didn't recognize Winstone and would only do so if he defeated Cuban-born Spanish national, Jose Legra. Winstone had defeated Legra several years earlier in Blackpool, England on a close points decision but had his title ripped away from the Cuban in his first title defense in front of a somber Welsh crowd in Porthcawl, Wales. Legra was then pitted against French-born Australian Johnny Famechon at the Royal Albert Hall in London on January 21, 1969.

In an entertaining, highly skilled battle, it appeared that Legra had done enough to retain his title, but the decision went to the Australian when referee George Smith, acting as the sole judge, lifted his arm in victory at the end of the 15th round. It appeared that while Famechon performed better than almost anybody outside of the Aussie camp predicted he would do; the champion had done enough to retain his title. He was arguably deprived of a few extra points when Smith seemed to miss knockdowns that appeared to come from clean punches.

Fighting Harada had moved into the featherweight division following the loss of his bantamweight crown and was given a mighty scare in his first bout campaigning as a featherweight when he escaped with a razor-thin decision against Dwight Hawkins.

Famechon carried his good fortune from the Legra bout into his maiden title defense when he welcomed the challenge of Harada in Sydney, Australia. Harada, having outgrown the bantamweight division, was attempting to become the first triple division world champion since the legendary Henry Armstrong, and to most observers appeared to have done so when he floored Famechon three times and had the better of the action. Just like the rules in Britain, Australia also used the referee as the sole arbiter. The referee, former featherweight world champion, Willie Pep surprised the audience when at the end of the bout, he appeared to declare the match a draw. The decision brought boos from the crowd, and in a confusing moment, Pep then amended his score and announced Famechon as the winner, which further displeased the audience. The hometown crowd felt that the visiting boxer had received a raw deal.

Since Saldivar had retired, the titles became fragmented with the WBC recognizing the winner of Winstone vs. Seki as their champion, The Ring then accepted the Winstone vs. Legra II winner as the division's lineal champion, and the WBA anointed the winner of the Raul Rojas vs. Enrique Higgins fight as their champion. Rojas won that bout in March 1968 but was defeated in his first title defense when Shozo Saijo defeated him on points at the Memorial Coliseum in Los Angeles in September that year. Up to this point, Saijo had been an active champion, having defended his title four times. Among his victims were the well-regarded Chilean Godfrey Stevens, and Frankie Crawford of Los Angeles.

The Comeback

Fight 54, vs. Rudy Corona, August 27, 1969

The decision for Eder to come back wasn't easy. Most of the family felt that Eder should stay retired. The popular opinion among the Jofres and Zumbanos was that Eder had enough money and that the sacrifices needed and the pressure that his high-profile career demanded was too much. They felt he would be better served spending his time playing football with his friends and brothers, relaxing with his family, and enjoying the fruits of his labor. Waldemar Zumbano and Aristides were the only ones who were adamant that Eder should return to the ring.

Eder went back to the gym with the enthusiasm of his younger years and was up early doing his morning runs. His first sparring partner was junior middleweight Pompilio Genico, who said he was astonished by Eder's performance. "Can you imagine if he was in a real fight?" asked Genico. Within a week, Eder ran up to four miles each morning, and his performances in sparring were described as "excellent" in *Estadão* on June 5. After a month back in training, Eder was ready to fight, and Bel-Boxe, a newly formed promotional outfit he partnered with, sent a contract offer to Spain for Jose Bisbal. The proposal was that the fight would take place in São Paulo on August 8. The contract never came back.

The date of Eder's return was postponed to August 27 when his opponent would be the experienced Rudy Corona from Mexico.

A VOLTA DE EDER JOFRE

PELA

RÁDIO BANDEIRANTES

hoje a partir das 21 h
do Ibirapuera

EDER JOFRE

VS.

RUDY CORONA

transmissão – JOSÉ CARLOS SILVA
comentários – BARBOSA FILHO
reporter – CHICO DE ASSIS

a semifinal também é muito boa,

LUIZ FABRI vs. RENATO REALI
com Borghi Jr.

patrocínio	presenças
MARTINI a marca mundial	**O ESTADO DE S. PAULO**
CAFEZINHO o seu companheiro	**JORNAL DA TARDE**
de tôdas as horas	

BOX É COM A BANDEIRANTES

At age 31, 80-fight veteran Corona was a couple of years younger than Eder, but he was on a miserable streak of form, which saw him losing more than he was winning. At his best, he performed well against the likes of Manny Elias, Jose Medel, Toluco Lopez, Lionel Rose, Eloy Sanchez, and others. Though mostly on the losing end, he was usually reliable for a good test for his opponent. That is precisely what he was brought in for when he traveled to São Paulo to be Eder's first opponent in a little over three years away from the ring. Corona felt he should be favored to win as he had been an active fighter and was the younger of the two boxers. "I don't believe Eder will be able to come back the way he used to be. Aging is pretty tricky in sports. We lose the reflexes and a bunch of other things that are important to a boxer. Eder can get in shape, but he will never be the same as four years before," he said.

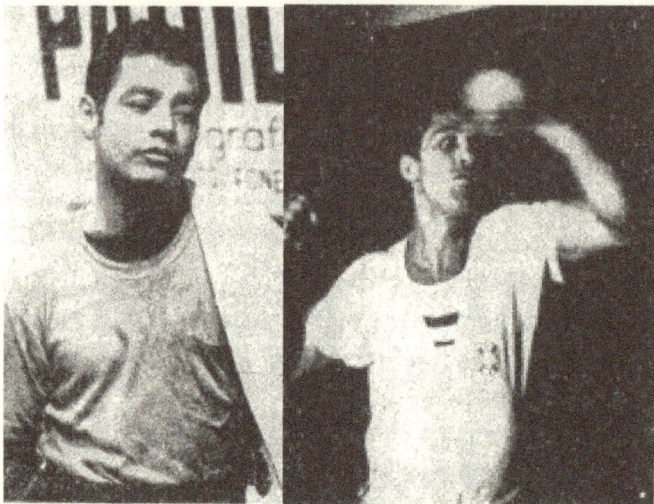

Corona and Eder in training

Fittingly, just as his professional debut had taken place at Ibirapuera, so too did his comeback bout, where he received a great reception from 4,000 fans. Eder worked behind his jab and peppered Corona at will during the first round while avoiding the wild swings of his Mexican opponent. In the second round, a nasty clash of heads left Eder worse off as blood gushed from his eye. It was immediately ruled by the referee to have been a head butt, and the fans booed the Mexican. Corona, undeterred, continued to use rough tactics, which brought warnings from referee Serafim Pereira. Eder continued to attack with his jab and became more comfortable putting his punches together in combinations. In the sixth round, Eder scored a knockout, which the fans applauded with great enthusiasm, reminding them of when Eder was working his way up the bantamweight ladder. *Estadão* reported: "The Brazilian boxer fought a good fight, but he still needs to calibrate his control of distance. Rudy took advantage of that several times by counter-attacking his attacks. Eder showed the same aggressive spirit that made him a world champion."

The victory over Corona came at a price as Eder bruised his left knuckle on his opponent's head during the second round. "I think I did well, but it would have been much better if I had fought against a taller opponent instead of Corona. It obviously made a difference that I haven't been in a ring for three years but only until the second round. What damaged me a little was my eyebrow wound. In many cases, I would prepare the sequence in which I would fight with my left hand, but I had to clean my eye off with my left hand. That got in the way," he said.

Eder had his injured hand examined the following day and had to rest for the remaining part of the year to allow the hand time to heal. After the bout, Corona dropped down to bantamweight to challenge for the North American title but fell short, losing against Rudy Villgonza on points before retiring with a record of 49 wins, 28 losses, and 1 draw with 31 knockouts.

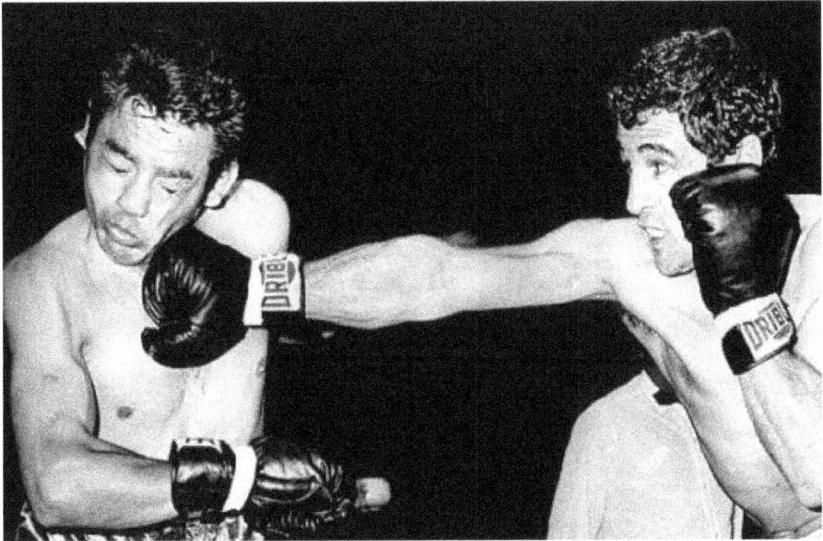

President Costa e Silva suddenly suffered cerebral thrombosis and was relieved of the presidency on August 31, 1969, before dying in December of a heart attack. A military junta took over in the interim with Vice-President Pedro Aleixo appointed as acting president before Emílio Garrastazu Médici was sworn in as President on October 30. The violence did not stop under Médici. The tortures and abuse of human rights escalated.

The public would not learn about the details until more than a decade later, but Médici signed off on some of the most significant human rights abuses of this era. Within the first year of Médici's tenure, Brazil suffered the embarrassment of many foreign diplomats being kidnapped and held for ransom. In 1970, Médici was an immensely popular president for his contribution to the growth of the Brazilian economy. It increased by 10% each year, and he appeared to carry an every-man appearance. It wasn't until the Catholic vicariate of São Paulo exposed Médici through thousands of classified documents in 1985 that people saw the atrocities he had committed.

1969 Results

Eder Jofre KO6 Rudy Corona

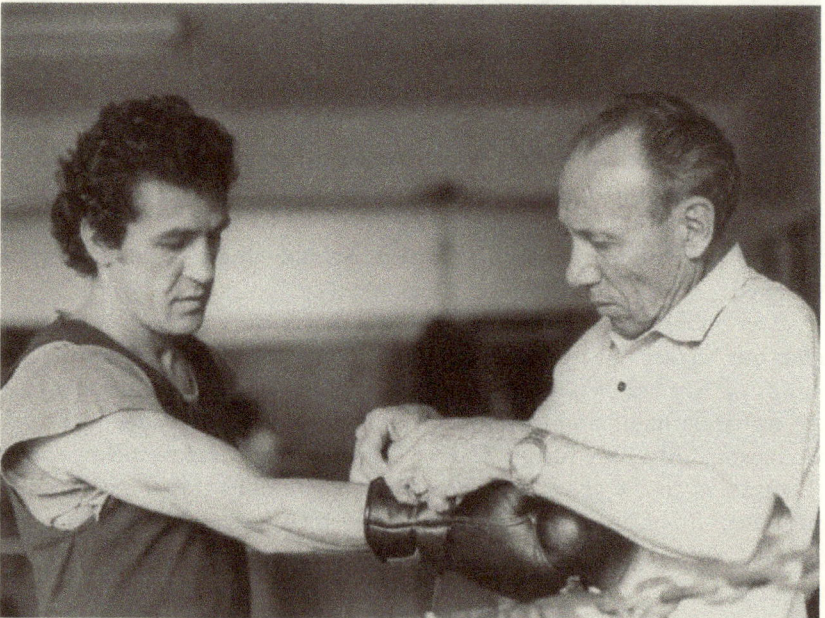

1970

On January 6, 1970, defending WBC world champion Johnny Famechon traveled to Tokyo to put his title on the line against Fighting Harada since most were not satisfied with the controversial decision in Famechon's favor the previous year. Famechon laid any doubts to rest as he scored an emphatic knockout victory over the local hero, and Harada retired shortly after the fight. Harada was only 26, but he had amassed a record of 55 wins against 7 losses and had won world championships at flyweight and bantamweight. To this day, he remains almost without dispute, the greatest Japanese boxer in history and is remembered as one of the finest fighters of his generation.

Fight 55, vs. Nevio Carbi, January 30, 1970

It had been six months since Eder's last fight, not an ideal start to the comeback. Eder was raring to go when Italian Nevio Carbi was brought over to Brazil. Carbi, at 29, had mixed with some high-class opposition, but much like Rudy Corona, had often fallen short at the highest level. He had been defeated on points in Australia against Johnny Famechon and Lionel Rose. He had recently lost a decision in a bid for the Italian featherweight title against Giovanni Girgenti. Carbi dropped a decision in Spain for the European title against Manuel Calvo (whom he would later knockout), so he was not expected to give Eder many problems. Still, he stood to be a useful opponent who would give Eder important rounds.

The two contestants met for the first time a week before the scheduled contest when they were brought together at the Italian consulate on Paulista Avenue. Eder and Carbi shared many laughs as they were entertained by comedian Alberto Sordi. Aristides was also at the meeting and discussed Eder's preparation and said that training was a lot easier than it had been. Eder concurred with his father: "I'm much more comfortable. I don't have to sacrifice to lose weight anymore the day before the fights."

Eder's training had consisted of three days of roadwork each week and five afternoons of gym work where he would focus on hitting the heavy bag, the speed ball, jumping rope, and sparring against three separate boxers to keep him fresh. His diet was a little less strict than his bantamweight days as he revealed he would eat pasta, yogurt, cheese, whole grain rice, bread, cooked vegetables, lots of fruit, and vitamins.

Carbi impressed the local media with his physical strength and his willingness to go toe-to-toe at short distances during his sparring sessions at the gym of Palmeiras Football Club. Some also noted that while he had short arms and a minimal reach, he moved well and could prove an elusive target for a rusty and older former champion. Eder worked with amateur bantamweights Antonio Franca and Jose Bendito to gain more quickness. Eder displayed improvement in his speed from the Corona fight when he worked out in front of the press, and his use of the bolo punch thrilled onlookers as he tried different methods of attack.

On the eve of the bout, Eder was put through his paces by his father as he was subjected to a long morning run by the river Tietê followed by a two-hour afternoon training session which saw him spar 12 rounds with three sparring partners. At the end of the training session, he appeared dry and showed no signs of fatigue. The Jofres were taking the Italian seriously since he had performed well against other world champions younger than Eder. Carbi was also reputed to have never been on the canvas in his career. The Italian closed off his final training session to most of the media. In his last session, it was rumored he looked powerful, but his style might play into the hometown heroes' hands as he liked to get inside and fight aggressively.

Round By Round from *Estadão*

Round 1
Carbi went first and tried to trap Eder against the ropes. Halfway into the round, Eder lands a powerful right-hand on Carbi's head, who answers with a head butt.

Round 2
Carbi tried to trap Eder against the ropes again, but Eder smartly dodged and landed punches at his midsection. Another powerful right-hand hook shakes Carbi up.

Round 3
Eder makes the Italian's nose bleed by landing a good shot at it. Carbi goes crazy on the head butts, especially when fighting inside the pocket.

Round 4
Carbi keeps harping on the same string, giving head butts at every opportunity. The referee warns him against it.

Round 5
It's time for the Italian's left eye to close because of Eder's right hand. Eder's jabs are enough to put Carbi away now. Carbi even decreased the number of head butts.

Round 6
Carbi avoided the fight; he clinched to stop Eder.

Round 7
Picking up the pace, Eder lands several shots at Carbi. At the end of the round, a straight right puts Carbi down on the canvas. He bounces back up as quickly as he could.
Round 8
Besides the nose, now Carbi is bleeding from his eyes.
Round 9
Eder hunts Carbi around the ring; the Italian is trying to avoid his right hand at all costs.
Round 10
In terms of boxing, this round was a disgrace. Even though the whole crowd was booing, Carbi couldn't help but push Eder away against the ropes; he was avoiding the fight by doing that. The final bell rings

Eder won a lopsided decision on the scorecards but had fallen just short of ending the bout inside the distance due to Carbi's survival tactics. Once again, Eder suffered a few minor injuries, and they didn't come as the result of his opponent's punches. He damaged the little finger on his left hand and also suffered from swollen knuckles to the same hand. He brought in Dr. Iva Ferrareto, a specialist who had worked with other boxers before on such injuries.

Eder raised a concern that the gloves perhaps didn't have the right padding to protect the hand while dismissing a theory floating around that he had a calcium deficiency. He took no chances, however, and did a thorough treatment, which would put him back on the shelf for three months.

While he had time off, Eder had surgery on his eyes since they had been injured again because of head butts. He was put under anesthesia while the doctors went to work on his damaged eyes and removed excess tissue that had built up. He rested at home for three days, and from then, went running every day besides his workout, but he refrained from sparring to allow his injuries the necessary time to heal.

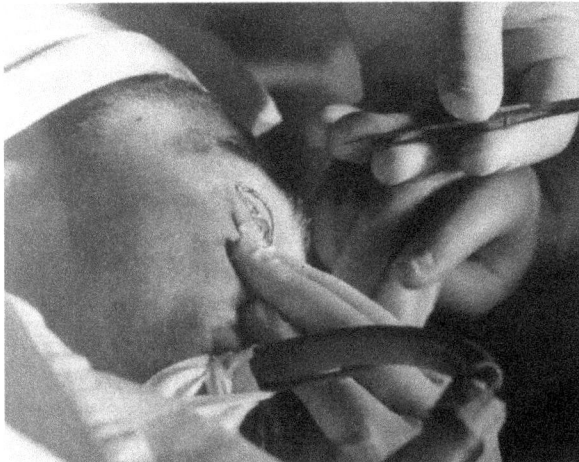

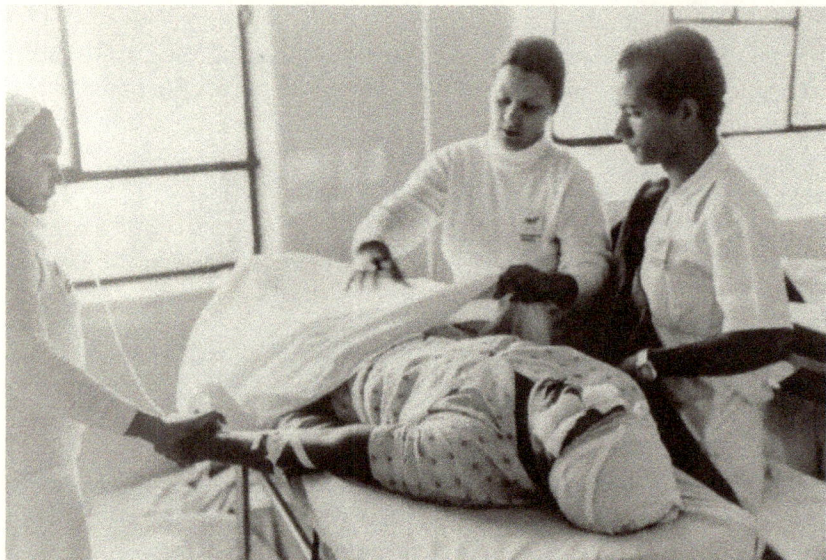

Eder undergoes eye surgery

Eder's management team touted Manny Elias as his next opponent. Elias had a little cache when it came to Eder due to their 1965 draw. "My last fight with Manny was the worst of my career," Eder said on February 1 as he was recovering from the Carbi bout.

Vicente Saldivar dethroned Johnny Famechon as WBC champion on May 9 in the second bout of his comeback. Having retired at the age of 24, Saldivar still had a lot to offer and had returned in 1969. The first opponent he met upon his return to the ring was former champion, Jose Legra. The Cuban had dropped Saldivar in the third round and appeared to be on his way to victory, but Saldivar finally had his rhythm back and took over during the second half of the contest and dominated down the stretch to earn a clear cut ten round decision victory. This win earned Saldivar the title shot against Famechon. In a quality fight in Rome, Saldivar earned a unanimous decision victory and sat atop the featherweight division once again.

Famechon disagreed with the verdict, believing he had done enough to retain his title. "I'm sure I won. I never thought Saldivar got on top. I have no marks. Saldivar's got a black eye and a swollen cheek. He is a good fighter, a good puncher, but none of his punches hurt me," he said after the bout. Famechon's trainer Ambrose Palmer was also in disbelief over the verdict. "The decision shocked me," he said. "Perhaps I look at these things with one eye, but I can't see where Johnny lost. He repeatedly landed straight lefts on the Mexican. Have you seen the other fellow? He can hardly see out of one eye. I didn't think he could lose after the 14th round," he added. Saldivar, for his part, was gracious in victory. "Famechon was good. He was difficult to hit because he moved very intelligently. Very often, he managed to evade my punches to the point where half-way through, I thought I would not win," he said.

Fight 56, vs. Manny Elias II, May 29, 1970

Elias and Eder signing the fight contract

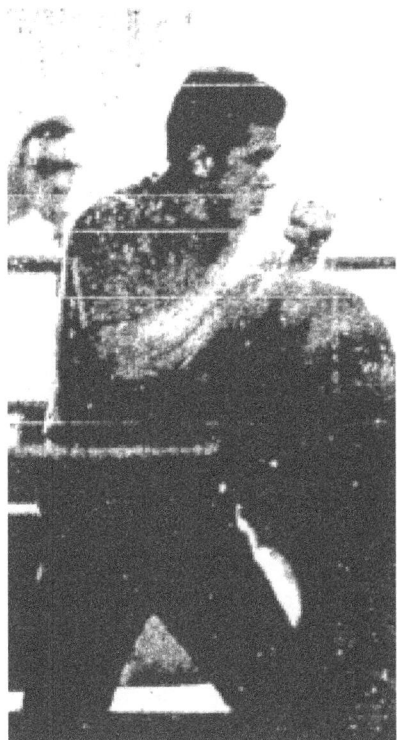

A fight with Manny Elias was a natural given they had fought to a draw in 1965 and the fact that Elias was a big step up in competition from Carbi and Corona. Since their previous meeting, Elias had claimed the North American bantamweight championship when he defeated Manuel Barrios in 1966, and he still held that championship. Elias arrived a week before the rematch and proclaimed himself to be in even better condition than for the previous fight against Eder. Elias worked out for the press on May 23 and appeared in excellent physical condition as he worked 12 rounds jumping rope, hitting the heavy bag, and shadowboxing. "Jofre fights really hard, but I think I won the 1965 fight. I know he is solid and may become featherweight champion, but I won't change my style. I will always come forward," said Elias.

Eder gave a spectacular performance in this fight. Elias provided a challenging target with his intelligent defensive moves, but after a feel-out opening round, Eder dominated the bout. Eder was faster and stronger than Elias throughout the contest. Every time Elias tried to get in close or force Eder to the ropes, he would face an onslaught of punches from the Brazilian, which put the American on the defensive.

"Eder didn't disappoint. Truth be told, Eder's performance lived up to the expectations. The former 'Galo de Ouro' gave the impression he was playing with his opponent at certain points because he had three or four opportunities to finish the fight before the final bell. Rounds like the fifth and the seventh, Eder seemed to let Elias try his game; he was just bobbing, weaving, and counter-attacking," *Estadão* reported.

As though by fate, just as Eder was starting back up after retirement and scoring successive victories, Brazil won the 1970 World Cup in Mexico by defeating Italy 4-1 in the final on June 21. With Pele back in action and in fine form, Brazil was so impressive that many still argue this was the finest national team in the history of the sport with Pele, joined by the likes of Tostao, Rivelino, Jairzinho, and Carlos Alberto. Eder knew that he needed more ring work to reclaim his championship form, especially now that he was older and competing at a higher weight class.

Fight 57, vs. Roberto Wong, September 25, 1970

Roberto Wong arrived on September 20 to fight Eder and was introduced to the press the following day at Terrazza Martini Cocktail Bar in São Paulo. Wong, a 27-year-old boxer of mixed Mexican and Chinese heritage, told the press he was no longer a featherweight but could sweat down the last few ounces to make weight for this fight. Aristides complained about Wong's weight and had his doubts he could get down to the featherweight limit. "That Chinese guy is not a featherweight, for he is weighing 130 pounds, four above the limit. That's why Eder has been sparring with heavier men, and I want to see if we can get this right so that Wong will enter the ring within the weight category, or at least just a little bit above it. Four pounds is a lot, especially since Eder has been inactive for so long," he said.

The bout had been scheduled on two weeks' notice, and it was difficult to get any ranked opponent to come to São Paulo on this date. Wong, at 5 feet 9 inches, was the tallest opponent Eder had faced to this point in his career. Wong stated to the press he was not impressed with the Brazilian's credentials or history. He looked sharp in his training sessions as he showed a nice jab and hook. He even dropped sparring partner Miguel Araujo in a public training session, which caused people to wonder if Eder would have difficulty cutting him down to size. Aristides wasn't concerned with the reports and insisted that it is what goes on in the ring that counts. As always, Eder was in fantastic condition and ready to go. "The important thing is to fight according to the opponent whom I still don't know. I am not worried about that because I had time to prepare," Eder said.

On the eve of the fight, Eder was in excellent form and felt good about his future beyond Wong when he worked out at his father's gym and had a massage. When Eder was asked if he was ready to go for the world championship already, he replied, "The way I feel right now, I am sure I could give it a try, but we are taking it easy. Who knows, maybe within six months I'll fight for the title," he said.

Eder realized that consistently strong performances went hand-in-hand with obtaining a high ranking from the sanctioning bodies. "Not that it's important to be in the ranking, but it works for getting contracts to fight against more famous names until I challenge for the title. I already know the process used by managers well, and I know I can get to the featherweight title. This fight is critical. I have to win it and win well to get up in the rankings. If I lose, I will not be ranked, and the contracts will be harder to get, and the opponents wouldn't be as important, which would make things complicated financially too," he said.

Eder was ranked fifth by the WBA and sixth by the WBC at this point and was informed that if he scored a victory over Wong, he would be ranked third by each governing body. "If Eder wins this fight, we want a fight with Ecuadorian Miguel Herrera, who has been running for a year, always making excuses. He is an interesting boxer for Eder in this preparation phase for the dispute of the title. There is also Shozo Saijo, but our true goal is to face Vicente Saldivar, the best in this weight category," Aristides said.

Eder had worked for two months non-stop in the gym, so he took it easy on the eve of the bout as he focused on breathing exercises and had a massage at the gym. While Eder was heavily favored to win the contest, he was warned by many that Wong appeared to be very capable and hit hard during his workouts. The local press believed that Wong would try to force his size advantage on Eder early and that he would be gunning for an early knockout, so Eder should focus on taking his time and fighting cautiously in the early going.

Round By Round from *Estadão*

Round 1
Not a lot of studying. Wong goes first, with his left hand upfront jabbing. Eder adopted the same strategy. He goes forward, jabbing with his left hand. Eder misses two right hooks and tries to close distance, but Wong uses his reach and doesn't let him. Wong lands two good straight right-hand punches and wins the first round.

Round 2
Wong comes forward and tries to finish the fight. Eder hits the backpedal and gets caught by a right cross and a left hook. But the Brazilian responds with a hook to the chin and the Asian falls to the ground. Furious, Wong bounces back up, looking for revenge, and again gets caught by a right cross and a left hook and goes down again. The round goes to Eder.

Round 3
Wong is groggy already and can't stand on his feet. He just gave up imposing his strategy and gave in to Eder's inside fighting. Wong hits Eder with a cross, and Eder responds with a strong uppercut right to the chin. That's the knockout.

After the contest, Wong said he was confident that Eder would get back to the top and win a world title again. "He is too powerful," he said. Eder had performed tremendously, exceeding expectations by scoring the quick knockout. Wong had brought the action as anticipated. Eder showed that he had carried his legendary power up from bantamweight with this impressive knockout over a fighter who was almost too big to be a featherweight.

Fight 58, vs. Giovani Girgenti, November 6, 1970

Italian featherweight champion Giovani Girgenti would be Eder's final opponent of 1970, and on paper presented the most challenging foe on the comeback trail. Girgenti, popular in his homeland, had beaten Nevio Carbi for the national championship and had earned a draw with former world champion Johnny Famechon before dropping two decisions against the talented Aussie.

Girgenti, 27, was respectful and made no pre-fight boasts about how he would perform. At the same time, his trainer Andrea Giaccio also spoke cautiously, saying that Girgenti was in his best physical and technical condition to date and that everything pointed to a good fight between the two men. "We have never seen Eder Jofre fight, but we know his record. This is Girgenti's most important fight, for he needs to win to fight Jose Legra for the European title. Girgenti is in good shape and can train for 20 rounds without getting tired, and Eder will have to do a lot to avoid defeat," said Giaccio.

Eder and his father pointed to the condition they had trained themselves into and did not offer any real predictions as they had not seen the Italian in action. For Eder, the focus was simply on winning and moving up the world rankings before he could beat the drums for a shot at the featherweight world champion Vicente Saldivar. "I keep calmly doing my thing, my fights, without worrying about the goal that is Saldivar. If everything works out, they will have to fight a lot to defeat me. I don't know my opponent, but I'm going through a great phase, and I see no problems. I haven't stopped training since my last fight with Roberto Wong, and I feel like my athletic status is very close to the ideal," Eder said.

The fight with Girgenti was more challenging than most anticipated. The Italian proved to be a very awkward and resourceful opponent. Girgenti was not opposed to bending the rules as he initiated a lot of clinches and pushed Eder off when he tried to close the range. Girgenti also taunted Eder occasionally, and this drew boos from the crowd. The fight began with Eder coming out behind his jab while Girgenti backed away. These defensive tactics continued throughout the opening rounds before Eder stepped up his attacks. Even on the occasions where Girgenti found Eder in the corner of the ring, he preferred to go back to the center of the ring and have Eder chase him. After dominating the first five rounds, Eder did get caught in the next round, which caused his eye to bruise up and bleed a little. Girgenti went after the eye in the seventh round, but Eder was more than willing to trade shots with the Italian, landing some hard body blows and bolo punches, which caused Girgenti to go back into his defensive shell.

In the last three rounds, Girgenti was simply fighting to survive and was relieved to hear the final bell. After Eder was announced as the winner on a unanimous decision, he stated, "The Italian is excellent. He knows how to effectively clinch and moves extraordinarily. He was never a threat to me, but the fight was balanced, and I never had the necessary distance to put my punches together. The truth is he proved that his name deserves to be among the best in the featherweight division."

In the locker room, Eder's eye was almost closed shut, and he was asked if the rapid swelling came from a head butt, but Eder was honest and confirmed it was a punch. "The truth is I was hit with a right cross when I got out of a clinch," he said. Eder took great pride in getting his revenge back on Girgenti in the final round by severely damaging the Italian's eye. The last round had been a thrilling performance by Eder in what had been his most challenging fight since his comeback began.

The Italian wasn't too generous in his appraisal of Eder's performance after the bout saying: "At 34 years old, I don't think Eder has any more possibilities to think about a title fight. His qualities are obvious, but he has to defeat his opponent by KO before the fifth round. Without a KO, his breath starts going away, making his ring game harder. Despite the punch to my eye by a hook in the last round, I finished well. I guarantee you guys that Eder is only a good local fighter. He doesn't stand a chance overseas."

The WBC title changed hands as Vicente Saldivar was dethroned in the first title defense of his second reign as champion when he was upset by Kuniaki Shibata of Japan in a thrilling contest in Tijuana.

1970 Results

Eder Jofre W10 Nevio Carbi
Eder Jofre W10 Manny Elias
Eder Jofre KO3 Roberto Wong
Eder Jofre W10 Giovanni Girgenti

1971

Fight 59, vs. Jerry Stokes, March 26, 1971

The Los Angeles native Jerry Stokes was Eder's first opponent of the New Year as he was now ranked number two in the division and closing in on a world title shot. Stokes had once been a promising young fighter out on the California circuit but had become a journeyman by this time and was coming off a decision defeat against the South American featherweight champion Godfrey Stevens of Chile. Stokes owned a barbershop to supplement his income when he was not fighting and was already prepared for life after boxing.

The Stevens fight had taken place on January 8 in Chile, and after that bout, Stokes went back to Los Angeles, where he helped Frankie Crawford prepare for his WBA world title shot at Shojo Saijo. Stokes also put in quality rounds with popular former lightweight world champion Mando Ramos and came to Brazil, claiming this was his last chance. "I don't know Eder, but he must be good since he's been world champion. This is a decisive fight for me. If I lose it, I'll leave boxing, if I win, I'll try to fight for the world title," said Stokes.

Outside sources were already reporting that although Eder had only fought a handful of bouts since his return to boxing, he was closing in on a world title shot. Waldemar Zumbano shot down speculation they were in advanced talks for a shot at the title. He said that it was Eder's choice when he would fight for the title, and only he could make that decision. "The challenge for the world title depends exclusively on Eder himself. He has stated that he will only fight for the title when he feels he is at an appropriate physical and technical condition to be successful," Waldemar said.

Eder acknowledged he felt he was close to fighting for the championship but admitted the three years he had been away from boxing had taken their toll on him and that he needed to be careful and not rush things despite his advanced age. For Eder, the most important thing at this point was remaining active and to keep training so he would be ready to fight for the championship when called upon. Eder trained 60 days for Stokes and appeared noticeably confident since he had completed the equivalent of ten rounds every day during this training camp.

Aristides was upbeat but had a healthy respect for the American and felt those predicting an early finish for his son could be in for a surprise: "Eder is very well prepared; however, I disagree with those predicting a knockout in the fourth or fifth round because Jerry Stokes might be a tough opponent. He punches hard with his left hand and is an experienced boxer." Aristides said that his son's training would be easing up on the eve of the bout with light exercises and a massage since he was in no need to lose any weight and had trained hard for this fight.

Eder entered the ring on his 35th birthday to rapturous applause the night he faced Stokes. The American was never in the fight as Eder showed his old bantamweight form as he moved elegantly and showed great technique as he took Stokes out in the second round. "Eder was insanely good. He didn't give Jerry a chance. From the first bell, Eder came up to him as a contender looking for the world title. The Ibirapuera gym shook again, like the old days filled with excited fans. The crowd screamed for the knockout, which Eder got sooner than he thought. Eder didn't wait for the referee to make the final count. As soon as Jerry went down, Eder immediately ran to his corner and started celebrating with the whole gymnasium full of people," *Estadão* reported.

The party began, as Eder came to the ring smiling, soaking in the atmosphere; and after the bout, he was carried from the ring by members of the audience as the crowd sang happy birthday all the way back to the locker room. Katzenelson said that he received a telegram saying that Eder will get a title shot against Shozo Saijo within five months.

Dona Angelina

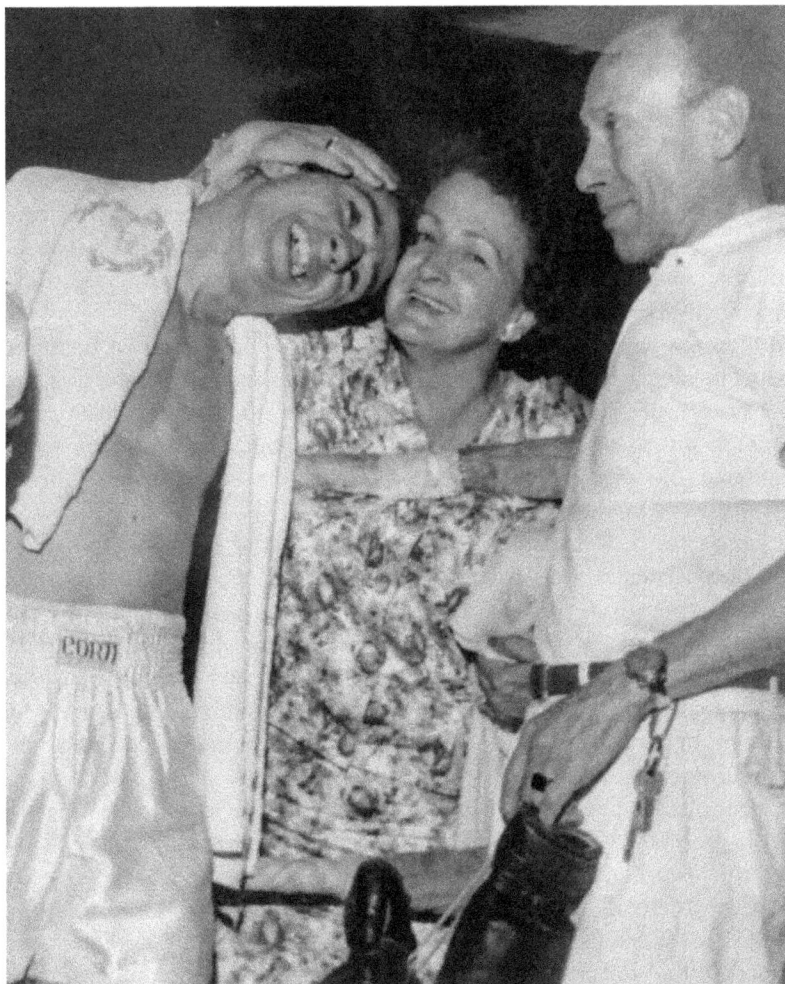

Everything seemed back on track in Eder's career. Then tragedy shook the family as his dear mother, Dona Angelina, was hospitalized with kidney stones. After running tests on her, they found she was also diagnosed with hepatitis. On May 1, Eder was training at the gym when the telephone rang with news from the hospital that Angelina's health had become worse. Aristides answered and shouted: "Eder, it's your mother!" and then they immediately cut the training session short and raced to the hospital. Angelina was hardly breathing, and her eyes were closed as the family sat around. Lucrecia leaned over to Angelina to tell her that the whole family was there to see her. Angelina briefly opened her eyes, smiled at them one last time as if to say goodbye, and then closed her eyes as she passed away quietly. While Aristides had always been the stern parent, ever serious and strict, Angelina was the opposite. "My mother was funnier. She was always playful and tried to cheer everyone with her jokes. She was always in a good mood and telling jokes," Lucrecia recalled.

Fight 60, vs. Domenico Chiloiro, July 9, 1971

The title shot was close for Eder as Katzenelson had spoken of how the WBA had assured him he would be getting a shot at Saijo's crown, but the Japanese champion had scheduled a voluntary title defense in Japan. Eder had to stay busy and maintain his top form so a bout was scheduled with experienced Italian Domenico Chiloiro. It surprised many that Eder worked his way up the rankings so soon as he had only participated in six bouts since his return after his break. "I am not to blame if I am placed second in the rankings," Eder said with modesty. He added that because of his age, he didn't feel he had a long time to wait around, but he also knew the game. Eder had been long overdue for the bantamweight world championship when he finally received his shot, but it was also believed that because of the great name and recognition he earned, he wouldn't need to lobby too hard to get a title shot this time.

Just as Nevio Carbi and Giovani Girgenti had done, Chiloiro extended Eder the full ten rounds. Eder showed excellent poise and boxing skills, which the spectators enjoyed. The Italian showed great endurance despite suffering a lot of facial damage from Eder's constant attacks. Generally, Chiloiro was on the defensive as he was chased all over the ring and showed particular concern for Eder's strong left hook to the liver. The Italian was in retreat mode for most of the evening, and when cornered, he resorted to clinching to catch his breath.

Eder pushed for the knockout as he varied his offense from working in combination behind the jab when he could and tearing into Chiloiro's body when in close. The Italian's attacks were easily blocked or dodged by Eder, who moved around his punches with relative ease.

Most of Chiloiro's attacks were countered effectively by Eder, which persuaded the Italian to fight more defensively as the fight wore on. Chiloiro was outclassed but held on, showing courage. He was losing the rounds as Eder had his way throughout the contest. In the third round, Chiloiro first felt Eder's powerful liver punching when he was forced to the ropes. While Chiloiro was protecting his body at all costs, Eder then switched his attack, focusing on the Italian's face as he tagged him multiple times with hard right-hands upstairs. Those shots shook up Chiloiro, who soon retreated to slow the pace of the fight. Eder was patient at the beginning of the fifth round as he appeared to let Chiloiro recover, but this was only temporary as he then closed the distance in the last minute of the round, bringing down the Italian's guard with some hard liver shots which opened up his head for Eder to tee off with quick left-right combinations.

While the fifth round was the most action-packed stanza of the bout with Chiloiro mustering up the strength to go toe-to-toe, the next two frames were comparatively slower. Eder landed hard right-hand punches in the sixth round, which forced the Italian into a defensive shell, which continued into round seven. During these three minutes, Eder was content to control the action behind a stiff left jab as he tried to find an opening with which he could land a bomb with his right hand.

Chiloiro was tired entering the final three rounds but still showed excellent assimilation to the punishment he received. Each time Eder cracked him, he shook the Italian up, and Chiloiro would back up to get away as the crowd roared for Eder to finish him. Eder tried everything he could to score the knockout, especially in the final round, when he landed several punishing blows that rocked Chiloiro. Still, the Italian held on and was out of range as Eder tried to apply the finishing touches to the bout. Chiloiro made it to the final bell but lost a lopsided decision on the scorecards of the judges.

Eder's next opponent, Tony Jumao-As of the Philippines, was not particularly famous but had mixed with excellent opposition such as Frankie Crawford and Ruben Navarro in Los Angeles. The Filipino was not seen as much more than a stopgap fight for Eder. Still, he was an extremely aggressive boxer with little regard for defense. He did not make a good impression with the local press as he was tagged a lot during his sparring sessions in the build-up to the fight.

Eder did not put too much stock into any word that came out of those sparring sessions; instead, he prepared for the hardest possible opponent and was not taking any shortcuts. "Practice is practice," Eder said regarding the sessions when Jumao-As appeared easy to hit and

AS 21H.30M.

DO GINÁSIO DO IBIRAPUERA

ÉDER JOFRE

x

TONY JAMAO

Narrador – HAMILTON GALHANO

Comentários – CLÁUDIO CARSUGHI

Repórter – ALUANI NETO

fought with his hands by his sides. Eder also told how he holds back in training to save his best for when it mattered most.

"There is no need to try hard during practices for what matters is the fight itself, and I know that he (Jumao-As) will show his qualities and not leave the audience disappointed," said Johnny Billaflor, coach of Jumao-As. Billaflor was full of praise for Eder and told the press how he had been on hand in the audience the night Eder made his American debut by defeating Jose Medel. "Eder lives a modest life and has the conditions to go for the featherweight title. His age is not an obstacle," he added.

Talk of a title shot for Eder was a constant in the lead-up to his fight with Jumao-As. The Brazilian refused to get too far ahead of himself and spoke with indifference, citing that the most important thing was to stay sharp and keep his activity up. "I still have to have another three fights until December. I don't want to say I'm in no condition to fight the Venezuelan (champion Antonio Gomez) now. I want to practice more to show everything I can do," he said.

The Filipino proved to be a livelier opponent than Stokes and Chiloiro had been. He was outclassed but proved to be durable and spirited. Often throughout the contest, Eder appeared to be on the verge of closing the show, but Jumao-As refused to fall. Early in the fight, Eder landed powerful left hooks to the Filipino's body, which forced him to carry his hands by his sides. Each round started with Jumao-As racing to the center of the ring, where he would throw hard shots before Eder took control and hammered him around the ring. "It was like hitting a stone," Eder later said. The Filipino said that he paid special attention to Eder's liver shots. In *Estadão*, they said that "Tony just didn't fall. Tony was not a total flop; he showed great power in his left hand. Despite the heavy punishment delivered by Eder, he finished the ten rounds on his feet."

Jumao-As never reached further than journeyman status but proved a durable foe for world-class opponents such as Ruben Navarro. He scored a significant victory in the next bout after his loss in Brazil. He defeated Raul Cruz, fresh off a win over Godfrey Stevens. Cruz owned victories over former and future world champions such as Lionel Rose, Chucho Castillo, Rafael Herrera, and Alfredo Marcano, so this was an impressive victory for Jumao-As, who had also gained a measure of pride in extending Eder the full distance.

Fight 62, vs. Robert Porcel, October 29, 1971

Robert Porcel, a 32-year-old French-based Algerian of Spanish and French descent, was next up for Eder and was more of a keep busy opponent than an actual test. It was widely believed that Eder was likely to confirm his intention to sign on for a championship bout once he disposed of Porcel. Antonio Gomez from Venezuela was now the WBA holder of the title, having knocked out Saijo Shozo in Japan on September 2.

Porcel, a truck driver by trade, came from a family of four brothers; all were boxers. Porcel told the press he had seen Eder fight once before in 1959. However, it seems unlikely as he said Eder's opponent was Alphonse Halimi, someone Eder did not oppose despite multiple offers and attempts to lure him. *Folha* reported that Porcel's record was 40 wins against one defeat and one draw, but that differs dramatically from Boxrec, which shows a far more modest ledger. His most recent bout had been when he dropped a points decision in a bid for the French featherweight title against Daniel Vermandere. Waldemar Zumbano saw Porcel up close in a training session and said he felt he was a competent boxer who could pose a challenge to his nephew. He said Porcel possessed a varied offense with good punching power.

Eder performed exceptionally against the Frenchman and clinically dismissed him, needing just under two rounds. In the opening round, the two boxers felt each other out, with Porcel trying to attack the body, but Eder was too smart and blocked those attacks as the two got in close. Eder opened his arsenal in the second round and attacked Porcel from different angles until a right cross dazed his foe, forcing him to the ropes. From there, Eder moved in, while the Frenchman tried desperately to fight back. Eder timed a perfect left hook that laid Porcel out for a full ten count, and the fight was over at 2:37 of the second round.

When Porcel came around, he said, "Eder Jofre, with that power in his punch, will soon be the featherweight world champion. Remember what I said." Eder did not commit to fighting for the championship but did say, "I did really great today. I would have defeated any opponent. It's a shame it wasn't (Antonio) Gomez."

Estadão reported that the fight had been a "waste of time" because the Frenchman could not defend himself and was in no condition to be fighting someone of Eder's ability. Despite the excellent performance, Eder was a little disappointed that the fight ended so quickly and felt it wasn't a great indication of how a fight with Antonio Gomez would transpire. "It was just two little rounds," he said.

In early November, just days after the Porcel fight, Katzenelson did start a dialogue with the representatives of Antonio Gomez for a challenge of the Venezuelan's world championship and offered them as much as $70,000 for a bout in March, 1972, at Ibirapuera. "Eder agreed to fight against Gomez, under the condition that the match is not held in Venezuela," Aristides told *Folha*.

It was widely believed that such a handsome sum would entice the Venezuelans and Aristides already started plotting the next moves. "Until March, Eder will have enough time to prepare. First, he will have two fights, and then he will start a rigorous training period. Eder would never refuse an offer to fight for the world title. He demanded only that the fight isn't in Venezuela. Here or another country, he accepts it," he said.

Eder was jaded from his 1961 experience in Venezuela, where they did everything from spiking his drink to pulling a knife on Cidinha. They had significant concerns that their affairs in Venezuela lacked integrity and understandably sought after a more appropriate venue for such a significant bout. That stance was reiterated by Bel-Boxe director Glicerio Mattei when he said, "To be able to win, Eder will have to fight with a lot of seriousness. In Venezuela, it might not be possible to win because they make things awfully hard for foreign boxers."

O Globo reported that the best counter-offer Eder received for a fight with Gomez was for $10,000 in Caracas. The Jofre camp dismissed this as not a serious offer, and stated they would not fight for less than $20,000, and it was clarified that he would not be fighting in Venezuela. Eder said,

"If I fight, it will have to be in Brazil or a neutral country, for a good amount. But I firmly say that nothing has been decided, not even about Luna Park (Buenos Aires) as it has been published."

The Jofre side was firm, and reiterated their stance they could provide Gomez with $70,000 to fight in Brazil. Ultimately a deal could not be reached as Gomez would not accept the $70,000. Instead, he signaled his intention to make a few defenses of his title in his homeland.

Eder lost a few months when he could have been fighting and instead had to make do with the work he put in at the gym and on his morning runs. He spent a lot of time enjoying summer and relaxing on the beaches in Guarujá and felt that the time away from the ring wasn't detrimental to his future chances. "I can say I don't depend on fights, but on the spirit necessary for disputing a world title," Eder said. He believed that his self-discipline and experience were just as important as squeezing in extra bouts.

Despite spending time vacationing, Eder still worked out twice each day. He expressed that he felt better physically after his workouts than when he ruled the bantamweight division. "Before, I had to avoid eating for 24 hours before the fight to be within the weight. That would give me many complications because it would make me dizzy at fight time and take all my energy. Now I can eat well, I'm not on a diet, and I feel strong."

Katzenelson was out of town, but Eder communicated with him in case some good news came in on the world title front. Eder spoke with indifference about getting the title shot, perhaps not wanting to appear overeager. "It's not easy. I've gotten used to a sort of comfortable life in which the importance of order is my private business first and then boxing. Besides, I have disputed a world title, I've won it, I know what it's like, and I'm not as eager as a beginner."

1971 Results

Eder Jofre KO2 Jerry Stokes
Eder Jofre W10 Domenico Chiloiro
Eder Jofre W10 Tony Jumao-As
Eder Jofre KO2 Robert Porcel

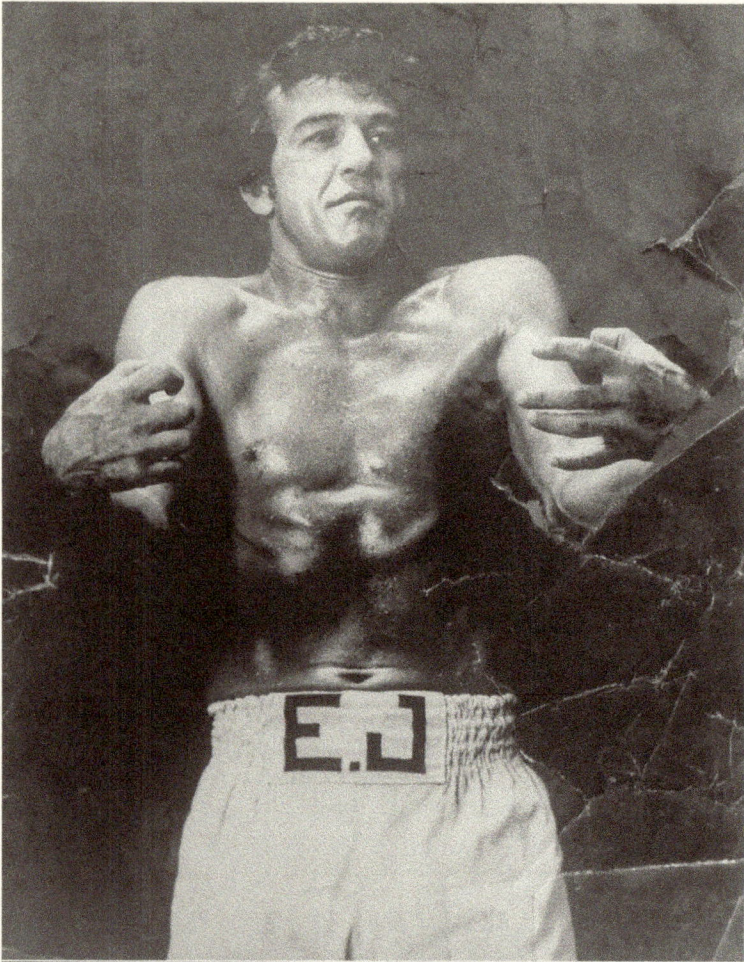

1972

Fight 63, vs. Memo Morales, March 24, 1972

As Eder's 36th birthday approached, he signed to face a Mexican boxer named Guillermo Morales of Mexicali on March 24 at Ibirapuera. It was disappointing for Eder not to be meeting Antonio Gomez, and he even appeared somewhat bored when he worked out for the press and showed frustration when interviewed. "I have been apathetic these days. I don't know what is going on with me, but I think this is natural for everyone. There are always days when we are not willing to do something," he said. His frustration was also partly because he could not fight for five months due to issues beyond his control. "In December, when I needed a fight the most, the venue was being used for other activities that had nothing to do with sport. I think Brazilian boxing will have more resources when it has a venue of its own. With no place and always struggling, no one can say they are a professional boxer," he added.

Eder had appeared indifferent just months before the lack of movement on getting his world title shot. Now he seemed to sing a different tune. This was because he was at a point where he realized time was not on his side, and the boxing politics began to wear thin. At 36, he didn't have the luxury of time. Eder said that he wasn't motivated by the purses that boxing was bringing him. His biggest priority was his family and his personal business. Eder was also frustrated and disillusioned by the lack of quality opponents available. His patience, which helped him as he worked his way up the ladder in the late 1950s, was waning, leading to boredom, and taking his mind away from boxing.

Morales was to be the 10th opponent of his comeback. With the title in Venezuela and the champion unwilling to accept great money to fight in a neutral venue, Eder appeared no closer to a title opportunity than when he returned from retirement in 1969. Eder was the highest-ranked contender in the world at this point and the biggest name in the division. He came out of retirement and had worked his way back up the rankings and had handily defeated all his opponents, so it didn't sit well that he was on the outside looking in when it came to getting a crack at the title.

Folha incorrectly reported Morales' record as 41 wins, three defeats, and 2 draws with one defeat being against Antonio Gomez on points. *Estadão* said Morales had three losses in 41 total fights. In reality, Morales was knocked out by Gomez and lost roughly as many bouts as he won. Frankie Crawford had recently defeated him on points in Los Angeles. In the corner for Morales was Fernando Serrano Villa. He had trained Rudy Corona for Eder's initial comeback fight in August 1969.

Morales confessed that he had never seen Eder in action but was impressed by what Villa had told him before expressing his belief in his abilities. "My favorite punch is my left hook, which is what I have used to take down most of my opponents," he said. Morales' camp noted that they were delighted with their treatment in Brazil. They praised the public, the weather, and the quality of the food provided.

Eder's mood improved in the last couple of days before the fight, and he delivered some incredible spectacles when working out before audiences at his father's gym. Glicerio Mattei felt that if Eder showed the same form he had displayed in his last bout against Robert Porcel, the fans would be pleased. "Even if I didn't consider Eder outstanding at boxing, I would trust him tonight. By how he's been doing the last few days, with so much enthusiasm, he looks more like an amateur getting ready for his first fight. I consider Morales a great test of Eder's intentions, but even so, I don't have any doubts that Eder will be OK. I hope he gives me the satisfaction to reach out for the Venezuelans as soon as possible," he said. Mattei was hoping that the WBA would act reasonably and force Gomez to defend his title against Eder.

Round By Round from *O Globo*

Round 1
Eder didn't do the traditional studying and started to attack. He landed good punches on Memo's liver, who felt it and tried to run a lot. Eder's round.

Round 2
Morales had a spectacular fall, with the counting coming to eight. Eder worked well with hooks on the liver, crossing the right, knocking down the Mexican. Eder's round.

Round 3
Twice Morales was about to fall. However, he recovered and took Eder to the ropes, where he could lock the Brazilian for a while. Eder's round.

Round 4

Morales tried to take Eder to the ropes, stopping the Brazilian's movement, who let go of good punches but was also hit back. The Mexican gave a head butt that caused a small hematoma to Eder. Tie.

Round 5

Eder looks to be very tired due to the punches he took from Morales, causing a small cut to his eye. Eder targets Memo's liver, but he misses the punches. Memo's round.

Round 6

After having bad moments, Eder got himself together, and after a left hook and a straight right-hand punch, he drops the Mexican to the ground, scoring the KO spectacularly.

Despite being out of the ring for five months with apparent signs of mental frustration, Eder looked sharp and was dominant during the first two rounds. He attacked his Mexican opponent at will as he threatened an early stoppage victory. In the second round, he put Morales down for a count courtesy of a quick right-hand. Morales got up groggily and appeared on the verge of a knockout defeat but made it out of the round. "During the first six minutes of the fight, the former world bantamweight champion was close to perfection. Floating like a butterfly and stinging like a bee in the right moments. Eder provoked a bruise to the Mexican's left eye and the first knockdown in the second round," *Estadão* reported.

Eder's performance took a drop in the next round. The Mexican forced the fight from the third to the fifth round. He recouped a lot of energy and charged out of his corner at the start of every round. Morales moved Eder to the ropes on multiple occasions. Eder was methodical and landed his fair share of counterpunches. By the halfway point, it appeared this would be a difficult evening for Eder. Morales was a little more tired in the sixth round. Eder allowed the Mexican to maneuver him to the ropes and then used his experience to set Morales up for a knockout. Eder avoided the shots coming from Morales as he landed uppercuts and then cracked him on the liver with a hook that lowered the Mexican's guard. Then Eder had an open target, where he landed a hard right-hand cross, which ended the bout at 2:38 of the sixth round.

Eder said, "The silence that the audience had from the third round on, feeling that I was at a disadvantage, made me emotional. Everyone trusted me, and I was letting them down. But I gathered all my strengths and was able to bring Morales down, giving them the joy they deserve."

Morales and his cornermen sat dejected in the locker room after the bout when members of the press asked for their take on the fight. Morales was still feeling a little tired and dizzy. Morales stated, "I felt that I hurt Eder in the fifth round, and then he hit me with two hard punches, on the liver and then the chin in the next round, and I couldn't recover." What impressed Villa the most besides Eder's great shape at his age, was the power of his punches. He further stated, "Eder always waits for his opponent to let his guard down to get his punches in. His punch is still excellent and the most important: his fighting is clean."

Villa was asked who he thought would win a title fight between Eder and Antonio Gomez. He said he thought both were equally skilled and could not call a winner. He felt his vantage point was valid because he had trained his fighter to face both men already.

Eder was not impressed by his performance despite scoring the knockout and felt that it wasn't at the level he needed to fight for the world title. "I can't let my audience down. It would be crazy to fight for the title now," he said at the post-fight press conference. He felt he had faded early and felt too sluggish. Eder stressed how important it was for him to be ready and in the best shape possible because he thought if he was at his sharpest, he could beat whoever they put in front of him. Luckily for him, he would not be sitting on the sidelines this time as his next appointment was already set up for just a month away when he would be back at Ibirapuera. Aristides was not quite as downcast as Eder was. He offered his praise of the Mexican's resilience and insisted that his son would continue to work towards getting in peak condition if a title shot would come.

Newton Campos said that he had it on good authority that a wealthy family in Rio was prepared to offer Antonio Gomez $90,000 to defend his title against Eder at the Maracanãzinho. Upon hearing this news, Eder said, "I still need to have other fights but let's do it."

Eder goes through his paces

Fight 64, vs. Felix Figueroa, April 28, 1972

Eder's next opponent was supposed to be Michel Jamet of France. For undisclosed reasons, the French Boxing Federation would not permit Jamet to fight. Glicerio Mattei had to reach out to some of his connections in America to see if an opponent would come to Brazil on short notice. The boxer offered as an opponent was Felix Figueroa, a Puerto Rican featherweight based in New York.

Mattei was satisfied with the opponent and the scouting report. "When a fight is scheduled within short notice, there are always problems like this. Jamet's canceling got in the way, and I had to get in touch with managers all over the world to get an opponent. I am happy because we found a great one to test Eder to see if he is in condition to fight for the world title," he said.

Eder put himself through the paces as he prepared for this bout, taking little time off since the Morales fight. He was determined to put in an excellent performance after admitting that he was below par and felt he only scored the knockout because of the difference in experience between himself and the Mexican. "I will only go for a world title when I feel I'm well physically and technically. I don't want to disappoint people who believe in me. I can assure you one thing: If I challenge for the title and I lose, I would like everyone to know that I accepted the fight because I felt capable," he said.

It still appeared that Eder was not happy at this point based on several comments he gave to the press in the build-up to this bout. He said that he wasn't even sure how he had arrived at the position of being the number one ranked contender and lamented that he could not face other fighters rated in the top 10 featherweights in the world. It was frustrating to him that Antonio Gomez and his team were so hell-bent on fighting in Venezuela and not even attempting to consider the lucrative sums of money to come to Brazil or explore the possibility of a neutral venue.

It appeared that some of Eder's hunger was going away and that he was beginning to dislike the rigors of training. "I need to have the focus necessary to dispute a world title. I don't have that enthusiasm anymore. I have a comfortable financial situation. I have a family, and half of my life is dedicated to private business."

Eder said that challenging for the title meant he would have to train harder, focus more, travel, and promote the event. "Everyone knows I don't like doing roadwork anymore. To say it clearly: I have to stop being lazy and do roadwork every morning, take a strict diet seriously, and practice every day. Only then I'll be able to fight well. Everyone says I'm doing well, that I can defeat anyone, but it's up to me to decide it. I'll only do something more ambitious when the right moment comes," he said.

Eder did say he wanted to get into the rhythm of fighting once a month and said that would excite him again. He also emphasized that he wanted to bring in top-level opponents rather than continue to face unranked opposition.

Another issue of discontent for Eder was the state of Brazilian boxing and what appeared to be a shrinking audience. *O Globo* reported: "Eder Jofre wants before anything else to promote Brazilian boxing. He wants to rebirth a sport that started fading, possibly when he lost the bantam world title to Harada. He remembers when he would drag crowds to Ibirapuera when the sport was practically the second in Brazil, right below football, and then it fell. He knows why: A lack of gyms, fighters, audience, lack of an appropriate place for great fights to take place at, and a lack of advertisement. Eder thinks; however, there are possibilities of boxing coming back again. João Henrique goes to Italy at the end of May, disputing a world title that Eder considers his. Miguel de Oliveira is second in the rankings and will try the South American title. And there is also himself, Eder Jofre, who one day will have to get into the ring to face Antonio Gomez. Actually, there was never structure in Brazilian boxing. These days when a boy comes to learn boxing at a gym, we considered this a true miracle."

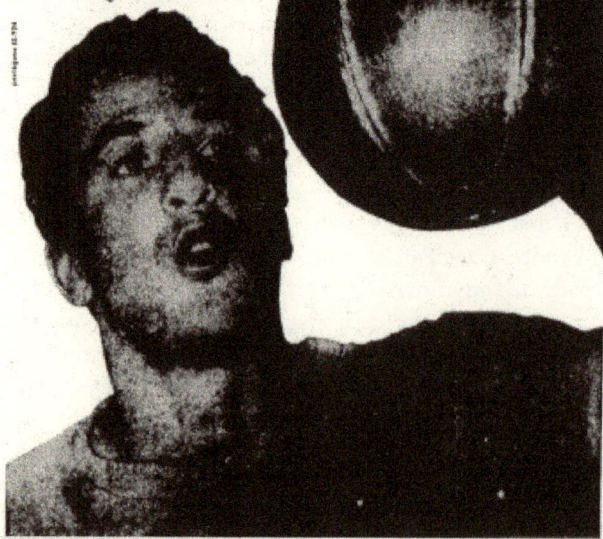

Felix Figueroa arrived on April 25, just three days out from the bout, and beamed at what he considered an incredible opportunity for his career. "I accepted the fight with Eder in Brazil because it is a great opportunity to get a world ranking, for he is first in the rankings. I know it won't be easy, but I don't think it's impossible. In the 50 fights I have had, I faced opponents as good as Eder and won," said the Puerto Rican. It was difficult to verify anything close to that number of bouts for Figueroa, nor could the validity of claims that Figueroa had scored a victory over former bantamweight champion Lionel Rose four months before this bout be proven. *O Globo* reported Figueroa's record as having 43 victories with 15 knockouts in his 50 fights. "My goal is to grow in boxing. I have fought important fights; I tied with Miguel Herrera, I defeated Lionel Rose on points, and Sammy Goss, but I've never been in a better position. I don't know Eder Jofre well, for now, he must be a lot different, but I'm very confident and believe in the victory," Figueroa said. Those results don't appear to be correct when looking through Boxrec, which doesn't list the Rose fight and has the Herrera and Goss fights as defeats.

Figueroa had youth on his side at 24, and despite arriving tired that evening, he went to Bel-Boxe headquarters and did a full training session. He jumped rope, worked the punching bag, shadowboxed, and sparred with an amateur boxer, Jose de Souza. His performance impressed onlookers and de Souza, who said, "Figueroa understands a lot about boxing. He hits hard with both hands and is dangerous at a short distance. He will be a great opponent for Eder Jofre."

Figureoa didn't feel the perceived age advantage he held over Eder would be a significant factor. Instead, he credited his famous opponent on the condition he was in at 36. "I don't believe age influences that much in a boxer if he prepares well and seriously. Of course, within certain limits, Eder is a good example of that. Even leaving boxing for a while, he went back to fighting and is here, in great condition. I respect him very much for that, honestly," he said. "Eder is a great fighter who excited the boxing world," the Puerto Rican added.

Carlos Rodriguez, one of the co-trainers of Figueroa, briefed the local scribes on the background of his charge. "Figueroa is a boxer like few I have seen. He trains every day even when he doesn't have scheduled fights. We were in New York when we were invited to come to Brazil. Since he is always in his best shape, I had no doubt to accept it, for a victory over Eder will establish him as a force," Rodriguez said.

Rodriguez had been Figueroa's coach since he started boxing and said proudly: "Everyone can find his big number of fights strange because he is only 24. It's because he started at 18, and since then, he fought a lot, and you guys will be able to see how much experience he took from that."

The two boxers met the following day at a small press banquet at Chamon Restaurant as they signed official articles for the bout. Eder revealed that for the previous match, he had a brief health scare, which prompted him to visit a doctor. He said he felt unusually tired in training and suspected he might have cysts on his kidneys. "I didn't tell anyone so that thousands of people who believed in me and went to Ibirapuera wouldn't worry. But everyone saw how my performance was lessened in the fourth and fifth rounds. If I didn't take Morales down in the sixth, things could have got ugly," he said.

Eder went for exams after the bout and received treatment and was back to normal in a week. "I don't feel anything else. I'm not worried, and I feel more confident than ever. My audience can rest their minds in peace because I'll give them more joy in this fight," he added. Waldemar Zumbano assessed the match by saying that he thought the Puerto Rican was likely to be Eder's toughest challenge of recent times.

On the eve of the bout, Eder did not put the gloves on; instead, he chose light exercises such as jumping rope and shadowboxing. Aristides told the press, "For his age (36), Eder doesn't need to push the training too much. I didn't want him to leave all his vitality here at the gym." In the other corner, Rodriguez knew that his fighter had a big challenge ahead of him but did say he was confident that they could get the victory and pointed to what they heard was a poor performance from Eder the last time he fought.

Five-thousand fans made their way into Ibirapuera to watch Eder face his younger foe, and they were given a treat as both boxers showed excellent technical skills going ten fast rounds. Eder was in control the whole way and showed great versatility as he moved with quickness, defended in close, and beat Figueroa to the punch on the outside. While the Puerto Rican performed admirably and even exceeded expectations by avoiding a knockout defeat, which looked almost certain late in the bout when Eder attacked his body, he was never really in the fight.

Eder started the bout by letting Figueroa take the center of the ring. Eder mixed in hooks to the liver, right uppercuts, and bolo punches to push the Puerto Rican back. Eder's early attack forced Figueroa into a defensive strategy, and Figueroa tried to keep a distance between himself and Eder by pumping his jab out.

In the third round, the Puerto Rican came out stronger again but got caught with hooks and crosses, which put him back on the back foot. Eder landed a powerful left hook to Figueroa's liver in the fifth round, which dropped his guard. That was an opportunity for Eder to punish him with some dangerous right-hand shots. Eder paused in the sixth round but appeared to play with his opponent. He used his superior boxing skills to work around Figueroa's long jab.

Eder had swept the first eight rounds but wanted to deliver a knockout for the fans, so he moved quickly in the ninth and tenth rounds. He doubled up on the jab while landing hard shots over the top, but the Puerto Rican made it to the final bell. Eder won every round on the judges' scorecards.

As Figueroa was walking out of the ring, he was interviewed and was full of admiration for his conqueror. "When I was a boy, Eder was a champion already. He is the best boxer I have fought in my career. Standing up to him was my greatest joy. I do not doubt that he will become the featherweight champion of the world," he said.

Figueroa felt he had given his best performance and suggested that it was perhaps because he was inspired by the magnitude of the occasion. "I think if we fought again, I wouldn't be able to overcome Eder's punching power. He hits hard and fast, destructive, especially when he hits the liver and the spleen. That's enough for me. I would like to come back to Brazil where I was treated very well but not to face Eder Jofre," he added. Figueroa had enjoyed his experience in São Paulo and the opportunity to oppose a legend. Still, he conceded that he could never beat Eder, and it was satisfaction enough to have gone the distance with him.

In the locker rooms, both parties were happy with what had transpired in the ring. Aristides said that he felt it had been a big test and that "he's still Eder Jofre." Eder thought it had been one of his finest performances of recent times and the performance filled him with confidence in his prospects. "I was happy with my performance, and I will ask Bel-Boxe to get me another fight for the end of May or the beginning of June. Figueroa surprised me. He was one of the best opponents I faced in the last few years. He is quick, hits hard, and is brilliant," Eder said.

Eder emphasized that he had tried to score a knockout but found Figueroa difficult to break down while admitting that he had to be smart when on the offensive. While he was happy with his performance, Eder still felt he had an extra level to go. "This proves that I still need more preparation, but in no way takes Figueroa's value away. He is a boxer with a lot of mobility, good footwork, and great ability," he said. Jose Bisbal of Spain was confirmed as the next opponent for Eder.

In the Figueroa locker room, Rodriguez was talking up Eder's chances should he challenge for the world title soon. "In a fight between Eder and (Antonio) Gomez, I lean towards Eder a lot more. He is more experienced, hits a lot harder, and doesn't look 36 years old. Today was the biggest proof of that as Figueroa is 12 years younger, and Eder is the one who looked like a young man," he said.

Fight 65, vs. Jose Bisbal, June 30, 1972

At 36, there had been many grumblings that Eder should follow the example set by Pele and get out while leaving his prestige and faculties intact. Pele had retired from the Brazilian national team as a World Cup winner in 1971. "I didn't promise titles and didn't take the responsibility to save Brazilian boxing. I came back because I couldn't stand not fighting, and if I get to the world title, it will be natural and not in a pre-established way. It's not indispensable for my career that I become the world champion. After all, I'm getting old, no?" Eder stated.

Jose Bisbal was experienced but brought little else to the table. He had been battle-worn over time but did have the experience of sharing the ring with many outstanding fighters. The most high-profile were Howard Winstone and Ruben Olivares, both of whom defeated him years earlier. Since João Henrique had failed in a bid to bring Brazil another world title when he was knocked out in Italy against Bruno Arcari for the WBC super lightweight championship, there was an added pressure put onto Eder to bring another title to Brazil. Eder was not concerning himself too much with this and asked, "Did I get any younger by chance that João Henrique lost?" Henrique had been the third Brazilian to attempt to win a world title since Eder lost his bantamweight title in 1965, and all three came up short, including Raimundo Dias and Jose Severino.

Antonio Gomez was still the name that kept coming up as it was clear Eder was at an age where he needed to fight for the title or consider retirement, but Gomez was scheduled to fight Ernesto Marcel of Panama in defense of his world title. For the Panamanian, it was his second attempt at a world title, having drawn in Japan the prior year when he challenged WBC champion, Kuniaki Shibata. That bout had been controversial as it appeared to those present, that Marcel, who displayed an incredible array of skills, had done enough to win the title but had to settle for a disappointing draw and was not given a rematch.

The Gomez vs. Marcel contest was scheduled for two months after Eder's bout with Bisbal. "If I perform well on the 30th this month against Jose Bisbal at Ibirapuera, I will be waiting for the result between Gomez and Marcel. Just one thing I decided: If I fight for the title, it's either going to be this year or never. If Marcel wins, maybe I'll go to Panama. If Gomez keeps his title, only if he comes to Brazil. Not in Venezuela ever," he said about his championship aspirations.

As the 30th drew closer, the organizers were worried about the Spanish team's whereabouts. They didn't hear from them, could not track their location, and missed out on staging some of the bout's promotional work. Finally, on June 27, they showed up with Bisbal at the offices of Bel-Boxe. Rather than scolding them, Mattei, in a typically jovial Brazilian manner said, "Welcome to Brazil."

Bisbal confirmed that representatives of Antonio Gomez had contacted him and promised that if he defeated Eder, then he would be given a shot at the world title in Madrid. For the Spaniard, the trip to Brazil was a golden opportunity. "I know it will be hard but fighting against Eder Jofre is an honor for any boxer. Beating him would be the consecration," Bisbal said at the offices of Bel-Boxe.

Bisbal said that while he held Eder in the utmost esteem, he would use the Brazilian's age as an advantage as Bisbal was the younger man by five years. The noise out of his training camp was that not only was Bisbal a stylish boxer, but he could stand the heat if a firefight broke out, and they were prepared for anything that Eder may bring to the table. "I came to Brazil only to try to beat Eder Jofre and get in the world rankings. I didn't come to tell lies. If I didn't trust my boxing, I would never expose my face for Eder to hit. I wouldn't be crazy," Bisbal said.

Eder displayed symptoms of a cold a few days before the fight, but he looked impressive in his last workout on the eve of the bout. He did four rounds of jumping rope, two rounds of shadowboxing, and then relaxed with a massage that his father gave him. He appeared confident and free of any illness.

Eder performed spectacularly against Bisbal. He scored a brutal second-round knockout, which saw the Spaniard knocked out of the ring. After a relatively quiet first round, which Eder controlled as he crowded Bisbal, he put his punches together in the second round and overwhelmed his overmatched opponent. Bisbal appeared scared in round two, and his strategy mainly consisted of trying to hold Eder's arms. The referee gave him a warning and told him to box, and then when the Spaniard tried to jab with Eder, he was punished, which caused him to desperately back up. Eder chased him down and then landed a straight right-hand, which dumped Bisbal out of the ring where he banged his head on the floor.

The referee counted him out and raised Eder's hand in victory, which sent the crowd into a wild frenzy. Bisbal was knocked out for two minutes and thirty seconds. When he woke up, the Spaniard said that he hoped the audience wasn't disappointed in his effort but insisted that he did not expect Eder to hit so hard or perform so well at his age. Bisbal's coach Fernando Carvalho confessed he was glad the fight ended in the second round because the gulf in class between both fighters was so big. He also said that he was nervous when Bisbal had to be assisted into the ring by the ringside press after the knockout blow. He said that if the fight had gone more than two rounds, "Eder could kill him."

After the fight, the first question Eder was asked pertained to a world title shot, but Eder did not get too carried away or promise that such a fight was looming. "What I want you to understand is that I can't announce a challenge to Gomez now. What I'm most afraid of is harming the image it took me so many years to build," he said. He clarified that he was prioritizing a title shot but that it wasn't straightforward in securing the bout. "You may think I don't want to fight for the title, but that is not true. My biggest dream now is to fight for the featherweight world title. I'll ask my manager for a fight in July and another one in August. If I perform like today, I won't have any doubts," he added. He did add that he was a little bit upset that his opponent could not last long as he felt himself warming up and wanted to get more work in, but the fight ended too quickly.

Fight 66, vs. Shig Fukuyama, August 18, 1972

Shig Fukuyama, a Los Angeles-based Japanese contender, accepted an offer to come to Brazil to face Eder the day before the Gomez vs. Marcel title bout in Panama. Fukuyama, a wild brawling type, was only 21 years old and had recently hit a difficult run of form after an initial purple patch in California. For Fukuyama, Eder provided the ideal springboard to move closer toward the world title.

The fans packed into Ibirapuera to see Eder take on Fukuyama and were treated to one of the most entertaining fights ever staged on Brazilian soil. After the bout, Eder admitted it was arguably his most significant victory on the comeback trail. He had to rely on the fans' support to get him through the most challenging moment of his career when he was hurt badly from a body shot in the sixth round.

The first three rounds were going exactly to script as Eder boxed Fukuyama silly and controlled the bout. He stepped up the offense in the fourth round, and the young Japanese fighter's punch resistance surprised everyone as he would not fall under the force of Eder's attacks. After the bout, Eder would admit that he felt he was about to force a knockout in the fifth round as he hurt Fukuyama. The Japanese made it out of the round and showed no fatigue despite taking a hammering over the bout's first half.

In the sixth round, disaster nearly struck as Eder was hurt badly from a left hook directly to his liver, which almost folded him up. He visibly winced from the effects of the punch and retreated as his Japanese opponent went in for the kill. "For the first time I saw Eder feel a punch so much, but after a few massages, he recovered. I told him to get off the ropes and start jabbing. I confess I was anxious," Aristides stated after the bout.

The fans chanted Eder's name, encouraging him through the pain barrier. Gradually, he recovered his senses and threw punches back. The fans were still nervous as the seventh round began, but it appeared Eder had passed this moment. Eder was cautious as he chipped away at Fukuyama to take control of the fight once again.

Fukuyama was tired, but Eder was still having a hard time moving him with his onslaughts until he switched his attack to the body of Fukuyama, which then brought immediate results as he dropped Fukuyama with a hard left hook to the liver. The punch came after Eder had worked him to the ropes and attacked his head, causing him to raise his guard before he slammed him with the body punch, which put him out for the count. Eder explained that he was in disbelief at the punishment Fukuyama could take. Though he felt his opponent tiring, he was still concerned that he could not move him during the first eight rounds.

"Listen, guys; if I wasn't macho, I would have gone to the ground in the sixth round. Fukuyama hit me with violence on the liver, and I completely lost my strength. You have no idea how much pain you are in when someone hits your liver hard. I'm sure that tonight I'll vomit a lot of bile," Eder told the assembled press in the locker room after the fight.

Eder felt a double joy from the match, which was the thrill of victory and the pure relief of avoiding defeat in what looked like a potentially disastrous situation. "It wasn't only my victory, but for all the audience that screamed my name when I needed them the most. I get easily carried away, and when everyone asked me not to fall when I had no strength against the ropes, I slowly got it together. I was able to recover, not so much for me or the defeat that seemed certain, but for the fans." Eder confessed that Fukuyama's liver shot had been the "hardest of my career."

Fukuyama never did win a world title, but he caused a big upset in 1974 when he stopped future world featherweight champion Danny "Little Red" Lopez in a thrilling contest. That victory earned him a title opportunity against Ghana's David Kotey, which ended in a TKO loss. Many years later, Eder said that the victory over Fukuyama was one of his proudest moments in the ring.

Fight 67, vs. Djmai Belhardi, September 29, 1972

Djmai Belhardi, a 28-year-old Algerian-born German citizen, was next up. Despite ranking second in Germany, he was expected to be a much easier opponent than Fukuyama the previous month. The focus of the bout was to stay busy as the title fight was believed to be the only bout Eder would accept next. According to his manager, Jupp Thelen, Belhardi had participated in 40 fights, of which he won 25, tied 10, and lost 5 in a career that began in 1964.

Eder knew he wouldn't challenge for the world title until 1973 because Ernesto Marcel had dethroned Antonio Gomez and promptly scheduled a defense of his WBA title against Enrique Garcia in his native country, Panama. "My understanding for the world title challenge is that Antonio Gomez lost to a Panamanian. There is a proposition for the current champion to come to fight in Brazil from what I know. Also, from what I heard; his coach doesn't want to agree with that. The thing is; I won't fight there. So, we are only waiting for a better proposition able to bring him over here," Eder said. It was becoming abundantly clear that Eder wanted to have home advantage when the title shot arrived. The money in Brazil was good, so optimism remained high.

On the Monday of fight week, Eder worked out in front of a packed gym. *Estadão* reported: "The training session draws some attention. If the interest in Eder's next fight lives up to the number of people watching his training, the event will be a success. Aristides said that only his son could drag so many people to the gym. Eder corresponded to the expectations, going four rounds against his sparring partner Luis Correia, who was caught with two hooks to the liver. Eder declared that he'd be doing more roadwork today, right after it, he's going to go sign the contract and finish the day with more sparring."

Belhardi arrived in São Paulo three days before the scheduled September 29 contest and talked a good game. He said he had extreme focus, fast legs and that he loved to brawl. "He (Jofre) is just like anybody else. I don't care if he was a champion. For those of you who doubt me, just tune in to see what happens," he said.

Estadão compared the bravado and attitude of the Algerian with that of Muhammad Ali. Word leaked out of the Belhardi camp; they were focusing on Eder's body since he had been troubled so much by Fukuyama's body punches in August. Belhardi refused to believe that Eder's age would give him an advantage and instead said that it could help him since he had so much experience.

Jupp Thelen said that his pupil was a fighter with a lot of will and one who loved to go toe-to-toe. "He never gives up, and he prefers to spend all of his strength rather than preserving himself. I have a lot of faith in him." It was reported that Belhardi had fought Jose Legra and came close to defeating the Cuban, but that fight was never verified. *O Globo* reported that Belhardi wasn't convincing when they saw him training at the gym. "Dijeamr Hardy (sp), who will face Eder, wrapped up his practices on Wednesday, in sparring practice, but didn't really convince. He showed speed in his arms, good waist movement, but his leg movement was a little bit deficient."

Eder was not taking any chances and was training hard to avoid the drama that came up in the Fukuyama fight. He was doing two full training sessions each day until the day of the fight and switched his sparring partners every day. Once again, he spoke about his disdain for doing his roadwork but understood the necessity. "I need to convince myself that without roadwork every morning I can never fight. Challenging the world champion means to take a life of diet and focus, a lot of practice. My private life will not always allow for that. I confess that it depends almost exclusively on my conscience to train every morning, but it's hard to change the life rhythm I got used to."

On fight night Eder attacked Belhardi like the bantamweight version of himself and received little resistance. According to *Folha*, "Eder looked like he was in his twenties" as he scored a punishing third-round stoppage over the Algerian. In the first round, Belhardi tried to attack Eder's body but was quickly in trouble as those shots were evaded. Then he was punished when Eder successfully went to his body, in particular the liver.

Eder continued to attack the body in the second round and mixed in some bolo punches as it was apparent Belhardi was out of his depth and could not last. Belhardi, sporting a cut eye, was analyzed by the doctor between rounds but was deemed OK to continue. He already had the look of a physically and mentally beaten fighter.

Eder continued the onslaught in the third round as he stalked his wounded prey before dropping the Algerian with a bolo punch. Belhardi barely survived the count but did not last much longer as Eder followed up with a punishing body attack, which saw the brave but overmatched opponent counted out for the full ten seconds. The fans met the finish with excitement, and many rushed into the ring to hug Eder before hoisting him into the air.

Eder said, "I realized Belhardi was instructed to hit my liver and repeat what happened to me against the Japanese last month. So, I was better prepared and hit Belhardi using my own body attack, which paid dividends. He got his payback in a hurtful way." Belhardi had been punished severely and wore the signs of a beaten fighter and was rather frank when asked for his assessment of the bout. "Eder almost killed me," he said.

Shortly after the Belhardi bout, in November, Aristides fell sick and had to stay at Santa Catarina Hospital for 20 days with a lung infection. He requested that he stay in the same room in which his wife stayed when she had been sick the previous year. Aristides was still depressed about Angelina's death and even spoke about how he didn't want to live anymore. "At that time, I really wanted to die and stay with my wife, but you also need to think of your children. They are very attached to me, and that's why I fought to survive," he told *Placar* magazine. The strength he knew his children would need was what saw him fight through his illness, and he was back in the gym before he had even made a full recovery. "They opened a meter of my body. To recover my energy, I was obliged to eat nine eggs a day. I almost turned into a chicken," he said.

It had been reported by *O Globo* in early November that "a special messenger" was sent to Mexico to negotiate a world title fight for Eder against Clemente Sanchez for the WBC version of the crown, but nothing came out of this. It isn't clear whether Aristides' health had caused the talks to die or whether this was simply a rumor created in the press. Sanchez soon accepted a challenge from former champion Jose Legra. Sanchez had shocked Kuniaki Shibata with a third-round knockout to win the title and had opted to take a title defense at home in Mexico.

1972 Results

Eder Jofre KO6 Guillermo Morales
Eder Jofre W10 Felix Figeuroa
Eder Jofre KO2 Jose Bisbal
Eder Jofre KO9 Shig Fukuyama
Eder Jofre KO3 Djiemai Belhadri

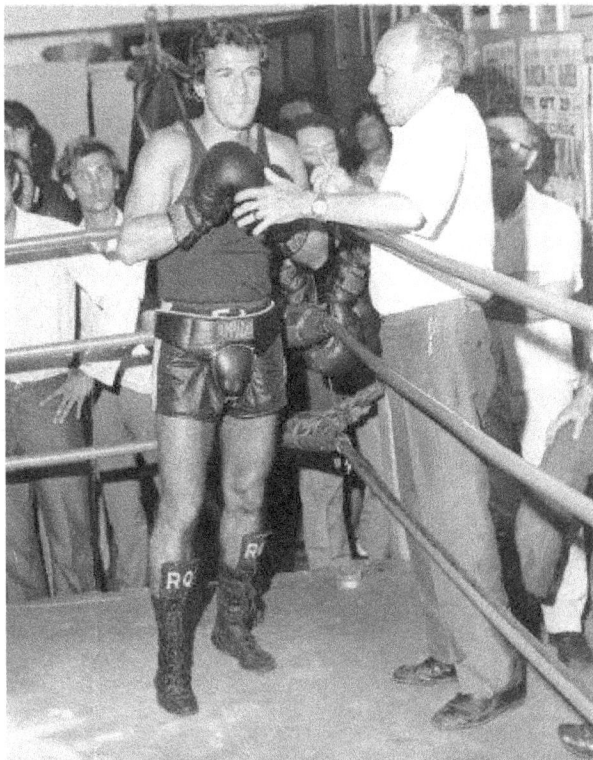

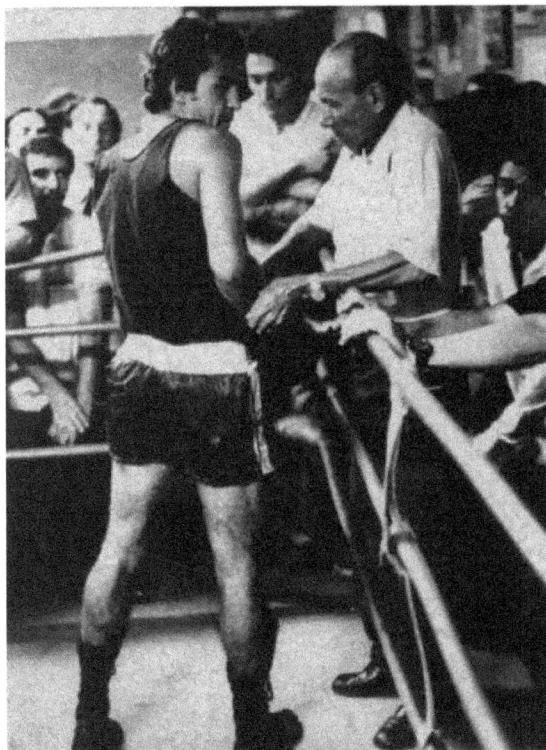

1973

Fight 68, vs. Jose Legra, May 5, 1973

Jose Legra was in his second reign as the featherweight world champion and was widely acknowledged as the top man in the division at this time. He had defeated Clemente Sanchez in a one-sided mismatch in Mexico to regain the world championship he insisted was wrongly taken from him against Johnny Famechon in 1969. Eder was close to his title shot at last, and it would come down to Legra to decide who he wanted to fight next.

The options were attractive in two legendary former bantamweight world champions, Eder Jofre and Ruben Olivares. In early March, Legra told *ABC Espana* he didn't care who he fought between the two legends. Although Eder, at 37, was 11 years older than Olivares, he had the better form of the two. Olivares had recently lost his bantamweight title by knockout to Rafael Herrera and, in his last bout, dropped a ten-round decision in a non-title rematch.

Jose Legra

Since that controversial loss to Famechon, Legra was defeated over the ten-round distance against Vicente Saldivar in a final eliminator the same year. Legra felt he had been the victim of a bad decision. "My defeat was unfair. I saw the film many times, and I know it was unfair. I'm man enough to recognize a defeat. I know I'm not God, and I can lose, but the defeat against Saldivar I can't accept. In boxing, there are many interests, money especially, and they gave the victory to Saldivar."

This viewpoint was not commonly shared outside of the Legra camp since he had been hanging on at the end of that contest, and it was reported by just about every news outlet as a clear-cut win for the Mexican. Legra was upset with the verdict but didn't let it hold him back. He then went on an impressive run that saw him reign as the European champion for three years before the Sanchez bout. He had lost a couple of non-title bouts above the featherweight limit, but Legra remained a formidable fighter who'd always had an excellent record in championship bouts.

Legra originally hailed from Baracoa, Cuba, and lived in Havana, before the Cuban revolution in 1959 outlawed professional sports. That is when he tried to settle in Miami. But he couldn't adapt to life there. He also attempted to settle in Mexico, but it didn't work out there either. It was in Cuba where Legra learned how to box and found he was a natural. "When I was a boy, I polished shoes and sold peanuts, and if a partner took one of my clients, I fought with him. I always fought in the streets until I was found and guided by Rene Castro Garcia, a coach from Guantanamo. He supported me in everything. He gave me my first boxing gloves and took me to his brother's house to eat because I was penniless," Legra said.

From there, he was taken to the gym, where he instantly fell in love with boxing and was part of a team of boys brought to Havana to compete in a tournament at age 18. Legra's parents did not know he was fighting, and he had to sneak around them to hide it from them. The competition at home in Baracoa was not good enough for him to keep his skills sharp, so he eventually settled in Havana and turned professional.

He ultimately settled in Madrid, Spain, where he became a sporting idol. He connected with former middleweight contender Kid Tunero, a fellow Cuban living in Barcelona training fighters. "I did not know what to do. Kid Tunero had settled in Spain and talked to me. He asked if I wanted to box there," he said. "With him, I became the champion of Europe and the World. That's how I compensated for the care he gave me when I got to Spain, where he paid for everything until I started making money," he added.

Legra moved to the capital but would travel back and forth between the two cities training and fighting. He kept up a high level of activity much like a lot of the Spanish boxers of that era. Legra ran up a big winning streak of 27 bouts before dropping a close decision in England to Howard Winstone. Undeterred, Legra then won his next 50 fights before he would meet Winstone again.

In the rematch, Legra relieved Winstone of his WBC title as he pummeled the Welshman. Spanish boxing historian Jose Vicente Flos said that Legra's level of fame and popularity in Spain exceeded that of any other athlete. This indicates the level of his popularity because, as everyone is aware, football is far and away, the most popular sport in Spain.

During this era, Spain was under the communist regime of General Francisco Franco. Legra was close with Franco, often by his side at public events and on television programs. General Franco told Legra in 1969, after losing his title to Famechon, "What they did to you is not fair. The world championship must come back here to Spain because Spain trusts you."

When Legra did regain that title, the streets were blocked off near Madrid's Gran Via as Legra was given a procession to the Royal Palace. To supplement his boxing income, he also owned apartments, parking lots, and beauty institutes in Madrid and the Canary Islands. He said he didn't intend to fight for much longer. "I will stop within a year, for I'm disillusioned with boxing. Boxing is a sport only for those who like it, like in my case, but when I first started, I didn't know of many things that now amaze me. I want to stop next year, but as a world champion," he said.

Legra was a stylistic nightmare for many, given he was tall for a featherweight at 5 feet 9 inches and had a long reach of 73 inches. He had excellent legs, which allowed him to move around the ring with grace and speed, and his hands were quick too. He felt that his biggest strength as a boxer was his ability to move around the ring and that he mastered the art of timing an opponent's jab when he would nail them with a shot to the throat.

Eder received a telegram from Katzenelson in late February while resting in the coastal town of Guarujá. "I was surprised when I got the proposition saying that Legra wanted to fight me and that they offered me a nice payment," he said. The proposal was that Eder challenge for the title in April. He said that he would like to take his time and make the right decision, but he was training with his father in early March. Aristides had been in hospital due to further issues with his lungs. "I was undecided, but now my father is OK to work, so there is no problem anymore. Only the time for preparation is brief, for I've been inactive since October. That is why I will try postponing for 30 days trying for May 15 or later," he added.

On March 7, Legra agreed to go to Brazil to defend his title against Eder. Eder signed his contract to face Legra for an April 15 date, although the exact venue was not identified. The possibility of staging the bout outside of São Paulo was discussed since they could make more money from television. Eder also liked this idea as he did like to get away from São Paulo occasionally as the atmosphere could get too intense at home and distractions easy to come by.

Glicerio Mattei, Eder's partner at Bel-Boxe, was opposed to the timing of the Legra vs. Jofre championship match: "At his age and having not fought in five months, he is taking a big risk, and I don't know why he accepted it. It was the pressure of managers who consider themselves smart that led him to it," he said. Mattei was upset with Katzenelson and accused him of misrepresenting a letter from WBC president Ramon Velasquez.

Velasquez said Legra vs. Jofre was a great fight, but he understood that Eder had been out of action, and his father had been having health issues. "Katzenelson ripped the letter off Eder and pressured Kid Jofre when he was still very ill at the hospital, and then he said I was too childish and couldn't promote boxing," Mattei said. This claim by Mattei appears to lack credibility since Eder had confirmed two weeks before the announcement, he had received a telegram and confirmed his father's health had improved, and he was returning to training. Eder had said that he would accept no fights until his father was ready to train him again.

Mattei's stance was that he wanted the fight, but he also felt that Eder deserved a tune-up and should make no big decisions while Aristides was sick. "I would only promote that fight if there was time for a warm-up fight. Not to mention Eder's age, and he's been inactive for five months. Going 15 rounds out of the blue is risky. Eder has a lot of grit and can overcome all obstacles, but Legra is not an easy opponent. He takes advantage of constantly being active and in great shape technically and physically," Mattei said.

Katzenelson and Marcos Lazaro worked together with the world-famous pianist João Carlos Martins, now acting as a director of União Comercial Bank, to schedule the fight with Enrique Cesena and Jose Lobato, co-managers of Jose Legra. "It's one of the most expensive sports events ever done in Brazil. And we have to follow the USA example. They do great events in small cities to explore TV broadcasting. That's why we will do it in Brasilia, Juiz de Fora, or Salvador, wherever there is a gymnasium for 20,000 people. We will sell the radio and television broadcasting rights to whoever pays most. And of course, the city needs to have good hotels, regular airlines, and other attractions," Katzenelson explained.

By March 23, Legra was haggling over particulars in the contract and claimed that he had not agreed to anything. This caused the date, April 15, to be delayed to April 28, as the managers sought to work out the differences. Legra had signed the contract, which was presented to him by his manager, Enrique Cesena, which gave him $30,000 in advance with an agreement he would receive an additional $55,000 48-hours out from the bout. Katzenelson pointed to the signed documents they had which were legally binding. They stipulated that if Legra defaulted on his agreement, the WBC would strip him of his title for breach of contract. "Legra cannot avoid this fight," Katzenelson said. Although Eder was the attraction to this event, his purse was believed to be around $20,000 since he was the challenger.

Eder signs for the title fight

One crucial aspect was quickly settled, and that was the venue of the bout, which would be the newly built Ginasio Presidente Médici in the capital city of Brasilia. Médici used sports and athletes to display his power while simultaneously demonstrating that he was a man of the people. As he was an instrumental part in getting the fight in Brasilia, Médici requested that Eder give him the gloves from the fight as a gift. There was one problem, and that was that Eder had promised his mother on her death bed that if he won another world championship, he would bury the gloves in her grave. "It was a rather embarrassing situation, and they proposed that my father only give up one glove. Médici would get one of the gloves, and the other would go in my grandmother's grave," Marcel Jofre remembered.

Another sticking point for Legra was he would not defend his title on the road if there was not at least one Spanish judge, a neutral judge, and a neutral referee. He believed that he was robbed when he lost the first bout to Howard Winstone in England, that his title was stolen against Johnny Famechon in England in 1970, and that he was robbed in his fight against Vicente Saldivar in Los Angeles the same year. He also wanted a guarantee from the WBC that should he defeat Eder; he would get a title fight in Mexico against Enrique Garcia for $45,000.

The loose ends were finally ironed out on April 6, and the bout was made official with a date for May 5. Legra had been training intensely for the match and was confident about his prospects despite Eder's history. Legra said, "If I don't knock him out, he's going to have a worse time than Clemente Sanchez. Poor Jofre, he has been bewitched to take the beating. I admire him because he has been a great champion, and his record is there, but I'm going to knock him out. It's going to be a bitter end for Jofre." Eder said Legra would be in for a disappointing evening if he believed he would score the knockout. He stated he never came close to being knocked out in well over 100 fights as an amateur or professional. "I don't know if I'll manage to beat the champion. But if it depends on the illusion, preparation, enthusiasm, and ambition, Legra must defend himself well; otherwise, he's going to suffer an unforgettable disappointment," Eder said.

Eder said it felt great to know he had no issues getting down to the featherweight limit. He could decide to rest for a couple of days before a fight rather than wrap-up in sweaters and sit in saunas to try to drop weight—the way he did when his bantamweight title was on the line. "I need the victory, and I am prepared to go 15 rounds. I will try to corner him and shorten the distance to lock him in. I am under the impression that Legra could impose his game in the center of the ring," Eder said regarding what tactics he was planning.

Eder trained in São Paulo with Joel Gomes, who said he was in awe of Eder's ability and how well he performed at age 37. "It's incredible how Eder keeps up. His attacks are hard, and his reflexes are still very efficient. He never applies a single blow. Sometimes, when he escapes from his left, I have a hard time avoiding the right, and if I succeed, he hits again with the left." Gomes also said that Legra would be in for a nasty surprise if he expected Eder to fight like any other 37-year-old boxer and felt that the champion was not taking Eder seriously as an opponent.

For the first time since he started his training camp for the Legra fight, Eder trained in two sessions on April 11. In the morning, he did his usual roadwork, and in the afternoon, he worked 12 rounds at the gym. He sparred six rounds with Roberto Santana before winding down by working two rounds on the heavy bag, two rounds shadowboxing, and two rounds on the speed ball. Eder said, "Now we need to train in the morning and the evening. I even got to a point in which I can't make excuses not even for a day, for I would be throwing away a two-month preparation."

Eder confirmed he would be keeping a strict training schedule of two workouts per day before he traveled to Brasilia on April 26, where he would be staying at Hotel National.

In Brasilia, he would train in a military partition and would be greeted by military officer and politician, Jarbas Passarinho. Brazilian television was broadcasting the film of Legra's defeat at the hands of former champion Vicente Saldivar in the build-up, and Eder confirmed he would be tuning in. "I am not too worried to see him fight, but it will be nice to watch the fight."

Eder said that his brother Mauro was watching films of Legra's fights and would take a look at him in the gym. He said it was the same for every fight in that he would get ready and listen to the scouting reports but felt that viewing film this time could come in handy. "This is the first time I concern myself about seeing an opponent in action. What I know of Legra can be useful, but I could learn more," he added.

On April 17, Eder participated in a public training session, but he restricted himself to light exercises. He worked three rounds on the heavy bag, two rounds on the speed ball, and performed two rounds of shadowboxing but did not partake in any sparring because he said he was losing too much weight. There was the belief that Eder could have been overtraining much as he did for the Harada rematch in 1966. "I have been losing an average of 500 grams each sparring match, and that's why I decided to change the days around. I feel terrific physically and now on the opposite of what used to happen; my biggest concern now is not to lose weight. I need to keep myself in the ideal weight until the day of the fight with Legra," he said. He confirmed that he was not skipping any roadwork but that he would spar every other day. "He knows everything about boxing. I don't need to explain anything. If he practices with gloves every day, he winds up saturated. Practice is different from fighting. On May 5, he will show what he knows," Aristides said.

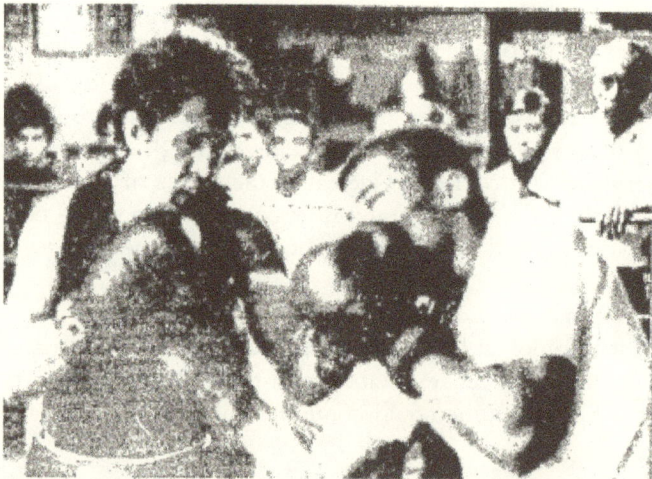

Legra told the Spanish press in Madrid: "I will massacre him. I don't believe the fight will go past the fourth round, and even if that happens, only the judges can take the title from me. Eder Jofre is a boxer with a great history, and he deserves better luck than having to fight me." The Cuban had been preparing in the mountain town of Torrelodones, roughly 18 miles outside of Madrid. He said that he had been training 14 rounds each day and was in the prime condition of his career.

Despite the promoters of the show wanting Legra to arrive 20 days out from the fight for publicity purposes, he arrived 15 days before the bout. He exited the plane looking well-dressed and flashed a big ring with a stone on his index finger. From the airport, he went to his hotel, where he rested for three hours before going to a restaurant in downtown São Paulo. He was full of confidence, to the point of dismissing his famous opponent. "I understand that Eder was the bantamweight of his time, but he's 37 years-old now. He's done, and won't be a difficult fight for me," Legra said.

The Brazilian press compared the pre-fight boasts and arrogance of the Cuban with that of Muhammad Ali. "I'm going to destroy Eder Jofre. I'm not fooling myself. I'm not stupid. When I get my mind focused on something, I know what I can do. I know that I will destroy him," he added.

On April 23, Legra had his first training session in Brazil, but it did not go smoothly as he was left stranded at his hotel for two hours when his driver failed to show. Legra eventually arrived at the gym and worked out for 90 minutes but did not spar. After his training session, he fielded questions from journalists for about 45 minutes.

When pressed on whether he had a genuine disdain for Eder, he said that he considered him a "perfect gentleman who was a phenomenon," emphasizing the *was*. "I really look up to him. He is a gentleman, but there is no chance he can win. I've been practicing for two months, climbing mountains, sweating a lot at the gym. I know that I am in condition to win, and if I say so, it's because I'm convinced of it. If I lose, there will be no contest. I have never been so well. If I lose, I will be the first one to shake Eder Jofre's hand," the champion said.

Legra said that he had seen two of Eder's fights recently on television back in Spain: "I saw Eder in action against Italians Giovanni Girgenti and

Domenico Chiloiri, when he won on points, while I defeated both by KO. When Eder faces a fighter who doesn't fight toe-to-toe, he loses his mind a little bit, trying for the KO all the time. That's when I'll show all my qualities."

Eder worked out the same day over at his father's gym and was said to be focused and looking very strong as he went through all of his exercises and looked sharp in his sparring sessions. Eder conceded that he was not the favorite to win the bout and said that while the crowd support would help him, ultimately, it wasn't a huge difference. "The main thing is to be physically well. Of course, that so many people will be screaming my name will be good for me, but I already said that the fight is decided up there," he said while pointing to the ring.

He was asked what he felt about the boasts coming out of his opponent's mouth and the bravado that the Cuban showed. Eder insisted that he didn't watch television or read newspapers in the build-up to his fights and only heard about what Legra said through friends. He said he felt Legra was imitating Muhammad Ali and that anyone with experience knows that fights are only won and lost in the ring. Aristides noted he heard Legra's comments that Eder was too old and will be knocked out, and it did not concern him. He said that he liked it when a boxer talked a lot before a bout. "Usually, those who talk a lot don't do much. I like it when Eder faces opponents full of themselves. He is even more motivated. If Legra is really underestimating my son, that's even better," he said.

Aristides joked that they might as well stop training since Legra would win in the fourth round. Mauro went to see Legra, and while he said he looked like an excellent fighter who possessed a lot of speed, he said that he observed several weaknesses that his brother could take advantage of. Mauro said that Eder should take his time and focus on attacking Legra's body since that is how Saldivar was successful against him.

The fighters met for the first time on April 25 in São Paulo at Bandeirantes Palace, São Paulo State Government, where the boxers met the governor Laudo Natel. At the palace entrance, Eder offered to let Legra pass first. "You go first. You are the world champion," Eder said. Legra said that it would stay that way after the fight. Eder said that while he had been helpful to Legra as he was a visiting guest, "Of course, I will not treat him well when we meet in the ring." Legra told Eder, "Take care of yourself because I am going to treat you worse." Then the two broke out into laughter and embraced and posed for photographs before going into the palace.

The champion said anyone interested in seeing him was welcome to watch his workout at the gym. "When I practice, anyone can watch, so they'll see a great boxer in action. I'm in the sustaining phase, which means I don't have to force it as much," he said. Legra didn't think that it would be an issue for him to fight in an environment where everybody would be rooting for his opponent because they can't get in the ring. "I've been warned that the Brazilian audience is boisterous during the fights, and I don't care about that too: in the ring, I'm the boss who dictates the rules," he added.

The fight was generally viewed as an even contest in Brazil, but once onlookers were able to see Legra up close and the more that was reported from his training sessions, the odds seemed to shift ever so slightly to Legra. The champion spoke about how he felt Eder left his guard open and that his jaw was an easy target he would take advantage of. He stood firm on his prediction of a fourth-round knockout victory.

Miguel Araujo, a local boxer sparring with Legra, was extremely impressed with the champion, "Legra's right hand is like a whip, and I have to cover myself up a lot so that I don't find myself on the canvas and this is just training. He only played with me. In the locker room, he told me not to worry, for he would practice very lightly," he said. "He only asked me to imitate Eder's style. I've seen Legra fight twice in Europe against Italians Chiloiro and Girgenti, winning both by KO. Against Girgenti, he did the same thing as the practice: opened his guard, left his face exposed, but was never hit. His quickness is impressive."

Mauro had a close look at this training session and acknowledged Legra's qualities but did not see the champion as being unbeatable: "He is good, but his guard doesn't look so good to me. He has a very dangerous right hand but not his left jab, which is slightly deficient. If he takes a well-hit counterpunch, he will easily fall. I don't believe he has shown everything in this practice, for everyone is watching, but it's not much better than that. He trusts his sidestep, but today he took a few punches from Miguel."

Legra was very confident and felt Eder could only do damage with his left hand, and that view was shared by the Spanish media who watched the film of Eder's fight with Giovani Girgenti. Suffice to say, to anybody that had seen much of Eder, that bordered on overconfidence given Eder's well-rounded and well-respected skill set, which consisted of a complete arsenal of different punches.

On May 3, *Estadão* reported that Legra appeared on edge, whereas Eder seemed calm and in control of his emotions.

"Jose was nervous, and Eder looked overly calm yesterday in their last training session. Pissed about the local papers, which published a story about him getting knocked down by his sparring partner, Legra screamed and shouted cuss words while sparring and smashing Miguel Araujo (his partner), and affirmed, 'I'm going to kill Eder.' Yesterday's Legra was a little different than what we got used to seeing. Instead of playing and kidding around the gym, right off the bat, he warned Miguel Araujo that the sparring would be harder than usual. Legra started by attacking and putting a lot of pressure on Miguel, always screaming and looking intimidating. Miguel got knocked down. In the third round, Legra came even harder and angrier, screaming the words: 'I'm going to bury Eder Jofre!' After that, he was still demonic while doing rounds on the punching bag."

"Eder trained yesterday, with the same attention of the press and fans, but a lot calmer. After the warm-up, he went three rounds against sparring partners, Roberto Santana and Joel Gomes."

While many doubted Eder's chances to win the title, nobody was as confident as Aristides about his son's prospects. "This is Eder's thing. He was born to do this. My son is so well prepared that if the black man decides to push the fight, he won't go past seven rounds," he boldly claimed. He said that Eder was as calm as always and was looking as good as he had in a long time. Eder did have some nasal congestion and seasonal allergies back in São Paulo but appeared to be clear of any infections in the fresh air of Brasilia. Eder said he would "do the impossible" to win the title, and stated that this fight meant so much to him since he had retired and had to work his way back up to the top. He said that he felt this fight was even bigger than the Eloy Sanchez fight back in 1960 because "it's about preserving the name."

FOLHA DE S. PAULO

É hoje, no ringue, sem conversa

ou Éder   ou Legrá

On the eve of the bout, Eder spent his time relaxing with his family after they joined him at his hotel. He didn't want to spend too much time talking about the fight. He spent the day relaxing and said that he just wanted to eat a fruit salad and get a massage. Legra was much more animated and worked out for the press. He put in some work on the heavy bag and then hammered away until it fell off its hinges. "That's how he's going to fall. He has only 24 hours," Legra said.

Legra had not endeared himself to Brazilian boxing fans with his aggressive trash talk and how he treated his training partners. On the way to the ring on fight night, Legra walked to the ring mocking the fans and his opponent, which caused further disapproval from the Brazilian fans. He flashed four fingers and pointed to the ground, once again letting everyone know his prediction.

Round By Round from *Estadão*, *A Folha* and *O Globo*

Round 1

(*Estadão*) Eder was looking overly calm as usual. It's up to Jose Legra to pick up the pace, showing all his physical strength: long arms - which kept Eder at a safe distance, in addition to his height and speed. Fighting in an American style, sort of a Spanish version of Cassius Clay, guard down, and shooting quick shots as Eder comes closer. Legra gets the best of the round, showing a lot of confidence in himself.

(*Folha*) As everyone expected, Legra started the round observing. The Brazilian was rooted to a spot, moving his waist and the world champion was faster with long left jabs. Legra guarded his stomach low; he even offered his face to the Brazilian, provoking Jofre. Eder maintained a distance to allow Legra to lower his guard and extend his arms in front. (*O Globo*) It was the traditional study phase between the boxers. Jose Legra tried to keep Eder Jofre at a distance. The Brazilian always tried to approach the Spaniard to land his punches. It was a balanced round, with Legra opening his guard on two opportunities which Eder did not take advantage of.

Round 2

(*Estadão*) Legra goes first again, throwing his fast left jabs, looking for an opportunity to drop the right hand, his secret weapon. Eder stays safe, protecting himself. His guard is up high, and (he) misses a powerful cross. Round goes to Legra.

(*Folha*) Legra comes back more aggressively and even slightly hits the Brazilian a few times. Legra sped up his legs, shifting, and Eder couldn't use his left. Eder let go of one of his arms, and Legra kept on running around the Brazilian. Eder landed his first two straight left-hand punches, but the world champion absorbed the punches well. The round ended with both boxers letting go short and powerful punches. Eder couldn't find the right distance, and Legra was staying away.

(*O Globo*) Eder attacked, trying to open Legra's guard, and initially landed a left hook on the solar plexus. But the champion reacted well, and counter-punched. From the first minute on, the round was balanced, with Legra keeping his distance to avoid the punches to his spleen. Eder Jofre landed a punch on his opponent's chin again.

Round 3

(*Estadão*) Legra keeps up with his pace, pressuring Eder. At the end of the round, Legra catches Eder by surprise, landing a powerful shot to his chin. Eder goes down as he hears the bell ring, announcing the end of the round.

(*Folha*) Legra came back even faster for the third round, letting go long left-handed punches. They both diminished the rhythm of the fight, trying to save their energy since they couldn't get past each other's guards. Eder closed the distance and got past the Spaniard's guard a few times. Legra tried to initiate his first clinch, but Eder resisted by moving swiftly. Almost at the end of the round, Legra's counterpunch hit Eder's chin, who fell to the ground. There was no counting because the bell rang, but Eder already had a bloodied eye.

(*O Globo*) Jose Legra's constant ironic smile had Eder annoyed, and at the start of the round, he landed a hook. Legra reacted with a strong

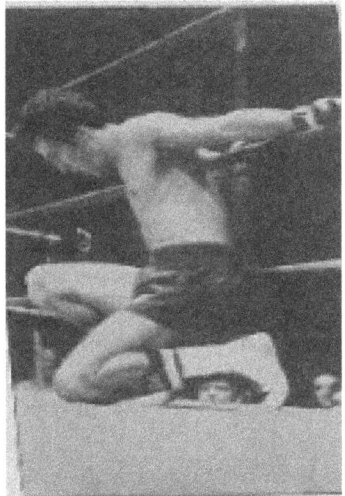

crossed punch, well defended by Eder. A Legra right cross punch caught Eder, who was unbalanced and went down. Round favorable to Jose Legra.

Round 4

(*Estadão*) Something has changed. Eder comes back in a different mood. He's furious. Legra tries his jabs, opens space for his right hand but misses. Eder goes after him and lands a strong shot to his liver. Legra feels the punch and sought to clinch. The Spaniard tries two crosses and misses again. Eder lands two jabs, Legra clinches him again. Eder keeps hitting him with anger; Legra is scared and begging for the referee (to) help. Round goes to Eder.

(*Folha*) Eder came back more carefully and Legra more confident, due to the Brazilian's fall. Eder tried more to hit the Spaniard on his waistline, but the world champion was still quick. Eder landed a good left hook on Legra's liver, and the champion felt it. The Brazilian went back to his attack, and Legra made his first mistake. He accepted the open fight and was violently punched by the Brazilian, who (had) recovered from the fall. Twice the world champion felt the punches and, dizzy, tried to clinch a bunch of times and pushed the Brazilian. Legra tried to push Eder with his elbows every time Eder approached. The bell rang and saved the Spaniard.

(*O Globo*) Jose Legra started with the initiative, and Eder showed to be confused. From the first minute on, everything changed. With three to four right cross punches, the world champion felt the punches to his face and solar plexus. Jose Legra had to use clinches. Round favorable to Eder.

Round 5

(*Estadão*) Eder comes back a little calmer now, after a crazy last round. Legra keeps running around Eder and trying to work out his angles, but Eder hits him in the midsection. Another clinch by Legra. Eder keeps landing punches. The referee registers one more clinch by the Spaniard.

(*Folha*) Legra came back, now more careful, and Eder was very aggressive. Eder's first dangerous punch was a right-hand, then a left hook. The combination hit Legra hard, and he grabbed. Eder could let no punch loose because the Spaniard clinched. He was so dizzy that he used his head, and referee Jay Edson told the judges to take a point off the champion. Legra didn't have the same movement anymore, and Eder was even more confident. At the end of the round, a straight right-hand punch, not so strong, also shook the champion, who once again finished the round very dizzy and nervous.

(*O Globo*) All the initiatives came from Eder Jofre, and Jose Legra grabbed onto the Brazilian, being warned by the referee. Legra's ironic smile faded with a good left hook from Eder. Legra used clinches and, after the third time, was punished with a point deduction. The champion only hit a crossed punch on Eder's face, but without shaking the Brazilian, who did better in this round.

Round 6

(*Estadão*) As usual, Legra starts by throwing his left jabs, looking for an opportunity to release his right hand. Both fighters are fighting at long-distance now with no effectiveness. Another clinch by Legra is registered after Eder lands a shot to his face. End of the round.

(*Folha*) Legra came back, not as quick. Eder realized that his legs were moving much less. He looked for a better opportunity to land a more powerful punch. With waist feints, Eder would already arrive with more openings to the opponent's chin, and Legra would try in every way he could to keep a long distance. The champion, much better, danced in front of the Brazilian but soon took a perilous one-two sequence. At the end of the round, they tried to rest, since the previous round was the most hectic one. They finished the sixth round well, which didn't give an advantage to either one of them.

(*O Globo*) It was a balanced round, with the two fighters slowing down. Eder Jofre continued taking the initiative and landed a right cross to Legra's face. Legra answered the same way. For most of the round, they exchanged punches without reaching the goal. Eder hit Legra's face, but the champion answered with a cross.

Round 7

(*Estadão*) Jose is not the same confident fighter from the beginning of the fight. The Spaniard is overly cautious and limits his performance to left jabs. Clinches are his favorite secret weapon when threatened by Eder's attack. But he still opens a cut on Eder's eyebrow.

(*Folha*) Eder, with good waist movement, tried not to let Legra hit him with left jabs. The champion, recovered from the punishment he received in the fifth round, tried to hit the Brazilian's spleen. Eder covered well with his elbow. Mid-way through the round, the referee warned Legra to desist from head butting but didn't deduct points. The fight was slower, with the two looking for an opportunity to start an attack. Legra tried a few clinches, and Eder, a little bit nervous, complained about the Spaniard's clinching. Before the bell rang, Legra's last clinch came. He used his elbow. Eder complained again.

(*O Globo*) Jose Legra took the initiative, with Eder trying to shorten the distance to throw his favorite punches. But Legra knew how to sidestep well and even hit a good straight punch to the Brazilian's face. Eder's answer didn't shake the former world champion. It wasn't a hectic round.

Round 8

(*Estadão*) Eder is winning the fight now. Eder is forcing all the action. He lands a good shot to Legra's jaw, who takes it. Eder's dominance is not in doubt.

(*Folha*) The two came back again, slowly. Eder tried to attack faster and hit the champion's stomach, who felt the punch a little. Eder tried a hook to the liver, but Legra got away from the ropes quickly. The Brazilian looked for the opportunity to land his right hand, but Legra did OK. Legra finished the round trying to clinch, scared by the threat of body punches from Eder.

(*O Globo*) A good punch by Eder and a nice sidestep from Legra got the audience excited, in a round in which the Brazilian hit a right cross that shook the champion. Eder took the initiative and landed a good left hook, answered by Legra with a strong right-hand punch. Before Eder's impetus, the world champion tried to initiate clinches. Round favorable to Eder.

Round 9

(*Estadão*) Adding to the clinches, Legra resorts to using head butts now, trying to stay in the fight. Eder is desperately seeking the knockout. Which he couldn't get because Legra does well counter-attacking him.

(*Folha*) Eder went back to the ninth round attacking, with good movement of the head and waist, while the champion still showed good physical shape and reasonably good movement on his feet. In the round, Eder hit Legra and tried hooks and crosses to his head. Legra grabbed him and ran. He did more clinches, especially when he would land a punch on the Brazilian. At the end of the round, the fight was violent, with Legra hitting a few punches on the Brazilian's head and receiving hooks and uppercuts to his body. Eder was looking good physically, while the champion appeared a little bit tired.

(*O Globo*) Another round favorable to Eder Jofre, who went on with the initiative, trying to open Legra's guard to land his right hand. Eder didn't worry about the distance, and after missing a hard punch, he hit Legra with other shots. Legra tried to hit his opponent underneath. Jose Legra insisted on clinches.

Round 10

(*Estadão*) Both fighters are fading away, Eder is still dominating. Legra used jabs and clinches to avoid the fight. Eder lands a good hook.

(*Folha*) Legra came back to the tenth round recovered and with good movement. Eder kept a tight guard and tried to attack the Spaniard. Once or twice, Eder would throw a straight punch or a hook. Legra showed signs of tiredness, and the Brazilian took advantage of that. He went after him. Legra went on dancing around Eder until the Brazilian connected an excellent right-hand punch on his chin, and he stopped jumping. At the end of the round, Legra got a little bit desperate and pushed forward, as if he realized he had a points disadvantage.

(*O Globo*) Right initially, Eder Jofre landed a right cross to Legra's face. Legra continued keeping a good distance from his opponent. Legra landed two good punches, but not with too much violence: a straight and a crossed punch. Eder's answer was a left hook thrown with little power. Eder tried, but couldn't get to Legra's body.

Round 11

(*Estadão*) Legra tries to aim at Eder's midsection, but seeing he can't get anything out of it, he comes back to his mediocre left jabs. Lots of clinches by Legra. Eder lands a liver shot, which is well absorbed by Legra, who counters it with a cross. The round ends with the referee heatedly warning Legra against the clinches.

(*Folha*) Eder and Legra were planted in the center of the ring, carefully boxing. Soon, Eder stopped the fight due to a Legra head bump, but the referee decided not to take any points, considering it accidental. Eder's eye bled since it was cut in the third round. The world champion tried to hit Eder's eye, who had slowed down, every way he could. When Eder tried to attack, the Spaniard clinched. Eder tried to attack at the end of the round, but couldn't close the distance, since Legra would either grab or run from the ropes. Both boxers sat down on their stools, tired.

(*O Globo*) A Jose Legra head bump caught Eder's left eye and scared the audience. It was a round with little technique, with both boxers entering clinch after clinch. Eder and Legra limited themselves to exchanging weak punches, highlighting the good work of Legra to keep a reasonable distance to work his left jabs.

Round 12

(*Estadão*) Legra is exhausted now; his only mission is to keep Eder at a distance and try to avoid the combat. Eder lands a beautiful uppercut towards the end of the round.

(*Folha*) Legra continued with quick left jabs but always worried about Eder quickly attacking him, with his left and right, up and down. Legra, much more aggressive, scored essential points for his initiative, and Eder got a little bit lost. In the middle of the round, the clinches were made again, and the Brazilian tried to keep a short distance. Legra used his head again and was warned by the referee. In the last 30 seconds, Eder often hit on the champion's waistline, and Legra pushed Eder against the ropes. Eder tried left and right uppercuts, but Legra didn't let him and finished the round better.

(*O Globo*) The first round in which Eder worked well to Jose Legra's waist, who, feeling the punches, used clinches. Initially, the champion used two jabs but wound up being surprised by a violent left hook punch, followed by another one, and his response was to clinch. In the final seconds, Eder also landed two good jabs.

Round 13

(*Estadão*) Both fighters are gassing out now; Legra wants to re-open Eder's cut on the eyebrow. At this point, the odds of a knockout are low because both fighters are tired.

(*Folha*) Once again in the center of the ring, both boxers tried to open up ways for a violent punch. They were trying to establish the right distance, but exhaustion kicked in, and the first two clinches appeared. Little by little, Eder attacked, stimulated by the cheering. He landed an excellent right-hand punch on Legra's chin. Eder, looking for the pendulum to get to the Spanish boxer, landed a few good punches, but that didn't undermine the world champion to where he would be attacked further. At the end of the round, Eder was more alert.

(*O Globo*) A round that surprised the audience for the lack of initiative. Legra always keeping the distance from Eder and what was seen was a few simultaneous exchanges of punches, with little effect. Eder tried to go under, but when approaching his opponent, he refrained with clinches.

Round 14

(*Estadão*) Contrasting from all the rounds, Legra almost knocks Eder out. Eder knew how to keep his guard at the position. The American referee Jay Edson has to break Legra's clinches all the time now.

(*Folha*) The round started violently, with Legra attacking Eder quickly, with his right and his left, up and down. The Brazilian kept himself guarded well, but he was inferior near the ropes. Legra, much more aggressive, won important points for his initiative, and Eder got a little bit lost. In the middle of the round, the clinches were used again, and the Brazilian tried to shorten the distance. Legra used his head again and got a warning from the referee. In the last 30 seconds, Eder often hit the champion's waistline, and Legra pushed Eder to the ropes. Eder tried left and right-hand punches, but Legra wouldn't allow him and ended the round excellently.

(*O Globo*) A strong right-hand punch and well-placed hook on Eder Jofre's spleen ended any possibility for the Brazilian fighter to take any initiative. Eder was cornered on the ropes for a few seconds, and the clinch saved him. Later, even feeling the previous punch, he reacted, but without discounting the world champion's advantage.

Round 15

(*Estadão*) There wasn't really a fifteenth round because the referee spends the entire round, breaking Legra's clinches, who, by the way, couldn't even stay on his own feet.

(*Folha*) In the last round, Legra came back not to fight toe-to-toe, for a tie would guarantee him the world title. Eder punched the Spaniard hard, cornered him on the ropes, and Legra grabbed him. In the last minute, with Legra running from the fight, Eder hit the Spaniard's liver a lot, and he would push him back. Jay Edson took off another point from Legra because of his fouls, and the last round ended with loud cheering from the audience. Eder continued attacking, while the Spaniard would grab and push.

(*O Globo*) It was a round favorable to Eder Jofre, who started the round with a spectacular left-hand punch, smashing Legra's face. The world champion tried to sidestep and wound up taking another two straight punches, which made him dizzy and obliged him to foul. Eder Jofre tried the KO as much as he could, but Jose Legra defended himself with all the clinches.

The bout had been closely fought and had plenty of momentum changes. At times Eder struggled to deal with Legra's movement and had difficulty closing the distance on the taller man. However, Eder succeeded because he was stronger and hit harder than the Cuban, in addition to possessing superior technique. He worked his way inside enough to do some damage as Legra didn't know how to deal with the infighting, which is why he could not land much inside and received points deductions and various warnings for holding and other infringements.

The early rounds were tentative as both men tried to figure out what the other possessed, but the task did appear to be a big one for Eder when Legra floored him at the end of the third round briefly. Eder turned the tables on Legra in the next round as he hammered him around the ring to gain the upper hand.

Like many great champions who respond well to adversity, Eder came out for the fourth round with revenge on his mind. Despite trailing, he had seen something in Legra he felt he could capitalize on and stepped up his offense. He had crashed several punishing blows into Legra's head and body, which forced Legra back into a more defensive approach.

The slower pace that ensued slightly favored Legra as he made use of his height and reach advantage to edge the majority of the next few rounds. As Legra slowed down, Eder once again gained a foothold and was dominant over the latter stages.

Legra struggled when the action got in close and resorted to clinching and smothering as he struggled to push Eder off. Legra did create some late drama in the 14th round when his body punch had Eder in pain. The Cuban could not follow up and, once again, showing that champion's spirit, Eder was soon in control as he ended the round in the ascendancy. In the final round, Eder had more strength left and forced the action, coupled with the point Legra had taken off, and it made the victory somewhat of a formality before the cards were read.

If the crowd was anything to go by, there was no sense in waiting for the verdict to be read, but they held hands as the announcer took the microphone to read the official decision. American referee Jay Edson scored the bout for Eder by the score of 146-141, Spanish judge Lorenzo Sanchez Villar scored the contest even at 143-143, but Brazilian judge Newton Campos had Eder out in front 148-143, which gave Eder the championship as the audience went wild.

Bo Zaine covered the event ringside for *The Ring* and wrote: "About 25,000 witnessed the biggest boxing show ever held in this country, and saw Eder Jofre win the WBC featherweight title from ex-Cuban, now Spanish, Jose Legra over fifteen rounds. Jofre was decked in the third round just as the bell sounded but started to come on in the following round. Jofre piled up the points as he chased Legra and tried to nail him, but Legra fled away. Legra was warned twice for holding. The last moment of glory for the ex-Cuban was when he had the Brazilian in trouble in the opening of the 14th round when he hit Jofre with a crashing right hook to the liver. Jofre survived, however, and won by 146-141, 148-143, and 143-143. A good referee, Jay Edson, worked."

Eder felt that the critical point in the fight had been the fourth round. This had been the round in which Legra predicted he would end the fight and having scored a knockdown at the end of the third round, he stood up between rounds and taunted the fans, pointing to the floor. Eder had another thing in mind and dominated the round, which altered Legra's tactics. "From that point on, he was on his bike," Eder said. Regarding the grappling tactics that Legra used, Eder joked: "He grabbed me so much that my wife almost asked to separate from me."

Predictably, Legra cried foul and felt he had been the victim of a hometown decision although he brought one judge over (the judge who scored it even) besides getting his request granted of a neutral referee and judge. "Indeed, I wasn't like I was on other occasions, but Jofre did not do enough to win the championship. The referee penalized me two times for no reason. And he didn't count it when Jofre went to the canvas in the third round," he said.

Legra acted like he wasn't too concerned about the verdict and appeared to be in denial: "I won the fight, as everyone could see. What they did outside the ring and later announced doesn't concern me. I know what happened between Eder and me. I told you guys Eder was good, but I was better. And I proved it by winning. The rest doesn't concern me." Legra always felt he had been the victim of a robbery in fights he didn't win on the scorecards such as when he was defeated by Vicente Saldivar in 1969 but was still crying foul four years later.

The Spanish team was not happy; Enrique Cessena called WBC president Ramon Velasquez a "thief and a scoundrel" and said that he doubted whether the judges even wrote their scores down. This is hard to believe since even the Spanish judge scored the bout even.

O Globo reported that Legra appeared to have been humbled and on the verge of tears when he said: "I told you guys I would win, and I did. I warned that you guys would hug me after the fight, and you are here with me, being very nice, joining me to the exit. I think if I had lost, you guys would be with Eder Jofre, who would have a lot of stories to tell. What I know and concerns me is this: I said I would win, and I did. You guys saw it."

Eder's son, Marcel was only ten years old when he attended this bout but remembers with fondness. "I am proud of all of my father's fights, but

I think the one of which I am most proud is the fight which made him the world featherweight champion against Jose Legra. I was ten years old and had more understanding of what was happening, which made it special. It was thrilling to see my champion father and also my grandfather's happiness," he reflected. Marcel left his seat before the end of the bout as he was too nervous about what the outcome would be. When Eder came back to the locker room with the world title belt, he handed it to Marcel and said, "This is for you."

President Médici celebrates Eder's win

Eder was greeted by President Médici backstage, and the newly crowned champion presented Médici with one glove from the bout. The spectators stayed in their seats and were singing and dancing in the arena while Eder received hugs and congratulations in the locker room. "I'm sure that you guys understand what I feel right now. Everything has been very hard so far, but I had to come back. It's my victory, as it is of all Brazilians, but I dedicate it entirely to my father, who even gave up his health to make me world champion again," Eder said.

Eder sported a few badges of honor from the fight but nothing too gruesome. He had a small cut on his inner lip, nose, and between his eyes and a cut over his left eye. "That was a head butt," he said. The champion explained that Legra's tactics had made it difficult to do everything he wanted to: "It was really hard taking the man in the late rounds. He would try and counterpunch, see he couldn't, and then would throw himself hard on me. I went through at least five rounds carrying him on my lap. But it ended up pretty well, and I didn't have problems breathing, despite a recent cold having clogged one of my nostrils."

Eder left the venue wearing a São Paulo football shirt he put on in the ring and was escorted from the locker room to his hotel room. He was applauded and acknowledged joyfully by everyone who got a glimpse of him. It had been an emotional victory for Eder and lost in all the celebrations was that Aristides had almost passed out. He had stomach and chest pains and was having breathing difficulties. He was seen by the medical staff in the arena after the fight and was recovering well, but this was still on Eder's mind.

This was not only an excellent triumph for Eder but also Aristides. The latter had to overcome the loss of his wife and his serious illness to inspire his son's training to pull off the upset victory and make history. It was a wonderful moment. The glove which Eder had promised to his late mother was covered in bronze and placed in her grave when they arrived back home in São Paulo.

"After my Angelina died two years ago, on May 1, 1971, I lost the will to live. At home, I wouldn't eat much and always thought of her. One day I decided to get a partner, but it didn't work out. After a while, I asked (her) to split up and invited my sister to come to live with me. My children helped me a lot, but it's tough to forget the one we love," he told *Placar Magazine*.

Here is the report which appeared in *Estadão* the morning after the bout:

THE WORLD HAS A NEW FEATHERWEIGHT CHAMPION

"Eder Jofre defeated Jose Legra by decision, achieving his second world title at 37 years old, after keeping for many years the bantamweight crown. It was a clear victory: the American referee Jay Edson gave it 146 to 141 for Eder, the Brazilian judge 148 to 143, the Spanish Lourenco Sanchez Villar had it a draw, 143 for both. In the end, amid the mayhem that took over the place, Legra's manager, Lobato Hernandez, ripped off the Brazilian judge's score card. Because of Lobato's bad attitude towards the fight result, Legra will suffer some disciplinary consequences, like his purse will be on hold for a while. It wasn't just Lobato's attitude that disappointed the crowd in

Brasilia. Legra himself couldn't live up to his promises before the fight. Even in his walkout, he was full of himself, downplaying Eder in front of the crowd. After showing off his skills in the training sessions to the journalists, he didn't have the guts to express it to Eder. He preferred to use clinches to stop the Brazilian. Not even when he got the only knockdown of the fight, was he able to keep on attacking, showing that he respected Eder way too much. Whereas Eder was the one who really fought like a champion, considering that he had to re-think his approach going against someone much taller, having to give up his left hook to the liver."

FOLHA DE S. PAULO 4
Esporte

Eder ressuscitou

Chegaria, cansado, Eder Jofre explica a vitória

Ele é o novo campeão dos penas: venceu Legrá por pontos

Esta é a contagem dos três jurados da luta

Saiba por que houve justiça na vitória de Eder

Empresário de Legrá diz que houve fraude na contagem

A luta, assalto por assalto: é a prova da vitória de Eder

Eder spent the day after the fight relaxing with his friends and family. He admitted that he felt worn out but had trouble sleeping after the fight. He spent the morning by the pool at Brasilia Palace Hotel and attended a barbecue at the hotel owner's country house in the evening. He said that he had made no future plans to fight and only wanted to eat and sleep and wasn't interested in hearing the proposals for bouts in Venezuela, America, and other places. "I am resting and getting to know the tourist points in this town, which I still haven't had a chance to really take a look at, although I've been here for a few days," he said.

Eder spent the following day relaxing by the pool in an area surrounded by trees and fresh air. He played football with Marcel, played with Andrea, and spent time swimming with Cidinha. The cleanliness and fresh air of Brasilia made him consider purchasing a vacation home there.

Eder spoke about having financial freedom and the luxury of only fighting when he wanted to. While Eder wasn't interested in talking about future fights, he was happy to talk about the Legra fight.

He said he could hear all of his father's advice in the corner and how he adjusted what mistakes Aristides was noticing but said that he missed hearing the screams of encouragement from his mother at ringside. He said that he felt he won by a comfortable margin and felt he had Legra on the brink of a knockout twice. "Twice, I felt him falling. A jab would be enough, but the bell saved him both times," he said. Eder and Cidinha were happy in Brasilia but had to get back home to São Paulo because Marcel and Andrea had to get back to school.

Katzenelson said Legra had proven to be a great fighter and deserved a rematch and would discuss possible terms for a return bout perhaps as early as September. Legra was bitterly disappointed the day after the match and would not leave his hotel room, simply saying he felt he had been robbed of his title.

Both fighters traveled back to São Paulo on May 8 on separate flights. Eder was tired and just wanted to get home and spend time close to his family. He thanked the press and public for their support and said that he wanted to rest for ten days and return to the gym. Legra was in a much more talkative mood when he touched down at the airport, but he complained about the verdict. "Eder is a great champion, a gentleman, but this time around, they gave him the title. I didn't lose the fight and those who watched it know that. If it were anywhere else in the world, I would still be a champion. They said I bumped my head (against his), but it's a lie. I only used my head to show my intelligence. I won the fight, and that's why I'm not upset. We will have a rematch, and I will defeat Eder anywhere in the world. I don't think of ending my career because of that defeat. I'll recover the title soon," Legra said.

On Thursday, May 10, both fighters collected their paychecks from the headquarters of Banco União Commercial, and Legra initiated a conversation with Eder:

"It's not because I'm in your presence, but I'll say again that I fought against a gentleman, a great quality boxer. I would like to cut your left arm off, which stayed in my way a lot during the fight," Legra said.

Eder replied in the same tone: "Then I'll cut your right arm off, which also gave me some serious trouble. I know your threatening statements before the fight were made to provoke me, for, in the ring, you also knew how to be a gentleman. That grabbing all the time is part of boxing."

Legra didn't take long at the bank and said that he was immediately going to Rio for a couple of days before flying back to Madrid on Monday. He said that he would probably be back in Brazil in two months to fight Kid Pascualito in a fight promoted by Eder's management team. Katzenelson said that he held preliminary discussions with Vicente

Saldivar's management team about a Jofre vs. Saldivar bout for some time later in the year.

When Legra departed Galeão Airport in Rio, he was very communicative to fans and media. He signed autographs and gave praise to the man who had taken his championship. "The title is in good hands. Eder showed he is a good fighter and out of the ring, a gentleman. I have my reasons to complain about the judges' decision, but that's a matter (to discuss) for another time and place," he said.

The legendary pianist and conductor João Carlos Martins cited Eder's triumph as a key motivator in his own life. Martins had achieved global fame as a teenager when he performed to critical acclaim in Washington D.C. before he would entertain the likes of John F. Kennedy and Fidel Castro, and a sold-out Carnegie Hall. He had settled in New York City and received rave reviews, but injuries, accidents, and botched operations had forced him to put his piano away and move back to Brazil.

His fingers weren't moving the same, and his performances had lost their luster. He met Eder in São Paulo and had told him he had to win another world title for Brazil. Martins had been distraught over his situation and had wanted to work in a field he felt couldn't be any further from being a pianist.

He decided he wanted to get into boxing management and expressed an interest in working with Eder. They struck up a close friendship, and few were more overcome with joy than Martins was that evening and he credited Eder's comeback against the odds with being an influencing factor in his own revival. "When I saw the referee raise Eder's hand, I said to myself: 'I am a coward. This man recovered the title, and I did not try the piano.' That was when I went back to the music," he said.

Post-Fight from Spain

The media in Spain did not share Legra's view that he had been accosted of his world title. "After the victory of the Brazilian Jofre over Jose Legra in Brasilia, it showed once again that our champions are only good for showing off. An incoherent boxing policy has left us without any champions," Manuel Alcantara wrote in *Blanco y Negro Madrid* following the bout. "We were not surprised by this decision. But it also happens that this time it was not unfair, in our opinion. The victory of Eder Jofre, Brazil's 'Golden Bantam,' was not a 'robbery,'" he added.

Legra turned down Katzenelson when he was asked if he was interested in trying to get his title back. In his 1975 autobiography *Golpe Bajo* (Low Blow), Legra appeared very bitter when discussing this loss. "I came out determined to not let him coax me into a dirty fight. I expected the reactions of my opponent. He wasn't a rival. I maintained him at a distance. I landed more and better than he did. I moved him into the position that I was interested in him being. The crowd was absolutely silent. Jofre was a puppet in my hands. My better form, my greater boxing skill was shining through, and the montage I thought had gone to hell, despite all the black magic they had placed on me to hunt me down," he wrote.

Legra did not fight much longer, saying that his hunger and passion for the sport had gone. He defeated Jimmy Bell in Spain but was blasted out in one round by a young up-and-coming fighter by the name of Alexis Arguello in Nicaragua. Legra said that he took the Arguello bout strictly for the money and was already effectively a retired boxer by the time the fight started that night. He remains one of the most accomplished and skilled fighters that has yet to be inducted into the International Boxing Hall of Fame.

Fight 69, vs. Godfrey Stevens, July 21, 1973

On July 15, *O Globo* took a look inside Aristides' gym and spent some time talking to the Jofres. Here is a section of that piece:

"At the gym on Santa Efigênia, Kid Jofre speaks, after screaming every five minutes the insistent warning: 'time.' Over 20 young men out of the over 200, who go to gyms in São Paulo, train in the modest place where Kid's gym is. Kid has hopes to get a new champion for his family. He thinks

Marcel, Eder's son, doesn't have what it takes to live on with the Jofre-Zumbano dynasty: 'He wants to be an astronaut. I have another grandson called Eder; he is 14 years old and a good puncher. He can be a good fighter, but he lives in São Vicente and can't practice there. I'm old, and when Eder fights for the title two more times, I can retire if I want. Who knows, in another 19 years, if I'm still alive, I can see another one in my family as a champion?'

Kid doesn't have as much autonomy as he did in the 1940s when he told Eder to hit whoever looked for a fight. Today he listens more to Eder than his son listens to him. That's why he welcomes him with a smile for the restart of practices, even if the champion is late.

Eder walks up the three flights of stairs and is welcomed with a smile by his father. He excuses himself to get changed and start the practice. Between a scream and another 'time,' he talks to his father's students. Others, younger, lean on the wall, watching, astonished, the champion jumps rope over 500 times.

'Eder, I'll fight on Saturday, will you come and watch me?'

'I think so if a cocktail party doesn't come up. Even so, I'll work it out. Listen, be careful with the opponent. Hit him.'

The others smile. It's another conversation for Eder with his father's students. He just doesn't like it when people ask how he keeps in shape:

'You know, I sleep in an oil barrel to lubricate the tissues. In the morning, when I get up, I'll carefully sand my lucky star, so it won't fade.'

His biggest resentment: the lack of trust from friends and journalists who didn't believe in him. Not even the 'shorty' pet name he got when he was young – he is only 5 feet 4 inches tall – displeases him as much. His revolts got even bigger when Rudy Corona, the Mexican he defeated in 1969, stated before the fight, 'I don't know how Eder is, but I can beat him.'

'The truth is people started talking about me, with no basis. They never saw me fight or watch my practices. They are very wrong. This thing to say that one can't fight at 37 is for those who spend their lives behind a desk.'

After two hours of exercise, Eder explains he will leave boxing at his peak. That's why he may fight another three or four times before he leaves the ring. For the masseur, he could take another four years. Eder did it all alone; it was also his initiative not to eat meat anymore: 'it's an addiction like any other.'

'When I left Brazil, not even a masseur was offered to me. I suffered a lot, and I want to leave boxing as a champion. But I won't say when. After all, I don't want to be like Silvio Caldas, who everyone keeps saying will stop singing.'"

Eder had been eager to defend his title in his next bout instead of taking a non-title match. He had felt great in going the 15 rounds with Legra and was ready to put his title on the line. Some names put forward were Ruben Olivares, Vicente Saldivar, and Arnold Taylor. Taylor, a South African contender, was thought to be the frontrunner because it was believed that a bout with him would have the most global appeal since Taylor was given good exposure by the BBC (British Broadcasting Corporation) and was popular within the British Commonwealth countries.

George Parnassus had been keen to stage a Jofre vs. Olivares super fight in Los Angeles. Katzenelson was clear that Eder would only defend his title in Brazil. Katzenelson felt the best route would be to take a couple of non-title bouts with high-profile foes not ranked in the world's top 10, then defend the title against a superstar opponent around September or October. There had been offers from as far away as Portugal, where there was some demand to see the champion fight in Europe for the first time. Ultimately, Katzenelson felt that showcasing Eder to different Brazilian cities would be the best way of cashing in on the title win and thanking the public of not only São Paulo but also the whole country for their support and belief in their hero.

It was on July 21 that Eder was scheduled to return to the ring in São Paulo in front of an adoring hometown public at Ibirapuera. The opponent was Chilean Godfrey Stevens, who at 35 had been around for a while. He proved to be one of the best fighters on the continent with a record of 71-5-3. Stevens possessed an awkward style of boxing. His movements could appear a little herky-jerky and unconventional. With his lanky frame, he was a competent user of distance in the ring. Throughout his career, he had generally fought in his homeland. He took impressive scalps like Don Johnson, Jose Jimenez, Kid Pascualito, Antonio Herrera, Bobby Valdez, and Jose Smecca.

Before his bout with Eder, Stevens had given a decent showing against the legendary Ruben Olivares when he extended the Mexican hero the full ten-round distance in a bout in Monterrey, Mexico. A couple of years before that bout, Stevens had given a good showing in Japan for the world title, albeit in a losing effort against the excellent Shozo Saijo.

Eder and Stevens came face-to-face for the first time when the fight contracts were signed on July 16. Stevens was said to be elegantly dressed and well-mannered at the cocktail luncheon. He brought attention to his crooked nose but informed those gathered that it was an injury he had sustained playing basketball 12 years ago.

The Chilean said that he liked to play basketball, football, and hockey and enjoyed skiing. Eder arrived with a suitcase full of his training gear since he said he would drive straight to the gym after the contract signing. Stevens greeted the champion cordially, "Very nice to meet you. I hope to see you Saturday night." Stevens said that he had already run four miles and boxed 12 rounds in the morning and intended to work out later in the afternoon. "Since I knew there would be a contract signing and these events take a little while, I decided to train in the morning. But I would like to train in the afternoon around three o'clock," he said.

When Eder fielded questions from the media, he was asked what he knew about his next opponent and confessed he didn't know a great deal. "I don't know Stevens. I only know he likes to fight openly and gives very little space for his opponents' punches. I particularly like boxers like that. You don't have to chase them around the ring; we know where to find them. I'm very well physically and I am calm for the fight. After facing Legra, I learned a lot, like being more patient and not trying for the KO as much, for points also decide a fight. If some opportunity comes up, we have to be alert too, but we can't force the situation."

In the days leading into the bout with Stevens, Eder confessed that he was close to retirement. "I haven't set a date to stop fighting, but I can guarantee that it will be very soon," he said. He explained that at 37, he wanted to "live a little." He noticed that he was gaining weight a little easier than in the past. "I was overeating and drinking too much soda, and then I thought, 'why do I have to get back to those unbearable diets?'" He also said that he didn't return to fight for the money and that the main reason for his comeback and his continued motivation was his father. Now that he had won the world title again and was back on top of the boxing world, he felt he was in a position to retire happily.

The champion was in perfect condition and had been training hard and was very satisfied with the sparring he had completed with Joel Gomes. "I have some info on Stevens. He is swift and likes fighting against aggressive fighters, who want to decide the fight quickly. Then he imposes all his technique," Eder said on what he had been told about the Chilean. "My tactic will be to hit him in the waist area during the early rounds, to mine his resistance so he won't be as fast. I think then I can get a KO, although I'm not too worried about it," he added.

Press members asked Stevens about his 1970 title challenge against Shozo Saijo, and Stevens said that he felt he had performed well. "Although the judges gave Saijo the victory, I think I deserved at least a tie, for I fought very well. But I don't usually discuss the judges' decision. I came here to defeat Jofre, despite the 11 months in which I haven't fought. That doesn't cause me a lot of trouble: I've been getting ready since December, waiting for an opportunity to fight for the title, which is my greatest goal," he said. The title was not on the line in this bout, but Stevens had a guarantee in his contract that if he scored a victory, he would be fighting Eder for the title later in the year.

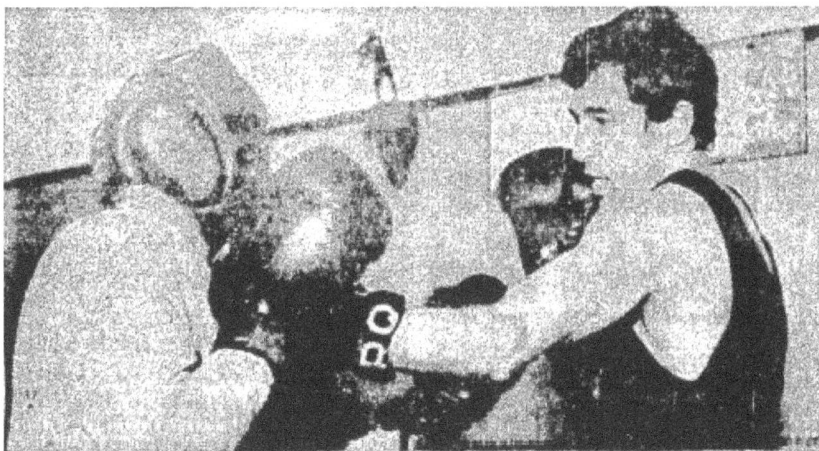

Stevens revealed little during his workouts for the press, but he took great pride in telling those on hand he had never been knocked down as a professional. He had serious doubts this would change even after the fight with Eder.

On the eve of the fight, Eder sparred three rounds with Arlindo Borges and one round apiece with Joel Gomes and João dos Santos before wrapping up his practice with some jump rope exercises and shadowboxing before getting a massage. He was in excellent condition since he knew that Stevens had so much to gain and had come to Brazil to win. Borges, who was scheduled to fight Stevens' sparring partner, Raul Estorga, went through some rough moments in his three rounds with Eder. In the second round, Eder pinned Borges on the ropes and put a beating on him, but some noted that Borges gave a good account of himself and was very appreciative of the chance to work with the champion. Eder made the point to explain that he had given Stevens the utmost respect and took his challenge seriously. "I know he is excellent, but it seems like he likes to fight at half distance, which favors me. I heard he's been hiding his game in practices, but I'm not concerned. In the fight with Legra, everyone said he would massacre me, that his style was very hard, that I wouldn't be able to get my hands on him. But in the fight, everything changed, and thank God I was able to get over myself and give an excellent fight."

Aristides was already looking beyond the bout with Stevens and onto a potential title fight with former champion Vicente Saldivar in September. "My son is OK. He doesn't have to worry for this fight isn't for the title. We only need to keep him in shape," he said. Saldivar, being a southpaw, would require slightly different preparation from Stevens, but again, Aristides didn't concern himself too much with that matter. "There is no problem. The only problem is to adjust him to a left-handed boxer. But traditionally, Eder always handles that kind of opponent well," he said.

A weather forecast of heavy rain and an announcement that the bout would be shown on tape delay meant that the crowd came in at less than 10,000 for Eder's first bout back as a world champion. Stevens wasn't expected to upset the apple cart when he took on Eder in an all-South American clash, but he was supposed to offer more resistance than he did against the returning legend.

Eder came out using his left jab to perfection from the onset. Stevens could find no way past it, nor could he defend himself as Eder worked his way down with a painful liver punch in the second round. The effects of this punch took the wind out of Stevens, who did well to avoid a knockout though the blow caused him to kneel. The bell ended just in time for him to avoid Eder's follow-up assault, but the writing was on the wall for the Chilean. Round three saw Eder immediately on the hunt, mixing in an array of body punches that forced Stevens back. When Stevens summoned the courage to fire back, he couldn't hit Eder, who displayed excellent head movement before swiftly moving forward to drop Stevens with a strong right-hand. This knockdown was followed up with a left hook, which put Stevens down again before the bell saved him. The expectant crowd cheered in celebration into the fourth round as Eder finished his courageous opponent with a flurry of punches that sat him down for the full count. It was an impressive show by the champion. He defied age by showing he was still one of the most dominant and aggressive fighters on the planet 13 years after winning the bantamweight world title.

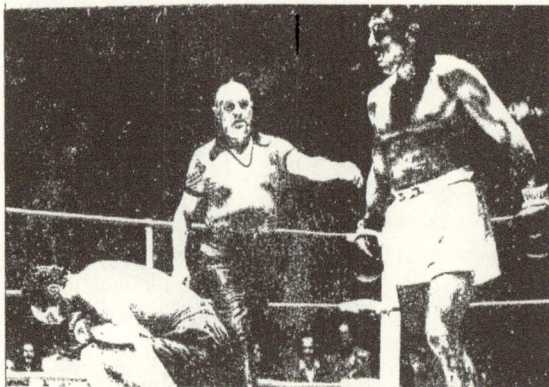

Fight 70, vs. Frankie Crawford, August 25, 1973

Eder was in high demand and was tempted by an offer to take his show on the road when he went to the southeastern town of Bauru, where he took on former world title challenger Frankie Crawford of Los Angeles. The 28-year-old Crawford was a skillful boxer who, like Stevens, had gone to Japan to take the crown from Saijo. Crawford came closer than Stevens when he lost a razor-thin majority decision in 1970. Crawford had scored a first-round knockdown and, despite some rocky moments, believed he had done enough to take the title. He had another opportunity at Saijo's title and once again came up short in another hotly contested close affair.

Throughout his career, Crawford was a popular fixture in Los Angeles. A split pair of decisions between him and Mando Ramos proved popular ticket sellers. He also came close to defeating the great Vicente Saldivar in an entertaining fight at The Olympic Auditorium. Saldivar ran out a deserved winner in a good, hard fight, but for a moment, Crawford had the Mexican out on his feet in the fourth round before weathering Saldivar's customary late rounds assault.

Crawford enjoyed himself in Baaru, where he was very playful with the media and talked about how he felt he was at the right age and point in his career where he

Frankie Crawford

could defeat any featherweight. He impressed onlookers as he sparred with Joel Gomes in front of a large crowd and told how he envisioned himself knocking Eder out in the third round. "I am in condition to win this fight, and Baaru was marked as the city that Eder Jofre was knocked out in the third round," he said.

Crawford brought a crucifix along with him and asked a Bishop to bless it for Eder's sake. Crawford teased about Eder's age and told how he respected the champion but felt he was too old. Eder arrived in Baaru the evening before the fight and went straight to his hotel to get some rest. He said that he had been in intense training for three weeks and hoped that Crawford would be a better opponent than Godfrey Stevens had proven to be. Eder's brother, Mauro, did get a glimpse at Crawford's last training session. He did not feel he carried a particular threat. "Crawford hid his game so much he'll never find it again," Mauro said.

Before this engagement with Crawford, there had been discussions about whom Eder would make his first title defense against. Three names mentioned were Ruben Olivares, Jose Legra, and Vicente Saldivar. Olivares' name was thrown into the mix on the strength of an impressive knockout

victory over Bobby Chacon for the North American Boxing Federation title, but Saldivar, as a former featherweight champion, was deemed a more logical opponent. Olivares was still building his reputation as a featherweight contender, and Legra said he was not interested in another fight. Saldivar was the most willing of those mentioned and was at a stage in his career where he only wanted to compete in big matches. A title shot in Brazil against Eder Jofre appealed greatly to the Mexican.

The Jofre vs. Crawford bout took place at Estadio Dr. Alfredo de Castilho on a humid Saturday afternoon, August 25. Crawford proved to be a resilient opponent and gave the champion a good fight. Eder found Crawford to be more difficult than Stevens as he landed some shots of his own and handled the body attacks of the Brazilian well enough to not be in any dramatic danger throughout the bout.

The fans enjoyed the spectacle as both men excellently exhibited beautiful boxing skills. In the final round, Eder attempted to put on a show for the crowd as he displayed excellent defensive skills when Crawford tried to maneuver him to the ropes. Eder followed up that show with some clean counter shots as Crawford pressed the action. The verdict was unanimous in Eder's favor, but he knew he'd been in a fight, and that is a sentiment echoed by his son Marcel, who remembers when he attended the bout as a youngster. "Frankie was a very durable opponent, and he gave my father good work in that fight," he said.

Here is the report by *Folha*: "To sum up the fight was like this: In the first three rounds Eder punished Crawford over and over even though without threatening to knock him out. The North American's promise to beat him in the third round was already over. In the fourth round, after a start with no news, with Eder attacking and Crawford exhibiting good agility and an extraordinary capacity to sidestep, there was a slight change in the action. After they were split and came back to the center of the ring, Crawford launched an attack at Eder's nose with a violent left hook. The champion's nose bled and it would keep on bleeding until the end. Excited by his action, Crawford kept doing the same thing repeatedly, attempting to reach and hurt the Brazilian again. But Eder knew how to keep calm, recover from the punch, and impose his technique again. The fifth round didn't have any news. The sixth was worse for Crawford, who was cornered on the ropes for a long time, suffering punishment that another opponent would not be able to get through. But the bell saved him, giving him good time to recover, with no other news in the next rounds up to the tenth, after which the two boxers would still look capable of fighting. Eder's arm was up. The champion had just obtained a new victory in his brilliant career."

According to Rick Farris, Crawford was often dismissive when discussing the merits of his former opponents. When asked who his most formidable opponent was, Crawford said, "Eder Jofre in Brazil. That guy was a fucking master." After the bout, Crawford apologized for what he said about Eder in the build-up and gave credit to the Brazilian. "I always believed that Eder fought well. He wouldn't be a champion if he didn't. I had in mind that he would have lost his strength due to his age. But he punches hard."

While the fans had been happy with the show they had seen, and Eder added the name of another valuable opponent, he was not satisfied with the effort he had put forward. "It was the worst fight I did. I don't know what was happening to me. I tried to hit Frankie's liver time and again, but only hit it once. My arms weren't as quick as I wanted. Despite everything, it was a good practice for me to fight Saldivar for the title."

Two days after the win over Crawford, it was reported that Eder's first defense of his featherweight crown would take place, likely on September 22 against Vicente Saldivar in a clash between the two greatest boxers of their respective divisions in the 1960s. Upon the announcement of this big fight, Eder said that he would be taking a week off to rest and heal from the fight with Crawford and then he would get down to business and start his training camp for what he and many anticipated would be one of his biggest challenges. A fight date of October 19 was ultimately confirmed.

The city chosen to host the Eder Jofre vs. Vicente Saldivar mega fight was Salvador, which was also showcasing the WBC annual convention. Eder wanted to take more fights out of São Paulo to have a change of scenery. Marcel recalled, "My father told me that he often liked to fight outside of São Paulo because the environment was sometimes a bit heavy." From a promotional viewpoint, it made financial sense as they would not have to blackout the fight in São Paulo for the live TV audience. Hence, they stood to make more money from television. Eder's purse was set at $60,000 whereas Saldivar was to receive $30,000.

During the convention, one topic of discussion was that Brazil wanted to host George Foreman's next defense of his heavyweight world championship against Ken Norton. Saldivar brought with him a fearsome reputation, having been the featherweight champion twice and undoubtedly one of the greatest fighters in the history of the weight class.

He ruled the division with an iron-clad fist from 1964-1967, defeating a slew of excellent fighters. Saldivar was a respected and highly regarded champion in his native Mexico but lacked popularity compared to some of the more outgoing Mexican boxing idols such as Ruben Olivares and even the adopted Cubans Jose Napoles and Sugar Ramos.

He was a recluse by nature and often would keep his private life behind closed doors and dedicate himself only to his family and his craft. According to Stephen D. Allen in his book, *A History of Boxing in Mexico: Masculinity, Modernity, and Nationalism*, it was often said that Saldivar appeared to lack passion in his fighting style and didn't have enough friends in the "Cantinas." His love of the fine arts and education caused many fans to turn against him despite his excellent results in the ring and the glory he brought to Mexican boxing.

Vicente Saldivar

Saldivar retired young but came out of retirement and looked as good as ever when he defeated Jose Legra in Los Angeles in 1969 before regaining the championship against Johnny Famechon in a close battle in Rome. His first defense was an unexpected defeat against Kuniaki Shibata in a thrilling contest in December of 1970. He bounced back with a solid decision win over Frankie Crawford the following year but had not fought since. That did not concern the Mexican who maintained his physical condition and always trained hard. "I try not to have pointless, silly fights. I'll only fight when I believe I am technically and physically well. I'm always training for that and try not to wear out uselessly," he explained.

Ironically, Saldivar's popularity increased since his retirement in 1967, perhaps lending to the fact that the fans had not realized what a great champion they were missing out on but because he also showed more vulnerability than in the past and he became more fan-friendly. Mexican boxing fans often get behind an underdog, such as when Rodolfo "Baby" Casanova was such an idol despite falling short of winning a world title.

O Globo reported that the fight against Saldivar could be Eder's last bout since the champion was unhappy that he was subjected to 50% taxation on the payment of each contest. There was speculation that he was entertaining fighting abroad once more to offset this tax issue. "It will all depend on government support. If there isn't a change in the taxes for the fights, or at least on the regulation of professional boxing, I will definitely leave boxing, and this will be my last fight," he said.

On October 3, it was reported from Mexico that Saldivar weighed around 134 pounds and intended to intensify his training and change his diet at home before arriving in Brazil under 130 pounds with the last few pounds to come off in Salvador. Saldivar was also subjected to a battery of medical exams and put his visa application in on that day too. The following day the fight was pushed back from Friday (19th) to Sunday (21st) due to a lack of available hotel rooms.

On a more positive note, Saldivar's medical exams came back fine, and the tests were then sent to the Brazilian Federal District Athletic Commission. The Mexican was supposed to leave on October 8, but his departure was delayed by 24 hours when his manager only received three of the promised four airline tickets. Eder missed a day of sparring since his two sparring partners, Joel Gomes and João dos Santos, didn't show up at the gym, but it was no issue for the champion. He went through his usual exercise routine under his father's guidance and shrugged off the fight delay as "just a couple of days." There was a rumor that the Mexicans would delay the fight even further due to accommodation issues, but Saldivar's manager Jose Lazaro denied this: "We reserved three apartments at Ondina Praia in the name of the tourism company."

Saldivar arrived from Mexico City via Guatemala City at Viracopos Airport at 6:50 am on Friday, October 12, where he went directly to Jaraguá Hotel in downtown São Paulo. Saldivar's team had not made their mind up on when they would be leaving for Salvador, and the decision depended on what the former champion wanted to do. Later that day, Saldivar went to sit in a sauna for over an hour with his brother Guillermo and his coach Adolfo Perez. He didn't want to make any promises or predictions on what would happen when he challenged for Eder's title. He said that he was surprised Eder was about the same height as he was since he expected he would be looking up at the champion during the bout. Saldivar said that one of his greatest victories was convincing his wife Maria de la Luz Reyes to allow him to get back into the ring. "Now she's interested in boxing but never when I fight. I was able to make her understand that I only know how to fight, so I ended up winning that fight too."

Eder was determined to head over to Salvador on Monday, but his management team tried to talk him out of it. They said that he needed to promote the fight more in São Paulo since they relied on a large television and radio audience to tune in. Over 100 participants from the WBC convention arrived in Salvador on Saturday, and Bahitursa, the tourism company in charge, confirmed that they had everything ready for fight week.

Eder took the Sunday to rest, whereas Saldivar woke up at 5:30 am and went for a brisk walk. The Mexican came back to his hotel, where he had a nice breakfast before taking a rest. He went to the gym at 1 pm and trained for eight rounds with only two rounds of sparring. Saldivar appeared to be in tremendous spirits, and onlookers said that he appeared to train with a lot of will and enthusiasm. In the evening, the Mexican team went to Morumbi Stadium to watch a football match between São Paulo and Cruizeiro.

Eder's preparation for the Saldivar fight was less than ideal. His training camp had started on September 10. Though he had looked sharp, there were several personal issues he had been dealing with at home with his father's deteriorating health. Aristides was looking like an old Kid Jofre, and it was hard for Eder to get his mind straight and be optimistic. To add to his fragile mental state, he had to deal with many issues on fight week. Bad weather meant that the plane from São Paulo to Salvador could not land, so he and his team had to land in Recife, some 500 miles away from Salvador.

The next day, they tried to leave Recife, but once again, bad weather kept them there for another day. Both boxers had been on the same midday flight from São Paulo and then crossed paths when they finally arrived in Salvador. "They both arrived optimistic and at the airport hugged each other wishing success to one another. Later, Eder, joined by his father, his brother Mauro Jofre and sparring partner João dos Santos, went to Oxumaré Hotel while Vicente Saldivar and his escort stayed at Ondina Praia Hotel," *O Globo* reported.

Eder and Saldivar meet at the airport

In Salvador, Eder's team then discovered that the hotel they had booked did not have a restaurant, so there was an issue finding suitable food, which Eder said was a problem. It differed greatly from what they were used to back home in São Paulo. To top it all off, the inclement weather made its way from Recife down south to Salvador, and this meant that Eder could not get in enough roadwork, so he struggled to get his weight down.

Saldivar, at 30, was seven years younger than Eder, and with only 39 fights, he was perceived to be the fresher boxer of the two. "To you Brazilians, I can say that I am equal to Eder when it comes to professionalism. I am always practicing, always eating well and sleeping early," he told an assembled media scrum before his public workout at Acropole Gym a few days out from the bout. Saldivar said that he had received a warm welcome in Brazil and was looking forward to facing what he considered a "great champion."

Saldivar stressed that he was not concerned about the all-Brazilian judging panel selected as he had fought abroad before and always received a fair shake. He was asked if he had any predictions for the fight, but he said that he preferred to do his talking in the ring. The press told him he differed greatly from Jose Legra in this respect. He was asked what he felt of Legra's pre-fight trash talk when he came over to Brazil to fight Eder and said, "He should have kept his mouth shut."

Three days before the bout, Eder's spirits were raised when Cidinha arrived with Marcel and Andrea. They spent the afternoon around the pool of the Bahia Hotel. The kids played in the water as Eder relaxed and was in good spirits. "With Cidinha and the kids close to me, I am calmer. I practice calmer, certain that my family is OK," he said. Eder was forbidden to go into the pool so he wouldn't soften his body. He complained a lot about the heat, so Andrea and Marcel helped cool him down and refreshed him by throwing buckets of water on him as he tried to rest.

Eder and Aristides talk by the pool in Salvador

Eder gave little away as to what kind of strategy he planned, simply stating that he was in the best shape he could be in and that he felt confident. He said that he thought since Saldivar's style of boxing was to stay in the center of the ring and fight with his feet planted, he could be an easy target. The following day Eder performed well for onlookers at the Acropole Gym. The press noted how he appeared enthusiastic and energetic, where he had looked a little labored in the first sessions in Salvador and that he looked sad, no doubt, due to his father's condition.

Saldivar was feeling the heat but remained focused on winning his title back. "Saldivar, who complained about the excessively hot weather that is upon them in Salvador, didn't let this affect his mindset nor his preparation for the title shot. He woke up at 4:45 am and went straight to the stadium for a morning run, with his coach Adolfo Perez and the doctor Armando Zamora. He's looking confident in his victory but didn't want to give any conclusions about the fight. Avoiding muscular fatigue, Eder did morning roadwork, ground exercises, and sparring sessions," *Estadao* reported.

Saldivar vs Jofre

The Mexican press who came to town was very confident that Saldivar would regain his title and defeat Eder. Eder's age and Saldivar's natural size advantage were the perceived differences in what promised to be a fascinating battle. Here is a sample of some of the press picks:

Antonio Hernandez, a Mexican journalist who had been writing about boxing for 20 years, picked Saldivar to win on points. "Saldivar is well prepared, and when he attacks, he always punches continuously. Eder Jofre can't do that, maybe because he is used to fighting, sparing himself as much as he can, like the old days. These days, the boxer who throws more punches in combinations always wins. The big enigma for me is Eder's age because he is 37 already. When you lose some of your leg strength, you slightly diminish your punching power. The advantage of his weight also favors Saldivar. Like it always favored Eder when he was a bantam. Saldivar has problems keeping himself within the weight limit. At the official weigh-in, he should be 126 pounds, and at night, when he gets into the ring, he should be 130 pounds. Eder always keeps himself around 123 pounds. That weight difference needs to be well considered. With his (Saldivar's) weight up, his punch should also be bigger."

Mario Ortiz (*El Universal*), Ramon Marquez (*Excelsior*), and David Navarro (*UPI*) also believed that Saldivar would win. Ortiz believed that Saldivar would knock Eder out. Marquez forecasted a knockout in the eighth round. He explained: "Saldivar is in much better shape, and by nature, he takes punches better than Eder does. Eight rounds will be enough so that Eder Jofre is physically worn out and suffers a knockout."

Navarro agreed Saldivar would win and stated:

"Eder will lose all his aggressiveness and leave the moment he gets tired. This should happen in the ninth round. I believe that Saldivar will win the fight, but I think this will happen on points."

Eder's last workout with gloves was on the Friday before the fight. After he ran in the morning, he went to Acropole Gym, where he worked the bags, jumped rope, and did some shadowboxing. A gym fly named "Kid Cachetada" claimed he had watched Saldivar often in the previous couple of days in the gym and told Edgar Alves of *Folha* all about his strengths and weaknesses. "Saldivar is an excellent fighter. He punches well from underneath, and he knows how to work up top with both arms. He is quick on the counterpunches, but he has a flaw that will favor Eder. He fights planted in the center of the ring, making it much harder for him to retreat.

Not moving, he will be a fixed target. Eder is far superior to Saldivar technically. I believe that after six rounds, Eder will completely control him," Cachetada said.

Some had suggested that Aristides had planted Cachetada as a spy, but they shrugged off the claim, and Aristides said: "Kid Cachetada shouldn't be taken too seriously." Newton Campos, President of the São Paulo Boxing Federation, did not quite have the conviction that Cachetada had and said: "I cheer for Eder. I have confidence in him, but in these times, I have to leave my fanaticism aside. I trust Eder, but I really fear this fight."

Eder said that he was excited about this fight and felt that Saldivar had a more crowd-pleasing style than Jose Legra, which should provide a better fight for the public. "Although he (Legra) is more technical and has a lot of experience, I'd rather fight Saldivar. He is more of a fighter, he opens up more with his guard when he punches," he said.

It was becoming increasingly difficult for Eder to focus on the bout as much as he would like due to his father's condition. Aristides' health deteriorated many months after he was diagnosed with lung cancer. The situation worsened and required a blood transfusion two days out from the fight. Aristides had been a heavy smoker for several years. He had also not recovered from the emotional heartbreak suffered when his wife died two years prior.

Despite his ailing health, Aristides insisted that he be the one to walk with Eder to the ring, be in the corner on fight night, and he would not have it any other way. Dogalberto pleaded with his father to stay at the hotel, but Aristides told him, "I am going to the fight no matter what!"

Eder wound down on the eve of the fight, spending the time with his family close by. He walked on the beach as Saldivar put another workout in. The tranquility that Eder showed in the days leading into the bout carried through to fight night when he arrived at the Ginásio de Esportes Antônio Balbino around 8:30 pm and went directly to the locker room. He didn't even care to use the separate locker room reserved for him, instead going into a shared locker room with the other Brazilian boxers featured on the evening's show. Cidinha and the children were checked in and shown to their seats as Eder relaxed in good spirits as his hands were wrapped.

Eder did not care there was no bathroom in the locker room and little ventilation as he joked with members of his entourage about the trunks he wore to the fight. "I'm a panther tonight. Pink Panther!" he shouted in reference to the light pink trunks he would be wearing into the ring. His friend, Osvaldo Forte, was not quite as relaxed and said, "It makes me crazy how calm he is. It feels like I am about to fight. He keeps on as if nothing is about to happen."

Saldivar had opted to take advantage of his own locker room and was in good spirits as he warmed up. "What can I say about Eder? He is a great fighter, and I hope he has a good fight. I think we are two fighters in the same class," he said.

On the eve of the fight, it was reported that the event had not been the blockbuster expected at the gate. The promoters even made sure that the bout was blacked out on local television to bring in as many spectators as possible, but only $15,000 in ticket sales were reported. Ringside seats were going for $20, which was considered high for Brazilian standards. "I expected a greater interest from 'Baianos' for the fight," Katzenelson admitted.

At around 9 pm, Saldivar made his way from his locker room first, and there was a knock on the door that Eder was up next. When asked if he had any specific plan or strategy, Eder said: "I am not a robot. I'll find out how he intends to fight, and then I'll define my own game." The crowd raised the roof for Eder's ring walk as he soaked in the applause before the two boxers met in the ring and exchanged their countries flags before the national anthems were played.

Marcel remembers this particular fight, above any, was the one that his father appeared most determined to finish quickly due to the precarious health of his grandfather. Aristides was tired, and even walking to the ring exhausted him further. Eder was worried that every time his father would have to pick up the stool and carry it to the ring would be a struggle. Aristides was determined he would be the one handling the corner. "I said to him to relax and let someone else carry the stool into the ring, but he said, 'No. I am OK,'" Eder recalled.

Despite the slow ticket sales reported in the days leading up to the event, a crowd of 11,000 eventually made their way into the venue on fight night, thus packing the arena to capacity. It is possible this could have been due to a drop in ticket prices on the day of the event or simply a last-minute surge in ticket sales.

Round By Round from *Folha*

Round 1

Saldivar takes the first punch to his stomach. They study each other for some time. Saldivar tries to risk a timid jab. Eder only watched. The next one was Eder's, also a little bit shy. The Brazilian approaches more, and they both get excited, starting their confrontation. Eder, much more efficient and showing incredible quickness, opens the Mexican's guard and hits his stomach with a powerful left hook. Saldivar, despite having absorbed it well, still expressed the pain, and Eder took him to the ropes punching him in the face. Saldivar reacted with quick blows to Eder's face, but they had no effect. The impression was that the Brazilian was in his best shape, such was the quickness of his punches.

Round 2

Eder throws strong right-hand punches. A short-left punch, not too strong, was enough for Eder to open the round. Saldivar accepted a toe-to-toe fight, trying to reach the waistline, while Eder would try his jabs. Left hand in front of him, Eder turned around, tried the hammer, saw Saldivar duck, leave the corner, and go back to middle distance, running away from toe-to-toe combat. Two right-hand punches hit the Mexican's face. He seemed not to feel it and then punched left and right against Eder's body. He felt the mistake of fighting openly, gave his back to Eder, and turned around. The answer was another strong right-hand punch (from Eder). Saldivar backed up, trying to use the ring better. The round is over.

Round 3

Saldivar reacts, but Eder hits better. Visibly worried about Eder Jofre's punishment and spectacular performance in the previous round, Saldivar went to the center of the ring carefully. Eder accepted to be studied again and, only walking towards him, he attacked with a long jab that hit Saldivar's face, who backed up to the ropes. Eder advanced quickly and applied a one-two up and under combination that shook the Mexican. After getting away from the ropes, Saldivar tried the toe-to-toe fight and tried to test Eder's resistance with lower punches and uppercuts to the face, but he suffered more than he wanted, for Eder accepted, and using the same technique, was much more potent.

Round 4

Eder shoots the stomach: it's the end. The third-round beating made Saldivar change his tactic. He spun around the ring, pursued by Eder. Saldivar raised his guard with his arms as Eder attacked aggressively. He fired a series of short left and right-hand punches against the Mexican's stomach. With no notion, Saldivar answered desperately. A few punches hit Eder on his face. Eder lands a straight punch to Saldivar's stomach. Saldivar still had enough strength to fight back. Eder went on. Two punches up and a well-timed right-hand entered the center of the Mexican's stomach like a firecracker. With no breath, Saldivar backed up, staggering, and then took a left hook to his face. A follow-up right-hand didn't even hit him, for he was already falling, knocked out.

Estadao reported: "What else could a 37-year-old boxer want, after achieving two world titles, and defeating a younger boxer in the fourth round? It was like in the good old days, when Eder was a world bantamweight champion: in the fourth round, Saldivar pushed Eder to the ropes and started throwing combos, trying to find a way to connect a punch. Smartly, Eder exchanged positions and put Saldivar against the ropes. The Mexican was blocking the blows well but couldn't expect a stomach hit. Eder landed a strong right hook; Saldivar put the guard down immediately, in a lot of pain. That was the beginning of the knockout at 1:40 in the round. Eder didn't waste time, quickly applied a one-two sequence at him, Saldivar still mustered some energy to run away from Eder, but at this point, he was completely groggy. Eder had time for one more combo, putting him to the ground. Saldivar was flat on the canvas, and Eder was jumping around celebrating like ten years ago when he got his first world title. His happiness has an explanation: not even he believed in his skills anymore. When he defeated Jose Legra, he brought back the confidence from his earlier years as a boxer."

Eder was overcome by emotion at the end of the fight as tears rolled down his face, and he embraced his father. "Thank you, Dad! This fight is for you and Mom. Everything I have achieved in life is thanks to both of you. I wish she were here," he told his father. Aristides felt such pride and told Eder, "You have made me feel so proud. The joy you gave me today is worth a lifetime. You've achieved everything boxing has to offer. If you want to quit, you can quit right now because this is it. You've done everything."

Eder celebrated as he had never done before. This victory had certain emotional elements attached to it that were not there when he had defeated Legra or won the bantamweight title all those years ago. In the locker room after the fight, Eder summarized what had transpired in the ring. "I was really confident. I knew I couldn't get too tired. Then I decided to make him tired of doing feints and sidestepping. Saldivar would try to punch me, and I would punch right away, surprising him. The fight was decided like that. I cheered like never. Not even when I won the bantamweight title. I was so happy. I mean, when I arrived in Salvador, I didn't quite adjust to the city air or the food. But by fight time, I had already overcome it all," he said.

Eder also explained that he overheard instructions from Saldivar's corner, telling him to jab and go underneath to attack Eder. "I immediately took care of myself. In the third round, we came to the corner together, and I heard Perez tell Saldivar to throw uppercuts. That was when I landed a hook on his liver with a lot of strength. I realized what he had felt. I could also take advantage of his quickness: if he was quick, he would open up, leaving a few openings. I took advantage of those openings to hit him," he added.

Newton Campos admitted before the bout he had been nervous about Eder's chances and was in awe of what he had seen. "He (Eder) had an impeccable performance. All eyes were on him. It was a great moment to show that Eder, even though boxing for many years, was still in excellent shape," he said. This sentiment was echoed by many of Eder's followers. Due to his pedigree, Saldivar was expected to be a particularly challenging opponent and the quick knockout shocked even the most fervent admirers.

Eder mentioned his father had seen the effect the body punch had on Saldivar in the third round and told him to push more in the next round, believing that would open the Mexican up more. Eder suggested that his next opponent might be Art Hafey from Canada since he had been told by George Parnassus he was interested in staging the bout at the Great Western Forum in Inglewood, California. "It all depends on my father's health. If he gets better, I will fight this year," he said. Saldivar said that he had not recovered from Eder's shots in the third round and explained how the body punch took a lot of wind out of him and that a left hook dizzied him. "After that punch, I didn't feel anything else. Not even the punch that knocked me down. Eder was a deserved winner," the Mexican explained.

Leaving the arena, Eder and his family took Aristides to the hospital as he was in a weakened state. After he was given the OK, they went back to the hotel, where they celebrated the victory in the swimming pool. The following day, Eder and Saldivar both boarded the same plane into Congonhas, and as they came off the plane, they were met by the press. Understandably feeling down, Saldivar looked a figure of dejection as he said little and was unsure if he would fight again, insisting he needed some time to work out what he would do with his future. "I have already spoken too much about the fight," Saldivar said. "If it were on me, I would keep fighting, but I must meet with my managers and see what they think. If they choose to retire me, so that will be," he added.

Eder came off the plane carrying a big trophy, which was given to him by the WBC for winning the bout, and he was beaming from ear to ear as he greeted the media. "I've done everything for Brazilian boxing. Another champion will rise to replace me soon. I'll stop. I don't know when, but I will retire soon. If a champion does not show up, there is nothing I can do," Eder explained to the journalists. He spoke of the sacrifices he had to go through for this victory. There was the news he would be offered a large sum of money to fight in Los Angeles. Eder said that he would strongly consider retirement if the tax situation in Brazil didn't change. Katzenelson had wanted to keep Eder in Brazil and display him to the public as much as possible, but the income tax issue was getting worse, and Eder said that he might have to fight abroad again to make it worthwhile.

Eder was not only fighting this cause for himself but other boxers. He felt that the sport would not be attractive to enough people the way things were being handled. He had made a lot of money through boxing and made that money grow through investments, but he knew not everybody was fortunate enough to get as far as he had done in the sport. "The only thing I ask is that the government takes a good look at our situation," he said.

He pointed out that when a boxer graduates from amateur to professional, he doesn't have time to work other jobs and has to consume himself so much with training full-time, otherwise it would be impossible to succeed. "I am not fighting and talking about my own case. I made some money, and I don't need any more to live for the rest of my life. I fight for other people. Most are not as lucky as I was. I only want that the situation is studied like they are doing with football players," he added.

Eder confessed that making the featherweight limit was becoming a problem. While it was never as challenging as it had been in making the bantamweight limit, it was becoming a sacrifice once again. "I didn't say anything to anyone, but in nine title defenses, at least six of them I had to go through the same sacrifice. In 1962, when fighting Caldwell, I was late to the official weigh-in. I told them I had a flat tire on my way over there. That was not true; I was training to lose the last grams left. Little by little, the weight cutting became my biggest opponent," he said.

Eder signed autographs, posed for photographs, and hugged fans as he was giving his answers. He praised his defeated Mexican opponent, "There were days of so much concern, but it ended well. I was prepared physically and technically. Saldivar is an excellent boxer," he said. Despite the euphoria surrounding what had been a signature victory of sorts and the offers coming in, Eder explained that he would only fight again once his father had recovered from his illness. "My father's disease won't leave me calm enough to fight. That's why I was even happier with the victory in a short time. I had the feeling of finishing my nervousness earlier," he said.

Eder, one more time Eder

The circumstances around this fight prompted Eder to count this among his most significant victories: "The weather was bad in São Paulo, which stopped me from doing roadwork regularly. That also happened in Salvador, and I was afraid my leg muscles wouldn't be so resistant. There was also trouble with the flight from São Paulo to Salvador, which made me stay a night in Recife. Even worse was the case of the first hotel I stayed in. There was no restaurant service, and I was forced to eat fruits and drink juice for two days. Besides, I was scared at the state of my father's health. I think with all these troubles; I have enough reasons to consider this was the greatest victory of my career."

A couple of weeks after the bout, Eder confessed to *Placar Magazine* he was concerned about the match with Saldivar. "I thought I was going to lose the fight. That may be surprising, but it's just that I went through so many problems before this fight, like the trip, the hotel, the weight, psychological pressure, and physiological disturbances, I couldn't help but have those thoughts."

The great Vicente Saldivar retired shortly after this bout and would never be tempted back into the ring again. He had saved a lot of his money and was content that his children would lack nothing and could get the best education possible. He would rarely be seen in the boxing circles in Mexico after his career, preferring to be out of the spotlight. Raul Macias said Saldivar was paranoid that people were trying to get gossip out of him. "Saldivar changed a lot, and we couldn't talk to him because he thought people were pursuing him for publicity reasons," said Macias.

"Unfortunately, in his life, he moved away from many of us," said Sugar Ramos. "I lived close to him, and many times I went to find him to walk around the block, chat for a while, or go to play soccer with other boxers, but he always declined. I knew he would run every morning, but later, he shut himself in," he added.

Saldivar suffered his own personal tragedies as he was involved in a messy divorce from his wife. He became an alcoholic and fell into a depression, which intensified when his mother died in 1984. For several years already, Saldivar had said that he wanted nothing to do with boxing or the past and didn't even watch it on television.

He told his closest friends that he wanted only his family at his funeral when his day comes. Under no circumstances would he want any publicity. Sadly, Saldivar died on July 18, 1985, of a heart attack. As he wished, there was almost no publicity as the funeral parlor used the name Samuel Saldivar Garcia and he was cremated shortly after. Although not as revered as some other Mexican legends, Saldivar remains one of the all-time great featherweight champions and finest Mexican boxers for those familiar with his career and accomplishments.

In early November, Katzenelson said that they had a lucrative offer to fight Japanese contender, Sensuke Utagawa, in Nagoya on February 2. "I would go, but I don't want the same problems with the judges like the ones in my fight with Harada when I lost the title. If the payment is the same in another place, then I'll go because it's a really good deal," Eder said.

Katzenelson contacted the WBC in Mexico City towards the end of the month to see if there were any promoters elsewhere willing to pay Eder $120,000 for a title fight.

Eder opted to take the rest of the year off and take his mind away from boxing while his management team found a date and an opponent for him to put his title on the line against. He also reaffirmed his stance he did not want to fight in Japan, citing the difficulty in getting a fair shake with the judges in addition to the freezing temperatures in February.

In early December, Eder received an exciting proposal to box in a non-title bout on the undercard of the upcoming Muhammad Ali vs. Joe Frazier rematch on January 28 at Madison Square Garden in New York. The opponent proposed for Eder was Carlos Hernandez of the Dominican Republic, and the purse was to be $20,000. While appearing on such a big show was appealing, it was an offer that had to be declined since Aristides had been hospitalized again. Eder did not want to fight without his father by his side.

1973 Results

Eder Jofre W15 Jose Legra
Eder Jofre KO4 Godfrey Stevens
Eder Jofre W10 Frankie Crawford
Eder Jofre KO4 Vicente Saldivar

1974

On January 5, Estadão reflected on the year in Brazilian sports, and Eder was referenced as the high point of the year. "The loss of a world title, the conquering of another, the death of a champion, some remarkable victories, and some disappointments: that's how 1973 went down for Brazil. It was a year without the Olympic and Pan-American Games, but we had some ups and downs in pretty much every sport. The title lost was Emerson Fittipaldi, our great Formula 1 driver, he lost to the Scottish Jackie Stewart. Whereas Eder Jofre brought back the spotlight to Brazilian boxing by conquering another world title, becoming the new world featherweight champion."

Eder was awarded the "Sports Personality of the Year" by O *Globo* for the magnificent year he had in 1973. Rather than take the stage to talk about his own success, Eder used this opportunity and award to make things easier for other boxers and the overall dynamics of the sport in Brazil. He had spoken to Minister Antônio Delfim Netto about the tax situation and financial difficulties that held the sport back and was given assurances, but Eder was still waiting. "He (Delfim Netto) guaranteed me he would protect the boxers with a law that would be approved in November or December 1973. I think the law would have a lot of what I suggested back then. I want the Government to let go of the tax in fights for the South American or World titles. Of course, I don't want paternalism – I know very well it doesn't fix the problem – and that's why I think the fighter should pay taxes in regular fights. They should be dismissed when it's for a title that will help advertise the country. I don't want anything for myself. I only ask for the men who are in the gyms eating beans and working to keep their shape in their free time," Eder said.

He explained that because he was held in such regard, he wanted to raise awareness of this situation, which he felt was holding the sport back and also affected the poorer class in general. "For a long time, Brazil will still rely on Pelé's, Eder's, Ademares Ferreira da Silva's, and Nelson Prudêncio's to appear in international sports. You can check, they all came from poor classes, but it wasn't by official support. The thing is, among all classes, the poor are the most crowded one, and with no doubt ends up showing some valuable people," he concluded.

Kid Jofre Loses His Battle

There were discussions for Eder to fight in Los Angeles in January, but Leonel Hernandez of Venezuela was the front runner for a February date in Brazil. The WBC proposed that Eder fight Hernandez on March 9 in a non-title match and then put his title on the line against Venezuelan Alfredo Marcano on April 21. Rafito Cedeño, manager of Marcano, had been lobbying the WBC to either mandate this bout or strip Eder since Eder was taking his time arranging his next title defense.

More important than the title was Aristides' health. Eder was spending a lot of time visiting his father in the hospital. Aristides had fallen ill with lung cancer, so understandably, Eder was pre-occupied and not putting in his usual training beyond his morning roadwork. On February 20, Aristides was released from the hospital after getting a lot better, so Eder went to Carnival in Rio with his mind in a better place. Eder said that he hadn't spoken to Katzenelson yet but was planning on doing so once he got back from Rio. Unfortunately, soon after Aristides had been discharged, he relapsed again.

On March 20, 1974, Aristides was taken to the hospital and was already in a coma state. His body battled for four days as the family sat around his bed, and Eder said to him, "Dad, please forgive me if I didn't do everything you expected from me." Sadly, Aristides passed away on March 24. The great Kid Jofre was gone. "Only my father could endure what he endured. He had been sick for some years. He had lung cancer for many years because of all the smoking. He smoked so much he got cancer," Eder said in *O Grande Campeao*. He remembered how he had wanted to finish the bout with Saldivar quickly, so Aristides would not have to keep climbing up to the ring to give his instructions between rounds. "Poor man. He was so pale and tired. He could not breathe well. He had to climb upstairs to the ring and then climb down again. I knew he'd have to do that on every round, so you can be sure I tried my best to win the fight by knockout so that my father wouldn't have to do that," he added.

Estadão reported on Aristides' death and said that he had been an invaluable part of Brazilian boxing history. "Jose Aristides Jofre was never a great boxer himself, but nevertheless he's a big part in the history of national boxing. Kid Jofre has a long and beautiful story. As an immigrant settling in Brazil, he worked hard for 40 years for Brazilian boxing and deservedly is credited as a champion maker. In 1928, his older brother, Armando Jofre, invited him to help in his boxing gym. Kid Jofre ran the gym like a tough general on a battlefield, but those who knew him closely can affirm that he was a man with a child's heart. More than a trainer, Kid always instilled in his fighters the confidence and the right mindset they needed, hence Eder's catchphrase in post fights interviews: 'I owe this victory to my father.'"

Henrique Matteucci preferred not to dwell on the sorrow of losing his friend and such a significant influence on Brazilian boxing. Instead, he focused on the image of Kid Jofre he wanted to have in his mind forever. The Kid Jofre who meant so much to so many people and was an example of integrity and courage. He wrote in the revised edition of *O Galo de Ouro* in 1977:

"I never sang sad songs for him; I never said the last funereal goodbye. Nothing like this. I didn't care if he was dying, or if physically, he wasn't around anymore. For me, Jofre was always a symbol of life. I did go to the funeral, but I refused to look at him that way. I wanted to remember the old Aristo with his bright and open eyes as I saw seven days before his death at his home in Parque Peruche. I went there to say goodbye (he noticed), we had a little conversation, and then I left. I was feeling destroyed inside. But the man on that bed kept fighting like he fought his entire life. I didn't see the dead Kid Jofre. I saw the living Kid Jofre. Like I always did. Shouting in the ring corner. And in my humble corner, after losing a fight against Manoel de Moraes, I had the pleasure to listen to his healing words:

- 'Well, at least you lost like a man, not like a coward.'

I want to remember him like this, dynamic and energetic in the gym. I saw Jofre in so many places, Montevideo, Chile, Lima, Rio, and Salvador. A living Jofre. One who gave his life for the sport. The old Aristo won a more difficult bout; he defeated the adversity, the ignorance, the misery, the pain. I think he beat death because she stayed a year and a half dropping low blows at him, trying to put him down. And when he fell, even the sky protested, a thunderstorm shook up the earth at the funeral. That's why I never said a funereal goodbye to my great friend. I didn't sing mourning songs. I waited. Jose Aristides Jofre suffered only a knockdown, and he's coming back someday, in some ring around the world, when the bell rings, calling the braves to fight."

A plaque commemorating Aristides "Kid" Jofre

Jose Aristides Jofre
12/31/1903 - 3/24/1974

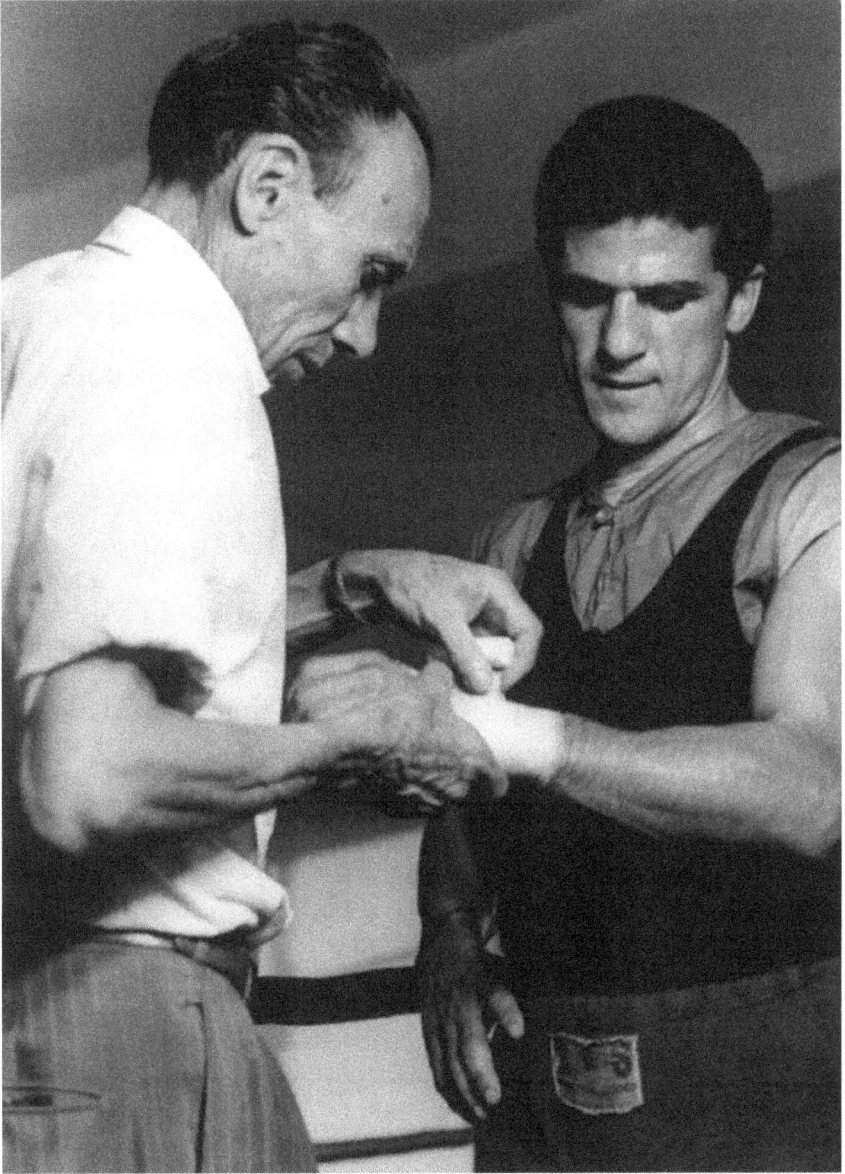

Unfortunately, Eder was also in the middle of an ugly battle between Katzenelson and Lazaro over money from the Saldivar bout. The two managers feuded over who was entitled to what, and this sabotaged Eder's championship. They allowed time to lapse, which led to the WBC stripping Eder of his title on June 17 for failure to schedule a title defense within a satisfactory time frame. Despite the sadness and depression over his father's passing, Eder was willing to defend his title and was ready to fight against the top contender Alfredo Marcano of Venezuela.

The issue between Katzenelson and Lazaro dragged on. It reached its boiling point when Lazaro did accept a deal to fight Marcano without his partner's consent.

Katzenelson would not accept the financial terms and told Eder that Lazaro was not looking out for his best interests and was ripping him off and jeopardizing his career. Katzenelson said that their partnership had been dissolved in November. Lazaro legally had no rights to any of Eder's fights abroad and, even in Brazil, had only a secondary role in the partnership.

This was a cruel blow for the champion as he had lost his father and his championship in a matter of only three months, and he was powerless in both instances. Eder reached out to one of Katzenelson's previous employees, Hugo Cinha, to help sort this mess. Cinha even traveled to Mexico on his own dime to petition the WBC not to strip Eder of his title due to an argument between two businessmen.

Unfortunately, he did not convince the WBC, and they took Eder's title and announced that a bout between Marcano and Bobby Chacon would be for the vacant championship. As Eder processed all happenings in his life, he lost the energy and passion for the sport and arranged no fights for some time. He spent more time close to home with his family and enjoyed some things he had missed due to his regular training schedule.

Eder reflected on this management rift, which cost him the title he had worked so hard to win in the ring. "I believed I was a good product because my managers fought upon the contracts all the time. They started to divide themselves from a team. So, I rebelled against it. They both were my co-managers, under a brand called Bel-Boxe, but they both claimed to be my exclusive manager, which meant Katzenelson used to bring me fights behind Marcos' back, and vice-versa. But if I agreed to fight one of those, I would have to pay a huge amount to the other for contract violation. That's what happened in Mexico when Marcos arranged a fight putting my title at stake. I was with my hands tied, so I just threw in the towel. I lost my world title without fighting for it. The press didn't understand what was going on because they didn't know about the huge penalty I had to pay if I accepted the fight. I went to the jury, later on, to try to recover my title, but I failed. My reign ended because of bureaucracy and politics, because of financial and managerial problems, not because of my boxing skills. There was a manager who tried to work with me, Hugo Cinha, but he didn't have enough money to cover all my expenses."

Fight 72, vs. Niliberto Herrera, December 21, 1974

Eder got back into the ring after 14 months away when he faced little-known Niliberto Herrera of Venezuela four days before Christmas. Katzenelson and Lazaro were still fighting, so Eder again approached Cinha to arrange this match for him. The bout took place in Jundiaí, about 35 miles north of São Paulo as Cinha conducted most of his business in Jundiaí and had various connections he felt could help the show.

This would be the first time Eder ever stepped into the ring without his father. Eder did not look far to find his new head trainer when he chose his brother Dogalberto to train him moving forward. To say the mood differed from usual would be an understatement as Eder was fighting without his best friend and his idol besides having lost his championship for reasons out of his reach.

Herrera impressed the press when he showed a good, efficient offensive game as he sparred Luis Correa. Dogalberto felt that Herrera's young age of 23 would not be a significant factor and that his style of boxing would play into his brother's hands. "Niliberto is the kind of opponent Eder likes," he said. Despite Herrera's relatively low profile, he had recently scored a knockout victory over Bernardo Caraballo. However, it must be acknowledged that Caraballo was no longer at the top level he had been a decade earlier when Eder went to Colombia to defend his bantamweight world title against him.

Dogalberto took a closer look at Herrera two days before the bout. While he said he had "no punch," he did admit that he presented stylistic issues. "His arms are longer (than Eder's), and he has a good counter-right punch. It is quick and unexpected," he said. Eder said that he had no opinion of his opponent since he left the scouting reports to his brothers. Herrera was beaming at the opportunity that had come his way, and he was full of praise for his illustrious opponent. "I was always an Eder admirer, for his style and his grit. It's hard to believe I will face him, but I intend to forget about all of that in the ring," he said.

Round By Round from *Folha*

Round 1
The first movements were to study each other with no exchange of punches. Only a few seconds away from the end of the round, Eder let a right-hand punch go over Niliberto's head. That was the only action moment of the round.

Round 2
Eder jabs with his left while Niliberto does the same with his right. Niliberto spins to Eder's right and keeps repeating that movement until the round is over. After trying to hit the opponent from underneath, Eder crosses the left and hits Niliberto on the head. He immediately landed a good straight right-hand punch. Eder tries and corners Niliberto, but desperate, the latter tries to run and gives him a head butt. Nothing serious. The round is over.

Round 3
Like in every other round, Niliberto does the cross sign before going into his opponent's direction. When he gets to the center of the ring, he

receives two straight left-hand punches to his head, which makes him fight at a distance again. Eder defines himself to the offensive game and hits Niliberto with a right cross. The Venezuelan absorbed the pain and clinched Eder, stopping the sequence of punches, thus avoiding more hits. Eder looks much better now. Niliberto is nervous and, therefore, a little bit uncontrolled.

Round 4

Eder starts the round by attacking his opponent. Trainer Giraldo Valdez is standing up in his corner, very nervous, yelling at his pupil to protect his waist. Eder crosses the left and lands well with the right hand. He lets his right go a little. Niliberto tries a straight right-hand punch and receives a counterpunch in return. Eder took advantage of that and closed the distance but got hit by a bump of heads that causes a wound on his scalp, a few centimeters above his left ear. A lot of bleeding due to the wound. The audience cheered Eder's performance and booed Niliberto due to the head butt. Even bleeding, Eder is still attacking, and apparently, his victory is guaranteed. Niliberto boxes with his guard high and Eder gives him hooks. The round is over. In the break, the audience cheers for Eder, screaming his name.

Round 5

Eder is still bleeding, and he takes another few seconds to come back. The distance is shortened, and Niliberto gives him another head butt. The referee calls a foul against the Venezuelan. Seconds later, the referee stops the fight again and looks at one judge, waiting for some information. Juan Diaz, the manager, protests in his corner: "What's wrong? What's wrong?"

Until the end of the round, Eder still hits Niliberto with a few light straight punches.

Round 6

Eder is in the center of the ring. From his corner, Dogalberto screams so he can watch his liver, telling Eder to be careful about Niliberto's body punches, which allows him to counterpunch his waist. Eder counter-attacks and Niliberto grabs him. The referee warns the Venezuelan. Niliberto is cornered against the ropes, and when he tries to throw his body against Eder's, he loses balance and hits the ground. The round is over.

Round 7

It starts with Eder's straight right-hand punch. Another straight one and Niliberto counter-punches with a hook that immediately is answered with a straight punch from Eder. The referee warns Niliberto again about the head butts. A hook by Eder and Niliberto appears to feel the punch. The round is over.

Round 8

In this round, both boxers only exchanged punches at a distance. The audience cheered only when Eder missed a right-hand punch that could have ended the fight.

Round 9

Eder attacks again. He corners Niliberto, and when he shortens the distance, he lets go straight punches and hooks. Niliberto feels the punches and clinched.

Round 10

Eder attacked with a straight punch and gets counter-punched. Niliberto keeps his distance. The wound on Eder's head bleeds again. But that doesn't diminish Eder's excitement, as he punches Niliberto, shortening the distance, throwing hooks. Niliberto feels the punches, and when it looks like he will be knocked out, he grabs Eder. The referee splits up Eder and Niliberto, and the bell rings within a few seconds. The fight is over.

Eder won every round, but he was disappointed that he couldn't give the fans a knockout. "I tried to find myself and get a knockout, but I couldn't do what I wanted, and I apologize for that," he said. Dogalberto was also apologetic that they could not score the knockout but was happy that Eder put in some good work. "He (Herrera) did exactly what he had to do; otherwise, he would have been knocked out. He avoided exchanging punches, and he showed a lot of agility and good leg movement. He is a great boxer," Dogalberto said.

The Herrera camp was happy that their man lasted the distance with his trainer Giraldo Valdez saying, "Eder proved that he is morally the world champion. At 38 years old, he fights as though he is 20. Eder is in excellent condition and is experienced. It was a spectacular fight. I'm happy because Niliberto knew how to fight a boxer as good as Eder and fought well." Herrera himself glowingly referenced the Brazilian when he gave his thoughts on the bout, stating: "I knew Eder's game and tried to avoid the fight as much as I could. If I stayed to fight him, it wouldn't end up well. Besides having a strong punch, he moves his waist very well. Today I really saw that Eder is the great champion I heard about ever since I was a boy. He was and still is the idol I dream about being someday. He is an idol back in my country." Based on Herrera's words, Eder's popularity in Venezuela had increased dramatically since 1961 when they wanted his blood for knocking out Ramon Arias in defense of his bantamweight world championship.

Eder did not feel like himself in this fight and said, "I can't do this anymore. I'm going to stop." He made no official announcements, but he did not fight in 1975. Eder felt Lazaro was the primary culprit behind losing his featherweight title and sat out as the managers bickered. Katzenelson came away with Eder's contract, but the champ was enjoying some time off with his family. "How great it is not having to take care of my weight, that's life!" he said, but just like when he had retired in 1966, he had the itch again and missed the sport.

Since Lazaro signed the contract for the Marcano fight without the consent of Katzenelson, he was dismissed from Eder's management team after losing a lawsuit. It had been a bitter end to what had been a mostly successful working partnership for over 15 years. Eder also was not happy with Katzenelson at this point. He knew that Katzenelson's ego and infighting with Lazaro had been at the root of the problem and was the primary reason he lost his title in the courtroom and not the boxing ring.

1974 Results

Eder Jofre W10 Niliberto Herrera

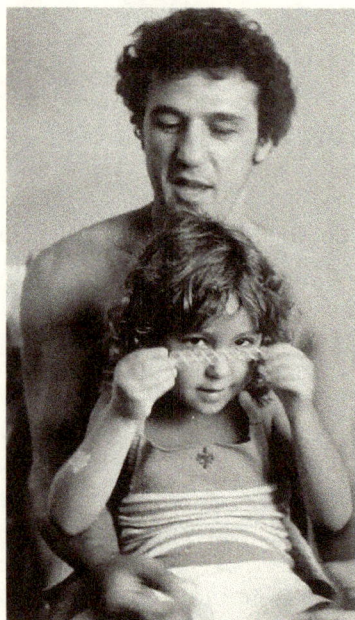

Eder and Andrea

Cidinha, Eder and Andrea

1976

As Eder entered his 40th year, sitting on the back of 12 months out of the ring, it may have seemed like the optimal time to make his retirement official, but an itch needed scratching. Eder had other business interests, but ultimately, he was a born fighter, and the ring was his home. "I'm a poet, I'm crazy, but my heart can't be away from a ring, from the gloves, from the smell of the ropes. If I get away from boxing, I'll die. And that's why I'm coming back for the second time, willing to get a new world title," he said upon announcing that he would make a return to the ring.

"In 1942, when I was six years old, I came up to the ring for the first time for an exhibition fight at my father's gym on old Rua Seminário. Since then, my love for this violent sport has only gotten bigger. Today, after seeing so many bad things in boxing and losing a title because of the managers fighting, I come back knowing I'm demanding a great achievement from myself," he added.

He felt healthy and said his body felt like it was closer to 20 than 40. "He may have lost a little in resistance, but he earned a lot of experience, and that can be a decisive factor to win back the title," said Waldemar Zumbano. Eder said that if his father was still alive, "he would try to talk me out of it but would wind up starting the basic exercises by my side."

Fight 73, vs. Enzo Farinelli, February 24, 1976

Doubts as to whether Eder could regain his old glory were understandable now that he was only a few weeks from turning 40, ancient by a featherweight's standards. It had been almost a decade since Eder had last failed to win a bout. Eder was determined to win a third world championship because he felt he was unjustly stripped of his world title. The opponent for the last bout of Eder's thirties was Italian Enzo Farinelli.

Farinelli, at 33, was a reasonably accomplished boxer who fought in a typically European style, which consisted of plenty of movement and a solid defense. The level of his competition was modest outside his winning of the Italian bantamweight and featherweight titles. He came up short when challenging for continental honors.

Orival Sapienza, now training Eder alongside Dogalberto, talked up Eder's prospects. "Despite his age, he has a lot of opportunities. Comparing him to other boxers, his technique is more than enough. He has grit, strength, courage, and champion instinct. The problem is staying in shape. He is currently doing well and should continue training and practicing, being careful not to get out of shape. Eder is methodical. For him, everything will be simple," he said.

Katzenelson said that he felt Farinelli would be an easy opponent for Eder. Even though Eder didn't fight in 1975, he had been in training for six months with his mind set on regaining the world title. The focus was to make sure Eder remained active and had little time off between fights. "Eder is in great shape, looking sharp. It's been six months of intense training; he should win this fight easily," Katzenelson said.

"This fight is a definitive mark in my boxing career. If I win like I expect to, I will be firmly working to get the title back. If I'm defeated, or even if I feel like I won by chance, I will immediately leave boxing," Eder said upon the announcement of his return to the ring.

Although scaling great heights and receiving great accolades, it had been a rough time for Eder in recent years. Despite being in a positive mindset coming into this comeback, he was hit by another family tragedy when his uncle Antonio Zumbano died from diabetes. Mauro told Eder at the funeral that his uncle was calling out Eder's name as he was slipping away. He wanted to speak to his famous nephew despite barely being cognizant of much else. When Eder was told about this, he remembered a strange dream he had just two weeks prior. Knowing what Mauro told him, Eder was convinced this image had something to do with his uncle wanting to communicate with him while lying on his death bed. Eder commented on this incident over 20 years after it occurred:

"I went to sleep one night, having my wife beside me, and suddenly I felt that my feet were tied up. I couldn't move, no matter what. I was locked in that position. So, I made a last effort, gave it all I got, and then I could move my legs again. I was relieved. So, I went back to sleep but woke up feeling immense pressure on my knees. I called God in desperate prayer, and I could free myself from that again. This time I got up to take some fresh air and drank water with sugar, spent some time pacing around the house before going back to bed, where my wife was still asleep. I laid down next to her again, then I felt the same pressure, but this time on my chest, like if there was something on top of me. I couldn't breathe; much less call my wife for help. I felt like someone was on top of me."

"I asked God to allow me to see what that was. So, I placed my hand on my chest and kind of pushed it away. That thing fell to the ground, next to me. I couldn't believe my eyes, it was terrible: it was a mouthless man looking at me, with a sort of feather on his head. Afterward, I told my wife what happened, but she acted like everybody else acted when this thing occurred to me, she told me that this was just a nightmare. Come on, a nightmare split into three parts! The first time it was on my feet, another on my knees, and again on my chest. God punishes me if I am wrong, but I've never heard of a dream that you can dream of being with your eyes wide open and awake like I was."

"A few days went by, and I went to visit my sister-in-law, right there in the entrance of her house, she said: 'Hey, did you know that Zumbanão wanted to talk to you before he passed away?' This man, Zumbanão, was my uncle, who recently had passed away. Then I realized: a mouthless man, speechless. Dead people can't talk, no matter how hard they try. Now I recognized that it was him, right in the dark bedroom, my uncle (very sick). He was trying to talk but failed to deliver the message, and I never came to know what he was trying to say."

"My interpretation, after being through this, is there is something beyond life and death. And I say that again, a three-part dream is too much to be something from this world. The visitor can't talk, but his desire to send the message still is in the air, somewhere in the universe. And I was this close to helping him, but he didn't have a mouth. A few hours before he died, he said to his wife, my aunt Roseli: 'I need to talk to Eder, I can't go without talking to him.' He passed on that same night. I still ask myself why I couldn't see any more of those visions after my uncle died."

Despite his fiery nature and penchant for getting into street brawls, Antonio was a much-beloved figure. "When he (Antonio) died, people from all over sent letters. They sent us their condolences," Ricardo Zumbano said.

Despite Eder's sadness, the bout with Farinelli was not postponed and was scheduled for Porto Alegre at the Gigantinho Ginasio on February 26. Within two hours of tickets going on sale, 8,000 had been snapped up, which pointed to the level of support Eder still had. "Despite not being as quick as I was when I became bantam champion, I'm doing well and am confident for the fight against Enzo Farinelli in Porto Alegre," Eder said on February 17.

Eder was working out at Orival Sapienza's gym and announced he would be departing for Porto Alegre the following day. Eder avoided sparring on this date. Instead, he did all of his other exercises and unveiled a new exercise he had been practicing with Marcel. This exercise involved bouncing a tennis ball quickly on the floor like a basketball which helped his hand speed. He told the press on hand he would be spending a week in Porto Alegre. "I just hope I can find an appropriate place so I can train peacefully and only at the stadium where the fight will be disputed at the 'Gigantinho' is where I'll be able to," he said.

Eder explained that he would be sparring with Brazilian featherweight champion Jose de Paula and that he would train every day until Monday when he would rest for the fight scheduled for Tuesday. "Considering how long I was inactive; I believe I'm in shape for the fight. I'm sure it will be a good presentation for the gaucho audience. I don't know much about Farinelli. Based on unreliable information, I thought he was much bigger than me and was surprised when I watched him on TV: I am actually bigger," Eder said.

Farinelli arrived in Porto Alegre the day before Eder and refused to allow journalists to view him train or visit him at his hotel. Farinelli's manager and trainer, Adriano Sconerti, told the press he had warned his pupil to be careful about Eder's famous punches to the liver. Word did get out of the Farinelli camp that the Italian had been sparring with Joel Gomes. In one incredibly challenging training session, he suffered a minor injury to his nose. Eder did his usual morning running before resting around lunch, working out in the afternoon, and relaxing in the evening. He did take in a football match between local team Gremio and Rio club Flamengo two days before the fight.

On fight night, Eder did not disappoint the spectators on hand as he delivered a dominating knockout victory. Eder closed the distance quickly in the first round as he took complete control of the contest. The first knockdown came from a perfect straight right-hand that came right down the middle and broke the guard of the Italian before the bell saved him after getting up on wobbly legs. Farinelli admitted after the bout he did not recover from the first-round punishment he received. "I lost the fight in the first round. Since that punch, I was dizzy and couldn't react anymore," he said.

The second knockdown came after Eder attacked with his right hand and landed cleanly multiple times as he moved Farinelli to the ropes, where he then dropped him with a hard left hook to the body at the end of the third round. The referee counted slowly while Farinelli tried to catch his breath and once the Italian got up the referee continued to count. This respite meant the Italian would survive the round as the bell went when the referee was finishing the second count. In the fourth round, Eder moved in quickly and punished Farinelli, who fell under an accumulation of blows. Once again, he courageously pulled himself up, but the towel was wisely thrown in from his corner, which gave Eder a fourth-round TKO victory.

"I want to fight again. I need to fight again and quickly. I feel like I am OK and that I can continue in the ring with no danger or fear. Look at me, 39 years old and still fighting and winning," Eder said after the fight. Farinelli also pointed to Eder's age and conceded that he was far too strong for him. "Eder doesn't look like he is 40 in the ring. He has the strength of a middleweight, and he is as quick as a 20-year-old. In Europe, there is nobody in this weight class that can beat him. His right-hand punch is extraordinary," the Italian said.

After the bout, Eder ordered Katzenelson to get him a fight the following month and said he would consider retiring for good if he could not secure a match. Eder realized that while his condition was good and his performance had been excellent, it was not easy to compete at the highest level if he didn't stay sharp by fighting often. The post-fight dinner was held at Barranco Churrascaria. Katzenelson said he had made a deal with Farinelli's manager to face another one of his pupils on March 31. Eder took a day off to enjoy the sights of Porto Alegre before getting back to São Paulo. He trained again on Monday, March 2, after a few days resting at home with his family. The March date didn't come to pass, but Katzenelson assured Eder he was close to securing a date and an opponent.

Fight 74, vs. Michel Lefevbre, May 2, 1976

Eder turned 40 on March 26 and spoke about how he still felt like a young man. "Who said I'm getting into my forties? I feel like I am 30 years old. The chronological age doesn't count. If I stopped fighting, then I think I would feel older," he said. The discipline that Eder still maintained surprised some given he had achieved everything the sport offered and had financial security and a happy family, but Eder cited his family and his childhood as the reason he was so disciplined. "I was lucky enough to be born in a family that was always connected to boxing. From an early age, I learned things in the ring. I think this just sticks in your head. At fight time, in a fraction of seconds, you just intuitively know what to do. It's fundamental to trust yourself and keep in shape. The rest you learn. I, for example, always think of a strategy to face my opponent. But at fight time, you always need to be open to change the tactic whenever necessary."

Eder's next opponent came from France and shared some similarities with him. Michel Lefevbre shared the same March 26 birth date as Eder but was born 14 years later, and he was also a vegetarian. Since the knockout victory over Enzo Farinelli, Eder had wanted to get back into the ring quickly. The layoff was a little over ten weeks, so when he was given a fight date, Eder completed 42 rounds of sparring, 18 rounds of jumping rope, 33 on the heavy bag, 80 miles of roadwork, and about 11 hours of general gym work. The Lefebvre fight would see Eder return to the site of his famous victory over Jose Legra, with the bout set for Nilson Nelson Gymnasium, which was formerly Ginasio Presidente Médici, in the nation's capital of Brasilia. The day before the fight, Eder did confess that he had recently been suffering from insomnia, but that didn't affect his training schedule.

Eder told *Estadão* he wakes up at 7 am every day, gets two and a half miles of roadwork in on an empty stomach before having orange juice, coffee, and toast for breakfast. That was followed by a nap until lunchtime when he would eat eggs, vegetables, and dessert, and then in the afternoon, he would go to the gym and get in his sparring.

Lefebvre was sparring with Brazilian Joel Gomes in training, and while Gomes said that he hoped Eder would win he was picking the Frenchman. "He's too fast, and better yet: knows how to connect his right hand. For sure, Eder's going to have a hard time trying to stop him. I hope I am wrong, but not this time, Eder," he said. Eder said that his strategy was simple and that he would follow the instructions his father used to give him: "I'll do what my father taught me: surround and hit, surround and hit, always dancing, until I get him."

Less than a minute into the first round, Lefebvre attacked Eder after a brief period of studying by both fighters. The Frenchman landed a straight left, which he followed up with a strong right-hand that connected. Eder got angry and accepted the aggressive fight which Lefebvre tried to force. "My original plan was to lead the fight until the fifth or sixth round, but I lost control over myself when he landed those punches," Eder said after the fight.

He attacked and landed four great shots to the head and body, which quickly put the Frenchman on the defensive. Lefebvre tried to clinch to avoid further punishment. In the second round, Eder landed a hard straight right-hand, which caused blood to stream through his opponent's nose

and mouth. He sensed the end was near and then followed up with a crunching left hook which dropped Lefebvre. The visiting fighter made it out of the round but was quickly trapped and battered in the third round. Eder mixed in two hard hooks to the liver and two clean headshots before referee Clovis Cataldi intervened to call off the bout giving Eder a TKO victory at 1:15 of the third round.

"If I let Eder land one more shot, he could have killed him," Cataldi said. Eder had been expecting a more difficult challenge based on what he had been informed on Lefebvre before the bout. "He tried to surprise me right in the second round, trying to knock me down. That's when things went bad for him. I had been told that he was a technical boxer, but he didn't show it."

Eder's management issues were still ongoing. Shortly after the bout with Lefebvre, Katzenelson said he might no longer be working with Eder due to too much interference from other parties. Katzenelson felt Eder's doctor, Fernando Cortez, was trying to get too involved in the promotional and managerial side of things. Also, there had been a heated argument between Orival Sapienza and Firmino Abate. Katzenelson felt it was ridiculous that people who had never stepped into the ring were trying to give Eder technical advice and tried to be the most important man in his camp in place of Aristides.

Eder looks on as Abe Katzenelson answers questions from the media

Hugo Cinha offered advice for Eder. Eder felt a sense of loyalty to Cinha because when the WBC stripped him of his featherweight title as

Katzenelson and Lazaro were fighting with each other, Cinha took the time out of his schedule and, with his own money, booked a flight and hotel in Mexico to meet with the WBC to make sure Eder kept his belt. Cinha, who was also working at Jundiaí City Hall as a financial counselor to the city's mayor, Mauro Pereira Cruz, also helped promote Eder's bout with Niliberto Herrera in December of 1974.

At Lago Restaurant in Brasilia, Katzenelson told press members he would walk away. This news came as a surprise to Eder when he was pressed on the subject the following day. He said that he preferred to rest and not read the press after his fights but was shocked to hear it from a friend since he said he spoke face-to-face with Katzenelson at the dinner. "Yesterday, when I got my paycheck, nothing was discussed about the future," Eder said. Eder was relaxed about the situation as he had several options if Katzenelson would no longer work with him. "If Katzenelson really intends to stop working with me, there won't be any problems. I will try and meet another manager. Here, among Brazilian managers, I'm well connected and don't have enemies," he added.

Katzenelson was tired of Brazilian boxing and did not have the most enthusiasm when it came to the future of the game in the country. He was considering working exclusively abroad. "I'm almost 61, and I don't want to kill myself anymore. In Brasilia, I worked like an animal, and they still wanted ten percent of my contract, besides the ten percent ticket profit they had the right to. I am exhausted, and instead of being encouraged, I still have problems with the Boxing Brazilian Confederation," he said.

Katzenelson added that he felt Dr. Cortez lacked ethics and lied about prescribed vitamins and went around the coaches' backs when it came to Eder's dietary supplements. He tendered his resignation on May 4 and insisted that he had no quarrel with Eder himself. "When he needs my advice, he can look for me. We talked in Brasilia, and I said I would think a lot before making my decision on the whole case. But actually, I just wanted not to hurt him. I hope he doesn't get upset about my decision, tries to understand it, and that he is pleased," Katzenelson said.

Katzenelson also said he had done the groundwork for Eder's next opponent and had spoken to the management team of Lefevbre, who claimed they had other fighters they would send to Brazil for a shot at Eder. "The manager who gets Eder, either Kaled Curi or Oscar Pedroso Horta Filho, or even another one, will have their job made easier in this promotion. There is already a great legacy," Katzenelson concluded. "Even with all the problems, I won't stop fighting, and I will continue with my goal to accomplish, for the third time, the world title. I need to detox my muscles and also my head," Eder said.

Eder chose Kaled Curi to be his manager, as Curi was a very trusted individual with a lot of power and knowledge of the boxing scene in Brazil. Curi had been one of Aristides' best pupils and, after his own career in the ring, would work in the media, manage fighters, and eventually authored his own book. Within Brazilian boxing circles, Curi was well-liked, and he was trusted. He knew the market and assured Eder he would maximize his profits in what was the twilight of his career.

Eder, Kaled Curi and Osvaldo Forte

Eder had a lot of faith in Curi. He would always do the right thing and look out for the interests of others. He made a clear and concise decision to hire a man who had been a close family confidant for decades. It had been discovered by Eder's friend Osvaldo Forte that after some investigation, Katzenelson had been taking a large portion of Eder's purses. Eder thought that the contract share he had with his management team was 50% for himself, 25% for his trainer, and 25% for his management team. Eder had been collecting a little under 20% of the recent purses. He would say years later that he wished he had paid closer attention to his contracts earlier and hired Curi years before. "I regret not having Kaled Curi by my side in my comeback. I would have made ten times more money," he said.

Fight 75, vs. Pasqualino Morbidelli, May 29, 1976

Just as Eder had wanted, there was a rapid turnaround for his next bout with less than four weeks between matches. His bout with 28-year-old Italian Pasqualino Morbidelli was scheduled for May 28, and significantly it was to be the first time Eder had fought in his hometown in three years. The last time fighting in São Paulo had been when he thrashed Godfrey Stevens, and now the time was right for him to bring the show back home. Two days before the bout, both boxers gave a good impression as they worked out at the Esperia Club. Eder sparred four rounds with Claudio dos Santos before winding down his training with some jump rope and bag work. There was a moment of fear when Eder was caught with an accidental head butt, but the damage was minimal. Eder had a little graze, but as a precautionary measure, he put on a head guard and covered his brows in Vaseline so that no more accidents could threaten the show.

Renzo Frizardi, coach of Morbideli, was impressed with Eder after seeing him workout. "With the qualities he has, he can easily fight until 50, as Archie Moore did," he said. For Morbidelli, it was his first bout outside of his homeland where he recently won and lost the Italian Featherweight title. Morbidelli was in the ring just after Eder and sparred three rounds with Javan de Oliveira. Morbidelli appeared strong and aggressive as he almost knocked his sparring partner out. "If Eder wants to win, he must fight with perfection using all of his knowledge," de Oliveira said.

The bout was Eder's first under the new management of Kaled Curi and was not broadcast on local television in an attempt to help boost the live gate. The event was a success at the gate with a near-sellout crowd, which created a loud atmosphere by the time of the main event.

The bout began with Morbidelli moving away. He tried to avoid being an easy target for Eder, who spent the first 30 seconds of the fight studying the Italian's moves. Eder soon cut the ring off on Morbidelli and landed two good punches, which slowed him down before he unloaded a right-hand punch directly to the gut. Morbidelli struggled to his feet and was saved by the jingle of the bell at the end of the round. Eder wasted little time in the second round, satisfied that he had the measure of his foe as he went in for the kill. Morbidelli tied Eder up when he moved in close to slow the action.

This pattern continued as the Italian tried to frustrate Eder and the crowd, which showed its disapproval. A small clash of heads re-opened Eder's training wound, but he did not appear bothered as he focused his attack more and more on Morbidelli's body. In the third round, the Italian started to try and jab and move and even landed two straight right-hand punches to Eder's face. Eder quickly stepped inside and exploded with a right-hand of his own, which dropped Morbidelli. The Italian abandoned his safety-first strategy and went toe-to-toe with Eder and even landed a strong body punch of his own. The two boxers met in the center of the ring in the fourth round and exchanged punches, but Eder was stronger as he was able to fell Morbidelli with a left hook to the body, which folded his opponent and laid him out for the count at 1:07 of the round.

Eder was carried from the ring to his locker room by his friends and admirers as he enjoyed the chanting of the crowd. In the crowded locker room, Eder sat beside famous Brazilian actors John Herbet and Renato Conseorte and said how he needed to have another fight shortly because his last three fights only lasted a combined 11 rounds. "Right at the start of the fight, I let my right hand go to see if he could take it. From his reaction, I thought to myself, 'Oh yeah, good for me.' Then he started running away and grabbing, but I was calm enough to wait for the right moment to get him. I heard all the instructions his coach shouted and had enough calmness to wait. It worked out. I only felt one punch during the entire fight. It was the hook to the liver," Eder said when assessing the bout.

"I used a technique I learned with my father and repeated many times by Orival Sapienza during the fight breaks: not getting desperate, waiting for the right moment to hit the ideal punch. Even so, I thought the Italian would take another few rounds," he added. He then looked briefly to the future, "We will wait for my next fight. We'll see if a 40-year-old boxer like me will come because these young guys can't take it," he joked. Morbidelli came into the locker room to congratulate Eder on his victory, shook his hand, and asked for an autograph and a photo.

Fight 76, vs. Jose Antonio Jimenez, July 2, 1976

Eder was signed to fight at Corinthians Gymnasium at home in São Paulo on July 2. Eder and Curi felt that with an eye on the world title, they needed an opponent who could withstand some punishment and provide Eder with a good, competitive fight. It was essential to get rounds in the bank and face an opponent who came into the ring confident of a victory. If Eder would ever fight the top boxers again, they probably would come into the ring with designs on beating him and adding the scalp of a legend to their resume, and not just come to survive or be used as cannon fodder the way Morbidelli, Farinelli, and Lefevbre had been.

The opponent that Curi reached a deal with was Spaniard Jose Antonio Jimenez after considering Scotland's Vernon Sollas. Known as "Gitano," Jimenez was a famous boxer in his native Spain. He had won the European featherweight title after Jose Legra had vacated that title in 1972 when he went for world honors. Jimenez came to Brazil with good credentials, having scored victories over fighters such as Tommy Glencross, Felix Said Brami, Daniel Vermandere, and Elio Cotena. Cotena, however, defeated Jimenez in a rematch and took Jimenez's European crown.

Jimenez arrived in São Paulo full of confidence with the belief that his age of 23 up against Eder's 40 years would make a big difference. He also spoke about getting revenge for his friend and idol, Jose Legra. "I'll fight for the justice of Legra, who unfairly lost to Eder. I'm confident in the victory for I'm younger, and I intend to challenge for the world title," the Spaniard said. Eder simply said that "I'm sure of one thing: Gitano will have to be very good to win the fight."

Eder said that while he didn't know a great deal about the Spaniard, he recognized his victory over the highly-rated Cotena. He hoped that Jimenez would prove to be a more durable opponent than Farinelli, Lefevbre, and Morbidelli had been. He also expressed some frustration and impatience in waiting for a title shot: "I confess I'm already impatient. Since the second fight after I came back, I already felt like I could fight for the title. The longer it takes, the older I get. The thing is to win the title now and get another achievement never done before for Brazilian boxing."

The two boxers trained at the same gym, and Eder was asked what he thought of Jimenez's words. "It is good that he thinks that way because he will have a surprise in the fight," Eder said. There was speculation that the Spaniard would struggle to get down to the weight limit, and he expressed surprise that the weather was cold in São Paulo. He packed no warm clothes, thinking it would be hot since he was just leaving a hot summer in Spain, but July is not summertime in São Paulo. Jimenez went out and bought a coat, which he then ran in. When he worked out for the press in a training session, he weighed himself and was slightly under the weight limit to his surprise and that of his team.

Eder sparred with Augusto Denys; a young boxer set to turn professional on the undercard. Another added attraction to the show was Servilio de Oliveira, who returned to the ring five years after being away from boxing. Still undefeated, Oliveira was once an upcoming young fighter, having landed Brazil's only Olympic boxing medal to this point when he won bronze at the Mexico City Olympics of 1968.

Unfortunately, he had an eye injury, which forced him to retire from boxing prematurely. There was great hope that Oliveira would become an idol of Brazilian boxing much in the manner Eder had become after his Olympics appearance. Oliveira had won the Brazilian and South American flyweight championships and was ranked third by the WBC and fifth by the WBA globally. He would now be starting from scratch in the bantamweight division, which Eder had dominated the previous decade. "Eder Jofre always was and still is my idol. He served as a mirror for me and much of my generation," Oliveira said regarding the impression Eder made on him as a youngster.

Although Jimenez had advantages in age and height, at 5 feet 8 inches against Eder's 5 feet and 4 inches, Eder was very calm and confident in his abilities. "If I can fight like the last few fights, I'll hardly be defeated. Jimenez may be younger and taller, but that doesn't impress me," Eder said. He added that if he finished this fight just as quickly as he had done the last three, he would instruct Curi to line up another fight and take only five days' rest. Jimenez said that while he knew Eder's reputation, he had "come to Brazil to win."

The day of the fight saw torrential rainfall in the city to where Eder told Cidinha and the kids, "there will be nobody in the arena today" after opening the curtains of their Jardins apartment on Alameda Ministro Rocha Azevedo and pointing outside. Much to his surprise, that scenario didn't materialize. When they pulled up outside the arena that evening there was a packed crowd waiting to get inside.

Eder was on a different level to Jimenez from the opening bell as the Spaniard appeared sloppy in his attacks and lacked technique. Eder quickly took the initiative and was in control, forcing Jimenez to fight on the back foot, where he struggled to create any distance. In the third round, the power supply went off in the arena as a transformer exploded on the eastern side of the city, cutting off power in the area. The venue had no backup generators, so the fight was paused before a TV network provided the venue with a generator, which they helped install to get the lights over the ring back on. "The arena was completely packed, and as though the day needed any more drama, the lights went out for two hours, and nobody left the arena. It was a really memorable night," recalled Marcel Jofre.

The two boxers remained in the ring patiently waiting for the restoration of the power, and the fans chanted Eder's name almost the whole time. "It was really a special night for my father who felt all the affection of his fans," Marcel added. The two-hour break did not cause many effects to Eder as he picked up where he left off and attacked as his opponent struggled to contain him. The Spaniard tried to attack in the fourth round but was knocked down and then went back to his defensive strategy, which consisted of moving and clinching.

Despite the spoiling tactics, Eder performed well, and the public was satisfied with the fight. Eder won all the rounds on the cards, and Jimenez admitted that he was defeated by a "phenomenon." Despite the dominant victory, Eder said he felt his performance was a little disappointing. "I thought I would hit him more," he said. This speaks to the level of perfection that Eder always aspired for. He was always his own worst critic throughout his career. Despite the comfortable victory over another highly-rated opponent, he was not satisfied. Perhaps this constant strive for perfection meant that he always remained in optimum shape and maintained an incredible level of consistency throughout his entire career.

Kaled Curi was thrilled at the sold-out crowd staying to watch the whole fight despite the power outage. "I consider Jofre the greatest idol of Brazilian sports currently. Despite the intense rain on Friday and the energy cut that delayed the fight for two hours, around 17,000 people packed Corinthians stadium," Curi said. Curi was set to meet WBC President Jose Sulaiman and WBA President Elias Cordoba in Lima, Peru, as he tried to work Eder towards a title shot. Eder and Cidinha took time off to enjoy Marcel and Andrea's school holidays up in the mountain resort of Campos do Jordão and left Curi to arrange for him two fights in quick succession.

Fight 77, vs. Juan Antonio Lopez, August 13, 1976

A quickly organized bout with 24-year-old Mexican Juan Antonio Lopez was scheduled next for Ibirapuera. After a few days' rest, Eder was back in the gym to keep himself in championship form. Lopez, from Culiacan, was not well known but had recently scored a victory over former bantamweight world champion Romeo Anaya and came into the contest with a respectable record of 32-5. Ramon Felix, the trainer of Lopez, declared that the bout was one between experience and youth and insisted that his charge was in fantastic condition and was ready for the challenge. "I respect Eder very much for his past, but I'm sure I'll defeat him. I just don't know in how many rounds," Lopez said. "Eder Jofre is world-famous. A victory over him will give me great prestige," he added.

For Eder, the task was simple: Win, and he would be in line to face David Kotey for the WBC featherweight title. Lose, and he would retire. It was believed by Newton Campos that since Eder was not the top-ranked opponent, it was a blessing and may entice the Ghanaian champion over to Brazil. "It's much better than if he was in second or third place. Then the champion would hardly agree to fight him in Brazil. If he's low in the rankings, they'll think he is not very good, and we won't need to pay much to bring David Kotey. I believe he will come to São Paulo for $80,000" Campos said.

Orival Sapienza, helping Dogalberto with training Eder, said that Eder would not be changing his way of fighting, and the plan was to attack the Mexican. "We don't know anything about the Mexican, besides the comments that he is very good, but it doesn't matter. Eder will enter the ring willing to finish the fight in the first round for he is basically an offensive fighter," Sapienza said. Eder's last training session consisted of no sparring, instead, he opted to jump rope, hit the heavy bag, work the speed ball, and shadowbox. "I am practicing very comfortably just to relax my muscles and detox," Eder said.

Lopez's last workout consisted of jumping rope and three rounds of sparring with Javani de Oliveira. "Juan is great, and if Eder beats him, it's because he's super gifted," Ramos Felix, trainer of Lopez said. "The age difference will favor Juan because the reflexes, the eyes, and the resistance are less than before, but Eder has powerful punches," he added. "Eder is a great fighter, he hits hard, but he can't have the same resistance at 40," Lopez chipped in.

Eder responded to the claims that his age was an issue: "I have defeated three opponents by KO this year. They all thought I was old, and when they saw me, they were on the floor."

Eder scored a clear victory over Lopez, but it proved to be a difficult fight. As early as the opening round, it was clear to Eder and the fans it would not be an easy fight. After taking a minute to study Lopez, Eder took the initiative in the first round and attacked. Lopez was the aggressor in the next round as he tried to attack Eder's body. Eder took command in the third round, with the highlight being a sweet right cross that connected hard on the Mexican.

Lopez proved to be a skillful and resourceful opponent and was competitive throughout the first six rounds. Eder's advantage became more apparent in the seventh round when he attacked Lopez and connected two great left hooks and other shots to his opponent's face. In the eighth stanza, Eder succeeded in dominating the action, closing the distance on Lopez as he hammered away with both hands. Lopez was still groggy in the ninth round, but he summoned up the courage to put forth a reasonable effort in the final round as he made it to hear the final bell.

Eder felt sorry that he couldn't deliver a knockout and was visibly frustrated in his performance as he apologized, shrugging his shoulders to the fans. "If I fight like that again in my next fight, I might leave boxing before the title shot," Eder said. The fans cheered him and picked him up and carried him out of the ring. Eder was always a winner to them, and he could never let them down with all that he had accomplished in boxing and for Brazilian sport.

In the locker room, Eder explained in more detail about the fight. "Right in the first round, Juan Antonio came up to me with everything he had. From then on, I felt like I owned the situation. I felt like I was doing well, loose and jumping a lot. But just like everyone has their job and knows when they have done everything they know, I felt today like I could have done much more than I was able to. I'm sorry I won by points. I am a puncher. I could have won by KO," Eder explained.

He confessed that in the sixth round, he had been stung by one of Lopez's punches and fought a lot more cautiously than he usually liked to fight: "It was then I got really nervous with myself. I heard the crowd shouting my name, and at the same time, I felt like I couldn't make them happy. I thought of going after him and decided it all soon, but it would mean to risk too much. The audience would be more frustrated if I lost. So, I preferred to be careful. But that's something I don't usually do, and it makes me furious."

Eder then went to take a post-fight massage, and the press outside were instructed that the locker room was now closed. Some press, still eager for a word, tried to show their credentials, but they were held back by security who told them, "If you wanted to interview him, you should have done it in the ring."

In the other locker room, Lopez had already showered and was about to exit the arena when he was interviewed about his views on the fight. "I think a tie would have been a fairer result. Eder is a great boxer, and I had to avoid a lot of his punches, but I think we both had the same chances to knock each other out. Eder doesn't have the same leg movement as before. He punches hard. I've had stronger opponents even though he is a great boxer like I said. I had to fight while on the move because if I had to be in front of him, I would definitely have been knocked out. I understand that the result, however, was natural. If the fight had been in Mexico, the victory would have been given to me," he added.

As Eder exited his locker room, the press did get a quick word with him. He told them that Lopez had been his most challenging opponent of the recent ones. "He is brilliant. He knows how to keep a distance well. He is an excellent boxer," he said. One of the press members told Eder that Lopez felt a draw would have been a fairer result, and Eder looked surprised as though somebody told him a joke. "He said that? Too bad I didn't knock him out," Eder concluded before walking out of the arena.

Lopez went on to two impressive winning streaks which saw him earn two world title shots. Unfortunately for him, they both came against the legendary Puerto Rican WBC super-bantamweight champion Wilfredo Gomez who stopped him in 1978 and 1982. Lopez retired with a record of 65-18 and would stay in the sport, training young fighters. One boxer he served as a mentor to was a young Julio Cesar Chavez in his hometown of Culiacan.

Fight 78, vs. Octavio Gomez, October 8, 1976

Despite being slightly disappointed by his performance against Lopez, Eder was determined to bring in an even better fighter to be his next opponent. Octavio Gomez of Mexico City fit the bill and was signed to be Eder's next foe in a highly anticipated bout at Ibirapuera.

"The colorful Octavio "Famoso" Gomez was one tough hombre from Mexico City who fought and defeated the best of his era. Former world champions such as Romeo Anaya, Danny "Little Red" Lopez, and Rafael Herrera, including formidable Canadian contender Art Hafey all took "L's" facing the clever Mexican journeyman Gomez. Though he began his career in 1964 as a flyweight, Gomez battled his way up to the featherweight division where he gained notoriety as an all-action fighter. His facial features eventually showing the effects of someone with over 80 fights. Known in boxing circles as an "upsetter," Gomez was victorious over upcoming featherweight Danny "Little Red" Lopez at the Anaheim Convention Center in 1975 by out-punching and cutting him up to win a 10-round unanimous decision. A few months later, "Famoso" confused former bantamweight champion Rafael Herrera by moving in-and-out while using a quick jab to pull out a unanimous points victory in their second meeting," wrote Gene Aguilera, boxing hall of fame author.

Octavio Gomez

Kaled Curi announced that the winner of the Jofre vs. Gomez match would be next in line to face the winner of the WBC championship bout between David Kotey and Danny Lopez. Gomez sparred with Javan de Oliveira, who had his own bout on the undercard against Danilo Batista, who was undefeated and closing in on a title shot with the great bantamweight champion Carlos Zarate of Mexico. In the gym, Gomez did not give up too much of his game plan and appeared to hold back as he mainly stuck to using the left hand. "He is still hiding his game, but I could see that he is quick and uses his punches well. I find this Mexican to be very dangerous, and Eder should be cautious to avoid surprises," de Oliveira said after the sparring session.

Gomez did more exercises before discussing the bout with a small gathering at the gym. "I really want the moment of the fight to come quickly so I can fight him and defeat him. In the meantime, I'll calmly wait more and more confident," he said before saying he would rest in his room and watch an exhibition football match between Flamengo Football Club and the Brazilian national team. Gomez was very respectful to Eder throughout the buildup to the fight and also spoke about his Catholic faith. He talked about how he also worked as an advertisement painter back in Mexico and that, much like Eder, he liked to paint in his spare time, and he enjoyed reading.

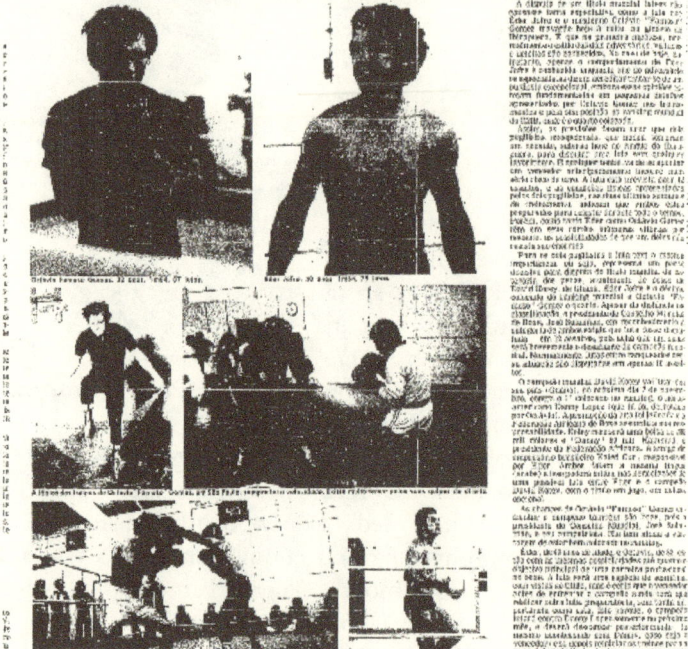

FOLHA DE S. PAULO

Éder enfrenta o misterioso Octávio

A minor controversy emerged before the bout when Dogalberto reported back to Eder he had seen Abraham Katzenelson in the Gomez camp, giving them advice on how to defeat Eder. Eder did not appear too disappointed with what many felt was an act of treason by simply saying "that attitude should be judged by the audience and not by me."

Eder was in a playful mood at his final public training session as he joked around with friends and members of the press and even sang songs. Eder appeared in excellent physical condition and looked to be sharp in his session. He said that he expected to have an outstanding performance, much better than his previous bout. "At 40, I'm still beating all the young men," Eder said.

One of Eder's sparring partners, Claudio dos Santos, said that Eder was in incredible shape and said that his form was better than he had remembered in recent times. "During the practices, he was cold, and it was hard to hit the target. He didn't forgive any of my mistakes, always hitting me with anger. I've practiced before with Eder, and I never got so beaten. This time he demanded a lot," dos Santos said.

Gomez was ranked number four in the WBC rankings, and the bout was scheduled for 12 rounds instead of the usual 10 for non-title bouts. The change was made by WBC president Jose Sulaiman, who said because of the quality of both boxers, and the fact that the winner would be fighting for the championship, it would be better suited for the boxers to box 12 rounds.

"I know he will be hard to fight with. He has a good background, and from his statements, when he got to Brazil, one can say he is smart and clever. An example was when he said he wouldn't consider the fact I'm 40, for, like he said, if I were old, I wouldn't fight," Eder said.

Gomez was confident coming into the contest and felt he was prime to score an upset victory. "I believe I'll be able to do everything that Eder can do in the ring. Of course, I will be nervous at fight time, but he will be too. Eder will have the audience's stimulation, but inside the ropes, it will only be the two of us, and I believe in the victory," Gomez said on the eve of the bout.

Gomez's trainer Pancho Rosales had no doubt that his fighter was going to leave Brazil with a significant victory. "I'm sure Gomez will win the fight. What he showed in his practices will be perfected during the fight. I respect Eder Jofre, who was a great champion but now he is old and stuck. Gomez will win," Rosales said.

Eder just wanted to relax and disconnect from boxing after he finished his last training session. "I have finished the practices, and I am OK, with no problems. All-day long today, I just want to stay at home because I'll keep thinking of the fight. I'll try to leave early, sunbathe, read a book, or do crosswords. I'll only think of boxing when I'm in the Ibirapuera ring in front of my opponent," he said after his workout. Kaled Curi told the press he felt Eder needed to score a knockout victory to send a big statement to the other boxers in the featherweight division.

Newton Campos said that he felt this bout was arguably the most important bout of Eder's career. "It's tough to see in Brazil a fight between two boxers in the world ranking like those two. It will be a high-level fight that will define the career of one or another, for whoever loses will have to leave boxing and could hardly start all over." Campos had faith in Eder since he had always come through challenging moments. He anticipated Gomez could challenge the Brazilian. "I consider tomorrow's fight to be one of the most dramatic in Eder's life. In my opinion, it's as important as the one he had with Joe Medel in LA. But it's in moments like these that Eder comes up stronger, transforming into the living legend of boxing that he is," he added.

Campos explained he could have chosen an easier opponent but felt it was essential to get Eder the best challenge available. "They said we (Campos and Kaled Curi) brought the wrong man to face Eder. That a weaker opponent should have come, that if he loses, Brazilian boxing is over and things like that. But this is the moment when a strong and powerful opponent is needed to definitively test Eder's condition to challenge for the world title. That opponent is exactly Octavio Gomez," Campos concluded.

On fight day Eder was clear that if he lost to Gomez, then he would finally retire from the ring. "Without sugarcoating it, this is all or nothing. I don't believe in a tie when two punchers meet in the ring. Even if in the future I face David Kotey, I consider tonight's fight decisive, for only after it I'll know if I finish my career after 19 years as a professional or if I still have conditions to try for the title," he said.

In Eder's locker room, he was surrounded by friends, family, and various well-wishers and barely had a chance to focus on the contest, whereas Gomez did 20 minutes of yoga before going to battle. Thirteen-thousand fans packed into Ibirapuera for what was expected to be Eder's most challenging bout in years.

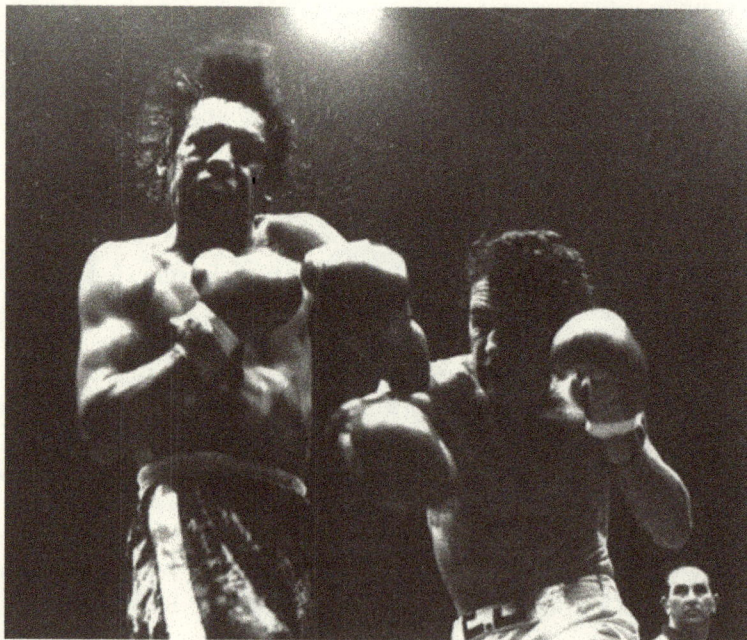

Eder raced out into an early lead as he landed several right-hand punches on Gomez's chin without receiving much fire in return. Eder did not press for a knockout, sensing that the Mexican was a dangerous opponent. Gomez worked his way back into the fight, starting in the third round as he became more comfortable with Eder's power and the atmosphere of the crowd. He showed good speed in his left hand and attacked Eder to the body.

The fight was close by the middle rounds when Gomez opened up a cut over Eder's left eye with a right-hand punch. Eder scored the bout's only knockdown towards the end of the seventh round, although the punch did not appear to hurt Gomez. Eder held the lead down the stretch but was hesitant about letting his hands go, which allowed Gomez back into the fight as the two fought on level terms by the end of the bout.

Neither fighter showed too much power, but the skill and craft on display did impress onlookers who were treated to a great boxing match. The scores were wide for Eder, as he won a unanimous decision by scores of 120-116, 119-115, and 117-116. The 117-116 was believed to be closer to reality as the contest had been balanced. Gomez said that he felt the knockdown was the difference in what he considered a close fight. Eder disagreed with the disparity of two of the scorecards. "I didn't win all of the rounds. I lost some," he said. He also admitted that he felt the knockdown he was credited with had not been a real knockdown as it was a glancing shot that caught Gomez on his shoulder, and his balance took him down and not the force of the punch.

O Globo reported on what had been a tough fight:

"After a brief period of studying, Eder took the initiative in the first round, trying to shorten the distance before the Mexican's height advantage. In the second round, Eder was able to take Gomez to the ropes several times. The third was more hectic, with the two boxers exchanging violent punches. Eder won the fourth and fifth rounds, but in the sixth, Gomez took the initiative, letting a hook go and then a right-hand punch on Eder's chin. In the end, another jab made Eder's left eye bleed. It was Gomez's round."

When in the seventh round, the Mexican tried to hit the Brazilian's hurt eye, he wound up cornered on the ropes, receiving a lot of punches until Eder hit a great uppercut with his right, knocking Gomez down.

Eder kept his advantage in the eighth round, and the ninth already showed both boxers more still, feeling tired. When Eder left from ninth to tenth, the audience started screaming his name, pushing him to try the KO: but this was the worst round of the entire fight. In the 12th, Gomez tried to have the initiative and got it, with two jabs in a row, making Eder's other eye bleed.

In the last round, punches were being exchanged consecutively. The round finished with a right hook from Eder onto Gomez's solar plexus."

Eder was asked if he would now move onto the title fight against the winner of the Kotey vs. Lopez fight, but he gave no kind of concrete answer about what he would do next. "This fight was a good lesson, and I think my life in boxing now will depend on my psychological condition. First, I'll let my injured eyes recover, and then I'll begin practice again. I'm thankful for all the work that is being done by my manager Kaled Curi, my brother Dogalberto and by Orival Sapienza in technical assistance. I feel like I am not well. My father is not by my side anymore. I think about him, but physically he is absent," Eder said.

Eder explained to *O Globo* he felt he was not hitting as hard as he used to and that his overall physical resistance had been declining.

Pancho Rosales, the manager of Gomez, was not happy with the verdict of the judges and asked Sulaiman if he would consider ordering an immediate rematch. Curi said that they would accept a rematch. "Rematch? Yes, we would accept it. But who

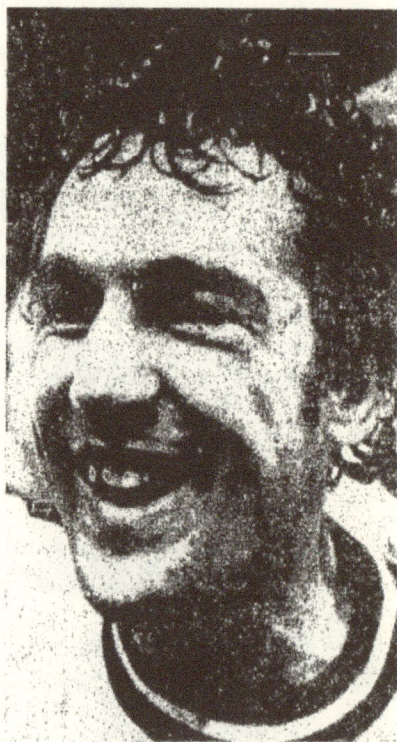

would do it and where? I believe that everything will depend on Eder himself. Despite the Mexican protests, Eder won the fight. The Mexican was frightened in the early rounds, but then Eder started showing some of the same faults as in the previous fights and got a little stuck, but I don't want to interfere in his practices, for he is a very experienced fighter and knows what he is doing," said Curi.

On October 13, Eder and Curi talked in depth about what his plans would be. They included the intention to move forward with the plan to fight for the championship again. Eder also sent himself for surgery to repair the damage accumulated on his eyes in recent fights. The intention was to fight once more before the year was up and then challenge for the WBC title in 1977.

Cornerman Orival Sapienza was released from the team due to complications. "I'll be back into practicing at the Sports and Recreation Coordination gym (CER), for the National Credit Bank Gym (BCN), my sponsor, still hasn't been set up. Doga will be my coach. He always accompanied my father's work and knows me very well. I won't work with Sapienza. With my contract with BCN and the practices I will need to have at CER Gym, Sapienza's life would be complicated. His profits come from his physiotherapeutic center. If he was joining me everywhere, he would wind up losing a lot of his clients. That's all that happened," Eder said on the adjustments made in the corner.

Further news emerged from the meeting. It was decided Eder would no longer have any bouts in São Paulo but that the next fight would remain in Brazil, with Rio being the most likely destination. "I can't say that people who go to the locker room before the fight will make the environment messy or that it influences my performance. I know everyone is friends with me and wants to see me. Despite that, I intend to fight outside São Paulo, for I'm convinced that it's better for me. Here I have many friends. The audience that went to Ibirapuera was excellent and supported me during my whole fight. I thank all the fans. If I have friends here, I think outside São Paulo I have many fans and will also have prestige. There always are people who enjoy watching the little man here fighting. People from São Paulo encourage me a lot. I don't know well how to explain this situation," Eder said.

Curi and Eder's close friend Osvaldo Forte, acting in an advisory role, felt that Eder was too easily distracted. Eder was always happy and willing to satisfy everybody, and that included drunken fans and friends that made the locker room a madhouse before fights. The feeling was that his attention and focus were diverted, and people in the locker room would smoke, so Eder didn't have the right environment to focus on his fights. Because Eder was a national celebrity and Brazilian sporting royalty, it was difficult for him to tell people "no" given his kind nature and natural inclination to want to please everybody.

Eder spoke about his ambitions as he left the meeting at Curi's office. "I'm in shape again. Now I'll submit myself to surgery on both eyes as fast as I can, and then I'll have another preparatory fight before I challenge the champion," he said.

The news of the surgery did surprise some, but Eder spoke about how there had been a lot of tissue damage and buildup over time, and it meant that his eyes became very susceptible to swelling and cuts. He did not want to take any chances and be in a title fight and then suddenly have blood running down into his eyes.

"Five years ago, I had to do an operation like this one. It's something simple. At the beginning of December, I'll be able to fight again. The eyes have been getting me worried. In the last fight against Famoso Gomez, the cuts made things very hard for me. I couldn't clean the blood that was running, and my vision was limited. I didn't take violent punches to my head. The eyes opened because the area is too sensitive. In the practices for the last fights, I had the same problem. The surgery will eliminate the callosity, and the wounds will only come up again with strong punches," he added. Eder said that while he wasn't pleased with the Gomez fight, he felt he had performed at a higher level than he did against Lopez in the fight prior.

Eder went for eye surgery on October 20 and was put under the knife by Dr. Carlos Pollini at Morumbi Hospital. The surgery lasted for an hour and fifteen minutes. It consisted of strengthening tissues and some minor plastic surgery. The first shot of anesthesia made Eder vomit, but he said he was not afraid of going under the knife. "I am only afraid of dentists," he joked. He said that the eye was expected to take ten days to heal. Then he would be fighting on December 3, perhaps in Rio against Elio Cotena of Italy.

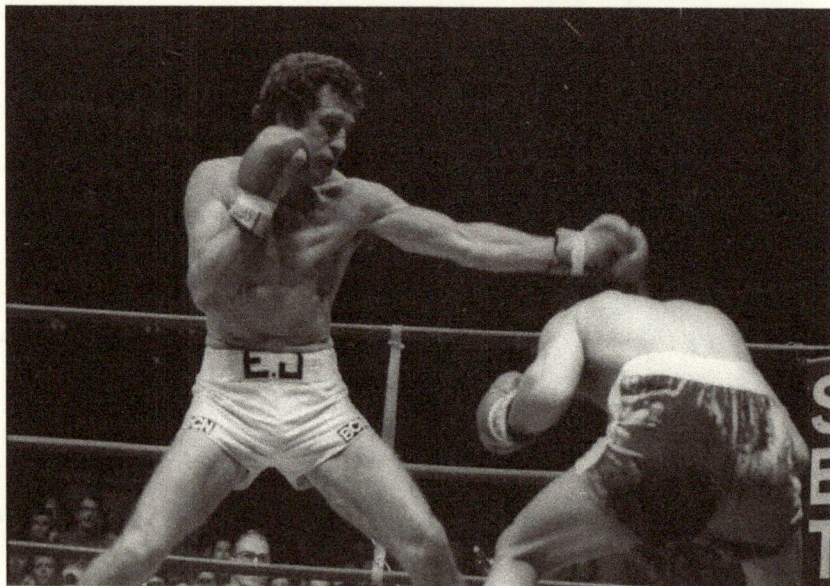

Retirement

It was not a failed title attempt that ended Eder's illustrious boxing career, nor was it boxing politics that turned him away. Another family tragedy simply proved one too many. Eder felt good and believed he was ready to contest another world championship, but then he received a phone call from his brother-in-law, Claudio Tonelli, from Santos in late October. "Eder, you should come here right now. It is Doga, he's not doing very well. We have hospitalized him." Eder and his friend Osvaldo jumped straight in his car and drove to Santos and arrived at the hospital, but it was already too late. By the time Eder arrived, Dogalberto had already passed away from internal intestinal bleeding. This was a consequence of the cancer that Dogalberto had when he was a young child.

Eder could only hold his brother and cry over his body. His mind flashed back to the beautiful moments they shared from their youth in Parque Peruche to the night Dogalberto was the first person in the ring to greet him the night he won the bantamweight world title to the recent fights where Dogalberto was proudly leading his corner in their father's absence. This was one tragedy too much for Eder. He felt he could not pick himself up emotionally to put his all into boxing anymore. Eder opted to step away from the sport that had given him and his family so much.

"It was a time to think hard, think about it. Now I do not know what was going on in my head at that moment, but it was difficult … I have a thousand words to praise my father. He gave me his competence, his teachings. Fortunately, as a son, I was able to assimilate everything and become a two-time world champion. Unfortunately, he had cancer from so much smoking. After my father passed away, my brother helped me. It was he who took care of the academy. Modesty aside, I knew more than he did, but having my brother's encouragement made the difference. My family, fortunately, was always united," Eder said regarding this challenging time in his life. Eder always had family in his corner, and now his father and brother were gone.

Marcel fondly remembered seeing his father in complete control when around the boxing ring. "I remember the fights that my father went to without my grandfather in the corner. Even with my uncle, he just didn't listen to anyone else. I heard it said a few times that he wouldn't need anyone else in the corner. I once witnessed this because I went to give him the mouth guard, I was all nervous when I was 9, 10 years old, and he looked at me, smiling and said: 'Why are you nervous? Calm down,' and I felt all the control he had when he was in the ring. It really was his universe."

It was not the technical aspect Eder would miss, but it was the family aspect and the team. He felt there was a chance he could go on and instructed Kaled Curi to secure a fight with Elio Cotena, but soon, the sadness overcame his ambitions again.

Eder felt physically and technically ready to go on, but emotionally he simply could not go any further, so he made his retirement from the ring official on February 15, 1977, at age 40. Eder was still winning fights and thrilling audiences, but this was the end of the road. Once again, it took a cruel act of fate for him to make that decision, but the champ also knew that he still had his prestige in place and his faculties intact and could offer a lot away from boxing.

In 1962 when he started considering his permanent retirement from the ring, it seemed an impossibility he would still be fighting and dominating high-quality opposition 14 years later. "Eder's last fights were not as world champion, but the public's love remained unshakable. Eder kept fighting in crowded arenas and always in great physical and technical form," said Brazilian boxing journalist Wilson Baldini Junior.

Marcel was a little too young to remember his father's fights in the 1960s, but he does remember attending several featherweight bouts during the 1970s. "Since being eight or nine years old, I was following my father's fights very closely. Each fight was a sensational event for a child who had a father that was a hero to many people. The best memories were being around relatives, especially my grandfather. Participating close to the big boxing show was a spectacular experience," he said.

Baldini was only nine years old when Eder retired for good, but he does remember the importance Eder held over a generation of sports fans. "In my house, Eder's presence was exceptionally large. My father was a publicist and worked in television, negotiating the broadcasting of Eder's fights. Everyone at home was a fan of Eder Jofre," he said. Baldini said that he always admired the qualities that Eder possessed on a human level. "He was from a straightforward family. Eder knew how to live well with fame. He never got himself involved in scandals or any kind of gossip. His name has always been linked to an example of citizens and sportsmen. His greatest qualities are his humility, gratitude, and honesty," Baldini added.

Eder attributed his discipline as being one of the major factors behind his longevity and his consistency. He spoke of having made many sacrifices to maintain a high level for so long. "My results in boxing came from my discipline. I was always relaxed in my early professional fights, I was always in perfect shape, despite some weight cuts that I was submitted to. But aging is not very helpful when you want to keep track of your body. I was getting heavier and worse, starving, and still had to content myself with just a salad and a piece of bread after my training sessions. No rice, no beans, no candies. It was torture for me. Picture that! I came from a poor family. After getting famous, I had money but couldn't eat what I wanted. My father, as my coach, wouldn't admit that I was out of shape; he was always very serious about it. I couldn't disappoint him. I suffered too much. One can say: 'Look at him; he's a champion, living a dream.' I was a champion but couldn't enjoy my life. I was invited to parties and couldn't eat and drink anything. My friends would invite me for a beer during weekends, and I just had to say no to that. I was young and full of life and didn't live those pleasures. It was hard," Eder would recall.

Newton Campos also pointed to this discipline being one of Eder's greatest strengths. He felt that this professionalism and his boxing brain are what made him the fighter he was. "Eder had always been a very responsible boxer. He had a lot of trouble getting his weight down to make bantamweight, but he always made weight. He always got it right and successfully defended the title many times. The greatest qualities he had were the discipline he had and the way he looked at boxing. Boxing was a religion for him. And it wound up becoming a religion for the Brazilian people as well, for we never had a fighter like Eder Jofre," Campos said.

Eder's place in Brazilian sports history had long been confirmed when he became the first world champion from Brazil in 1960. That he became the world's best fighter pound-for-pound in the 1960s as he staked his claim for being the greatest bantamweight of all-time and then completed one of boxing's greatest comebacks in the 1970s meant that his name immediately was etched into boxing history as one of the finest fighters of any era. His career had been an example of excellence, professionalism, and consistency. His style of boxing consisted of an almost flawless technique, but he was also an aggressive fighter who always knew it was a duty to leave a good impression on the audience. This is perhaps why, even today, Eder is revered by those who have seen him fight. "Most modern boxers use the tactic of hitting and not being hit, which is only natural, right? These days, they don't necessarily do what Eder used to do: He would attack and defend. He was an offensive boxer, he liked providing a spectacle. He wasn't only a puncher; he was a highly technical boxer. There is nobody who can be compared to Eder Jofre," added Campos.

Though it is always a great moment when a fighter retires on his own terms, Eder's retirement was bittersweet. For Eder, there was a hint of sadness because it was one tragedy too many which forced him to decide. For his fans, it was the end of an era, and there was reason to believe they could be waiting forever to see a champion so great again.

Here is the prepared retirement statement which Eder read:

"More than a simple farewell letter, I insist on making this a gratitude letter to all Brazilian people. Boxing is, at its foundation, an individual sport, but nobody can get to the top of this game without an excellent team behind them. I was well served with the best staff in the world: One hundred and twenty million people. I always had them in my corner. Here (in Brazil), in Los Angeles, in San Francisco, Tokyo, the Philippines, Caracas. In every ring I stepped in, I had them on my side.

I say I will not fight inside the ring anymore, but I will fight outside the ring, for the sport, for the boxers, and my people. That's my way of saying thanks to all of you. I'm talking to the ones who felt the punches I felt, who cried when I cried, the ones who won when I won, and to the ones who lost when I lost. I'm talking to the journalists that always encouraged me and treated me with fairness. Without you, nobody would know anything about me. I'm talking to my first manager Jacob Nahun, with whom I started my career and was a good and honest man. I'm talking to the manager Kaled Curi, with who I end my professional career. He was more than a manager for me. He was a friend, an adviser, who always over-delivered. I'm happy to know that national boxing is in his hands. With him, the nation and new boxers go.

I'm talking to the companies that sponsored me during my career. I'm talking to my dear friend Osvaldo Forte, since the beginning, he's been like a brother, always on my side in low moments and extraordinary moments. I'm talking to my training partners, my sparring partners: Ivan Cipriano, Oripes dos Santos, João dos Santos, Jose de Paula, Claudio dos Santos and more. I'm talking to the doctor Fernando Cortes, who gave me the best physical condition of my life. I'm talking to the lawyer Dr. Jurandir Scarcela Portella, who took care of my problems, giving me inner peace to fight calmly. I'm talking to my uncles Waldemar, Ralph, and Ricardo Zumbano, who I inherited my technique. I'm talking to Henrique Matteucci, the journalist who wrote my biography and the history of my family in such a moving way.

I request an excuse to discuss my mother, Angelina, and my father Aristides, to my brother Doga and my uncles Higino and Tonico. My kiss of gratitude and love will cross the curtains of death and find you wherever you are. My father – the Old Aristo, like they dearly called him – made me three times: He put me in this world, made me a man, and a champion. To him, my eternal gratitude, my career, my triumphs, my titles.

If I could, I would break my golden belt into a hundred and twenty million pieces and give a piece to each of you. I retire now, not because of my age. I'm feeling good and full of energy. I believe I could go on for a couple more years. My experience and history taught me that a man just gets old when he wants to. He gets old because he intoxicates the body with alcohol, tobacco, drugs, or excess of worrying, with his own evil, sloth, negative thoughts, and resentment. Every athlete can compete at an advanced age. And the fountain of youth is within us and is based on two things: simplicity and action. Sorry if I am conceited. I just believe that my personal experience can help the youth and all the simplistic men. If my advice helps at least one person, I will be happy.

I'm leaving boxing with a clean conscience and love for the sport. I always fought fairly and exhaustively dedicated myself to training because I wanted to deliver the best for the people. Boxing is a clean sport. Inside the ring, the odds are all the same for both fighters. Boxing is a complete sport; it molds the character of a man. Physically and psychologically. My son Marcel is already training. If he will turn out to be a boxer, that's his problem. But he will learn how to fearlessly fight for his life. I'm leaving boxing also because I have other projects – arts, for example – and because my presence is not very necessary right now. We have excellent boxers, like João Mendonca, Diogenes Pacheco, Danilo Batista, Valdemar Paulino, Expedito Alencar, Fernando Alencar, Fernando Martins, and so many others. Brazilian boxing is not Eder Jofre anymore. Now it belongs to this new generation. I am sure they will do well. I just hope that, like me, they can count on a hundred and twenty million people. I wish to add that I feel fulfilled and happy. I fought. I lived. Like the poet taught. To all, my affection.

February 16, 1977, São Paulo.

1976 Results

Eder Jofre KO4 Enzo Farinelli
Eder Jofre KO3 Michel Lefevbre
Eder Jofre KO4 Pasqualino Morbidelli
Eder Jofre W10 Jose Antonio Jimenez
Eder Jofre W10 Juan Antonio Lopez
Eder Jofre W12 Octavio Gomez

Brazilian Boxing after Eder's Retirement

Estadão reported on February 16: "National boxing is not going to be the same without Eder. The whole country came to this conclusion way before, when Eder lost the rematch to Harada and took time off from the rings: Without an idol to look up to, the nation was living amid frustrations.

People used to go to the Ibirapuera gymnasium not to watch a boxing match, but to watch their idol."

Miguel de Oliveira had been Brazil's second world champion when he won the WBC junior middleweight championship in 1975 but had lost that title the same year. He fought on for many years but could not fight his way back into championship contention. Danilo Batista was the next Brazilian boxer to fight for a world title when he would try to become a bantamweight champion just like Eder was, but he fell short when he traveled to Los Angeles to face the great Carlos Zarate in October of 1977. Despite performing well in the early rounds, Batista was stopped in the sixth round by the Mexican knockout artist. While the likes of João Mendonca, Diogenes Pacheco, and Waldemar Paulino won South American championships, they never made it to a world title fight like Batista.

It would be almost a decade later when the next Brazilian boxer contended for a world title when Claudemir Carvalho Dias fell short against Hilario Zapata for the WBA flyweight title in 1986. Francisco Tomas da Cruz was next to fight for world honors when he challenged the legendary Mexican champion, Julio Cesar Chavez, in Nimes, France, but he was knocked out in three rounds. Appearing on that undercard was Sidnei Dal Rovere, a fighter who held many hopes for Brazilian fight fans. Dal Rovere scored a decisive win on that show when he knocked out the French national champion, Bruno Jacob. Dal Rovere ran up an unbeaten 18-fight streak and won the national featherweight title before winning the South American title. He fought for a world title, but he was defeated by the great Ghanaian world champion Azumah Nelson for the WBC super featherweight title in 1988.

The following year, Dal Rovere's Olympic teammate Francisco de Jesus was next to challenge for a world championship when he contested the heavy-handed Julian Jackson for the WBA super welterweight title but was stopped in eight rounds. It was almost another decade later when the next Brazilian challenged a world title, this time Peter Venâncio faced William Joppy for the WBA middleweight title, and while Venâncio came closer than the others, he too was defeated, by a close decision on points.

Brazilian boxing fans had been spoiled that their first world champion had been such a great one. Eder had been good enough to hold world championships in two weight classes in an era when becoming a world champion was a mammoth task. He was arguably the greatest boxer in the history of the bantamweight division. With his unbeaten record as a featherweight, he had capped what many would argue was boxing's greatest comeback. He had not only been South America's finest fighter in the 1960s but was considered the world's greatest fighter pound-for-pound in an era where legends such as Emile Griffith, Carlos Ortiz, Dick Tiger, Luis Rodriguez, Sonny Liston, and Cassius Clay had been active.

This status was almost impossible for any Brazilian boxer to match, and it would not be until 1999 that Brazil saw another world champion in Acelino Freitas. The wildly popular Freitas gave the people a taste of the glory days and had a magnificent career, but he fell far short of even comparing to Eder Jofre. Freitas remains arguably the second-best fighter in the history of Brazilian boxing.

"Over time, the Brazilian Boxing Federation prioritized amateur boxing, focusing more on the Olympics," Dal Rovere said. While the years since Eder's boxing career have seen numerous successes for Brazilians in other sports such as football, Formula 1, and mixed martial arts, it has often been wondered why such a successful sporting nation of such a large population has produced a relatively small number of champion-level boxers. The easy answer would be to point to the popularity of football in Brazil. It is the national sport and is a huge part of Brazilian culture. Beyond the World Cup victories of 1958, 1962, and 1970 which all came during Eder's heyday, they also won the 1994 and 2002 World Cups in addition to multiple Copa America titles.

During the days of boxing in Brazil, when the Zumbanos were prominent figures within the sport, boxing was well attended, especially in São Paulo. Eder's arrival and dominance shone a bright light on the sport. Eder's greatness helped raise the profile of the sport even further, but in the subsequent years, after he left the ring for good, boxing fell to the back of the minds of many Brazilians.

"Brazilian boxing felt orphaned by the retirement of Eder Jofre. It was only to recover in the 80s when the journalist Luciano do Valle started to broadcast the boxing matches on TV. At that time, the highlight was heavyweight Adilson "Maguila" Rodrigues, who fought against Evander Holyfield and George Foreman," said Wilson Baldini Junior. Adilson Rodrigues was a big name in the 1980s and 1990s, but he never contested a world title despite winning the domestic and continental honors available in the heavyweight division.

Eder and Adilson Rodrigues

"There has always been a lack of investment in the sport and lack of opportunity. There is a lack of investment; there is no incentive in Brazil, unlike countries like the United States of America, England, Germany, and others," said Servilio de Oliveira. Oliveira had worked in boxing since the time he was forced to retire a second time in 1977. He was an assistant trainer at Clube Atlético Pirelli until 1992 when he became manager and technical supervisor at São Caetano Football Club in their boxing department. He managed several fighters and even saw one of his pupils, Valdemir Pereira win the IBF featherweight world title in 2006 when he defeated Thailand's Prayat Sawaingam. He left that role in 2010 and has worked for ESPN Brazil ever since. This lack of investment, which Oliveira said held Brazilian boxing back, was something Eder had talked about from the beginning of his career.

"Since 1957, when I became professional, whenever I could, I would tell the authorities to avoid the boxing decadence in Brazil. I would criticize, point out solutions, suggest alternatives, but very little was done. I've spoken too much. Today I consider myself a man disappointed at the future possibilities of Brazilian boxing. I think more support from the official area and private businesses is urgent. The big industries could invest in boxing, financing the building of gyms, keeping the coaches, and giving material to training. The expenses won't be more than four to five thousand Cruzeiros (roughly $300-400) a month. There will be a return for sure, with the presence of the names of those companies on the fighter's uniform, seen by millions of viewers due to the television broadcasting. With measures like that, the appearance of new fighters would be automatic," he said in an interview with *O Globo* in 1976.

When he gave his retirement speech, Eder did appear optimistic about the future of Brazilian boxing, but it did always appear close to his mind that the sport was not being run properly. One of Eder's biggest concerns was that without proper promotion of top-class managers, boxing in Brazil would fade to the back of people's minds. He said that his father died believing in boxing and that he always wanted to feel upbeat about what the sport had in store in Brazil but had his doubts.

Dal Rovere expanded on the direction that boxing headed in Brazil following Eder's retirement from the ring. "At the time that Eder Jofre was fighting, in the 60s and early 70s, here in Brazil, all boxers wanted to earn money, to be professional boxers. For many years, here in Brazil, the government has sponsored Olympic sports. The best Brazilian boxers are training daily, the Brazilian Boxing Confederation, the body responsible for developing Olympic-style boxing, receives money to keep the daily training, housing, and food. This means keeping the best Brazilian boxers in Olympic-style boxing. Here, at the moment, we don't have boxing promoters like Abraham Katzenelson. Now the best Brazilian boxers are training for the next Pan American Games and Olympic Games," he concluded. With the style of boxing between amateur boxing and professional boxing being so different, it would make sense it is slightly more difficult to produce a high number of genuinely top-class professional boxers.

Cuban amateur boxing teams, for example, have dominated many international championships and the Olympics, but those successes have seldom transferred to professional boxing. Some Cuban boxers have made it to world championships in recent years, but none of these fighters came close to the quality of the wave of Cubans which fled Fidel Castro's Cuba in the early 1960s when the likes of Jose Napoles, Jose Legra, Luis Rodriguez, and Ultiminio Ramos fled the island. "Brazilians don't like sports. They like winners," Baldini said. With so few Brazilian fighters getting to the world title fights or coming close to the level that Eder reached, it would naturally make sense that the crowds would grow smaller, and the interest in the sport would wane. There may have been many Zumbanos and Jofres in Brazilian boxing, but there was only one Eder Jofre.

Section Four: Champion Forever

This section focuses on Eder's life and career after he announced his retirement from boxing in 1977 up to today.

Life After Boxing

At age 40, Eder was considered old for boxing. In reality, he was still a young man. Eder had always cared for his body and lived like an athlete from a young age. Staying home all day, basking in his accomplishments, and growing his waistline was never an option, given he came from a family that set an example through hard work. With two young children at home, that example would be passed on to them as well, so the family values never died. Eder always showed a measure to treat people with respect. He raised his children with freedom but was conscious also to let them know that not everyone had the same privileges. He would make the point to show Marcel and Andrea other kids on the streets, cleaning cars, and selling fruits. His point was that while they had something, they were no better than other people.

"My father always tried to give me values to be a correct and dignified human being. These values certainly passed from my grandfather to him. My grandfather told him: 'don't steal, don't kill, help your family and help others when you can,'" Marcel said.

Andrea said that she always viewed him as "Dad" and not this legendary figure that was a hero to many. Andrea said Eder was her hero though she was older before she started to become genuinely interested in boxing and comprehend what a legacy Eder had created in the sport. Marcel was a few years older and remembered attending the fights. He has always maintained an interest in boxing.

Despite knowing they had a famous father held in high regard, the Jofre children never used this to get ahead or feel special. "My father passed on the teachings that his father taught. Be polite, humble, kind, and help whenever you can. Don't steal or kill. He taught us to be happy. To achieve things, you have to work. He never demanded a great job. The important thing was to have one that you liked and earned enough money," Andrea said.

Eder was financially intelligent. He made fruitful investments, like having a large share of properties in addition to the fabric store he co-owned. He had sponsors and never required a large entourage. "I got rich in boxing. There was a time that I remember fighting just once every two or three months because the payments were worthy. And with each payment, I used to buy a three-room apartment, sometimes even two apartments. But my family was big, so I always helped them, bought land for my brothers and stuff. My father always advised me to save money; about eight percent of my payments would be saved. I invested and helped my family," Eder said. Despite having other interests, boxing was innate to Eder, and it seemed impossible to him that he would no longer be training for fights. He had no clear idea of what he wanted to do when he finally stepped away from the ring for good.

Although boxing has a relatively low profile compared to football in Brazil, Eder retained his popularity. "After his retirement, the schedule of appointments remained great, with plenty of television, newspapers, as well as commercials. He even participated in a television show on Globo T.V., the largest in Brazil, with questions and answers where the theme was Muhammad Ali," Marcel said.

Eder was comfortable with the money he earned through boxing, but because most of his career was in South America with only occasional U.S. bouts, he knows he missed out on some of the mega paydays associated with the sport in America.

"I don't know where to start but, I can tell you that a professional boxer in the U.S. has a chauffeur that brings him to train, he can choose his sparring, etc., and he lives like a celebrity. In Brazil, I didn't have any of those things. A fighter like me, who had achieved so much, in the United States, I would have been a millionaire. No doubt about it, but I can't complain, because I got a little rich in Brazil too, I mean not a lot, but a little rich," Eder reflected.

Despite Eder's status as a national icon, he missed several endorsement deals offered to football players in Brazil. Boxing does not enjoy the popularity and attention that football does. "My best contract was with Goodyear, but it was almost at the end of my career. During my prime times, I was with Bitônico Fountoura (an anti-anemic medicine) and with a tea brand. The sports brands were too busy sponsoring football players. Shoemakers were looking at Maria Ester Bueno, Wimbledon champion. It was a glory time for Brazil," he added. Eder was never bitter about this. He came from little and made enough to make things comfortable for himself and his family and to be in a position to have his money work for him. He was smart and lived well within his means, which put him in this position.

Eder ensured his family was secure and wealthy. They lived without the fear of poverty, which existed when he was young. This differs greatly from most boxers of Eder's generation. They boxed too long and stayed around for one last payday to recover lost funds from futile investments or shady managers. Eder did not live the playboy lifestyle of many athletes. Eder came from a simple family and he stayed close to those roots. His intelligent financial decisions gave him a comfortable retirement.

Andrea, Cidinha, Eder and Marcel

Eder had been so involved in his boxing career he never had the time to further his education beyond high school. Still, he learned a lot about life, the world, relationships, and what is right and wrong. These traits are what he would use as his tools in his post-boxing life. Eder remained close to boxing and encouraged young boxers. He even tried his hand at training young fighters and teaching boxing classes just as his father and uncles had done so successfully. However, like many great fighters, becoming a full-time head trainer was never going to happen for Eder.

"He did not like to teach. He preferred to fight," Marcel said. One of Eder's most remarkable characteristics was always his willingness to help others and give to people from all walks of life, his time and respect. Eder derived pleasure in talking to his supporters. He gave them attention, whether it was in the gym where people would come off the street to get a glimpse of him or in the supermarket while shopping.

"My father always helped his neighbor in any way he could. When he was training at the academy on Santa Ifigênia, many people went to look for him with many different requests. Despite my grandfather trying to guard against it, the heart spoke louder, and my father would always give his time to them," Marcel said. The interaction with the fans had always been warm, no matter where he encountered them. "My father always knew the importance of fans in his career," he added.

Spiritual House

Eder always connected with his spiritual side. He had always maintained a strong Catholic faith, and God always had a strong presence in his life. His visions affected him greatly. There had been the one with his uncle Antonio shortly before his passing, but Eder also had these visions since he was a child, and they have always stayed with him.

The first vision he recalled was when he was about six or seven years old. He woke up one cold evening shivering, with his teeth clattering together. He was startled when he saw a local lady who would sell candy sat next to his bed. Eder had never spoken to the lady, but he had seen her around the neighborhood selling coconut sweets to the children around Parque Peruche. Her name was Dona Maria Balleira, a popular lady in the neighborhood said to give off an air of grace. When Maria finished her sales of candies, she would gather the parents together and divide the remains and entertain the children and parents with stories. When Eder saw her next to his bed, he recalled feeling his heart racing as he became scared and hid under his blanket, hoping that she would go away. He peaked from under the blanket, and Dona Maria remained with the candy on her lap. Eder ran to get his mother, and by the time they entered the room, Dona Maria had disappeared. But just a few days after this dream of Eder's, Dona Maria was found dead in Rio Tietê with a big rock attached to her feet. She had committed suicide. Marcel recalled his father narrating this story and said that it appeared to have a significant effect on Eder and that it gave him chills just talking about it.

There was another story Eder recalled from his childhood when he stepped outside the family home to use the toilet in the backyard. Through a crack in the wood, he saw a figure that was the body of an old man. He became scared by this and ran back inside the house and never saw the man again. There was another incident when he said he was picking fruit from the trees in the backyard, and as he looked up, he saw an old lady picking fruit from the same tree. "One time I went down to pick up some fruits, as I look upwards at the tree's canopies, I saw an old lady. What was that? She was shining as the sunlight touched her. I ran to tell my family, told my mother and my grandmother. They came to see it, but it was gone, and everybody remarked that my face had gone pale," Eder said.

Eder believed it wasn't a coincidence of dreams. He felt there were messages behind these visions of his. "My interpretation after being through all of this is that there is something beyond life and death," he said. This belief in spirituality reinforced his desire to help others. Eder volunteered at a spiritual house named "House Transitional Fabiano de Cristo," also known as "Casa Transitoria." The house was named after a Portuguese friar named João Barbosa. Barbosa migrated to Brazil, where he became known as Fabiano de Cristo for his charitable work and kindness towards his fellow man. Eder shared similar sentiments, so he would help

1958 World Cup-winning captain Bellini and Palmeiras Football Club icon Dudu shortly after his retirement announcement in 1977.

"I was invited by my friend Eloy dos Santos Teixeira, who took me to Casa Transitoria. The Casa at that time had 20 children, and I started to dedicate myself to these kids," Eder said. The Casa provided workshops, courses, shelter, a cafeteria, and sports facilities for the youth. He was proud he provided these children with the opportunities that were not there when he was young. Also, because he wanted to see young people gravitate towards respectable careers. "I dedicated myself to these kids because I think they have to dedicate themselves. I learned that children should participate in sports, and they have to get educated instead of smoking cigarettes, drinking alcohol, and getting into toxic substances," he added. Eder promoted a healthy lifestyle for young people. He wanted to make sure the neighborhoods were full of sporting opportunities for the kids that would also help keep them out of trouble.

Ultimately Eder played a big part in forming the sports board of the association. "For the children, they did several structural works on a piece of land that was in the back of the property," Marcel said. Eder always maintained his passion for football, so he worked with Bellini and Dudu to have a football field made beside locker rooms on the facility. "I got them a grass football field and a dressing room. All of this contribution came through an entity that provided us with material that we built and grew it to more than 300 children. It then had pre-professional courses, primary school, and secondary school education," Eder said.

One facility they provided was a mechanical cow which they would use with the object to feed the young athletes soy milk. Eder was a volunteer, so he did not get paid for this work. Despite that, he worked hard on many projects. He created an extensive network of friends in the political field because the Casa required fundraising to complete certain projects.

Politics

Brazil was entering a new era politically. The military regime that had been in effect since 1964 was softening its stance and wasn't quite at the same dictatorial level as it had been. Eder was informed that with his profile and good reputation, he could help many people if he went into politics. Although this appealed to Eder, he confessed that he did not know a lot about politics and that his focus was to help the Casa as much as possible. In 1978 he was invited to meet with Eduardo Suplicy, one founder of the Brazilian Workers Party (P.T.), a heterogeneous collection of union workers, liberation theologists, militants, intellectuals, and left-wing artists. Suplicy had been an amateur boxer trained by Higino Zumbano and even competed at the 1962 Forja de Campeões.

The P.T. party was founded in opposition to the military regime. Eder helped Suplicy run for state representative, and Suplicy succeeded in his campaign and was elected on March 15, 1979. Eder decided he would enter politics with his focus on providing more opportunities for the Casa and a better environment for the whole population. When he approached Suplicy about getting a place in the council, things became a little complicated, and Eder was not given the position he desired. "Being recognized as a champion draws attention in society. I had once helped a friend be elected as a senator. That same friend turned me down when I was looking for a place in the council," Eder said. Eder's decision to accept this was difficult since he had believed lending his name to a friend's campaign would be reciprocated. "When I first went into politics, I was too naïve to think that being Eder Jofre they would be friendly with me, I was wrong. Once you get there, you are on your own," he said. Marcel's interpretation of these events was that Suplicy was looking out for his friend and perhaps wanted to guide him away from entering the political world.

After the treatment he received from the P.T. party, Eder was enticed with an offer to attend meetings with the Democratic Social Party (PDS). Eder had two cousins, Francisco and Luiz Pacces, who were close to Armando Pinheiro, one founder of the PDS party. The PDS party was founded in January 1980. Pinheiro was a politician who was closely aligned with the former governor of São Paulo, Paulo Maluf.

Because Eder was upset at the P.T. party, he would hear what the opposition party had to say. He was told that ultimately, he would be the one ruling on decisions but that he would have advisors working for him. "He (Pacces) knew that I always tried to help my community. He said: 'Instead of going to the major office or going door-to-door looking for sponsorship from companies, you would be one who opens the door for the people.' When he told me that, I answered: 'That's true, I would be inside, doing something meaningful for the people,'" Eder said.

Eder contested under a newly formed party which hurt his chances of emerging as the councilor, but he had his foot in the door. "The choice of a party considered conservative was a tough decision for my father because the family had arms in the communist party. Another problem in the election was at the time, there was a tied vote, where the voter could only vote for candidates from the same party. From councilman to the mayor, governor, etc. this was decisive for my father not to have won at first because his electorate was much more progressive. If he had left, for example, for the MDB, (the Brazilian Democratic Movement), he would certainly have twice as many votes," Marcel said. "At that time, the brothers Luiz and Francisco Pacces, affiliated to the PDS, directed the campaign that at the end obtained 20,542 votes, leaving my father as the first substitute," he added.

Although this movement was not aligned with the politics Eder was raised around, he did see it as a chance to help many people. Eder was not as involved in politics as his uncles had been, but this decision to go with "the other party" was met with a heavy heart. It was a difficult decision because he knew how passionate the Zumbanos were about the communist party. Eder said that his uncles did not understand his reaction, telling him "those people are oppressors, they hunted us, spanked us."

Apart from his political career, Eder was reminded of his boxing accomplishments when he was inducted in the inaugural class of the World Boxing Hall of Fame in 1980. This hall of fame no longer exists, and they had no physical location. They hosted a dinner annually in Los Angeles. While Eder was not present to attend, this was a nice accolade for the champion to be recognized in America 18 years after he had last fought there.

In September of 1983, Eder received recognition from the WBC as their selection for the greatest bantamweight of the previous 20 years at an event at the United Nations in New York City. Eder attended this ceremony and was on hand to collect his award. The event was graced by Muhammad Ali, Joe Frazier, Roberto Duran, Nino Benvenuti, Carlos Zarate, Alexis

Arguello, Ruben Olivares, Carlos Monzon, Emile Griffith, Jose Napoles, Gabriel "Flash" Elorde, and Eder's old rival, Fighting Harada. Unfortunately for Eder, there was no Brazilian press on hand to see him collect his award. Still, it was an excellent chance for Eder to catch up with some of his old boxing friends and rub shoulders with some of the greatest fighters in history. As the only Brazilian there, this gave him an added sense of pride. "I was the only Brazilian among all the big stars, including Muhammad Ali. I was there representing Brazil by myself with that huge accolade. I expanded the image of my country around the world. What really excites me after all those years of boxing is being recognized as the best bantamweight of all-time," he said.

Eder was set to take office on October 11, 1983, in place of Nelson Guerra Junior. There was a rumor he could not be sworn in because he had signed a membership form with the Brazilian Democratic Movement Party (PMDB). In reality, the document did not exist. Between 1983 and 1986, Eder occupied the seats of Nelson Guerra Junior, João Aparecido de Paula, Celso Matsuda, Osvaldo Giannotti, and Alfredo Martins, and in 1986 he assumed a starting seat after receiving 9,541 votes. Marcel worked alongside his father at Câmara Municipal de São Paulo (Municipal Chamber of São Paulo). He had enrolled in Mackenzie University studying law the previous year before joining his father in the chamber. Marcel quickly worked his way up and was extremely busy shuffling between this work and studying for his degree. "I headed his political office, and we practically stayed together 24 hours every day, because I still lived with him. It was a very nice period of our lives. I was able to assist him on several issues, always trying to protect him from the political world," Marcel remembers.

Once again, Eder was reminded of his glorious boxing career when he was inducted into *The Ring* Boxing Hall of Fame class of 1986. This provided him with further recognition for his boxing career, and the documentary *Quebrando a Cara*, directed by Ugo Giorgetti, was released. This documentary gave Brazilian sports fanatics insight into Eder's career. Also, it covered the story of the Zumbano family. Sadly, Walter, the one Zumbano brother who didn't box, passed away this year at the age of 75 from diabetes.

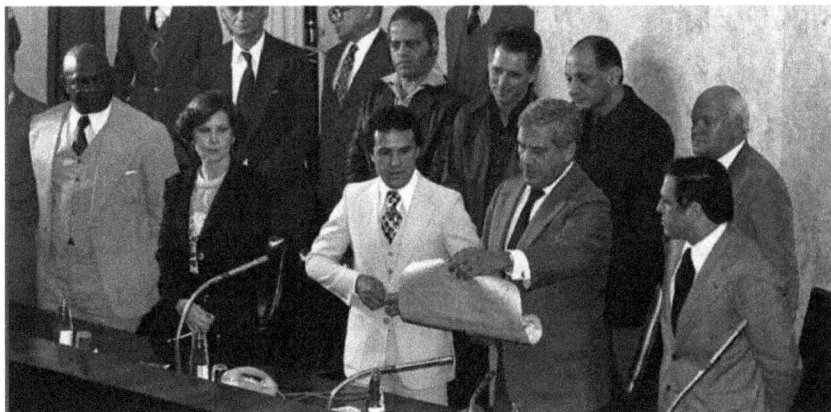

This was also the year Eder took over as a councilman after Celso Matsuda left for the secretary of supply, and this is a position where Eder made a lot of positive changes. The public responded positively to Eder, and he was never too busy to stop and chat in the streets when people would ask him for things or tell him what they felt was needed. Eder built a good team around him, and he authored over 25 laws that passed. The majority were related to health and education. "The advice he offered was for life, but he followed his convictions," said Osmar de Oliveira, parliamentary adviser. "I'm not saying he was a visionary, but a simple guy who knew the whole world and stored the information to try to apply it here in Brazil," Osmar added.

Eder was generally admired, but he did say that the most frustrating aspects of his life in politics were when others did not share visions or set out to harm others. "When you get into politics, to get your bills passed, you first need to create a project for that, and after that, you need to form allies; that's how it works: 'I support your project if you support mine.' So, I didn't really like this mechanism because there are few trustworthy people. Even though I wasn't part of this mechanism, I had 25 projects approved in fourteen years in the public service," he said. It was highly competitive as to who would enact the best laws and get the most laws approved. This is something Eder admitted would sometimes cause unnecessary stress and even jealousy.

Predictably, the opposing party probed Eder's political ambition. They accused him that his education did not go beyond high school and that he had taken too many blows to the head during his boxing career. Osmar de Oliveira pointed out that while many pointed this finger and ridiculed certain ideas, the proposals put forward by Eder eventually came to fruition and were heralded later. Eder had several ideas, including a ban on smoking in public places and the painting of different buses for different zones. He put other ideas in motion: a monorail service, reserved seats for elders on public buses, and a ramp to ease their boarding on and off the bus.

Eder visits Volkswagen

Eder still volunteered his time at the Casa all this time, so it was still a big passion of his to improve sporting facilities for the youth. "The project that I most liked is the one I created in 1990. It aimed at taking kids off the streets, putting them into a school able to serve lunch and provide professional courses like cooking, engineering, and sports." Eder revealed that his main goal was to have a sports center in each neighborhood of São Paulo so the youth could train. He knew the value of sports in young people's lives, and what it meant for the children he had grown up around. In the 1930s and 1940s, he said that "a thief was the one who stole fruit," compared to the modern-day problems with drugs, guns, and violence, which have become prevalent in many impoverished neighborhoods. Eder's clean life, while challenging, taught the type of discipline that adds value to young people and helps them in all walks of life and not only in sports. "Sport is a way of giving young people more conditions, it helps to keep them away from drugs," he said. Eder succeeded in approving laws related to education and sports created by the Municipal Sports Council in 1991.

Eder in his office

Ultimately the PDS party provided Eder with the vehicle for him to gain a seat in the chamber, but he did admit many years later that he felt it was a mistake. "I think I made the wrong move to join the PDS party because I've always carried the left-wing side in my vein," he said. "As a politician, sometimes you are forced to support all kinds of stuff your party presents to you. I didn't like that and had arguments with some of my partners because of this. So, I decided to leave this party and accepted another invitation to the PSDB party," he added. Eder joined the PSDB (Brazilian Social Democratic Party) in 1989 and was elected once again in 1992, with 14,565 votes.

In June of 1992, Eder was inducted into the newly formed International Boxing Hall of Fame in Canastota, New York. "I remember he was excited when he received the news that he was being inducted. It was like he had won another belt," Andrea said. The news of this recognition was big in Brazil as Eder still held a special place in his countrymen's hearts. "I remember I received the news from a friend. At the time, he didn't even know how important it was. I was overjoyed," Marcel said.

The Hall of Fame invites the inductee and one guest, so Eder brought his son along. Cidinha preferred that Marcel attend in her place because she knew how much Eder's legacy meant to him. She had traveled the world with her husband and attended all of his fights and many awards ceremonies. Eder remembered with fondness when he received this news and how he felt: "I felt thrilled to be extolling the name of Brazil once again."

Eder was inducted in the same class as Alexis Arguello, Charles Burley, Nino Benvenuti, Ken Norton, Billy Graham, and Max Schmeling, as the modern inductees. Fellow bantamweight great Panama Al Brown was among the "old-timer" inductees alongside Ted "Kid" Lewis, Packey McFarland, Harry Wills, Lou Ambers, Mike Gibbons, Battling Nelson, and Nonpareil Jack Dempsey. Except for Billy Graham, who had passed away in January, Charles Burley, who was in poor health, and Max Schmeling, all the other modern inductees were present as well as other boxing personalities such as Willie Pep, Archie Moore, Ike Williams, Sandy Saddler, Carlos Ortiz, Gene Fullmer, Carmen Basilio, Kid Gavilan, Vinny Pazienza, Hector Camacho, Bob Foster, and Sean O'Grady.

This was an exciting moment for Eder as he always held fond memories of his fights in America and the treatment he received. It was in America where he made

history by becoming Brazil's first world champion in boxing when he defeated Eloy Sanchez in 1960. Eder has always maintained a fondness for America and the American way of life. "When we had the opportunity to go to Canastota, New York, for him, it was like for a kid to go to Disneyland. The reunion with some boxing friends like Carlos Ortiz, Alexis Arguello, and Angelo Dundee was special in his life. He also had the chance to box in a mini-exhibition with Alexis (Arguello). Particularly for me, it was an incredible experience to see my father recognized in another country, who has always treated him with respect and recognition," Marcel said. 10,000 fans attended the event between June 4-7, and Eder had the time of his life feeling the fans' warmth and mingling with fellow boxing greats. With Angelo Dundee interpreting, Eder thanked everybody for attending the ceremony, talked about his father, and spoke with pride about how he was the first Brazilian boxer to make it to the Hall of Fame. "It is a great honor and a joy, after all this time to be remembered," he said.

Alexis Arguello and Eder

Eder's career in politics ended in the year 2000 when he did not get re-elected. "He didn't want to do it anymore. He was tired," said Osmar de Oliveira. Eder and his team had no new projects presented, and *Veja* magazine posted an article stating as much. That didn't leave his team with enough time to respond appropriately. Eder's biggest concern was that his team would be unemployed.

Eder had spent 18 years in politics and made his mark. He acknowledged, "I owe a lot to boxing for the votes I had," and he never hid from this. Eder was always grateful for the platform boxing provided for him. "I think my biggest victory is the friendships I made and the trips I took to many countries worldwide. As an artist or a factory worker, I would never get that far," he said.

Eder knew that his popularity gave him a unique position which helped overcome his lack of a political background. The successes he earned in the ring made him a national icon and thus a very recognizable figure that people looked up to. "I had been a world champion. I was known almost all over the world, and the people thought I could do anything and that I was the owner of the Chamber," he said. Despite having this prestige, Eder always maintained that everything he did was bettering the people who elected him. He always maintained the highest level of integrity and would not get caught up in badmouthing other politicians, nor would he bend for others with questionable-looking motives. "He didn't like to accept money from outside. The biggest asset was Eder's name and a team that worked hard. There was total dedication. He never wanted to take advantage of his position," de Oliveira pointed out. This integrity that Eder carried himself with showed the perfect example of leading by example in a profession where this is often exceedingly difficult to do.

While Eder was always trying to help sports at the grassroots level, he couldn't push much forward as far as boxing was concerned. He felt that the sport was in good hands under Newton Campos but the lack of Kid Jofre's was why Brazil struggled so much to replicate his own success. "I didn't have a chance to help my own sport. Every time I tried to introduce a new project; they said: 'we already built that gymnasium, what else do you want?' That's right, there is the gymnasium, but how is the maintenance? Last time I checked, they only served sandwiches to the athletes; how can you survive such hard training with a diet like that? The situation is still not good for the ones aspiring to be boxers in this county. The problem with this generation is they don't have a Kid Jofre looking out for them. He knew how to teach boxing. You must have a technique."

In an article written for the Municipal Chamber of São Paulo, author Sândor Vasconcelos explained some of Eder's most significant accomplishments in his time in office:

"Among the main projects that Eder approved in the São Paulo parliament are those related to education and sports. Law 11.118/91 created the Municipal Sports Council (Comesp). Law 11.383/93 determined that the activities developed in the gyms of São Paulo should be supervised by a physical education professional and that practitioners should present a previous medical examination.

During his work as a parliamentarian, he was a member of the Commission on Education, Culture and Sports, and the Commission on Traffic, Transport and Economic Activity. He was also President of the Economic Activity Commission. In public administration, Eder is the author of the project that culminated with Law 11.351/93, which obliges the Municipal Executive to honor contracts signed in previous administrations, establishing criteria. Eder is also the author of the project that created Law 11,603/94, authorizing the use of natural gas as fuel in the fleet of official vehicles in public and collective passenger transportation.

Another law of great importance was 12.093/96, which made it mandatory for the maintenance of Mobile Medical Assistance Units with first-aid equipment, a multi-professional health team, and adequate devices for removal in football stadiums, sports gyms, and places with a great concentration of people.

Eder is the author of the bill that instituted the São Silvestre Trophy, granted to the winners of the International Race held on the last day of the year in the streets of São Paulo."

By the time Eder retired from his political career in 2000 his children had grown and started their own families. Andrea had married an Argentine and moved to Rosario, Santa Fe, Argentina with her husband's family. Her son Axel Damian Martinez was born on July 7, 1993, but Andrea's marriage was breaking down, and she moved back home to São Paulo. Her second child, a girl, Lanika Jofre, was born on January 4, 1995. She moved back to Argentina a few months after Lanika was born but was again in São Paulo after six months.

Eder and Cidinha lived on Alameda Ministro Rocha Azevedo in the Jardims district of the city when Andrea came to live with them again. "I was living with my two small children, Axel and Lanika. There I was doing things as a daughter and mother," Andrea said. Andrea had opened her own variety store but opted to close the business after two years because her children were young, and it was becoming impossible to balance time between raising them and running the store.

Marcel was still working at Camara Municipal and welcomed a son on July 28, 2000, which he named Eder Neto Jofre in honor of his father. When Eder Neto was born at the hospital, Marcel and his wife told Eder they would name the boy Kleverson Carlos, and Eder could not hide his outrage at what he clearly thought was a horrible name. Marcel was playing a joke on him, and once it dawned on Eder, he laughed. Marcel told him what the child would be named, and suddenly Eder was overcome with emotion and had a hard time fighting back his tears of joy.

Olga Zumbano passed away on September 3, 2000, of heart failure. She was 84 years old. Ralph Zumbano died on November 8, 2001, of a stroke at the age of 76.

Marcel still works at Camara and is the parliamentary adviser. Andrea moved out when she married for the second time, on January 11, 2003, with her current husband, Antonio Oliveira. After Eder left Camara Municipal, he went to work in public relations for Dersa. This state-funded company managed and maintained the roads in the state of São Paulo. He worked at Dersa before retiring from the workforce to settle down and enjoy more time at home and around his family.

Waldemar Zumbano lived the longest life of all the Zumbano siblings, making it to the age of 91, before he passed away on January 2, 2004, after a battle with prostate cancer. Later that year there was the release of *O Grande Campeao*, which was released on DVD. This was the second major feature documentary released on the great champion after *Quebrando a Cara* was released in 1986. The film featured several highlights and went through his life and boxing career.

Eder's boxing accolades did not stop as he was inducted in the virtual Boxing Hall of Fame inaugural class of 2012.

Cidinha

Cidinha was suffering from rheumatoid arthritis at this point, so Eder and Andrea took care of the chores around the house. Andrea was living close by and always visited her parents three times a week because Cidinha was struggling more and more with her illness. On May 10, 2013, on the Friday before Mother's Day, Andrea visited her parents. She had a feeling that something wasn't right. She seldom would visit on a Friday, but something told her to go over to see her parents.

Unfortunately, that impulse proved to be serious because Cidinha was having chest pains. She said that the previous evening was painful. Andrea felt upset and asked why she didn't call her and tell her she was having problems, but Cidinha said she didn't want to bother her. Cidinha then had chest pains again. "I was scared and started trying to get her attention. She reacted for a moment, and I called my father, who was calling an ambulance, to help me put her in bed. She passed out, so we took her to her room. I called my husband, and then my brother (Marcel), who soon arrived with my sister-in-law and an ambulance," Andrea said.

Cidinha was then taken to nearby Hospital das Clinicas, and as the family gathered, Eder could not stop crying. "This was one of the most difficult moments of my life. I was losing my mother and seeing the imposing figure of my father, whom I always sought refuge in, so fragile, and I had to support him," Andrea said. Cidinha passed away that evening, and she was buried the next day. Eder cried non-stop from the cemetery back to his home.

Eder and Cidinha had been married for 52 years. They first met in 1953 when it was love at first sight back in Parque Peruche. They had traveled the world together, and Cidinha had been by Eder's side at his highest highs and for the tragic moments in his life. Now Eder had to come to terms with his beloved being gone. This was a tough time for Eder as he suffered a lot. Eder asked God to take him too since he didn't want to live without her. Eder's mental state was at a worrying point, and he was breaking down.

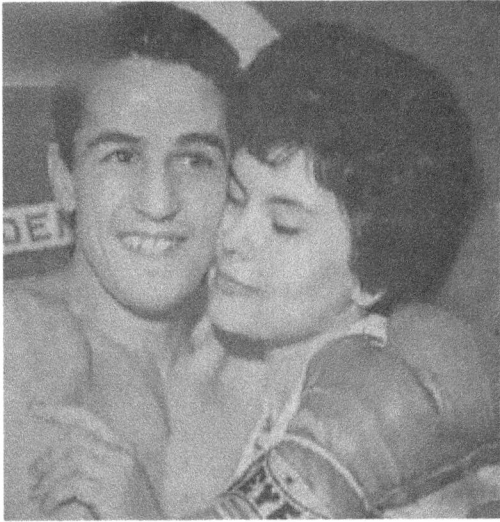

"The situation worsened to the point that he stopped recognizing us and our house for a moment and asked why we were doing this to him. He sometimes had explosive disorders, screaming and punching the walls. After three days like this, we had to seek medical help. He was hospitalized for 15 days for psychological treatment, thus providing medications and tranquilizers to stabilize him emotionally," Andrea remembered.

Eder was depressed, and this accelerated some symptoms he was suffering from his boxing career. It was believed that Eder had Alzheimer's or Parkinson's disease, but this proved to be false. Dr. Bernardino Santi had seen Eder on television and noticed how his illness was being reported. "When he first became sick, I started to pay attention to the diagnosis and noticed that he never got better," Dr. Santi said. Dr. Santi had formed a friendship with Eder and his family over the years. Dr. Santi had roughly 30 years of experience dealing with athletes who had suffered head traumas, and this experience and expertise prompted Dr. Santi to see a neurologist. "The family believed in what I told them. When I took them to the university to my friend who is a specialist, they immediately accepted and agreed to all of the tests and were very important in the recuperation," said Dr. Santi.

The neurologist that Dr. Santi brought in was the renowned Dr. Renato Anghinah. Dr. Anghinah also had a lengthy history of working with boxers and assisting people with diseases like Eder's. Dr. Santi recommended to the Jofres they all meet with Dr. Anghinah to get to the root and gain a more accurate diagnosis.

Dr. Santi had been in touch with Andrea's husband, Antonio Oliveira, and he was then introduced to Dr. Anghinah. After some preliminary research, Eder and his family went to see Dr. Anghinah. "About two weeks after the contact, he was in my private office, and we changed the diagnosis. They thought it was Alzheimer's. I thought it could be CTE. He was very, very weak and I prescribed a different medication," Dr. Anghinah said.

"I believe his condition nowadays, maybe 70-80% related to boxing and CTE (chronic traumatic encephalopathy), also known as 'pugilistic dementia,' is the consequence of the condition. The brain suffered the consequences of how many times he was hit," said Dr. Anghinah. Dr. Santi shared this view: "This condition is related to athletes who received punches or get their head hit. It is because of a protein called TAU. It's related to a repetition of hits to the head."

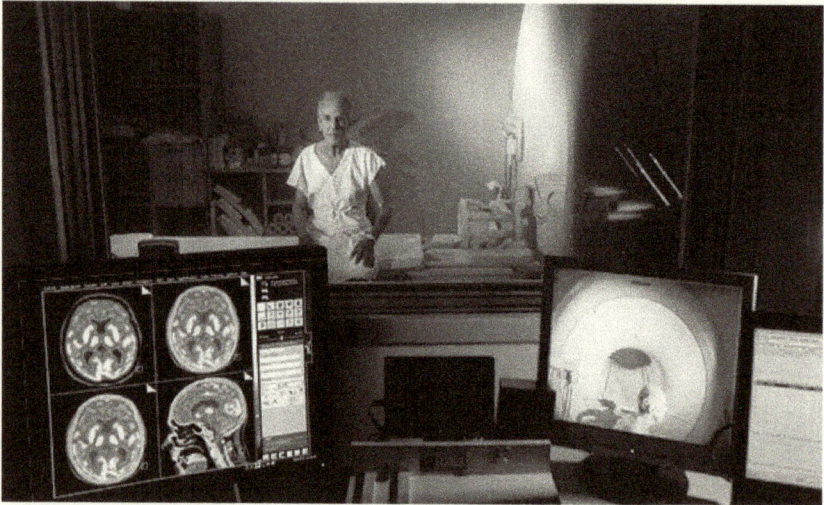

The doctors did take Eder off the medications he did not need since it was clear the diagnosis had been incorrect. Soon, Eder's health began to improve, and his nutrition and cognition improved. He remembered things again, and he got his humor back. He no longer appeared depressed and frail. The initial phase stabilized Eder's mental and physical health. "Immediately, we started the treatment, and we changed the medication because the medication prescribed before I saw him was not working. After the change in medication and approach, he started to become healthy," said Dr. Anghinah. "We prescribed medicine which stimulated healthy cells in his brain. Before, they were only treating the consequences of the disease. They thought it was Alzheimer's and Parkinson's, and it wasn't. The medicine we prescribed improved the stimulation of the brain cells," said Dr. Santi. After about six weeks, the results were good, and Eder's reflexes and responses improved.

Eder moved in with Andrea and Antonio. "I was his little princess, and he was my hero. I became a woman, and now it was time for me to take his mother's place," Andrea said. Andrea has dedicated her life to making sure her father is happy and well cared for. "When I was about six or seven years old, I was playing catch, and I fell into the pool. I didn't know how to swim, so my father jumped in and saved me. He was my hero," she said. She soon began to take a further interest in the details of his career and the sport in general. "I started going to CNB (National Boxing Council of Brazil) events and often went up to the ring with my father. I thanked the fans and friends for their affection," she said. Andrea does not work in boxing but is a connection point between the WBC and her father. "I just want more and more people to know the name Eder Jofre and that his legacy is eternalized so that today's youth know his history and what he has done for Brazil," she added.

Today

Over time, Eder was back in the gym working out and was happy again. He maintains a healthy diet still and trains twice a week with family friend Harry Rosenberg. Rosenberg, a personal trainer, started training with Eder in the 1990s and has maintained a close friendship with the family. "He has always been kind, polite, and playful. He has always been disciplined and dedicated," Rosenberg said. It has been a great pleasure for Rosenberg to help Eder with keeping his body and mind sharp during private sessions at The Renaissance Hotel in São Paulo. "Andrea is very affectionate and dedicated to her father. They (the Jofre family) are extraordinary people," Rosenberg added.

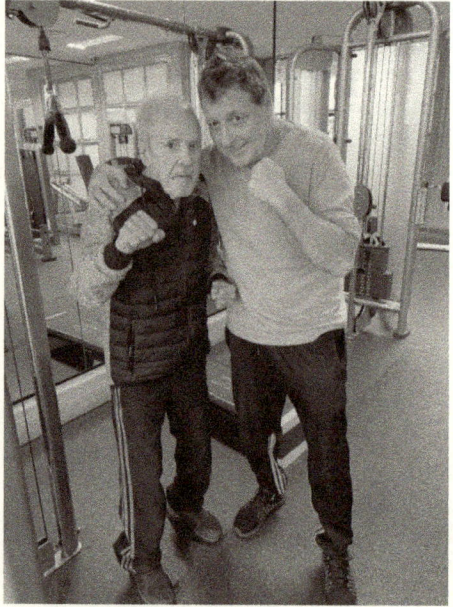

Eder and Harry Rosenberg

Marcel and his second wife Janete Oliveira welcomed a daughter into the world in 2016 when Maria Eduarda Jofre was born on August 4.

Eder received a medal of honor for sports merit on October 9, 2017, because of the prestige he had brought to Brazil and São Paulo. "I am ecstatic to receive a tribute like this. There have been many victories that I have already achieved, and today is another moment of joy," he said. That year also a tribute was made to him in the movie *João, o Maestro*, a film about the life of his old friend João Carlos Martins. Martins had always referenced Eder's comeback and victory over Jose Legra as an inspiration to himself, and this part was acted out in the movie. Martins was on hand when Eder received the medal of honor and said, "As a human being, as a father, as a husband, Eder is an example for Brazil. And I think today is a glorious day for this auditorium." Councilor Dr. Milton Ferreira was the main speaker at this ceremony. "It is a relevant tribute that the Chamber pays to this athlete. A person recognized in Brazil and worldwide. One of the best that the country has ever had, and one who took us to the top."

In 2018, a movie based on Eder's life titled *10 Segundos Para Vencer* (*10 seconds to win*) was released in cinemas across Brazil. Actor Daniel de Oliveira played the role of Eder, with Osmar Prado playing his father, Aristides. The movie was created by Thomas Stavros, who had worked passionately for many years making it.

Eder had the following to say upon the release of the movie: "Many thought it was impossible, but in all my life, the word 'impossible' was never part of my vocabulary. Yesterday was the premiere day of the movie *10 Segundos Para Vencer* which counts all my professional and family history beautifully until I was 37 years old when I won the featherweight world title. I knew it would be exciting, but I never imagined a movie as beautiful as this. Thank you to my family and everyone involved. Daniel De Oliveira made me look very handsome on screen. I could see my father as Osmar Prado. It was terrific. My special thanks to Thomas

Eder and Antonio Oliveira at movie premiere

Stavros, who, 15 years ago, came to me and promised me that he would write a movie for me and that he would launch it in the theaters. He fulfilled his promise with a lot of struggle and perseverance, and the result could not be better. It's not a simple boxing film; it's a movie also about family, love, and above all, about overcoming. And if there's something Brazilian people understand, it's about overcoming."

Marcel was delighted with the finished product seeing his father's story told on the big screen. "The film was a long project of more than ten years until it materialized. Here in Brazil, the only sport that matters is football, and making a movie about boxing was difficult. But it worked, and it was a great emotion to see the story of my family on the screen," he said. This film later became a mini-series that appeared on *TV Globo* in four chapters.

Eder had an exciting reunion with Pele on November 28, 2018, in a meeting between Eder's son-in-law, Antonio, and Santos Football Club. On November 18, São Paulo Football Club paid tribute to Eder, honoring the 58th anniversary of his bantamweight world title win. Andrea and Antonio heard somebody say that it had been 60 years since Brazil's first World Cup win and there really hadn't been any kind of celebration honoring their team, or star player, Pele. "At that moment, my husband had the idea of promoting their meeting to exchange congratulations. He contacted Pele's advisor, who liked the idea and said Pele would be at the Santos museum on November 28," Andrea said.

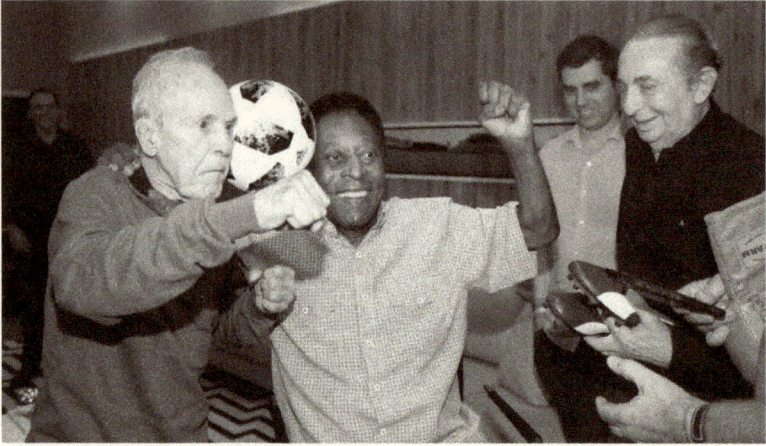

Eder and Pele

When Pele arrived, he was moved and cried as the two legends embraced each other and exchanged gifts. Eder presented "The King of Football" with an autographed boxing glove, and Pele gave Eder a signed football, a football boot, and a shirt from the Brazilian national team. "At this moment, my father said to him, 'Thank you very much Pele for your history,' and immediately Pele replied: 'Eder, you don't have to thank me for anything. We are the ones who have to thank you for everything you did for Brazil,' and then they embraced again," Andrea said.

There was an emotional day for Eder with the opening of the Fight Club Academy in São Paulo, which is a school for boxing and martial arts. It was inaugurated in May 2019, and Eder was on hand to unveil a large photograph honoring his father and did an autograph session. It is one of several gyms around the city which honors the memory of Kid Jofre. In October of that year, Eder received the Necklace of Honor Merit of Legislative Assembly from the state of São Paulo alongside comedian Carlos Alberto de Nóbrega. "I feel very happy to receive this honor. It is a great thing, a great merit. I keep the happy moments I spent with people,"

Eder said when presented with his necklace. Carlos Alberto gave an emotional speech and spoke with the joy he felt in being honored alongside Eder, who he said had always been one of his idols.

Eder and Carlos Alberto de Nobrega honored

Eder was invited to the WBC's annual convention in Cancun in October 2019, where Andrea, Antonio, and members of the CNB were on hand as Eder received a new world title belt and received a trophy in recognition of his extraordinary career. At the event, Eder brushed shoulders with some of the greatest boxers in history, such as Julio Cesar Chavez, Carlos Zarate, Lupe Pintor, Oscar De La Hoya, and others.

Eder is greeted in São Paulo after WBC convention in Cancun

In May of 2020, Rick Farris announced he would be inducting Eder into the West Coast Boxing Hall of Fame class of 2021. This was a big moment for Farris, who has long held Eder in the highest regard. "As President of the West Coast Boxing Hall of Fame, I am honored to induct this all-time great boxing legend into our organization. The first world bantamweight and featherweight world champ to join our Honor Roll," Farris said. For Eder's children, this was of great joy to see him still being recognized by the boxing world. Andrea said that she feels great satisfaction in seeing his happiness. "I feel delighted to be extolling the name of Brazil once again. It is great that people still remember me after all this time," Eder said upon hearing this news.

Today Eder has his physical and neurological limitations, but he fully knows who he is. He remembers certain fights and moments but will sometimes struggle with the details and mixes things up. He always gets emotional when talking about his father. He loves to attend boxing events throughout the city where he is still treated like royalty after all these years. It is always a great emotion for him to hear the public's applause and see the appreciation his fans still have for him.

At home, he likes to relax and watch boxing and football on television. Eder's doctors said these activities are great for his health. He enjoys watching his beloved São Paulo Football Club at Morumbi Stadium. Eder visits the club museum which displays some of his boxing items like fight-worn gloves, the belt he received from *The Ring* when he defeated Piero Rollo in 1961, and some of the clothing he wore to his fights.

"Whenever he gets the opportunity, he likes to watch his old fights and other fighters as well. That's for sure in his DNA. The passion for boxing is very much alive in him. I also have the same boxing virus in my veins. I like to watch his fights when I get a chance," Marcel said.

In the years since his retirement, Eder enjoyed the careers and styles of Sugar Ray Leonard and Julio Cesar Chavez. His favorite fighter has been Mike Tyson due to his many knockouts and the excitement he brought to the sport. "We should applaud Mike Tyson. He was not a boy like me, who had been fighting since he was a kid. Only after many problems did he dedicate himself and was the champion. A boxing phenomenon who made many people come back to fight and led the public to the gyms. It's these things that make boxing happen," he said. He maintains that the greatest boxer of all-time to this day is Sugar Ray Robinson, and even though he says he idolized Muhammad Ali for what he stood for, he thinks Joe Louis was the greatest heavyweight champion.

Eder always lived a life based upon hard work, constant striving for perfection, leading by example, and sacrifice. These principles saw him reach greatness in the profession that brought his father to Brazil. It was boxing which brought his parents together. Eder put everything into boxing and became a legend and national hero. From that platform, he sought to help others and maintained those principles through life. He has never lost touch with where he came from and has been an example of excellence and dignity. Eder never suffered the horror of a messy divorce or tedious lawsuits. He didn't go down the all too familiar route of many former greats who end up broke and drunk. Eder never had to come out of retirement to recoup lost funds or lend his name to some up-and-coming fighter hungry to get a legend's name on their record. He entered and left the murky world of politics unscathed.

There have been tragedies he had to contend with, but the respect and love Eder always gave to others has been reciprocated. Today he lives happily and content with his status and his place in history because above all, he always sought to do the right thing.

Tributes From the Boxing World

Authors, Historians, and Media

Even his nickname – "The Golden Bantam" – hearkens back to the golden era of not only his division but of the sport itself. Bantamweight king Eder Jofre was a complete fighter, a dream fighter, who would have been favored against Bud Taylor, Charley Phil Rosenberg, Kid Williams, Pete Herman, and 50/50 against Panama Al Brown. Jofre confirmed that he belongs among the all-time best when he ended his retirement, competed eight pounds north of his natural division, and took the featherweight crown. He was 37 when he had his last great victory, and it was a legend-builder. There's a veritable army of formidable fighters that have emerged out of Latin America, but only Roberto Duran has exceeded these achievements. Brazil's Eder Jofre stands alongside Panama's Duran and Mexico's Julio Cesar Chavez—the three greatest living fighters on the planet.

-   **Springs Toledo, USA**

Eder Jofre carried himself with quiet dignity. The accounts of his ring prowess disclose him as a fighter close to perfection. The late legendary ring historian Nat Fleischer, the founder, and editor of *The Ring* magazine, favorably compared Eder Jofre with the old-timers of the past and declared him pound-for-pound the best fighter of his era. He repeatedly referred to Jofre as the bantamweight Sugar Ray Robinson. This is high praise when you consider that Fleischer in his long and distinguished career personally witnessed in their prime ring immortals such as Sugar Ray Robinson, Joe Louis, Sam Langford, Harry Greb, Joe Gans, Benny Leonard, Terry McGovern, Jack Dempsey, Gene Tunney, Jack Johnson, Harry Wills, Mickey Walker, Tiger Flowers, Willie Pep, Henry Armstrong, Tony Canzoneri, Jimmy McLarnin, Barney Ross, Kid Chocolate, Sandy Saddler, and countless others.

In a career that spanned nearly 20 years Jofre met the best of his era and captured two world titles – 13 years apart. The second title occurring at the amazing age of 37. Jofre, like Robinson, was a supreme stylist and a picture book boxer with a big punch. Ray was more a stand-up boxer, while Eder used a bobbing and weaving semi-crouch style. He was a very intelligent fighter who could change his style to adjust to any kind of opponent. Eder was very patient in the ring and liked to feel his way during the early rounds looking for weaknesses. He was adept at working the body to wear opponents down before moving upstairs and unloading his terrific left hook or straight right-hand. Moreover, he possessed perfect balance in the ring and there seemed to be no apparent effort when he launched his

power punches. Additionally, he was a defensive genius with fast hands, reflexes, stamina, and a cast-iron chin.
- **Dan Cuoco, USA**

Eder Jofre was only 20 when his name first hit U.S. newspapers during the 1956 Olympics, but he'd already given his life to boxing. The gym was his kindergarten, he once said. We've been given more than 60 years since his U.S. print debut to contemplate Jofre's significance to Brazil and South America, and to the world of boxing. On the veritable eve of Jofre being rightly recognized for his many accomplishments, it's clear the world of boxing wishes to confirm its respect and adoration for such a champion and man. Two separate title reigns in two divisions over 10 years apart say more than any writer ever could. Eder Jofre is truly great, and that's plenty.
- **Patrick Connor, USA**

Eder Jofre, this name is still special for a lot of boxing fans in Japan. The name will never fade away. Every time Fighting Harada sees me, he always tells me how Jofre was great, and he tells me there have been many boxers in the world, but Eder Jofre is the best. Harada tells me Eder Jofre is the greatest boxer of all-time and that he respects him, misses him greatly, and considers him one of his greatest friends.
- **Akihide Ishi-I, Japan**

I first heard of Jofre when I read Nigel Collins' profile in *The Ring's* August 1986 issue. The Brazilian was being inducted into *The Ring's* Hall of Fame in the Modern Category, and in it, Collins wrote: "He boxed out of a classic, stand-up stance with his chin ducked down behind his shoulder. His footwork was economical but effective. However, it was when he hooked off the jab or crossed his right, that the secret of his success was truly revealed. Simply stated, Jofre was one of the hardest punching bantams to ever lace on the gloves." That caught my attention, but legendary matchmaker Teddy Brenner sealed the deal when he said "Jofre fought a little bit like Alexis Arguello." Arguello was one of my favorite fighters growing up, so when I began my video collection in 1986, I had to get Jofre footage. Although the only available fights at the time were his two losses to Masahiko "Fighting" Harada, Jofre fought well enough to justify the glorious descriptions. And what a glorious career it was: A 72-2-4 (50 KO) record, undisputed titles at 118 and 126, and the consensus choice as the best pound-for-pound fighter during the early 1960s.

While his record at bantamweight was exceptional, his legend was secured when he assembled arguably the greatest comeback in boxing history: He won all 25 fights and improbably captured his second championship by scoring an off-the-floor majority decision over the 129-9-4 (49 KO) Jose Legra. At 37 years 49 days, Jofre remains the oldest fighter ever to win a widely recognized belt at 126 and he never lost it in the ring as the WBC stripped him for not fighting mandatory challenger Alfredo

Marcano. Jofre's all-around excellence is his everlasting legacy, and that legacy is explained in this book.

- **Lee Groves, USA**

"They sure don't make them like they used to." I know you've heard this oldie but goodie, have assuredly muttered it yourself a time or two, in relation to automobiles, electrical appliances, construction materials, what have you. The same can be said for prizefighters, and Eder Jofre is a perfect example. The man was literally born in a boxing gym, for crying out loud. Fighting was a proud tradition within the Jofre family, so much so that Eder's Aunt Olga was a wrestler.

Extraordinarily powerful for a diminutive bantamweight, Jofre packed a hell of a punch in both hands and possessed stamina that seems almost superhuman. That uppercut of his is a thing of brutal beauty to behold, particularly when it connected with his opponent's liver or solar plexus, prematurely ending many an evening inside the prize ring. If, like me, you maintain a special appreciation for boxers who occupy the lower weight classes, I'm sure you delight in watching old fight films of Eder Jofre and saying to yourself, "They sure don't make them like they used to."

- **Christopher Benedict, USA**

Historically, the bantamweight division has always been phenomenal, but perhaps often living in the world of anonymity in the sense of mainstream sports. Known as the little-men division, the eclectic skills of these fighters have come in all shapes and sizes. The scientific brawling of the likes of Ruben Olivares and Carlos Zarate, the marvelous ring technician that is Orlando Canizales, the pure originals that are Terry McGovern and George Dixon, the mainstream run of the aesthetically pleasing Jeff Chandler. And then there is Eder Jofre; the total package. How good was he? A fighter most known for his defense at the lower weight classes is indeed rare, Eder did it better than them all. And he could fight a little bit too.

- **Anthony "Zute" George, USA**

Eder Jofre never fought in the UK and he met only one British opponent, but he has left an indelible mark upon my boxing consciousness. I particularly remember his victory, in 1973, over Jose Legra. It seemed amazing to me at the time that a 37-year-old could win a title after he had first held one some thirteen years before. The early seventies saw many prestigious comebacks but there were none as good as this one. His victory over Johnny Caldwell in 1962 was achieved with boxing artistry, destructive punching power, and clear-minded ring ruthlessness.

It was this combination of qualities that place him apart from every other bantamweight in the history of the sport, for Eder Jofre was, quite simply, the best bantamweight to have ever laced the gloves.

- **Miles Templeton, England**

That Eder Jofre has not, until now, received the common courtesy of a dedicated analysis in the shape of a book in English is one of the more inexplicable shortfalls in boxing's literature. No sport, aside from perhaps cricket and baseball, has such a deep well of readable work on the greats down the ages but boxing falls short in the strangest places; Chris Smith sets out to put that right with the book you hold in your hands. Jofre, among the greatest of bantamweights, the greatest of boxers, will prove fertile ground for exploration. The Brazilian icon, as technically flawless as any fighter ever to don the gloves, is in possession of perhaps the most under-told boxing story post World War Two. You know, but you don't know; you're familiar, but not intimately so. Jofre, though, did it all. And it is nice now to have it all told.

- **Matt McGrain, Scotland**

Once upon a time, a long time ago, boxing pundits finally got it right. They heralded the passing of the "pound-for-pound" torch from one Sugar Ray Robinson to a Brazilian bantamweight named Eder Jofre. Sometimes called "The Miniature Ray Robinson," Jofre is possibly the least known and least talked about all-time great world champion. But it's time that history gets caught up to "The Golden Bantam" - he was that dominant a force - and one of the few world champions that never got knocked out in the ring.

In touring the world during his many title defenses, he proudly wore his country's flag on his sleeve; and as the first world champion from Brazil, Jofre was nothing less than pure South American royalty. Just as Jofre was starting his career in the late 50s and blossoming during the swinging 60s; the invaluable U.S. television market simply did not exist for the smaller superstar boxers. Big networks had no interest in buying a main event that featured a 118-pounder from Brazil. And even when New York was the boxing capital of the world, Eder Jofre could not get booked at Madison Square Garden. As a result, he only fought three times in the United States (all in California), and precious few videos of his fights exist today. Jofre retired with a scintillating ring record of 72 wins (50 by knockout), 2 losses, and 4 draws. And those nagging four draws? Based on South America's "unique" scoring at the time, a fight was declared a draw if a boxer did not lead by at least four points on two of the judges cards. The time is now for all good boxing historians to do the right thing and call them victories!

I was honored to meet the classy Eder once in 1997 when I accompanied Ruben Olivares to *The Ring Magazine's* 75th-anniversary celebration in Atlantic City, New Jersey. Both Eder and Ruben allowed each other the greatest of respect, somehow in their minds wondering how a big-money battle would have looked between the two. Eder seemed a very quiet and humble man - a direct contrast to the slashing, daring boxer that he was - and reminded me of a long-lost uncle that I hadn't seen in ages. To that, I stand up and say: God bless "The Golden Bantam" and God bless Eder Jofre.

- **Gene Aguilera, USA**

When I think back about Eder Jofre, I perhaps am guilty at times of not remembering how great he really was. It seems fighting and winning came so easy to him. I knew back then he was an elite fighter. I also read he was a vegetarian. I found that odd because I always pictured a fighter eating a big steak before a fight. Little did I know. Most of the glory years of Eder Jofre were before I began to write about boxing. However, I had already been following boxing long before I began to write about it. I knew many of the names of his opponents, so I knew he was very good. It turns out the word good should have been great.

I could rehash his career fight-by-fight but there is no reason to do that. His record is there for all to see. There is also plenty of video. For those who have never seen him in action, it will be an amazing treat. For those of us who did witness some of his fights back in the day, it never gets old. Eder Jofre was a class act, with skills beyond comprehension. The fact he lost twice to a very good fighter, Japan's Fighting Harada, shocked me at the time. Not to take anything away from Harada I just thought Jofre was a better fighter. I was equally surprised when Jofre retired after the second Harada fight. However, when he came back, he returned to glory and never lost another fight. What a record, what a fighter, what a man!

-   **Jerry Fitch, USA**

Like Harry Greb, Eder Jofre fought at a time when information on fighters was not readily available. But based on word of mouth and footage from his fights with Fighting Harada (against whom he lost two close decisions) and Jose Medel (on August 18, 1960)—and a documentary titled O Grande Campeao, it's clear that he had everything a legendary fighter must possess including fighting the best opposition, being a highly-skilled stylist, being a boxer-puncher, having a rock-solid jaw, and bookending a career in which he went undefeated in his first 50 fights and undefeated in his final 25. Historians know that "The Golden Bantam" was one of the absolute best pound-for-pound fighters of all time, but not all fans are historians. Let's just call him the greatest fighter who fought under the radar.

-   **Ted Sares, USA**

Not known by the younger generation or by many American boxing fans is Eder Jofre. He was the first world champion from Brazil and truly one of the greatest boxers of all time. A two-weight division champion, Jofre began his professional career in 1957, and compiled a record of 34-0-3, before he won the NBA bantamweight title in November 1960, and in 1962, he won the world bantamweight title. Jofre won his next ten fights, all by knockout, before traveling to Nagoya, Japan to defend his title against Fighting Harada on May 18, 1965. He would lose a 15-round split decision. In a rematch, the following year on May 31, 1966, in Tokyo, Japan, Jofre would lose again by a 15-round unanimous decision. After the second loss to Harada, Jofre retired, only to return to the ring three years later, in 1969,

at the age of 33. After going undefeated in 14 bouts, on May 5, 1973, he defeated Jose Legra by 15-round decision to win the WBC featherweight title. Jofre would fight another two years, going unbeaten in 10 bouts, before officially retiring for good at 40 years old. His ring record was outstanding: 72 wins, 2 losses, 4 draws, and 50 wins by knockout, with Harada the only fighter to ever beat Jofre as a professional. At 118 pounds, I rank Jofre as the #1 greatest bantamweight, and he is #11 on my list of the greatest pound-for-pound boxers of all time.
-   **David Martinez, USA**

Latin America has had many great fighters. One of the best would be Eder Jofre. Arguably the best fighter from South America, the pride of Brazil would not only defeat his opponents on his way to a 72-2-4 career record, he would destroy them. Jofre was a savage in the ring, a bantamweight champion for half a decade and is a member of the International Boxing Hall of Fame. I could go and list other accomplishments, but the best way to appreciate the man is to view his fights and study his career. If you are a boxing fan do yourself a favor and check out some of his fights that can be found online and see for yourself why he was named the 19th greatest fighter of the past 80 years by *The Ring* in a 2002 publication.
-   **Jose Martino, USA**

A legend comes to light! Finally, a biography of Eder Jofre, the best bantamweight boxer ever and one of the greatest fighters of all-time. A bear myth whose career - for Americans - was consigned to boxing magazines or the agate type at the bottom of the sports pages. Regardless of the dateline, the headline was invariably the same: "Jofre wins," "Jofre by KO," "Jofre retains his title." Buttressed in an era between Latin American ring legends, predecessors Luis Firpo and Pascual Perez and successors, Carlos Monzon and Roberto Duran, Jofre never had the opportunity of worldwide television exposure or exhibiting his talents on the grand stages of Madison Square Garden, Yankee Stadium or at Las Vegas' casinos, his reputation of greatness among hardcore fans and historians of the ring never wavered over the course of his three-decade career.

Eder was the most contemporary boxer ranked by *The Ring* publisher Nat Fleischer, an observer of boxing for 70 years - having personally witnessed world champions from Terry McGovern to Roberto Duran. The founder of *The Ring* rated Jofre higher (#4) in his weight class (bantam) than he did Joe Louis, Sugar Ray Robinson, and Henry Armstrong in their respective divisions. Never knocked out, he lost only two bouts - to Japan's greatest boxer, two-division world champ Fighting Harada in his victor's homeland. A chronicle of the life and times of this two-division Hall of Fame world champion who is the bantamweight division's equal of heavyweights Muhammad Ali and Joe Louis, welterweight Sugar Ray Robinson, lightweight Roberto Duran and the featherweight Willie Pep, is long overdue. I hope this informs and educates a new generation about the career and life of this remarkable athlete.

- **Don Majeski, USA**

Eder Jofre is one of the greatest bantamweight and featherweight champions ever. Undisputed champion in two weight divisions back in the days when there were only 10 weight divisions and one recognized world champion per division. He only lost two fights in a 78-fight career and his two losses were to another undisputed two-weight division world champion Fighting Harada. Although Eder Jofre never fought an Australian boxer, he had a very interesting boxing career and an interesting part in Australian boxing history. Fighting Harada, after winning the bantamweight title from Eder Jofre, lost the title in his fifth defense to Australian Lionel Rose. Lionel Rose became the first Aboriginal to win a world title in any sport. Shortly afterward, Australian Johnny Famechon won the world featherweight title from Jose Legra then defended the title twice against Fighting Harada before losing the title to Vicente Saldivar. In 1973 Eder Jofre came back to win the world featherweight title from Jose Legra and defeated Vicente Saldivar in a world title defense. I think Eder Jofre's story will be a must-read for all boxing fans.

- **Gary Luscombe, Australia**

I grew up listening to my father and grandfather commenting on Eder Jofre's fights. The heroic and brave way in which the "Golden Bantam" was characterized gave the impression to a boy of six, seven years old that he was a huge and destructive monster. With that, I learned to admire him. His fights broadcast in the seventies on television were an unmissable and mandatory event in our home. After some time, I became a sports journalist and soon I had a mission given by my father: "When you interview Eder Jofre, have a lot of respect. You will be talking to a legend."

- **Wilson Baldini Junior, Brazil**

Eder Jofre's career as a fighter spanned 19 years (1957-1976) with a hiatus that lasted 3 years after losing his bantamweight title (his first loss in 50 fights) and then the rematch, both by decisions, to Fighting Harada. Within that 19-year period, Eder Jofre was the best fighter in the world, Ali might have been "The Greatest" (according to Muhammad), and there were names more common to recall and because of the media hype seemed more spectacular, but when it all came out in the wash, Eder Jofre was better than them all, and if I have to use the cliché "pound-for-pound" to make my point, there you have it.

The great ones made their comebacks but were paler images of their once magnificent selves. Ray Robinson struggled with middleweights and lost 16 fights. Ali had slowed to a walk. Joe Louis had to fight because he owed the government. That was the hardest of all to take. But when Jofre came back to a division a step higher, he hadn't missed a beat. He never lost again and, in the process, won the featherweight title and retired undefeated. Maybe it was because he fought at a lower weight. Maybe it was because he only fought three times in the U.S. Eder Jofre never got the credit he deserved. He made no kick about it because he knew, and the fighters knew where he stood. Now Chris is letting everybody know. It's overdue. Better late than never.

- **Roger Esty, USA**

When I was growing up, Eder Jofre was the man in the bantamweight division. He picked up his first world championship in 1960, and two years later, the WBA and WBC version of the bantamweight crown. I was fascinated by this little man from Brazil, no bigger than a jockey, reading everything I could about his amazing boxing ability.

When he lost a razor-close decision, after going undefeated in 50 professional bouts, I was stunned. His desire was lacking went the story. Defeated in a rematch, he hung up his gloves. Then he shocked me again when he came out of retirement. Jofre was 33, old for a little man, but his skills were still sharp. He won 14 fights in succession, scoring eight knockouts - securing a world title shot against the talented Jose Legra. Jofre had turned 37 a few months before. Legra had recently won the title and was considered the favorite going into the bout. Jofre went down in round three and was bleeding from cuts near his eyes. No matter. He dug down deep and punished Legra's body, winning the fight, and the WBC featherweight world title.

He fought 10 times more, posting victories over tough Frankie Crawford, and former champion Vicente Salvador before hanging up the gloves for good in 1976. Jofre was classy, savvy, gutsy, and tough – one of the best fighters ever, and the greatest bantamweight to ever lace up the gloves.

- **John Raspanti, USA**

Boxers

In my opinion Eder, by his perseverance and pleasure in fighting overcame all his difficulties to get where he wanted to get. I think that to get to the top is not easy. You must have a hard conviction, to have faith that it is possible. When you have a target and adapt training to your conditions, you find a way to do a better job. When a boxer gets to this level in training and competition, he is very strong by the fact of always working with the absolutes of life. Responsibility, fidelity, patience perseverance, and humility.

- **Miguel de Oliveira, Brazil, WBC super welterweight world champion 1975**

Eder Jofre was and always will be the greatest idol of Brazilian boxing and one of the best boxers in the world of all-time. Eder Jofre, after winning his first world title on November 18, 1960, against Eloy Sanchez, from Mexico, encouraged the great majority of young Brazilians of that time. I met Eder Jofre personally in 1962, at the Ibirapuera Gymnasium in São Paulo, at the age of 14; I confess that it was the biggest emotion I felt in my entire life.

- **Servilio de Oliveira, Brazil, Olympic Bronze Medalist 1968**

Eder Jofre is a boxing idol. Brazil's first champion of the world. I had the honor of knowing him and I mirrored him. Not only to me but to other fighters he is a very big reference for Brazil and the World. I have so much to say about Eder Jofre, this great man and great warrior.

- **Valdemir Pereira, Brazil, IBF featherweight world champion 2006**

Eder Jofre is considered the best bantamweight of all time. As a person, he's a great human being. I've always heard many stories about him. Brazilian boxing has to value our first world champion, who represented boxing very well, inside and outside the ring. Eder is always a champion in boxing and life.

- **Patrick Teixeira, Brazil, WBO super welterweight world champion 2020-2021**

Eder is the greatest Brazilian boxing idol of all-time. He is a very charismatic person. He is our eternal golden bantam, our eternal three-time champion. For me, it is always an honor to be near Eder Jofre. I didn't see him fight, but Eder Jofre's era was glorious. Eder Jofre is a reference for young people, and he is an icon of boxing.

- **Acelino Freitas, Brazil, WBO super featherweight world champion 1999-2003, WBA super featherweight world champion 2001-2003, WBO lightweight world champion 2004-2005, 2006-2007**

There's one thing about Eder Jofre that needs to be said: HE WAS ALWAYS THERE. Here in Brazil, this is very important because you don't have any kind of support from no one, but Eder was always there. He was there for my first fight and was also for my last one - always cheering at ringside. His inspiring presence did more for Brazilian boxing than any public authority has ever done.

- **Adilson Rodrigues, Brazil, heavyweight contender**

In the mid-1960s, when I began my boxing career in Los Angeles, I was well aware of the bantamweight champion of the world, an unbeaten Brazilian named Eder Jofre. The 118-pound division was well stocked in L.A. and this was due to two great promoters and Southern California's proximity to the Mexican border. Mexico has long claimed to have the best bantamweights and featherweights on the planet, but this was not true during the two decades that Eder Jofre was active between 1957 to 1976 and held undisputed world titles in both divisions.

Having grown up in Los Angeles, a city that showcased the great Ruben Olivares, Carlos Zarate, Vicente Saldivar, Chucho Castillo, Rafael Herrera, Jesus Pimentel and Jose Medel (to name a few) that says a lot. As I learned of the great Mexican fighters, I also was aware of the great Brazilian legend who had come to the City of Angels in 1960 to win his first world title, knocking out another brilliant Mexican bantam to win the 118-pound world title. He would only lose to one boxer in a 78-bout career, finishing with an amazing 72-2-4 record with 50 knockouts. His two losses were both the product of weight issues, and the first loss (in Japan) was considered an international robbery.

- **Rick Farris, USA, professional featherweight and founder and President of The West Coast Boxing Hall of Fame**

When I was young, I admired Eder Jofre. He was a great boxer, a great champion. I had heard whispers that a fight with Jofre was in the works, but it never panned out. If we would have fought, I would have knocked him out . . . I'm sorry to say this. He was on his way out, and "Puas" was on his way up. I was still an active fighter . . . younger, and stronger than Jofre. His manager knew this. Even though Jofre would have loved to tangle, as all great fighters do, his manager using common sense would have stopped it.

- **Ruben Olivares, Mexico, world bantamweight world champion 1969-1970, 1971-192, WBA featherweight champion 1974, WBC featherweight champion 1975, International Boxing Hall of Fame inductee**

What I know about him is he was a great champion. I have guided myself by his record and videos of his fights. He is 15 years older than me. He has a great record and was very strong. The fights he had with Jose Medel and Vicente Saldivar without doubt were dramatic. I had the pleasure of meeting him at the WBC convention in Cancun in 2019. It was a pleasure to meet him and chat with him. The organization gave him a belt to recognize him as a great champion. I was very pleased with the fact that he recognized me after his kids talked to him about me. I could see that he was happy to meet me and I took the moment to take a photo that also united me with Julio Cesar Chavez.

- **Carlos Zarate, Mexico, WBC bantamweight world champion 1976-1979, International Boxing Hall of Fame inductee**

There is no doubt Eder Jofre was the greatest boxer I faced in the ring in my boxing career. I had two fights with Jofre. Throughout the long and tough 30 rounds I was suffering from his strong punches. In the first bout between us, as you know I won the bantamweight title from Jofre somehow. Jofre lost for the first time during his professional career. The decision was close. He should have had a very hard time with it. I'll never forget the next moment in my lifetime. He walked across the ring, and he came up to me and lifted me up, and said, "Congratulations Harada." No one except Jofre can act like this.

Jofre is a real champion not only for his great boxing skill but also for his gentle heart. I respect him. And one more thing I would like to tell you, Eder Jofre is a man with his own dignity. He is a gentleman. Throughout my lifetime, I'd like to have him as my best friend. I miss him very much; I would like to see him one more time. Eder Jofre is a real champion of the world; he is the best of all the boxers.

- **Masahiko "Fighting" Harada, Japan, world flyweight champion 1962-193, world bantamweight champion 1965-1968, International Boxing Hall of Fame inductee**

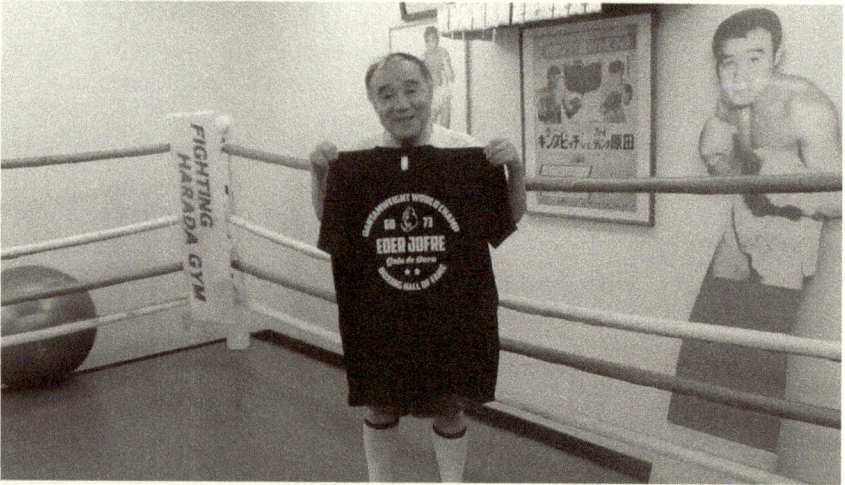

Harada proudly displays his Eder Jofre shirt

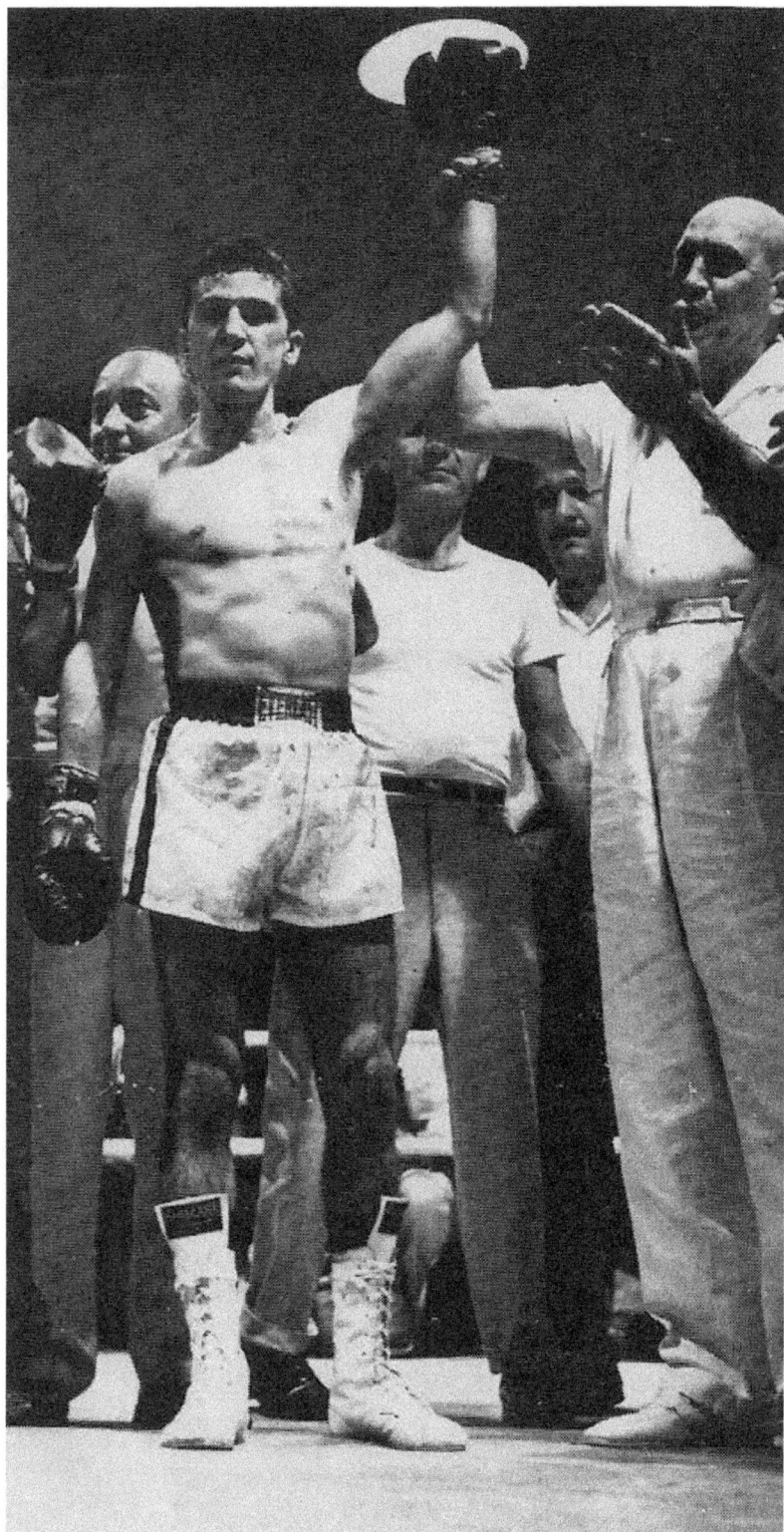

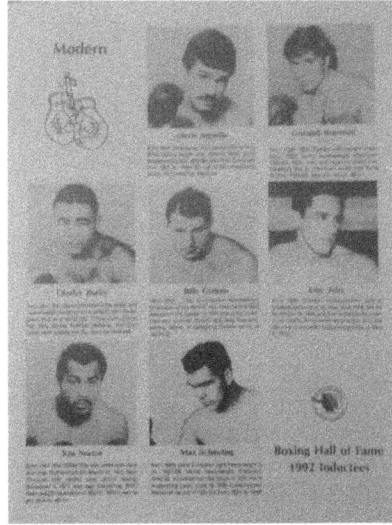

1992 International Boxing Hall of Fame program

Eder featured in Japanese Manga cartoon

Éder Jofre mostra os golpes

Jab — É um golpe rápido, que visa o rosto; o punho estende-se em linha reta e não requer muito esforço físico. É o golpe mais usado, exceto pelos boxadores baixos.

Swing — É um golpe longo, que visa atingir um alvo localizado acima da cabeça do pugilista que o desfere. Na foto, Éder abriu o golpe para facilitar a compreensão.

Hook (gancho) — É um golpe curto, que pega o fígado (com a esquerda) ou o baço, coração ou estômago (com a direita). As costas da mão estão voltadas para o adversário.

Bôlo punch — É um golpe de trajetória longa, usado mais como exibicionismo. É aplicado quando o adversário está dominado, porque ao lançá-lo o pugilista se descobre.

Cross (cruzado) — É um golpe em que o punho descreve trajetória semicircular, de fora para dentro, com levantamento do cotovêlo. Atinge geralmente embaixo do queixo.

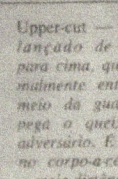

Upper-cut — Golpe lançado de baixo para cima, que normalmente entra no meio da guarda e pega o queixo do adversário. É usado no corpo-a-corpo e a meia-distância.

Direto — É um golpe reto, pouco mais longo que o jab. O pugilista canhoto (punho e pé direitos à frente) lança diretos de esquerda; o pugilista destro lança diretos de direita.

ÉDER O" MESTRE"

DÁ UMA AULA DE BOX

"Realidade", S. Paulo.

Eder shows the moves

Eder sparring in Tokyo for Aoki clash

The champ shows off his cars

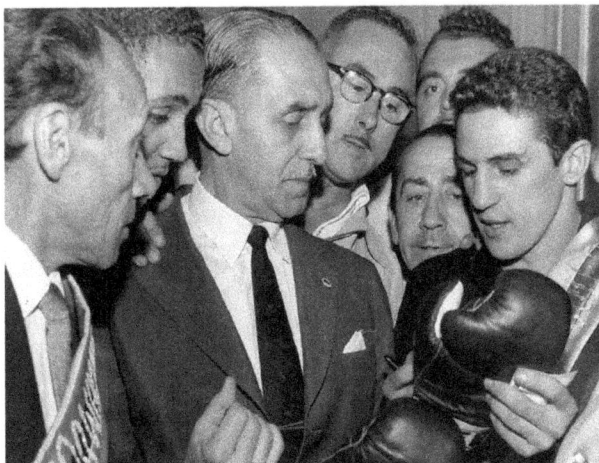

Teaching Governor Carvalho Pinto to put on gloves

Ademar de Barros, governor of São Paulo presents Eder the Medal of Honor of Merit

Botão (Button Game)

<u>Artwork</u>

Here is a small collection of some of Eder's artwork.

Cidinha and Marcel

Cidinha

Andrea

Eder and his mother (top), in action landing a hook (below)

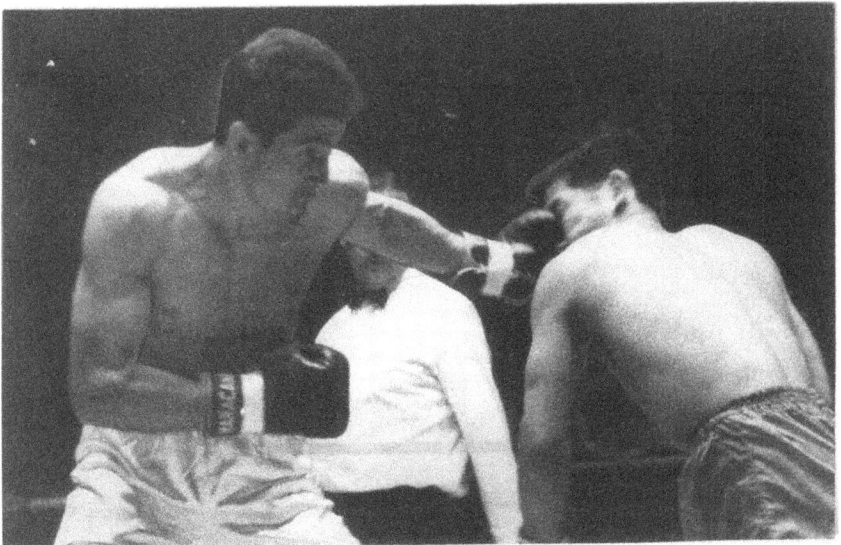

Eder and Aristides with Pele

Eder shares a magazine cover with Maria Esther Bueno, Pele and Bruno Hermanny

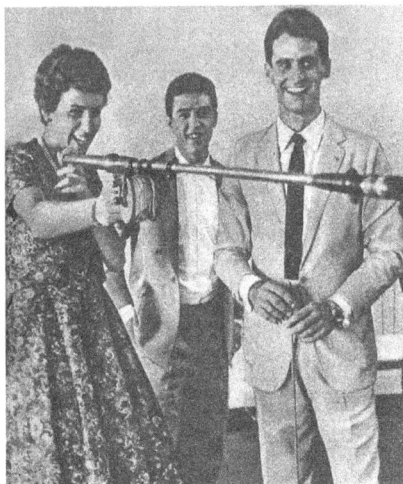

Maria Esther Bueno, Eder and Bruno Harmanny

Pele and Eder in a car commercial

With Nelson Gonçalves

With Roberto Carlos

Eder and Aristides attend a Santos vs. São Paulo match

Perfil

Éder Jofre

O boxe trouxe-lhe fama e a certeza que é preciso sempre continuar na luta para conquistar respeito e espaço para novos projetos de vida. Sai de cena o pugilista. Entra o político que, aos 63 anos, tem grande preocupação com o futuro de nossa juventude. Qual a saída? Educação e esporte.

With Fighting Harada

With Acelino Freitas and Miguel de Oliveira

With Servilio de Oliveira

Dream fight! Eder and Carlos Zarate

Eder receives an award from São Paulo Municipal Sports Department in 2019

Eder receives the Adhemar Ferreira da Silva Trophy from the Olympic Committee

Eder plays with Andrea's children
Lanika and Axel Damian

Lanika Jofre, Eder, Andrea, Axel Damian Martinez and Antonio Oliveira

Marcel, Eder, Eder Neto, Janete (Marcel's wife) and Maria Eduarda

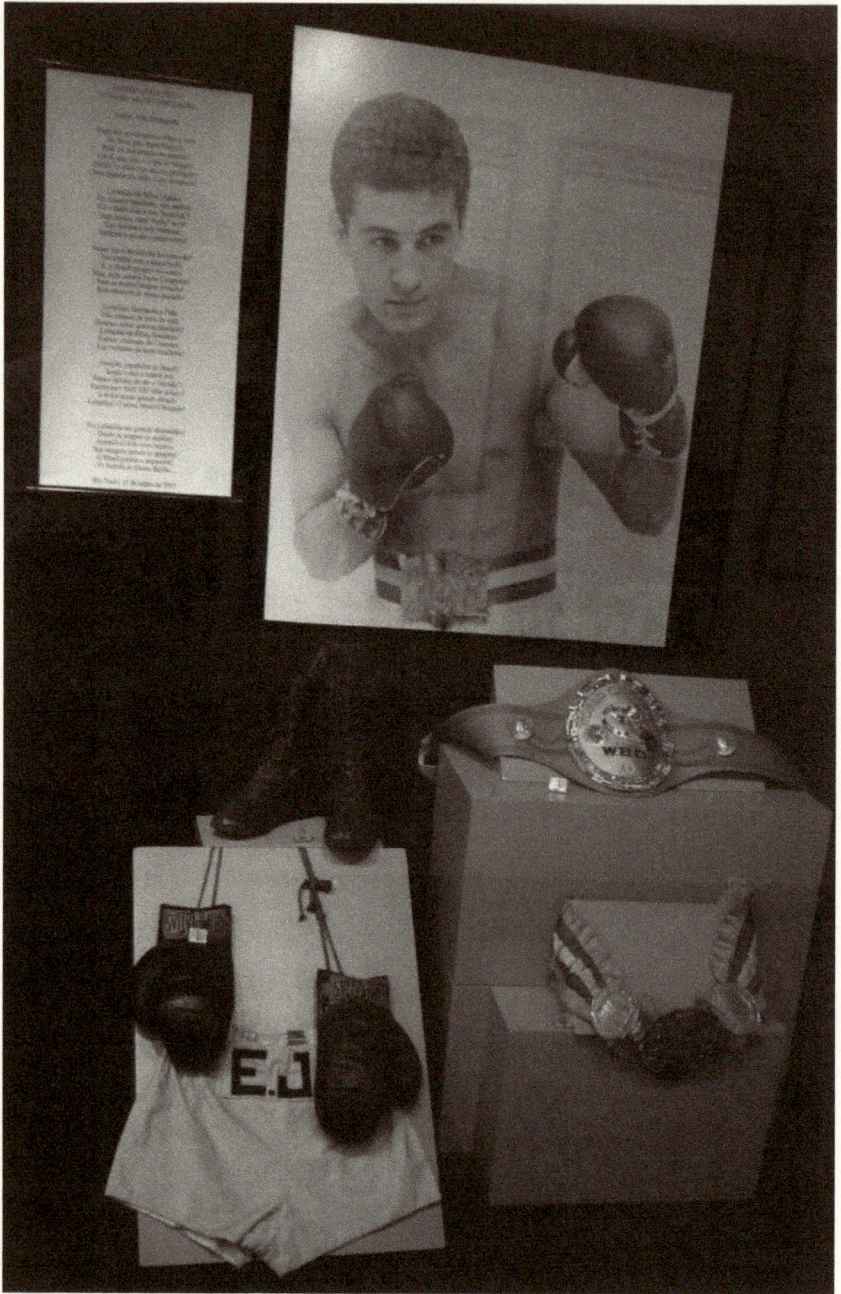

A display at São Paulo Football Club museum

Newton Campos seated next to Eder

Itamar Zumbano, Andrea, Antonio Oliveira, Marcel, Janete, Maria and Eder

Eder Jofre in December 2020

Professional Record

TOTAL FIGHTS: 78
WON: 72 (50 KO's)
LOST: 2 (0 KO's)
DRAWS: 4
TOTAL ROUNDS: 555
AVERAGE ROUNDS PER FIGHT: 7.11
KO PERCENTAGE: 64.1 KO %

DATE	OPPONENT	VENUE	RESULT
March 29, 1957	Raul Lopez	Ginásio do Ibirapuera, São Paulo	WON TKO 5
April 26, 1957	Raul Lopez	Ibirapuera, São Paulo	WON KO 3
May 24, 1957	Osvaldo Perez	Ibirapuera, São Paulo	WON TKO 10
June 7, 1957	Osvaldo Perez	Ibirapuera, São Paulo	WON KO 2
June 14, 1957	Juan A. Gonzalez	Ibirapuera, São Paulo	WON TKO 5
July 5, 1957	Raul Jaime	Ibirapuera, São Paulo	WON POINTS 10
July 19, 1957	Raul Jaime	Ibirapuera, São Paulo	WON POINTS 10
August 16, 1957	Ernesto Miranda	Ibirapuera, São Paulo	DRAW POINTS 10
September 6, 1957	Ernesto Miranda	Ginásio do Estádio Pacaembu, São Paulo	DRAW POINTS 10
October 30, 1957	Luis Angel Jimenez	Ibirapuera, São Paulo	WON KO 8
December 13, 1957	Adolfo Ramon Pendas	Ibirapuera, São Paulo	WON POINTS 10
December 22, 1957	Cristobal Gavisans	Auditório da TV-Rio, Río de Janeiro	WON POINTS 10
January 29, 1958	Avelino Romero	Ibirapuera, São Paulo	WON KO 2
March 7, 1958	Cristobal Gavisans	Ibirapuera, São Paulo	WON TKO 6
May 14, 1958	Ruben Caceres	Palacio Peñarol, Montevideo, Uruguay	DRAW POINTS 10
June 21, 1958	German Escudero	Ibirapuera, São Paulo	WON KO 2
June 29, 1958	German Escudero	Auditório da TV-Rio, Río de Janeiro	WON KO 2
July 18, 1958	Juan Carlos Acebal	Ibirapuera, São Paulo	WON KO 2
August 8, 1958	Roberto Olmedo	Ibirapuera, São Paulo	WON TKO 5
September 12, 1958	Jose Casas	Ibirapuera, São Paulo	WON POINTS 10
October 10, 1958	Jose Casas	Ibirapuera, São Paulo	WON KO 3
November 14, 1958	Jose Smecca	Ibirapuera, São Paulo	WON TKO 7
December 12, 1958	Roberto Castro	Ibirapuera, São Paulo	WON KO 2
March 23, 1959	Aniceto Pereyra	Ibirapuera, São Paulo	WON POINTS 10
April 20, 1959	Salustiano Suarez	Ibirapuera, São Paulo	WON KO 4

June 4, 1959	Leo Espinosa	Ibirapuera, São Paulo	WON POINTS 10
June 19, 1959	Angel Bustos	Ibirapuera, São Paulo	WON TKO 4
June 28, 1959	Salustiano Suarez	Auditório da TV-Rio, Río de Janeiro	WON KO 1
July 31, 1959	Ruben Caceres	Ibirapuera, São Paulo	WON KO 7
October 9, 1959	Angel Bustos	Ibirapuera, São Paulo	WON KO 3
October 30, 1959	Gianni Zuddas	Ibirapuera, São Paulo	WON POINTS 10
December 12, 1959	Danny Kid	Ibirapuera, São Paulo	WON POINTS 10
February 19, 1960	Ernesto Miranda	Ibirapuera, São Paulo	WON POINTS 15
	(Won South American Bantamweight title)		
June 10, 1960	Ernesto Miranda	Ibirapuera, São Paulo	WON KO 3
	(South American Bantamweight title)		
July 15, 1960	Claudio Barrientos	Ibirapuera, São Paulo	WON TKO 8
August 18, 1960	Jose Medel	Olympic Auditorium, Los Angeles, California	WON KO 10
September 30, 1960	Ricardo Moreno	Ibirapuera, São Paulo	WON TKO 6
November 18, 1960	Eloy Sanchez	Olympic Auditorium, Los Angeles, California	WON KO 6
	(Won NBA & Lineal Bantamweight world title)		
December 16, 1960	Billy Peacock	Ibirapuera, São Paulo	WON KO2
March 25, 1961	Piero Rollo	Estádio de General Severiano, Río de Janeiro	WON TKO 9
	(NBA, Lineal and The Ring Bantamweight title)		
April 18, 1961	Sugar Ray	Ibirapuera, São Paulo	WON KO 2
July 26, 1961	Sadao Yaoita	Ibirapuera, São Paulo	WON KO 10
August 19, 1961	Ramon Arias	Estadio Universitario, Caracas, Venezuela	WON TKO 7
	(NBA, Lineal and The Ring Bantamweight title)		
December 6, 1961	Fernando Goncalves	Ibirapuera, São Paulo	WON KO 8
January 18, 1962	John Caldwell	Ibirapuera, São Paulo	WON TKO 10
	(Undisputed World Bantamweight title)		
May 4, 1962	Herman Marquez	Cow Palace, Daly City, California	WON TKO 10
	(Undisputed World Bantamweight title)		
September 11, 1962	Jose Medel	Ibirapuera, São Paulo	WON KO 6
	(Undisputed World Bantamweight title)		
April 4, 1963	Katsutoshi Aoki	Kuramae Kokugikan, Tokyo, Japan	WON KO 3
	(Undisputed World Bantamweight title)		

May 18, 1963	Johnny Jamito	Araneta Coliseum, Quezon City, Philippines	WON TKO 11
	(Undisputed World Bantamweight title)		
November 27, 1964	Bernardo Caraballo	Estadio El Campin, Bogota, Colombia	WON KO 7
	(Undisputed World Bantamweight title)		
May 18, 1965	Fighting Harada	Aichi Prefectural Gymnasium, Nagoya, Japan	LOST POINTS 15
	(Undisputed World Bantamweight title)		
November 5, 1965	Manny Elias	Ibirapuera, São Paulo	DRAW POINTS 10
May 31, 1966	Fighting Harada	Nippon Budokan, Tokyo, Japan	LOST POINTS 15
	(Undisputed World Bantamweight title)		
August 27, 1969	Rudy Corona	Ibirapuera, São Paulo	WON KO 6
January 30, 1970	Nevio Carbi	Ibirapuera, São Paulo	WON POINTS 10
May 29, 1970	Manny Elias	Ibirapuera, São Paulo	WON POINTS 10
September 25, 1970	Roberto Wong	Ibirapuera, São Paulo	WON KO 3
November 6, 1970	Giovanni Girgenti	Ibirapuera, São Paulo	WON POINTS 10
March 26, 1971	Jerry Stokes	Ibirapuera, São Paulo	WON KO 2
July 9, 1971	Domenico Chiloiro	Ibirapuera, São Paulo	WON POINTS 10
September 10, 1971	Tony Jumao-As	Ibirapuera, São Paulo	WON POINTS 10
October 29, 1971	Robert Porcel	Ibirapuera, São Paulo	WON KO 2
March 24, 1972	Memo Morales	Ibirapuera, São Paulo	WON KO 6
April 28, 1972	Felix Figueroa	Ibirapuera, São Paulo	WON POINTS 10
June 30, 1972	Jose Bisbal	Ibirapuera, São Paulo	WON KO 2
August 18, 1972	Shig Fukuyama	Ibirapuera, São Paulo	WON KO 9
September 29, 1972	Djemai Belhadri	Ibirapuera, São Paulo	WON KO 3
May 5, 1973	Jose Legra	Ginasio Presidente Médici, Brasília	WON POINTS 15
	(WBC & Lineal World Featherweight title)		
July 21, 1973	Godfrey Stevens	Ibirapuera, São Paulo	WON KO 4
August 25, 1973	Frankie Crawford	Estádio Dr. Alfredo de Castilho, Bauru	WON POINTS 10
October 21, 1973	Vicente Saldivar	Ginásio de Esportes Antônio Balbino, Salvador	WON KO 4
	(WBC and Lineal World Featherweight title)		
December 21, 1974	Niliberto Herrera	Ginásio Municipal de Jundiaí, Jundiaí	WON POINTS 10
February 24, 1976	Enzo Farinelli	Ginásio Gigantinho, Porto Alegre	WON KO 4
May 2, 1976	Michel Lefevbre	Ginásio de Esportes Nilson Nelson, Brasília	WON KO 3

May 29, 1976	Pasqualino Morbidelli	Ibirapuera, São Paulo	WON KO 4
July 2, 1976	Jose Antonio Jimenez	Ginasio do Corinthians, São Paulo	WON POINTS 10
August 13, 1976	Juan Antonio Lopez	Ibirapuera, São Paulo	WON POINTS 10
October 8, 1976	Octavio Gomez	Ibirapuera, São Paulo	WON POINTS 12

Amateur Record

This is not a complete amateur record but this is the documented dates of some of Eder Jofre's amateur bouts and tournaments. Some reports indicate a record of 148 victories and 2 defeats. Data compiled by Bob Yalen.

DATE	OPPONENT	LOCATION	RESULT
January 31, 1953	Jose Duran Garcia	São Paulo	UNKNOWN
March 15, 1953	Alberto Rodrigues	São Paulo	WON TKO 1
	(Torneio Operario de Boxe)		
August 12, 1953	João dos Santos Pinto	São Paulo	UNKNOWN
August 16, 1953	Manoel Medina	São Paulo	UNKNOWN
September 16, 1953	Luis B. Dias	São Paulo	WON TKO 2
October 14, 1953	Luis B. Dias	São Paulo	WON POINTS 3
November 3, 1953	Armando Leme	São Paulo	WON
	(Campeaonato Brasil)		
November 23, 1953	João Santana	São Paulo	WON KO 1
	(Campeaonato Brasil)		
November 28, 1953	Raimundo Alves	Rio di Janeiro	WON
	(Campeaonato Brasil)		
November 29, 1953	Walfrido Tourinho	Rio di Janeiro	WON KO 1
	(Campeaonato Brasil)		
December 17, 1953	Valdomiro Torres	Montevideo, Uruguay	WON POINTS 3
	(Torneio Ramon Platero)		
December 23, 1953	Valdomiro Torres	Montevideo, Uruguay	WON POINTS 3
	(Torneio Ramon Platero)		
April 7, 1954	Acyr Mendonca	São Paulo	WON POINTS 6
April 16, 1954	Acyr Mendonca	Pacaembu, São Paulo	WON POINTS 4
	(listed as "Profissionais")		
May 19, 1954	Ari dos Santos	São Paulo	WON KO 3
September 27, 1954	Ari dos Santos	São Paulo	Did not compete due to fractured hand in preliminary
December 18, 1954	Ari dos Santos	São Paulo	WON TKO 2
January 19, 1955	Claudio Silva	São Paulo	WON POINTS 3
April 27, 1955	Claudio Silva	São Paulo	WON POINTS 3

May 4, 1955	Orlando Brito	São Paulo	WON TKO 1
August 28, 1955	Jose Neves Martins	São Paulo	WON POINTS 3
	(Campeaonato Brasil)		
August 29, 1955	Ari dos Santos	São Paulo	WON KO 1
	(Campeaonato Brasil)		
September 10, 1955	João Santana	Salvador	WON TKO 2
	(Campeaonato Brasil)		
September 14, 2020	Geraldo Magalhaes	Salvador	WON POINTS 3
	(Campeaonato Brasil)		
September 17, 1955	Valdemar Santos	Salvador	WON POINTS 3
	(Campeaonato Brasil)		
October 23, 1955	Pedro Praxedes	Rio di Janeiro	WON POINTS 3
	(Torneio 'Luvas de Oure')		
October 30, 1955	Luiz Augusto da Silva	Rio di Janeiro	WON
	(Torneio 'Luvas de Oure')		
November 18, 1955	Frrancisco de Lima	São Paulo	WON POINTS 3
December 19, 1955	Francisco de Lima	São Paulo	WON POINTS 3
February 18, 1956	Acir Sereno	São Paulo	UNKNOWN
March 27, 1956	Acir Sereno	Rio di Janeiro	WON KO 1
April 6, 1956	Walter Valentim	Pacaembu, São Paulo	WON POINTS 6
April 27, 1956	Pedro Praxedes	São Paulo	WON TKO 5
	("Profissionais")		
June 20, 1956	Francisco de Lima	Pacaembu, São Paulo	WON TKO 4
June 30, 1956	Luis Augusto Silva	Rio di Janeiro	WON POINTS 3
July 13, 1956	Ataide de Oliveira	São Paulo	WON POINTS 6
July 28, 1956	Aniceto Pereyra	Rio di Janeiro	UNKNOWN
August 10, 1956	Aniceto Pereyra	Pacaembu, São Paulo	WON POINTS 3
September 21, 1956	Osmar Crocicchia	São Paulo	WON TKO 3
October 9, 1956	Manuel Vegas	Montevideo, Uruguay	WON TKO 2
	(Campeaonato Latino Americano)		
October 14, 1956	Guido Granizo	Montevideo, Uruguay	WON
	(Campeaonato Latino Americano)		
October 20, 1956	Goncalo Chavez	Montevideo, Uruguay	WON POINTS 3
	(Campeaonato Latino Americano)		
October 23, 1956	Aniceto Pereyra	Montevideo, Uruguay	LOST POINTS 3
	(Campeaonato Latino Americano)		

November 26, 1956	Thein Myint	Melbourne, Australia	WON POINTS 3
		(Olympic Games)	
November 28, 1956	Claudio Barrientos	Melbourne, Australia	LOST POINTS 3
		(Olympic Games)	

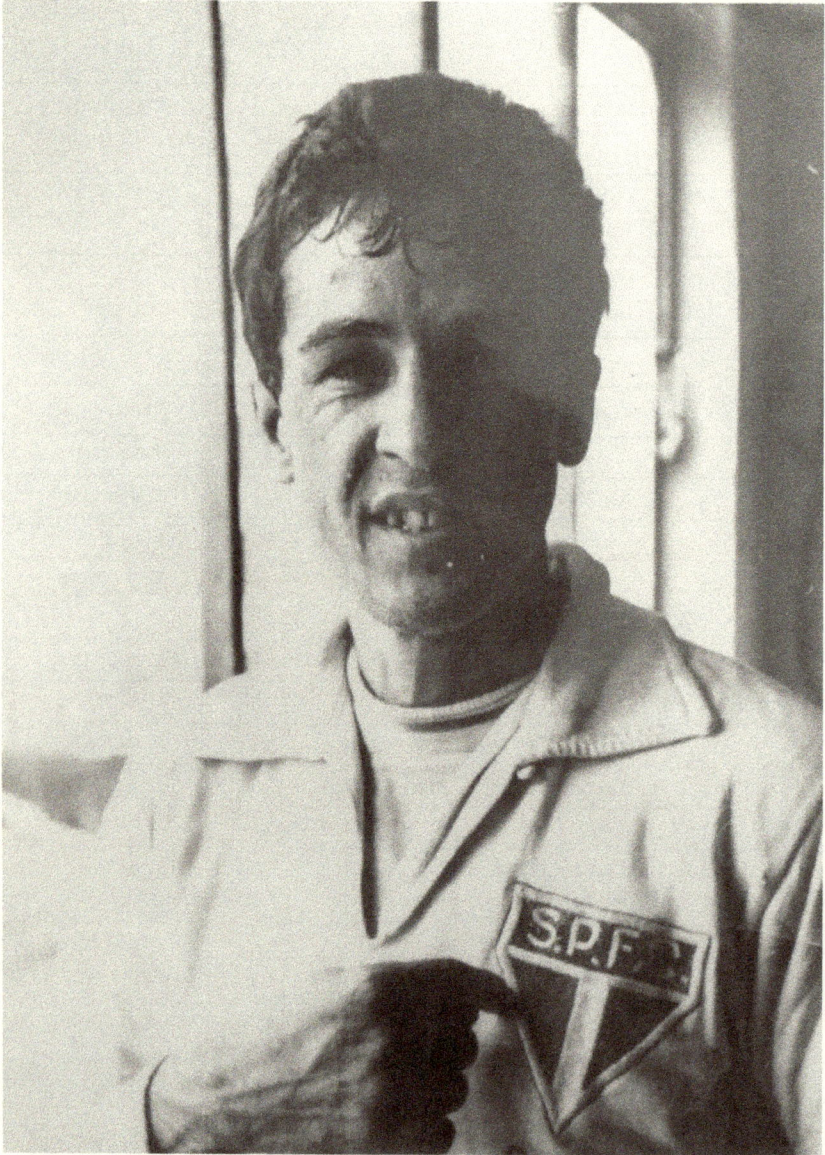

Honors Received

Titles won

NBA World Bantamweight Championship (lineal) 1960
The Ring Bantamweight Championship 1961
Undisputed World Bantamweight Championship 1962
Inaugural WBC World Bantamweight Championship 1963
WBC Featherweight World Championship (lineal) 1973

Hall of Fame

World Boxing Hall of Fame 1980
The Ring Hall of Fame 1986
International Boxing Hall of Fame 1992
California Boxing Hall of Fame 2015
West Coast Boxing Hall of Fame 2021

Recognition

#1 Greatest Bantamweight of all-time *Inter American Press Association* (1985)
#9 50 Greatest fighters of the last 50 years *The Ring* (1996)
#19 80 Greatest fighters of the last 80 years *The Ring* (2001)
#1 Bantamweight of all-time by *Bert Sugar & Teddy Atlas Ultimate Book of Boxing Lists* (2011)
#1 Greatest boxer of the 1960s by *The Ring* (2011)
#16 Greatest pound for pound fighters of all-time by *IBRO* (2019)
#1 Bantamweight of all-time by *IBRO* (2019)
#1 Greatest Bantamweight of all-time *WBC*
All-time Super Champion *WBA*

Awards

Boxer of the Year *Grand Award of Sports New York World's Fair* (1964)
Anchieta Medal and Diploma of Gratitude *City of São Paulo* (1978)
Silver Salute 50 year Anniversary Brazil's first Boxing World Champion *Municipality of São Paulo* (2010)
Adhemar Ferreira da Silva Trophy (lifetime award) *Brazilian Olympic Committee* (2010)
Medal of Honor Sports Merit *Municipal Chamber of São Paulo* (2017)
Medal of Honor for Merit *Braz Cubas Municipality of Santos* (2019)
Hall of Fame Department of Sports *Municipality of São Paulo* (2019)
Necklace of Honor Merit of Legislative Assembly *State of São Paulo (2019)*

Sources

Here is a list of the various newspapers, magazines, and websites used. In brackets is the country of publication for newspapers and magazines.

ABC Espana (Spain)
Al Folha (Brazil)
A Gazeta Esportiva (Brazil)
Association Press (USA)
Belfast Telegraph (Northern Ireland)
Blanco y Negro (Spain)
Boxing News (England)
Boxing Illustrated (USA)
Boxrec
Coventry Evening Telegraph (England)
Cyber Boxing Zone
Daily Express (England)
Daily Herald (England)
Daily Mirror (England)
ESPN Brasil (Brazil)
ESPN Deportes
International Boxing Research Organization
Japan Times (Japan)
Joe Rein.net
Liverpool Echo (England)
Los Angeles Times (USA)
London Evening News (USA)
Nippon (Japan)
Oakland Tribune (USA)
O Globo (Brazil)
O Estadão São Paulo (Brazil)
Pacific Stars and Stripes (USA)
Premier Tempo (Colombia)
Terceiro Tempo (Brazil)
The Long Beach Independent (USA)
The Ring (USA)
São Paulo Camara Municipal Revista
Sacramento Bee (USA)
San Francisco Examiner (USA)
Sports Illustrated (USA)
Sydney Morning Herald (Australia)
Ultimas Noticias (Venezuela)
Universal (Colombia)

Here is a list of the books used:

Allen, Stephen D. Allen, A History of Boxing in Mexico: Masculinity, Modernity, and Nationalism (2017)
Aguilera, Gene, Latino Boxing in Southern California (2018)
Costa de Macedo, Bruno, Boxing in São Paulo from 1928-1953 (2019)
Flynn, Barry, Best of Enemies: John Caldwell vs. Freddie Gilroy (2014)
Hernandez Blasquez, Benjamin, Arte en el cuadrilátero (2019)
Legra, Jose, Golpe Bajo (1976)
Lisboa, Luiz Carlos, Gente: Eder Jofre, (2002)
Matteucci, Henrique, O Galo de Ouro (1962)
Matteucci, Henrique, O Galo de Ouro (1977)
Matteucci, Henrique, Boxe: Mitos e Historia (1988)
Roberts, James B. & Skutt, Alexander G., The Boxing Register: International Boxing Hall of Fame Record Book (1997)
Smith, Joseph, A History of Brazil (2002)

Acknowledgments

The subject of this book began as a curiosity to me a little over 20 years ago. That curiosity turned into a hobby and ultimately a passion project. For years I had collected any information I could on Eder Jofre without knowing that all along it was directing me to this path and the book you are holding in your hands. Though this project bordered on an obsession and became a full-time job, not for one moment did I ever feel it was a chore. The long hours between working full-time on this book and my day job have resulted in a project I am proud of. To write a book requires time, passion, and help. It would only be right to thank everyone who helped me along the way as this would have been impossible without such support and assistance along the way.

I would like to thank my parents, David and Elaine Smith & Geoff and Gillian Allen as well as my brothers Michael and Adam Smith for their support and encouragement.

My publisher Win By KO Publications and Adam Pollack for his excellent guidance and for always being available to help. Dan Cuoco, Clay Moyle, Vivian Jimenez, and Christopher Benedict for their generosity with their time, their insight, and structural and technical advice. A big thank you to Chris Miller and Javier Serrano for their design and technical work on the book. I am incredibly grateful to my wonderful editor Godsfavor Robinson whose promptness, excellence, and efficiency helped a great deal.

A huge thank you to Colleen Aycock, for holding my hand through this project, sharing my passion, and for being there every step of the way. I couldn't ask for a better mentor and I have so much gratitude for the work she put in to make this project above and beyond what I initially imagined it would be.

My translators Bruno Yuni Canthende, and Carolina Massote. I do not believe I am exaggerating when I say that without them this book would not have been possible. Initially, when I had a collection of roughly 2000 separate newspaper articles from old Brazilian archives, I figured it would be too mammoth a task to get through it, but I got lucky finding these two individuals. They shared my enthusiasm for this subject and that helped tremendously, and I cannot thank them enough for being so efficient and available.

Akemi Irie, Akihiko Honda, and Nobu Ikushima for taking their time out to go above and beyond in getting me to Fighting Harada. Bob Yalen, for his amazing ability to find dates, archives, and his connecting me with Akemi, and for his incredible researching skills. A huge thank you to Akihide Ishi-I, who is my absolute go-to on all things Japanese boxing. Akihide is a dear friend of Harada and it was through connecting with him that I was able to have regular contact with Harada, who I would also like to thank for being so generous both with me and with the affection he showed Eder. What a genuinely great fighter he was and such a wonderful, humble, and warm person. Shoji Tsue, who alongside Akihide, stands as my encyclopedia for Japanese boxing, especially Harada, and Eder's other Japanese opponents. Shoji has been generous in dedicating ink to this project and our plans for Eder and Harada beyond the release of this book in his Kyodo News columns and Japan's "Boxing Magazine."

A huge thank you to Rick Farris who really helped me understand the era, the history of the bantamweight and featherweight classes, and many of Eder's opponents in a greater light. The enthusiasm and support I received from Rick when I told him about this project was something that always kept me motivated and excited.

Gary Luscombe, for giving me access to his incredible magazine collection. Dr. Yoshihiro Suenaga, for his generosity with his prized fight film collection. Tony Hood, another individual who shared my passion and really went above and beyond in his efforts to help in every which way possible and being about as generous a soul as you could ever wish to encounter. Harry Rosenberg, Eder's personal trainer, and Dr. Bernardo Santi and Dr. Renato Anghinah, both of whom helped the champ recover from his illness in 2013 and were so helpful in sharing their experiences with me. The super talented Jun Aquino, who has captured Eder's image so spectacularly through his incredible artwork and has supported this project and the champion with great enthusiasm.

A big thank you to Paul Caldwell who helped recall many of his father's memories from his fight with Eder in 1962 and also connected with John's brother, also named Paul, who was there in Brazil that evening and remembers the event well. I want to thank one of the greatest bantamweights ever in my friend Carlos Zarate for sharing his knowledge and for being pure class and a big thank you to Gene Aguilera for his insight on many of Eder's opponents and for connecting me with his friend Ruben Olivares. Alejandro Sanchez and Pablo Sanchez Velazquez, sons of Eloy Sanchez, and Juan Carlos Medel, son of Jose Medel, for helping me with additional information on their late fathers.

I would like to thank the following individuals who contributed in many ways: Jeff Fenech, Michael Nunn, Tracy Callis, Jose Vicente Flos, Lee Groves, Kyle McLachlan, Springs Toledo, Jerry Fitch, David Martinez, Miles Templeton, Ted Sares, Anthony George, Matt McGrain, Patrick Connor, Jose Martino, Don Majeski, Roger Esty, Michael Flanagan, Gustavo Estrada, Adam Quigley, Anthony Coleman, Chris Thacker, Andrew Thacker, Alan Rudkin, Steve Lott, Matthew Hallinan, Matt Chudley, Nick Christofides, Bryan Martin, Melvin Perez, James Dowe, Akbar Abdul Muhammad, Hector Duarte Junior, Brad Young, Lou Arriazola, Donovan Kasp, Trisha Morrison, John Martin, Masahito Kawaguchi, Tim Jimenez, Leo Zambrano, Carlos Zambrano, Oscar Venegas, Art Venegas, Javier Campos, Jennifer Venegas, Chris Zambrano, Michelle Zambrano, Claudia Duarte, Rick Gagne, Donald Ankofski, Imran Iqbal, Chris Haddadi, Robert Ambrose, Brian Duncan, James Neill, Marcio Freitas, and Zé Dassilva.

A big thank you to Servilio de Oliveira, Wilson Baldini Junior, Sidnei dal Rovere, Miguel de Oliveira, Acelino Freitas, Patrick Teixeira, Valdemir Pereira, Antonio Oliveira, Adilson Rodrigues, Gilney Munoz Braz, Newton Campos, Fernando Tucori, Gabriel Leão, and Yul Briner Freitas for helping me understand Brazilian boxing and what Eder means to Brazilian sport beyond what I had previously imagined. Itamar Zumbano, grandson of Walter Zumbano, for being an excellent source of information regarding the Zumbano family and helping me connect many dots. I would also like to thank Waldemar Zumbano's grandson, Breno Altman, who was of tremendous help with the Zumbano family information. Also, a warm thank you to Eder's son-in-law, Antonio Oliveira, and his daughter-in-law, Janete Oliveira.

A tremendous and heartfelt thank you to the family that made this book a possibility. It was a few years ago that I got in communication with Marcel and Andrea Jofre. They have always been incredibly generous with their time, their insight, and their support. There were a lot of dots that I felt I needed to connect when it came to the career of Eder Jofre. Through this reason and my constant communication, I started to get into depth about the life of Eder Jofre. Marcel and Andrea have been fantastic in that if they didn't have the answer, they would connect me with the person that would have the answer. The access they have given me to their father has been invaluable and really helped turn a small feature piece into a thoroughly written book which I hope will be used as a reference in the future.

Lastly, a big thank you to the subject of the story himself, Eder Jofre. Thank you for being the fighter you were and the person you are. A career and life which I felt deserved this much of my time and I am proud to be able to present this book on your life. Thank you for putting your trust in me and allowing me this privilege. It is my biggest honor and I am eternally grateful and proud beyond anything words can truly comprehend. Muito obrigado, campeão.

About the Author

Christopher J. Smith is a member of the International Boxing Research Organization (IBRO), a contributor on BoxeoMundial, and is on the board of directors for the West Coast Boxing Hall of Fame. He is an avid boxing history enthusiast and friend of the Jofre family. He was born in England and resides in Los Angeles, California.